The Blackwell
Philosoph
and Legal Theory

Blackwell Philosophy Guides

Series Editor: Steven M. Cahn, City University of New York Graduate School

Written by an international assembly of distinguished philosophers, the *Blackwell Philosophy Guides* create a groundbreaking student resource – a complete critical survey of the central themes and issues of philosophy today. Focusing and advancing key arguments throughout, each essay incorporates essential background material serving to clarify the history and logic of the relevant topic. Accordingly, these volumes will be a valuable resource for a broad range of students and readers, including professional philosophers.

The Blackwell Guide to the
Philosophy of
Law and Legal Theory

Edited by

Martin P. Golding and William A. Edmundson

Blackwell
Publishing

© 2005 by Blackwell Publishing Ltd

BLACKWELL PUBLISHING
350 Main Street, Malden, MA 02148-5020, USA
108 Cowley Road, Oxford OX4 1JF, UK
550 Swanston Street, Carlton, Victoria 3053, Australia

First published 2005 by Blackwell Publishing Ltd

Library of Congress Cataloging-in-Publication Data

The Blackwell guide to the philosophy of law and legal theory / edited by
Martin P. Golding and William A. Edmundson.
p. cm. — (Blackwell philosophy guides; 18)
Includes bibliographical references and index.
ISBN 0-631-22831-4 (hardcover : alk. paper) — ISBN 0-631-22832-2 (pbk.: alk. paper)
1. Law—Philosophy. I. Golding, Martin P. (Martin Philip), 1930– II. Edmundson,
William A. (William Atkins), 1948– III. Series.
K235.B58 2004
340′.1—dc22
2004012895

A catalogue record for this title is available from the British Library.

Set in 9/11.5pt Galliard
by Kolam Information Services Pvt. Ltd, Pondicherry, India
Printed and bound in the United Kingdom
by TJ International, Padstow, Cornwall

The publisher's policy is to use permanent paper from mills that operate a sustainable
forestry policy, and which has been manufactured from pulp processed using acid-free and
elementary chlorine-free practices. Furthermore, the publisher ensures that the text paper
and cover board used have met acceptable environmental accreditation standards.

For further information on
Blackwell Publishing, visit our website:
http://www.blackwellpublishing.com

Contents

Notes on Contributors

Larry A. Alexander is Warren Distinguished Professor of Law, University of San Diego. He is editor of *Constitutionalism: Philosophical Foundations, An Anthology* (1998) and coauthor (with Paul Horton) of *Whom Does the Constitution Command?* (1988) and (with Emily Sherwin) of *The Rule of Rules* (2001). His *Is Freedom of Expression a Human Right?* is forthcoming in 2005.

Brian H. Bix is the Frederick W. Thomas Professor of Law and Philosophy at the University of Minnesota. He is author of *Jurisprudence: Theory and Context* (3rd edn. 2003) and *Law, Language and Legal Determinacy* (1993).

Jes Bjarup is Professor in Jurisprudence, Juridiska Institutione, Stockholms Universitet, Stockholm, Sweden. He is author of *Skandinavischer Realismus, Hagerstrom, Lundstedt, Olivecrona, Ross* (1978, Dutch translation 1984). His essay, "Kripke's Case" is collected in *Law and Legal Interpretation* (2003).

William A. Edmundson is Professor of Law and of Philosophy at Georgia State University. He is author of *Three Anarchical Fallacies* (1998) and *An Introduction to Rights* (2004), and editor of *The Duty to Obey the Law* (1999).

Claire Finkelstein is Professor of Law and Philosophy at the University of Pennsylvania, where she is Director of the Institute for Law and Philosophy. She is currently writing a book entitled *Contractarian Legal Theory*. She is also the editor of a collection of essays entitled *Hobbes on Law*, forthcoming in 2004.

Martin P. Golding is Professor of Philosophy and Professor of Law at Duke University. His books include *Philosophy of Law* (1975, Japanese translation 1985, Chinese translation 1988), *Legal Reasoning* (1984), and *Free Speech on Campus* (2000). He is also editor of *Jewish Law and Legal Theory* (1994).

Alvin I. Goldman is Professor of Philosophy at Rutgers University, New Brunswick. His many books include *Epistemology and Cognition* (1986), *Knowledge in a Social World* (1999), and *Pathways to Knowledge* (2002).

Guy Haarscher is full professor (*professeur ordinaire*) at the Université Libre de Bruxelles (ULB) and visiting professor at the Duke University School of Law and at the Central European University in Budapest. He also teaches at the College of Europe in Bruges. His books include *L'ontologie de Marx* (1980), *La raison du plus fort* (1988), *Philosophie des droits de l'homme* (4th edn. 1993), *La laïcité* (3rd edn. 2004), *Le fantôme de la liberté* (1997), *Philosophie du droit*, with B. Frydman (2nd edn. 2001), and *Les démocraties survivront-elles au terrorisme?* (2002).

Alon Harel is Walter E. Meyer Professor of Law at Hebrew University of Jerusalem. He has been a Faculty Fellow at Harvard University and a Visiting Professor at Columbia Law School and at the University of Toronto Law School. His article "What Demands are Rights? An Investigation into the Relations Between Rights and Reasons" appeared in the *Oxford Journal of Legal Studies* (1997).

Douglas Husak is Professor of Philosophy at Rutgers University, New Brunswick. He is author of *Legalize This! The Case For Decriminalizing Drugs* (2002), *Drugs and Rights* (1992), and *Philosophy of Criminal Law* (1987).

Lewis A. Kornhauser is Alfred B. Engelberg Professor of Law at New York University. His essay, "Preference, Well-Being, and Morality in Social Decisions" appeared in the *Journal of Legal Studies* in 2003.

Matthew H. Kramer is Professor of Legal and Political Philosophy at Cambridge University, where he is also a Fellow and Director of Studies in Law at Churchill College. His many books include *A Debate Over Rights: Philosophical Enquiries* (1998) (with Nigel Simmonds and Hillel Steiner), *In Defense of Legal Positivism: Law Without Trimmings* (1999), and *The Quality of Freedom* (2003).

Brian Leiter is Joseph D. Jamail Centennial Chair in Law, Professor of Philosophy, and Director of the Law and Philosophy Program, University of Texas at Austin; and Visiting Professor of Philosophy, University College London. He is the author of *Nietzsche on Morality* (2002) and *Naturalizing Jurisprudence* (forthcoming), and editor of *Objectivity in Law and Morals* (2001).

Stephen R. Munzer is Professor of Law at the University of California, Los Angeles. He is the author of *A Theory of Property* (1990) and editor of *New Essays in the Legal and Political Theory of Property* (2001).

Mark C. Murphy is Professor of Philosophy at Georgetown University. He is the author of *Natural Law and Practical Rationality* (2001) and *An Essay on Divine Authority* (2002), and is editor of *Alasdair MacIntyre* (2003). He is currently at work on *Natural Law in Politics and Jurisprudence*.

Eric A. Posner is Kirkland and Ellis Professor of Law at the University of Chicago. He is the author of *Law and Social Norms* (2000) and the editor of *Chicago Lectures in Law and Economics* (2000).

Joseph Raz is Professor of the Philosophy of Law, Oxford University and fellow of Balliol College, and Professor of Law, Columbia University. His many books include *Practical Reason and Norms* (1975, 2nd edn. 1999), *The Morality of Freedom* (1986), and *The Practice of Value* (2003).

Patricia Smith is Professor of Philosophy at Baruch College and the Graduate Center, City University of New York. She is editor of *Feminist Jurisprudence* (1993) and *The Nature and Process of Law* (1992) and is coeditor of several other volumes. She is the author of *Liberalism and Affirmative Obligation* (1998) and is currently working on a book titled *Omission, Law and Responsibility.*

Nicos Stavropoulos is University Lecturer in Legal Theory at Oxford University. He is the author of *Objectivity in Law* (1996) and contributed "Hart's Semantics" to *Hart's Postscript* (ed. Jules Coleman, 2001).

Mark V. Tushnet is Carmack Waterhouse Professor of Constitutional Law at Georgetown University. He was the secretary of the Conference on Critical Legal Studies from 1976 to 1985, and is author of *Red, White, and Blue: A Critical Analysis of Constitutional Law* (1988), and *The New Constitutional Order* (2003).

Jeremy J. Waldron is Maurice and Hilda Friedman Professor of Law and Director of the Center for Law and Philosophy at Columbia University. His many books include *Liberal Rights: Collected Papers 1981–91* (1993), *Law and Disagreement* (1999), and *God, Locke and Equality* (2002).

Richard Warner is Professor of Law and Faculty Director of the Center for Law and Computers at Chicago-Kent College of Law of the Illinois Institute of Technology. He has edited the papers of philosopher Paul Grice, and is author of *Freedom, Enjoyment, and Happiness: an Essay on Moral Psychology* (1987) and "Pragmatism and Legal Reasoning" in *Hilary Putnam: Pragmatism and Realism* (2002).

Benjamin C. Zipursky is Professor of Law at Fordham University. Among his articles in torts and jurisprudence are, "Civil Recourse, not Corrective Justice" in the *Georgetown Law Journal* (2003), "The Model of Social Facts" in *Hart's Postscript* (ed. J. Coleman, 2001); "Pragmatic Conceptualism" in *Legal Theory* (2000), and "The Moral of *MacPherson*" (with J. Goldberg) in the *University of Pennsylvania Law Review* (1998).

Introduction

William A. Edmundson

The purpose of this volume is to offer the reader a guide to the most important topics of current discussion in the closely related fields of philosophy of law and legal theory. Each of the chapters attempts to convey what is currently agreed upon with respect to its topic, what is in dispute, and the more prominent positions that have been taken in disputed areas. Each chapter also attempts to assess the importance of what is in dispute – the "stakes" – and the prospects of some resolution being reached. In some instances, matters of agreement and of disagreement may be found to rest upon what the author believes is some shared mistake. In others, the historical progress of dialogue is examined to diagnose the sources of dispute and prospects for resolution. In every instance, the author has had the option to take and defend a particular position – evenhandedly of course.

At the outset, a remark is in order on the implied contrast between "philosophy of law" – on the one hand – and "legal theory" – on the other. The verbal distinction between the two has come about largely as a historical accident. The philosophy of law has – as its name implies – its base of operations within the study of philosophy, and therefore shares with philosophy certain traditional methods of inquiry and investigative priorities. The term "legal theory" tends to connote an enterprise having its operational base within the legal academy – an enterprise that has tended to concentrate on rationalizing and legitimating whole departments of legal doctrine – such as tort and contract – and the role of unrepresentative and typically unelected judges as *de facto* law-

makers in a democratic polity. As such, legal theory might seem to have a somewhat narrower set of concerns than the philosophy of law, but in fact the distinction between the two is evanescent: one that is no more useful than that between "general" jurisprudence (as a separate academic subject) and philosophy of law. It has been the editors' hope to rise above arbitrary divisions of academic turf and to produce a valuable reference for philosophers and academically minded lawyers that will, in addition, be a suitable primary or secondary text for introductory, upper-level undergraduate and postgraduate courses in moral philosophy, political philosophy, law, legal philosophy, political science, political theory, and government.

Contending Schools of Thought

The natural law tradition in the philosophy of law can be traced back at least as far as the writings of Thomas Aquinas in the thirteenth century. Mark C. Murphy reads Aquinas as having formulated the central natural law thesis that, "*necessarily, law is a rational standard for conduct*." Though it is not so easily refuted as many have thought, Murphy acknowledges that natural law theory is nonetheless "marked by ambiguity and unclarity at its core" – a condition that he attempts to correct. Murphy defines and defends an intermediate "Weak Reading" of the central thesis – one also advocated by John Finnis – according to which irrational or insufficiently rational laws are treated as laws, but defective laws, in the same way that the existence of lame cheetahs is to be reconciled with the truth that, necessarily, cheetahs are fast runners. Natural law differs from legal positivism (whose "generic thesis" is that the status of a social rule as a law is entirely independent of its status as a rational standard) in holding that there is a rational standard *internal* to law that makes an irrational law a *defective* though valid law.

Parting company with Finnis, Murphy argues that the better line of defense of natural law begins with the idea that law is a functional kind, that is, a kind of thing characterized by its function. Murphy treats several objections to this functionalist approach, and concludes that law need not have a characteristic end (such as social order, or justice) to serve as a functional kind, so long as law employs certain characteristic means to achieve what ends it serves. What remains is to describe those characteristic means as essentially involving a background in which humans are engaged in their characteristic activity as rational beings, namely, acting for reasons. Law's characteristic means, Murphy concludes, are "to provide dictates backed by compelling reasons for action, and . . . law that fails to do so is defective as law."

Legal positivism has a shorter history than its natural law rival, as Brian H. Bix points out. The nineteenth-century lectures of John Austin contain the classic statement of the legal positivist project: to establish the study of law free of entanglement with proposals for its reform. Bix sets aside the ambition (often associated with Austrian legal positivist Hans Kelsen) for a "science" of law measuring up to the standard of rigor set by the physical sciences, and concludes that the more modest Austinian proposal to study law in a disinterested and scientific spirit is "neither misguided nor naïve," even if unattainable. But this raises, for Bix, the question of what legal positivism's distinctiveness can consist of today, when its modest aim is so widely shared, and the goal of a separate science of law has been foresworn.

Bix identifies various strains of contemporary legal positivism, but concentrates on the strain that derives from H. L. A. Hart and focuses on law as a social convention that must be grasped from a "hermeneutic" or participant's perspective. Within the Hart-inspired strain, contending

"inclusive" (or "soft") and "exclusive" (or "hard") schools have emerged. The two schools divide over the understanding of the fundamental tenet of legal positivism, that there is no *necessary* linkage between law and morality. For exclusive positivists – such as Joseph Raz, Andrei Marmor, and Scott Shapiro – the fundamental tenet of legal positivism means that no moral criteria can ever be needed, nor suffice, to identify a rule as a legal rule. For inclusive positivists – counting David Lyons, Jules Coleman, and the later Hart among this group – some legal systems may as a matter of convention incorporate certain moral criteria among their criteria of legal validity, as either necessary or as sufficient conditions. As Bix points out, "the debate is still evolving" but, as legal positivists respond to criticisms from within their camp and from without by repeatedly adding qualifications, the theory "may be able to beat off all attacks, but the fortified product is one that sometimes seems to be neither recognizable nor powerful" (a predicament akin to that in which Murphy finds contemporary natural law theory).

The distinction between the philosophy of law and legal theory is illustrated by the contrast between American Legal Realism and its Scandinavian cousin. As Brian Leiter explains, the latter resulted from the application of a wider philosophical program to law, while the former grew out of the early twentieth-century reaction of an influential but loosely affiliated group of lawyers and law professors to a dominant "formalist" ideology propagated by Christopher Columbus Langdell at Harvard Law School in the late nineteenth century. The "core claim" of the American Legal Realists (or "Realists," here, for short) was that an appellate decision is better understood as a response to the factual nuances of the case, rather than as a mechanical application of legal rules. The Realists attacked "mechanical jurisprudence" in order to open the way to reform, whether by encouraging a more detailed restatement of the responses of courts to facts, or by opening legal argument to economic and social scientific facts that would not otherwise have been relevant. Although the Realists argued that the legal rules that formalism held to determine outcomes were, in fact, often indeterminate, most were on Realism's "Sociological Wing," which found that appellate outcomes did fall into predictable patterns, although these patterns – according to the "core claim" – were to be explained not by the rules but by looking to patterns within the underlying facts, whether or not those facts had been deemed legally relevant. Few went as far as Jerome Frank, who believed that judicial responses were entirely individual, and whom Leiter places on Realism's "Idiosyncratic Wing."

Leiter traces the impact Realism has had on American legal practice, and the diminution of its influence on legal theory and the philosophy of law due to the work of the "Legal Process School" at Harvard in the 1950s and H. L. A. Hart's attack on Realism (*sub nomine* "rule skepticism") in the early 1960s. After a detailed examination of Hart's critique Leiter concludes that its merits do not fully justify its influence.

One of the legacies of Realism has been an increased interest in the economic dimension of legal decision making. Lewis A. Kornhauser describes how economic analysis, which was confined even during the Realists' heyday to subjects of legislation, burst in the latter half of the twentieth century into the precincts of the common law, offering both descriptive accounts of doctrine and prescriptions for its interpretation, reform, or replacement. Kornhauser argues that the *normative claim* of economic analysis – that common law rules should be evaluated solely by the degree to which they promote welfare (or "efficiency" in any of its technical economic senses) – is not essential to the practice of economic legal analysis. What is, however, distinctive about economic analysis is its approach to the normative nature of law: while traditional legal scholarship proceeds upon the assumption that legal rules are normative (i.e., action-guiding, motivating), economic analysis makes no such assumption, seeking instead to place legal rules within causal patterns that need not reflect H. L. A. Hart's "internal point of view" – the point of view taken by officials and others who regard the law as a rational standard worthy of guiding conduct. The "strong" (unlike the "modest") research program of economic analysis simply repudiates normativity.

Kornhauser distinguishes a policy analysis school and a political economy school of economic analysis. Both apply microeconomic

theory and its technical conception of preference to the law; but while the former treats private individuals as self-interested preference maximizers, the latter treats public officials in this manner as well. Even if "self-interestedness" is given a wide scope (allowing for, e.g., altruistic preferences), the core concept of economic analysis – that of preference – is at odds with the mainstream understanding of law as normative, that is, as purporting to obligate rather than merely to coerce. Kornhauser examines the concepts of preference and of obligation in order to determine how economic analysis might reconcile its theories, elaborated in terms of preference, with the mainstream legal theory's insistence upon the idea of legal obligation.

Another of Realism's legacies is Critical Legal Studies ("CLS," for short), which, as Mark V. Tushnet recounts, emerged in the 1970s in the United States as a left-wing opposition to the consensus-assuming Legal Process school and the perceived scientism of an emerging "Chicago School" of economic analysis. The CLS slogan, "law is politics," reflected a rejection of institutions as repositories of settled wisdom, and of law as a reflection of some "immanent rationality." CLS was largely inattentive to traditional disputes about the nature of law and its relation to morality, but was instead concerned to open up avenues of reform that were closed off by the "false necessity" attributed to traditional legal categories and their assumed determinacy. CLS took up the Realist critique of determinacy, but innovated by offering explanations of the undeniable predictability of most legal outcomes by drawing upon the concept of *hegemony* as elaborated in the work of Antonio Gramsci and other humanist Marxists.

Contrary to the widely held view that CLS was killed by the question, "What would you do?" Tushnet points to the many policy initiatives supported (if not precisely entailed) by CLS, and to the critical race and critical feminist theories it engendered. Because of its fruitfulness, it was perhaps inevitable that intramural disputes would begin to divide CLS. Tushnet instances the "critique of rights": while many critical legal scholars suspiciously view the concept of rights as a double-edged instrument of bourgeois individualism, critical race theorists have come to the defense of the capacity of rights to counter subordination and to advance the interests of racial minorities. Critical race and critical feminist scholars have also innovated by employing narrative as a way of exposing and countering the processes of hegemony, by which a persuasion of the inevitability and justice of subordinate social positions is instilled in the minds of those who occupy them. CLS is not moribund, Tushnet concludes, but an analytical technique very much at the disposal of legal scholars.

Four themes in feminist legal theory form the subject of Patricia Smith's chapter. The respect due differences between men and women is the first theme. Equal treatment and identical treatment have been distinguished at least since Carol Gilligan's *In a Different Voice* (1982). As in the case of pregnancy leave, ignoring differences may lead to an unjust allocation of burdens. But Smith warns against allowing the celebration of putatively feminine virtues, such as caring and nurturing, to reinforce traditional gender roles. Care and nurture, because valuable, are to be inculcated equally in men and women, Smith argues. The pervasive, socially constructed relation of male dominance and female subordination is Smith's second theme. Drawing upon Stephen Schulhofer's recent work on rape law, Smith argues that male dominance systematically dampens the legal system's response to the crime of rape, and manifests itself in a number of "futilitarian" responses (to borrow Peter Unger's phrase) to the persistence of male violence toward women.

Domesticity, Smith's third theme, concerns the institutionalization of gender roles by superficially gender-neutral mechanisms. The stereotypical "perfect worker" and "breadwinner" roles cannot readily be filled by the stereotypical "perfect mother," who must be ever ready to answer the demands of children and spouse. Smith argues that gender bias can masquerade as neutral meritocracy only because the role of worker and the criteria of evaluating workplace performance are themselves shaped by bias. Smith seconds Joan Williams's proposal to allow discrimination suits against employers who impose masculinized norms in the design of work schedules and leave policies. Threaded throughout Smith's chapter is her fourth theme: the commonplace denial that the injustices targeted by feminist jurisprudence

exist or deserve further attention – what Deborah Rhode has labeled "the 'no problem' problem."

Doctrinal Domains and their Philosophical Foundations

The "general part" of the criminal law deals with issues such as culpability, voluntariness, attempt liability, and defenses of justification and excuse, in contrast to the "special part," which treats specific offenses such as murder, rape, or – as Douglas Husak informs us – exhibiting deformed animals. Both theory and law school pedagogy concentrate on the general part almost to the exclusion of the question: what *ought* to be criminalized? Husak finds this misdirection of interest to be both puzzling and deplorable in light of the proliferation of statutory and regulatory offenses in recent years, and the related explosion in the number of prison inmates over the last quarter-century – much of the increase attributable to drug offenses unknown to the criminal law of a century ago. Husak devotes his chapter to an effort to begin to correct this imbalance.

Addressing *criminalization*, the basic question of criminal law theory, presupposes an analysis of what is distinctive of criminal law. Husak defends the "orthodox position" that punishment is the hallmark of criminal law, and a serviceable one despite the existence of borderline cases. The theory of criminalization is thus tied to the task of justifying punishment – a task which, under examination, is not satisfactorily performed by standard theories, such as utilitarianism in its modern, law-and-economics incarnation, nor by Joel Feinberg's elaboration of John Stuart Mill's "harm" principle, nor by H. L. A. Hart's hybridization of utilitarian and retributive approaches. The problem is that legislatures have been so prolific in enacting punitive statutes that no theory of punishment stands a fair chance of fitting the law on the books. In the United States, the constitution allows legislatures huge latitude to criminalize conduct so long as – as is typically the case – fundamental rights such as free speech and privacy are not infringed. Husak concludes by boldly proposing that legislatures subject criminal statutes to the kind of "strict scrutiny" that courts employ in fundamental-rights cases.

The term "tort theory" may seem oxymoronic, Benjamin C. Zipursky warns, because torts are so much a practical and everyday business. Nonetheless, philosophical methods have much to tell us about the structure of tort doctrine and, reciprocally, tort doctrine can illuminate moral philosophy. The leading problem for tort theory during the twentieth century was that of making sense of the rationale and respective domains of the fault principle ("No liability without fault!") and the principle of strict liability, which holds causers of harm liable irrespective of the degree of care they have taken. Zipursky describes the spectrum of leading views: from Richard Epstein's libertarian advocacy of strict liability to Ernest Weinrib's formalist insistence on a negligence regime. In the middle, allowing scope to both negligence and to strict liability, fall George Fletcher's account based on the idea of reciprocity of risk, and the several accounts advanced by Jules Coleman, perhaps the leading tort theorist writing today.

The debate over strict liability and fault is not the only discussion going on in tort theory, however. Zipursky instances the effort to understand the concept of duty, and the relative standing of the "monadic" and "dyadic" forms it can take. Because of tort's nature as a microcosm of social life, tort theory illuminates wider issues in legal philosophy, such as the ongoing debate between instrumental and deontological normative accounts of law. Tort theory is, Zipursky observes, of value to philosophy "as a form of moral anthropology." Recent work by Coleman, Weinrib, Stephen Perry, and others has, moreover, placed corrective justice once again in its proper position with respect to its Aristotelian counterpart, distributive justice, given such prominence by political philosopher John Rawls. Despite its simplicity, Zipursky tells us, tort law stimulates and sustains the philosopher's deepest inquiries.

Contract law forms, with torts, the doctrinal area known as *private law*, and is the subject of Eric A. Posner's chapter. Although contract law has affinities to the morality of promising, it diverges in a variety of ways, such as its doctrine of consideration: it is, Posner writes "the institutional form that gives people the power to make commitments when reputation and other nonlegal sanctions are insufficient." Normative theories of contract divide into welfarist and nonwelfarist types, with the latter further dividing into ones that stress the centrality of promising to autonomy, and ones that stress instead the justice of protecting reliance. Posner focuses on the descriptive adequacy of the normative theories currently in play, setting aside the related but separable issue of whether contract doctrine can be unified under a single conceptual theme.

Welfarist or economic theory of contract portrays doctrine as a set of default rules duplicating the efficiency that contracting parties ideally would achieve, were they able to completely specify terms. Posner reviews the reasons why most scholars have concluded that welfarist theory is descriptively inadequate, raising the question whether doctrine should be reformed on a basis of welfarist principles. Nonwelfarist theorists resist the economists' call for reform, and offer instead what they believe to be descriptively and normatively superior accounts. Posner examines a variety of nonwelfarist theories: Fried's "contract as promise," Randy Barnett's "contract as consent," Peter Benson's "contract as transfer," S. A. Smith's "contract as property," and Tim Scanlon's account – all of which he finds to have descriptive shortcomings. Posner then turns to historical accounts, such as Grant Gilmore's and Patrick Atiyah's, and to certain general topics implicated by contract law: formalism, distributive justice, and paternalism. He concludes with the observation that the theories that have been brought to bear on contract doctrine may be inherently too coarse to account for its distinctive rules, which, like rules of the road, may be serviceable even though incapable of rigorous derivation.

Most lawyers find it congenial to think of property as a "bundle of sticks," where the sticks consist of the various "legal advantages" analyzed by Wesley Newcomb Hohfeld a century ago, and later specified by Tony Honoré. Stephen R. Munzer shows how the traditional understanding is intertranslatable with the framework of property, liability, and inalienability rules proposed by Calbresi and Melamed in the early 1970s. But Munzer's focus is on "something new under the sun" – the idea of the *anticommons*, an area (literal or figurative) from which many have a nonexclusive right to exclude others, in contrast to the commons, typically (and often confusedly) conceived as an area which many have nonexclusive rights to enjoy. The very idea of an anticommons stirs worries about wasteful underuse, just as wasteful overuse was the theme of Garrett Hardin's 1968 article, "The Tragedy of the Commons."

Munzer evaluates the conceptual and practical promise of the idea of the anticommons. M. Heller has proposed that private property be understood as a middle position between a commons and an anticommons – a proposal that Munzer finds promising as a way of untangling the US Supreme Court's "takings" jurisprudence (although, as Munzer explains, Heller and Krier's recent work, drawing on Calabresi and Melamed, has advantages as well). The anticommons may help explain the "*numerus clausus*" principle that limits the recognized forms of ownership to a traditional few (although, as Munzer notes, the idea of information costs may be just as illuminating, and it may be that the principle itself is overstated). Finally, Munzer describes and assesses the idea of a *liberal commons* – defended by Dagan and Heller as a way of honoring liberal values of autonomy and free exit while at the same time securing the social benefits of cooperation – and the application of the liberal commons to marital property. Although these recent innovations involve difficulty, they could set the agenda for both theoretical and doctrinal development in property law over the coming decades.

The topic of evidence in the law is broadly construed by Alvin I. Goldman to include not only the rules of evidence at trial but also civil discovery rules and the adversary system itself. Goldman defends the thesis that adjudication is best justified and explained by reference to substantive justice as its ultimate value, while truth-seeking – as a necessary but subordinate value – governs the law of evidence, subject to side constraints determined by values other than truth, such as administrability and the fostering of certain relationships. Despite exceptions and complications, the truth rationale for the rules of evidence has, Goldman concludes, no serious competitors. Judged from the perspective of "social epistemology," Goldman points out that

the adversary system has both advantages and disadvantages vis-à-vis alternative "inquisitorial" systems, in which the facts are developed by neutral agents of the court rather than by the parties.

Turning to philosophical fundamentals, Goldman explores the role of Bayesianism in the theory of legal evidence. Bayesianism holds that factfinders, upon exposure to evidence, should adjust their degree of belief in a given hypothesis according to the conditional likelihood, against their background of prior beliefs, of there being such evidence if the hypothesis were true. The standard interpretation of Bayes's theorem to this effect is, however, a subjective one, taking the factfinder's conditional probability estimates as they are found. But the rules of evidence – and the landmark *Daubert* decision on the admissibility of expert testimony – are better served by requiring an objective rather than a subjective interpretation. Because subjective Bayesianism cannot guarantee that truth is approached, Goldman proposes what he terms a "quasi-objective" Bayesian alternative, which requires that the factfinder reason in Bayesian fashion upon a set of subjective likelihoods that are related in a certain way to objective likelihoods, which are to be given a modal interpretation along lines suggested by the work of the late David Lewis. This approach has practical implications: in particular, it favors court appointment of expert witnesses over the predominant practice of allowing the parties each to hire experts.

Perennial Topics

As Matthew H. Kramer notes, questions concerning legal and moral obligation (or duty) are of long standing. Kramer considers these questions as they divide into three sets. The first set concerns whether and how legal obligations engender moral ones or, more precisely, how there can be a "prima facie, comprehensively applicable, universally borne, and content-independent" duty to do what the law requires. Kramer reviews efforts to ground such a duty as a species of promissory obligation or consent, as an instance of a wider duty of fairness (or, as H. L. A Hart termed it, of fair play), as a duty of gratitude, or as a utilitarian rule. Each of these efforts have fallen short, leading some to revisionism, as in the case of Ronald Dworkin's "associative obligations," which lack content independence and comprehensive applicability.

A second set of questions concerns whether the law *purports* to impose moral duties – an issue sometimes cast in terms of the nature of law's authority. Kramer examines the arguments of Joseph Raz representing law as necessarily, if only implicitly, claiming to impose moral duties of compliance. Kramer concludes that Raz fails to rule out the possibility of wicked legal regimes that disdain rather than disown the moral claim. Law, for Kramer, differs from mere coercion not by adding a moral claim but by the generality, temporal extension, and consequent regularity of its commands.

Kramer's third set of questions focuses on the logical characteristics of moral and legal obligation and, in particular, on the reach of the "correlativity thesis" propounded in the early twentieth century by legal theorist Wesley Newcomb Hohfeld. Kramer defends the view that legal duties may lack correlate legal rights – may, in that sense, be "nominal" – but that moral duties and moral rights are mutually entailing. Thus, although legal rights are not strictly tied to remedies, moral rights are: where morality is at issue "there is no room for nominal duties."

Hohfeld's analysis is taken up in the first section of Alon Harel's chapter, but with emphasis on filling out the "underdefined" feature that distinguishes X's having a right (moral or legal) from there merely being a duty concerning X on another's part. Harel compares the *choice theory* of rights, which conceives rights as a "protective perimeter" for the rightholder's autonomy, with the *interest theory*, which sees rights as tied to the promotion of the rightholder's interests more generally. Both theories fall short of Harel's criteria of adequacy for a theory of rights, in that each either contradicts or leaves unexplained certain entrenched features of rights discourse. Choice theory, for example, has trouble accommodating inalienable rights; while interest theory has difficulty explaining why only some, not all, interests generate rights. Harel considers the prospects of the hybrid theory recently proposed by Gopal Sreenavasan, before turning to the question: *why* take rights (so) seriously? – a

question Harel explores with reference to the notoriously difficult "trolley" problem.

The second half of Harel's discussion is an effort to locate rights within moral theory generally. Are they foundational, or reducible to more basic terms? Harel discusses Joseph Raz's view that rights are mediary between values and duties, and proposes instead a "nonreductionist" account emphasizing that new values emerge from social practices that, on a superficial view, may seem merely to serve a more abstractly described value. Only such an account can explain why the right to free speech varies so from nation to nation even though it everywhere serves, in an abstract sense, to protect autonomy. The practice of protecting speech for the sake of autonomy – and not merely, say, to promote the general welfare – endows speech with an intrinsic value it lacks in societies whose practices do not single out speech as a preferred vehicle for autonomy. Harel considers also Marxist, antineocolonialist, communitarian, and feminist critiques of the very idea of rights, and finds that although it is important that there be certain "rights-free zones, in which spontaneity may flourish," it is also true that in a world without rights "an intangible human sensitivity would be lost."

The justification of punishment is a topic of perennial dispute in the philosophy of law. Claire Finkelstein surveys the candidate theories – deterrence and retribution chief among them – and catalogues their strengths and weaknesses. Deterrence theories are notoriously objectionable insofar as they do not require that the recipient be guilty of any crime – a defect that is often assumed to be cured by "mixed" theories such as H. L. A. Hart's, which fix deterrence as punishment's "general justifying aim" while requiring desert as its "principle of distribution." By means of an ingenious series of examples, Finkelstein shows that the mixed theory still violates the Kantian prohibition of treating others as mere means. But honoring the dignity of the punished cannot be satisfied by embracing retributivism; for, as Finkelstein shows, retributivism is unable to explain the proper measure of punishment.

Both retributivism and deterrence provide important partial insights into the justification of punishment, Finkelstein concedes, but "it is the voluntary nature of the system of punishment that is required to give both deterrence and moral desert their proper place." The voluntary nature of the system of punishment can only be captured, she argues, by a contractarian account along broadly Rawlsian lines. Rational agents will view life under a regulated system of punishment as preferable to the perils of a state of nature, and will not willingly gamble away the security that system provides. The contractarian approach can account for salient features of criminal punishment that elude competitor theories, she argues, and it also has the not unwelcome consequence that certain forms of punishment – such as torture and execution – are irreconcilable with it.

The theory of responsibility – a major theme of the "general part" of criminal law – is the subject of Martin P. Golding's chapter. The focal issue is that of how far criminal law ought to reflect our ordinary notions of moral responsibility. In law, as in everyday life, Golding points out, questions of responsibility are often the "flip side" of excuses offered on behalf of an agent whose conduct has caused harm or otherwise varied from relevant norms. One approach is that of Oliver Wendell Holmes, Jr., who advocated imposing liability on an "objective" basis that would ignore the mentality of the defendant except where the "reasonable man" would have done as the defendant did. Golding questions Holmes's utilitarian rationale for curtailing the common law *mens rea* requirement, which after all reflects distinctions that matter in everyday life, as Holmes well knew. Aristotle's distinction between innocently excusable ignorance of facts and inexcusably wicked ignorance of norms raises, but does not settle, the long-disputed question as to whether ignorance of fact must be objectively reasonable if it is to excuse.

The influential Model Penal Code effectively created a presumption that mistake of fact exculpates, but in doing so did not resolve the moral question. H. L. A Hart's early, "negative" view was that mental elements are in effect nothing but summaries of recognized defenses. Antony Duff has taken the quite different position that *mens rea* is a positive notion, and that intention is its "central species." Duff, in turn, has been criticized by Alan Norrie for failing to appreciate the self-contradictoriness of criminal law's emphasis on a formalistic notion of intention while, at the same time, dismissing motive as irrelevant to guilt. In light of this dissension, Golding turns to Barbara Wootton's proposal to dismiss *mens rea* altogether from the definition of offenses. Why have excuses at all? Golding concludes by sympathetically recounting the later view of Hart, which locates the rationale for excuses in considerations of fairness to individuals and respect for their capacity for choice.

Legislation is the practice by which law is made in formal ways by institutions that present themselves as dedicated to that very task, Jeremy J. Waldron explains. This is not to deny that other institutions – courts and agencies, for example – often make law. But characterizing legislation in this way draws attention to its special source of legitimacy: its representativeness. Legislation arouses antipathy because "the very thing that attracts democratic theorists – the involvement of ordinary people in lawmaking – tends to repel the legal professional." Antipathy is especially high in the United States, where standards of legislative craftsmanship and deliberation are low. Antipathy or ambivalence is also found in legal theory, where legislation tends to be treated as merely an input to the judicial process. While H. L. A Hart depicted legislative institutions as marking a society's progress from a prelegal to a legal order, Joseph Raz has argued that the essence of a legal order is not a norm-creating but norm-applying institution. Legal Realists and the Legal Process School portrayed legislation as at most a stimulus or input for other, more genuinely effective, organs of government, and more recently Ronald Dworkin has identified the judiciary – rather than the legislature – as the abler "forum of principle."

Waldron thinks legislation deserves more respect. He sketches how a more affirmative account of legislation will emphasize its role as mediator between democratic values and rule-of-law values. The diversity of typical legislative assemblies is a feature unique to them, one which assures a degree of representativeness that supports law's claim to impose duties of obedience upon ordinary citizens, and enriches the pool of opinion and information upon which deliberation operates. It is diversity, Waldron emphasizes, and not majoritarian procedure, that sets legislative assemblies apart. Diversity helps to explain the "textual focus" of the legislative process, and why statutory texts must be read constructively rather than as expressions of a univocal purpose. Waldron concludes with a cautionary discussion of judicial review of legislation, especially where matters of constitutional interpretation are involved – for where a judicial and a legislative body differ, it is the opinion of the legislative body that represents and is accountable to the views of the citizenry.

Larry A. Alexander explains what constitutions are, what they can do, and why we should want one. What constitutions are is explained by a story that takes us through a series of steps. It begins with whatever views about justice and politics we happen to have; it proceeds, then, by taking into account the "circumstances of politics," that is, our need to reach agreement with others who hold contrary views – at which stage we agree with others on second-best principles that are preferable to anarchy (though not, from one's own perspective, to dictatorship by oneself). At a further stage, a distinction becomes possible between the constitution, which is the set of agreed-upon symbols, and the metaconstitution, which is the agreed-upon mode of identifying and interpreting those symbols. Constitution and metaconstitution can vary independently, as Alexander indicates with examples from US history. The task of distinguishing the constitution, the metaconstitution, and ordinary legislation is best achieved by reference to degrees of entrenchment. Although the "whole edifice" ultimately rests upon acceptance, the metaconstitution most clearly does, and so is the least entrenched; ordinary legislation is more entrenched; while the constitution is the most entrenched – although the picture is more intricate, as Alexander explains.

Constitutions serve to entrench rules for making and changing ordinary law, and so serve the vital purpose of assuring that these rules are not themselves drawn continually into dispute. Entrenchment can also curb legislative shortsightedness and protect minority representation. But are these desiderata enough to justify curtailing democracy? The question is especially acute when the interpretation of the constitution itself is at issue. When constitutional rules are indeterminate, judicial review of legislation arguably becomes "judicial despotism." But Alexander takes

issue with Jeremy Waldron's view that the legislature has better moral standing than the judiciary to decide how the constitution is to be interpreted. Alexander takes up a series of arguments that might favor Waldron, but finds that none of them rules out the possibility that the "just so" story, which explained what constitutions are, could be continued by settlement upon a metaconstitutional rule of judicial review rather than one of majoritarian democracy.

Legal reasoning is a species of practical reasoning distinguished by the influence of legal rules, Richard Warner explains. We insist that courts confine themselves to applying legal rules, but why? A state is legitimate only if its citizens have a duty to obey, but such a duty exists only when the state represents the citizen. Courts, however, are impartial, not representative. Thus, valuing freedom seems to entail what Warner calls the "confinement claim," namely that judging is legitimate only to the extent that it enforces "obligations that have been encoded in laws through prior representative political processes." This is the heart of what turns out, however, to be a "Mistaken View." Authoritative legal materials underdetermine outcomes, and judges must and do rely on moral principles in their decisions. Since condemning judging as illegitimate is not attractive, one of two options must be chosen. The first, worked out by Ronald Dworkin, broadens the confinement claim so that the authoritative legal materials include the morally best theory of the settled law.

The shortcomings of Dworkin's answer lead to the second option, which Warner calls the "Received View" that abandons the confinement claim and holds adjudication legitimate if it supplements authoritative legal materials with selected moral principles no more than necessary. The "necessary means" conception of legitimacy built into the Received View invites controversy about what is to count as necessary. Controversy is unsurprising because the Received View tells us that adjudication can be legitimate even if its outcome adversely affects persons who profoundly disagree with the moral principles applied by the court. Respect for freedom counsels that this "second-best" legitimacy be invoked sparingly, and courts ideally will confine themselves to moral reasons that everyone can freely acknowledge *as reasons* even if not all agree about those reasons' relative weight. Warner argues that the concept of a *person* encourages the hope that "shared reasons" are typical of cases of second-best legitimacy. To the extent that self-defining commitments are the grounding of the reasons that guide our lives, we have reason to acknowledge others' similar reasons, however contrary to our own.

Privacy as a moral right and as a claimant for legal protection is the topic of William A. Edmundson's chapter. Legal protection of privacy is a modern arrival that comes by way of a multifaceted cause of action in tort, by legislative command, and – most controversially – by judicial recognition of "nontextual" constitutional rights. Some have argued that privacy is, or reflects, a univocal value, while others view it as merely instrumental to various unrelated interests. Privacy can, however, usefully be seen as having three different dimensions. Physical privacy consists of a right to the exclusive enjoyment of certain areas of space. Informational privacy has to do with control over information about oneself. Decisional privacy is related to the right to liberty, and concerns the right to do something, in contrast to the right to do it in seclusion, or to do it without others' knowledge.

A right to liberty can be distinguished from a right to decisional privacy by stipulating that the latter rests on the idea that the actor has a right to be free of interference regardless of the moral merits of the action at issue. The constitutional right to abortion is better seen as a decisional privacy right than a liberty right, for example, in the sense that it need not be understood as commending abortion. A right to decisional privacy is, in this sense, a *right to do wrong* – a paradoxical notion to many, insofar as wrongness seems to connote a permission on the part of others to impose sanctions upon wrongdoing. Edmundson explores the apparent clash between decisional privacy rights and the "Enforcement Thesis," which holds that moral wrongness at least pragmatically entails permissible sanctionability. Appeals to neutrality, autonomy, dignity, and "self-defining" choices are examined, but do not relieve the conflict. This puzzle takes on added importance in light of the US Supreme Court's *Lawrence v. Texas* decision,

which can be understood to formulate constitutional liberty and privacy alike as decisional privacy rights.

Continental Perspectives

For over a century, anglophone legal philosophers have supposed that their "analytical" approach gives them advantages denied to their counterparts on the European continent, Jes Bjarup writes. But the analysis of legal concepts has not been neglected on the Continent, nor has Jeremy Bentham's distinction between expository and censorial jurisprudence – that is, between "what the law is" and "its merit or demerit," as John Austin put it. Bjarup uncovers strains of legal positivism in the thinking of Immanuel Kant, whose influence is undimmed even today. Kant accepted the legal positivist's thesis that law is identifiable by its source, but located the normativity of law not in the command of the sovereign but in the "categorical imperative" of practical reason, and its purpose not in securing the greatest happiness, but the greatest freedom. Hegel's philosophy of law also has affinities to legal positivism, if only because Hegel dismissed the possibility of a censorial jurisprudence altogether, leaving only the task of setting forth the organic law of the community – a view developed by von Savigny.

The diminished but not extinguished torch of natural law was carried forward into the twentieth century, in Germany, by the Catholic philosopher Viktor Cathrein, but was not readily received by Protestant hands. Rudolf Stammler's doctrine of law as a "social ideal" represented, in the 1920s, an effort to go beyond "technical legal science" to develop a natural law, but one with "a changing content" not fixed *a priori* in Kantian fashion. Gustav Radbruch – who endured the Nazi era – criticized Stammler's effort and proposed instead the "Radbruch formula," according to which law is to be identified in legal positivist terms, subject to the proviso that law that does not even attempt to do justice is to be dismissed as "false law." Bjarup concludes that the post-World War II revival of natural law thinking has been a multifaceted one not usefully analyzed in terms of "continental" and "noncontinental" approaches.

Guy Haarscher similarly finds that the boundary between continental and anglophone philosophy of law has become harder to draw over the past 30 years – a trend that the catchphrase "globalization" does little to illuminate. Thirty years ago Marxism and a "deconstructionist" postmodernism seemed dominant in Europe; while in English-speaking countries there reigned a broadly pragmatist and neopositivist attitude of trust in the sciences. Today, postmodernism and neo-Marxism have made inroads in the anglophone academy while, on the continent, Marxism has been cast aside, translations of Rawls and Ronald Dworkin are widely debated, and law itself has become "a respectable, and even trendy, philosophical subject." Moreover, the global dominance of liberal ideas has been accompanied by an "ascent of the judges" within civil law systems, eroding the familiar contrast to common law systems, with the result that "the fundamental regulation of society becomes . . . less political and more legal." Haarscher critically assesses these trends but suggests that basic differences of approach endure.

Haarscher examines an argument advanced by Belgian scholars François Ost and Michel van de Kerchove, that the shape of European law no longer resembles a pyramid having the sovereign state at its apex, to which all other norms are subordinate and have reference. Rather, it has transformed itself into a network of norms continually under negotiation among a plurality of private and public actors. Haarscher argues that the structure of the law of the European Union, as shaped by the European Court of Human Rights in Strasbourg, seen in this way, poses a philosophical question about the relationship of hierarchy and equality. Rather than being straightforward contraries, equality and hierarchy may be mutually necessary components of the rule of law. Via an analysis of recent freedom of expression decisions by the Strasbourg court, Haarscher cautiously concludes that judicial "balancing" of rights can introduce a perverse uncertainty into the domain of fundamental values upon which the law's legitimacy depends.

Methodological Concerns

The objectivity of law is the subject of Nicos Stavropoulos's chapter. The notion of objectivity (which some theorists have tried to relativize to particular domains) is itself in need of clarification, he explains. One approach represents a domain as objective to the extent that truth in that domain tracks the way things are in the world independent of the mind; while another approach (advanced by Thomas Nagel) represents objectivity as a process of detachment from any particular perspective on the world. Stavropoulos fixes upon a theme common to the two: objectivity must create a logical space for the possibility of error. Applied to law, the objectivity question becomes: "Is there an objective fact about what the law requires?" – or, put differently, does the nature of law admit a logical space for possible error about what is legally required?

Stavropoulos distinguishes the objectivity question from a concern with determinacy. Although related, the two ideas are not identical: what is determinate may be subjective and what is indeterminate objective. He surveys leading theories of law and assesses their stances toward law's objectivity. H. L. A. Hart's legal positivism, which is not baldly skeptical of objectivity, encourages us to distinguish the objectivity of the process of identifying legal norms from the objectivity of the application of those norms to particular facts. Both aspects are fundamentally social, for Hart, and thus on his view there is space for error between what law requires and any particular official's judgment, but none between what law requires and the "settled collective judgment" of officials. In contrast, Ronald Dworkin's account of law implicates objective values both in the identification of legal norms and in their application. Variant forms of legal positivism might treat norm identification as not allowing space for massive social error, while allowing such space in the matter of norm application. But, to the extent that such variants of legal positivism are "inclusive" in the sense of allowing that official practice may employ objective values, it is a live question whether they thereby destabilize the legal positivist tenet that the nature of law is fundamentally social.

"Can there be a theory of law?" asks Joseph Raz. To succeed, a theory of law must propound a set of necessary truths that explain what law is. But law is a human institution that varies with place and time. Moreover, the *concept* of law is not unary, but is subject to similar (if less extreme) variation. How, then, can any theory of law succeed? Raz undertakes the task of showing that admitting the parochial nature of law – and even the parochial nature of the concept of law – does not ordain failure for the theory of law. Although his chapter does not purport positively to show that such a theory is possible (much less, to exhibit the theory itself) it aims to clear away a number of seductive misunderstandings that have suggested the contrary.

The major misunderstanding proceeds from the undeniable fact that the concept of law is parochial. General observations about the nature of concepts show how and why explaining the concept of law is secondary to the study of the nature of law, and is a component of that study

only with respect to societies that possess the concept. A society need not possess our concept of law – nor any concept of law nor, indeed, *any* legal concept – in order to possess a legal system, Raz argues. Hart correctly emphasized that a legal system's existence depends in a special way upon people's awareness of the role of legal rules in their lives, but – Raz cautions – that is not to say that they must possess a concept of law in order to be aware of rules which, by our account, serve them as legal rules. Raz challenges Ronald Dworkin's contrary insistence that law is an "interpretive practice," which presupposes the self-conscious possession of a concept of law. For Raz, "law can and does exist in cultures which do not think of their legal institutions as legal." Thus, various arguments from parochialism – as well as arguments objecting to "essentialism" – fail to reveal any serious obstacle in the way of progress toward a theory of law. Indirectly, Raz illustrates why the pursuit of such a theory is worthwhile; for, in his words, "in large measure what we study when we study the nature of law is the nature of our own self-understanding."

Part I
Contending Schools of Thought

Chapter 1

Natural Law Theory

Mark C. Murphy

Natural law theorists claim that, necessarily, law is a rational standard for conduct: it is a standard that agents have strong, even decisive, reasons to comply with. This is the central thesis from which their developed theory of law takes its starting point. My aim here is to make clear how we might understand natural law theory's central thesis, how it can be deployed in a fruitful theory of law (see CAN THERE BE A THEORY OF LAW?) and why one might take it to be true. I will proceed by first examining briefly the way that this thesis surfaces in the work of Thomas Aquinas, the paradigmatic natural law theorist: aside from providing a salutary glimpse of the history of natural law theorizing, this will help us to see in Aquinas's work the ambiguities and tensions that form the problematic of recent natural law thought. I will then proceed analytically, examining some of the various formulations that the natural law thesis might take, considering the extent to which each of these formulations is incompatible with the legal positivism (see LEGAL POSITIVISM) with which natural law theory is typically contrasted, and asking what sorts of arguments can be offered for the natural law thesis.

It will no doubt be wondered why a thesis that concerns a connection between law and reasons for action bears the seemingly uninformative label "natural law theory." It bears this label because the most historically important defender of this central thesis is Thomas Aquinas, and Aquinas identified the principles of rational conduct for human beings as the principles of the natural law. Thus, given Aquinas's theory of reasons for action, the thesis in question can be

stated as asserting a connection between human law and natural law. A danger with this label, of course, is that one might confuse theses of Aquinas's theory of practical rationality with theses of his theory of law, and take objections to one of these theories to constitute objections to the other. A different label might have been better at describing the view at the level of abstraction that we will treat it. But the label "natural law theory" has stuck, and I will not attempt to detach it here.

Aquinas's Theory of Natural Law

Brian Bix has remarked that it is, in general, a bad idea to read texts on law from the distant past with the assumption that the concerns of the authors of those texts are the concerns of contemporary analytical jurisprudence (Bix 1996: 227). Bix, and others, have suggested that this is particularly true of Aquinas: Aquinas, they write, was not interested in providing a descriptive theory of the nature of human law; he was, rather, concerned to provide a theory of political obligation (see LEGAL AND MORAL OBLIGATION), that is, an account of the source and limits of the moral requirement to comply with the demands of law (see, for example, Bix 2002:63; Soper 1983:1181). Aquinas *was* concerned with the problem of political obligation. But that does not mean that he was not *also* concerned to provide a correct description of what law essentially is. Here is a helpful comparison. In the work in which Aquinas's mature thoughts on law are to be found, the *Summa Theologiae*,[1] the set of questions that is labeled by commentators the "Treatise on Law" (ST IaIIae 90–107) is preceded by sets of questions labeled by commentators the "Treatise on Virtue" (ST IaIIae 55–70) and the "Treatise on Vice" (ST IaIIae 71–89). These considerations of virtue and vice are primarily descriptive – they are meant to provide an account of the concept, nature, and causes of virtue and vice. This is a speculative, not a practical, enterprise, however much one may draw upon Aquinas's answers here to get a better grip on (for example) how tasks of moral education ought to be carried out. So just because Aquinas later draws practical conclusions about the law and the requirement of obedience to it, that does not mean that he was not trying to come up with a theory of (human) law – an account of law that is both necessarily true and which provides an explanation of it (see CAN THERE BE A THEORY OF LAW?).

That Aquinas is indeed concerned with the task of providing an adequate descriptive theory of law is clear when we examine the structure of his argument to the conclusion that human law is a rational standard for conduct. This conclusion is a straightforward implication of his view that *all* law is a rational standard for conduct. The thesis that all law is a rational standard for conduct is defended in the first article of the first question of the Treatise on Law (ST IaIIae 90, 1) and it is a thesis that applies not only to human law but to the (for the most part unknowable) eternal law, that law by which God exercises providence over all creation (ST IaIIae 91, 1). No practical issues are being addressed and no such issue has even been raised. Only later does Aquinas make the further argument that human law is capable of binding in conscience (ST IaIIae 96, 4), and only much later does Aquinas provide a full account of obedience to authority, including political authority (ST IIaIIae 104–105). There is little reason to follow Bix and others in holding that Aquinas's theory of law is primarily a theory of the obligation to obey it.

To return, then, to the natural law theorist's central thesis, and Aquinas's defense of it. Why does Aquinas think that all law is a rational standard for conduct?

Law is a sort of rule and measure of acts, according to which one is induced to act or restrained from acting, for *lex* (law) is said to be from *ligare* (to bind) because *obligat* (it binds) one to act. But the rule and measure of human acts is reason, which is the first principle of human acts, ... for it belongs to reason to order things to the end, which is the first principle in practical matters, according to the Philosopher [that is, Aristotle]. However, that which is the principle of any given genus is the measure and rule of that genus, like unity in the genus of number and the first motion in the genus of motion. Hence it follows that law is something pertaining to reason. (ST IaIIae 90, 1)

Though this argument is couched in unfamiliar terms, its gist is, I think, plain enough. Aquinas's idea is that, no matter what else we think about law, we agree that it consists in rules, mandatory standards by which our conduct is to be assessed. Furthermore, the sort of assessment involved is essentially practical: the standard that law sets is a standard by which one is "induced to act or restrained from acting." But the only standards that can induce rational beings to act, *qua* rational beings, are rational standards. So law necessarily is a rational standard for conduct.

Aquinas's full, famous definition of law is that law "is nothing other than [1] an ordinance of reason [2] for the common good, [3] issued by one who has care of the community, and [4] promulgated" (ST IaIIae 90, 4). The latter three elements of this definition are subordinate to the first element, in that Aquinas employs the claim that law is an ordinance of reason to show that law is for the common good, issued by one who has care of the community, and promulgated. Why does Aquinas write that law must be for the common good? Because law is a rule not concerning an individual *qua* individual, but for the governance of *group* conduct; and just as what determines reasonable conduct of an individual is that individual's good, what determines reasonable conduct for members of a group is the common good of that group (ST IaIIae 90, 2). Why does Aquinas write that law can be made only by one who has care of the community? Because while anyone can make *suggestions* about how it is reasonable to order group conduct, only one who is charged with making such determinations can render an *authoritative* ruling on what is to be done, thereby setting the standard that members of that group must follow (ST IaIIae 90, 3). Why does Aquinas write that law must be promulgated? Because rational beings cannot act on a rational standard as such unless they have the means to become aware of the existence of the standard, its status as authoritative, and its content, and the promulgation of the rule provides for this awareness (ST IaIIae 90, 4). The essential character of both the nonpositive and the positive elements of law are explained through the master thesis that law is a rational standard for conduct (cf. Finnis 1996: 205).

Aquinas is aiming at descriptive adequacy in providing his theory of law. It is not a statement that, or of the conditions under which, people are obligated to obey the law, but an account of what law is: a rational standard. But it turns out that the *content* of this descriptively adequate statement of what law is entails that one must draw on one's normative views, whether theorized or not, in order to provide a fuller, more descriptively adequate account of law (cf. Finnis 1980: 16). From the fact that law necessarily is a rational standard for conduct it follows that (in some sense, to be explored further in the following section) a rule that cannot be a rational standard for conduct for beings like us cannot be law for beings like us. But which rules can be rational standards for conduct for beings like us is something that cannot be grasped without drawing on one's normative views.

Here is an analogy. Suppose that I attempt to build a "reason-backed rule" machine. When a person pulls the handle of the machine, the machine is supposed to display on its screen a rule, in the handle-puller's language, that the handle-puller has strong reason to comply with. Now, it is an accurate description of the machine to say that its function is to exhibit rules that those who operate it have strong reason to comply with. But if one is going to provide a fuller account of when the machine is functioning as it is designed to function and when it is not, one is going to have to draw on one's views, theorized or not, about what one has strong reasons to do. If you pull the handle on the machine and it displays "you should give one-third of your income to Oxfam," you will not be able to say whether the machine is functioning as designed unless you can say whether one in circumstances such as yours has reasons to make sacrifices of this sort.

The same holds true with law, on Aquinas's natural law view. In offering further claims on the nature of law, Aquinas draws upon a wide range of his normative beliefs, some already defended in the *Summa*, some later to be defended in the *Summa*, some undefended in the *Summa* but assumed in virtue of the context of the work. (The *Summa* is a teaching tool for those training for the religious life: Aquinas's intended primary audience consists of those who share his Christian commitments, some of which are normative commitments.) These normative beliefs concern, in part, what agents have reason to do. Aquinas relies on this stock of claims about reasons for action in defending more specific theses about what the essential features of law are.

Here is one example of how Aquinas draws on claims about reasons for action in drawing more specific conclusions about the nature of law. Aquinas holds that there is a "natural law," consisting of the fundamental principles of practical rationality, which govern all human conduct, individual and collective (ST IaIIae 91, 2; 94, 1–6). (It is important to keep in mind that there are natural law *moral* theories and natural law *legal* theories. The two are logically separable: one can affirm either one while rejecting the other. For a quick overview of natural law moral theory, see Murphy 2001: 1–3, and Murphy 2002.) All reasons for action are rooted in the natural law. Thus one of the conclusions that Aquinas can reach, given the abstract connection between human law and reasons for action previously established, is that all human law is rooted in the natural law (ST IaIIae 95, 2). This does not mean, Aquinas emphasizes, that all human law simply reproduces the contours of natural practical rationality (ST IaIIae 96, 2–3); while some of it does (for example, laws against murder, rape, etc.), some of it goes beyond the natural law by fixing, by making determinate, the vague requirements of the natural law (for example, "drive no more than 65 miles per hour" determines the vague "when driving, proceed at a reasonable speed") (ST IaIIae 95, 2).

So Aquinas is clear that the human law is not just a mirror that reflects in whole or in part the demands of the natural law. The view that the natural law theorist holds that φ-ing's being independently morally required is necessary for φ-ing's being legally required (or, even worse, necessary and sufficient for φ-ing's being legally required) is a common caricature of natural law theory, but Aquinas's emphasis on the way that human law can make determinate what the principles of practical rationality leaves indeterminate shows that he does not hold that view. Finnis has also responded to this caricature explicitly (see his 1980: 28), but it continues to be attributed to the natural law view. Consider, for example, the following argument from Jules Coleman and Brian Leiter:

> [According to natural law theory,] in order to be law, a norm must be required by morality. Morality has authority, in the sense that the fact that a norm is a requirement of morality gives agents a (perhaps overriding) reason to comply with it. If morality has authority, and legal norms are necessarily moral, then law has authority too. This argument for the authority of law, however, is actually fatal to it, because it makes law's authority redundant on morality's. . . . Natural law theory, then, fails to account for the authority of law. (Coleman and Leiter 1996: 244)

This argument assumes the premise that the natural law theorist claims that φ-ing's being independently morally required is necessary for φ-ing's being legally required. But Aquinas rejects this thesis, as does the natural law jurisprudential tradition generally.

Here is another example of how Aquinas draws on independent theses about reasons for action in drawing specific conclusions about law. Aquinas accepts as a matter of Christian moral orthodoxy, and later argues in philosophical/theological terms, that there are some moral absolutes, norms that it is unreasonable for one ever to violate (ST IIaIIae 33, 2). There can never be adequate reason to kill innocent persons (ST IIaIIae 64, 6), or to blaspheme (ST IIaIIae 13, 2). But it follows, given the connection between law and reasons for action, that a rule, promulgated by one who has care of the community, that requires one to kill the innocent or to blaspheme would fall outside the definition of law that Aquinas offers (ST IaIIae 96, 4).

Aquinas's natural law account of human law, influential as it has been in defining the natural law program, is marked by ambiguity and unclarity at its core. First off, how are we to understand the claim that law is a rational standard for conduct? Does it follow from this claim that – as many critics of natural law theory have supposed – wicked or unjust or otherwise unreasonable rules cannot be valid law? And if it does not follow from the natural law thesis that unreasonable rules cannot be valid law, what on earth does it mean to claim that, *necessarily*, law is a rational standard for conduct? Second: against Aquinas, it seems as if there are plenty of systems of rules that in some way apply to rational beings for which there does not exist an internal connection between those standards and reasons for action. Consider, for example, rules of games, or certain outdated codes of honor; it does not seem that it is essential to these systems of rules that there be sufficient reason for rational beings to comply with them. Why, then, should we think that this particular kind of system of rules, a legal system, exhibits this internal connection between law and reasons for action? Can we get an adequate account of the warrant for claiming that there is indeed this internal connection?

The Meaning of the Natural Law Thesis

How should we understand Aquinas's natural law thesis? In asking this question, I am not primarily asking how we ought to interpret Aquinas's texts, but rather what is the best way to formulate the connection between law and reasons for action that Aquinas and natural law theorists that followed him were impressed by.

The formula that we are to understand is: *necessarily, law is a rational standard for conduct*. The most straightforward understanding of this thesis – and the understanding that was fixed upon by critics of the natural law view in order to expose it as absurd – is an understanding on which *necessarily, law is a rational standard for conduct* is a proposition of the same form as *necessarily, a square has four and only four sides*. Just as a figure with five sides simply is not a square, this strong reading of the natural law thesis – I will henceforth call it the Strong Reading, or the Strong Natural Law Thesis – holds that a rule that is not a rational standard for conduct is no law at all. Legality is strictly limited by rationality: *lex sine rationem non est lex.*

Why do I formulate the Strong Reading as *lex sine rationem non est lex* (that is, law without [adequate] reason is no law at all) rather than as the better known natural law slogan, *lex iniusta non est lex* (an unjust law is no law at all)? The latter is sometimes attributed to Augustine, sometimes to Aquinas, but as Kretzmann notes, that precise formulation occurs in neither Augustine's nor Aquinas's work (Kretzmann 1988: 100–1). It continues to be common to formulate the natural law thesis in terms of a connection between law and justice, or between law and morality more generally. I have chosen to formulate the view in terms of the connection between law and reasons for action because it is clear that the tradition of the natural law theorizing connects law with practical rationality generally, and that same tradition has treated a failure with respect to justice as simply one way that a purported law can fail to be backed by decisive reasons for compliance. It is of course controversial to characterize injustice as simply a species of rational failure, but it is uncontroversial that this is how Aquinas saw it (ST IaIIae 58, 4), and it is because Aquinas saw unjust action as rationally defective action that he was willing to affirm claims very like "*lex iniusta non est lex.*"

The Strong Reading of the natural law thesis is the usual target of positivist criticism. As John Austin wrote,

> To say that human laws which conflict with the Divine law are not binding, that is to say, are not laws, is to talk stark nonsense. The most pernicious laws, and therefore those which are most opposed to the will of God, have been and are continually enforced as laws by judicial tribunals. (Austin [1832] 1995, Lecture V: 158)

Presumably Austin would say the same about the formulation of the natural law thesis under consideration here: to say that laws inadequately backed by reasons for compliance are not laws is to talk stark nonsense. Again, and much more recently, here is Brian Bix on the Strong Natural Law Thesis:

> The basic point is that the concept of "legal validity" is closely tied to what is recognized as binding in a given society and what the state enforces, and it seems fairly clear that there are plenty of societies where immoral laws are recognized as binding and enforced. Someone might answer that these immoral laws are not *really* legally valid, and the officials are making a mistake when they treat the rules as if they were legally valid. However, this is just to play games with words, and confusing games at that. "Legal validity" is the term we use to refer to *whatever* is conventionally recognized as binding; to say that all the officials could be wrong about what is legally valid is close to nonsense. (Bix 2002: 72–3)

Even self-labeled natural law theorists have endorsed objections of these sorts. John Finnis, whose work has clearly been at the forefront of the revival of natural law theory in the late twentieth century, has written that the Strong Reading is "pure nonsense, flatly self-contradictory" (Finnis 1980: 364); and Robert George has remarked that the fact that Aquinas was perfectly willing to talk about unjust laws shows that the paradigmatic natural law position does not affirm the Strong Reading, for to affirm the Strong Reading while being willing to refer to "unjust law" would be inconsistent (George 2000: 1641).

There are two distinguishable criticisms here. One of these is the "self-contradiction" criticism: the Strong Natural Law Thesis either is internally inconsistent or is inconsistent with other claims that natural law theorists are willing to affirm. The other is the "officials' say-so" criticism: the Strong Natural Law Thesis is inconsistent with the practice of legal officials. How serious are these criticisms for the Strong Reading?

The "self-contradiction" criticism is far from decisive. It need not be stark nonsense to affirm claims of the form "a ___ X is no X at all." David Lyons has noted that "counterfeit dollars are no dollars at all" is simply true (Lyons 1984: 62). One might also add that "glass diamonds are no diamonds at all" is simply true. The cases in which "a ___ X is no X at all" makes perfect sense are those in which the blank is filled with an *alienans*, a certain class of adjective (Geach 1956: 33–4). "Fake" is always an *alienans*: fake Rolexes are not Rolexes, fake dog doo is not dog doo, fake flowers are not flowers. "Counterfeit" is always an *alienans* as well. But there are some adjectives that count as instances of the *alienans* only with respect to particular nouns: while "glass" is obviously not always an *alienans* (glass sculptures are sculptures), it can be (glass diamonds are not diamonds). The strong natural law theorist can hold that "unable to serve as a rational standard" is, when applied to "law," an *alienans*, and thus avoid the charge that the Strong Reading is incoherent. (See also Kretzmann 1988.)

The "officials' say-so" objection is also far from decisive. Bix's claim is that since the consensus of legal officials is that there are laws that are inadequately backed by reasons for compliance, it would be flying in the face of the word of experts and indeed courting incoherence to assert the contrary. But it can hardly be a criterion for the truth of a legal theory that it make impossible divergence between official say-so and the implications of that theory. On Austin's general jurisprudence, every law is a command, issued by a sovereign and backed by a sanction (Austin [1832] 1995, Lecture I: 21). A sanction is a credible threat of harm to a subject attendant on a violation of the order (Austin [1832] 1995, Lecture I: 22). It follows from Austin's view that there is no law that is not backed by a sanction. But, possibly, all of the legal officials in some society might hold that some particular norm, a norm unbacked by a sanction, is law. If Austin's view is true, law without sanction is no law at all. Thus Austinian positivism violates Bix's constraint.

Even on a more sophisticated view like Hart's, Bix's constraint is violated. On Hart's general jurisprudence, whether something is law in a given society depends on whether it is recognized as such by the rule of recognition, the usually tremendously complex rule that guides legal officials in making, identifying, and applying law (Hart [1961] 1994: 94–5). It follows from Hart's view that there is no law that is not acknowledged as such by the rule of recognition. But, possibly, all of the legal officials in some society might hold that some particular norm, a norm not acknowledged by the rule of recogni-

tion, is law. (The rule of recognition might hold that if norm N was part of the originally adopted constitution, then it is law; but they might all hold a false view about whether norm N was part of the originally adopted constitution.) If Hart's view is true, law unacknowledged by the rule of recognition is no law at all. Thus Hartian positivism violates Bix's constraint.

Now, one might say that the *actual* (as opposed to the merely possible) practice of legal officials is not at odds with the Austinian or Hartian view. While I have extremely strong doubts about the former and strong doubts about the latter, we can note, first of all, that the actual convergence is not enough to rescue the incoherence claim: whether the view is incoherent cannot depend on contingent facts. The incoherence charge could be revised, even in the face of this sort of contingency, by holding that law is *conventional* and that therefore to deny that officials' say-so is dispositive is to assert an incoherent view. But that law is conventional is a substantial claim, indeed the substantial claim that the natural law theorist is concerned to deny (or, better, to qualify). While it is often hard to tell when a claim that a rebuttal is question-begging is warranted, this would seem to be one of those warranted cases: any appeal to the status of law as conventional to rescue the claim that the officials' say-so argument is decisive would beg the question against the natural law theorist. One can, of course, still make the point that the say-so of legal officials is not to be gainsaid in a theory of law. But that is a much weaker point, as much weaker as an appeal to authority is weaker than a *reductio ad absurdum*.

Suppose though, that one continues to be suspicious of the Strong Reading of the natural law thesis, noting that officials' say-so seems to run contrary to the view. What alternative formulations of the view are available? One alternative is that suggested by those who would hold that the primary concern of Aquinas in the Treatise on Law is to provide an account of political obligation: on this view, the claim that law is necessarily a rational standard is a disguised normative claim. On this formulation, what we may call the Moral Reading of the natural law thesis, the natural law theorist's central thesis is just a dramatic way of saying that one ought to obey the law only when it is adequately reasonable. As George proposes,

"What is being asserted by natural law theorists [is]...that the moral obligatoriness which may attach to positive law is *conditional* in nature" (George 1996: viii). All that the natural law theorist wants to do in affirming a connection between law and reasons is to issue a reminder that adherence to some laws would constitute such a departure from reasonableness that there could not be adequate reason to obey them; the only law that merits our obedience is law that meets a certain minimum standard of reasonableness. Whatever the intrinsic merits of this claim, I will immediately put it to the side as a candidate formulation of the natural law thesis. If the Moral Reading were all there is to the natural law thesis, the natural law theorist would have almost no one to disagree with in the entire history of philosophy. And whatever other desiderata a formulation of the natural law thesis must satisfy, a candidate formulation must be one that preserves the status of natural law theory as a contentious position.

There is, however, a contentious natural law position that is nevertheless not prone to some of the initial deep misgivings to which the strong formulation is prone. Recall that the strong formulation is to be understood in such a way that *necessarily, law is a rational standard for conduct* is a proposition of the same form as *necessarily, squares have four and only four sides.* A weaker but still interesting version of the natural law thesis – call it the Weak Reading, or the Weak Natural Law Thesis – affirms that *necessarily, law is a rational standard* while holding that it is not of the same form as *necessarily, squares have four and only four sides*; rather, it is of the same form as *necessarily, cheetahs are fast runners.* A figure with only three sides is no square at all; but it is not true that an animal that is not a fast runner cannot be a cheetah. Rather, an animal that is not a fast runner *either* is not a cheetah *or* is a defective cheetah. The necessity attaches to the *kind* cheetah rather than to *individual* cheetahs: while one might fail to be a fast runner while remaining a cheetah, belonging to the kind *cheetah* sets a standard such that those that are not fast runners fall short as cheetahs (cf. Thompson 1995 and Foot 2001: 30; Robert Alexy makes such a distinction, which he labels a distinction between "classificatory" and "qualificatory" connections between properties and kind-membership, and employs it

with respect to theories of law in Alexy 1998: 214 and 1999: 24–5).

This seems to be the approach taken by John Finnis, the most influential contemporary defender of natural law theory. Finnis roundly rejects the natural law thesis in its stronger formulation, labeling the Strong Reading paradoxical and inconsistent and incoherent and self-contradictory (Finnis 1980: 364–5). But he affirms the Weak Reading. According to Finnis, regardless of whether one is inclined to take a natural law view in jurisprudence, it is a mistake to look for necessary and sufficient conditions for legality (Finnis 1980: 6, 9–11). Rather, we ought to proceed by looking for the conditions that define the central, paradigmatic case of legality (Finnis 1980: 9–11). On Finnis's view, the paradigmatic case of legality is the rule or norm that is not only socially grounded but also grounded in a correct understanding of what reasons for action agents have. While there may be laws that are unreasonable for agents to follow, Finnis allows, these laws are laws only in a secondary, derivative, incomplete sense. Their status as laws is parasitic on the primary, fundamental, complete sense of law, that notion of law on which laws bind rational agents to compliance (Finnis 1980: 14). (I say more on Finnis's argument for this view in the final section below.)

It might be supposed that the Weak Reading of the natural law thesis just is the Moral Reading that I set to the side as trivial. If this were the case, it would surely be damaging to defenders of the Weak Reading. But these readings are not identical. The defender of the Weak Reading wants to make a claim about what counts as a *defect* in law – and the conditions under which some objectionable (or even otherwise unobjectionable) aspect of a thing counts as a defect in it are very specific, tied to the kind of thing at stake. It is, after all, a commonplace that a feature of some object can be objectionable without that feature's being a defect in that thing. The flourishing of the rodent in my attic is objectionable, all right, but I wouldn't presume to claim that its flourishing makes that rodent defective. Similarly, all the defender of the Moral Reading can say is that there is some way in which unreasonable laws are objectionable; the Moral Reading of the natural law thesis does not itself make the further claim that law that is not rationally binding is defective as law. Thus the defender of the Weak Reading has an extra argumentative burden, that of showing that law is the kind of thing that is backed by decisive reasons, so that an individual law unbacked by decisive reasons is substandard.

We should also note that while the distinction between the Strong and Weak Natural Law Theses – between a view on which reasons for action are connected to the legal validity of a norm, and a view on which those reasons are connected to legal nondefectiveness – is very important, and thus the distinction that I will focus on for the remainder of this chapter, it is not the only relevant distinction one could make. One could distinguish among natural law theories on the basis of the strength or sort of reasons for action to which legal validity or legal nondefectiveness is allegedly connected. For example: while I have focused on how we ought to understand claims like *lex sine rationem non est lex* – does it mean that unreasonable laws really lack validity, or does it mean that while such can be legally valid, they are in some way defective as law or perversions of law? – one might also focus on the *nature* and *extent* of the departure from reasonableness involved. Assuming for a moment the Strong Reading, one might ask, that is, whether *any* unreasonableness in law is sufficient to undermine legal validity, or whether perhaps the unreasonableness must reach some *extreme* pitch before legal validity is precluded. Thus, for example, Gustav Radbruch's famous formula is about legal validity but kicks in only in cases of severe injustice: on Radbruch's view, enactments the injustice of which are at "an intolerable level" have "no claim at all to legal status" (Radbruch 1946, cited in Alexy 1999: 16; see also CONTINENTAL PERSPECTIVES ON NATURAL LAW THEORY AND LEGAL POSITIVISM). He would surely have said, though, that any level of injustice in law makes it legally defective, even if not necessarily legally invalid.

Natural Law Theory and Legal Positivism

Legal positivism has defined itself by setting itself in contrast with natural law theory. This is as true of Austin's and Bentham's positivist views as it is of Hart's and Raz's. But we have seen that the natural law view – like the positivist view – admits of a variety of formulations. To what extent is the opposition between natural law theory and legal positivism a real opposition?

Suppose that we take as the generic legal positivist thesis the view that the status of some social rule as law is logically and metaphysically independent of the status of that social rule as a rational standard of conduct. This is close to what Austin had in mind when he delivered his pathbreaking lectures on jurisprudence: "The existence of law is one thing; its merit or demerit is another" (Austin [1832] 1995, Lecture V: 157). It is close to the thesis that Hart defends, in contrast to the natural law position, in "Positivism and the Separation of Law and Morals": "In the absence of an expressed constitutional or legal provision, it could not follow from the mere fact that a rule violated standards of morality that it was not a rule of law" (Hart [1958] 1983: 55). It is close to Coleman's *Separation Thesis*, which on his view defines the positivist outlook: "There exists at least one conceivable rule of recognition (and therefore one possible legal system) that does not specify truth as a moral principle among the truth conditions for any proposition of law" (Coleman 1982: 141). It is, with proper qualifications, entailed by Raz's *Sources Thesis*: "A jurisprudential theory is acceptable only if its tests for identifying the content of the law and determining its existence depend exclusively on facts of human behaviour capable of being described in value-neutral terms, and applied without recourse to moral argument" (Raz 1979d: 39–40).

If we take this to be the generic positivist position, it is obvious that there is no incompatibility between the Moral Reading of the natural law thesis and the positivist standpoint. The positivists, after all, were concerned to defend their position on the nature of law not merely for the sake of conceptual clarity but also for reasons of moral psychology: by demystifying law, one will be less likely to obey simply because it is the law and more likely to obey only when there is adequate reason to do so. (For a critique of this line of argument for positivism, see Soper 1987.) This is entirely consistent with, and even complementary to, the Moral Reading's insistence that law is to be obeyed only when it falls within the domain of the reasonable. (As I mentioned above, it is the overwhelming plausibility of the Moral Reading that is its undoing: it is so plausible it is uninteresting and nondistinctive.) On the other hand, the Strong Reading of the natural law thesis is just as clearly incompatible with generic positivism. For the positivist wants at least to take a stand on legal validity: social rules can be legally valid though there be far from adequate reason to comply with them. Austin and Bentham took as their primary targets Blackstone's seeming affirmation of the Strong Natural Law Thesis, and it is the seeming affirmation of versions of the Strong Natural Law Thesis by Radbruch and by Fuller that Hart took as his primary target. So the strongest version of natural law theory is necessarily at odds with positivist views.

With respect to the Weak Reading, matters are less clear. One is tempted to say that the Weak Natural Law Thesis, according to which any law either is an adequate rational standard for conduct or is defective, is entirely compatible with the positivist thesis. For the Weak Reading does not deny that there can be valid law that only an unreasonable person would comply with. It says only that, be it valid, it nevertheless falls short of some standard internality to legality. This is a view endorsed both by Finnis and by MacCormick (who describes himself as a positivist; MacCormick 1992: 108). But while positivists have been willing to allow that their views require them to employ evaluative judgments in providing their theory of law (for example, judgments about what phenomena are more important than others in the categorization of human institutions), some may be less sanguine about the notion that the provision of an adequate theory of law requires one to take a stand on highly disputable and disputed questions of practical reasonableness. Thus the Weak Natural Law Thesis might well be taken to be a departure from the positivist program, even if it is compatible with the most influential formulations – for example, Austin's, Bentham's, Hart's, Raz's, and Coleman's – of first-order positivist theses.

Defending the Natural Law Thesis

On the basis of what sorts of arguments can the natural law view be defended? I will put to the side the Moral Reading of the natural law thesis: it is too uninteresting and uncontroversial to bother with. It is the Strong and Weak Readings, both of which aim to provide an account of the nature of law, that are of interest here. I will proceed by pursuing two argumentative strategies: the 'legal point of view' argument, initially defended by Finnis in his 1980 *Natural Law and Natural Rights* and continually reaffirmed by him since then, and the "function" argument, defended (with reservations) by Michael Moore in a couple of recent papers.

Finnis's argument for the natural law thesis is inspired by Hart's methodology in *The Concept of Law* (see LEGAL POSITIVISM). We should not, Finnis writes, hope to provide an account of the necessary and sufficient conditions for law, such that some legal systems and individual norms and decisions in cases will count as law through exemplifying these conditions, whereas the remainder will not. Rather, we should hope for an account that provides us with the central, paradigm instances of law and legality. With this account, we will be able to classify some social systems and social norms as clearly law, some as entirely extra-legal, and some as simply falling short of or distinct from the central case in one or another specific way.

So the task of the legal theorist is to provide the central case of law. But centrality is an evaluative notion, and this particular evaluative notion is always from a point of view. The question, then, is whether there is a point of view that is *privileged* within legal theory. Again Finnis, following Hart, holds that there is such a privileged point of view: it is the point of view of those who take the internal point of view with respect to a legal system. People who take the internal point of view with respect to a legal system are those who take its rules as such to be a guide to their conduct. Hart emphasizes that he does not mean to privilege any particular motivation or rationale for taking the internal point of view: those that treat the law as a standard for conduct based on moral considerations and those that treat it as such based on "calculations of long-term interest" or "disinterested interest in others" or "an unreflecting inherited or traditional attitude" or "the mere wish to do as others do" all equally take the internal point of view (Hart [1961] 1994: 203). But Finnis argues that the internal point of view, as characterized by Hart, is not sufficiently differentiated for analytical purposes. The argument is by elimination: none of these species of the internal point of view, save the point of view of the person who obeys the law because it is a matter of moral requirement, can be the privileged legal point of view, for "All these considerations and attitudes are manifestly deviant, diluted or watered-down instances of the practical viewpoint that brings law into being as a significantly differentiated type of social order and maintains it as such" (Finnis 1980: 14). The central legal viewpoint is that in which legal systems are seen as morally worthy, worth bringing about and preserving, and in which the demands of law are justified and binding; and indeed the clearest case of this central viewpoint is that of the person whose moral judgment is correct (Finnis 1980: 15–16). Given this most privileged point of view, it is clear that law in its central or "focal" meaning will be law that is a rational standard for conduct.

This strategy is meant only to establish the Weak Natural Law Thesis, and it is obvious that it can establish no more than that: its appeal to the central, paradigmatic notion of law is not meant to preclude the presence of a limited, technical sense of legal validity, a sense explicable without reference to moral or practical considerations. But it is hard to see why we would follow Finnis even this far in his extension of Hart's methodology on the basis of this argument. Hart has good reason for taking the burden of proof to be on those who wish to make some particular version of the internal point of view more privileged. For while his arguments against the legal realists show that legal theory must account for the datum that people can take the internal point of view with respect to a system of legal norms (Hart [1961] 1994: 88–91), this datum just is that people treat the existence of legal rules as reasons or constituent parts of reasons for action.

The datum does not, however, extend further to the *basis* on which they so treat those norms. Far from the internal point of view just being an "amalgam" of different viewpoints, Hart's undifferentiated take has a clear rationale, and so is not unstable; it is up to Finnis to destabilize it. But nothing he says in the crucial stretch of argument discussed above succeeds in destabilizing it. The law tends not to care a whit for the motivations that one has for complying with it; and while Finnis appeals to the great efficacy of some points of view in generating a legal system, one might rightly retort both that the tasks of explaining how a legal system comes into being and explaining what it is for a legal system to be in place are, while interestingly related, different questions and that there are some points of view that may have greater efficacy in generating and sustaining a legal system than that of the person of full practical reasonableness – for example, that of the person who holds a false tribal or nationalistic morality.

By so closely identifying the task of characterizing law with the task of saying what a fully practical reasonable person should be interested in when dealing with the law, Finnis's view seems to become simply applied ethics – he is asking what features of the law the fully reasonable citizen, or the fully reasonable judge, should be interested in responding to, and in particular what features of the law are such, when present, for the fully reasonable citizen or judge to treat the law as authoritative. But this seems to make Finnis's view too much like the uninteresting Moral Reading, leaving his critics to wonder what all the fuss was about natural law theory (Bix 1996: 226).

A more promising line of argument, to my mind, takes as its starting point the common notion of *function*. According to this line of argument, once we see that some legal systems or individual legal norms have functions, and see what those functions are, we should recognize that those systems and norms have nondefectiveness conditions that include the presence of reasons for action. One might worry that this sort of argument for the natural law thesis is doomed to triviality: what could be easier, one might ask, than to assign a morally charged function to law, and then, on the basis of such an ascription, hold that law that does not perform this function, or perform it satisfactorily, is either no law at all or is law only defectively? It is obvious that no interesting argument for the natural law thesis that proceeds from the idea that the law has a function can follow this pattern. But the ascription of a function to an object is a much more constrained matter than such an argument would suggest. I cannot simply assign the function "keeping New Haven populated" to law professors, and then declare that law school faculty that do not reside in New Haven are no law professors at all, or are law professors only defectively. What *are* the conditions that must be met to ascribe a function to some object or institution, and how can these be brought to bear to show that one or another formulation of the natural law thesis is correct?

Roughly, and not at all originally, and not entirely uncontroversially, we can say that for an object or institution x to have the function of φ-ing, the following conditions must be satisfied:

(*characteristic activity*) x is the kind of thing that φ-s
(*goal productivity*) x's φ-ing tends to bring about some end-state S
(*teleology*) x φ-s because x's φ-ing tends to bring about some end-state S
(*value*) S exhibits some relevant variety of goodness.

There is reason to think that each of these conditions is individually necessary; and there is reason to think that they are jointly sufficient. A heart has a characteristic activity: it pumps. Its pumping tends to bring about the circulation of the blood; and, indeed, the heart pumps because its pumping contributes to the circulation of the blood. (This is so in two ways: in animals with hearts there is a feedback loop such that the circulation of the blood is in part what causes the heart to be able to continue pumping; and the very structure and activity of the heart was selected because of efficiency in causing the circulation of the blood.) Some would take these first three conditions to be jointly sufficient, but it seems to me that it is also important that the circulation of the blood is beneficial for the animal. As Mark Bedau has noted, a stick pinned

against a rock in a stream by the backwash that very stick has created may exhibit the first three features: it is pinned against a rock, its being pinned against a rock causes the backwash, and it is pinned against the rock because its being pinned against the rock causes the backwash. But no one would be tempted by the view that it is the stick's function to be pinned against the rock (Bedau 1992: 786). One way to accommodate such cases is to emphasize that functions are ascribed when there is, in some sense, a good realized through the activity: either an end sought out by the designer of the object, or simply the self-maintenance of the thing in question, or the like.

To show, then, that the natural law thesis is true in virtue of the law's function (or one of the law's functions) one needs to show that these various conditions are satisfied, and that a particular legal system or law fails to perform its function when it fails to serve as a rational standard for conduct. An instance of this strategy is the argument offered by Moore. Moore suggests that the essence of law might reside in its function rather than in any distinctive set of structures. To find out what law's function is, we look at the sorts of cases that we pretheoretically label instances of legal systems and laws, and try to identify some distinctive good that they serve; we can then use that tentative identification of a distinctive end served by law to identify other instances of laws and legal systems. If it turns out that there is some good distinctively served by law, and that law can serve this good only if those under that law are practically required to comply with it, then we have reason for thinking that the natural law thesis is true. Indeed, Moore suggests that this argument, if successful, would be sufficient to establish the Strong Natural Law Thesis (see Moore 1992, 2001).

Moore worries about whether there is any distinctive end that law serves: he doubts that there is any such distinctive end – though he notes some candidates, such as John Finnis's notion of the common good – and thinks that if there is no such distinctive end, then we must give up on the idea that law is to be understood in terms of its function. But this is too hasty. For recall that the ascription of a function to some thing brings into play not just the goal brought about by the thing's activity (S) but the characteristic activity of that thing (φ-ing). So even if law does not serve an end that is distinctive to it – and how could it, given that all of the goods that we take to be served by law can be served better-or-worse by extralegal institutions? – it might be distinctive at least in part through the characteristic activity that it employs to serve those ends. And it might turn out that the (or a) characteristic activity of the law makes it the case that law that fails to serve as a rational standard for conduct does not perform its characteristic activity well and is therefore defective or perhaps even not law at all.

One might, for example, simply argue *directly* that one of law's characteristic activities is to provide dictates with which the agents to whom the dictates are addressed have decisive reason to comply. One might note the features of legal systems to which Raz has drawn our attention, that is, that they claim to be authoritative (see Raz 1979b: 30) and that, characteristically, their dictates go with the flow of normative reasons rather than against them (Raz 1985, 1986: 53-69). One might further note the way that law characteristically ties sanctions to certain activities in order to give agents further reason to abstain from them. One might also take notice of Fuller's eight ways to fail to make law: on his view, putative legal rules can fail to achieve legality when they are *ad hoc*, inadequately promulgated, retroactive, incomprehensible, contradictory, or require conduct adherence to which is beyond the powers of subjects, or are ephemeral, or insincere (see Fuller 1964: 39). For our purposes, what is relevant about Fuller's eight ways is that each of them indicates some way in which law can fail to serve as a reason for action for those living under it. On the basis of such considerations, one might well come to the conclusion that it is part of law's characteristic activity to lay down norms with which agents will have sufficient reason to comply. Even, then, if the end that law's characteristic activity serves is itself not an obviously obligatory end – if it is, to follow Hart and Fuller, something like that of realizing social order, or social control – the natural law thesis could be sustained if law's characteristic activity is to provide dictates that are rational standards for conduct and that it provides these dictates as a means to, and because they are a means to, realizing social order.

Now, one might retort: it can hardly be that it is law's characteristic activity to provide dictates that are rational standards for conduct, when it is clear that so many dictates of law are no such thing. To take the low road, we can appeal to cases as dramatic as the Fugitive Slave Law or as banal as parking ordinances. To take the high road, we can appeal to the growing literature in support of the claim that the law lacks authority, that its dictates do not in fact typically constitute decisive reasons for agents to comply with them. (This literature is large and growing. Influential pieces include Simmons 1979; Raz 1979c; Smith 1973; and Green 1990. The literature has been surveyed in Edmundson 1999a and 1999b, and will be again in Edmundson forthcoming.)

The initial response here is just that to say that φ-ing is X's characteristic activity is not to say that all Xs always φ. It is to say that Xs are the kind of thing that φ, and this is compatible with there being instances – even perhaps in the majority of cases – where Xs fail to φ. (Up until relatively recently the activities of the medical profession probably did more to undermine health than to promote it. That does not entail that the characteristic activity of physicians, up until relatively recently, was the undermining of their patients' health.) But the retort does raise an important question, which is: how do we know that these cases in which law fails to provide dictates that are backed by decisive reasons for action count not as counterexamples to the claim that this is law's characteristic activity but rather as cases in which law is failing to perform its characteristic activity?

With artifacts, often the answer is easy: our source of information about what kind an object belongs to, and what is the characteristic activity of that kind, is determined at least in large part by the maker's intentions. But with law, as with other large-scale social institutions, we have something that is not the product of some thinker's intentions. Here the more apt analogies are the systems of organisms. We know that a heart's characteristic activity is to pump blood, and that this is its function; and we can know this without appeal to a designer's intentions. We can know this in spite of the fact that animals can have heart attacks. We say that the heart's characteristic activity is to pump blood not just because of statistical frequency – again, we can imagine states of affairs in which heart attacks were disastrously more frequent, and this would give us reason to say that hearts were malfunctioning all over the place, not that its characteristic activity had changed or that we were wrong about what its characteristic activity is. We persist in the judgment that the characteristic activity is pumping blood because judgments of characteristic activity are made against a background, a privileged background of normalcy. An object's departure from its characteristic activity is to be accounted for through appeal to a change in the normal background.

To sustain the claim that law's characteristic activity is to provide dictates with which agents have decisive reason to comply – even in the face of divergences of this activity – we have to say that in such cases the privileged background for the description of institutions like the law does not obtain, and that departures from the activity of providing dictates that agents have decisive reason to comply with is to be explained by reference to the departure from this background. Here is the crucial move: the background from which human institutions are to be assessed, so far as possible, is one in which humans are properly functioning. But human beings are rational animals, and when properly functioning act on what the relevant reasons require. And so law would not be able to realize the end of order by giving dictates in a world in which humans are properly functioning unless those dictates were backed by adequate reasons. Thus we should say that it is law's characteristic activity to provide dictates backed by compelling reasons for action, and that law that fails to do so is defective as law.

To accept this understanding of the function of law is to affirm the Weak Reading of the natural law thesis. It does not, I think, give anyone reason to affirm the Strong Reading. Objects with functions can badly malfunction without ceasing to exist: whether an object that essentially bears some function exists depends on its structure and origin, not on its continued capacity to perform its characteristic activity. So just as a malfunctioning heart is a heart, a law that is not a rational standard can still be law. The "function of law" argument should aim no higher than the Weak Natural Law Thesis.

Note

1 Cited as ST with part, question, and article number.

References

Alexy, Robert. 1998. Law and correctness. In Michael Freeman (ed.), *Current Legal Problems 1998: Legal Theory at the End of the Millennium*. Oxford: Oxford University Press, 205–22.

Alexy, Robert. 1999. A defense of Radbruch's formula. In David Dyzenhaus (ed.), *Recrafting the Rule of Law*. Oxford: Hart Publishing, 16–39.

Austin, John. [1832] 1995. *Province of Jurisprudence Determined*, ed. Wilfrid Rumble. Cambridge, UK and New York: Cambridge University Press.

Bedau, Mark. 1992. Where's the good in teleology? *Philosophy and Phenomenological Research* 52: 781–806.

Bix, Brian. 1996. Natural law theory. In Dennis Patterson (ed.), *A Companion to Philosophy of Law and Legal Theory*. Oxford: Blackwell, 223–40.

Bix, Brian. 2002. Natural law theory: The modern tradition. In Jules Coleman and Scott Shapiro (eds.), *Oxford Handbook of Jurisprudence and Philosophy of Law*. Oxford: Oxford University Press, 61–103.

Coleman, Jules. 1982. Negative and positive positivism. *Journal of Legal Studies* 11: 139–64.

Coleman, Jules and Leiter, Brian. 1996. Legal positivism. In Dennis Patterson (ed.), *A Companion to Philosophy of Law and Legal Theory*. Oxford: Blackwell, 241–60.

Edmundson, William. 1999a. Introduction. In William Edmundson (ed.), *The Duty to Obey the Law: Selected Philosophical Readings*. Lanham, MD: Rowman and Littlefield, 1–15.

Edmundson, William. 1999b. Introduction: Some recent work on political obligation. *APA Newsletter on Law and Philosophy* 99: 62–67.

Edmundson, William. Forthcoming. Political obligation. *Legal Theory*.

Finnis, John. 1980. *Natural Law and Natural Rights*. Oxford: Oxford University Press.

Finnis, John. 1996. The truth in legal positivism. In Robert P. George (ed.), *The Autonomy of Law*. Oxford: Oxford University Press, 195–214.

Foot, Philippa. 2001. *Natural Goodness*. Oxford: Oxford University Press.

Fuller, Lon. 1964. *The Morality of Law*. New Haven, CT: Yale University Press.

Geach, Peter. 1956. Good and evil. *Analysis* 17, 33–42.

George, Robert P. 1996. Preface. In Robert P. George (ed.), *The Autonomy of Law*. Oxford: Oxford University Press, vii–viii.

George, Robert P. 2000. Kelsen and Aquinas on "the natural-law doctrine." *Notre Dame Law Review* 75: 1625–46.

Green, Leslie. 1990. *The Authority of the State*. Oxford: Oxford University Press.

Hart, H. L. A. [1958] 1983. Positivism and the separation of law and morals. In H. L. A. Hart, *Essays in Jurisprudence and Philosophy*. Oxford: Oxford University Press, 49–87.

Hart, H. L. A. [1961] 1994. *The Concept of Law*, 2nd edn. Oxford: Oxford University Press.

Kretzmann, Norman. 1988. *Lex iniusta non est lex*: Laws on trial in Aquinas' court of conscience. *American Journal of Jurisprudence* 33: 99–122.

Lyons, David. 1984. *Ethics and the Rule of Law*. Cambridge, UK and New York: Cambridge University Press.

MacCormick, Neil. 1992. Natural law and the separation of law and morals. In Robert P. George (ed.), *Natural Law Theory: Contemporary Essays*. Oxford: Oxford University Press, 105–33.

Moore, Michael. 1992. Law as a functional kind. In Robert P. George (ed.), *Natural Law Theory: Contemporary Essays*. Oxford: Oxford University Press, 188–242.

Moore, Michael. 2001. Law as justice. *Social Philosophy and Policy* 18: 115–45.

Murphy, Mark C. 2001. *Natural Law and Practical Rationality*. Cambridge, UK and New York: Cambridge University Press.

Murphy, Mark C. 2002. The natural law tradition in ethics. *The Stanford Encyclopedia of Philosophy*, ed. Edward N. Zalta. <http://plato.stanford.edu/archives/win2002/entries/natural-law-ethics/>.

Radbruch, Gustav. 1946. Gesetzliches Unrecht und übergesetzliches Recht. In Gustav Radbruch, *Rechtsphilosophie*, 8th edn., ed. Erik Wolf and Hans-Peter Schneider. Stuttgart: Koehler, 339–50.

Raz, Joseph. 1979a. *The Authority of Law*. Oxford: Oxford University Press.

Raz, Joseph. 1979b. The claims of law. In Joseph Raz, *The Authority of Law*. Oxford: Oxford University Press, 28–33.

Raz, Joseph. 1979c. The obligation to obey the law. In Joseph Raz, *The Authority of Law*. Oxford: Oxford University Press, 233–49.

Raz, Joseph. 1979d. The social thesis. In Joseph Raz, *The Authority of Law*. Oxford: Oxford University Press, 37–52.

Raz, Joseph. 1985. Authority, law, and morality. *Monist* 68: 295–324.

Raz, Joseph. 1986. *The Morality of Freedom*. Oxford: Oxford University Press.

Simmons, A. John. 1979. *Moral Principles and Political Obligations*. Princeton, NJ: Princeton University Press.

Smith, M. B. E. 1973. Is there a prima facie obligation to obey the law? *Yale Law Journal* 82: 950–76.

Soper, Philip. 1983. Legal theory and the problem of definition. *University of Chicago Law Review* 50: 1170–200.

Soper, Philip. 1987. Choosing a legal theory on moral grounds. *Social Philosophy and Policy* 4: 31–48.

Thompson, Michael. 1995. The representation of life. In Rosalind Hursthouse, Gavin Lawrence, and Warren Quinn (eds.), *Virtues and Reasons*. Oxford: Oxford University Press, 247–96.

Chapter 2

Legal Positivism

Brian H. Bix

History and Context

The history of ideas is often written in terms of
schools of thought, that come in and out of fashion, that prevail in struggles over particular issues,
or are defeated. In legal philosophy, as elsewhere
in the history of ideas, we have schools of thought
that have risen and fallen, sometimes with little
explanation. Some have faded from the scene but
without any obvious reason – such as historical
jurisprudence (whose prominent advocates included Friedrich Carl von Savigny (1779–1861)
and Sir Henry Maine (1822–88)). As Joseph Raz
has written: "Because legal theory attempts to
capture the essential features of law, as encapsulated in the self-understanding of a culture, it has
a built-in obsolescence, since the self-understanding of cultures is forever changing" (Raz 1996:
6). While some schools of thought have faded in a
matter of decades, by contrast at least one approach to legal theory, natural law theory, has
been around literally for millennia, yet remains
vibrant. See NATURAL LAW THEORY. Legal positivism is neither thousands of years old nor the
product of recent fashion. As a recognizable approach to the nature of law, legal positivism is
almost two centuries old, though aspects of the
approach can be traced back further, certainly to
Thomas Hobbes (1588–1679), and perhaps even
to Thomas Aquinas (c.1225–1274) (Finnis 1994:
195–200). While in some circles, legal positivism
now seems the dominant approach to the nature
of law, this dominance has never meant that the
approach was without critics. This chapter will

outline the current state of legal positivism, consider major criticisms, and reflect on what may be
necessary for this approach to remain a vibrant
part of the debate about the nature of law.

There is a danger whenever one speaks about a
"school" or "general approach," and the danger
may be particularly acute with discussions of legal
positivism. The risk arises from the effort to speak
in general terms about a wide variety of theorists,
whose views overlap but may diverge sharply on
any particular question. As will be mentioned
later, some quite distinct approaches to law
share the label "legal positivism," and any effort
to create a quick summary representation of the
approach faces the chance of constructing a
weakened perspective and one that no single theorist would adopt in full (Raz 1998: 1). Nonetheless, an effort will be made to speak about this
collection of theories and theorists, making all
efforts to be respectful of the differences between
the theorists that share this label.

The first task is to place legal positivism into a
historical context: one that refers both to its own
history of development, and to the larger history
of ideas within which it evolved. The usual summary of legal positivism comes from a few lines
stated in 1832 by John Austin (1790–1859), the
person frequently seen as the founder of legal
positivism:

> The existence of law is one thing; its merit or
> demerit is another. Whether it be or not be is one
> enquiry; whether it be or be not conformable to
> an assumed standard, is a different enquiry.
> A law, which actually exists, is a law, though we

happen to dislike it, or though it vary from the text, by which we regulate our approbation and disapprobation. (Austin [1832] 1994: 157)

If one looks at Austin's work – and, similarly, if one prefers to trace the roots of legal positivism to the early writings of Jeremy Bentham (1748–1832) (Bentham 1970; Bentham [1789] 1996) or the work of the English political theorist Thomas Hobbes (Hobbes [1651] 1996) – then the purpose of proposing a legal positivist position seems straightforward: it is an effort to establish a study of the nature of law, disentangled from proposals and prescriptions for which laws should be passed or how legal practice should be maintained or reformed.

One might push a little further, and discuss how Austin ([1879] 2002, vol. 2: 1107–8), and, some decades later, Hans Kelsen (1881–1973), emphasized the objective of making law into a "science" (though, as regards Kelsen's work, it should be noted that *Wissenschaft* in German has a much broader extension, and fewer implications, than "science" in English). Kelsen was reacting against sociologists of law; he sought a way of studying law "as such," purified of history, social theory, and so forth (Kelsen [1934] 1992: 7–8). Kelsen was thereby taking the concerns of Austin and Bentham a step further: to exclude not only practical and theoretical disquisitions about how governments should be organized, but also to exclude more academic discussions about the history or sociology of the law, and the like. These were times when there was great optimism that the same sort of rigor and objectivity could be applied to the study of human behavior that had been applied to the physical sciences, and that perhaps the same level of progress could be made. While this sort of optimistic "delusion" about the human sciences is at least as old as the Enlightenment (e.g., Berlin 1997: 326–58), a similar sort of optimism has dominated thinking about law at various more recent periods – not only in Christopher Columbus Langdell's (1826–1906) quasi-scientific thinking about law and legal education that notoriously grounded his new "case method" at the end of the nineteenth century and the beginning of the twentieth century (see Twining 1985: 11–12), but also in the writings of American legal realists (and the post-

realists) of the early and middle decades of the twentieth century, when these writers offered "policy science" as the way to make law "modern" and "objective." See AMERICAN LEGAL REALISM.

We may treat such views as naïve, or at least misguided; we may think that it only tends to hide or disguise the political aspects of law and the inevitable biases of its commentators to use a term like "science" which (in English at least) implies a level of objectivity and disinterestedness that we are unlikely to attain in the study of how societies regulate their citizens through rules and institutions. However, if we consider the search for a "science" of law at a more general or more metaphorical level, the objective is simply a *separate study* of law – a study in the "scientific spirit" of independent observation and analysis, separate from the important, but quite different, striving for legal reform and justice. And, so understood, the objective seems neither misguided nor naïve – though it may yet turn out to be unobtainable.

There seems less significance (and less urgency) today than there was two hundred years ago to an argument urging the separate study of "law as it is." We are living at a time where we are surrounded by law schools – almost certainly too many rather than too few – devoted to the graduate-level study of law and legal practice, and journals devoted to every aspect of law and every conceivable approach to its investigation. It should be remembered that things were much different as recently as two hundred years ago (around the time when legal positivism had its beginnings) – a time when there was little university-based legal education, either in the United States or in England. The first time a law school appeared as a professional school within an American university was in 1817 (at Harvard University). Prior to that date, law schools were largely proprietary institutions, set up independent of university education – though there was a *professorship* in law somewhat earlier, at the College of William and Mary in 1779 (Warren 1908, vol. 1: 1). In England, the first university instruction in the common law came as late as 1753, with Sir William Blackstone's Oxford University lectures (Holdsworth 1903–38, vol. 12: 91); the first Chair in Law outside of Oxford and Cambridge was given to John Austin at University

College London in 1826, and it was Austin's lectures there that would eventually form the foundation of modern legal positivism. (In looking at the contemporary situation, one could comment that though there are now many institutions, academics, and journals devoted to law, there are arguably few signs of a "pure science of law" or a study of law "as it is" separated sharply from "law as it ought to be." However, that is a topic for another day.)

If legal positivism is not about the importance of the separate and "scientific" study of law, or at least not about that *today*, one might wonder what its purpose and meaning is. One suspects that legal positivism's distinctiveness and its point have become more elusive, even as it has become more established within English-language analytical jurisprudence – perhaps *because* it has become more established in analytical jurisprudence. Maybe "we are all legal positivists now" much the way "we are all legal realists now" – in both cases the approaches to law have prevailed to so great an extent that their views have been coopted by the mainstream, leaving it hard to recall or discern what their distinctive point is or was.

Clarifications

It is important, as an initial matter, to clear up what legal positivism *is not*. During the early decades of the twentieth century, legal positivism was accused of advocating a wooden perspective on judicial decision making and legal interpretation – a view of legal positivism that has re-emerged with regularity in the decades since (e.g., Cover 1975: 28–9; Sebok 1998: 17, 107), though rarely with much basis in fact. This picture is a bad mischaracterization of legal positivism, or, at best, a pejorative borrowing of the label for an entirely dissimilar perspective in a different area (Bix 1999b: 903–15). The mistake is arguably attributable to a certain American bias: because judicial review is so important to the legal and political life in the United States, American legal theorists tend to ask of *all* legal theories what they have to tell us about judicial reasoning in general and constitutional interpretation in particular; and they tend to see legal theories through that

lens even when the theories do not purport to touch those subjects. (This tendency to misread legal theories as theories of judicial reasoning has in fact caused misunderstandings of natural law almost as often as it has caused misunderstandings of legal positivism (cf. George 1999: 110–11).) Legal positivism is a theory about the nature of law, by its self-characterization a descriptive or conceptual theory. By its terms, legal positivism does not have consequences for how particular disputes are decided, how texts are interpreted, or how institutions are organized. At most, the theory may have something to say about how certain ways of operating are *characterized* (is it "law" or is it, for some reason, "not law"?), but not on how they should be evaluated or reformed.

Legal positivists have also been accused of asserting some version of "might makes right" as applied to law. Or, the indictment softened slightly upon confrontation with the facts, critics sometimes claimed that if the legal positivists did not actually assert such positions, this is nonetheless where their views led. Legal positivism was attacked for causing legal professionals to be too deferential to the government, and thus too willing to obey even unjust laws. After World War II, a strong debate ensued on what role German legal positivism played, if not directly in the rise of the Nazis, at least in the way that German lawyers and judges did so little to resist the creation and application of evil Nazi laws (e.g., Paulson 1994). This too reflects, at best, a misunderstanding of what is claimed and what is at stake in the debate about legal positivism. (One should remember that most of the key early figures in legal positivism were law reformers, not apologists for the status quo.) In the context of such accusations, the famous 1958 debate between H. L. A. Hart and Lon Fuller (Hart 1958; Fuller 1958) was, to a large extent, a discussion about the role that legal positivism did play, and could play, in the resistance to evil laws and evil regimes. Some have even portrayed both theorists as trying to *ground* the arguments for legal positivism and the alternatives on which approach would be best, instrumentally, in encouraging the resistance to evil laws (Schauer 1994a). Hart argued for what would then have been considered a paradoxical position: that legal positivism is in fact *better than* natural law theory in encouraging resistance to evil. The argument went that a legal positivist knows that the validity of law is one thing, its merit another (pointing to the roots of legal positivism in the work of the law reformer, Jeremy Bentham), while natural law theory, with its equation of legal status with moral status ("an unjust law is no law at all") encourages a confusion among the populace between whether a rule is moral just because it happens to be treated as valid. As it happens, upon closer inspection, there are probably no strong arguments, either logical or psychological, for favoring legal positivism *or* natural law theory (or any other alternative) for the resistance to evil law (Soper 1987; Schauer 1996). Similarly, though one might find a political motivation behind the development of legal positivism (Dworkin 2002: 1677–8) – however, even here, the argument is much easier to make for Bentham than for Austin – it remains more misleading than helpful to evaluate legal positivism in terms of its political motivations (or effects) rather than its status as a theory about the nature of law.

Recently, some commentators have lamented that legal positivism is irrelevant to important debates within law or legal philosophy (e.g., Wright 1996; Dyzenhaus 2000; cf. Dworkin 2002: 1678–9). The complaint is that legal positivism does not entail any particular answer to the important questions of law and practical reasoning: questions relating to constitutional interpretation, the proper response to evil laws, the objectivity of morality, and the role of judges within society. This complaint is not so much wrong as a misunderstanding. One should no more expect theories about the nature of law to guide behavior or answer difficult ethical questions than one should expect day-to-day guidance in life from theories of metaphysics (and, many would add, an inability of general philosophical theories to answer mundane ethical questions is no reason to dismiss such inquiries as worthless).

While it is true that one prominent legal theorist, Ronald Dworkin, has argued that there should be no sharp line between a theory of the nature of law and views about legal practice in a particular legal system, and that one's jurisprudential theory will and should have implications for daily legal practice (Dworkin 1987: 14), that

view is exceptional among theorists writing on the nature of law. The burden seems naturally to be placed on those who would maintain that an investigation into the (abstract) nature of a social practice has immediate implications for how individuals should live their lives, or how practitioners within a practice should resolve difficult disputes within that practice. To claim otherwise is to challenge, at least in this instance, many entrenched views about keeping "is" and "ought" ("description" and "prescription") separate, understanding that the second cannot be derived from the first. (Dworkin has arguments for why these presumptions and distinctions should not be given deference in jurisprudence, but this is not the place to consider in detail the merits and shortcomings of those arguments.)

Alternative Legal Positivisms

In Anglo-American legal theory, legal positivism has become, in a sense, merely a series of elaborations, emendations, and clarifications of H. L. A. Hart's work, in particular his work, *The Concept of Law* (1994), which was first published in 1961. Though, like the claim that modern Western philosophy is "merely" a series of footnotes on the works of Plato and Aristotle, this need not be seen as a dismissal, just a recognition of the importance of Hart's remaking of the legal positivist tradition.

If the dominant strand of English-language legal positivism clearly follows the work of Hart (subdividing into "inclusive legal positivism" and "exclusive legal positivism," as will be discussed below), there remain other strands in legal positivism that deserve mention. Historically, the first strand is the command theory which both Austin ([1832] 1995, [1879] 2002) and Bentham (1970, [1789] 1996) offered. This approach reduced law to a basic picture of a sovereign (someone others are in a habit of obeying, but who is not in the habit of obeying anyone else) issuing a command (an order backed by a threat). Though the command theory (in particular, Austin's version of it) was subjected to a series of serious criticisms by Hart and others (e.g., Hart 1994: 18–78), this approach continues to attract adherents. (Moles

1987; cf. Schauer 1994b; Cotterrell 2003: 49–77). Its potential advantages compared to the mainstream theories are: (1) it carries the power of a simple model of law (if, like other simple models of human behavior, it sometimes suffers a stiff cost in distortion); (2) its focus on sanctions, which seems, to some, to properly emphasize the importance of power and coercion to law; and (3) because it does not purport to reflect the perspective of a sympathetic participant in the legal system, it does not risk sliding towards a moral endorsement of the law.

The second strand is that of Hart and his followers. Hart's approach can be summarized under its two large themes: (1) the focus on social facts and conventions, and (2) the use of a hermeneutic approach, emphasizing the participant's perspective on legal practice. Both themes, and other important aspects of Hart's work, are displayed in the way his theory grew from a critique of its most important predecessor. Hart built his theory in a conscious contrast with Austin's command theory (Hart 1958, 1994), and justified the key points of his theory as improvements on points where Austin's theory had fallen short. Where Austin's theory reduced all of law to commands (by the sovereign), Hart insisted on the variety of law: that legal systems contained both rules that were directed at citizens ("primary rules") and rules that told officials how to identify, modify, or apply the primary rules ("secondary rules"); and legal systems contained both rules that imposed duties and rules that conferred powers – conferring powers not only on officials, but also on citizens, as with the legal powers conferred in the ability to create legally binding contracts and wills.

A key element of Hart's theory, "the Rule of Recognition," will be discussed in greater detail in the next section. For present purposes, it is sufficient to understand that this is a secondary rule that specifies the criteria of legal validity within a legal system. For Hart, a legal system exists if there is a Rule of Recognition *accepted* by the system's officials, and if the rules valid according to the system's Rule of Recognition were *generally obeyed* (Hart 1994: 116).

As earlier mentioned, Austin's work can be seen as trying to find a "scientific" approach to the study of law, and this scientific approach included trying to explain law in empirical terms: an empirically observable tendency of some to obey the commands of others, and the ability of those others to impose sanctions for disobedience (e.g., Austin [1832] 1994: 21–6). Hart criticized Austin's efforts to reduce law to empirical terms of tendencies and predictions (an effort that would be duplicated in different ways in the work of the Scandinavian legal realists (e.g., Olivecrona 1971); and Hart would criticize those theorists for those attempts (Hart 1983: 161–9)); for to show only that part of law that is externally observable is to miss a basic part of legal practice: the acceptance of those legal norms, by officials and citizens, as giving reasons for action (Hart, 1994: 13, 55–8, 82–4, 88–91, 99). The *attitude* of those who accept the law cannot be captured easily by a more empirical or scientific approach, and the advantage of including that aspect of legal practice is what pushed Hart towards a more "hermeneutic" approach. The possibility of popular acceptance (whether morally justified or not) is also what distinguishes a legal system from the mere imposition by force by gangsters or tyrants.

While Austin and Hart sometimes made casual references to their theories as "scientific" (e.g., Austin [1879] 2002, vol. 2: 1107–8) or "descriptive" (e.g., Hart 1994: v, 1987: 37), it would be left to some of the later theorists working within this tradition to work out the extent to which one could or could not claim "descriptive" – or at least "morally neutral" – status for a legal theory. In recent work, it has become almost a commonplace that legal theory cannot be "descriptive," if by that it is meant that there is no evaluation of the data considered. Description without evaluation would become, in the words of John Finnis, "a conjunction of lexicography with local history" (Finnis 1980: 4).

Some basis is required for selection, and this is a point realized even by Hart: that law should be analyzed in its fullest and richest sense (not what is universal to all instances we might be inclined to call "law"), and that the analysis of a legal system should take into account the perspective of someone who accepts the legal system (Hart 1994: 98; Finnis 1980: 6–7). Finnis recharacterizes the process (using ideas from Aristotle and Max Weber) as one of seeking the "ideal type" or "central case" of law (Finnis 1980: 9–11). Other theorists emphasize other aspects of the process of selection within theory production: for example, that one should prefer theories that are simple, comprehensive, and coherent (Waluchow 1994: 19–29), and that a legal theory should strive to identify the "central, prominent, important" features of law (Raz 1985b: 735; cf. Raz 1994: 219–21; Dickson 2001). Legal positivists emphasize that such evaluation should not be confused with moral evaluation (e.g., Coleman 2001: 175–97; Dickson 2001); this argument, and the question of whether a morally neutral form of legal positivism is possible, will be revisited below.

To return to the typology, the third strand of legal positivism is that of Hans Kelsen (Kelsen 1967, [1934] 1992), who published much of his work in German, and remains better known and more influential on continental Europe (and in Latin America and South America) than he ever has been in the United Kingdom and the United States. Kelsen's work has certain external similarities to Hart's theory, but it is built from a distinctly different theoretical foundation: a neo-Kantian derivation, rather than (in Hart's case) the combination of social facts, hermeneutic analysis, and ordinary language philosophy. (Kelsen's ideas developed and changed over the course of six decades of writing; the claims made about his work here apply to most of what he wrote, but will generally not apply to his last works (Kelsen 1991), when he mysteriously rejected much of the theory he had constructed during the prior decades (Hartney 1991: xxxvii-liii; Paulson and Paulson 1998: vii; Paulson 1992a).)

Kelsen applied something like Kant's Transcendental Argument to law: his work can be best understood as trying to determine what follows from the fact that people sometimes treat the actions and words of other people (legal officials) as valid norms (e.g., Paulson, 1992b). Kelsen's work can be seen as drawing on the logic of normative thought. Every normative conclusion (e.g., "one should not drive more than 65 miles per hour" or "one should not commit adultery") derives from a more general or more basic normative premise. This more basic premise may be in terms of a general proposition (e.g., "do not harm other human beings needlessly" or "do

not use other human beings merely as means to an end") or it may be in terms of authority ("do whatever God commands" or "act according to the rules set down by a majority in Parliament"). Thus, the mere fact that someone asserts or assumes the validity of an individual legal norm ("one cannot drive faster than 65 miles per hour") is implicitly to affirm the validity of the foundational link of this particular normative chain ("one ought to do whatever is authorized by the historically first constitution of this society").

Like Austin, but unlike Hart, Kelsen is a "reductionist" in the sense that he tried to understand all legal norms as variations of one kind of statement. In Austin's case, all legal norms were to be understood in terms of commands (of the sovereign); in Kelsen's case, all legal norms are to be understood in terms of an authorization to an official to impose sanctions (if the prescribed standard is not met). (There is a different sense of "reductionism" which applies to Austin, but not to Kelsen, in that Austin attempts to explain the normative aspects of law in empirical terms, while Kelsen is steadfast in asserting that the normative cannot be reduced to the empirical.)

As Kelsen's work comes from a different tradition and a different form of analysis than Hart's, Kelsen's work is not vulnerable to the same lines of criticism that are offered against Hart and his successors. However, Kelsen is (unsurprisingly) subject to a different set of criticisms, many related to the particular neo-Kantian approach he adopts (Tur and Twining 1986; Paulson and Paulson, 1998). Not least, Kelsen's work, because largely abstracted from the social facts and practices of existing legal systems, frequently struggles with the ontological nature of (legal) norms, along with the logical relations among them. For Kelsen, the validity of legal norms derives from a Basic Norm, and that Basic Norm is in turn "presupposed" by those seeing legal orders as normative. As a legal positivist, Kelsen does not mean to ground the normative force of his Basic Norm or his legal norms on their moral validity, but by making his theory "pure" even of sociological (or practice-based) elements, it is hard to see what it means to say that norms "exist" or are "binding" (e.g., Bulygin 1998). As regards the logic of norms, as the content of norms derives, however indirectly, from the actions of officials, within Kelsen's approach there is no basis for assuming that normal rules of logic and inference (e.g., rules of noncontradiction) apply (e.g., Kelsen 1973: 228–53; Conte 1998; Hartney 1991: xlii-lii).

As mentioned, most discussions of legal positivism in contemporary English-language legal scholarship skip over the Austinian and Kelsenian strands of legal positivism, and focus solely on the legal positivism of Hart and his successors. Unless otherwise noted, this will be the focus of the discussions in this chapter as well.

The Rule of Recognition and the Basic Norm

There are roughly analogous concepts central to both Hart's and Kelsen's work that have attracted a great deal of discussion – Hart's Rule of Recognition and Kelsen's Basic Norm (*Grundnorm*) – but the analogous general role of those concepts too frequently has gotten lost in fights over the details. It is certainly important to note the distinctly different natures of Hart's and Kelsen's theories of law (the difference between a theory grounded on social practices versus one grounded in a neo-Kantian analysis of legal normativity), but there is also something to be learned from certain convergent elements in the two theories.

As discussed above, H. L. A. Hart had argued that all (modern or mature) legal systems have secondary rules – rules about rules, rules that allow for the identification, modification, and application of "primary rules." As Hart saw it, these rules are necessary, for though some small or close-knit communities might survive on a set of primary rules alone, that community's rule system would be static, and there would likely be problems of uncertainty and inefficiency in the system, all problems that can be solved by the presence of secondary rules (Hart 1994: 92–5). Most significantly within Hart's analysis, legal systems have a "Rule of Recognition," which comprises the basic criteria of legal validity within the legal system in question: the Rule of Recogni-

tion "will specify some feature or features possession of which by a suggested rule is taken as a conclusive affirmative indication that it is a rule of the group to be supported by the social pressure it exerts" (Hart 1994: 94). The basic role or nature of the Rule of Recognition is established by the legal system's being a normative system: a structured system of "ought" statements. Any individual norm stating what individuals can and cannot do according to law, must be grounded on a more basic or more general normative statement, and so the chain of normative justification goes, until one reaches a norm for which there is no further justification. Under Hart's approach, one looks at the behavior of legal officials (especially judges) to determine what the ultimate criteria of validity are. (The sovereign plays a comparable role in Austin's command theory. All the valid norms in the legal system, according to this approach, can be traced back to a direct or indirect command by the sovereign (indirect commands include the sovereign's authorization that judges can make new law in the sovereign's name).)

Similarly for Kelsen: as discussed earlier, under his approach, one derives the Basic Norm from the citizens' treatment of certain acts as normative. However, Kelsen's Basic Norm is *derived* from treating rules as legal norms, while Hart's Rule of Recognition is discovered in the actual practices of legal officials. (As earlier noted, in his last works, Kelsen seemed to shift his views on many subjects radically, and this included moving from a neo-Kantian theory of the Basic Norm, to one based more on Hans Vaihinger's "as if" theory (Kelsen 1991; Paulson 1992a).)

Both the Rule of Recognition and the Basic Norm rest on the idea of chains of normative validity: a particular legal norm is only valid because it has been authorized by a more general or more basic legal norm. This chain of validity must end somewhere, with a foundational norm that carries no further justification, other than its "acceptance" (Hart 1994: 100–10) or its having been "presupposed" (Kelsen [1934] 1992: 59). It is again important to note the difference of approach and methodology here: Hart's theory is meant as an analytical description of actual practices, while Kelsen sought a theory purified even of sociological observation, and is best understood as a neo-Kantian transcendental deduction from the fact that we treat certain rules as legal norms (e.g., Paulson 1992b).

Both the idea of a (single) Rule of Recognition and a (single) Basic Norm derive from assumptions that societies' legal regulations occur or are viewed as occurring in a systematic way – all the norms fitting within a consistent, hierarchical structure of justification. If one does not think that legal systems must be systematic in this way, then one could conclude that there could be more than one Rule of Recognition (Raz 1980: 197–200) or more than one Basic Norm (Raz 1979: 122–45).

Hart's Rule of Recognition may play an additional general role in his theory which is not echoed in Kelsen's Basic Norm. For many theorists writing about Hart's theory, either in support or in criticism, the Rule of Recognition has come to be equated with the ability to determine the validity of a legal norm by recourse only to the process by which it was enacted or promulgated (the norm's "source" or "pedigree") without consideration of its content. When Dworkin famously offered the existence of legal principles as a purported rebuttal to Hart's theory of law, Dworkin argued that Hart's Rule of Recognition could not account for the legal status of such principles, or at least that any Rule of Recognition that *could* differentiate principles that were part of the legal system from those that were not would no longer be able to serve the purposes behind Hart's Rule of Recognition (Dworkin 1977: 39–45, 68–74). Hart, in his posthumously published postscript, rejected the claim (Hart 1994: 250–4, 259–68), mostly by adopting the "inclusivist" interpretation of his own work. As will be discussed in the next section, this is a defense that may carry significant costs.

The Divisions Within Contemporary Legal Positivism

In contemporary Anglo-American legal positivism, which has focused on elaborating the Hartian strand of legal positivism, much recent discussion has been on an internal debate between "inclusive legal positivism" (also sometimes called "soft" or "incorporationist" legal

positivism) and "exclusive legal positivism" (also known as "hard" legal positivism). The debate between the two camps involves a difference in interpreting or elaborating one central point of legal positivism: that there is no *necessary* or "conceptual" connection between law and morality. Exclusive legal positivism (whose advocates have included Joseph Raz (1994: 194–221), Andrei Marmor (2002), and Scott Shapiro (1998)) interprets or elaborates this assertion to mean that moral criteria can be neither sufficient nor necessary conditions for the legal status of a norm. In different terms: exclusive legal positivism states that "the existence and content of every law is fully determined by social sources" (Raz 1979: 46).

The most prominent argument for exclusive legal positivism is one offered by Joseph Raz based on the relationship between law and authority. This argument depends, in part, on accepting Raz's distinctive views on both the nature of law and the nature of authority (cf. Waluchow 2000: 47–52). First, as regards law, Raz argues that legal systems, by their nature, purport to be justified (legitimate) practical authorities (Raz 1994: 199, 1996: 16). (He does not say that it is in the nature of law *to be* justified practical authorities; that would be contrary to the basic tenet of legal positivism that one can determine status as law without recourse to moral tests; it would also be in tension with Raz's argument elsewhere that legal rules, even in generally just legal systems, do not impose a *prima facie* moral obligation (Raz 1994: 325–38).) Raz has argued for what is sometimes called "the service conception of authority": that the "role and primary normal function [of authorities] is to serve the governed" (Raz 1990: 21). Authorities are to consider the same reasons for action that would apply to the subject, and the subject ought to act as the authorities suggest if that person "is likely better to comply with reasons that apply to him...if he accepts the directives of the alleged authority as authoritatively binding and tries to follow them, rather than by trying to follow the reasons which apply to him directly" (Raz 1985a: 19 (italics removed)). This analysis of authority is by no means universally accepted; it has been challenged both on descriptive and normative grounds (e.g., Lukes 1990; Dworkin 2002: 1671–76).

Continually with Raz's approach to authority: those subject to an authority "can benefit by its decisions only if they can establish their existence and content in ways which do not depend on raising the very same issues which the authority is there to settle" (Raz 1994: 219). In the context of law, this means that with legal rules, which are meant to make authoritative decisions on matters on which citizens would otherwise be subject to various moral (and prudential) reasons for action, we must be able to ascertain their content without recourse to further moral evaluation. According to Raz, law purports to play a particular role in citizens' practical reasoning – legal rules are to be "pre-emptive reasons" or "exclusionary" reasons for action (Raz 1994: 199–204; cf. Raz 1990: 35–48, 73–84, 178–99). Following this analysis, inclusive legal positivism must fail, it is argued, because it is inconsistent with a core aspect of law, the legal system's purporting to be a justified practical authority.

Among the responses to Raz's attack on inclusive legal positivism have been the following: (1) that legal rules and legal systems may be authoritative even when the content of the rules are sometimes determined in part by moral reasons (e.g., Waluchow 1994: 129–40, 2000: 47–71); and (2) Raz's argument does not work where the moral criteria for validity (usually part of a constitutional standard) are different from the moral reasons that would normally apply to citizens (e.g., the reasons for not murdering are different from the equality or "no cruel punishment" reasons that may be the basis of invalidating a certain murder statute) (e.g., Coleman 2001: 125–7).

Another argument that has been offered for exclusive legal positivism derives from a claim about the nature of rules. Scott Shapiro (1998) has emphasized that it is in the nature of rules, including legal rules, that they make a difference in our practical reasoning, and that inclusive rules of recognition would fail to make a difference in this way, as they would merely point us towards moral evaluations already applicable to our choices. This claim has evoked a number of responses (e.g., Coleman 2001: 134–48; Waluchow 2000; Kramer 2000; Himma 2000), and

the debate is still evolving. One response is that it is sufficient that the legal system *as a whole* make a difference in our practical reasoning, and this will continue to be the case if the moral criteria of an inclusive Rule of Recognition were the sufficient conditions for *some* of the valid norms of the legal system, but not for all of them (e.g., Waluchow 2000: 76–81).

Inclusive legal positivism (whose advocates have included Jules Coleman (1982, 1998, 2001), Wilfrid Waluchow (1994), Philip Soper (1977), David Lyons (1977), and H. L. A. Hart (1994: 250–4)) interprets the separation of law and morality differently, arguing that while there is no *necessary* moral content to a legal rule (or a legal system), a particular legal system may, by conventional rule, make moral criteria necessary or sufficient for validity *in that system* (e.g., Waluchow 1994; Coleman 1982). In the posthumously published "Postscript" to *The Concept of Law*, Hart indicated that he saw inclusive legal positivism as better reflecting his own views and intentions (Hart 1994: 247–54).

The strongest argument for inclusive legal positivism seems to be its fit with the way both legal officials and legal texts talk about the law (though at least one advocate of the inclusive approach has disclaimed such reliance on "fit" (Coleman 2001: 109)). Morality seems to be *sufficient* grounds for the legal status of a norm in many common law cases (and decisions in which legal principles play a large role (Dworkin 1977: 14–45)), where a legal norm is justified only or primarily on the basis that morality requires it. (Of course, exclusive legal positivists have no objection to judges *declaring new law* based on moral considerations; it is the argument that something is *currently valid law because* of its moral merit that would run counter to exclusive legal positivism.) The more familiar example for inclusive legal positivism is not about *sufficient* grounds for legal validity, but *necessary* grounds: when constitution-based judicial review of legislation (e.g., in the United States and Canada) requires or authorizes the invalidation of legislation that runs afoul of moral standards codified in the constitution (e.g., regarding equality, due process, or humane punishment), this appears to make moral merit a necessary, but not sufficient, basis for legal validity.

Additionally, the inclusive view allows theorists to accept many of Dworkin's criticisms of legal positivism without abandoning what these same theorists consider the core tenets of legal positivism (its grounding in social facts and conventions). Inclusive legal positivism accepts that moral terms can be part of the necessary or sufficient criteria for legal validity in a legal system, but insist that the use of moral criteria is *contingent* – and derived from the choices or actions of particular legal officials – rather than part of the nature of law (and thus present in *all* legal systems).

Various legal positivist theorists have offered a series of modifications and clarifications to try to secure their views against the criticisms of Dworkin and of other legal positivists. For example, in response to Dworkin's argument that judges do not have discretion, but instead are obligated to apply legal principles (which are determined in part by their moral content, and thus could not be picked out by a Hartian Rule of Recognition), Joseph Raz has argued that not every norm judges are obligated to apply in deciding legal disputes is thereby "law" (Raz 1983: 83–85). Raz elsewhere (Raz 1994: 317) offers the example of a court being directed to resolve a dispute by reference to the laws of another country or the internal rules of an association; but whether such an analysis can fairly be applied also to (e.g.) the moral standards incorporated in constitutional requirements may raise a more difficult question. Another example: to Dworkin's argument that there is no Hartian Rule of Recognition in modern constitutional democracies that could adequately serve the purported function of such rules – helping citizens to identify what is and is not valid law – Jules Coleman and Brian Leiter have argued that the Rule of Recognition should be seen as having a validation function even if it does not have, within some legal systems, an identification function (Coleman and Leiter 1996: 252). And numerous other epicycles have been added to the basic legal positivist view to try to respond to critics within and without. The problem is that the defenders of legal positivism may have become too clever for their own good. With all the intricate modifications, clarifications, and addenda, the positivists may have won the battle but lost the war. The theory may be able to beat off all attacks, but the fortified product is one that sometimes seems to be neither recognizable nor powerful (cf. Dworkin 2002: 1656–65; Bix 1999a).

Debates and Distinctive Views

As already noted, a useful approach to understanding a theory or a school of thought is to consider its origins, seeing that to which it was reacting or responding. For Bentham and Austin, the key provocation for early legal positivism was the sloppy natural law thinking of William Blackstone: in Blackstone's claim ("no human laws are of any validity, if contrary to [the law of nature]" (Blackstone [1765–9] 1979, vol. 1: 41)), some discerned an implication that whatever was law (whatever rules the common law judges had developed over time) was right and reasonable. In response, Bentham in particular saw the need to distinguish clearly between the statement of what the law was, and the evaluation of its merits. Bentham as reformer could then present a clear case for *changes* in the law. (Bentham was thus also the strong advocate of codification and a strong opponent of the common law and judicial legislation; as for legal reform, Bentham was also one of the founders of Utilitarianism, so he had a moral system ready to guide the lawmakers in their reforms (Bentham [1789] 1996).)

The path of legal positivism in the decades after Austin and Bentham broadly followed this initial track: legal positivism as a contrast to natural law theory (see NATURAL LAW THEORY). However, the boundary lines and conflict lines between that great tradition and legal positivism tend to become elusive upon closer inspection (Bix 2000). It is hard to locate natural law theorists who actually disagree with the legal positivist position, when the position is carefully stated (cf. Finnis 1994). One can find some sloppy language by some peripheral figures which might be intended to equate legality and moral validity in a naïve way (or which at least invites that misreading) – John Austin ([1832] 1994: 157–9) pounces on just such a remark by Blackstone in his *Commentaries* (quoted earlier). However, such examples are rare, and fighting such occasional sloppiness is hardly enough to justify a whole school of jurisprudence. Most natural law theorists are as anxious as most legal positivists to separate questions of validity within a legal system and questions of moral value. Natural law theorists may argue that immoral laws are not "laws in their fullest sense" (in that they do not create *prima facie* moral obligations), but that is quite different from saying that they are "not 'law' at all" (Kretzmann, 1988). (Nor need a legal positivist disagree with that conclusion – at least in the sense that no disagreement seems required by the "tenets" of legal positivism (MacCormick 1992).)

There likely still are points of disagreement between legal positivism and natural law theory, but they tend to come on relatively peripheral or marginal points (for a characterization of the two schools of thought as more sharply divided, see Mark Murphy's discussion, NATURAL LAW THEORY). For example, modern legal theorists tend to agree that a theory of law should take into account the perspective of a participant in the legal process (Hart 1994: 89–91). The idea is that law, like other social practices, is a purposive activity, and an account of the nature of law that can take into account the views of participants is thereby a better theory than one that does not do so. While natural law theorists have come to agree with that view (e.g., Finnis 1980: 3–6), natural law theorists and legal positivists disagree on whether an ability to distinguish morally legitimate law and law which falls short of that mark should be built into that participant's perspective.

Both advocates and critics of legal positivism sometimes discuss the way in which legal positivism succeeds or fails in "explaining the normativity of law." There is a deep ambiguity to that phrase, which hides important questions about the nature of the claims legal positivist do and should be making about law. One view, following Kelsen and a possible interpretation of Hart, is that legal positivism is best understood as accepting the "fact" of normativity, that is, as starting from *the assumption* that some large percentage of officials and citizens within a legal community accept the law as establishing reasons for action (people viewing the legal norms as offering reasons for action means more than being "persuaded" to act by the coercive force

the system may use to enforce its standards; in that case, it would be the sanctions, and not the legal norms themselves, that would be the reasons for action). Hart famously criticized Austin's command theory for being unable to distinguish a legal system from a gunman's threats, writ large (Hart 1994: 20–5). Hart's line of argument, in the context of a critique of Austin's command theory, can be seen merely as describing better and worse descriptive theories: that a good descriptive theory will be one that can take into account the differences between a gangster's imposition and a system that is (rightly or wrongly) accepted as legitimate by some or most of its officials and citizens. Austin's theory, with its focus on the tendencies of sanction and obedience, cannot discern the difference; Hart's theory, incorporating the internal point of view, allows for this distinction. Thus, legal positivists *observe* the fact of normativity, and account for it only in the sense of constructing a legal theory that can take that fact into account. Under this view, legal positivists do not "explain normativity" in the sense of showing how such views can be justified or legitimate, for that sort of "explanation of normativity" is just the type of moral or evaluative judgment that legal positivism leaves to other types of analysis – for example, political theory or moral theory.

Some commentators, perhaps unwisely, have tried to read more into Hart's critique of Austin (and other similar comments), and have thought that it *was* legal positivism's task to "explain normativity," in the evaluative sense of explaining in what sense the legal system could legitimately give its officials and citizens additional reasons for action. Such explanations, when attempted, have tried various paths, including arguments about legal rules and standards as coordinating conventions (e.g., Coleman 1998) or as – in Michael Bratman's terminology (Bratman 1992) – a "shared cooperative activity" (Coleman 2001: 74–102; cf. Shapiro 2002; Bratman 2002). One suspects that these sorts of explanations may be doomed to failure – for whenever they venture from the sociological project of *observing* normative behavior to the task of *justifying* such behavior, they risk the error David Hume pointed out long ago, of improperly trying to derive an "ought" from an "is" (cf. Finnis 2000). There may be interesting work to be done in trying to ground moral obligations in the coordination of behavior, but intertwining these arguments with the core views of legal positivism may be more likely to invite confusion than insight.

Critiques of Legal Positivism

Every leading approach to law has its strong points and its weak points, aspects of legal practice it accounts for very well and other aspects less well. The parts of legal practice that legal positivism (or at least "exclusive" forms of legal positivism, see above), seems to account for or explain less well, and that sometimes motivate scholars towards alternative theories, include the following:

(1) Common law reasoning (e.g., Perry 1987; Postema 1996: 95–6) – while there are a variety of theories of what is or should be going on in traditional forms of common law reasoning, one could reasonably argue that this form of reasoning gives instances of a norm being valid law *because* of its moral content rather than being based on a social source.

(2) Purposive interpretation – the way that statutes and constitutional provisions are interpreted in line with their purposes (or with the broader purposes of particular areas of law) has seemed to some to be evidence that the distinction between "law as it is" and "law as it ought to be" is not as sharp as legal positivists make out (Fuller 1958: 661–9; cf. Hart 1958: 606–15).

(3) Customary law – legal systems which recognize "customary law" often characterize the judges applying such laws as merely recognizing already existing legal standards. Again, the question is whether to treat such "recognitions" at face value, or to treat them as judicial legislation. Austin ([1832] 1994: 34–6) wrestles awkwardly with fitting customary laws into a system based on commands (concluding that customary norms, because not commands, cannot be legal rules, but that they can become legal rules when adopted by judges – which he then characterizes as indirect commands of the sovereign).

(4) "Landmark cases" where courts change radically what most judges and commentators had assumed the law to require, but the courts insist that they are merely discovering or clarifying the existing law (e.g., Dworkin 1977: 22–31). The English tort law case, *Donoghue v. Stevenson* (1932), and a comparable American case, *MacPherson v. Buick Motor Co.* (1916), are paradigmatic examples. While a legal positivist (at least of the "exclusive" variety) could simply refer to these cases as instances of judicial legislation, the judges and commentators frequently resist such characterizations, preferring the view that the law "works itself pure" (*Omychund v. Barker* 1744 at 23), thus blurring the legal positivist's line between "what law is" and "what law ought to be."

As the above four categories exemplify, to varying degrees, in general legal positivism does better explaining those aspects of law that derive from "will," the choice of some identifiable lawmaker, and less well in explaining those aspects of law that seem to derive from "reason," the derivation of legal standards directly or indirectly from moral standards. Alternative approaches, like Ronald Dworkin's interpretive approach and some versions of natural law theory, tend to have the opposite problem: they are better with the "reason" side of law, and weakest in dealing with the "will" (or "authority") aspects of law (cf. Bix 2003a: 133–8, 2002: 68; see NATURAL LAW THEORY; ADJUDICATION AND LEGAL REASONING). This contrast may be most sharply visible in Hans Kelsen's work, where a judge's application of a general norm to a particular case (e.g., "no one may park on this street," therefore "James was not allowed to park on this street") was considered the creation of a new norm. That is, the specific norm was law because, and only because, it was so willed by the judge; prior to that act of judicial lawmaking the specific norm was not law, even though it might be connected to a general legal norm by the simplest of logical operations (Kelsen [1934] 1992: 67–8; cf. Finnis 2000: 1600–01).

Fuller summarized the will/reason distinction and its significance for understanding law:

> When we deal with law, not in terms of definitions and authoritative sources, but in terms of problems and functions, we inevitably see that it is compounded of reason and fiat, of order dis-

covered and order imposed, and that to attempt to eliminate either of these aspects of the law is to denature and falsify it. (Fuller 1946: 382)

As has been discussed elsewhere in this chapter, legal positivism *can* account for the "order discovered" aspect of law, on the basis that such "discoveries" do not become significant for a legal system until announced by the duly appointed officials (though the debate remains whether the standards should be thought of or treated as having been valid law *prior* to this promulgation). Legal positivism's focus on the authoritative sources and officials also has the virtue of accounting for the inevitable disagreement and fallibility in ascertaining what the implicit or eternal order is. On the other hand, Fuller's point, echoed by other critics of legal positivism, is that refusing to give equal emphasis to the (implicit or eternal) order which lawmakers aspire to ascertain and apply is to miss something basic in the nature of law.

To resume the list of objections:

(5) Significant disagreement – as Dworkin has pointed out (e.g., Dworkin 1986: 120–39, 2002), the appearance of pervasive disagreement among legal officials and legal scholars about even basic aspects of practice within many legal systems (including those in the United States and Britain) raises serious questions for a legal theory that seems to be grounded on conventional agreement.

(6) Legal mistake – the problem of "mistake" can cause problems for legal positivism, but probably no more than for almost any alternative theory. *Whatever* criteria one chooses for legal validity, there will be occasions when judges or other legal officials seem to act contrary to those criteria, most frequently from a sincere but mistaken application of the criteria, but sometimes from corruption or other wicked motives. The reality of such deviations can tempt theorists to say that the only criterion of validity is the decision of the ultimate decision maker (e.g., the most recent decision on the issue by the United States Supreme Court or the House of Lords). However, this recourse has even greater difficulties, difficulties which Hart satirized through his description of "scorer's discretion"

(an intentional misinterpretation of games which have rules for when a goal has been scored but where referees have the final word on whether a goal has in fact been scored). As Hart pointed out, it badly mischaracterizes what is going on to declare the relevant norm to be that a goal is scored if and only if the scoring judge declares it to have occurred (Hart 1994: 141–7). This ("scorer's discretion" or "what the judges say, is law") view of practices with final arbiters who purport to apply norms misses the extent to which the ultimate decision makers consider themselves bound by standards, and the extent to which other actors, or the same decision makers at a later date, may criticize the initial decision by reference to those standards.

There is no reason to believe that these items, individually or collectively, form a conclusive case against legal positivism. They are rather, as earlier noted, weak points, and competing approaches to the nature of law will have their own, different, weak points. (Roger Shiner (1992) has shown how the weak points in legal positivism could lead one towards a natural law approach, but that the weak points in natural law theories would lead one back to legal positivism.)

Two Critics: Ronald Dworkin and John Finnis

The most incisive criticisms of legal positivism in recent years have come, first, from Ronald Dworkin (1977, 1985, 1986, 2002) and some other prominent theorists (e.g., Stephen Perry (1995, 1996, 1998, 2002)), developing a comparable line of criticism, and, second, from the natural law theorist John Finnis. This section will offer a brief overview of these critiques.

Ronald Dworkin

Dworkin's challenge to legal positivism has had three general themes: (1) a challenge to the picture legal positivism gave (or seemed to give) that legal systems were merely systems of rules; (2) an argument that legal positivism was wrong in be-lieving that questions of legal validity are, by their nature, separate from considerations of the con-tent or the merit of purported legal norms; and (3) a challenge to the general belief that law and legal validity are conceptually separate from ques-tions of morality and moral worth. (Dworkin has also argued that legal positivism is best under-stood as a "semantic" theory (Dworkin 1985: 31–44) – attempting only to determine the mean-ing of the word "law" – but this has been rejected by all contemporary legal positivists as both un-charitable and unwarranted. Legal positivists have never been mere lexicographers: they have tried, if not always with success, to say something about a certain social institution or a certain concept (e.g., Hart 1994: 239–48).)

In his earlier works, Dworkin argued that Hart's version of legal positivism must be rejected because it assumes a view of a legal system that consists entirely of legal rules, when legal systems contain "principles" as well. Legal principles differ from legal rules, in Dworkin's critique, in that principles are moral propositions, grounded in the past actions of legal officials, that are not conclusive for the cases to which they apply: in-stead, they add varying levels of weight to the argument for the outcome one way or the other. There can thus be, and frequently will be, legal principles on both sides of a difficult case (Dworkin 1977: 22–8). Because the questions of whether legal principles apply in a particular case, and what weight they have in that case, are factors relating to the content of the principle, and not merely based on the principle's "source" or "pedigree," Dworkin argued that a Hartian Rule of Recognition could not identify valid legal principles and still play the role Hart needed the Rule of Recognition to play within a legal positiv-ist theory of law (Dworkin 1977: 28–31, 39–48, 64–8).

While there was much contemporary debate of Dworkin's rules/principles critique of legal posi-tivism (e.g., Raz 1983), that discussion has largely fallen away, in large part because Dworkin's later work offered a view of the law that did not turn on the distinction between rules and principles, but rather on a more nuanced interpretive theory of social practices (Dworkin 1986). However, vari-ations of Dworkin's initial critique, questioning

whether a legal positivist rule or recognition can account for all the valid norms within the legal system ("rules," "principles," or otherwise) sur-vives, though it has mostly been transformed into the detailed infighting between inclusive and ex-clusive legal positivism, which was discussed above.

A more productive line of critique has been offered by Stephen Perry, whose version of Dwor-kin's nonneutrality critique argues that Hart was wrong to believe that a "descriptive" – morally neutral, nonevaluative – theory of law was pos-sible (Perry 1995, 1996, 1998, 2002). Perry's argument, in rough summary, is that in the con-struction of a theory of law, choices must be made; theories cannot be just an accumulation of facts. These choices have often been justified by some argument regarding the *purpose* of law, but different theorists have put forward different purposes (e.g., Dworkin often refers to the justi-fication of state coercion, while a number of the legal positivists have preferred to see law's pur-pose as guiding citizen behavior). How can one choose between one purpose and another, a foun-dational question within the theory, except on the basis that one is morally superior to the other? To put the question differently, what morally neutral principle, what simple principle of theory con-struction, would be sufficient to adjudicate be-tween competing theories about the primary purpose of law?

There are a number of thoughtful responses as to how neutral principles of theory construction or conceptual analysis *could* be sufficient (e.g., Coleman 2001: 197–207; Waluchow 1994: 19–29; Dickson 2001). Whether these responses are adequate to rebut the Dworkin/Perry challenge regarding the impossibility of a neutral theory remains highly contested and unsettled.

Dworkin has raised other challenges to legal positivism: in his later work (e.g., *Law's Empire* (1986)), as mentioned earlier, Dworkin argued that legal positivism (at least in the Hartian trad-ition) could not adequately account for pervasive disagreement within legal practice. He argued that the model of law based on a pedigree-based (content-neutral, no moral evaluation) Rule of Recognition could at best be understood as a kind of "conventionalism" that placed great value on stability and predictability within legal practice, and that Hart's theory as a whole was most charitably understood as explicating the (often unstated) shared criteria officials and citizens have regarding the meaning of legal practices, concepts, and propositions. Dworkin argued that Hart's model of law falls short, both descriptively and morally, compared to his own interpretive theory of law (Dworkin 1986: 33–46, 114–50). In turn, Hart and others have rejected this interpretation of legal positivism, and Dworkin's critique of legal positivism more generally (e.g., Hart 1994: 238–76; Coleman, 1998). Again, it is the response to this line of criticism by Dworkin that has prompted the development of "inclusive legal positivism" and driven much of the debate between it and "exclusive legal positivism" (see above).

John Finnis

A different line of criticism has recently emerged from the traditional opponent of legal positivism – natural law theory. John Finnis (Finnis 2000, 2002), the most prominent legal theorist working within the natural law tradition, argues that law must be understood both in terms of (1) a description of the past acts of legal officials, and (2) reasons for action (for officials and citizens alike). However, a full and proper analysis of the second aspect of law, its giving reasons for action, cannot be accomplished without a focus on what constitutes *good* (moral) reasons for action. Only a theory (like a natural law theory) that takes into account moral argumentation can appropriately come to terms with the way that actions by officials *can* affect the moral obligations of citizens (and why such actions sometimes *fail* to change our moral rights and duties). And once the discussion of law becomes separated from questions about the law's (moral) authority, it can do no more than "report[] attitudes and convergent behavior" (Finnis 2000: 1611).

One possible response was touched upon earlier – that legal positivists should not worry about not being able to account for *the moral force* (if any) of law, because that was never the purpose of this approach. Finnis's challenge would remain: questioning whether there is any-

thing useful that can be stated about the nature of law *without* purporting to evaluate legal rules and legal systems normatively (and without being reduced to a mere sociology of law-related behaviors). This question is touched upon in the next section in a more general way, and can be summarized, briefly, as follows: should a theory about the nature of law focus (in a morally neutral way) on law's status *as a kind of social institution*, as legal positivism arguably does; or should it instead focus (as natural law theory arguably does) on law's status *as a reason for action* that can affect people's moral obligations (and is there any theoretical approach to the nature of law that can fully capture both aspects of law's nature)?

Methodological Questions and the Way Forward

This brief overview of the debates involving legal positivism connects to a question about the purpose of legal theory (and of philosophy). What do we expect legal theory *to do*? How can we distinguish good legal theories from bad ones? See CAN THERE BE A THEORY OF LAW? We cannot test theories about the nature of law the way we test scientific theories: by setting up controlled experiments to see if the events predicted by the theory come about or not. Nor can we even apply the test of historical theories: judging theories by the extent to which they match with the facts in the past. Neither conventional approach to verification or falsification works with theories about the nature of law, because such theories do not purport to be (merely) empirical theories, but rather conceptual claims, claims about what is "essential" to the concept (or "our concept" of) "law."

However, if legal positivism is not about some simply factual claim about the systems we call "law," the question returns more sharply: what are the criteria of success, and how do we tell a good or successful theory of law from a less good or less successful theory?

A good theory *explains*. A good theory would be one that tells us something significant – that says something interesting about the category of phenomenon we call "law." Even if it is not a claim that can be verified or falsified, one can still feel that a theory either does or does not give us an insight into the practice or phenomenon that we did not have before. A theory that offers to tell us something about the "nature of law" needs, of course, to reflect, to a substantial extent, the way citizens and lawyers perceive and practice law – it must "fit" our legal practice, though the fit need not be perfect; however, significant deviations from the participants' understanding of a practice must be justified by some insight offered. This relates to the second point: a theory should offer more than general descriptive fit – it should also tell us something about the practice that even regular participants in the practice might not have been able to articulate, but which they would recognize when confronted with the theory.

Legal positivism, if it is to continue to be a tenable and valuable theory of law, must seek out a position that offers insight, and this must also be a position with which reasonable persons might disagree (otherwise the theory reduces to an everyday truth, unworthy of discussion). This is the advantage that exclusive legal positivism has over inclusive legal positivism: whatever its relative merits in the debates with natural law theory and Dworkinian theory, exclusive legal positivism has the advantage of a distinctive statement about the nature of law and its role in society. Exclusive legal positivism emphasizes the differences between law as it is, and law as it ought to be (a distinction Dworkin's theory fogs, when it does not erase it entirely), and it emphasizes the connection between law and the role of authority in governance (in democratic regimes, that officials make choices in the name of the people, which other officials must then enforce). This is not a conclusive argument for exclusive legal positivism, but it is a significant factor in its favor (exclusive theorists still face the challenge that they maintain a distinctive view of law at the cost of too large a gap between their characterization of the practice and how practitioners understand their own legal systems).

If legal theories in general, and legal positivism in particular, are merely a contestable way of characterizing the nature of law, if there is no clear "right" or "wrong," and no sense in which "fitting the facts" is a strict criterion of success, there is a temptation to ask why anyone should care about such things. If theorizing about the nature of law is not a search for "the truth," narrowly understood, like pure physics, and it is not meant to respond to some particular view of social justice, what is the point? Here one must assert the intrinsic value of explanation and understanding.

The controversial claim and the interesting claim of legal positivism may be at its foundation: that it is both possible and valuable to offer a descriptive or conceptual theory of law. The claim that one can create a descriptive (or, at least, morally neutral) theory of law will be met by those (like Ronald Dworkin) who claim that nothing interesting can be said at the level of law in general, and thus that legal theory should be theories of *particular legal systems* (Dworkin 1987: 16). And, as already discussed, the claim that there can be a descriptive (or morally neutral) theory of law will also be met by those (e.g., Dworkin 1986: 31–113; Perry 1995, 1996, 1998, 2002) who argue that controversial moral choices are inevitable even in a purportedly descriptive theory. (Here, though, there is a thin line between evaluative standards which are selective, but arguably not morally evaluative, and standards that do seem morally evaluative or political.)

It is important for legal positivists – indeed, for all theorists about the nature of law – to spend more time thinking of their project in the broader context of social theory, and the problem of the social sciences. For example, the view that there can be a fully descriptive theory of law may be open to attack on the grounds that social theory can never be neutral in that way (e.g., Lucy 1999). Legal positivists are well advised to look to the nature of comparable debates within social theory, when making their arguments in defense of their approach to the nature of law.

While law can be seen as a subset of social institutions and practices on one hand, it is also, on the other hand, a subset of reason-giving practices (along with religion, morality, and perhaps etiquette), as mentioned in the previous section, in discussing John Finnis's critique of legal positivism. For this broader category of theorizing about reason-giving practices, there would be obvious tensions in any effort to create a "descriptive" or "neutral" theory of an intrinsically evaluative practice. At the least, there are evident arguments for preferring a perspective on reason-giving practices that would reflect on their merits according to their ultimate purposes (cf. Finnis, 2000, 2002). It may well be that law's double nature – as a social institution and as a reason-giving practice – makes it impossible to capture the nature of law fully through any one approach, with a more "neutral" approach (like legal positivism) required to understand its institutional side, and a more evaluative approach (like natural law theory) required to understand its reason-giving side.

Finally, legal positivists who offer a *conceptual* theory of law will be met by those (like Leiter) who challenge the possibility, or at least the value, of conceptual analysis (Leiter 1998a, 1998b, 2002; cf. Harman 1994). Once again, the question should not be seen as one peculiar to *legal* theory. Brian Leiter (1998b) has rightly reminded legal theorists that they are part of a larger world of philosophy, and the abandonment of conceptual analysis elsewhere in philosophy (abandoning "armchair metaphysics" for more empirically grounded inquiries) should give legal theorists pause. However, while conceptual analysis may have been largely discarded in some areas of philosophy, like epistemology, the direct comparison is not whether conceptual theory is still considered useful for a theory of knowledge, but rather whether conceptual theory is still considered useful for *social theory* – for that is arguably the closest topic in general philosophy for theorists working on the nature of law. Some legal theorists have already offered reasons for believing that the attack on conceptual analysis in social theory generally, and jurisprudence specifically, can be rebutted (e.g., Coleman 2001: 210–17). However, even if conceptual analysis is considered appropriate for jurisprudence, there is still work to be done to elaborate what is meant by speaking of the "nature" or "essence" of law; to explain whether or in what way there are "necessary truths" about law; and to analyze whether there has only been one concept of law throughout history or, to the contrary, different societies

have had different concepts (many of these issues are discussed by Joseph Raz (See CAN THERE BE A THEORY OF LAW?); see also Bix, 2003b).

Conclusion

Many people approach legal positivism with a strong presumption in its favor. After all, how could one reasonably be against having a descriptive (or at least morally neutral) study of a social institution and practice, separating what is from what should be, and allowing other disciplines to discuss normative or historical or sociological aspects of the same social institution and practice? However, as this chapter has indicated, under further critical examination, there are questions that can and should be asked about the possibility and value of this type of inquiry. First, approaches to the nature of law should be understood within the context of larger debates regarding theories of other social practices and institutions, and theories of other reason-giving practices. Broader inquiries will include, on the one hand, the question of the possibility of a morally neutral theory, and, on the other hand, the viability of "conceptual" theory.

A more precise set of questions might be derived from the above general considerations: What does it mean to talk about the nature of law, and what does it mean to succeed or fail in having a theory of law? To answer these questions, in light of the general concerns outlined, is the challenge that legal positivism must meet if it is going to warrant our continuing attention. If this challenge is not met, legal positivism will become, one fears, just another interesting topic in the history of ideas, rather than a vibrant debate in our current reflections on what it means to have and maintain a legal system.[1]

Note

1 I am grateful to the comments and suggestions of William A. Edmundson, Daniel A. Farber, Miranda Oshige McGowan, Brian Z. Tamanaha, and those who heard earlier versions of this chapter when they

were presented at the University of Minnesota and the University of Stockholm.

References

Austin, J. [1832] 1994. *The Province of Jurisprudence Determined*, ed. W. E. Rumble. Cambridge, UK: Cambridge University Press.

Austin, J. [1879] 2002. *Lectures on Jurisprudence or the Philosophy of Positive Law*, 2 vols., 4th edn., rev. and ed. by R. Campbell. Bristol: Thoemmes Press.

Bentham, J. 1970. *Of Laws in General*, ed. H. L. A. Hart. London: University of London, The Athlone Press.

Bentham, J. [1789] 1996. *An Introduction to the Principles of Morals and Legislation*, ed. J. H. Burns and H. L. A. Hart. Oxford: Clarendon Press.

Berlin, I. 1997. *The Proper Study of Mankind*, ed. H. Hardy and R. Hausheer. London: Random House.

Bix, B. 1999a. Patrolling the boundaries: Inclusive legal positivism and the nature of jurisprudential debate. *Canadian Journal of Law and Jurisprudence* 12: 17–33.

Bix, B. 1999b. Positively positivism. *Virginia Law Review* 85: 889–923.

Bix, B. 2000. On the dividing line between natural law theory and legal positivism. *Notre Dame Law Review* 75: 1613–24.

Bix, B. 2002. Natural law theory: The modern tradition. In J. L. Coleman and S. Shapiro (eds.), K. E. Himma (assoc. ed.), *Oxford Handbook of Jurisprudence and Philosophy of Law*. Oxford: Oxford University Press, 61–103.

Bix, B. 2003a. *Jurisprudence, Theory and Context*, 3rd edn. London: Sweet and Maxwell.

Bix, B. 2003b. Raz on necessity. *Law and Philosophy* 22: 537–59.

Blackstone, W. [1765–9] 1979. *Commentaries on the Laws of England*, 4 vols. Chicago: University of Chicago Press.

Bratman, M. E. 1992. Shared cooperative activity. *Philosophical Review* 101: 327–41.

Bratman, M. E. 2002. Shapiro on legal positivism and jointly intentional activity. *Legal Theory* 8: 511–17.

Bulygin, E. 1998. An antinomy in Kelsen's pure theory of law. In S. L. Paulson and B. L. Paulson (eds.), *Normativity and Norms: Critical Perspectives on Kelsenian Themes*. Oxford: Clarendon Press, 297–315.

Coleman, J. L. 1982. Negative and positive positivism. *Journal of Legal Studies* 11: 139–64.

Coleman, J. L. 1998. Incorporationism, conventionality, and the practical difference thesis. *Legal Theory* 4: 381–426.

Coleman, J. L. 2001. *The Practice of Principle: In Defence of a Pragmatist Approach to Legal Theory*. Oxford: Oxford University Press.

Coleman, J. L. and Leiter, B. (1996). Legal positivism. In D. Patterson (ed.), *A Companion to the Philosophy of Law and Legal Theory*. Oxford: Blackwell, 241–60.

Conte, A. G. 1998. Hans Kelsen's deontics. In S. L. Paulson and B. L. Paulson (eds.), *Normativity and Norms: Critical Perspectives on Kelsenian Themes*. Oxford: Clarendon Press, 331–41.

Cotterrell, R. 2003. *The Politics of Jurisprudence*, 2nd edn. London: LexisNexis.

Cover, R. 1975. *Justice Accused: Antislavery and the Judicial Process*. New Haven, CT: Yale University Press.

Dickson, J. 2001. *Evaluation and Legal Theory*. Oxford: Hart Publishing.

Donoghue v. Stevenson. 1932. A.C. 562.

Dworkin, R. 1977. *Taking Rights Seriously*. Cambridge, MA: Harvard University Press.

Dworkin, R. 1985. *A Matter of Principle*. Cambridge, MA.: Harvard University Press.

Dworkin, R. 1986. *Law's Empire*. Cambridge, MA.: Harvard University Press.

Dworkin, R. 1987. Legal theory and the problem of sense. In R. Gavison (ed.), *Issues in Contemporary Legal Philosophy*. Oxford: Clarendon Press, 9–20.

Dworkin, R. 2002. Thirty years on. *Harvard Law Review* 114: 1655–87.

Dyzenhaus, D. 2000. Positivism's stagnant research programme. *Oxford Journal of Legal Studies* 20: 703–22.

Finnis, J. 1980. *Natural Law and Natural Rights*. Oxford: Clarendon Press.

Finnis, J. 1994. The truth in legal positivism. In R. P. George (ed.), *The Autonomy of Law: Essays on Legal Positivism*. Oxford: Clarendon Press, 195–214.

Finnis, J. 2000. On the incoherence of legal positivism. *Notre Dame Law Review* 75: 1597–1611.

Finnis, J. 2002. Natural law: The classical tradition. In J. L. Coleman and S. Shapiro (eds.), K. E. Himma (assoc. ed.), *Oxford Handbook of Jurisprudence and Philosophy of Law*. Oxford: Oxford University Press, 1–60.

Fuller, L. L. 1946. Reason and fiat in case law. *Harvard Law Review* 59: 376–95.

Fuller, L. L. 1958. Positivism and fidelity to law – a reply to Professor Hart. *Harvard Law Review* 71: 630–72.

George, R. P. 1999. *In Defense of Natural Law*. Oxford: Clarendon Press.

Harman, G. 1994. Doubts about conceptual analysis. In M. Michael and J. O'Leary-Hawthorne (eds.), *Philosophy in Mind: The Place of Philosophy in the*

Study of Mind. Dordrecht: Kluwer Academic Publishers, 43–8.

Hart, H. L. A. 1958. Positivism and the separation of law and morals. *Harvard Law Review* 71: 593–629.

Hart, H. L. A. 1983. *Essays in Jurisprudence and Philosophy*. Oxford: Clarendon Press.

Hart, H. L. A. 1987. Comment [on Dworkin]. In R. Gavison (ed.), *Issues in Contemporary Legal Philosophy*. Oxford: Clarendon Press, 35–42.

Hart, H. L. A. 1994. *The Concept of Law*, 2nd edn. Oxford: Clarendon Press.

Hartney, M. 1991. Introduction. In H. Kelsen, *General Theory of Norms*, ed. M. Hartney. Oxford: Clarendon Press, ix–liii.

Himma, K. E. 2000. H. L. A. Hart and the practical difference thesis. *Legal Theory*, 6: 1–43.

Hobbes, T. [1651] 1996. *Leviathan*, ed. R. Tuck. Cambridge, UK: Cambridge University Press.

Holdsworth, W. S. 1903–38. *A History of English Law*, 12 vols. London: Methuen.

Kelsen, H. 1967. *Pure Theory of Law*, trans. M. Knight. Berkeley: University of California Press.

Kelsen, H. 1973. *Essays in Legal and Moral Philosophy*, ed. O. Weinberger, trans. P. Heath. Dordrecht: D. Reidel Publishing Co.

Kelsen, H. 1991. *General Theory of Norms*, ed. and trans. M. Hartney. Oxford: Clarendon Press.

Kelsen, H. [1934] 1992. *Introduction to the Problems of Legal Theory*, trans. B. L. Paulson and S. L. Paulson. Oxford: Clarendon Press.

Kramer, M. 2000. How moral principles can enter into the law. *Legal Theory* 6: 83–108.

Kretzmann, Norman. 1988. *Lex iniusta non est lex*: Laws on trial in Aquinas' court of conscience. *American Journal of Jurisprudence* 33: 99–122.

Leiter, B. 1998a. Naturalism and naturalized jurisprudence. In B. Bix (ed.), *Analyzing Law: New Essays in Legal Theory*. Oxford: Clarendon Press, 79–104.

Leiter, B. 1998b. Realism, hard positivism, and conceptual analysis. *Legal Theory* 4: 533–47.

Leiter, B. 2002. Naturalism in legal philosophy. In E. N. Zalta (ed.), *Stanford Encyclopedia of Philosophy* <http://plato.stanford.edu/archives/fall2002/entries/lawphil-naturalism/>.

Lucy, W. 1999. *Understanding and Explaining Adjudication*. Oxford: Oxford University Press.

Lukes, S. 1990. Perspectives on authority. In J. Raz (ed.), *Authority*. New York: New York University Press, 203–17.

Lyons, D. 1977. Principles, positivism, and legal theory. *Yale Law Journal* 87: 415–35.

MacCormick, N. 1992. Natural law and the separation of law and morals. In R. P. George (ed.), *Natural Law Theory: Contemporary Essays*. Oxford: Clarendon Press, 105–33.

MacPherson v. Buick Motor Co. 1916. 217 N.Y. 382, 111 N.E. 1050.

Marmor, A. 2002. Exclusive legal positivism. In J. L. Coleman and S. Shapiro (eds.), K. E. Himma (assoc. ed.), *Oxford Handbook of Jurisprudence and Philosophy of Law*. Oxford: Oxford University Press, 104–24.

Moles, R. N. 1987. *Definition and Rule in Legal Theory*. Oxford: Basil Blackwell.

Olivecrona, K. 1971. *Law as Fact*, 2nd edn. London: Stevens & Sons.

Omychund v. Barker. 1744. 26 E.R. 15.

Paulson, S. L. 1992a. Kelsen's legal theory: The final round. *Oxford Journal of Legal Studies* 12: 265–74.

Paulson, S. L. 1992b. The Neo-Kantian dimension of Kelsen's pure theory of law. *Oxford Journal of Legal Studies* 12: 311–32.

Paulson, S. L. 1994. Lon L. Fuller, Gustav Radbruch, and the "positivist" theses. *Law and Philosophy* 13: 259–84.

Paulson, S. L. and Paulson, B. L. (eds.). 1998. *Normativity and Norms: Critical Perspectives on Kelsenian Themes*. Oxford: Clarendon Press.

Perry, S. R. 1987. Judicial obligation, precedent, and the common law. *Oxford Journal of Legal Studies* 7: 215–57.

Perry, S. R. 1995. Interpretation and methodology in legal theory. In A. Marmor (ed.), *Law and Interpretation*. Oxford: Clarendon Press, 97–135.

Perry, S. R. 1996. The varieties of legal positivism. *Canadian Journal of Law and Jurisprudence* 9: 361–81.

Perry, S. R. 1998. Hart's methodological positivism. *Legal Theory* 4: 427–67.

Perry, S. R. 2002. Method and principle in legal theory. *Yale Law Journal* 111: 1757–1813.

Postema, G. J. 1996. Law's autonomy and public practical reason. In R. P. George (ed.), *The Autonomy of Law: Essays on Legal Positivism*. Oxford: Clarendon Press, 79–118.

Raz, J. 1979. *The Authority of Law*. Oxford: Clarendon Press.

Raz, J. 1980. *The Concept of a Legal System: An Introduction to the Theory of Legal System*, 2nd edn. Oxford: Clarendon Press.

Raz, J. 1983. Legal principles and the limits of law. In M. Cohen (ed.), *Ronald Dworkin and Contemporary Jurisprudence*. Totowa, NJ: Rowman and Allanheld, 73–87.

Raz, J. 1985a. Authority and justification. *Philosophy and Public Affairs* 14: 3–29.

Raz, J. 1985b. The morality of obedience. *Michigan Law Review*, 83: 732–49.

Raz, J. 1990. *Practical Reason and Norms* 2nd ed. Princeton, NJ: Princeton University Press.

Raz, J. 1994. *Ethics in the Public Domain.* Oxford: Clarendon Press.

Raz, J. 1996. On the nature of law. *Archiv für Rechts- und Sozialphilosophie* 82: 1–25.

Raz, J. 1998. Postema on law's autonomy and public practical reasons: a critical comment. *Legal Theory* 4: 1–20.

Schauer, F. 1994a. Fuller's internal point of view. *Law and Philosophy* 13: 285–312.

Schauer, F. 1994b. Critical notice of Roger Shiner, *Norm and Nature. Canadian Journal of Philosophy* 24: 495–510.

Schauer, F. 1996. Positivism as pariah. In R. P. George (ed.), *The Autonomy of Law: Essays on Legal Positivism.* Oxford: Clarendon Press, 31–55.

Sebok, A. J. 1998. *Legal Positivism in American Jurisprudence.* Cambridge, UK: Cambridge University Press.

Shapiro, S. J. 1998. On Hart's way out. *Legal Theory* 4: 469–507.

Shapiro, S. J. 2002. Laws, plans, and practical reason. *Legal Theory* 8: 387–441.

Shiner, R. 1992. *Norm and Nature: The Movements of Legal Thought.* Oxford: Clarendon Press.

Soper, E. P. 1977. Legal theory and the obligation of a judge: The Hart/Dworkin dispute. *Michigan Law Review* 75: 473–519.

Soper, E. P. 1987. Choosing a legal theory on moral grounds. In J. Coleman and E. F. Paul (eds.), *Philosophy and Law.* Oxford: Basil Blackwell, 31–48.

Tur, R. and Twining, W. (eds.). 1986. *Essays on Kelsen.* Oxford: Clarendon Press.

Twining, W. 1985. *Karl Llewellyn and the Realist Movement.* Norman: University of Oklahoma Press.

Waluchow, W. J. 1994. *Inclusive Legal Positivism.* Oxford: Clarendon Press.

Waluchow, W. J. 2000. Authority and the practical difference thesis: A defense of inclusive legal positivism. *Legal Theory* 6: 45–82.

Warren, C. 1908. *History of the Harvard Law School and of Early Legal Conditions in America,* 3 vols. New York: Lewis Publishing.

Wright, R. G. 1996. Does positivism matter? In R. P. George (ed.), *The Autonomy of Law.* Oxford: Clarendon Press, 57–78.

Further Reading

Bix, B. 1993. *Law, Language and Legal Determinacy.* Oxford: Clarendon Press.

Bix, B. 1999. H. L. A. Hart and the hermeneutic turn in legal theory. *SMU Law Review* 52: 167–99.

Bix, B. 2001. John Austin. In E. N. Zalta (ed.), *Stanford Encyclopedia of Philosophy* <http://plato.stanford.edu/archives/sum2002/entries/austin-john/>.

Bix, B. 2003. Law as an autonomous discipline. In P. Cane and M. Tushnet (eds.), *The Oxford Handbook of Legal Studies.* Oxford: Oxford University Press, 975–87.

Campbell, T. D. 1996. *The Legal Theory of Ethical Positivism.* Aldershot, UK: Dartmouth Publishing.

Campbell, T. D. (ed.) 1999. *Legal Positivism.* Aldershot, UK: Ashgate Publishers.

Coleman, J. L. (ed.). 2001. *Hart's Postscript: Essay on the Postscript of the Concept of Law.* Oxford: Oxford University Press.

Endicott, T. A. O. 1998. Herbert Hart and the semantic sting. *Legal Theory,* 4: 283–300.

Fuller, L. L. 1969. *The Morality of Law,* rev. edn. New Haven, CT: Yale University Press.

Gardner, J. 2002. Legal positivism: $5\frac{1}{2}$ myths. *American Journal of Jurisprudence* 46: 199–227.

George, R. P. (ed.). 1994. *The Autonomy of Law: Essays on Legal Positivism.* Oxford: Clarendon Press.

Green, L. 1996. The concept of law revisited. *Michigan Law Review* 94: 1687–1717.

Green, L. 1999. Positivism and conventionalism. *Canadian Journal of Law and Jurisprudence* 12: 35–52.

Green, L. 2003. Legal positivism. In E. N. Zalta (ed.), *The Stanford Encyclopedia of Philosophy* <http://plato.stanford.edu/archives/spr2003/entries/legal-positivism>.

Green, M. S. 2003. Hans Kelsen and the logic of legal systems. *Alabama Law Review* 54: 365–413.

Himma, K. E. 2002. Inclusive legal positivism. In J. L. Coleman and S. Shapiro (eds.), K. E. Himma (assoc. ed.), *Oxford Handbook of Jurisprudence and Philosophy of Law.* Oxford: Oxford University Press, 125–65.

Kramer, M. H. 1999. *In Defense of Legal Positivism: Law Without Trimmings.* Oxford: Oxford University Press.

Kramer, M. H. 1999. *In the Realm of Legal and Moral Philosophy.* London: Macmillan.

Kramer, M. H. 2002. Throwing light on the role of moral principles in the law: further reflections. *Legal Theory* 8: 115–143.

Leiter, B. 2003. Beyond the Hart/Dworkin debate: The methodology problem in jurisprudence. *American Journal of Jurisprudence* 48: 17–51.

Lyons, D. 1984. *Ethics and the Rule of Law.* Cambridge, UK: Cambridge University Press.

Lyons, D. 1993. *Moral Aspects of Legal Theory.* Cambridge, UK: Cambridge University Press.

MacCormick, N. 1985. A moralistic case for a-moralistic law? *Valparaiso University Law Review* 20: 1–41.

MacCormick, N. 1994. *Legal Reasoning and Legal Theory*, rev. edn. Oxford: Clarendon Press.

MacCormick N. and Weinberger, O. (eds.). 1986. *An Institutional Theory of Law*. Dordrecht: D. Reidel.

Marmor, A. 2001. *Positive Law and Objective Values.* Oxford: Clarendon Press.

Marmor, A. 2002. The pure theory of law. In E. N. Zalta (ed.), *Stanford Encyclopedia of Philosophy* <http://plato.stanford.edu/archives/win2002/entries/lawphil-theory/>.

Moore, M. 1998. Hart's concluding scientific postscript. *Legal Theory* 4: 301–27.

Murphy, L. 2001. The political question of the concept of law. In J. L. Coleman (ed.), *Hart's Postscript: Essay on the Postscript of the Concept of Law*. Oxford: Oxford University Press, 371–409.

Perry, S. 1989. Second-order reasons, uncertainty and legal theory. *Southern California Law Review* 62: 913–94.

Postema, G. J. 1998. Jurisprudence as practical philosophy. *Legal Theory* 4: 329–57.

Raz, J. 1998. Two views of the nature of the theory of law: A partial comparison. *Legal Theory* 4: 249–82.

Schauer, F. 1998. Positivism through thick and thin. In B. Bix (ed.), *Analyzing Law: New Essays in Legal Theory.* Oxford: Clarendon Press, 65–78.

Shapiro, S. J. 1998. The difference that rules make. In B. Bix (ed.), *Analyzing Law: New Essays in Legal Theory.* Oxford: Clarendon Press, 33–62.

Shapiro, S. J. 2000. Law, morality and the guidance of conduct. *Legal Theory* 6: 127–70.

Soper, E. P. 1998. Two puzzles from the postscript. *Legal Theory* 4: 359–80.

Stavropoulos, N. 1996. *Objectivity in Law.* Oxford: Clarendon Press.

Summers, R. S. 1968. Legal philosophy today – an introduction. In R. S. Summers (ed.), *Essays in Legal Philosophy.* Oxford: Basil Blackwell, 1–21.

Waldron, J. 1996. Kant's legal positivism. *Harvard Law Review* 109: 1535–66.

Waluchow, W. J. 1998. The many faces of legal positivism. *University of Toronto Law Journal* 48: 387–449.

Chapter 3

American Legal Realism

Brian Leiter

Introduction

American Legal Realism was the most important indigenous jurisprudential movement in the United States during the twentieth century, having a profound impact not only on American legal education and scholarship, but also on law reform and lawyering. Unlike its Scandinavian cousin, American Legal Realism was not primarily an extension to law of substantive philosophical doctrines from semantics and epistemology. The Realists were lawyers (plus a few social scientists), not philosophers, and their motivations were, accordingly, different. As lawyers, they were reacting against the dominant "mechanical jurisprudence" or "formalism" of their day. "Formalism," in the sense pertinent here, held that judges decide cases on the basis of distinctively *legal* rules and reasons, which justify a unique result in most cases (perhaps *every* case). The Realists argued, instead, that careful empirical consideration of how courts *really* decide cases reveals that they decide not primarily because of law, but based (roughly speaking) on their sense of what would be "fair" on the facts of the case. (We shall refine this formulation of the "core claim" of Realism shortly.) Legal rules and reasons figure simply as *post hoc* rationalizations for decisions reached on the basis of nonlegal considerations. Because the Realists never made explicit their philosophical presuppositions about the nature of law or their conception of legal theory, one of the important jurisprudential tasks for Realists today is a philosophical reconstruction and defense of these views, especially against the criticisms of legal philosophers, notably H. L. A. Hart.

But Realism also bore the marks of an intellectual culture which it did share with its Scandinavian cousin. This culture – the dominant one in the Western world from the mid-nineteenth century through at least the middle of the last century – was deeply "positivistic," in the sense that it viewed natural science as the paradigm of all genuine knowledge, and thought all other disciplines (from the social sciences to legal study) should emulate the methods of natural science. Chief among the latter was the method of *empirical testing*: hypotheses had to be tested against observations of the world. Thus, the Realists frequently claimed that existing articulations of the "law" were not, in fact, "confirmed" by actual observation of what the courts were really doing. Also influential on some Realists was behaviorism in psychology – John Watson's version, not the later, and better known, brand associated with B. F. Skinner – which was itself in the grips of a "positivistic" conception of knowledge and method. The behaviorist dispensed with talk about a person's beliefs and desires – phenomena that were unobservable, and thus (so behaviorists thought) not empirically confirmable – in favor of trying to explain human behavior strictly in terms of stimuli and the responses they generate. The goal was to discover laws describing which stimuli cause which responses. Many Realists thought that a genuine science of law should do the same thing: it should discover which "stimuli" (e.g., which factual scenarios) produce which "responses" (i.e., what judicial decisions). This understanding of legal "science" is most vivid in the work of Underhill Moore, to whom we return below. For most of the Realists, however, the commitment to "science" and "scientific methods" was more a matter of rhetoric and metaphor than actual scholarly practice: one sees it, for example, in the common Realist talk about the necessity of "testing" legal rules against experience to see whether they produced the results they were supposed to produce.

American Legal Realism claimed Oliver Wendell Holmes, Jr., as its intellectual forebear, but emerged as a real intellectual force in the 1920s at two law schools in the Northeastern United States, Columbia and Yale. Karl Llewellyn, Underhill Moore, Walter Wheeler Cook, Herman Oliphant, and Leon Green were among the major figures in Legal Realism associated with these two schools (though Green ultimately spent most of his career at Northwestern and Texas, while Cook soon departed Columbia for Johns Hopkins). Not all Realists, however, were academics. Jerome Frank – who has had a disproportionate impact on the long-term reception of Realism – was a lawyer with considerable trial experience, who (like many Realists) later worked in President Franklin D. Roosevelt's "New Deal" Administration during the 1930s, and eventually served as a federal judge; he never held an academic appointment. Among legal theorists, the Realists are certainly notable for the sizable number who also enjoyed distinguished careers in the practice of law, including, for example, William O. Douglas (appointed to the US Supreme Court by Roosevelt), and Thurman Arnold, founder of a prominent Washington, DC law firm that still bears his name.

Legal Indeterminacy

The Realists famously argued that the law was "indeterminate." By this, they meant two things: first, that the law was *rationally* indeterminate, in the sense that the available class of legal reasons did not *justify* a unique decision (at least in those cases that reached the stage of appellate review); but second, that the law was also *causally* or *explanatorily* indeterminate, in the sense that legal reasons did not suffice to explain why judges decided as they did. Causal indeterminacy *entails* rational indeterminacy on the assumption that judges are responsive to applicable (justificatory) legal reasons. Of course, that assumption is not a trivial one, and at least one Realist, Jerome Frank (1931), drew attention to the indeterminacy that results from judicial incompetence or corruption. From a jurisprudential point of view, of course, this indeterminacy is trivial, since no legal theorist, of any school, denies that the law does a poor job of predicting what courts will do when courts are ignorant of or indifferent to the law!

Realist arguments for the rational indeterminacy of law generally focused on the existence of conflicting, but equally legitimate, canons of interpretation for precedents and statutes. Llewellyn demonstrated, for example, that courts had endorsed *both* the principle of statutory construction that, "A statute cannot go beyond its text," but also the principle that "To effect its purpose a statute must be implemented beyond its text" (Llewellyn 1950: 401). But if a court could properly appeal to either canon when faced with a question of statutory interpretation, then the "methods" of legal reasoning (including principles of statutory construction) would justify at least two different interpretations of the meaning of the statute. In that case, the question for the Realists was: why did the judge reach that result, given that law and legal reasons did not require the judge to do so?

Llewellyn (1930a) offered a similar argument about the conflicting, but equally legitimate, ways of interpreting precedent. According to Llewellyn's (incautiously) strong version of the argument, *any* precedent can be read "strictly" or "loosely," and either reading is "recognized, legitimate, honorable" (1930a: 74). The strict interpretation characterizes the rule of the case as specific to the facts of the case; the loose interpretation abstracts (in varying degrees) from the specific facts in order to treat the case as standing for some general norm. But if "each precedent has not one value [that is, stands for not just one rule], but two, and ... the two are wide apart, and ... whichever value a later court assigns to it, such assignment will be respectable, traditionally sound, dogmatically correct" (Llewellyn 1930a, 76), then precedent, as a source of law, cannot provide reasons for a unique outcome, because more than one rule can be extracted from the same precedent.

One difficulty with these Realist arguments is that they rely on a tacit conception of *legitimate* legal argument. The assumption is that if lawyers and courts employ some form of argument – a "strict" construal of precedent, a particular canon of statutory construction – then that form of argument is *legitimate* in any and all cases. Put this incautiously, the assumption cannot be right: not *every* strict construal of precedent will be legally proper in every case. Even Llewellyn must recognize this, as suggested by his famous – but clearly facetious – example of the "strict" reading that yields, "This rule holds only of red-headed Walpoles in pale magenta Buick cars" (1930a: 72). But that is hardly likely to ever be a legitimate construal of a precedent, barring some bizarre scenario in which all these facts turned out to be legally relevant, and Llewellyn surely knows as much. The claim cannot be, then, that *any* strict or loose construal of precedent is *always* valid. It must only be that lawyers and judges have this interpretive latitude often enough to inject a considerable degree of indeterminacy into law.

There is a related difficulty, pertaining to another suppressed assumption of the Realist argument. For notice that the Realist argument for the indeterminacy of law – really the indeterminacy of law and legal reasoning – is based on an implicit view about the *scope* of the class of legal reasons: that is, the class of reasons that judges may properly invoke in justifying a decision. The Realists appear to assume that the legitimate sources of law are exhausted by statutes and precedents, since they focus, almost exclusively, on the conflicting but equally legitimate method for *interpreting* statutes and precedents in order to establish law's indeterminacy. Unfortunately, the Realists themselves never gave arguments for this assumption. Later writers, like Ronald Dworkin, have argued that much indeterminacy in law disappears once we expand our notion of what constitute legitimate sources of law to include not only statutes and precedents, but also broader moral and political principles. The Realists, consistent with their positivist intellectual culture, largely presumed that moral principles were sub-

jective and malleable. There are certainly reasons to think the Realists were right, and Dworkin wrong, in this regard (cf. Leiter 2001), but the topic is, unfortunately, unaddressed by the Realists themselves.

One final point about the Realist indeterminacy thesis bears emphasizing. Unlike the later Critical Legal Studies writers, the Realists, for the most part, did not overstate the scope of indeterminacy in law. The Realists were (generally) clear that their focus was indeterminacy at the stage of appellate review, where one ought to expect a higher degree of uncertainty in the law. Cases that have determinate legal answers are, after all, less likely to be litigated to the stage of appellate review. Thus, Llewellyn explicitly qualified his indeterminacy claim by saying that, "[I]n any case doubtful enough to make litigation respectable the available authoritative premises ... are at least two, and ... the two are mutually contradictory as applied to the case at hand" (Llewellyn 1931: 1239). And Max Radin noted that judicial "decisions will consequently be called for chiefly in what may be called marginal cases, in which prognosis is difficult and uncertain. It is this fact that makes the entire body of legal judgments seem less stable than it really is" (Radin 1942: 1271).

The Core Claim of American Legal Realism

All the Realists agreed that the law and legal reasons are rationally indeterminate (at least in the sorts of cases that reach the stage of appellate review), so that the best explanation for why judges decide as they do must look beyond the law itself. In particular, all the Realists endorsed what we may call "the Core Claim" of Realism: in deciding cases, judges respond primarily to the stimulus of the facts of the case, rather than to legal rules and reasons. It is possible to find some version of the Core Claim in the writings of all the major Realists.

Oliphant, for example, gives us an admirably succinct statement when he says that courts "respond to the stimulus of the facts in the concrete cases before them rather than to the stimulus of over-general and outworn abstractions in opinions and treatises" (1928: 75). Oliphant's claim is confirmed by Judge Joseph Hutcheson's admission that "the vital, motivating impulse for the decision is an intuitive sense of what is right or wrong for that cause" (1929: 285). Similarly, Frank cited "a great American judge," Chancellor Kent, who confessed that, "He first made himself 'master of the facts.' Then (he wrote) 'I saw where justice lay, and the moral sense dictated the court half the time; I then sat down to search the authorities ... but I *almost always found principles suited to my view of the case*' " (Frank 1930: 104 note). Precisely the same view of what judges really do when they decide cases is presupposed in Llewellyn's advice to lawyers that, while they must provide the court "a technical ladder" justifying the result, what the lawyer must really do is "on the facts ... persuade the court your case is sound" (Llewellyn 1930a: 76). Similarly, Frank quotes approvingly a former ABA President to the effect that " 'the way to win a case is to make the judge want to decide in your favor and then, and then only, to cite precedents which will justify such a determination' " (Frank 1930: 102).

Several points bear noting about how we should understand the Core Claim of Realism. First, it is not simply the trivial thesis that judges must take account of the facts of the case in deciding the outcome. Rather, it is the much stronger claim that in deciding cases, judges are reacting to the underlying facts of the case, *whether or not those facts are legally significant*, that is, whether or not they are relevant in virtue of the applicable legal rules. Second, the Core Claim is not the thesis that legal rules and reasons *never* affect the course of decision; rather it is the weaker claim that they generally have no (or little) effect, especially in the sorts of cases with which the Realists were especially concerned: namely, that class of more difficult cases that reached the stage of appellate review. Llewellyn is representative when he asks, "Do I suggest that ... the 'accepted rules,' the rules the judges say that they apply, are without influence upon their actual behavior?" and answers, "I do not" (Llewellyn 1930b: 444). The Realist approach, says Llewellyn, "admits ... *some* relation between *any*

accepted rule and judicial behavior" but then demands that *what* that relation is requires empirical investigation, since it is not always the relation suggested by the "logic" (or content) of the rule (1930b: 444). As he puts the point elsewhere: realists deny that "traditional ... rule-formulations are *the* heavily operative factor in producing court decisions" (1931: 1237, emphasis added). But to deny only *this* claim is to admit that rules play *some* causal role in decisions.

Third, many of the Realists advanced the Core Claim in the hope that legal rules might be reformulated in more fact-specific ways: this, more than anything, accounts for the profound impact Realism had on American law and law reform. Thus, for example, Oliphant (1928) spoke of a "return to *stare decisis*," the doctrine that rules laid down in prior cases should control in subsequent cases that are relevantly similar. Oliphant's critique was that the "legal rules," as articulated by courts and scholars, had become too general and abstract, ignoring the particular factual contexts in which the original disputes arose. The result was that these rules no longer had any value for judges in later cases, who simply ignore the abstract official doctrine in favor of a situation-specific judgment appropriate to the particular facts of the case. Oliphant argued that a meaningful doctrine of *stare decisis* could be restored by making legal rules more fact-specific. So, for example, instead of pretending that there is a single, general rule about the enforceability of contractual promises not to compete, Oliphant suggested that we attend to what the courts are really doing in that area: namely, enforcing those promises, when made by the seller of a business to the buyer; but not enforcing those promises, when made by a (soon-to-be former) employee to his employer (1928: 159–60). In the former scenario, Oliphant claimed, the courts were simply doing the economically sensible thing (no one would buy a business, if the seller could simply open up shop again and compete); while in the latter scenario, courts were taking account of the prevailing informal norms governing labor relations at the time, which disfavored such promises. (The *2nd Restatement of Contracts*, produced by the American Law Institute (ALI), later codified something very close to Oliphant's distinction.)

Two Branches of Realism

Although all Realists accepted the Core Claim, they parted company over the question of how to explain why judges respond to the underlying facts of the case as they do. The "Sociological" Wing of Realism – represented by writers like Oliphant, Moore, Llewellyn, and Felix Cohen – thought that judicial decisions fell into *predictable* patterns (though *not*, of course, the patterns one would predict just by looking at the existing rules of law). From this fact, these Realists inferred that various "social" forces must operate upon judges to force them to respond to facts in similar, and predictable, ways.

The "Idiosyncracy Wing" of Realism, by contrast – exemplified most prominently by Frank and Judge Hutcheson – claimed that what determines the judge's response to the facts of a particular case are idiosyncratic facts about the psychology or personality of that individual judge. Thus Frank notoriously asserted that "the personality of the judge is the pivotal factor in law administration" (1930: 111). (Note, however, that no Realist ever claimed, as popular legend has it, that "what the judge ate for breakfast" determines his or her decision!) Or as Frank formulated the point elsewhere: the "conventional theory" holds that "*Rule* plus *Facts* = *Decision*," while his own view is that "the *Stimuli* affecting the judge" plus "the *Personality of the judge* = *Decision*" (1931: 242). It is, of course, Frank's injection of the "personality of the judge" into the formula that puts the distinctive stamp on his interpretation of the Core Claim: drop that and you have the Core Claim itself.

Now notwithstanding the behaviorist rhetoric in the preceding formulation, Frank was, in fact, primarily influenced by Freudian psychoanalysis, a doctrine anathema to behaviorists since it dispenses with the behaviorist prohibition on reference to what goes on in the "black box" of the mind: beliefs and desires – *unconscious* ones no less! – are the very stuff of psychoanalysis. Despite that difference, Freudianism retains the scientist self-conception characteristic of behaviorism, and so Frank could still think of his approach as contributing to a science of law.

Influenced by Freud's idea that the key to the personality lay in the buried depths of the unconscious, however, Frank felt that it would be impossible for observers of judicial behavior to discover the crucial facts about personality that would determine a judge's response to the facts of a particular case. As a result, Frank concluded that prediction of judicial decision would be largely impossible; the desire of lawyers and citizens to think otherwise, Frank suggested, reflected merely an infantile wish for certainty and security.

Frank's skepticism about our ability to predict how judges will decide cases flies in the face of the experience of most lawyers. While the outcome of some cases is hard to fathom, most of the time lawyers are able to advise clients as to the likely outcome of disputes brought before courts: if they weren't, they'd be out of business! Yet despite the fact that Frank's skepticism sits poorly with practical experience, a striking feature of the long-term reception of Realism is that Frank's view is often taken as the essence of Realism (cf. Leiter 1997: 267-8, and the sources cited therein). This "Frankification" of Realism does justice neither to the majority of Realists who felt that judicial decision was predictable – because its determining factors were identifiable social forces, not opaque facts about personality – nor to those Realists who envisioned a refashioned regime of legal rules that really would describe and predict judicial decisions, precisely because they would take account of the particular factual contexts to which courts are actually sensitive.

Recall Oliphant's example of the conflicting court decisions on the validity of contractual promises not to compete. Oliphant claims that in fact the decisions tracked the underlying facts of the cases:

> All the cases holding the promises invalid are found to be cases of employees' promises not to compete with their employers after a term of employment. Contemporary guild [i.e. labor union] regulations not noticed in the opinions made their holding eminently sound. All the cases holding the promises valid were cases of promises by those selling a business and promising not to compete with the purchasers. Contemporary economic reality made these holdings eminently sound. (Oliphant 1928: 159–60)

Thus, in the former fact-scenarios, the courts enforced the prevailing norms (as expressed in guild regulations disfavoring such promises); in the latter cases, the courts came out differently because it was economically best under *those* factual circumstances to do so. Llewellyn provides a similar illustration (1960: 122–4). A series of New York cases applied the rule that buyers who reject the seller's shipment by formally stating their objections thereby waive all other objections. Llewellyn notes that the rule seems to have been rather harshly applied in a series of cases where the buyers simply may not have known at the time of rejection of other defects or where the seller could not have cured anyway. A careful study of the facts of these cases revealed, however, that in each case where the rule seemed harshly applied, what had really happened was that the market had fallen, and the buyer was looking to escape the contract. The court in each case, being "sensitive to commerce or to decency" (1960: 124), applied the unrelated rule about rejection to frustrate the buyer's attempt to escape the contract. Thus, the commercial norm – buyers ought to honor their commitments even under changed market conditions – is enforced by the courts through a *seemingly* harsh application of an unrelated rule concerning rejection. It is these "background facts, those of mercantile practice, those of the situation-type" (Llewellyn 1960: 126) that determine the course of decision.

Underhill Moore tried to systematize this approach in what he called "the institutional method" (Moore and Hope 1929). Moore's idea was this: identify the normal behavior for any "institution" (e.g., commercial banking); then identify and demarcate deviations from this norm quantitatively, and try to identify the point at which deviation from the norm will *cause* a judicial decision that corrects the deviation from the norm (e.g., how far must a bank depart from normal check-cashing practice before a court will decide against the bank in a suit brought by the customer?). The goal is a predictive formula: deviation of degree X from "institutional behavior (i.e., behavior which frequently, repeatedly, usually occurs)" (1929: 707) will cause courts to act. Thus, says Moore: "the semblance of causal relation between future and past decisions is the result of the relation of both to a third variable,

the relevant institutions in the locality of the court" (Moore and Sussman 1931: 1219). Put differently: what judges respond to is the extent to which the facts show a deviation from the prevailing norm in the commercial culture.

The thesis of Sociological Wing Realists like Llewellyn, Oliphant, and Moore – that judges enforce the norms of commercial culture or try to do what is socioeconomically best on the facts of the case – should not be confused with the idea that judges decide based, for example, on how they feel about the particular parties or the lawyers. These "fireside equities," as Llewellyn called them (1960: 121), may sometimes influence judges; but what more typically determines the course of decision is the "situation-type," that is, the general pattern of behavior exemplified by the particular facts of the disputed transaction and what would constitute normal or socioeconomically desirable behavior in the relevant commercial context. The point is decidedly not that judges usually decide because of idiosyncratic likes and dislikes with respect to the individuals before the court (cf. Radin 1925: 357). So, for example, Leon Green's groundbreaking 1931 textbook on torts was organized not by the traditional *doctrinal* categories (e.g., negligence, intentional torts, strict liability), but rather by the factual scenarios – the "situation-types" – in which harms occur: for example "surgical operations," "traffic and transportation," and the like. The premise of this approach was that there was no general law of torts *per se*, but rather predictable patterns of torts decisions for each recurring situation-type that courts encounter.

But why would judges, with some degree of predictable uniformity, enforce the norms of commercial culture as applied to the underlying facts of the case? Here we must make an inference to the best explanation of the phenomenon: there must be features of the "sociological" (as opposed to the idiosyncratic psychological) profile of the judges that explain the predictable uniformity in their decisions. The Realists did little more than gesture, however, at a suitable psychosocial explanation. "Professional judicial office," Llewellyn suggested, was "the most important among all the lines of factor which make for reckonability" of decision (1960: 45); "the *office* waits and then moves with the majestic power to shape the man" (1960: 46). Echoing, but modifying, Frank, Llewellyn continued: "The place to begin is with the fact that the men of our appellate bench are human beings. . . . And one of the more obvious and obstinate facts about human beings is that they operate in and respond to traditions. . . . Tradition grips them, shapes them, limits them, guides them. . . . To a man of sociology or psychology. . . this needs no argument. . . ." (1960: 53). Radin suggested that "the standard transactions with their regulatory incidents are familiar ones to him [the judge] because of his experience as a citizen and a lawyer" (1925: 358). Felix Cohen, by contrast, simply lamented that "at present no publication [exists] showing the political, economic, and professional background and activities of our judges" (1935: 846), presumably because such a publication would identify the relevant "social" determinants of decision. "A truly realistic theory of judicial decision," says Cohen, "must conceive every decision as something more than an expression of individual personality, as . . . even more importantly. . . a product of social determinants" (1935: 843), an idea taken up at length in recent years by political scientists studying courts (cf. Cross 1997).

In sum, if the Sociological Wing of Realism – Llewellyn, Moore, Oliphant, Cohen, Radin, among others – is correct, then judicial decisions are causally determined (by the relevant psychosocial facts about judges), and at the same time judicial decisions fall into predictable patterns because these psychosocial facts about judges (e.g., their professionalization experiences, their backgrounds) are not idiosyncratic, but characteristic of significant portions of the judiciary. Rather than rendering judicial decision a mystery, the Realists' Core Claim, to the extent it is true, shows how and why lawyers can predict what courts do.

We can now see, also, that only the Sociological Wing Realists could hold out the hope of crafting legal rules that *really* would "guide" decision, or at least accurately *describe* the course of decision actually realized by courts. This is precisely why Oliphant, for example, spoke of a "return" to *stare decisis*: the problem for Oliphant, as for most of the Realists in the Sociological Wing, wasn't that rules were pointless, but rather that the existing rules were pitched at a level of gener-

ality that bore no relation to the fact-specific ways in which courts actually decided cases. Where it was impossible to formulate situation-specific rules, the Realists advocated using general norms, reflecting the norms that judges actually employ anyway. This formed a central part of Llewellyn's approach to drafting Article 2 of the Uniform Commercial Code in the United States – an undertaking that would seem pointless if Realists didn't believe in legal rules! Since the Sociological Wing claimed that judges, in any event, enforced the norms of commercial culture, Article 2 tells them to do precisely this, by imposing the obligation of "good faith" in contractual dealings (Sec. 1–203). "Good faith" requires, besides honesty, "the observation of reasonable commercial standards of fair dealing in the trade" (Sec. 2–103). For a judge, then, to enforce the rule requiring "good faith" is just to enforce the norms of commercial culture – which is precisely what the Realists claim the judges are doing anyway! (For discussion, see White 1994.)

Naturalized Jurisprudence?

Sociological Wing Realists – who were, recall, the vast majority – thought that the task of legal theory was to identify and describe – *not* justify – the patterns of decision; the social sciences were the tool for carrying out this nonnormative task. While the Realists looked to behaviorist psychology and sociology, it is easy to understand contemporary law-and-economics (at least in its descriptive or "positive" aspects) as pursuing the same task by relying on economic explanations for the patterns of decision. See ECONOMIC RATIONALITY IN THE ANALYSIS OF LEGAL RULES AND INSTITUTIONS.

As a result of this Realist orientation, there is a sense in which we may think of the type of jurisprudence the Realists advocated as a *naturalized* jurisprudence, that is, a jurisprudence that eschews armchair conceptual analysis in favor of continuity with *a posteriori* inquiry in the empirical sciences (cf. Leiter 1997, 1998). Just as a *naturalized* epistemology – in Quine's famous formulation – "simply falls into place as a chapter of psychology" (Quine 1969: 82), as "a purely descriptive, causal-nomological science of human cognition" (Kim 1988: 388), so too a naturalized jurisprudence for the Realists is an essentially descriptive theory of the causal connections between underlying situation-types and actual judicial decisions. (Indeed, one major Realist, Underhill Moore, even anticipates the Quinean slogan: "This study lies within the province of jurisprudence. It also lies within the field of behavioristic psychology. It places the province within the field" (Moore and Callahan 1943: 1).) There are, of course, competing conceptions of what it means to *naturalize* some domain of philosophy, and we cannot enter here the debates on their merits and demerits (see Leiter 1998, 2002). What bears emphasizing is that the *method* that the Realists bring to bear in legal theory (at least, in the theory of adjudication) might, fruitfully, be thought of as a *naturalistic* method, akin to Quine's proposal for naturalizing epistemology.

Notice, in particular, that both Quine and the Realists can be seen as advocating naturalization for analogous reasons. On one familiar reading, Quine advocates naturalism as a response to the failure of the traditional foundationalist program in epistemology, from Descartes to Carnap. As one commentator puts it: "Once we see the sterility of the foundationalist program, we see that the only genuine questions there are to ask about the relation between theory and evidence and about the acquisition of belief are psychological questions" (Kornblith 1994: 4). That is, once we recognize our inability to tell a *normative* story about the relation between evidence and theory – a story about what theories are *justified* on the basis of the evidence – Quine would have us give up the normative project: "Why not just see how [the] construction [of theories on the basis of evidence] really proceeds?" (Quine 1969: 75).

So, too, the Realists can be read as advocating an empirical theory of adjudication precisely because they think the traditional jurisprudential project of trying to show decisions to be *justified* on the basis of legal rules and reasons is a failure. For the Realists, recall, the law is rationally indeterminate; that is, the class of legitimate legal reasons that a court might appeal to in justifying a decision fails, in fact, to justify a *unique* outcome in many of the cases. If the law were determinate,

then we might expect – except in cases of ineptitude or corruption – that legal rules and reasons would be reliable predictors of judicial outcomes. But the law in many cases is indeterminate, and thus in those cases there is no "foundational" story to be told about the particular decision of a court: legal reasons would justify just as well a contrary result. But if legal rules and reasons cannot *rationalize* the decisions, then they surely cannot *explain* them either: we must, accordingly, look to other factors to explain why the court actually decided as it did. Thus, the Realists in effect say: "Why not see how the construction of decisions really proceeds?" The Realists, then, call for an essentially *naturalized* and hence *descriptive* theory of adjudication, a theory of what it is that causes courts to decide as they do.

We should not overstate, though, the force of the analogy (though it will prove helpful in seeing shortly where later legal philosophers have gone wrong in assimilating Realism to the paradigm of philosophy-cum-conceptual-analysis). For one thing, we should not think that the Realists are committed to proto-Quinean doctrines across the boards. We can see this at two places. First, as we will see shortly, the Realists end up presupposing a theory of the concept of legality in framing their arguments for law's indeterminacy; thus, while they may believe the only fruitful account of *adjudication* is descriptive and empirical, not normative and conceptual, they themselves need a concept of *law* that is not itself empirical or naturalized. The analogy with naturalized epistemology, in other words, must be localized to the theory of adjudication, and not the whole of jurisprudence.

Second, the crux of the Realist position (at least for the majority of Realists) is that nonlegal reasons (e.g., judgments of fairness, or consideration of commercial norms) *explain* the decisions. They, of course, explain the decisions by *justifying* them, though not necessarily by justifying a unique outcome (i.e., the nonlegal reasons might themselves rationalize other decisions as well). Now clearly the descriptive story about the nonlegal reasons is not going to be part of a nonmentalistic naturalization of the theory of adjudication: a causal explanation of decisions in terms of reasons (even nonlegal reasons) does require taking the normative force of the reasons *qua reasons* seriously. The behaviorism of Quine or Underhill Moore is not in the offing here, but surely this is to be preferred: behaviorism failed as a foundation for empirical social science, while social-scientific theories employing mentalistic categories have flourished. Moreover, if the non-legal reasons are themselves indeterminate – that is, if they do not justify a *unique* outcome – then any causal explanation of the decision will have to go beyond reasons to identify the psychosocial facts (e.g., about personality, class, gender, socialization, etc.) that cause the decision. Such a "naturalization" of the theory of adjudication might be insufficiently austere in its ontology for Quinean scruples, but it is still a recognizable attempt to subsume what judges do within a (social) scientific framework.

How Should Judges Decide Cases?

The naturalism of the Realists – as manifest in the Core Claim and their desire to achieve a sound empirical understanding of how courts *really* decide cases – leaves unaddressed the *normative* question that has most often interested legal theorists in recent years: how *ought* courts to decide cases? The Realists do not speak univocally on this score, but two dominant themes do emerge. Some Realists (Holmes, Felix Cohen, Frank on the bench) think judges should simply adopt, openly, a legislative role, acknowledging that, because the law is indeterminate, courts must necessarily make judgments on matters of social and economic policy. These Realists – let us call them "the Proto-Posnerians," to mark their anticipation of a view familiar in our own day (Posner 1999: 240–2) – would simply have courts make these judgments openly and candidly. Rather than engaging in the facade of legal reasoning, judges would tackle directly exactly the kinds of political and economic considerations a legislature would weigh.

Another prominent strand in Realism, associated especially with Llewellyn and Frank in his theoretical writings, embraces a kind of "normative quietism," according to which it is pointless to give normative advice to judges, since how judges decide cases (as reported by the Core

Claim) is just an irremediable fact about what they do: it would be idle to tell judges they *ought* to do otherwise. The strongest form of this doctrine is apparent in Frank, who views hunch-based decision making as a brute fact about human psychology: "the psychologists tell us," he says, that "no human being in his normal thinking process arrives at decisions by the route of any... syllogistic reasoning..." (1930: 108–9). (No actual psychological evidence is cited.) Similarly, Frank says regarding what he dubs "Cadi justice" – essentially justice by personal predilection – that "the true question... is not whether we should 'revert' to [it], but whether (a) we have ever abandoned it and (b) we can ever pass beyond it" (1931: 27). Advocating a "'reversion to Cadi justice'" – as some critics wrongly accuse Realism of doing – "is as meaningless as [advocating] a 'reversion to mortality' or a 'return to breathing'" (1931: 31). This is because "the personal element is unavoidable in judicial decisions" (1931: 25).

Alas, Frank had no sound empirical support for his strong assumptions about hunch-based decision making and the role of the "personal element." Indeed, the Sociological Wing of Realism, as we have seen, criticized Frank precisely on the grounds that these assumptions weren't plausible, given the predictability of much of what courts do.

A more subtle version of quietism, however, is apparent in Llewellyn's work. Here the Realists are not entirely silent on normative questions; they simply give as *explicit* advice that judges *ought* to do what it is that they largely do anyway. So, for example, if judges, as a matter of course, enforce the norms of commercial culture, then that is precisely what Realists tell them they ought to do. That, as we have seen, is exactly the view that informed Llewellyn's approach to the Uniform Commercial Code (cf. White 1994 on this topic).

This weaker version of quietism – tell judges that they *ought* to do what they by-and-large do anyway – resonates with the views of at least some of the Proto-Posnerian Realists. Holmes, for example, complains that "judges themselves have failed adequately to recognize their duty of [explicitly] weighing considerations of social advantage" (1897: 467). But having just noted that what is really going on in the opinions of judges anyway is "a concealed, half-conscious battle on the question of legislative policy" (Holmes 1897: 466), it follows that this "duty" is in fact "inevitable, and the result of the often proclaimed judicial aversion to deal with such considerations is simply to leave the very ground and foundation of judgments inarticulate, and often unconscious" (1897: 467). Thus, what Holmes really calls for is for judges to do explicitly (and perhaps more successfully, as a consequence) what they do unconsciously anyway.

In a striking case of the divide between theory and practice, Frank on the bench was much more clearly a Proto-Posnerian – at least of the Holmesian variety – than a believer in the inevitability of Cadi justice. For example, in his concurring opinion in *Ricketts v. Pennsylvania R. Co.* (1946), Judge Frank, now sitting on the US Court of Appeals for the Second Circuit, rejected the majority's doctrinal analysis of the case (which involved an injured employee, who had, unwittingly, and as a result of bad legal advice, signed away his right to sue the railroad):

> I think we should . . . reject many of the finespun distinctions [invoked by the majority that are] made by Williston [in his treatise on contracts] and expressed in the Restatement of Contracts. . . .
>
> As Mr. Justice Holmes often urged, when an important issue of social policy arises, it should be candidly, not evasively, articulated. In other contexts, the courts have openly acknowledged that the economic inequality between the ordinary employer and the ordinary individual employee usually means the absence of "free bargaining." I think the courts should do so in these employee release cases. . . .
>
> Such a ruling will not produce legal uncertainty, but will promote certainty – as anyone can see who reads the large number of cases in this field, with their numerous intricate methods of getting around the objective theory [of contracts]. Such a ruling would simply do directly what many courts have been doing indirectly. It is fairly clear that they have felt, although they have not said, that employers should not, by such releases, rid themselves of obligation to injured employees, obligations which society at large will bear – either [by taxes or charity]. (*Ricketts v. Pennsylvania R. Co.* 1946 at 760, 768, 769)

Note that the familiar, contemporary questions about the legitimacy of unelected judges engaging in this kind of policy-driven "legislating from the bench" were not questions that concerned the Proto-Posnerians. Indeed, they would likely regard such questions as pointless and distracting: "Legitimate or not," one can imagine Judge Frank saying, "this is what judges are really doing – so let's just do it openly and directly."

Of course, some Proto-Posnerians among the Realists had no quietist pretensions. Cohen (1935), most notably, recommended that judges address themselves to questions of socioeconomic policy *instead* of the traditional doctrinal questions he claimed they had been addressing.

Keep in mind, too, that the "quietism" of some Realists is quietism about normative guidance *for judges*. It is quite clear, of course, that quietists like Llewellyn thought it was *good* that judges were inclined in commercial disputes to try to enforce the norms of commercial culture. That, of course, is a normative view about how judges *ought* to decide cases; the quietism emerges in the fact that these Realists don't think there is any point to a normative theory that tells judges they ought to decide in some different way. Llewellyn, like other Realists, was a New Deal liberal, and offered no explicit theoretical rationale for his normative preferences. Yet, as has been recently argued (Schwartz 2000), one can understand Llewellyn's preference for judges who attended to the norms of commercial culture as reflecting a kind of nascent appreciation of efficiency norms in legal rule making.

Legacy of Legal Realism I: Legal Education and Scholarship in the United States

Within American law and legal education, the impact of Legal Realism has been profound. By emphasizing the indeterminacy of law and legal reasoning, and the importance of nonlegal considerations in judicial decisions, the Realists cleared the way for judges and lawyers to talk openly about the political and economic considerations that in fact affect many decisions. This is manifest in the frequent discussion – by courts, by lawyers, and by law teachers – of the "policy" implications of deciding one way rather than another. The modern legal textbook is largely an invention of the Realists as well. The "science" of law envisioned by Christopher Langdell, Dean of Harvard Law School in the late nineteenth century, was to be based exclusively on a study of the opinions issued by courts: from these, the scholar (or student) could formulate the rules and principles of law that governed decisions. The Realists, who very much shared the ambition of making the study of law "scientific," disagreed profoundly with Langdell over what that entailed. For if the Realists were correct that judges' published opinions at best hint at and at worst conceal the real nonlegal grounds for decision, then the study only of cases could not possibly equip a lawyer to advise clients as to what courts will do. To really teach law, the Realists thought, it was necessary to understand the economic, political, and social dimensions of the problems courts confront, for all these considerations figure in the decisions of judges. Thus, the modern legal teaching materials are typically titled, "Cases *and Materials* on the Law of...," where the materials are drawn from nonlegal sources that illuminate the various nonlegal factors relevant to understanding what the courts have done.

Realism has also had a significant impact upon law reform, including the work of the American Law Institute. This may, at first, seem surprising, since the Realists were famously hostile to the ALI at its inception. Leon Green declared that, "The undertaking to restate the rules and principles developed by the English and American courts finds in the field of torts a most hopeless task" (1928: 1014). And no student of Legal Realism or the American Law Institute can forget Yale psychologist Edward Robinson's impassioned denunciation in the pages of the *Yale Law Journal* in 1934:

And so the American Law Institute has thought that it can help simple-minded lawyers by giving an artificial and arbitrary picture of the principles in terms of which human disputes are supposed to be settled.... [But] [s]uch bodies of logically consistent doctrines as those formulated by the

experts of the American Law Institute are obviously not to be considered as efforts to understand the legal institution as it is. When one considers these "restatements" of the common law and how they are being formulated, one remembers how the expert theologians got together in the Council of Nicaea and decided by a vote the nature of the Trinity. There is a difference between the two occasions. The church fathers had far more power than does the Law Institute to enforce belief in their conclusion. (Robinson 1934: 260–1)

Yet the real worry of these Realists was the one articulated by Oliphant (1928), discussed earlier. The Realist critics of the ALI feared that the Restatements would simply codify "over-general and outworn abstractions" (Oliphant 1928: 75) that courts might recite but which shed no light on what they were doing. Yet, in practice, the Restatements have been pursued in precisely the spirit in which Oliphant called for a return to *stare decisis*: namely, as a way of restating legal doctrines in ways that were more fact-specific, and thus more descriptive of the actual grounds of decision. (Recall that the *2nd Restatement of Contracts* in fact incorporates something very close to Oliphant's distinction between different kinds of promises not to compete.)

The paradigm of scholarship established by the Realists – contrasting what courts say they're doing with what they *actually* do – is one that has become so much the norm that distinguished scholars practice it without even feeling the need, any longer, to self-identify as Realists. Consider the classic modern debunking of what courts call "the irreparable injury rule" (Laycock 1991). The irreparable injury rule states courts will not enjoin misconduct when money damages will suffice to compensate the victim. According to Professor Laycock, however:

Courts do prevent harm when they can. Judicial opinions recite the rule constantly, but do not apply it ... When courts reject plaintiff's choice of remedy, there is always some other reason, and that reason has nothing to do with the irreparable injury rule.... An intuitive sense of justice has led judges to produce sensible results, but there has been no similar pressure to produce sensible explanations. (Laycock 1991: vii)

Like the Realists, Laycock finds a disjunction between the "law in the books" and the "law in action," and, also like the Realists, he invokes as an explanation for that disjunction the decision makers' "intuitive sense of justice." Like Oliphant before him, Laycock seeks, in turn, to reformulate and restate the rules governing injunctions to reflect the *actual* pattern of decisions by the courts following this intuitive sense of justice.

Legacy of Legal Realism II: Legal Theory

Although the Realists profoundly affected legal education and lawyering in America, they have had less influence within recent Anglo-American jurisprudence. The history of Realism in this respect is complex. With the advent of World War II, many scholars (especially at Catholic universities) criticized the Realists on the grounds that their attacks on the idea of a "rule of law" simply gave support to fascists and other enemies of democracy. At the same time, scholars at Yale (notably Harold Lasswell and Myres McDougal) propounded a watered-down version of Realism under the slogan of "policy science." These writers emphasized the Realist idea of using social scientific expertise as a way of enabling legal officials to produce effective and desired results. "Policy science" is now, happily, defunct, since it had far more to do with rationalizing American imperialism than it did with science.

In the 1950s, American legal education was swept by the "legal process" school, which largely suppressed the lessons of Realism. The Legal Process School, associated with the work of Henry Hart and Albert Sacks at Harvard, identified the distinctive institutional competence of judges as providing "reasoned elaboration" for their decisions; this could be done well or poorly, and it was the business of legal scholars to monitor the performance of judges in this regard, and thus to help ensure that judicial opinions would provide a reliable guide to the future course of decision. Absent in all this was any principled response to the Realist argument that the law

and legal reasoning were essentially indeterminate. (Within Anglo-American jurisprudence, the work of Ronald Dworkin is usefully understood as a philosophical defense of the Legal Process conception of adjudication.)

The decisive blow for Legal Realism as a jurisprudential movement, however, was dealt by the English legal philosopher H. L. A. Hart. In his seminal 1961 work, *The Concept of Law* (2nd edn. 1994), Hart devoted a chapter to attacking "rule-skeptics," by whom he meant the Realists (though he did not, unfortunately, distinguish carefully between the American and Scandinavian versions of Realism). Early on, Hart characterizes rule-skepticism as "the claim that talk of rules is a myth, cloaking the truth that law consists simply of the decisions of courts and the predictions of them" (1994: 133). Indeed, much of the discussion is devoted to attacking this version of rule-skepticism. But Hart identifies a second type of rule-skepticism: "Rule-scepticism has a serious claim on our attention, but only as a theory of the function of rules in judicial decision" (Hart 1994: 135). This second rule-skeptic claims, in particular, "that it is false, if not senseless, to regard judges as themselves subject to rules or 'bound' to decide cases as they do" (135). Let us call the former doctrine "Conceptual Rule-Skepticism" and the latter "Empirical Rule-Skepticism."

Conceptual Rule-Skepticism proffers a skeptical account of the concept of law. The account is skeptical insofar as it involves denying what we may call, for ease of reference, "the Simple View" of law. This is the view that certain prior official acts (like legislative enactments and judicial decisions) constitute "law" (even if they don't exhaust it). (The view is simple to be sure, but not false!) A Conceptual Rule-Skeptic offers an account of the concept of law which denies the Simple View: according to this rule-skeptic, rules previously enacted by legislatures or articulated by courts are not law. This follows from the skeptic's own account of the concept of law, according to which, "The law is just a prediction of what a court will do" or "The law is just whatever a court says it is on the present occasion." Positivism, by contrast, is a nonskeptical account, since the Legal Positivist notion of a Rule of Recognition – a rule constituted by a practice among officials of deciding questions of legal validity by reference to certain criteria – is fully compatible with the insight captured in the Simple View. See LEGAL POSITIVISM.

Empirical Rule-Skepticism, by contrast, makes an empirical claim about the causal role of rules in judicial decision making. According to this skeptic, rules of law do not make much (causal) difference to how courts decide cases. In Hart's version of this type of skepticism, skeptics are said to believe this because of their view that legal rules are generally indeterminate, an argument to which we return below.

Hart's refutation of Conceptual Rule-Skepticism is swift and devastating, as a modified version of just one of his counterexamples will illustrate. Suppose a judge must decide the question whether a franchiser can terminate a franchisee in Connecticut with less than 60 days' notice. The judge would presumably ask herself something like the following question: "What is the law governing the termination of franchisees in this state?" But according to the Conceptual Rule-Skeptic, to ask what the "law" is on termination and notice is just to ask, "How will the judge decide this case?" So a judge who asks herself what the law is turns out – on the skeptic's reading – to really be asking herself, "What do I think I will do?" But this is clearly *not* what the judge is asking, and so the skeptical account has missed something important about our concept of law. As Hart puts it: the "statement that a rule [of law] is valid is an internal statement recognizing that the rule satisfies the tests for identifying what is to count as law in [this] court, and constitutes not a prophecy of but part of the *reason* for [the] decision" (1994: 102; cf. 143).

Now one of the American Legal Realists arguably was a Conceptual Rule-Skeptic: Felix Cohen. (Some of the Scandinavian Realists were also Conceptual Rule-Skeptics, but that was a consequence of their commitments in metaphysics and semantics.) But Cohen is nowhere cited by Hart; Hart's Realism is an amalgamation, largely, of Frank, Holmes, and Llewellyn. It is undeniably true that these writers, like most Realists, talk about the importance of "predicting" what courts will do. The question is whether, in so talking, they are fairly read as offering an analysis of the concept of law. Only Hart's grossly ana-

chronistic reading suggests an affirmative answer. The idea that philosophy involves "conceptual analysis" via the analysis of language is an artifact of Anglo-American analytic philosophy of the twentieth century; indeed, as practiced by Hart, it really reflects the influence of fashionable views in philosophy of language current at Oxford in the 1940s and 1950s. The Realists were not philosophers, let alone analytic philosophers, let alone students of G. E. Moore, Russell, and Wittgenstein, let alone colleagues of J. L. Austin. The idea that what demands understanding about law is the "concept" of law as manifest in ordinary language would have struck them as ludicrous. While the Realists had much to say about adjudication and how legal rules work in practice, they had nothing *explicit* to say about the *concept* of law.

How, then, do we understand their talk about "predicting" what courts will do? Frank (1930: 47 note) cautions the reader early on that he "is primarily concerned with 'law' as it affects the work of the practicing lawyer and the needs of the clients who retain him." Holmes begins "The Path of the Law" by emphasizing that he is talking about the meaning of law to lawyers who will "appear before judges, or . . . advise people in such a way as to keep them out of court" (1897: 457). Against this background, infamous statements like Llewellyn's – "What these officials do about disputes is, to my mind, the law itself" (1930a: 3) – make perfect sense. This is not a claim about the "concept" of law, but rather a claim about how it is *useful* to think about law for attorneys who must advise clients what to do. For your client the franchisee in Connecticut doesn't simply want to know what the rule on the books in Connecticut says; he wants to know what will happen when he takes the franchiser to court. So from the practical perspective of the franchisee, what one wants to know about the "law" is what, in fact, the courts will do when confronted with the franchisee's grievance. That is all the law that matters to the client, all the law that matters to the lawyer advising that client. And that is all, I take it, the Realists wanted to emphasize.

In fact, there is a deeper theoretical reason why the Realists could not have been Conceptual Rule-Skeptics. For the Realist arguments for the indeterminacy of law – like *all* arguments for legal indeterminacy (cf. Leiter 1995) – in fact presuppose a nonskeptical account of the concept of law. Indeed, they presuppose an account with distinct affinities to that developed by the Legal Positivists. The central claim of legal indeterminacy, recall, is the claim that the "class of legal reasons" fails to justify a unique outcome in some or all cases. The "class of legal reasons" is the class of reasons that may properly justify a legal conclusion (and thus "compel" it insofar as legal actors are responsive to valid legal reasons). So, for example, appeals to a statutory provision or a valid precedent are parts of the class of legal reasons, while an appeal to the authority of Plato's *Republic* is not: a judge is not obliged to decide one way rather than another because Plato says so. Any argument for indeterminacy, then, presupposes some view about the *boundaries* of the class of legal reasons. When Oliphant argues, for example, that the promise-not-to-compete cases are decided not by reference to law, but by reference to uncodified norms prevalent in the commercial culture in which the disputes arose, this only shows that the law is indeterminate on the assumption that the normative reasons the courts are actually relying upon are not themselves *legal* reasons. So, too, when Holmes chalks up judicial decisions not to legal reasoning but to "a concealed, half-conscious battle on the [background] question of legislative policy" (1897: 467) he is plainly presupposing that these policy concerns are not themselves *legal* reasons. The famous Realist arguments for indeterminacy which focus on the conflicting, but equally legitimate, ways lawyers have of interpreting statutes and precedents only show that the law is indeterminate on the assumption either that statutes and precedents largely exhaust the authoritative sources of law or that any additional authoritative norms not derived from these sources conflict. It is the former assumption that seems to motivate the Realist arguments. Thus, Llewellyn says that judges take rules "in the main from authoritative sources (which in the case of law are largely statutes and the decisions of the courts)" (1930a: 13).

What concept of law is being presupposed here in these arguments for legal indeterminacy: a concept in which statutes and precedent are part of the law, but uncodified norms and policy argu-ments are not? It is certainly not Ronald Dworkin's theory, let alone any more robust natural law alternative. Rather, the Realists are presupposing something like the Positivist idea of a Rule of Recognition whose criteria of legality are exclusively ones of pedigree: a rule (or canon of construction) is part of the law in virtue of having a source in a legislative enactment or a prior court decision. The Realists, in short, cannot be Conceptual Rule-Skeptics, because their arguments for the indeterminacy of law presuppose a nonskeptical account of the criteria of legality, one that has the most obvious affinities with that developed by some legal positivists.

That leaves us with Hart's attack on Empirical Rule-Skepticism. Hart's version of the doctrine (1994: 135) involves two claims: (1) legal rules are indeterminate; and, as a result, (2) legal rules do not determine or constrain decisions. Notice that Hart's way of framing the skeptical argument makes it depend upon a philosophical claim about law, namely, that it is indeterminate. But (2) could be true even if (1) were false (that would be *pure* Empirical Rule-Skepticism, we might say). Yet Hart is surely correct that most Realists (Moore may be the main exception) argue for both (1) and (2). But he is wrong about the Realist argument for (1), and thus underestimates the amount of indeterminacy in law.

Hart's central strategic move is to concede to the skeptic, right up front, that legal rules are indeterminate, but to argue that this indeterminacy is a marginal phenomenon, one insufficient to underwrite far-reaching skepticism. The skeptic is portrayed, accordingly, as having unrealistically high expectations for the determinacy of rules, as being "a disappointed absolutist" (1994: 135). The strategy depends, however, on Hart's account of the source of indeterminacy, an account that is, in fact, quite different from the arguments given by the Realists.

According to Hart, legal rules are indeterminate because "there is a limit, inherent in the nature of language, to the guidance which general language can provide" (1994: 123). Language is, in Hart's famous phrase, "open-textured," in the sense that while words have "core" instances – aspects of the world that clearly fall within the extension of the word's meaning – they also have "penumbras," cases where it is unclear whether the extension includes the aspect of the world at issue. (A Mercedes-Benz sedan is clearly a "vehicle"; but what about a motor scooter?) In cases in which the facts fall within the penumbra of the key words in the applicable legal rule, a court "must exercise a discretion, [since] there is no possibility of treating the question raised ...as if there were one uniquely correct answer to be found, as distinct from an answer which is a reasonable compromise between many conflicting interests" (Hart 1994: 128).

The Realists, however, located the indeterminacy of law not in general features of language itself, but – as we saw above – in the existence of equally legitimate, but conflicting, *canons of interpretation* that courts could employ to extract differing rules from the same statutory text or the same precedent. Indeterminacy, in short, resides for the Realists not in the rules themselves, but in the ways we have of characterizing what rules statutes and precedents contain. Thus, even if we agreed with Hart that the open texture of language affects rules only "at the margins," the Realists have now given us an *additional* reason (beyond Hart's) to expect indeterminacy in law. If the Realists are right, then not only do legal rules suffer from the open texture that Hart describes, but statutes and precedents will frequently admit of "manipulation" – legally proper manipulation, of course – and thus be indeterminate in this additional respect as well. The *combination* of sources of interdeterminacy (the open texture of language, and the conflicting canons of interpretation) seems sufficient to move indeterminacy from the margins to the center of cases actually litigated.

Hart, of course, is not entirely insensitive to the Realist arguments, though he treats them extremely cursorily. In response to Llewellyn's point, for example, that a court can interpret a precedent both "loosely" and "strictly" and thus extract two different rules from the same prior decision, Hart says simply this: "in the vast majority of decided cases there is very little doubt [as to the rule of the case]. The head-note is usually correct enough" (1994: 131). But every first-year litigation associate knows that this approach to precedent would be a recipe for disaster. To extract "holdings" without regard to the facts of the case – which is all a head-note typically pro-vides – is mediocre lawyering. Skillful lawyers know exactly what Llewellyn describes: that the "rule" of a prior case can be stated at differing degrees of specificity, and so made to do very different rhetorical work depending on the needs of the case at hand.

Now there does remain a genuine point of dispute between Hart and the Realists. While both acknowledge indeterminacy in law, and while both acknowledge, accordingly, that rules do not determine decisions in some range of cases, they clearly disagree over the *range* of cases about which these claims hold true. Theirs, in short, is a disagreement as to *degree*, but it is a real disagreement nonetheless. While Hart would locate indeterminacy, and thus the causal irrelevance, of rules "at the margin," Realist skepticism encompasses the "core" of appellate litigation.

So how does Hart, in the end, respond to the Realist contention that, at least in appellate adjudication, rules play a relatively minor role in causing the courts to decide as they do? Here is, I take it, the crux of Hart's rejoinder:

> [I]t is surely evident that for the most part decisions ...are reached either by genuine effort to conform to rules consciously taken as guiding standards of decision or, if intuitively reached, are justified by rules which the judge was antecedently disposed to observe and whose relevance to the case in hand would generally be acknowledged. (Hart 1994: 137)

Alas, the argument here consists in just four words: "it is surely evident." But that is no argument at all. Hart simply denies what the Realists affirm, but gives no reason for the denial other than his armchair confidence in the correctness of his own view. Of course, Hart *may* be correct, but given the devastating impact Hart's chapter had upon Realism among legal philosophers, it is surely more than ironic that on the crucial point of dispute with Realism – to what extent rules matter in appellate adjudication – Hart never offers any argument at all.

Meritorious or not, Hart's critique had the effect of turning the attention of professional philosophers away from Legal Realism. In the 1970s, and continuing into the 1980s, nonphilosophers associated with the Critical Legal Studies

("CLS") movement brought the Realists back to prominence within American legal thought. CLS, however, invented its own version of Realism, one more congenial to its distinctive theoretical ambitions. See CRITICAL LEGAL THEORY. For example, while claiming to embrace the Realist claim that the law is indeterminate, CLS writers went beyond Realism in two important respects. First, unlike the Realists, many CLS writers claimed that the law was "globally" indeterminate, that is, indeterminate in all cases (not just those that reached the stage of appellate review). Second, unlike the Realists, CLS writers generally grounded the claim of legal indeterminacy not in the indeterminacy of methods of interpreting legal sources, but rather in the indeterminacy of all language itself. Here they took their inspiration – albeit very loosely (and often wrongly) – from the later Wittgenstein and deconstructionism in literary theory.

CLS writers also made much out of an argument against the "public–private" distinction, due to the Columbia economist Robert Hale and the philosopher Morris Cohen. (Both were marginal figures in Realism; indeed, Cohen was primarily known at the time as a critic of Realism!) The argument runs basically as follows: since it is governmental decisions that create and structure the so-called private sphere (i.e., by creating and enforcing a regime of property and contractual rights), there should be no presumption of "nonintervention" in this "private" realm (i.e., the marketplace) because it is, in essence, a public creature. There is, in short, no natural baseline against which government cannot pass without becoming "interventionist" and nonneutral, because the baseline itself is an artifact of government regulation. This argument has proved popular with legal academics in recent years – including non-CLS writers like Sunstein (e.g., Sunstein 1987) – yet it involves a blatant non sequitur. It simply does not follow that it is normatively permissible for government to regulate the "private" sphere from the mere fact that government created the "private" sphere through establishing a structure of rights; the real question is whether the *normative* justification for demarcating a boundary of decision making immune from governmental regulation is a sound one. Nonetheless, this flawed argument became cen-

tral to the CLS version of Legal Realism (a version well represented by the introductory materials and selections in Fisher et al. 1993).

References

Cohen, Felix. 1935. Transcendental nonsense and the functional approach. *Columbia Law Review* 35: 809–49.

Cross, Frank B. 1997. Political science and the new legal realism: A case of unfortunate interdisciplinary ignorance. *Northwestern University Law Review* 92: 251–326.

Fisher, W. W., Horwitz, M. J., and Reed, T. A. (eds.). 1993. *American Legal Realism.* New York: Oxford University Press.

Frank, Jerome. 1930. *Law and the Modern Mind.* New York: Brentano's.

Frank, Jerome. 1931. Are judges human? Parts I & II. *University of Pennsylvania Law Review* 80: 17–53, 233–67.

Green, Leon. 1928. The duty problem in negligence cases. *Columbia Law Review* 28: 1014–45.

Green, Leon. 1931. *The Judicial Process in Torts Cases.* St. Paul, MN: West Publishing.

Hart, H. L. A. 1994. *The Concept of Law*, 2nd edn. Oxford: Clarendon Press.

Holmes, Oliver Wendell, Jr. 1897. The path of the law. *Harvard Law Review* 10: 457–78.

Hutcheson, Joseph. 1929. The judgment intuitive: The function of the "hunch" in judicial decision. *Cornell Law Quarterly* 14: 274–88.

Kim, Jaegwon. 1988. What is "naturalized epistemology"? *Philosophical Perspectives* 2: 381–405.

Kornblith, Hilary. 1994. Introduction: What is naturalistic epistemology? In H. Kornblith (ed.), *Naturalizing Epistemology*, 2nd edn. Cambridge, MA: MIT Press, 1–14.

Laycock, Douglas. 1991. *The Death of the Irreparable Injury Rule.* New York: Oxford University Press.

Leiter, Brian. 1995. Legal indeterminacy. *Legal Theory* 1: 481–91.

Leiter, Brian. 1997. Rethinking legal realism: Toward a naturalized jurisprudence. *Texas Law Review* 76: 267–315.

Leiter, Brian. 1998. Naturalism and naturalized jurisprudence. In B. Bix (ed.), *Analyzing Law: New Essays in Legal Theory.* Oxford: Oxford University Press, chapter 4.

Leiter, Brian. 2001. Objectivity, morality, and adjudication. In B. Leiter (ed.), *Objectivity in Law and Morals.* Cambridge, UK: Cambridge University Press, 66–98.

Leiter, Brian. 2002. Naturalism in legal philosophy. In E. Zalta (ed.), *The Stanford Encyclopedia of Philosophy* <http://plato.stanford.edu/archives/fall 2002/entries/lawphil-naturalism/>.

Llewellyn, Karl. 1930a. *The Bramble Bush*. New York: Oceana.

Llewellyn, Karl. 1930b. A realistic jurisprudence – the next step. *Columbia Law Review* 30: 431–65.

Llewellyn, Karl. 1931. Some realism about realism – responding to Dean Pound. *Harvard Law Review* 44: 1222–64.

Llewellyn, Karl. 1950. Remarks on the theory of appellate decision and the rules and canons about how statutes are to be construed. *Vanderbilt Law Review* 3: 395–406.

Llewellyn, Karl. 1960. *The Common Law Tradition: Deciding Appeals*. Boston: Little, Brown & Co.

Moore, Underhill and Callahan, Charles. 1943. Law and learning theory: A study in legal control. *Yale Law Journal* 53: 1–36.

Moore, Underhill and Hope, Theodore. 1929. An institutional approach to the law of commercial banking. *Yale Law Journal* 38: 703–19.

Moore, Underhill and Sussman, Gilbert. 1931. Legal and institutional methods applied to the debiting of direct discounts – VI. The decisions, the institutions, and the degree of deviation. *Yale Law Journal* 40: 1219–50.

Oliphant, Herman. 1928. A return to stare decisis. *American Bar Association Journal* 14:71–6, 107, 159–62. Also in W. W. Fisher et. al. (eds.), 1993. *American Legal Realism*. New York: Oxford University Press, 199–201.

Posner, Richard A. 1999. *The Problematics of Moral and Legal Theory*. Cambridge, MA: Harvard University Press.

Quine, W. V. O. 1969. Epistemology naturalized. In W. V. O. Quine, *Ontological Relativity and Other Essays*. New York: Columbia University Press, 69–90.

Radin, Max. 1925. The theory of judicial decision: Or how judges think. *American Bar Association Journal* 11: 357–62.

Radin, Max. 1942. In defense of an unsystematic science of law. *Yale Law Journal* 51: 1269–79.

Ricketts v. Pennsylvania R. Co. 1946. 153 F2d 757.

Robinson, Edward S. 1934. Law – an unscientific discipline. *Yale Law Journal* 44: 235–61.

Schwartz, Alan. 2000. Karl Llewellyn and the origins of contract theory. In J. Kraus and S. Walt (eds.), *The Jurisprudential Foundations of Corporate and Commercial Law*. Cambridge, UK: Cambridge University Press.

Sunstein, Cass. 1987. Lochner's legacy. *Columbia Law Review* 87: 873–919.

White, James J. 1994. The influence of American Legal Realism on Article 2 of the Uniform Commercial Code. In W Krawietz, D N MacCormick and G H von Wright (eds.), *Prescriptive Formality and Normative Rationality in Modern Legal Systems*. Berlin: Duncker and Humbolt.

Further Reading

Leiter, Brian. 2001. Legal realism and legal positivism reconsidered. *Ethics* 111: 278–301.

Schlegel, John Henry. 1995. *American Legal Realism and Empirical Social Science*. Chapel Hill: University of North Carolina Press.

Twining, William. 1973. *Karl Llewellyn and the Realist Movement*. Norman: University of Oklahoma Press.

Chapter 4

Economic Rationality in the Analysis of Legal Rules and Institutions

Lewis A. Kornhauser

Introduction

In the first half of the twentieth century, lawyers and legal academics referred to economic concepts and theories only to elucidate areas of laws such as antitrust, the regulation of public utilities, and taxation that had an explicit economic content. Even the suggestion that economics should play a role in the understanding of core doctrinal subjects of the common law would have been rejected as ludicrous.

In the early 1960s, however, Ronald Coase (1960) and Guido Calabresi (1961) began the systematic application of the techniques of microeconomic analysis to the study of legal rules and institutions including common law legal rules and institutions. Within 15 years, the tools of microeconomics had been applied to virtually every area of law (Posner 1973). By the end of the twentieth century, serious scholarship in almost every area of law had to address issues and arguments raised by the economic analysis of law.

During the 1970s, Richard Posner (1973, 1979, 1980) claimed first that common law rules were in fact efficient (the *positive claim*) and second that common law rules *ought* to be efficient (the *normative claim*). Around 1980, the proliferation of economic analyses spawned great controversy in the legal academy. The controversy centered on the second of Posner's claims: that common law rules *ought* to be efficient. The controversy has had two primary com-

ponents. The first, at least in part internal to the community of economic analysts of law, concerns the appropriate understanding of the term "efficient." On one interpretation, "efficient" simply means "Pareto efficient"; that is, a legal rule is Pareto efficient if and only if there is no other rule that would induce behavior such that no person was worse off and at least one person in society was better off. On a second interpretation, "efficient" means "wealth-maximizing" where "wealth" is the sum of the compensating or equivalent variations of the individuals in society. This second interpretation essentially adopts cost–benefit analysis as an implementation of the Kaldor–Hicks welfare criterion. (On Kaldor–Hicks see Coleman 1980 or Kornhauser 1998b.) On the third interpretation, offered most recently by Kaplow and Shavell (2002), "efficient" means only that the evaluation of legal rules should be welfarist; evaluation should depend only on the well-being of the individuals in society. This third interpretation is the most general as both Pareto efficiency and the maximization of the compensating or equivalent variations are welfarist criteria. (For more extensive discussion of these claims, see Kornhauser 1998b, 2003b.)

The other focus of controversy over Posner's normative claim concerned its moral validity. Various authors, for example, Dworkin (1980a, 1980b), asserted that "wealth," understood either as Pareto efficiency or as the "consumer surplus" generated by a legal rule, was not a value or, at least, a value that the law ought to promote. In its current incarnation, the dispute has turned to the more general moral issue of the validity of welfarism as the exclusive social goal.

A commitment to economic analysis of law, however, does not entail a commitment to welfarist evaluation of legal rules and institutions. The denial of the normative claim in any of its three formulations does not undermine much of the practice of economic analysis of law. Consequently, the dispute over the normative claim has not much influenced either the internal development of the discipline or the acceptance of its approach by its critics. The dispute has merely diverted attention from the principal difference between economic analysis of law and more traditional enquiries concerning legal rules and institutions. This difference reflects distinct approaches to the normativity of law. Within the legal academy, scholars start from the premise that legal rules are norms; they primarily study the content and interpretation of those norms. By contrast, economic analysis of law, at its core, analyses the causes and effects of legal rules and institutions. Consequently, it must explain and predict how private citizens and public officials will respond to legal rules and institutions. These explanations, however, generally ignore, and sometimes deny, the normative features of legal rules.

This chapter seeks to elucidate the contrasting approaches to normativity and to determine the extent to which they are incompatible. The argument, however, is complex and tentative for two reasons. Within law and jurisprudence, the concept of the normativity of law itself is controversial and elusive. Moreover, economics has substantial resources for modeling diverse phenomena. The failure of economic analysis of law to account for the normative aspects of law may be a contingent rather than a necessary feature of the practice used to explain legal behavior.

The chapter proceeds as follows. In the following section, I formulate the question. I then distinguish between two distinct research programs in economic analysis of law: a modest and a strong one. The modest research program poses little or no challenge to traditional questions concerning the normativity of law. The strong research program rejects normativity. The next section sets jurisprudential accounts of the normativity of law. Then, in the central section of the chapter, I elaborate and assess the resources available to economic analysis of law to capture jurisprudential conceptions of normativity.

A Characterization of Economic Analysis of Law

Practitioners and critics describe a very diverse set of projects as "economic analysis of law." These projects include (1) explanations of how a legal rule or institution influences individual behavior; (2) explanations of why particular legal rules or institutions arose or persist; (3) the design of legal rules or institutions to accomplish particular aims; (4) the evaluation of legal rules or institutions; and (5) the interpretation of specific legal doctrines.

These projects have in common the application of microeconomic theory to understanding of legal rules and institutions. To begin, I briefly outline the core concept of these microeconomic analyses, the concept of preference. I then sketch two distinct schools of economic analysis of law.

The concept of preference

"Preference" in microeconomic theory is a technical term that refers to a mathematical structure over a domain of "objects." Specifically, a preference is a relation R over a domain that is *symmetric*, *complete*, and *transitive*. Symmetry means that, for every x in the domain, xRx; completeness means that, for every x and y in the domain, either xRy or yRx; and transitivity means that, for any x, y, and z in the domain, if (xRy and yRz) then xRz.

The relation R is often expressed as "at least as good as" or "at least as preferred as." The term "preference" and these locutions suggest a psychological content to the concept of preference. This suggestion is often misleading. The interpretation of this structure varies with the context and purpose of application. The mathematical structure has no inherent psychological content. Indeed, the mathematical structure has no inherent economic content. Many physical relations are preferences in the technical sense. The relation "at least as tall as" over the domain of mountains on earth satisfies the formal conditions of a preference. Similarly, an economic interpretation of this structure need not have a psychological content, though it may.

For example, in evaluating a legal institution, one might interpret each agent's preference as his or her well-being; moreover, one might understand well-being as an objective list so that the degree of agents' well-being may be largely independent of their psychological state. On the other hand, a model of the effects of a negligence rule on the behavior of agents engaged in a risky activity may invite an interpretation of the agents' preference as their motivation, a psychological concept. As these two examples suggest, evaluative preferences understood as well-being may be distinct from explanatory preferences understood as motivation. Further confusion may arise because the domain over which agents choose may also differ from the domain over which either their explanatory or evaluative preferences are defined. Voters, for example, may have basic or fundamental preferences over legislative programs. When they vote, however, they must choose among candidates for a single seat in the legislature. Though their choices are governed by their preferences over legislative programs, they may not in fact have well-defined preferences over candidates (for further discussion see Kornhauser 2003a).

In many applications, preferences, either explanatory or evaluative or both, are assumed to be *self-interested*. Self-interest may be understood narrowly as a concern only for the agent's own consumption of goods and services. Or it may be understood more broadly as any concern of the agent. Interpreted broadly, then, a self-interested agent may act out of an altruistic motivation or evaluate his or her well-being in part in terms of the well-being of others. The formal concept of preference, of course, is consistent with both broad and narrow understandings of self-interest.

Much of the critical debate about economics generally and economic analysis of law in particular suffers from the four confusions suggested here. The confusion between explanation and evaluation plagues not only the interpretation of

preference but elaboration of ideas of normativity. The varying extent to which economic analysis of law relies on psychological interpretations of preference also muddies discussions of the issues. Third, analyses often equivocate between narrow and broad interpretations of preference as self-interest. Again, the consistency of an economic analysis of law and a more traditional analysis may depend on the breadth of interpretation of the idea of preference. Finally, discussions generally ignore the discrepancy between the domains of choice and of preference.

Two schools of economic analysis of law

Economic analysts of law share a commitment to the application of microeconomic theory to the analysis of legal rules and institutions. A wide variety of different projects and approaches are nonetheless consistent with this commitment. One may, however, usefully distinguish two schools. I shall call one school the *policy analysis* school and the other, the *political economy* school. These two schools adopt identical assumptions concerning the behavior of private individuals but differ in their assumptions concerning the behavior of public officials.

The *policy analysis* school investigates the effects that legal rules have on the behavior of private individuals. Policy analysts assume that private individuals respond to legal rules in an economic fashion. Private individuals, that is, have predominantly self-interested preferences, narrowly understood. In the most straightforward analyses, a legal rule on this account simply specifies some proscribed behavior or behaviors and a sanction that is imposed for noncompliance with the legal rule. Alternatively, a legal rule, such as a farm subsidy (or a tax), may identify a permitted behavior and attach a reward (or, respectively, a penalty), to that behavior. More sophisticated analysis considers the role that a legal rule plays in coordinating behavior or the role it plays in transmitting information among asymmetrically informed parties.

The influence of legal rules on behavior is mediated through the rational calculations of agents seeking to maximize their preferences. Analysts generally invoke one of two primary mediating paths of influence. The first, and most common, path assumes that a legal rule directly influences behavior through the price it sets on behavior that does not conform to the legal rule. The sanction for engaging in proscribed behavior increases the cost of choosing that action. The second path assumes that the legal rule conveys information concerning the appropriate action to agents. This path might explain, for example, the role of law in solving coordination problems. A third, largely unexamined path that is suggested by the framework of microeconomic theory would investigate the effect of legal rules on the preferences that the agents have. (For further discussion, see Kornhauser 1997.)

Policy analysis assumes that public officials, in contrast to private individuals, are conscientious; they faithfully perform their legal obligations. When public officials face resource constraints and cannot meet *all* their legal obligations, or when their legal obligations are ambiguous or otherwise unclear, the policy analyst generally assumes that they act to maximize social welfare. Conflict with more jurisprudential approaches to law thus arises at two points. First, the lawyer objects to the presumption that conscientious legal officials seek to maximize social welfare; the law might not have welfarist aims. The controversy over the normative claim arose out of this objection. Second, a lawyer might object to the assumption that private individuals are solely motivated by self-interest. One should note, though, that philosophers of law as diverse as Holmes (1897) and Hart (1961) explicitly acknowledged that nothing in the concept of law requires private individuals to have anything but a self-interested response to law.

Political economy extends the assumption of narrowly self-interested action by private individuals to public officials. Public officials on this account only meet their legal obligations if it is in their (self-) interest to do so. The extension of the assumption of narrowly self-interested action from private individuals to all actors reflects both a different, and perhaps more ambitious, research program and a more radical approach to law.

The research programs of the two schools differ in at least two respects. First, the policy analysis school seeks to explain the effects of legal rules and institutions on the behavior of citizens; the political economy school seeks also to explain the structure and content of the legal rules and institutions themselves. Second, the policy analysis school generally seeks not only to explain the effects of legal rules and institutions but also to influence the design of legal rules and institutions. This project of design adopts an instrumental view of law; it sees legal rules and institutions as tools for the promotion of specified aims.

The political economy school has a more equivocal attitude towards design. In some incarnations, sometimes called constitutional political economy, this school proposes the design of constitutional institutions. In this guise, the political economy school shares the instrumental view of law of the policy analysts but the nature of the instrumentalism differs. While the policy analysts are *rule instrumental*, the political economists are *institutionally instrumental*. The policy analyst views each legal rule as intentionally designed to promote the aim of the policy makers but the constitutional political economist views only institutions as intentionally designed to promote given aims. Particular legal rules produced by those institutions may not have coherent aims. A constitutional designer who saw legislation as inevitably the product of interest group politics would still seek institutional forms that molded and directed the formation of coalitions among interests. (For further discussion see Kornhauser 2000.)

The logic of the political economy school, however, argues against any design project at all and the denial of the instrumentality of law. Carried to its extreme, the political economy approach thus adopts a much more radical approach to the study of legal rules and legal institutions than policy analysis. Constitutional designers are not in principle exempt from the self-interested motivations that political economists attribute to all other private and public actors. For political economy, then, law consists solely of a set of incentive structures that ensure an equilibrium in which both private individuals and public officials comply with their legal obligations. Legal rules are simply equilibrium phenomena that have no causal force. Only the structure of the institutions that sanction individuals have any explanatory power.

Political economy thus pursues a project radically at odds with, and rejected by, the jurisprudential approach to legal rules and institutions. In *The Concept of Law*, H. L. A. Hart (1961) attacked the sanction theory of duties that underlies the conception of obligation implicit in political economy. Though citizens might regard legal rules simply as sanctions, Hart argued that public officials who apply the law required a different attitude towards the rule of recognition and to legal rules generally.

Hart argued that the imposition of a sanction was neither necessary nor sufficient for the existence of an obligation. Violation of some legal rules, such as those that structure the enabling regimes of contract or corporations, do not impose sanctions. Conversely, some rules, such as those that impose taxes for undertaking certain actions, impose costs on agents without creating legal duties. The nature of legal obligation, on Hart's account, lies not in sanction, but in the attitude – the "internal aspect" – that the public official holds towards the rule. See LEGAL POSITIVISM.

Hart's objections to the sanction theory of law have most force against the project of political economy if one adopts a narrow interpretation of self-interested preferences. Under the narrowest interpretation of self-interest, public officials care only about their own consumption of standard economic goods and services. Often, however, economic models of legal institutions interpret the preferences of public officials more broadly. Judges, for instance, in models of judicial politics are generally assumed to have preferences over policies. When preferences are understood this way, the force of Hart's objection is less clear. The following investigates how one might reconcile preference theories to Hart's objections.

Normativity

Understanding the relation between law as a social institution and law as a set of normative requirements preoccupies legal philosophy and much legal theory. Much of the debate within legal philosophy concerns the relation between law and morality, another normative system. Though legal norms might differ essentially from moral norms, an understanding of legal normativity often begins with a discussion of general conceptions of normativity.

Several questions arise. The first, an ontological one, addresses the nature of norms in general and of moral norms in particular: do norms exist "objectively" or not? A related question, of more interest to social scientists, is epistemological: how do individuals know what norms exist?

A third set of questions posed by norms and normativity is specific to law. Under what conditions does law impose obligations? What is the source of law's normativity? This chapter will not address questions about the specific nature of legal normativity.

A fourth set of questions concerns the role that norms and obligation ought to play in practical reason. H. L. A. Hart, who traced his view back to Hobbes in *Leviathan*, argued that two features characterized the role of legal norms in practical reasoning: a legal norm is *peremptory* and it is *content-independent*. A peremptory reason displaces the agent's normal deliberative process of articulating and weighing all reasons for and against possible courses of action. A content-independent reason derives its force and relevance not from the content of the reason but from the nature of its issuer. The peremptory nature of legal rules means that a legal rule should displace an agent's own reasons for action; the existence of the legal rule itself should provide the agent with both necessary and sufficient reasons to act as directed.

Hart's account of peremptory reasons in Hart (1982) corresponds to Raz's account of exclusionary reasons (Raz 1975). Raz offers his analysis within a more general account of practical reason that distinguishes between first-and second-order reasons for action. First-order reasons for action bear directly on the appropriateness of the options that the agent faces; second-order reasons guide agents in their deliberations over the relevant first-order reasons. An exclusionary reason is both a first- and second-order reason; it gives agents a reason to act or not to act and it directs agents not to consider all (or some) other first-order reasons that bear on their decision. On Raz's account, all rules, including legal rules, function as exclusionary reasons.

Philosophers of ethics and practical reason do not generally offer accounts of norms as elements of an explanatory theory of behavior. One of the central questions in their enterprise, however, concerns the motivational role that reasons play in determining an agent's actions. For philosophers of practical reason, the key question is: does an individual have a reason to act even if he or she has no motivation to act on that "reason"?

Economists treat their preference theories of action as both normative and explanatory theories. They claim both that an agent's decisions ought to conform to the demands of maximizing a preference and that agents' decisions do in fact conform to the demands of preference theory. But economists rarely address explicitly the normative or motivational questions that occupy philosophers because "reasons" play no explicit role in their models. The economic models, however, do not obviously preclude a discussion of reasons. As elaborated in Kornhauser 1998c, we might interpret an agent's preference ordering as an integration of that agent's reasons for action into an all-things-considered set of judgments.

The assumption of narrowly self-interested preferences restricts the set of reasons behind the agent's preference ordering. When studying market behavior, self-interest generally means that agents care only about their own consumption and not the consumption of others. In the nonmarket contexts studied in the economic analysis of law, the concept of "self-interested preferences" is often given a broader interpretation to include the "policy preferences" of a public official. Though an interpretation of preference as narrow self-interest is apparently at odds with Hart's and Raz's account of practical reason, this more expansive interpretation seems to allow more room for obligation because the broader interpretation of self-interest admits a wider set of reasons that agents integrate into their preference ordering understood as a summary of their all-things-considered judgments.

Preference and Obligation

Preference theories and practical reason

Is the logic of obligation incompatible with any explanatory theory that relies on preference? An inconsistency might arise from at least two different sources. It might arise because obligations do not motivate agents to act. Alternatively, obligation and preference might be incompatible because the structure of decision governed in part by obligation is logically inconsistent with the demands of preference theory.

Controversy over the incompatibility of obligation and preference has long existed among moral and political philosophers. Some philosophers, notably Plato and Hume, offer accounts of ethics that are compatible with preference theory. On these accounts, the obligations one has are distinct from the springs of actions; meeting one's obligations, however, is in the self-interest of the agent either directly or indirectly. For Plato, acting rightly is directly in the self-interest of the agent; it is better for the agent to act justly than to act unjustly. Of course, the conception of well-being underlying this Platonic account differs from the subjective account of well-being and motivation that underlies the economic analysis, but resolution of the question of compatibility rests on the formal structure of preference, not on its interpretation.

For Hume, conformity to moral obligations either directly or indirectly promotes the agent's self-interest. Some moral virtues are natural in the sense that the individual has an inherent motivation, or preference, to comply. Other moral virtues are artificial; adherence to them is beneficial to the agent conditional on others' adhering. This account is fully consistent with the economic account of preference maximization that provides a narrowly self-interested interpretation of the agent's preference.

Other philosophers, among them many legal philosophers (and many other legal scholars), deny the relevance of preference theory to the analysis of obligation. This claim might have a strong and a weak form. The weak form of the claim denies only that obligation can be captured within a preference theory that interprets preference in narrowly self-interested terms. Obligation might then be reconciled with preference if the ordering incorporates other-regarding concerns or other concerns that are excluded by an assumption of narrow self-interest.

The strong form of the claim denies that obligation can be reconciled with any preference theory, even one that interprets preference in broadly self-interested terms. This claim denies that the expansive conceptions of the concerns reflected in an agent's preferences can capture the role of obligation in practical reason. We might understand this more radical claim as a claim that normative motivations cannot be integrated with self-interested and other-regarding interests into a coherent preference. It is not clear, however, what argument the critic of economic analysis of law offers to support this more radical rejection of preference theory.

Ironically, this radical rejection of preference theory does suggest a way to reconcile the projects of legal philosophy and economic analysis of law. The philosophical project to articulate the role of obligation in practical reason differs from the explanatory project of economic analysis of law for which preference theories are deployed. The difference goes beyond the normative aim of the philosopher of practical reason and the explanatory aim of the economic analyst. The two projects differ even if one adapts the normative theories of practical reason and of preference theory to empirical uses.

When economists assume that an agent has a preference over some domain, they prescind from the question of the origin or source of those preferences. One might thus understand a preference as the summary of the results of the operation of practical reason in all possible decision contexts that the agent may face. On this interpretation of a preference, the philosophical inquiry into the role of obligation must have already been resolved in order to construct the preference ordering of the agent. After all, that ordering summarizes the choices the agent would make; to the extent that obligation weighs in the agent's calculations, its importance would already be integrated into the preference.

A conflict between the projects will then only exist if obligation plays a role in practical reason that is somehow inconsistent with the demands of a preference theory. Incompatibility might arise in at least three distinct ways. The first two forms of incompatibility concern behavior. First, if the demands of obligation somehow induced behavior that violated the transitivity requirement on the preference ordering, the two projects would be incompatible. But, as I suggest in the following subsection, such a conflict is unlikely. At the very least, its existence will depend on what one seeks to achieve with a preference model that seeks to incorporate normativity. Second, obligation might not influence behavior. Narrow self-interest might, in fact, explain all behavior adequately. The subsection 'Does obligation motivate?' below suggests, however, that this argument confronts both problems of interpretation and conflicting empirical evidence. The third incompatibility concerns the structure rather than the result of practical reasoning. Even though one might attribute preferences to the agent that led to choices that reproduced the conclusions of the agent's practical reasoning from obligations, the preference structure would misrepresent the logic (and perhaps the psychology) that led to the choices. The strength of this case also rests on the nature of the evidence concerning reasoning and action and on questions of interpretation.

Obligation within preference

The conflict between preference and obligation is at least partially interpretive rather than formal. This statement follows almost immediately from the earlier distinction between narrow and broad interpretations of the concept of self-interested preferences. A broad interpretation of self-interest offers several routes for the partial reconciliation of obligation and preference that may even be acceptable to a political economist who adopts a relatively restricted interpretation of self-interest. This subsection briefly discusses two routes: the possibility of norm internalization and formal redefinition of the domain of preference.

The reconciliation offered here may be partial because it provides an account only of obligations that the agent accepts in some sense. On some philosophical accounts of obligation, agents may have obligations regardless of their acceptance of them. These obligations may fail to motivate them or, on other accounts, they may motivate through reason.

Internalization

One might further assert that an agent's preferences reflect normative concerns. The agent may have *internalized* various obligations where we understand the process of internalization as incorporation of a concern for compliance with obligations in general or with a particular obligation into the agent's preference ordering. An agent might internalize a norm, however, in very different ways; and the method of internalization might influence our evaluation of the role of obligation in the determination of action.

Consider, for example, a norm against littering. Internalization of the norm might mean incorporation into a preference in one of at least three different ways. The agent might value compliance with norms generally so that compliance with the norm against littering satisfies this more general concern. The agent might value compliance with the specific norm against littering. Or the agent might value uncluttered landscapes. In the first two instances, internalization means that the agent has developed a preference for compliance to the norm; obligation would appear, then, to play a direct role in the explanation of the agent's behavior. In the third instance, however, the agent does not internalize the norm as norm; the agent develops a taste for uncluttered landscapes. The obligation not to litter now plays no direct role in explaining the agent's actions.

Redefinition

With an adequate description of the obligations to which the agent is committed, one may incorporate these obligations into a complete, transitive preference. This conclusion follows directly from the observation that the definition of a preference requires implicit or explicit criteria that identify which options are identical. Agents who meet their obligations distinguish options in part in terms of features that indicate the existence (or nonexistence) of an obligation to act in a specified way. The relevance of the existence of obligations to the agents' decisions will thus be reflected in their preference ordering.

Consider for example the problem discussed in Anand (1993) and Sen (1993) in which the agent, from the pair (orange, small apple) chooses the orange; from the pair (orange, big apple) chooses the big apple; and from the pair (big apple, little apple) chooses the little apple. This agent apparently violates transitivity as she prefers big apple to orange to small apple to big apple. She is, however, following a simple rule: never choose the largest exemplar of a given type of fruit. We might understand this rule-following behavior as conforming to an obligation not to take the largest fruit. In any case, the agent distinguishes options in part in terms of the set of alternatives with which they are presented. Attention to this feature of her preferences rationalizes them and avoids the intransitivity. Her choices are in part contingent on the menu of options from which she chooses; once we understand the dependence we may redescribe her options appropriately to avoid the intransitivity. The incompatibility between preference and obligation formally disappears.

Several considerations, however, make this formal compatibility an insufficient response to the objections of a sanction theory of law. First, in many cases, one cannot fully specify the content of the agent's obligation. Consider the obligation of judges in common law jurisdictions to abide by *stare decisis*. (A fuller discussion appears in Kornhauser 1998a.) The obligation is defined by a judicial practice that involves both the obligation of lower court judges to abide by the rulings of higher court judges ("vertical" *stare decisis*) and the obligation of the judges of a given court to abide by the prior rulings of their own court ("horizontal" *stare decisis*). Consider the easier case of vertical *stare decisis*, an obligation we may take to be strict and not overridable. Suppose that the lower court must decide two cases, A and B. Each case may be decided in one of two ways: for the plaintiff or against the plaintiff, which we shall label A and not-A in the first case and B and not-B in the second case. The court has preferences over states of the law, that is, over each of the four possible outcomes of the cases (described as an ordered pair). Assume the court prefers (A, B) to (not-A, not-B) to (A, not-B) to (not-A, B). A court unconstrained by vertical *stare decisis* would, when asked to decide the first case, choose A over not-A. If, however, a superior court has dictated an outcome of not-B in cases of type B, then a lower court that adheres to its obligation of vertical *stare decisis* will choose not-A over A. If we ignore the obligation, the court may appear to have inconsistent preferences. Once we account for the obligation appropriately, however, its behavior is consistent with a preference theory. The example, however, assumed that we could clearly determine which cases were governed by a prior decision. The criteria that determine when one case is identical to a prior case are difficult to articulate. Consequently we cannot redescribe the agent's options to eliminate "apparent" conflicts with transitivity.

Second, incorporation of the content of the obligation into the preference ordering will not explain violations of the obligation. Agents rarely conform to all their obligations; more interestingly, they may sometimes conform to a given obligation and sometimes breach that obligation. An agent might keep one promise and break another. A judge may adhere to *stare decisis* in one case but abandon it in a second.

One might reconcile this complex behavior to preference theory in two unsatisfactory ways. One might redefine the obligation so that it is defeasible; under appropriate conditions the obligation is excused or no longer obtains. Alternatively, one might identify the conditions that trigger breach of the obligation and characterize these options as distinct from the conditions under which the agent conforms. Either strategy is fruitful only if we can characterize the defeasing or triggering conditions *ex ante* so that our

theory of behavior has both predictive and explanatory force. When obligations are not fully specified, such characterization will fail. Moreover, we may provide more perspicuous and powerful explanations when we combine an understanding of obligatory action with a cruder specification of options.

Does obligation motivate?

Before one asks how obligation motivates, one must accept that obligation does in fact influence behavior. This claim seems obvious to a legal scholar but the radical interpretation of the project of political economy denies that obligation has causal efficacy. Phrased differently, the political economist denies that obligation ever gives an agent a reason for action except through the sanction imposed for noncompliance or some information that the rule communicates. More strongly, the political economist apparently contends that self-interest provides the only source of reasons for action, and argues that obligations never influence behavior; only incentive structures determine action. Action is better explained through an assumption of self-interested preference than through an assumption of a more complexly derived ordering. In this subsection, I review reasons that both support and contradict this denial.

Empirical tests alone cannot resolve the question of the superiority of self-interested explanation to normative explanation of behavior. Formulation of empirical tests require that we specify clearly how obligation in theory influences behavior and that we can disentangle self-interested from normative motivations. In this subsection, I first discuss the difficulty of attributing motivations. I then address the empirical questions more directly.

Interpretive problems

Our explanation of behavior requires an interpretation of the behavior that requires the attribution of some motivation to the agent; but many interpretations are possible. Consider, for example, Liza who does not eat meat.

Explanations of Liza's behavior might refer to any of a number of distinct motivations. An economic explanation will refer to both her beliefs and to her preferences. The claim that self-interested explanation does not refer to obligation means that obligation is not relevant to the characterization of either her beliefs or her preferences.

Of course, in some possible explanations, obligation plays no role in either preference or belief. Thus, Liza's failure to eat meat results from narrowly self-interested preferences in at least two distinct ways. Liza might simply dislike the taste of meat; she prefers vegetarian cuisine. On the other hand, Liza might enjoy meat but face a budget constraint that induces her to eat vegetarian meals. After all, Liza must allocate her resources not only to food but also to housing, education, and other activities that she also values.

On other explanations, obligation plays no role in explaining the content of Liza's preferences but its role in Liza's belief system might still partially explain her actions. Liza might have a vegetarian diet because she seeks to conform to the behavior of those in her circle, all of whom are vegetarians. We might try to explain this conformity by assuming a taste for conformity directly (see e.g., Jones 1983), or through a taste for reputation (Akerlof 1980), or some positional good (Bernheim 1994). In these explanations Liza has self-interested preferences understood more broadly but obligation still plays no role in the content of her preference.

In these explanations, however, obligation might enter an explanation as a belief rather than a preference. Liza might believe that she has an obligation not to eat meat. She conforms to the community's vegetarianism because she understands that the practice is grounded in obligation. Consequently, not eating meat has special importance for each member of the community, and conformity is expected. Other common practices may not trigger expectations of conformity. Everyone, for example, might habitually go to the movies on Saturday night. If Liza does not go, her reputation will not suffer. People may notice her absence, remark on it, or speculate as to its causes. They may call concerned about her health, wonder about the demands of her job, or whether she has lost her taste for films. Comment will not

be critical. In this instance, the existence of an obligation marks specific behaviors as socially important and hence ones that are relevant to tastes to conform or for reputation. This reduction of the role of obligation to a signal, however, does not appear to capture the distinctive role of obligation in assessing options and making decisions. See PRIVACY.

Real experiments and thought experiments

Evidence should guide a choice between explanatory theories. The discussion above suggested that the evidence did not speak plainly for one theory over another because the theories relied on the attribution of competing motivations; the attribution of motivations presented problems of interpretation. Nonetheless, proponents of both preference and obligation theories of explanation may point to phenomena for which they believe their theory provides a clearer explanation.

Political economy seems to explain differences in legal behaviors across countries better than theories that rely on normative obligation. The normative theories may point to differences in cultural norms, but the theories have no apparent resources for explaining the emergence of different norms in those cultures. The political economist, by contrast, will point to differences in incentive structures or environmental conditions that over time led to the emergence of different behaviors.

Consider for example a question of current academic and practical concern: why do public officials conform to the rule of law in some societies but not in others? The legal (and moral) obligations that in theory bind public officials in the United States and the Netherlands do not differ dramatically from those that apply to public officials in Argentina or Nigeria. Yet most agree that officials within the former countries conform to the "rule of law" – that is, commonly meet the express legal obligations of their systems – while the officials of the latter countries frequently do not. It is not clear how the legalist explains these differences. The difficulty for the legalist may simply reflect the more general problem of explaining noncompliance within a normative framework. For the economist, noncompliance presents no explanatory difficulties; an agent will fail to comply with a norm when the costs and benefits of noncompliance exceed those of compliance. Thus, the economist explains the behavior of public officials in different countries either by pointing to differences in the incentive structures within the countries, by identifying differences in the circumstances in which the officials act, or by elaborating models with multiple equilibria, in only some of which public officials comply with their obligations in equilibrium. This approach of course raises the problem of explaining why one equilibrium is chosen rather than another.

Of course, the mere fact that individuals do not comply with a norm does not imply that the norm has no influence on the individuals' behavior. Moral commitments or legal rules may influence behavior in many indirect ways. Consider, for example, legal rules that limit the speed at which motorists may drive on a given thoroughfare. Widespread violation of the legal obligation, however, does not alone imply that legal obligation plays no role in an explanation of motorist behavior. Obligation might explain the *pattern* of noncompliance. When the speed limit is raised from 55 miles per hour to 65 miles per hour, the distribution of speeds at which motorists travel changes predictably: a limit of 55 miles per hour may yield a modal speed of 60 miles per hour with most motorists traveling between 50 and 65 while a limit of 65 miles per hour yields a modal speed of 70 miles per hour with most motorists traveling between 65 and 80 miles per hour. Several standard economic accounts might explain this shift in distributions. Different speed limits lead to different enforcement practices by police and judges; these different enforcement practices then lead to different choices by motorists. Of course we must now explain why the enforcement practices of police and judges change in response to changes in the legal speed limit. Or we might assume that the speed limit carries information about the safe speed, and individuals then use that information to adjust their own behavior (e.g., posted limits for mountain curves).

From within legal culture, it appears obvious that obligations provide distinctive reasons for action to agents, particularly to public officials. The existence of these obligations seems to pro-

vide clear, concise, and cogent explanations for a number of pervasive phenomena. A convincing legal response to the project of political economy, however, must identify real phenomena that the political economist cannot explain but that are explained by reference to obligation. Here I sketch two potential legal challenges to the approach of political economy. The first concerns adjudication; the second concerns the difference among legal forms.

Social scientists and legal scholars have long adopted different approaches to adjudication. Legal scholars study judicial opinions and seek to explain and predict judgments in terms of the content of the opinions that judges write to accompany their judgments. As the obligation of *judges* to provide reasons for their decisions lies at the core of adjudicatory practice, the legal scholar's intensive scrutiny of the given reasons implicitly assumes that these obligations will explain judicial behavior.

The "attitudinalist" approach to judicial politics contends that the judge's preferences over policy outcomes better explains judicial decision than the expressed reasons of the judges. Moreover, they proffer extensive evidence in support of this claim. Spaeth and Segal (2000; Segal and Spaeth 1993), for example, test their claim against a claim that judicial adherence to *stare decisis* explains judicial decisions. They conclude, using a narrow definition of horizontal *stare decisis*, that Supreme Court justices only rarely adhere to *stare decisis*. This empirical demonstration, however, is not fully convincing. For one thing, as noted above, the obligation of *stare decisis* is difficult to specify precisely; the persuasiveness of the empirical test depends on the adequacy of the specification. Moreover, one may question the validity of the tests that Segal and Spaeth use. As one broadens their narrow definition of *stare decisis*, adherence to the obligation increases. More importantly, they measure adherence to *stare decisis*, narrowly defined, in a problematic way. Adherence is defined in terms of movement relative to the status quo. But a prior decision redefines the status quo; it determines the terms of future debate and this itself influences the development of the law.

The traditional legal scholar has a more sweeping response. The reasons judges offer in their opinions refer centrally to the obligations of the judge as well as to the obligations of the parties to the dispute. Often these opinions assume that private individuals or public officials will take legal obligations seriously. The attitudinalist and the political economist who denies the motivational force of obligation must view the entire practice of judicial opinion writing as a charade, and the public to whom the opinions are addressed as deluded. This conclusion renders ironic the motivation behind the adoption of the assumption of self-interested action of public officials. The political economist sought to simplify and unify the theory of public and private behavior by attributing the identical motivations to private and public actors; this unified framework, however, apparently renders private actors irrational.

Consider next the differences among legal forms. Regulation may take many forms. One might regulate air pollutants, for example, by a tax, a criminal fine, or a civil fine. Consider the difference between a tax and a fine, either criminal or civil, for exceeding prescribed levels of emission of air pollutants. Suppose that the tax and the fine impose equal penalties for exceeding these prescribed levels by any amount. The economist would regard these two legal forms as economically equivalent: they impose identical incentives. The legal scholar, and many lay individuals, view the legal forms very differently. A tax *permits* the agent to emit more than the prescribed levels but the fine prohibits excessive emission. Excessive emissions violate the norm and are at best inappropriate but more exactly wrong. This distinction might explain why some environmentalists resist market-based regulatory schemes; they resist the legal characterization of environmentally destructive behavior as permissive either for symbolic reasons or for instrumental reasons.

A similar distinction appears in the difference between regulating scarce parking space at a town center through parking meters that permit a driver to park for a fee and through a fine that punishes drivers who park in the identical spot with an identical fee. The fee permits parking but the fine prohibits it; to the philosopher of practical reason a permission coupled with a price provides a very different type of reason for action than a prohibition tied to a sanction of

equivalent size. The two regulatory approaches might also have different distributional consequences.

Legal theorists thus predict that embedding identical sanctions in different legal forms will produce different behaviors. Reference to the existence of an obligation *explains* at least in part individual action. Their claim is compelling, however, only if two conditions are met. First, the empirical prediction must be true; individuals indeed respond differently to a tax than to a fine. Second, the political economist cannot explain the predicted pattern of behavior.

Concluding Remarks

Modern jurisprudence has generally presumed that legal obligations have normative force. Though current theories usually admit that private individuals often – perhaps always – meet their obligations because it is in their self-interest to do so, the theories generally assume that public officials meet their obligations because they ought to. Economic analysis of law, particularly its political economy branch, has challenged this presumption. This chapter attempted to determine the gravity of this challenge to traditional conceptions of law.

In economic theory, the agents' preferences explain their actions. The formal concept of preference, however, places no restrictions on the features that agents may consider relevant to their decisions. Consequently, I have argued that there is no formal incompatibility between the economic approach to law and current jurisprudential theories. The analyst may incorporate the normative force of legal obligation within the formal structure of preference if the obligation is sufficiently well specified. Incompatibilities may arise, however, when the theorist restricts the features of an option that are relevant to the agent's decision either because the obligation is not sufficiently well defined or for other reasons.

Economic analysis of law generally does place restrictions on the preferences of agents. It assumes that self-interested preferences are sufficient to explain the behavior of both private individuals and public officials. I have argued that the evidence for the truth of this claim is equivocal for two reasons.

First, the motivations underlying action are not self-evident. They require interpretation and frequently both self-interested and nonself-interested interpretations may be attributed to identical behavior. Distinguishing between these interpretations may require further evidence. Moreover, the concept of self-interest is itself ambiguous. The political economist slides between narrower and broader interpretations of self-interest.

Second, both the political economist and the traditional legal theorist may point to phenomena that seem to support their position. Perhaps most problematically, the political economist has no adequate account of the variety of legal forms that regulation may take: tax, civil liability, or criminal responsibility. An incentive-based explanation fails because the size of the sanction is independent of the legal form of the regulation.[1]

Note

1   I benefited from the comments on an earlier draft of Liam Murphy and Bill Edmundson. The financial support of the Filomen d'Agostino and Max E. Greenberg Research Fund of NYU School of Law is gratefully acknowledged.

References

Akerlof, G. 1980. A theory of custom of which unemployment may be one consequence. *Quarterly Journal of Economics* 94: 749–75.

Anand, P. 1993. The philosophy of intransitive preferences. *Economic Journal* 102: 337–46.

Bernheim, D. 1994. A theory of conformity. *Journal of Political Economy* 102: 841–77.

Calabresi, G. 1961. Some thoughts on risk distribution and the law of torts. *Yale Law Journal* 70: 499–553.

Coase, R. 1960. The problem of social cost. *Journal of Law and Economics* 3: 1–44.

Coleman, J. 1980. Efficiency, utility and wealth maximization. *Hofstra Law Review* 8: 509–51. Reprinted in J. Coleman, 1988. *Markets, Morals and the Law*. Cambridge, UK: Cambridge University Press, 95–132.

Dworkin, R. M. 1980a. Is wealth a value? *Journal of Legal Studies* 9: 191, 194–10.

Dworkin, R. M. 1980b. Why efficiency? *Hofstra Law Review* 8: 563–90.

Hart, H. L. A. 1961. *The Concept of Law*. London: Oxford University Press.

Hart, H. L. A. 1982. Commands and authoritative legal reasons. In H. L. A. Hart (ed.), *Essays on Bentham*. Oxford: Oxford University Press, 243–68.

Holmes, O.W., Jr. 1897. The path of the law. *Harvard Law Review* 10: 457–78.

Jones, S. 1983. *The Economics of Conformism*. Oxford: Blackwell.

Kaplow, L. and S. Shavell 2002. *Fairness vs. Welfare*. Cambridge, MA: Harvard University Press.

Kornhauser, L. A. 1997. How law influences behavior. In B. Garth and A. Sarat (eds.), *Justice and Power in Socio-Legal Studies*. Evanston, IL: Northwestern University Press, 208–32.

Kornhauser, L. A. 1998a. Stare decisis. In P. Newman (ed.), *The New Palgrave Dictionary of Economics and the Law*, vol. 3. London: Palgrave Macmillan, 509–14.

Kornhauser, L. A. 1998b. Wealth maximization. In P. Newman (ed.), *The New Palgrave Dictionary of Economics and the Law*, vol. 3. London: Palgrave Macmillan, 679–84.

Kornhauser, Lewis A. 1998c. No best answer? *University of Pennsylvania Law Review* 146: 1599–1637.

Kornhauser, L. A. 2000. Three roles for a theory of behavior in a theory of law. *Rechtstheorie* 31: 197–252.

Kornhauser, L. A. 2003a. The domain of preference. *University of Pennsylvania Law Review* 151: 717–46.

Kornhauser, L. A. 2003b. Preference, well-being, and morality in social decision. *Journal of Legal Studies* 33 (1): 303–30.

Posner, R. A. 1973. *Economic Analysis of Law*. Cambridge, MA: Harvard University Press.

Posner, R. A. 1979. Utilitarianism, economics and legal theory. *Journal of Legal Studies* 8: 103–40.

Posner, R. A. 1980. The ethical and political basis of the efficiency norm in common law adjudication. *Hofstra Law Review* 8: 487–598.

Raz, J. 1975. *Practical Reason and Norms*. Princeton, NJ; Princeton University Press.

Segal, J. and Spaeth, H. 1993. *The Supreme Court and the Attitudinal Model*. New York: Cambridge University Press.

Sen, A. K. 1993. Internal consistency of choice. *Econometrica* 61: 495–521.

Spaeth, H. and Segal, J. 2000. *Majority Rule or Minority Will: Adherence to Precedent on The U.S. Supreme Court*. New York: Cambridge University Press.

Chapter 5

Critical Legal Theory

Mark V. Tushnet

Historical Background

Critical legal theory refers to a body of scholarship developed primarily in the United States starting in the 1970s. Critical legal theory originated when a group of younger legal academics reflected on their largely political disagreements with more senior scholars, focusing on issues of race, wealth inequality, and the then ongoing American war in Vietnam (Tushnet 1991). Politically, the early critical legal theorists identified themselves as substantially to the left of mainstream liberals, whom they associated with the Cold War and an unwillingness to take the steps necessary to rectify racial and wealth inequalities.

The political underpinnings of critical legal theory led its proponents away from concerns associated with jurisprudence understood in traditional terms. At least in the first instance, critical legal theorists were not interested in examining the question, "What is law?," for example, or the question, "What is the connection between law and morality?," although their narrower concerns ultimately intersected with these more traditional questions.

The critical legal theorists understood themselves to be in a world of legal theory where a consensus-based "legal process" school had eclipsed a conflict-based legal realism. They thought that the ongoing social conflicts over the war in Vietnam, racism, and poverty rendered implausible what they took to be the legal-process claim that well-designed institutions for taking social decisions could produce outcomes that people would generally accept despite their deep disagreements about what the outcomes *should* be. Critical legal theory took as its premise that disagreements were deep and ineradicable. They examined the legal system to see how those disagreements manifested themselves, and developed a critique aimed at undermining claims that law provided a distinctive and satisfying way of overcoming deep disagreement.

An Overview

The most general statement of critical legal theory was the slogan, "Law is politics" (Kairys 1982). This meant several things. First, the methods of legal reasoning were, in the end, indistinguishable from the methods of political argument: analysis would show that what legal theorists presented as distinctively legal arguments were reducible to arguments commonly made in general political discourse. Second, disputes within law were resolved in the same way that disputes within politics were resolved, by some fairly messy combination of coercion and reasoned argument, rather than by reason alone (as they understood their seniors to claim). Importantly, the claim was not that law, like politics, was a domain of coercion pure and simple; rather, it was that both domains mixed coercion and reason. This part of the claim about law and politics thus connected critical legal theory to traditional jurisprudential concerns about the relation between law and morality, although the connection was weak and never became a focus of attention within the work of critical legal theorists. Third, and perhaps most obvious, just as in politics we do not expect disagreement to disappear once some provisional resolution of a problem is located, so too in law we should not expect disagreement to disappear once an apparently authoritative decision has been rendered.

Critical legal theory drew from American legal realism the perception that an account of law must combine analysis of legal reasoning with social theory, loosely defined. See AMERICAN LEGAL REALISM. The legal realists had found themselves confronting what they, or at least their successors, described as a conceptualistic formalism, in which verbal formulations of rules were to be interpreted in ways that resolved concrete controversies. For the legal realists, *formalism* meant that legal rules could be justified by deduction from self-evident first principles. (To the extent that those principles are moral principles, the legal realists' understanding of formalism is loosely related to more contemporary definitions of formalism, which assert that the legal system has an immanent moral rationality.) Critical legal theorists appreciated – and perhaps may be said to have appropriated – the legal realists' rule-skepticism as a response to formalism. By examining the relation between particular rules and concrete problems, rule skeptics argued that the rules actually did not provide conclusive answers to any legal dispute; the formalist promise that answers could be deduced from agreed-upon premises failed, according to the legal realists, because alternative interpretations of agreed-upon rules, defensible by accepted methods of legal reasoning, were ordinarily available to support quite diverse outcomes.

Critical legal theorists confronted versions of formalism that had arisen after the legal realists developed their rule-skepticism, notably the legal-process school and the Chicago style of law-and-economics scholarship that played a large role in the legal academy when critical legal theory began to be developed. But, the critical legal theorists believed, legal-process theory reproduced formalism. Instead of deducing substantive rules from higher-level premises, legal-process theorists argued that legal tasks should be allocated to different institutions on the basis of higher-level principles identifying each institution's central characteristics. For critical legal theorists, this simply shifted the level on which formalism occurred from substantive law to the questions of institutional design and procedure. The scientism of Chicago-style law-and-economics was even more obviously formalistic; here substantive legal rules were to be deduced from extremely thin assumptions about individual motivation and self-interest.

Critical legal theorists also appreciated the legal realists' materialism. As the critical legal theorists read legal realism, rule-skepticism implied that one could not explain the outcomes actually reached in legal disputes by referring to the rules of law alone. Some social, not legal, theory would have to be invoked to explain outcomes. Again, as the critical theorists read legal realism, the relevant social theory for legal realists was fundamentally materialist in a loosely Marxist sense: class interests explained why judges (and, even more obviously, legislators) reached the results they did.

Critical legal theory modernized rule-skepticism, but probably did not add strikingly new arguments to the ones the legal realists had produced. The situation was different with respect to the explanatory social theory, though. Critical legal theory combined, sometimes awkwardly, a phenomenological account of social action with elements of the humanist rather than determinist Marxism that had become fashionable on the left in the 1960s and early 1970s.

The Indeterminacy Thesis

Critical legal theory's version of rule-skepticism gained the label, *the indeterminacy thesis*, and examining that thesis provides a useful entry point into the claims made by critical legal theorists (Tushnet 1996). Although the thesis was sometimes stated in entirely universal terms, to the effect that all imaginable legal questions were indeterminate, qualified versions played a more important part in critical legal theory and, of course, were more plausible. One could put a qualified version of the indeterminacy thesis in this way: in any legal dispute with some social significance, whether that significance arises from the legal rules at issue or from the problem generating the dispute, the legal resources available in any reasonably well-developed legal system were sufficient to justify any socially significant outcome, where *justify* refers to practices of justification generally regarded as available to a person well-trained in the system's methods of legal argument. Critical legal theorists defended the indeterminacy thesis with two general types of arguments. The first operated *within* specifically defined fields of law like property and contract, the second *across* fields.

Critical legal theorists argued that within any given field of law one could observe concepts grouped in pairs with one concept dominant over the other (Kennedy 1976). For example, in property law the predominant concept was the owner's sovereignty over the property owned, meaning that owners could do with their property what they wished, while one subordinate concept is nuisance, meaning that owners cannot do with their property something that interferes with another person's sovereignty interest in property. In contract law, the dominant concept of agreement is countered by subordinate concepts of force, fraud, and mistake. Critical legal theorists claimed that, given any problem (within the range specified by the indeterminacy thesis), a well-trained lawyer could produce arguments that in the circumstances the subordinate concept ought to prevail over the usually dominant one. Importantly, those arguments would draw on the very justifications for creating the "exception" or subordinate concept in the first place, so they operated on the terrain already identified as legally relevant.

Duncan Kennedy offered the clearest version of the argument supporting the indeterminacy thesis across fields (Kennedy 1986, 1997). Kennedy noted that sometimes lawyers experience difficulty in doing the work needed to elevate a subordinated concept. Instead of continuing to labor at *that* problem, Kennedy pointed out, the lawyers could turn to some other field of law, moving from tort to contract or from property to tort, and redefine the problem at hand as implicating a concept dominant in the neighboring field. Kennedy noted in passing that in United States law at least – and increasingly in other legal systems – moving from private law to constitutional law would often provide the resources lawyers needed to make their argument fit the norms of the profession, that is, to justify the result they sought.

The indeterminacy thesis implied that legal decision makers, including specifically judges, inevitably found themselves in a position of choice. The legal materials with which they worked did not require them to pursue one or another course, and so they could choose which to pursue. Critical legal theory's progressive impulses counseled decision makers to make the progressive choice, but this advice did not arise organically from the indeterminacy thesis itself. Indeed, as critics of critical legal theory noted, political conservatives could agree with the indeterminacy thesis unless they accepted some account of conservatism that required legal determinacy.

At least in qualified versions, the indeterminacy thesis has moved from the domain of critical legal theory into mainstream legal thought. Typically, though, the thesis is domesticated. Some accounts of law against which critical legal theory reacted claimed that legal disputes could be resolved by applying generally accepted methods of legal reasoning to the materials – statutes, cases, and the like – in the legal system. Accepting the indeterminacy thesis made it difficult to accept that claim. Instead, mainstream legal thinkers assert that acceptable outcomes result when decision makers exercise judgment or, in some variants, practical wisdom. When inspected carefully, this response reproduces the legal-process account, and therefore cannot satisfy proponents of critical legal theory.

A different response to a qualified indeterminacy thesis is also common, but it is a response that critical legal theory anticipated and worked into its own underpinnings. In an important way, the indeterminacy thesis is inconsistent with the experience of lawyers. Whatever might be true in the abstract, lawyers know that they frequently can predict, with a reasonably high level of accuracy, how a legal dispute will in fact be resolved. Indeed, they can make these predictions even within the range specified by a qualified indeterminacy thesis. How, then, can there be indeterminacy when accurate prediction is possible?

Another way of putting the point is that, while the indeterminacy thesis concludes by identifying a moment of choice in every legal dispute, what actually happens shows that the choices are somehow constrained. But what is the source or nature of the constraint?

Critical Legal Theory and Social Theory

Traditional Marxist and American progressive thought offered one answer to the question of the source of actual determinacy: the legal system is "tilted" in favor of the powerful. Those bodies of thought identified several possible sources of this tilt, but even in the aggregate the fact of tilt seemed not fully explained. One source was self-conscious action on behalf of the interests of the powerful, construed in traditional Marxist and progressive thought as referring to the interests of capital or the wealthy. Critical legal theorists did not deny the fact of occasional, and sometimes widespread, self-conscious action of this sort. They were concerned, however, with the inadequacy of an account relying on self-conscious class-conscious action comprehensively.

The reason for rejecting self-conscious action to explain "tilt" was that it failed to capture important parts of the phenomena in which critical legal theorists were interested. For one thing, judges regularly reported, both in their opinions and in their reflections on their work, that they paid attention to the law, not to class (or any other social) relations. Reflecting on their own legal training, and on their observations of lawyers at work, critical legal theorists believed that these self-reports were largely accurate.

Perhaps more important, critical legal theorists were interested in legal reforms designed, or so it seemed, to aid the working class and other subordinated groups (Klare 1978). One could design class-conscious accounts of these reforms; traditional Marxists could and did argue, for example, that liberal-seeming labor law reforms were aimed at staving off more substantial revolutionary transformations by buying off important segments of labor's leadership. Legal

sociologists offered alternative structural accounts for the fact that liberal reforms were deradicalized. Critical legal theory assimilated Marc Galanter's classic argument that the "haves" come out ahead because they have structural advantages in litigation over "one-shot" players, deriving from the haves' accumulated experience with and investment in repeated litigation over specific questions in contrast to the limited investments one-shotters could make (Galanter 1974).

While conceding that such explanations had some value, critical legal theorists found them seriously incomplete. They believed that liberal proponents of labor law, civil rights, and other reforms were sincere in their assertions that the reforms were designed to improve the conditions of workers and others. Further, critical legal theorists, along with many Marxist revisionists, were convinced that class domination explanations could not be fully satisfying when the working class and other subordinated groups were fully enfranchised. In democratic systems, why would not the legal system eventually come to reflect the interests of the largest groups, and specifically of workers?

Critical legal theorists relied on two strands of revisionist Marxism. First, they recalled the Italian communist Antonio Gramsci's account of hegemony, which referred to various social processes that led subordinated groups to accept the conditions under which they found themselves, or at least to believe that no alternatives were realistically achievable. Again, some of those processes, such as the domination of the mass media by capitalists, involved self-conscious action on behalf of a ruling class, but again the account seemed incomplete. Further, Gramsci's specific account was too tied to the social conditions of Italy in the 1920s to be helpful.

Critical legal theorists found the humanist Marxism rediscovered in the 1960s valuable in completing their social theory. That theory focused on the lived experience people had in society. Hegemony was maintained, according to critical legal theory, by accounts people came up with that made sense of their own experience. Particular social arrangements presented people with varying ways of experiencing the world, sometimes as participants in a group engaged in a common project but more often as individuals isolated from each other and pursuing their own projects. These experiences were supplemented by messages emanating from the media, and together experience and social reinforcement provided the basis for fantasies of social life that people internalized as real. Having internalized these fantasies, people came to experience existing social arrangements as natural (Gabel 2000).

This social theory retained its connection to its Marxist origins by its emphasis on the material substratum of experience. Materialism, however, did not mean determinism. Material experience structured the way people internalized understandings of social arrangements, but alternative understandings were always available and made choice possible.

As with the structure of legal doctrine, in social theory too critical legal theory found a predominant structure of understanding and a subordinate one. The predominant one was individualist, captured by Peter Gabel's description of people standing in line at a bank waiting for service and not connecting with each other. The subordinate one came to consciousness in moments of what Kennedy and Gabel called "intersubjective zap," and which were exemplified by the experience of participating in social movements like those of the 1960s (Gabel and Kennedy 1984).

The humanist Marxism that influenced critical legal theory's social theory was another reason critical legal theorists had for rejecting the traditional Marxist explanation for tilt as a result of self-conscious bias. Traditional Marxism was simply too determinist to be plausible to critical legal theorists. In the domain of law in particular, Marxist determinism was thought to be inconsistent with the implications of the indeterminacy thesis. According to traditional Marxists, the logic of capital – the material base – determined the superstructure, including law. The critical legal analysis of property law showed, however, that law was part of the base to the extent that it defined the property relations that constituted capitalism as an economic system. Humanist Marxism allowed critical legal theory to reject a determinism that seemed incompatible with the theory's analysis of law.

The Critique of the Public/Private Distinction

Aspects of the indeterminacy thesis converged with the phenomenological social theory in critical legal theory's critique of the distinction between a public world and a private domain. Critical legal theory attacked the distinction along many fronts (Kennedy 1982). Drawing on the analytical techniques used to develop the indeterminacy thesis, critical legal theorists noted that the so-called private sphere was defined by the actions of public agencies, and in particular by the courts as they spelled out the common-law entitlements held by actors in the private sphere. For example, "the family" and "the market" were identified with the private sphere, but what constituted a family and what market actors had power to do were the result of public definitions offered by the institutions of the law. A parent who abused a child might be the object of public intervention into the private sphere, but often a husband who abused a wife would be able successfully to claim that penalizing him would be an unjustified intrusion into the private (Olsen 1983). Wherever the line was located, public institutions would draw some line between the family understood as a private entity and the proper reach of public regulation. Again, the limits on contractual freedom identified by doctrines like fraud and mistake showed how market freedom resulted from actions in the public arena. In the study of constitutional law, critical legal theorists argued that the well-known incoherence of the state action doctrine resulted from that doctrine's inevitably unsuccessful effort to identify the line dividing the public from the private, when that line could be identified only by a public institution, the courts, in implementing the state action doctrine.

The phenomenological version of critical legal theory's social theory supported the critique of the public/private distinction. People experienced themselves as isolated individuals with private complaints that they could not, without substantial assistance, turn into public ones. Those who experienced racial discrimination saw themselves as victims, but doing so leads people to try to identify the perpetrators of their victim-hood (Freeman 1978). The phenomenology of discrimination, that is, leads to a focus on individual actors, both victims and perpetrators, rather than to a focus on the structural sources of discrimination of the sort that traditional Marxists might identify. An important argument by Alan Freeman pointed out that the courts tended to take the perpetrators' perspective in assessing claims of discrimination, but from the point of view of critical legal theory's social theory, it would have been equally problematic had the courts taken a perspective understood to be that of victims seen as individuals subject to discrimination one by one.

The phenomenological social theory also helped explain the component of the indeterminacy thesis emphasizing the juxtaposition of dominant and subordinate concepts. To take one example, critical legal theory found in contract law a dominant concept of free choice and a subordinate one of force and fraud. But, according to critical legal theorists, on analysis much that was characterized in the law as free choice could be equally well characterized as the result of force and fraud, depending only on the scope of what the analyst took into account in examining the problem. An impoverished worker could be said to have made a free choice to accept a job with unsafe working conditions, for example. It became possible to see the decision to take the job as one forced on the worker, once one's vision expanded to include the worker's material conditions. In repudiating its earlier jurisprudence enforcing a constitutionally based freedom of contract, the Supreme Court understood the point by characterizing a world without a minimum wage as one in which the community provided a "subsidy for unconscionable employers" (*West Coast Hotel v. Parrish* 1937). Workers did not freely choose to work for low wages; they were forced to do so by the distribution of property rights that gave their employers great wealth and the workers very little. The phenomenological social theory explained the concepts of *free choice* and *force and fraud* as social constructs arising from the way in which people interpreted their material conditions.

Policy "Implications"

That critical legal theory's recommendations about what to do at the moment of choice were ungrounded led to another line of criticism, this one a criticism to which critical legal theory's social theory responded. As one sympathetic observer put it, the question that killed critical legal studies was, "What would you do?" (Fischl 1992). That is, critics of critical legal theory wondered what concrete policy proposals critical legal theorists offered.

In several senses, the question was misplaced. Works in critical legal theory made scores of concrete policy suggestions, ranging from endorsing liberal versions of property/contract law such as finding an implied warranty of habitability in leases to impoverished tenants (Kennedy 1976), to suggestions about the way in which national labor law should be interpreted (Klare 1978), to proposals for large-scale constitutional changes that included creating a branch whose task was to be available to destabilize settled understandings of the law (Unger 1987). The difficulty, according to critical observers, was that these proposals were either entirely conventional, requiring nothing from critical legal theory to support them, or wildly utopian, unachievable in present circumstances or even in realistically foreseeable ones.

Proponents of critical legal theory made concrete policy proposals, but they did so on understandings quite different from those of their interlocutors. To some extent, the proposals were designed to expand the range of things that legal theorists could consider. Too often, critical legal theorists believed, law was seen as compelling particular policy choices, or at least as sharply narrowing the range of outcomes that could be achieved in a manner consistent with existing legal materials. The indeterminacy thesis demonstrated that these claims of necessity were false. One point of the policy proposals was to pose the question: what in the existing legal materials *rules out* this proposal? When the answer was, "Nothing," critical legal theorists turned to social theory to account for the unnecessary restriction of policy argument. Critical legal theory's distinctive policy proposals may have been utopian, but – although critical legal theorists would have been happy had the proposals been adopted – the proposals' point was to expose that their utopianism resided in social arrangements, not in the legal materials.

Critical legal theory's social theory had another implication, related as well to the question of policy proposals. The theory's interlocutors wondered what proposals flowed from critical legal theory. The indeterminacy thesis and the social theory associated with critical legal theory answered that *nothing* flowed from the theory in the sense required. The question assumed some degree of legal or social determinacy, an assumption that critical legal theory rejected. All that could be done in any specific situation was to engage in an extremely detailed analysis of the interests at stake, the possibilities of change, the social setting, and much more; serious policy proposals could emerge only from such fine-grained analyses, and even then decision makers were highly likely to find themselves at a point when they would simply have to make a pure choice. So the questions being asked of critical legal theory demonstrated, to the critical legal theorists, a deep lack of understanding of the theory itself.

The Critique of Rights

The indeterminacy thesis and the phenomenological arguments about the ways in which people created images of legality to reconcile themselves with their social positions combined in one of early critical legal theory's most controversial claims, described as the *critique of rights* (Tushnet 1984). Critical legal theory was created after the US Supreme Court had begun to repudiate its earlier interventions on behalf of liberal interests in cases involving race and social welfare. Those interventions remained important in the legal academy's understanding of the *possibilities* of legal, and particularly judicial, action in support of progressive visions of social justice. Among those possibilities was the use of the legal system

to vindicate rights – moral, constitutional, and other – on behalf of socially subordinated groups. *Brown v. Board of Education* (1954), the desegregation decision, and *Roe v. Wade* (1973), the abortion decision, loomed large in the minds of progressive legal scholars.

The critique of rights posed a sharp challenge to the prevailing image of legal possibility. It seemed to place *Brown* and *Roe* in question, suggesting that these triumphs of liberal legal activism were somehow inconsistent with enduring achievements for progressive law and politics.

The critique of rights questioned the utility of making claims of legal right on a number of grounds. First, the indeterminacy thesis suggested to critical legal scholars that rights-claims were a double-edged sword. There was no reason to suppose, they argued, that courts would vindicate only rights-claims made by subordinated groups. Seeing hints in the late 1970s and early 1980s of possibilities that came to fruition in the 1990s, the critique of rights worried that strong defenses of courts as rights-protectors would turn against progressives when the courts started to vindicate the rights of whites in affirmative action cases, and property owners in cases involving claims that government regulation amounted to a taking of primate property.

Second, the critique of rights found in the slogan, "Law is politics," another danger in reliance on rights-claims in the judicial arena. Such claims could trigger counter-claims of right-invasion by political opponents. More important, framing political claims in legal terms naturally induced activists to seek redress in courts, diminishing the attention they could devote to other arenas of political action such as legislatures and the streets. But, courts were not a reliable source of rights-protection. Even when courts took the progressive side in identifying rights-violations, actually implementing the courts' decisions required a mobilized political community whose development might have been impaired by the dominance of lawyers pursuing the rights strategy.

Third, the critical legal scholars' phenomenology led them to believe that, at least in the context of the United States in the late twentieth century, claims about rights were likely to reinforce an individualism that they believed stood in the way of developing community solidarities that could generate more substantial progressive change. The dominant concepts in constitutional law in particular were strongly individualist. The rhetoric of *Brown* focused on the rights of each individual African American child to attend school without regard to his or her race; *Roe* relied on an earlier case saying, "If the right of privacy means anything, it is the right of the *individual* . . . to be free from unwarranted governmental intrusion" (*Eisenstadt v. Baird*, 1972). Critical legal theorists believed that the individualism of a rights-based strategy occluded the underlying social conditions, including social mobilization, that actually induced courts to recognize rights.

Related to this last point was a fourth one, deriving from the phenomenological social theory. Rights-strategies on behalf of progressive interests took advantage of, but were also infected by, the prevailing view of people as individuals with rights that resided in themselves as embodied persons, a view most obviously compatible with the claims of women in the abortion cases. But, the critique of rights argued, rights-*claims* were made against the state, and led people to experience rights as something conferred on them by a fantasized "state" rather than as a set of lived experiences arising out of social relations of a particular sort.

The critique of rights elicited a strong reaction from minority legal scholars who were part of the rough social formation – leftist, non-liberal legal theorists – that included the early critical legal scholars (Williams 1987). The minority response was that the critique of rights undervalued the contribution rights-claims had made to reducing social subordination and, perhaps more important, failed to take account of the ways in which judicial recognition of rights provided minority communities with a sense of full membership in the nation even if the rights were imperfectly implemented. The latter point, if not the former, was actually compatible with the indeterminacy thesis and, indeed, with the critique of rights itself, and this aspect of the minority response to early critical legal theory became an accepted part of critical legal theory generally.

Critical Feminist Theory and Critical Race Theory

The minority response to the critique of rights was only the beginning of a proliferation of critical legal theories, including critical race theory and critical feminist theory. These theories developed in ways that led to some significant divergences from early critical legal studies, and here I emphasize only themes in later analyses that resonate with ones articulated in early critical legal theory.

Critical feminist theory and critical race theory generally accepted the indeterminacy thesis, but offered different social-theory accounts for the way in which legal outcomes were structured. Focusing on the subordinate position of women and racial minorities in society, they found it easier to accept accounts of domination cast in terms of the immediate self-interest of dominant groups, that is, men and whites. See FOUR THEMES IN FEMINIST LEGAL THEORY. Ideological domination was less important (relative to coercion) in accounting for the maintenance of the dominant position of whites and men over racial minorities and women than it was in accounting for class-based domination. Still, some notion of ideological domination or hegemony remained helpful to these theories, to deal with the ways in which apparent legal reforms nonetheless preserved existing relations of power (Siegel 1997).

Critical race theory and critical feminist theory also developed a better method than early critical legal theory had for conveying the role that phenomenology played in their theory's social theory. That method was the narrative of personal experience. Narrative and a phenomenologically focused social theory fit comfortably with the identity politics to which critical race theory in particular was connected. Mainstream critics of these theories derided the narrative method for failing to show that individual experiences were in some statistical sense typical of the experiences of members of the social groups from which the narratives emerged (Farber and Sherry 1997). That criticism, however, failed to appreciate the role that narrative played in critical theory. Early critical legal theory had presented its phenomenological accounts in highly theorized and abstract forms, invoking Freud and Sartre. The narrative form proved more effective in establishing the importance of phenomenology in constructing a social theory that made sense of claims about the processes by which ideological domination or hegemony was constructed.

Critical race theorists redirected the early critical legal theorists' concerns about the priority given a universalist individualism in mainstream legal theory. Early critical legal theory argued that individualism predominated over group-oriented approaches in much of existing law. Critical race theorists refined the analysis by pointing out that the subordinated concept of "group" actually identified a far more differentiated social reality. They were particularly effective in pointing out the importance of what they called *intersectionality*, by which they meant the legal treatment and social status of collectivities composed of people with two or more subordinated identities, such as African American women or Asian American gay men (Crenshaw 1989).

The idea of intersectionality reinforced another component of early critical legal theory. That theory's non-determinist component led proponents of critical legal theory to insist that one could not answer questions about what should be done, whether cast in terms of general policy-making or in terms of case outcomes, in the abstract. As I noted earlier, only a highly contextualized analysis could begin to provide decent guidance on those questions. The idea of intersectionality helped critical legal theorists appreciate again the complexity of social life by broadening the range of the groups whose social and legal subordination they opposed, thereby demonstrating why analysis had to be highly contextualized.

Critical race theory made another important contribution in clarifying and providing perhaps more persuasive examples of the social construction of legal concepts than early critical legal theory had. The critical race theorists' insight was captured by the term *race-ing* (introduced by Kendall Thomas at a conference on Frontiers of Legal Thought in 1990). The analysis offered by mainstream legal theory, and even by some early critical legal theorists, treated racial categories as natural, at least in their core meanings.

Critical race theorists argued that racial categories were constructed through processes by which people were "raced," that is, given races by the societies in which they were located. Skeptics of the argument that "free choice" was a socially constructed category may have found it easier to accept the idea that "race" was a socially constructed category.

The Legacy

By the late 1990s proponents and opponents of critical legal theory often observed that that theory was "dead." Precisely what they meant was unclear. Critical legal theory had generated an organization, the Conference on Critical Legal Studies, that had indeed passed from the scene. Yet writers who had been prominent in the development of critical legal studies continued to produce works that were plainly consistent with the premises of early critical legal theory. The claims notoriously associated with critical legal theory – that "law is politics," the indeterminacy thesis, the critique of rights, the critique of the public/private distinction – had entered into mainstream discourse, sometimes achieving widespread acceptance in modestly qualified forms (as with the indeterminacy thesis) and sometimes becoming at least a proposition that mainstream theorists had to take seriously (as with the critique of rights). Critical feminist theory and critical race theory were active areas of scholarship as well.

What it meant to say that critical legal theory was dead, then, was that critical legal theory did not appear to be generating distinctive new insights. Perhaps so, although much the same could be said of many well-established approaches to legal analysis, such as Chicago-school law-and-economics and even liberal legal theory. Some younger scholars applied the ideas and insights associated with early critical legal theory in their work on legal areas to which prior authors had devoted little attention, such as disability discrimination, copyright law, and local government law. In short, critical legal theory was not, I think, moribund relative to any other sub-field of legal thought. It had become one of many analytic techniques available to legal scholars.

References

Brown v. Board of Education. 1954. 347 US 483.

Crenshaw, Kimberle Williams. 1989. Demarginalizing the intersection of race and sex. *University of Chicago Legal Forum* 1989: 139–67.

Eisenstadt v. Baird. 1972. 405 US 438.

Farber, Daniel and Sherry, Suzanna. 1997. *Beyond All Reason.* New York: Oxford University Press.

Fischl, Richard Michael. 1992. The question that killed critical legal studies. *Law & Social Inquiry* 17: 779–820.

Freeman, Alan. 1978. Legitimizing racial discrimination through antidiscrimination law. *Minnesota Law Review* 62: 1049–1119.

Gabel, Peter. 2000. *The Bank Teller and Other Essays on the Politics of Meaning.* San Francisco: Acada Books.

Gabel, Peter and Kennedy, Duncan. 1984. Roll over Beethoven. *Stanford Law Review* 36: 1–55.

Galanter, Marc. 1974. Why the "haves" come out ahead. *Law & Society Review* 9: 95–160.

Kairys, David. 1982. *The Politics of Law,* 1st edn. New York: Pantheon.

Kennedy, Duncan. 1976. Form and substance in private law adjudication. *Harvard Law Review* 89: 1685–1778.

Kennedy, Duncan. 1982. The stages of the decline of the public/private distinction. *University of Pennsylvania Law Review* 130: 1349–57.

Kennedy, Duncan. 1986. Freedom and constraint in adjudication. *Journal of Legal Education* 36: 518–62.

Kennedy, Duncan. 1997. *Critique of Adjudication: Fin de Siècle.* Cambridge, MA: Harvard University Press.

Klare, Karl E. 1978. Judicial deradicalization of the Wagner act and the origins of modern legal consciousness, 1937–41. *Minnesota Law Review* 62: 265–339.

Olsen, Frances E. 1983. The family and the market. *Harvard Law Review* 96: 1497–1578.

Roe v. Wade. 1973. 410 US 113.

Siegel, Reva. 1997. Why equal protection law no longer protects. *Stanford Law Review* 49: 1111–48.

Tushnet, Mark. 1984. An essay on rights. *Texas Law Review* 62: 1364–1403.

Tushnet, Mark. 1991. Critical legal studies: A political history. *Yale Law Journal* 100: 1515–44.

Tushnet Mark. 1996. Defending the indeterminacy thesis. *Quinnipiac Law Review* 16: 339–56.

Unger, Roberto Mangeibera. 1987. *False Necessity.* New York: Cambridge University Press.

West Coast Hotel v. Parrish. 1937. 300 US 379.

Williams, Patricia J. 1987. Alchemical notes: Reconstructing ideals from deconstructed rights. *Harvard Civil Rights-Civil Liberties Law Review,* 22: 401–33.

Chapter 6

Four Themes in Feminist Legal Theory: Difference, Dominance, Domesticity, and Denial

Patricia Smith

Feminist jurisprudence is a comparatively new discipline that grew out of the women's liberation movement of the late 1960s and 1970s. At that time a relatively large number of women (as compared to previous decades) entered the profession of law and related academic pursuits, some with the idea of using law to correct the unjust and unequal treatment of women that was widely evident at the time. The puzzle of why women are treated unequally, why this injustice is so commonly invisible to so many in power, why it persists even when identified, and what it will take to change it has become the subject matter of feminist legal theory.

But the approach to this subject matter has evolved over time. In the 1970s activists argued that for all legally relevant purposes men and women were equal and should be so treated in law. By the 1980s feminist scholars undertook to analyze and evaluate the legal structures that retarded justice for women instead of promoting it. Thus, feminist legal theorists began by arguing simply for the inclusion of women in all social practices as they stood, and progressed to a critique of those practices and legal norms. Today feminist jurisprudence is focused on law in three distinctive ways: first, to identify sources of bias and injustice within it; second, to find ways to use it as a means to promote justice for women in other institutions and social practices; and third, to identify and overcome devices of denial, sub-

version, and containment that pose barriers to reform. This chapter will review three basic themes that have focused much feminist legal scholarship since the 1980s: difference, dominance, and domesticity.

These general themes, and especially certain particular issues within them, have at times been extremely controversial and public. We might call these public debates "spotlight controversies." Issues of abortion, pornography, affirmative action, sexual harassment and date rape have all had some share of the spotlight. But the level on which these issues have been debated in the public eye (as opposed to discussion in law journals or academia) has often been emotional and ill considered, pandering to the public enjoyment of sensationalism and oversimplification.

Many of these discussions illustrate clearly what Deborah Rhode calls the "no problem" problem. Date rape and sexual harassment are clear cases of one variety. Despite alarming statistics it is asserted that date rape and sexual harassment either are rare or are not harmful. Women exaggerate their claims about these matters, it is said.

Affirmative action represents a different sort of denial. Some opponents say it was always unjustified in principle as reverse discrimination, while glossing over the seriousness of the discrimination it is supposed to counter. Others claim that it was once justified as a countermeasure to sex discrimination, but now that sex discrimination is pretty much a thing of the past (at least as rare as sexual harassment and date rape) there is no more justification for affirmative action. In her book, *Speaking of Sex: The Denial of Gender Inequality* (1997), Rhode provides a well-documented and encyclopedic account of many sources of the continuing subordination of women and the denial of its existence. Hers is the most comprehensive treatment of a subject receiving increasing attention in recent scholarship, namely, the identification of sources of subversion and containment or reinterpretation and reversal of women's claims to equality. As I review the three major themes of difference, dominance and domesticity, I will also bring in the issue of denial as an emerging area, or fourth theme of increasing importance in feminist legal thought.

The Double Bind of Sameness and Difference

The debate over sameness and difference (of men and women) may be viewed as a question mark. It is either a complete diversion – that is, an instance of feminists themselves being sucked into traditional norms that we have all been socialized to value and perpetuate – or it is a primary instance of the double bind encountered by outsiders who seek to reform a system by criticizing the very procedures that they themselves must use to accomplish their desired reforms. Possibly it is both. I will begin with the latter.

Ann Freedman's 1983 essay, "Sex Equality, Sex Difference, and the Supreme Court," marked the beginning of an avalanche of articles debating claims of sameness and difference during the 1980s, that focused primarily on the issue of pregnancy leave. The double bind of that debate was that assuming equal treatment means identical treatment (i.e., sameness) then, if both men and women have no pregnancy benefits they are being treated equally; so equality in this case means disadvantage for women. On the other hand, if women argue against the disadvantage it is viewed as special pleading, asking for special treatment, which means better treatment, extra favors. This, obviously, is a no-win debate for women. It results from not being able to set the

terms of the debate, a common sign of outsider status.

Martha Minow (1987) characterized this kind of problem as "dilemmas of difference." Where difference means disadvantage, she pointed out, the courts reinforce the disadvantage either by ignoring the difference or by acknowledging it. If the disadvantage is acknowledged so as to address it or compensate for it, the acknowledgement reinforces stereotypes that perpetuate the disadvantage. If the court denies the stereotype, it is then prone to ignore the disadvantage, leaving the cost with the victim. Thus, we have something close to a no-win situation for courts as well as for women unless the issue is reformulated.

Minow argues that such dilemmas rely on unstated assumptions about the nature of difference that must be transcended to enable the courts to formulate more creative solutions to the problem of equal treatment in cases of difference. Courts typically reason from an unstated norm that uncritically assumes the status quo. This implies that the status quo is natural, uncoerced, and good, or perhaps inevitable, but in fact it is simply not considered. From this vantage point the perspective of the judge takes on the aspect of the impartial observer, neutral and objective, rather than one possible perspective among many; and the difference of the outsider to the norm seems to be a characteristic of the outsider rather than a relation between the outsider and the unconsidered insiders who represent the norm. Thus, women (or the disabled, or people practicing non-Christian religions) are characterized as different. But women are no more different from men than men are from women. Any difference is relational. If women appear to present "special" issues in the workplace, it is only because the norm from which they are being judged has been formulated by and for men (Minow 1987). From analyses like Minow's the insight emerged that there was no reason to call rights to pregnancy benefits "special rights" or "special treatment" unless the norm against which they were being judged was male. There is nothing extraordinary or "special" about a woman being pregnant, since most women do experience this condition at some time during their working lives. In that regard it is less extraordinary than, say, appendicitis or a broken leg. Thus, the very construction of the debate as a question of either equal or special rights is a false dichotomy that is slanted against women.

This is an important insight because it illustrates that norms themselves must be evaluated, and not just taken as given, or assumed to be neutral. So most feminists today view the idea of equal rights versus special rights as a misguided formulation of the problem that needs to be transcended. Yet the debate over sameness and difference has continued, and has influenced feminist legal scholarship in a broad range of areas.

In particular, the work of Harvard psychologist Carol Gilligan (1982) has had a certain impact in feminist jurisprudence, as it has had in all areas of feminism. What is positive in Gilligan's view is its defense of humane values associated with women's traditional roles: concern, sympathy, nurturing. These are indeed significant values that should not be abandoned in the quest for equality.

What is troubling about Gilligan's view is that it looks like a reinstatement of traditional norms. Not only does Gilligan celebrate traditional "female virtues," she specifically re-attaches them to women. She argues that men and women think differently and value differently, men tending to operate from an abstract "ethic of justice," while women tend to utilize a contextual "ethic of care" (Gilligan 1982).

There is nothing very new about this set of ideas. Pythagoras thought more or less the same thing. It fits quite nicely within his theory of oppositions. These ideas have been the foundation of sexist prejudice for thousands of years, except for one important difference. Gilligan's point is that thinking and valuing one way is no better than the other. We need to appreciate both. That is an important point, which unfortunately seems all too easily overlooked or ignored. Furthermore, Gilligan's view creates the impression that women as a class think and value differently from men as a class, which borders precariously on the old, discredited, essentialist idea that men and women necessarily think and value differently. While Gilligan denies that she is making any such essentialist claims, she uses language throughout her book that is easily mistaken for it.

How, exactly, such a view should be used in law to promote the rights of women is a good question. Unsurprisingly, it has in fact been used for the opposite end. For example, in the case of *EEOC v. Sears* (1986), testimony of feminist scholars citing Gilligan's work was used to counter a claim of employment discrimination for hiring and promotion practices that automatically funneled women into low paying, dead end clerking positions rather than higher paying commission sales positions, even when they applied for commission sales. The ground was that women are not interested in such work (even if they apply for it) because women (being nurturing and caring) do not like competition. Such cases show how close Gilligan's portrait of womanhood is to the Victorian standards of middle-class motherly matrons, and how easy it is to interpret them for exactly the same nineteenth-century effect: the subordination of women. Of course, it does not follow that Gilligan's theory is false (or true), but it does follow that it is dangerous.

Thus, the problem with Gilligan's view is that while it correctly identifies important values, it focuses the issue of difference in exactly the wrong direction. Values are learned, and it is not women who need more socialization to learn to identify with values of care and nurture, but men. (Women should be learning to identify with values of accomplishment and self-sufficiency.) All these values are universal and should be reflected in a balanced set of virtues for all people. Thus, the identification of certain values with women (especially the values associated with traditional motherhood) is much too susceptible to abuse to be useful in legal analysis. It reinstates the old self-reinforcing idea that certain virtues are natural for women and certain others are natural for men (no matter how many individuals do not really fit the paradigm). From there it is only one short step to the idea that it is only natural that roles should be different as well, and it follows that the requirements of justice will also be different. This was exactly the conclusion drawn in *Sears*, as applied to employment discrimination. Indeed, the idea of difference has manifested itself in the form of prejudice in virtually every area of life and law for centuries, and continues in the present day. Nowhere is this kind of problem more evident than in the ongoing war over abortion.

Abortion is the ultimate spotlight controversy. It is extremely important, rests on fundamental disagreement, and is prone to produce volatile, ill-considered, and generally unproductive debate, rather than thoughtful discussion. It is noteworthy, however, that abortion is much more controversial outside feminism than within it. Within feminist theory abortion is a fundamental issue of self-determination for women. If the determination of the use of one's body is controlled by someone else (such as the state), then every other source of self-determination is seriously jeopardized. The jurisprudential controversy is over whether the best foundation on which to base a right of self-determination in regard to abortion is privacy or equality. This is an interesting legal question, both sides of which have pros and cons that have been carefully explored in feminist legal scholarship (see e.g., Olsen 1989; Law 1984; see also PRIVACY).

Of course, the spotlight issue has not been this one, but whether abortion should be allowed or not in any case, an issue which is said to be determined by the answer to the question of when life begins. Most of this controversy is not about jurisprudence. The intensity and intractability of it does, however, represent the depth of underlying disagreement and ambivalence toward the entire agenda of feminism and feminist jurisprudence. The significance of the sameness/difference controversy in all this is that the "difference" of women is exactly what makes the requirements of justice "different" for them, and the idea of equality (supposedly) inapplicable. In the case of abortion it means that since women are "different" (namely, mothers), self-determination is not fundamental for them. They are precluded from it by nature.

Feminists argue that nature may make men and women different, but it is not nature that makes the difference redound to the advantage of men and the disadvantage of women. Nature made some human beings black and others white, but it was not nature that made some slaves and others masters. Such differential valuations and effects are created and maintained by unjustifiable physical, social, and legal structures premised on the excuse of difference. Consequently, what is important about feminist work on the issue of difference (despite its obvious inherent practical dangers for women) is that ultimately the meaning of equality and justice in cases of difference must be worked out. Some differences are real; yet difference should not mean disadvantage. It should not, but it certainly does at present, as is clearly displayed in the other two themes of feminist legal theory.

Dominance, Feminism, and Legal Protection

Not only are women traditionally viewed as different, but also as subordinate, and this subordinate status is enforced not only by institutional structures, but also by widespread personal interactions and social practices of coercion and violence. These attitudes and practices are being combated by activists, but are yet widely discounted in law and largely denied in popular discourse. "Male dominance" is often considered a laughable topic these days, reserved for radical feminist fanatics, but its effects – domestic violence, sexual harassment, and rape – are serious social problems. The theme of dominance in feminist jurisprudence reflects what early radical feminists called the "construction of gender" (or sexuality) as male domination and female subordination. It is manifested in the ancient game of the male predator and the female prey, in the identification of masculinity with power and femininity with submission. It implicates a deep-seated set of preconceptions about the nature of human life and the relative hierarchical positions of men and women within it.

This attitude is reflected in long-standing practices of violence and coercion that feminists have sought to correct through legal reform and educational programs. During the 1970s the primary focus of dominance feminists was rape and sexual harassment, but these issues were eclipsed in the public discourse of the 1980s by debates over the issue of pornography, a spotlight controversy that I will not dwell on here. While feminist concern over pornography is understandable, the political and practical effect of the public controversy can only be described as divisive and counterproductive for the cause of women's liberation. Furthermore, the theoretical positions espoused by feminists on this issue are so diametrically opposed to one another that there cannot be said to be a single feminist position on it. Finally, given its apparently irresolvable character (like the abortion controversy), it functions as a distraction from issues that might otherwise be confronted and addressed, despite their controversial nature.

I will accordingly concentrate on some of these other issues. Three serious problems that clearly represent three sources of entrenched enforcement mechanisms for male domination, as well as clear illustrations of the problem of denial are sexual harassment, domestic violence, and rape. In the interest of space I will focus primarily on feminist legal scholarship regarding the rape issue as representative of this area.

Sexual and marital arrangements reflect who we are as individuals and as a culture. They represent the most intimate of our personal relations, as developed over centuries of civilization. For all those centuries until the twentieth, male domination was a given. The natural order of social life and the proper relations between the sexes have always been viewed as hierarchical. The paradigm of manhood is power; and the paradigm of womanhood is subordination to that power.

These attitudes are manifested in both social and aesthetic norms: standards of beauty, style, manner, courtship, courtesy, masculinity and femininity, attractiveness, and appropriateness of behavior, as well as work roles, family responsibilities, social and political organization, the nature of authority, and the structure of institutions. They also manifest themselves in sexual harassment, domestic violence, and rape, and they are expressed in pornography as well as in mainstream media, especially commercial media. Those feminists (e.g., MacKinnon 1993; Dworkin 1979) who have been particularly concerned about pornography see it as an expression and reinforcement of the attitude of male dominance that results in rape, harassment, and violence. That these are manifestations of male dominance is a point that is widely ignored or denied, perhaps because it is more comfortable to marginalize these problems by disassociating them with "normal life," or perhaps because it is

hard to see what to do about such a global phenomenon as "male domination as such." But rape, battery, and sexual harassment are specific illegal behaviors. They can be addressed, if taken seriously. Recent scholarship suggests that radical feminists are correct that it is the pervasive entrenched tradition of male domination that makes the reaction to rape, harassment, and battery less than it should be, that facilitates attitudes of denial and dismissal, and consequently retards reform. However, the radicals are not correct to suppose that no social progress can be made until the worldview is changed. Progress is being made (slowly but actually). Furthermore, the only way to address the basic attitude – the largely unconscious presumption of male dominance as normal – is to attack its manifestations, while recognizing that they are effects of a pattern of normal life and thought that reformers must be dedicated to changing. Thus, the response to male domination as a worldview can only be to redouble reform efforts to counter its causes and effects, but those efforts must take the pattern of domination into account and address it in explicit measures designed to counteract the underlying attitudes that have undercut the effectiveness of previous attempts at reform.

Recognition of these points is well illustrated in recent feminist work on the issue of rape. Stephen Schulhofer's book, *Unwanted Sex: The Culture of Intimidation and the Failure of Law* (1998), is a good example. Schulhofer notes that reforms to rape law over the past 50 years have largely failed. For example, alarmingly low conviction rates in rape cases that prompted the American Law Institute to attempt to encourage reforms during the 1950s have not substantially changed despite decades of repeated reform efforts. In 1975 the National Task Force on Rape led to further statutory reform in some states, and continuing feminist activism has promoted widespread legal change in certain respects (e.g., the introduction of rape shield laws, the demise of the cautionary instruction to juries, and the easing of the resistance requirement). Yet studies in several states during the 1990s showed little impact: no increased reporting, prosecution, or conviction rates were indicated (Schulhofer 1998:18ff.).

Because of all this legal activity (and despite the recent reports of its ineffectiveness) there is a myth of radical change, Schulhofer explains. It is assumed that the legal problems have been corrected. So the social problem is denied. Backlash writers claim that women themselves are to blame for engaging in careless behavior. The behavior of abusive men is viewed as inevitable. Acquaintance (or date) rape is dismissed as simply bad sex. And the complaints of feminists are treated as special pleading. (See e.g., Paglia 1992; Roiphe 1993.) But in fact, as Schulhofer so ably demonstrates, the law has not been corrected effectively, the protection against rape is virtually as weak and restricted as it was in 1950, and consequently women are at risk of sexual assault in all areas of life without genuine recourse to legal protection of their basic interest in bodily integrity.

Schulhofer suggests that this situation is due to two factors that reinforce each other. First, the law as currently written is grossly inadequate to protect the interest it is supposedly designed to protect (namely, the interest in not being coerced into sexual intimacy). For one thing, the basic elements of the crime (namely, force and consent) are vague, and vagueness is resolved in favor of the defendant (as it should be, of course, in a criminal case). Furthermore, some sexual abuses, such as obtaining sexual submission by fraud, intimidation, abuse of authority, or any form of coercion short of serious physical force or the direct threat of it, are excluded from coverage by definition. Schulhofer points out that the law of theft was once this way. Property owners were protected only from direct physical taking by force and without consent (e.g., robbery) but not from losing their property by what are now called embezzlement, extortion, or fraud. During the sixteenth century this situation was gradually changed, and ownership is now protected by a comprehensive regime of legal mechanisms that recognize the loss of property as an addressable interest against a wide range of illegitimate infringements. But the law does not similarly protect bodily integrity from fraud, extortion or blackmail. It is still at the level of property loss in the sixteenth century. Because of these problems the law itself poses an obstacle to reform, entrenching traditional discriminatory attitudes that protect men but leave women with no effective legal recourse to protect themselves.

Second, social attitudes about sex, sexuality, and rape are ambivalent, confused, and pervasively biased to favor traditional notions of sexual relations. The result is that genuine legal reform (that is, legal reform that would reflect a recognition of equal rights to sexual autonomy) is almost precluded from possibility, and even the partial reforms that are instituted are interpreted to correspond to traditional ideas. This social ambivalence indicates the great need for clearer legal standards to counter harmful behavior, Schulhofer argues. And since attitudes are in flux, reform is not impossible.

Rape law is pervaded by two abiding concerns: protecting the male interest in pursuing sexual intimacy, and fear that women could bring false charges against them. These are legitimate concerns, but there is virtually no recognition of women's competing interest in self-determination of their own intimate relations. Thus, the major problem with rape law, according to Schulhofer, is its failure to recognize a right to sexual autonomy for all people.

Autonomy requires freedom of choice, which implies both the right to accept and the right to decline. But obviously when people engage in a shared activity one person's interest in pursuing it is limited by the other person's right to refuse to do so. As the law currently stands, it is so strongly slanted toward the protection of pursuing sexual intimacy and the protection against false charges that there is no effective legal right to refuse. This maintains and reflects what Schulhofer (1998) calls a culture of intimidation.

Addressing the culture of intimidation is no easy task (Schulhofer proposes a model statute to begin to do so), but identifying and describing it accurately in detail is a very important step. One gratifying feature of Schulhofer's work (and other such recent scholarship) is the clear documentation of the extreme bias that currently presumes male domination as normal life, and the complicity of law in failing to address it. The pattern is repeated in practices of sexual harassment and domestic violence, all of which are dismissed by repeated themes of denial. Deborah Rhode lists four such themes:

1   The general problem is not serious; serious instances are rare.

2 Common complaints are not about serious harms or real injuries (women are exaggerating).
3 Men are not responsible for the harm; the victim is (she provoked it, asked for it, deserved it, or enjoyed it . . .).
4 Law cannot deal with it (at least any more than it already has).

Rhode analyzes these claims in connection with her analysis of sexual harassment (Rhode 1997: 96ff.), but in fact they are illuminating for the issues of rape and domestic violence as well. The similarities are quite striking.

Consider the first two claims, since they rely on one another. That these dual claims are patently false as applied to domestic violence is easily verifiable with clear statistics. Domestic violence produces approximately four million victims needing medical treatment costing $5 to $10 billion each year in the United States alone, according to American Medical Association estimates. It is the leading cause of injury to women (see Rhode 1997: 108; Schneider 2000: 4). Four million serious injuries to women every year cannot be characterized as a few rare incidents. It is a social problem of large proportions.

The damage done by sexual harassment and date rape (and even their frequency of occurrence) are harder to document. There is, however, ample evidence that the behaviors referred to by the phrases "sexual harassment" and "date rape" are in fact common. (Whether they should be evaluated as harassment or rape is a separate issue.) The behavior itself (whatever we call it) is common. It is documented that every year millions of women are propositioned and pushed into having sex with their employers, supervisors, teachers, doctors, lawyers, psychiatrists, indeed with any man who has authority and is willing to abuse it to extort sexual favors (see Schulhofer 1998). And millions of women every year are subjected to ridicule, sexual innuendo, threatening confrontations, degrading remarks, pictures, posters, calendars, and attitudes, some of which are intentionally aimed (minimally) at making them uncomfortable, and (maximally) at driving them out of what some men see as "their world." All this – the behavior itself – is documented (see e.g., Rhode 1997: ch. 5).

So the real question is not whether the behavior is rare. The real question is whether it is harmful. Do women have a legitimate interest that is being violated? And is it an interest that should be legally protected? These questions are not that hard to answer. The clearest case, again, is that of domestic violence. The most basic and uncontroversial interest traditionally protected by the criminal law is the interest in physical security. Since being beaten can no longer be recharacterized as punishment, it is then assault. Assault is a recognized legal injury, and anyone has a legal interest in being protected from it.

Rape is more complicated, since it involves two interests. The clearest cases are those involving violence or the threat of it. These implicate again the uncontroversial interest in physical security that law is designed to protect.

The other interest, a much more controversial one, is the interest in sexual autonomy, or self-determination over the physical use of one's body. There is no legal recognition of this interest, but it is hard to see what could justify that. Who can deny that all individuals have an interest in controlling what happens to their own bodies? Thus, all people should have an enforceable right to refuse sexual intimacy, just as we have a right to refuse medical treatment, and a right not to be beaten. Sexual self-determination is a fundamental interest for any person, and violating it is a harm.

Finally, a few words on sexual harassment. This is a highly complex issue and I cannot begin to cover it adequately here. It reflects not only attitudes of domination, but also preconceptions about basic differences of gender, and assumptions of domestic work roles (that will be discussed in the next section). Yet, its status as a harm is not difficult to establish.

One form of sexual harassment (*quid pro quo*) involves an abuse of power in order to obtain sexual intercourse, and thus is indistinguishable from the nonviolent sexual abuse discussed under the heading of rape. If, as I argued there, an interest in sexual autonomy exists, undermining that interest by extortion is a harm, and a serious one. The other form of sexual harassment (hostile environment) is a particular version of workplace discrimination that is designed and intended to offend, ridicule, and demean women in order to drive them out of the workplace. As complex and interesting as this phenomenon is, it is a rather uncontroversial harm since it is a clear example of harassment (even if a specialized form of it) and harassment is a legally recognized injury.

Overall, then, the claim that (most) domestic violence, date rape, and sexual harassment are not real harms to women is not supportable. The kernel of truth is that all this behavior ranges from minor annoyance to serious harm, a continuum that facilitates denial, while statistics show that supposing serious infractions are rare is a mistake. So the dual claim that the truly harmful behavior is rare, and the common behavior is not harmful, is false.

The third claim – that men are not responsible for sexual harassment, date rape, or domestic violence because they are provoked by their victims – is such blatant rationalization that it hardly deserves a response. This is another manifestation of the bias that reflects an acceptance of male misbehavior as a subset of male dominance, viewed as inevitable human nature, while imposing the costs on female victims. Notice the implications.

First, it might suggest that such behavior would not occur if it were not provoked, which in turn suggests that women have control over preventing it. But that supposition is clearly false. Women do not have control over a hostile work environment or an overreaching supervisor – except to quit. That hardly qualifies as control. Similarly, women can avoid rape (insofar as it is possible at all) only by restricting their own activity. They have no control over restricting the behavior of men. Finally, battered wives do not have control over preventing their husband's violence. It can be brought on by anything or nothing, or at least nothing that wives can control (such as his unemployment, or his drinking, or his bad day at the office). Women do not control men's behavior; consequently, they cannot prevent it.

Second, and more importantly, shifting responsibility from men to women (i.e., from perpetrator to victim) accepts the legitimacy of gauging the limitation of women's freedom in terms of the misbehavior of men. It treats male behavior as if it were a force of nature, or that of a wild animal. If you go walking in a hurricane, or play with a lion, you can't blame the hurricane or the lion if you get hurt. The way to avoid the

harm is to restrict your own behavior. But men are not natural forces or wild animals. They are human agents with as much free will and control over their choices and actions as women have. Consequently, it is unjust to allow men to control or overpower women simply because they have the physical capability or social authority to do so. This recognition was reflected in a comment by Golda Meir some years ago in response to a suggestion that a curfew should be imposed on women temporarily because there was a rash of assaults against them. The men are committing the attacks, she responded; impose the curfew on them (quoted in Rhode 1997: 124).

Overall then, unless he is claiming incompetence, a man is an autonomous agent who is responsible for his own actions, whatever the behavior of others around him may be. Thus, the suggestion that men are not responsible for their own behavior makes no sense.

The fourth claim is that while the social situation may be unfortunate and the problems serious, the law is not the appropriate way to address them. Many critics and reformers alike have suggested that the law has already done all it can do in these areas. Domestic violence (assault and battery), rape, and sexual harassment are already illegal. What we need now are better educational programs, counseling, sensitivity training, consciousness raising, as well as more women's shelters, rape crisis centers, and the like.

There is much to be said for this view. Law alone will never solve these problems. Law is interactive with and dependant on social norms, presumptions, and practices, and these must be addressed by all the mechanisms and institutions just mentioned, as well as others. But it does not follow that law has done all it can do.

It may be precisely in showing what more law should be doing that some of the best work in feminist legal theory is being accomplished today. Schulhofer's work documents the deficiencies of rape law in detail and explicates reforms designed to correct the current bias. Elizabeth Schneider's recent book, *Battered Women and Feminist Lawmaking* (2000), lays out a feminist program of lawmaking to combat domestic violence, and documents in thorough detail the seriousness of the problem, as well as the failures and successes of processes intended to deal with it. Andrew

Taslitz, in *Rape and the Culture of the Courtroom* (1999), explains why the trial process itself, and especially our adversarial system, denies rape victims their day in court, and provides concrete suggestions for reform.

All these scholars and others emphasize the importance of acknowledging the culture of dominance that produces the problems they detail, as well as the legal environment that dismisses them. Only by situating these problems of coercion and violence within the overall context of domination and submission will we be able to understand and address them fairly, and thereby erode the culture of intimidation.

Domesticity and Institutional Organization

Physical coercion is not the only source of subordination, nor the most effective. Economic strength is the most certain and extensive form of control, as well as the surest source of independence. Money is power. As noted by Virginia Woolf, economic independence is a necessary condition of self-determination. Yet economic power is precisely what most women lack. And this condition is essentially insured in virtually all economic systems today, which reflect an organization of family and work that perpetuates the economic disadvantage and consequent subordination of women.

This organizational structure is a gendered system, often referred to as the culture of domesticity. It presupposes the older notions of difference discussed earlier: men and women are different. Women are domestic and men are not. Women are natural caregivers, innately nurturing, tidy, and oriented to the personal relations of family. Men, in contrast, are aggressive, competitive, and oriented to the impersonal relations of market and political life. This convenient image of masculinity and femininity reflects the organization of work and family in separate spheres of life, dominated by men and women respectively, and encourages precisely the attitudes and psychological characteristics that suit them for activity in their assigned spheres.

This form of social organization became especially prominent during the industrial revolution when masculinity became synonymous with "breadwinning," which meant leaving home to earn money in the market by which to provide for the material needs of one's family by one's purchases. A successful breadwinner (or real man perhaps?) could provide for the material needs of his family unaided. Therefore, a woman with an adequate breadwinner would be able to perform her correlative role of homemaking with total dedication. A woman forced to participate in the market was, thus, a sign of an inadequate breadwinner and a lower-class family. For about 200 years a nonworking wife has been a symbol of middle-class status. And, despite the great challenge to this norm since the 1970s, domesticity overall remains intact and entrenched today (see e.g., Olsen 1983).

Men are still breadwinners: their primary responsibility and source of self esteem is to "earn a living." In recent polls, for example, blue-collar workers expressed feeling threatened by stagnant wages that forced their wives to work. And their working wives characterized their own wages as "helping out." They were not themselves breadwinners. That is a male role, and a powerful source of masculine (but not feminine) identity (Williams 2000). Nor is this attitude confined to the working class. At every level of society success in the public sphere is the test of manhood. Men are breadwinners. That norm is unquestioned.

And women are still homemakers: their first responsibility is the care and maintenance of the home and children. Although this norm has become much more complex and contested for women, about 90 percent do become mothers, and all mothers are hard pressed to ignore the norm. Many middle-class women characterize their motivation for working as "self-fulfillment" (Williams 2000). So, working-class wives work to help out, and middle-class wives work for personal edification. Neither of them is a breadwinner, which suggests that there can only be one per family and it must be male if there is a man in the family. It also suggests that work (i.e., paid labor) for women is ideally optional, and acceptably temporary or intermittent – all possibilities that are not open to men, which in turn enables women to assume responsibility for the home and retards men from it. These social arrangements and expectations are still predominant in every society, and the attitudes that presume such social organization to be natural, normal, more or less inevitable, and basically right are pervasive (Williams 2000: ch.1).

There are two big hitches in this neat arrangement from the viewpoint of equality for women. The first, as just noted, is that the public sphere is a male domain: men are the breadwinners (as well as the leaders, specialists, authorities, etc.). Women may be allowed in the public sphere at this point but it is not theirs. They are visitors, there by choice and not by duty. And the male world of work is policed by extensive norms, presumptions, and overt rules that relegate women to subordinate status, unless they (individually) can emulate men without also alienating them. This is a tricky business that few woman are able to accomplish, thereby insuring that the public sphere remains a male domain, and that women remain (subordinate) visitors within it.

The second hitch is that domestic work (the domain of women) is unpaid. (At least in one's own home it is unpaid; and outside one's own home it is among the lowest paid forms of work in existence.) Furthermore, because it is unpaid it is not really recognized as work. Real work is paid labor. Domestic activity is an expression of love.

One result of this attitude is that domestic responsibilities are not recognized as relevant considerations in the public sector, or as the basis for monetary entitlement. Little or no allowance is made for them (either for men or women) in the market or in governmental programs. The domestic sphere is private and invisible. A second result is that caregivers (or homemakers) are necessarily dependent on breadwinners. Hence, the relationship (between breadwinners and caregivers) is not and cannot be economically equal. Domestic activity, as currently viewed, cannot be translated into market value (or at least, at current rates its market value is so ludicrously low that no rational person who could do otherwise would engage in it for the purpose of gainful employment). This attitude is reflected in divorce settlements that treat a man's wage as his property (not joint property) and a wife's domestic contribution as nonmonetary.

Her domestic work is not recognized as an investment in his future wage. Thus, the dependency and inequality of women is all but guaranteed by the correlative roles of caregiver and breadwinner, the implications of which are finessed by the language of domesticity, love, and marriage. Obviously, this institutional organization profoundly disadvantages women, and raises at least three issues of justice that are central concerns of feminists.

The first is the issue of freedom or equality of opportunity (in the minimal sense of open institutions). If all women are restricted to the profession of homemaking, while men are allowed to compete for all other pursuits available in the world, the disparity of freedom is obvious, and could only be justified (or supposedly justified) by old assumptions of innate difference: the innate domesticity of women. Once that presumption was denied the restriction of women from the public sphere could only be seen as injustice.

The second issue is that of equal treatment. If women do work in the public sphere, they should have the same opportunities for promotion and advancement, the same pay for equivalent work, the same benefits, and so forth. Since there is no reason to think of gender as a relevant basis for differential treatment in any such areas, discrimination on the basis of sex with regard to them is unjust.

The third issue is the structure of social organization. The current organization of family and work is structured to provide men with the benefits of both market and family life at the expense of marginalizing women in the market and reducing them to dependency as caregivers. But if social institutions and practices are organized in a way that inherently or systematically benefits one group at the expense of another then the organization itself is unjust. The particular concern of feminist legal scholars with regard to all this is how law is used to maintain these injustices, and how it could be used to alleviate them.

The first set of issues was the initial focus of feminists during the 1960s and 1970s (although it sounds like an eighteenth-century issue). In fact, the Civil Rights Act of 1964 made discrimination on the basis of sex a cause of action for the first time. In 1971 the Supreme Court recognized sex equality as a constitutionally protected interest, and overt barriers to women were generally dismantled over the next 10 years or so.

During this time the predominant ideal of feminism was the model of "full commodification." Excellent and affordable day care as readily available as libraries, school days coordinated with work days, on-site school doctors and clinics, and the possibility of a 35-hour work week would enable parents to share equally the responsibilities of home and family, and thus enable women to participate equally in the market. These were the visions of the 1960s. Women could "have it all," it was said.

Instead the work week increased; day care became more expensive, less available and often of poor quality; school days still do not match work days, and the possibility of school clinics that actually treat sick children is no longer even a dream; the image of shared parenting was replaced by the "supermom," who worked a "double day," on what often turned out to be the "mommy track," and overt barriers to the equal participation of women were widely replaced with informal and often unconscious ones. So overt legal barriers to women have largely been removed, and this represents a major improvement and enormous change in certain respects. But in other ways the change is minimal because society continues its long-standing assumptions and practices, like a horse long hobbled to trot continues its same measured pace as though the restrictions were never removed.

The result is that progress toward real equality has been disappointingly slow. Female participation in the work force grew from 35 to 75 percent between 1960 and 1992, but job segregation has remained at 75 to 80 percent (a reduction of less than 5 percent in over 30 years). Predominantly female occupations (such as nursing, teaching, secretarial, or clerical work) remain relatively low paying, with little advancement available. While a great many women have entered traditionally male professions (such as law, medicine, business, and higher education) they remain clustered in the lower ranks with disproportionately few reaching top level positions. And those who do reach the top positions are typically paid less than men in comparable spots (see e.g., Rhode 1997: ch. 6; Estrich 2001: ch. 4).

For example, 99.94 percent of CEOs and 97.3 percent of top earners in business are men, even though women have represented 25 percent or more of business school graduates for the past 25 years. Similarly, while women comprised at least one third of law school graduates since 1980, they represent only 13.6 percent of partners in the larger law firms, and half of those are not equity partners who share in profits. Only 8 percent of federal judges are women. Furthermore, while women make up more than half of all college graduates, they make up only 26 percent of faculty members, 11 percent of full professors, and less than 7 percent of department chairs and deans (see Estrich 2001: 72-7). It has been estimated that at our present rate of progress it will take three to four centuries for women to achieve equal representation in American executive suites, and about 500 years to accomplish it in Congress. In the early 1970s women wore "59" buttons to protest that women made only 59 cents to the male dollar. After 30 years the wage gap has stagnated at 72 cents (Estrich 2001: 79). So, despite substantial participation in the market for more than a generation, women who work full time still earn less than three-quarters of what men earn for the same work. (Woman who work part time, of course, earn much less than that.)

Thus, in pay, promotion, and advancement the disparity between men and women is substantial, and it cannot be explained (as it once was) by a lack of eligible female candidates in the pool. This raises the second set of issues. Unequal treatment is not only unjust, but illegal. What constitutes unequal treatment, however, is a complex matter, and the devices of denial are pervasive and strong.

The bulk of the public debate in this area has been focused on the spotlight issue of affirmative action. One major drawback of this issue is that it focuses attention (and questions) on one rather minor corrective measure rather than on the problem of discrimination itself, and the more substantial measures that might be taken to correct it. Issues like comparable worth or pay equity have been dismissed out of hand, and the deficiencies of policies like the Family and Medical Leave Act, or the Equal Pay Act are largely ignored, while the problems of discrimination and inequality are disregarded or glossed in the debate over the nature and legitimacy of affirmative action. As Deborah Rhode has pointed out, affirmative action would not correct the problem of discrimination even if it were fully implemented (which is not to say that it should not be fully implemented). Nevertheless, resistance to it illustrates the problem of denial in this area. There is no systematic evidence that beneficiaries of affirmative action are unqualified to perform their jobs (Rhode 1997: 168–70). Yet the persistent perception is that affirmative action programs pass over qualified candidates in favor of unqualified ones. The basis of this idea involves the denial of the problem of gender discrimination itself.

According to Deborah Rhode, this denial is based on two primary rationales. The first she calls "the myth of meritocracy." We live, it is said, in a meritocracy. Our system of rewards and benefits is based on individual merit, measured in terms of effort and productivity, through the mechanism of the free market. Consequently, once formal barriers to women's participation in the market were removed, the problem of discrimination was solved. The market is neutral. It simply selects on the basis of performance, so sex discrimination is irrational in market terms. It is inefficient to exclude competent workers on the basis of sex. So if women are excluded, they must not be competent, or at least as competent as those (men) who are selected instead (Rhode 1997: 144).

This is a nice argument in theory, but as Rhode notes, it simply does not accurately reflect the realities of the actual world, which includes a market originally constituted by men. As noted earlier, the culture of the public sector is traditionally male, so customers and coworkers may well prefer what they are used to. Many men are more comfortable in an all-male work environment, and some men will not work for women. Many studies (and court cases) have shown widespread bias in hiring. Women are systematically channeled into lower paying, more subordinate positions than those offered to men with the same qualifications. And women are consistently funneled into female-dominated occupations with lower pay and fewer opportunities for advancement. None of this indicates a neutral market (see Rhode 1997: ch.6).

Furthermore, stereotypes go against advancement for women, who are characterized as emo-

tional, indecisive, deficient in quantitative skills, lacking in commitment and leadership qualities. Conversely, women who do not fit the stereotype are penalized for being "unfeminine," "difficult," or "pushy." This Catch 22 affects evaluations of merit, which are hardly neutral. Many studies have shown that women's work, records, and potential are consistently rated lower than men's. One well known study switched the names on resumes from male to female and vice versa. The resumes with female names were rated lower than when they had male names. How does that fit into a neutral market (Rhode 1997: ch.6)?

It is well known that black baseball players were excluded from major league teams for many years despite the clear knowledge that their performance was undeniably superior to that of many white players who were hired instead of them. This is a very good counterexample to the claims of a neutral market because the criteria of quality performance are actually objective in this case. Yet they were ignored for years, even when it could have meant the difference between winning and losing games. Thus, market evaluations are not always rational in practice, even when criteria of performance are objective. And most professions and jobs do not have criteria of quality performance that are objective, even though we like to pretend that they do. Consequently, bias can easily and even unconsciously be built into the very criteria or process of evaluation. Furthermore, the higher level the job evaluation is, the more subjective the criteria become. Capacity for leadership, creativity, and intellectual promise are not objective criteria, and the male culture and mentoring system further undercuts the equal participation and the evaluation of women. It may be claimed that the market is neutral, but all the human beings who make the market evaluations in everyday life are not. Thus, the claim of meritocracy through the neutral open market is a rationalization that covers discrimination and denies its existence without adequate grounds to do so (Rhode 1997: ch. 6).

Rhode's second basis of denial she calls the myth of choice. The myth of choice raises the third set of issues, the injustice of certain forms of social organization, and notably the culture of domesticity. It is widely claimed that whatever their talents and abilities may be, women choose lower pay and less prestige as a trade-off for pleasanter working conditions and more convenient hours. Thus, their marginalization is a result of their own choice. It is what they prefer (Rhode 1997: ch.6).

In her recent book, *Unbending Gender: Why Family and Work Conflict and What to Do About It* (2000), Joan Williams provides a comprehensive explanation of the myth of choice in terms of the culture of domesticity. The culture of domesticity relies on two interrelated ideals: the perfect worker and the perfect mother. The perfect worker is available to work long hours, weekends, or overtime without distraction, to travel or even relocate. Work responsibilities are never intruded upon, interrupted, or restricted by personal responsibilities. Furthermore, employers are entitled to perfect workers, and men are both duty bound and entitled to be perfect workers. And since the perfect worker is exempt from family responsibility so that he can be totally dedicated to his work, his personal life depends on a flow of services provided by a wife. So, the male norm (whatever its deficiencies) is basically integrated and harmonious. The more successful a perfect worker is at work, the better he meets his most basic obligation, which is breadwinning.

Similarly, the perfect mother is totally committed to her family responsibilities. She is there, available or on call 24 hours a day, to provide the care and services needed by her children. She is unselfish, nurturing, and dedicated to her home and family above all. She also keeps up with the housework (about 30 hours a week of it on average). But the important job of a mother, of course, is child care, which has become increasingly time consuming during the past 30 years, as children have become more directed, protected, and less free. The organization of middle-class child life now requires a great deal of oversight and personal service. As a result of these duties, two thirds of all mothers do not work full time year round, and those who do work full time gravitate toward traditional female occupations that accommodate family responsibilities. This is characterized as a matter of choice. Women *choose* to marginalize themselves in the workplace because they *prefer* to spend more time with their children. It follows that they cannot be perfect

workers. Consequently, they cannot compete in the market, so they hold lower level positions (on average), they are promoted less, and are paid less because they merit less. That is what they choose (Williams 2000: ch.1).

Williams explains that as long as the culture of domesticity continues to divide labor into the traditional public and private domains of segregated responsibility, these choices will be unavoidable. But that means that the social organization that requires such unfair choices is itself discriminatory. The fundamental problem of inequality cannot be solved unless the norm of parental care is recognized as valuable, which requires the basic norms of perfect worker and perfect mother to be reconstructed. This is not an impossible task, Williams argues, but legal measures are needed to accomplish it. Williams proposes two sorts of measures: (1) those aimed at reconstructing the workplace and its current entitlements; (2) those aimed at reconstructing the role of caregiver, especially lack of entitlements.

These legal measures are justified in order to combat discrimination. However, a broader understanding of what constitutes discrimination is necessary. Currently, only sexual harassment and stereotyping are recognized as illegal forms of discrimination. But designing the workplace around male size and strength is also discriminatory. And designing work schedules around the flow of family services only available to men is discriminatory as well (Williams 2000: ch.3).

Legal mechanisms are available that could be interpreted to challenge these and related practices, including widespread discrimination against mothers. Title VII of the Civil Rights Act of 1964 provides two forms of action: disparate treatment and disparate impact. Disparate treatment has been widely used to challenge discrimination in cases where an individual woman can show that she was passed over for promotion despite performance that meets the standard of the perfect worker required by employers. The so-called "sex plus" theory of disparate treatment forbids discrimination against mothers even if equal opportunity is provided to nonmothers. This will not reconstruct any workplace norms, since it takes the norms as given, but it could at least lead to a reconceptualization of what constitutes discrimination against those mothers who are able to meet the norm. While recognizing that suing one's employer is a personally devastating way to encourage social change, Williams astutely notes that it is not the suit but the threat of it that leads to social modification. No one took sexual harassment seriously until the threat of suit encouraged a change of perspective. Disparate treatment could do the same.

Disparate impact analysis has considerable power for social reform, but (perhaps because of its potential power) it has thus far been interpreted very narrowly. Yet it could be used to challenge masculine norms in the workplace. Williams suggests that such suits could be used to challenge the "executive schedule" (or 80-hour week), the design of promotion tracks that require the executive schedule, relocation, mandatory overtime, training programs in off time, stringent sick leave policies that impair parental responsibilities, penalties for work interruptions, or the denial of part-time work. Disproportionate impact could also be used to challenge workplace design and equipment design over time.

Another possibility is the Equal Pay Act, which requires that two employees of the same firm must be paid the same for substantially equal work. This could be used to challenge the heavy penalty structure attached to part-time work. The goal would be to convince courts that "substantially equal" and "effort required" should be evaluated in terms of the effort required per hour, and thus to give up their own attachment to the perfect worker norm as the only test of a loyal and committed worker (Williams 2000: ch.3.).

The results of such challenges, if they succeeded would correspond to proposals made by unions and by time relief advocates (such as Juliet Schor in *The Overworked American*) that amount to quality of life proposals that would benefit men and children as well as women. Schor (1992) has pointed out that the workload requirements in the United States have become untenable over the past 30 years. Union gains of the 1940s and 1950s have been completely reversed. A 50-hour work week is now common for men, as is mandatory overtime. A man may be able to meet the 80-hour executive schedule, but in no way is it a benefit. Thus, the time may be ripe to challenge some workplace norms.

The second half of Williams's comprehensive proposal is to challenge family norms and entitlements. If we are serious about the value of parental care then caregivers should not be disadvantaged or impoverished for providing it. Given that men are able to perform as perfect workers only because they are supplied with a flow of family work by their wives, the income, including the future income that results, should be considered joint property. This means that in the event of a divorce, a fair split of the joint property would be required. After considering several possibilities, Williams suggests that the best alternative is to equalize the standard of living of the two households. This would help to counter the all too common impoverishment of women and children after divorce that results from the assumption that a man "owns" his wage, and owes his former wife and children only enough to provide for their basic needs.

This rationale should be changed, according to Williams, to reflect the idea that the primary caregiver "owns" a portion of the wage, because it was the flow of family work that enabled this earning potential to be manifested in the perfect worker, and precluded its manifestation in the caregiver. Family work and market work together should be viewed as a joint venture. The joint property proposal could be instituted by statute or by court action, Williams notes. Its intent is to change the way we think about property entitlements to income from wages that are produced by the labor of two people rather than one, and to counter the current assumption that child support and alimony are something like charity (Williams 2000: ch.4).

Williams calls her overall proposal "reconstructive feminism." Its purpose is to "deinstitutionalize domesticity by deconstructing the ideal-worker norm" (Williams 2000: 143). Like the recent work on dominance, Williams's comprehensive treatment of the work/family conflict lays out the systematic discrimination against women that is built into the very structure of social organization in the culture of domesticity, and details the legal action that could help to correct it. The insight displayed in all this work is that discrimination against women is systemic and imbedded in law. The best recent work illustrates in detail how this is so.

Conclusion

The object of this overview of feminist legal theory has been to lay out four major themes of analysis, and to attempt to represent the systematic nature of bias against women, as well as its pervasiveness, invisibility, and depth of entrenchment. I highlighted the work of three scholars (Rhode, Schulhofer, and Williams) as representing the best recent work on three of the most important topics. It is not the only outstanding work, but there is none better. And the topics are not the only important ones, but there are none more crucial that these. The culture of dominance and the culture of domesticity combine to produce the multidimensional subordination of women to men that is accepted as normal life, and the rationalization of difference is used to justify it.

Unfortunately, recognizing pervasive and systematic discrimination against women makes everyone uncomfortable (including women) because it illustrates that our society is fundamentally unjust. Indeed, it is organized on the basis of injustice. We do not want to recognize that, so we deny it. But as Deborah Rhode so clearly demonstrates, if we refuse to acknowledge the problem then we cannot adequately address it. Feminist jurisprudence is the gadfly that reminds us of this.

References

Dworkin, A. 1979. *Pornography: Men Possessing Women*. New York: Dutton.

EEOC v Sears. 1986. 628 F. Supp. 1264 (N.D.Ill. 1986), affd. 839 F. 2d. 302 (7th Cir. 1988).

Estrich, S. 2001. *Sex and Power*. New York: Riverhead Books.

Freedman, A. 1983. Sex equality, sex difference, and the Supreme Court. *Yale Law Review* 92: 913–83.

Gilligan, C. 1982. *In a Different Voice*. Cambridge, MA: Harvard University Press.

Law, S. 1984. Rethinking sex and the Constitution. *University of Pennsylvania Law Review* 132: 955–1030.

MacKinnon, C. 1993. *Only Words*. Cambridge, MA: Harvard University Press.

Minow, M. 1987. Justice engendered. *Harvard Law Review* 101: 10–127.

Olsen, F. 1983. The family and the market: A study of ideology and legal reform. *Harvard Law Review* 96: 1497–1612.

Olsen, F. 1989. Unraveling compromise. *Harvard Law Review* 103: 105–92.

Paglia, C. 1992. *Sex, Art, and American Culture*. New York: Vintage.

Rhode, D. 1997. *Speaking of Sex: The Denial of Gender Inequality*. Cambridge, MA: Harvard University Press.

Roiphe, K. 1993. *The Morning After*. Boston: Little, Brown.

Schneider, E. 2000. *Battered Women and Feminist Lawmaking*. New Haven, CT: Yale University Press.

Schor, J. 1992. *The Overworked American*. Cambridge, MA: Harvard University Press.

Schulhofer, S. 1998. *Unwanted Sex: The Culture of Intimidation and the Failure of Law*. Cambridge, MA: Harvard University Press.

Taslitz, A. 1999. *Rape and the Culture of the Courtroom*. New York: New York University Press.

Williams, J. 2000. *Unbending Gender: Why Family and Work Conflict and What to Do About It*. New York: Oxford University Press.

Further Reading

Allen, A. 1988. *Uneasy Access: Privacy for Women in a Free Society*. Totowa, NJ: Rowman and Littlefield.

Bartlett, K. and Kennedy, R. (eds.). 1991. *Feminist Legal Theory*. Boulder, CO: Westview Press.

LeMoncheck, L. and Sterba, J. 2001. *Sexual Harassment: Issues and Answers*. New York: Oxford University Press.

MacKinnon, C. 1982. Feminism, Marxism, method, and the state: An agenda for theory. *Signs* 7: 515–44.

Minow, M. 1990. *Making All the Difference: Inclusion, Exclusion and American Law*. Ithaca, NY: Cornell University Press.

Olsen, F. (ed.). 1995. *Feminist Legal Theory*, 4 vols. New York: New York University Press.

Rhode, D. 1989. *Justice and Gender*. Cambridge, MA: Harvard University Press.

Smith, P. (ed.). 1993. *Feminist Jurisprudence*. New York: Oxford University Press.

Part II

Doctrinal Domains
and their Philosophical
Foundations

Chapter 7

Criminal Law Theory

Douglas Husak

Surely it is pretentious to suggest that criminal law theory might be somewhat different from what the most distinguished criminal theorists have construed it to be. Can it possibly be true that virtually all of the acknowledged experts have tended to neglect the most central issues? Despite the implausibility of this suggestion, I will attempt to defend it here.

The Need for a Theory of Criminalization

Anyone who consults the writings of the recognized authorities in the field would come to believe that criminal law theory revolves around a number of questions that arise in the so-called "general part" of criminal law (Williams 1961). The exact nature of the general part is enormously controversial; commentators have provided very different accounts of what the general part of criminal law is thought to include and exclude (Lacey 1998). But everyone agrees that the doctrines of the general part consist in generalizations about the "special part" of criminal law – the many offenses that have been enacted by legislatures. The status of these generalizations remains a matter of heated scholarly debate.

Perhaps the nature of the general part is best introduced simply by describing the issues that criminal theorists have typically investigated. Most of these issues have both a conceptual and a normative dimension; I will mention only a

small number of them. What is the reason to require all crimes to include a voluntary act? When may persons be punished for their omissions? What mental states make agents culpable for performing criminal acts? Must each material element of every crime contain a culpability component, or is strict liability sometimes acceptable? Should persons ever be punished for negligence? What conditions must be satisfied before an agent can be said to have caused a result, and should results always, sometimes, or never be relevant to criminal liability? How should justifications be differentiated from excuses, and how useful is the contrast between these two types of defenses? Might defendants have a justification defense even though they were unaware of the circumstances that gave rise to the justification? Why should the state recognize excuses, and which excuses should it allow? Is the character of defendants ever material to their criminal liability? Needless to say, detailed positions on these matters invite further questions that have given rise to a massive literature.

Everyone admits the above issues are important and difficult. Each issue, however, pales in significance against a topic that criminal theorists have tended to neglect. This is the topic of criminalization – the conditions that must be satisfied before the state may enact a statute that subjects offenders to criminal liability. A theory of criminalization, in other words, describes the conditions under which criminal offenses are justified. In this chapter, I will confine my remarks to this basic issue.

I hope it is clear that the foregoing examples of controversies in the general part are less fundamental to criminal theory than the topic of criminalization. Most of the normative objectives sought by criminal theorists would be frustrated if we begin with a defective theory of criminalization. No doctrine in the general part can begin to compensate for the injustice that inevitably occurs when a state punishes conduct that should not have been subjected to liability in the first place. A few examples should illustrate the centrality of the problem of criminalization. Even if criminal theorists could persuade courts to reject strict liability, so that some degree of culpability were required for each material element of every offense, little would have been accomplished if the conduct for which liability is imposed should not have been proscribed. Or suppose that legal philosophers could produce an unproblematic account of causation. Almost no progress would have been gained if the state has no reason to prevent the particular results for which punishment is imposed. Or suppose that a persuasive defense of punishment could be provided. Surely the application of this theory presupposes that legislators have adequate reasons to select the conduct that subjects persons to liability.

In fact, several issues in the general part are barely intelligible when applied to criminal laws precluded by our best theory of criminalization. Consider the question of whether and under what circumstances defendants have a justification defense for committing a criminal offense. This question can be peculiar if the crime in question is unjustified, and lies beyond the legitimate reach of the penal sanction. On many occasions, we cannot understand what it could mean to ask whether and under what conditions a defendant is justified in committing an offense that should not have existed. No example to illustrate my point is unproblematic; each depends on agreement that legislatures should not have enacted the law in question. Suppose, however, we assume that the state should not have proscribed marijuana possession; this conduct creates no substantial harm or evil of a kind that should concern the criminal law. Many jurisdictions allow a generic justification defense when the "harm or evil sought to be avoided by such conduct is greater than that sought to be prevented by the law defining the offense" (Model Penal Code, §3.02(1)). If "the law defining the offense" prevents no substantial harm or evil of a kind that should concern the criminal law, what sense does it make to inquire whether this harm or evil is outweighed?

Much the same oddity arises in the context of excuses. Why suppose that an excuse is needed to engage in conduct that should not have been prohibited? Again, no example to illustrate my point is beyond controversy. But what sense does it make to demand an excuse for a defendant who violates a nineteenth-century statute proscribing the harboring of runaway slaves? Criminal theorists who provide accounts of defenses almost certainly assume that their views will be applied to defendants who commit criminal offenses that are themselves justified. If so, theorists must undertake a more basic inquiry into the conditions under which criminal offenses are justified – that is, into the criteria of criminalization. Further examples to demonstrate the normative priority of the topic of criminalization to most of the questions entertained in the general part of criminal law could be multiplied indefinitely.

Despite its central importance, however, relatively little progress has been made in defending a theory of criminalization. Indeed, no good theory of criminalization exists; few meaningful constraints on the scope of the criminal law are endorsed by commentators or observed by legislators. Because of this failure, states throughout the world have overcriminalized. Few scholars are prepared to estimate how many criminal laws actually exist. A decade ago, one commentator guessed that at least 300,000 existing federal regulations are enforced by criminal sanctions in the United States (Coffee 1991). A more recent estimate in England is that approximately 8,000 different criminal statues have been enacted (Simester and Sullivan 2000). These numbers rise each year. With no political constituency in favor of reform, criminal prohibitions are frequently created but seldom repealed. Partly because of too many criminal laws, too many people are punished. In the United States, approximately two million persons are currently jailed or imprisoned – four times the number in 1980. No other country resorts to incarceration so frequently; one-quarter of the world's prison population resides in the United States. Perhaps more alarming is the fact that 6.5 million

Americans are presently under the supervision of the criminal justice system – which includes probation and parole. Prosecutorial restraint is the main reason these totals are not even higher.

Anyone who peruses state or federal criminal codes would be astonished "at their scope, by the sheer amount of conduct they render punishable" (Stuntz 2001: 515). Most of the people sentenced to jails or prisons today are incarcerated for conduct that was not even criminal a century ago. Because crimes overlap so extensively, a defendant can violate six or eight statutes simultaneously by engaging in conduct that one would expect to constitute a single offense. Criminal laws are so ubiquitous and far-reaching that almost everyone has violated them at some time or another. The criminal law no longer distinguishes "us" from "them." What tends to characterize many of us who have escaped criminal liability is the good fortune not to have been caught, or the resources and social standing to avoid punishment in the event we are apprehended.

Criminal offenses have increased not only in number. The characteristics of criminal law are changing rapidly; whole new kinds of statutory schemes have been created. Largely in response to sensationalistic media accounts and the influence of political pressure groups, criminal laws are routinely enacted as though they were the natural response to any and all social problems. Many of these new crimes might be called "ancillary offenses" – statutes designed to support a complex regulatory scheme that persons find ingenious ways to circumvent (Abrams 1989). The features of many of these offenses – the absence of culpability requirements, the shifting of burdens of proof, the imposition of liability for omissions, the implicit trust in prosecutorial discretion to prevent abuse – are incompatible with fundamental principles long held sacrosanct by criminal law theorists (Ashworth 2000).

One would naturally hope to gain an understanding of these general trends by consulting any of the leading casebooks assigned in law schools. Yet there is a surprising (and almost inexplicable) gap between the reality of contemporary criminal law and the picture that is conveyed in these texts. Most notably, none of these casebooks contains a sustained discussion of drug offenses, even though the crimes of illicit drug possession and distribution are principal forces that drive the criminal justice system today. This fact is not reflected in the content of casebooks, and students are not given the resources to assess whether this development is welcome or unwelcome. More generally, the topic of criminalization is not included in a standard course in criminal law in most law schools. The most widely used casebook in courses in criminal law today devotes a scant 16 of its 1,138 pages to the topic of "what to punish?" In the accompanying Teacher's Manual, the authors recommend skipping these pages in a one-semester course (Kadish and Schulhofer 2001: 34). Of course, virtually all first-year courses in criminal law span only a single semester. Typically, students begin and end their study by applying existing statutes to real or imaginary fact patterns. Since the content of criminal offenses is regarded as given, scholarly inquiry begins somewhere near the middle. Students are seldom invited to think about why the statute came to be as it is, or how its content could be improved. These issues are no more likely to be explored outside than inside law schools.

If the criminal law has changed so dramatically, and grown so rapidly in size and shape, one would anticipate that contemporary theories of the criminal law would reflect these developments. Unfortunately, they have not. Contemporary theories are not very different from those that were in vogue 25 years ago. But a theory that might have been adequate to explain the content and function of the criminal law a generation ago is likely to be woefully deficient today. Legal philosophers sometimes avoid this problem by confining the scope of their views to cases of so-called core criminality. Since these crimes have not changed significantly in decades, a theory devised in the nineteenth century is just as viable today. But theorists pay a high price by restricting the application of their views to core criminality. The criminal law has expanded far beyond its core, and one would like to provide a perspective to assess this phenomenon. Consider, for example, the recent trend to shift the focus of the criminal law from the punishment of prohibited conduct to the incapacitation of dangerous persons (Robinson 2001). One way this transition has been achieved is by expanding the number of possessory offenses (Dubber

2001). A theorist who informs us that these crimes deviate from core criminality does not tell us anything we did not know already. Doctrines in the general part that are derived from core criminality are unlikely to offer the perspective needed to evaluate the most important trends in contemporary criminal law.

Any number of examples could be given from the criminal codes of different jurisdictions to illustrate the recent expansion of the criminal law. Since many statutory schemes in the United States are too complex to serve as useful illustrations, I will mention only a few of several possible examples. Federal regulations punish persons who bring dogs or other animals on the grounds of federal buildings, who include a member of the armed forces in a voter preference poll, or who disturb mud in a cave on federal land. States punish persons who sell untested sparklers or exhibit deformed animals. Can these crimes possibly be justified? What considerations should be invoked to answer this question? As I will show, philosophers of law have made disappointingly little progress in resolving this issue – in defending and applying principles to restrict the reach of the criminal sanction. This state of affairs is intolerable. We have too many criminal laws, too much punishment, and too little that differentiates criminals from noncriminals. In part, these phenomena are due (*inter alia*) to the absence of a viable theory of criminalization. We urgently need a better theory to identify the scope and limits of the criminal law.

The Nature of the Criminal Law

In fact, however, criminalization is not the most basic issue in criminal theory. We cannot begin to construct a theory of criminalization without criteria to identify its subject matter. In short, what is the criminal law? I will make the convenient (but jurisprudentially problematic) assumption that we are able to identify law. Therefore, the difficulty is to decide what makes a given law, or a body of law, criminal. Proposed solutions of this problem identify the nature of the criminal law.

Specifying the nature of the criminal law is important for conceptual, practical, and norma-

tive reasons. As a conceptual matter, we need to be clear what we are talking about when we produce theories of the criminal law. The theories we construct about the criminal law will differ depending on what we conceptualize as criminal. Consider traffic offenses, for example. Are they crimes? Are they merely violations that are properly included in criminal codes, even though they are not really crimes? As a practical matter, a number of safeguards become applicable when a law is labeled as criminal. Several provisions in the United States Constitution, for example, are operative only if a defendant is accused of criminality. For example, persons may be convicted of a criminal offense only after their guilt is established by proof beyond a reasonable doubt, and no persons may be required to incriminate themselves in a criminal case. These constitutional protections are inapplicable outside of the criminal arena. Finally, as a normative matter, a theory about the nature of the criminal law helps us to understand what it is about the criminal law that requires justification. All legal philosophers agree that criminal laws must satisfy demanding criteria of justification. They differ not only about the content of this justificatory standard, but also about why it should be imposed.

Theorists typically evade rather than address the problem of identifying the nature of the criminal law. As Henry Hart once lamented, a crime seems to be "anything which is called a crime" (Hart 1958: 404). This account might be called positivistic: laws are criminal if and only if they are denominated as such by legislatures. If we reject a positivist account, and search for characteristics that differentiate criminal laws from other kinds of laws, we find that no single feature suffices to draw the contrast. Admittedly, many characteristics are distinctive of core criminality – of what might be called the paradigm of criminality. Criminal law attaches special significance to culpability; it does not require actual harm, but only (at most) a risk of harm; it is enforced by the state rather than by private individuals; and it imposes higher burdens of proof in order to impose liability. Despite these important differences, I believe a better answer is available. The single feature that is most helpful to identify the nature of the criminal law is that laws are criminal when they subject persons who violate them to state punishment. I will call this view the *orthodox position* on the nature of the criminal law. The orthodox position identifies criminal laws by reference to the sanction that may be imposed on persons who violate them.

This answer, of course, gives rise to many difficult problems. Fortunately, not all of these problems must be resolved in order to believe the orthodox position to be correct. I will mention only two such controversies. First, in order to hold that laws are criminal when they subject violators to punishment, one need not produce an altogether satisfactory account of the nature of punishment. Perhaps no entirely adequate definition of punishment exists. Most philosophers probably agree that punishment necessarily involves hard treatment while expressing censure or reprobation, but concur about little else. Philosophers who accept the orthodox position need only believe that an adequate account would identify state punishment as whatever may be imposed on actual or supposed offenders of criminal laws. In other words, state punishment – regardless of its elusive nature – is a defining feature of the criminal law.

Moreover, one need not be able to categorize each borderline sanction on one side of the line or the other – as punishment or not as punishment – to accept the orthodox position. We are confident in our ability to identify clear instances of punishment, but many modes of treatment deviate from this paradigm and may or may not qualify as instances of punishment. Troublesome cases are increasingly familiar to constitutional scholars and probably have given rise to more ongoing dispute than any other issue in criminal law recently addressed by the Supreme Court. The Court's decisions about when a sanction amounts to a punishment are confusing at best (Logan 1998). Perhaps such confusion is inevitable. If we draw from the concept of punishment employed in ordinary language, we should not always expect a right answer to the question of whether each sanction is or is not an instance of punishment. The concept of punishment, like most concepts in ordinary language, is vague and allows for borderline cases. This conclusion creates problems for many of the uses to which the concept of punishment is put. Suppose, for example, that a statute requires persons previ-

ously sentenced for sex offenses to register with the police in the communities where they reside. A defendant alleges that this statute imposes a retroactive punishment. He would not be satisfied if he were told that the registration requirement is somewhat like but also somewhat unlike a paradigm case of punishment. Typically, legal purposes demand that questions of categorization be given a yes or no answer. Our ordinary language conception of punishment, however, does not always provide the means to sort these borderline cases onto one side of the line or the other. Therefore, answers to the question of whether a given mode of treatment is or is not an instance of punishment may be indeterminate. Theorists can continue to accept the orthodox position while remaining agnostic about whether given sanctions are or are not punitive. If forced to provide a definitive answer, they probably must resort to stipulation.

I dwell on this topic because the criterion by which laws are identified as criminal is absolutely crucial to theory construction. As I have indicated, different sets of data can, and do, produce radically different theories of the criminal law. Suppose, for example, that laws are (and not merely ought to be) criminal when they implement a principle of retributive justice (Moore 1997). On this account, a theorist of the criminal law need not be concerned with laws that do not serve this function. But if the orthodox position is correct, and laws are criminal when they subject offenders to state punishment, I doubt that a relatively simple theory about the aim or function of the criminal law will prove defensible. No account, I fear, can remotely fit the data. The hundreds of thousands of laws that subject violators to state punishment are sufficiently diverse to resist a unifying theory. A long line of distinguished theorists has contended that the criminal law is essentially concerned with wrongdoing and blame. Whatever may have been the case historically, however, I am less persuaded that this concern remains prominent in the criminal law today. Recent commentators have protested that theorists "mythicize" the criminal law when they construe it to require individualized moral blameworthiness (Bilionis 1998: 1279). It is easier to defend the claim that moral blameworthiness *ought* to be a defining feature of the criminal law. But judicial deference to legislative supremacy in the enactment of laws that subject offenders to state punishment all but ensures that no simple theory about the aim or function of the criminal law will closely fit existing practice.

Inadequate Theories of Criminalization

Clearly – or at least as I have assumed – we have too many criminal laws and too much punishment. Legal philosophers have not been especially helpful in suggesting how this trend might be reversed. In this section, I will describe four approaches that yield important insights, but produce defective or incomplete theories of criminalization.

First, consider the efforts of theorists to draw from other disciplines to identify the scope and limits of the criminal law. In particular, scholars in the law and economics movement have struggled to produce a theory of criminalization. If we begin by asking why the criminal law should ever be employed, we may come to identify the conditions under which its use is justified. When one person harms another – as in cases of core criminality – why not rely on the remedies available in tort? Typically, tortfeasors are required to make restitution to compensate their victims for the losses they cause. Why not treat criminals similarly? Different answers to this question suggest different limitations on the scope of the criminal sanction.

One kind of answer attempts to specify the kinds of losses for which the criminal sanction is uniquely appropriate. In particular, the losses caused by crimes might be noncompensable. When compensation is impossible or necessarily inadequate, tort remedies cannot substitute for criminal punishments. Homicide causes the most obvious noncompensable loss, and thus is a clear candidate for criminalization. But most of the losses caused by criminal conduct are compensable if we confine our focus to individual victims. Of course, translating losses such as pain and bodily injury into monetary terms is difficult. Somehow, however, tort law has managed to cope with this problem. In any event, a broad

range of harms may be noncompensable if we expand our horizon to include the impact of conduct on third parties. A system that permitted assaults if compensation were paid *ex post* might give rise to general fear and anxiety throughout the general population. It is hard to imagine (for both practical and theoretical reasons) how persons could be compensated for these losses. On this account, conduct should be criminalized when permitting it would spread fear and anxiety throughout society, even if individuals knew they would receive full compensation were they to be victimized directly (Nozick 1974).

The foremost difficulty with this answer is that it both contracts too narrowly and expands too broadly the scope of the criminal sanction. Consider the former objection. Whatever may be the case with assaults, undue fear and anxiety need not occur if theft is permitted in a state that requires compensation to be paid *ex post*. Why, then, should property offenses not be repealed? Or consider the latter objection. Many of the losses caused by torts give rise to enormous trepidation among potential victims. Any reasonable passenger in an automobile should be worried about the risk of a crash, but no one concludes that automobile accidents should be transformed into criminal offenses. The general problem is that the contrast between conduct that does or does not cause fear and anxiety maps poorly onto the contrast between conduct that should or should not be criminalized.

Tort remedies may be inadequate for a different reason. If criminals/tortfeasors were merely required to compensate victims for the losses they inflict, they would be indifferent between the option of buying goods *ex ante* on the market or taking them and paying their market price *ex post*. In addition, of course, the probability of detection is less than one, so a great many perpetrators would not be forced to pay compensation at all. In economic jargon, persons would lack an incentive to observe the distinction between property and liability rules – a distinction grounded in considerations of efficiency (Calabresi and Melamed 1972). To prevent criminals/tortfeasors from taking goods and compensating victims *ex post*, the amount of damages must be greater than the market value of the loss inflicted. A "kicker" is added to the damages to be paid by the defendant in order to induce the defendant to respect the distinction between property and liability rules.

But this kicker need not take the form of incarceration – the stigmatizing mode of hard treatment imposed for serious crimes today. Why is a monetary penalty not sufficient to deter? The sad but incontrovertible answer is that the majority of persons who inflict losses on others lack sufficient wealth to fully compensate their victims. As a result, most victims would not receive compensation, and the criminals/tortfeasors would have little to fear from the kicker imposed for their unlawful conduct. Impecunious defendants could be forced to labor, but this option encounters obvious practical and principled difficulties. Therefore, this view reserves criminal sanctions for "cases where the tort remedy bumps up against a solvency limitation" (Posner 1985: 1204). Of course, many tortfeasors are impecunious as well, but this problem is mollified by third-party insurance. No one would allow criminals/tortfeasors to buy insurance against the risk of performing conduct the state is trying to prohibit. A world in which "crime insurance" could be purchased would give rise to the phenomenon of "acute moral hazard"; more crimes would take place in this world than if crime insurance were not permitted. Since many criminals are unable to afford compensation, and cannot resort to insurance, nonmonetary sanctions are required to induce compliance. Thus, the state has little alternative but to resort to hard treatment.

But even if economic analysis were able to explain why the state selects some acts for punishment, its main deficiency is its inability to justify the extraordinary significance the criminal law attaches to culpability – the mental states of persons who commit criminal acts. Any sensible system of criminal law contains a principle of proportionality – a principle that makes the severity of the punishment sensitive to the seriousness of the crime. The seriousness of the crime, in turn, is partly dependent on the culpability of the offender (Von Hirsch and Jareborg 1991). Existing codes frequently punish persons with increasing severity when they commit criminal acts negligently, recklessly, knowingly, or purposely. Many theorists have argued that this culpability structure needs fundamental revision.

Perhaps the criminal law should increase or decrease the number of culpable states to be countenanced. But the basic question remains: why should a greater kicker be added onto the compensation that is required when a given defendant behaves more culpably than another? Economic analysis offers no plausible account of why the criminal law should care about culpability at all.

Attempts to produce a theory of criminalization that draw from moral philosophy rather than economics might seem to have the potential to remedy this deficiency. I am dubious, however, that the dominant approach among moral philosophers will prove satisfactory. Many theorists are utilitarians about criminalization, and contend that the state is justified in proscribing conduct that produces a net balance of disutility. They are far less likely, of course, to apply the same standard to punishment – to identify whom to punish, or to what extent. In these matters, desert plays a central role and the problems with utilitarianism are widely recognized. A utilitarian theory would justify the punishment of innocent persons, in violation of their rights and despite their lack of desert. Yet many theorists, under the enormous influence of H. L. A. Hart, attempt to combine a desert theory of punishment with a utilitarian approach to criminalization. This combination, I believe, is untenable. I will briefly argue that the same objection acknowledged to be decisive against a utilitarian theory of punishment – that it violates the rights of the innocent by imposing undeserved punishments – is fatal to a utilitarian theory of criminalization as well.

Conduct should not be criminalized solely on utilitarian grounds if we are serious about protecting the rights of persons who do not deserve to be punished. Otherwise, even our best efforts to protect the innocent could easily be circumvented by changes in the content of the substantive criminal law. Consider an example of a kind of punishment that only utilitarians could endorse: collective punishments. Punishments are collective when each member of a group is punished for an offense committed by a single member of that group. Collective punishments are commonly imposed in military training. When one soldier breaks a rule, the sergeant punishes all of the soldiers in the platoon. In the appropriate circumstances, no one doubts that collective punishments work; they can promote utilitarian objectives like deterrence. Nonetheless, these utilitarian practices are textbook examples of injustice; they punish persons who are innocent of the offense. Notice, however, how easy it is to evade this objection to collective punishments. Suppose the military were to create a new rule that proscribes membership in a platoon in which a soldier breaks a rule. After implementing this simple change in the content of the rules, every soldier punished by the sergeant would become guilty.

Comparable examples can be drawn from the law. Suppose the police get a tip that illicit drugs are being used inside a hotel room. They break in and find drugs, but none of the four people inside the room is willing to admit guilt. In this kind of situation, no individual can be convicted of the offense of drug possession beyond a reasonable doubt. To protect the innocent, it would seem that all four must be acquitted, despite the indisputable fact that one (or more) is guilty. Of course, the state can easily circumvent this problem by imposing collective punishments under a different name. The offense can be changed (prospectively, not retroactively) from actual possession to constructive possession, so that everyone in the room becomes guilty of the crime. To mitigate the unfairness, the new crime of constructive possession might include a culpability requirement, so that no one can be convicted unless he or she knows of the drugs in the room. I assume that this change in the law is defensible on utilitarian grounds; the objectives of deterrence and incapacitation are frustrated if everyone in the hotel room must be acquitted.

The above strategy can be employed in *any* case in which people are punished despite their innocence and lack of desert. A simple alteration in the content of the substantive law – defensible on utilitarian grounds – can instantly transform innocence into guilt. Can this strategy possibly be justified? After this change is implemented, can any of those people in the platoon or hotel room continue to complain that they are punished despite their innocence and lack of desert? One possible answer is that this objection evaporates. This answer might be called a legalistic (or positivistic) solution to the problem. Guilt and desert are solely matters of legality – of what the law says.

But legalism can't be correct. If we really believed that the persons in the original examples were innocent and did not deserve to be punished, would we always abandon this objection if we were informed that the rule had been revised to make each of them guilty? On many occasions, the objection would persist; we would now complain that the law is unjust. The law is unjust because it punishes persons who are innocent and do not deserve to be punished.

If the above argument is sound, it follows that utilitarianism is a defective theory of criminalization. Laws that are acceptable to utilitarians are vulnerable to the same difficulty that is decisive against a utilitarian theory of punishment – that it allows the innocent to be punished, in violation of their rights and despite their lack of desert. Persons may be innocent in the morally relevant sense, even though a law that is justified on utilitarian grounds pronounces them to be guilty. This result is not really so surprising. Utilitarianism has been widely discredited as a moral theory generally, and its application to issues of criminalization is no more plausible.

We still lack a viable theory of how criminal offenses can be justified. Yet another familiar attempt to limit the reach of the criminal sanction invokes the need for *harm* as a prerequisite to liability. I am inclined to endorse the harm principle. For several reasons, however, the harm principle has proved somewhat less helpful than theorists might have hoped. First, almost any conduct that anyone has ever proposed to criminalize could be said to cause harm. Are persons harmed when they are deeply offended, for example? Obviously, an account of harm is needed to answer such questions. Unfortunately, the term has proved stubbornly resistant to analysis. The most thorough and sophisticated account of harm has been defended by Joel Feinberg. According to Feinberg, "to say that A has harmed B [in any plausible formulation of the harm principle] is to say much the same thing as that A has wronged B, or treated him unjustly. One person wrongs another when his indefensible (unjustifiable and inexcusable) conduct violates the other's right" (Feinberg 1984: 34). Clearly, this analysis cannot be applied to decide whether one person has harmed another in the absence of a theory of rights. Needless to say, controversies about the nature and content of rights have proved every bit as intractable as disputes about harm. See THEORIES OF RIGHTS.

Second, the harm requirement encounters difficulties in attempts to differentiate the criminal from the civil law (Kleinig 1986). The latter, perhaps even more obviously than the former, presupposes harm. Why should the state not criminalize breaches of contract, for example? Presumably, A wrongs B and violates B's right whenever A defaults on an agreement with B. A resolution of this problem must distinguish criminal from noncriminal harms. According to Feinberg, the choice between criminal and civil responses to harmful conduct is "determined by such practical matters as the use of available resources, court facilities, police time, enforcement costs, effects on individual expectations, and the like" (Feinberg 1986: 17). One might hope, however, for a principled rather than a merely pragmatic reason why persons who breach their agreements should not be subject to criminal liability. Some theorists have argued, for example, that crimes are unlike civil offenses in that the former cause *public* harm, or are wrongs against the community (Marshall and Duff 1998). But it is notoriously difficult to explain the sense in which crimes involve public or communal harms.

Third, it is clear that the primary motivation for embracing the harm requirement is to preclude *legal moralism* – criminal legislation designed to punish harmless wrongdoing. Legal moralism continues to attract contemporary defenders. But the recent growth of the criminal law is fueled less by statutes designed to proscribe immorality (harmless or otherwise) than by statutes that do not seem to involve immorality at all. The main expansion of the criminal law into controversial terrain is in the area of risk prevention. All theorists concede that the risk of harm, and not harm itself, may warrant the enactment of a criminal offense. But nearly all conduct creates risks of some kind or another. Without principles to limit the use of the criminal law in proscribing risk, the harm requirement is of little value in restricting state power. The task of identifying, defending, and applying these principles has proved enormously difficult (Husak 1995).

Finally, we need to understand how the harm requirement should be construed. According to a

suggestion by John Gardner and Stephen Shute, "it is no objection under the harm principle that a harmless action was criminalized, nor even that an action with no tendency to cause harm was criminalized. It is enough to meet the demands of the harm principle that, if the action were not criminalized, that would be harmful" (Gardner and Shute 2000: 216). Depending on how this idea is explicated, a great deal of criminal legislation might turn out to be compatible with the harm principle. Suppose citizens were inclined to retaliate violently against persons who were perceived as having escaped their just deserts for engaging in conduct that the state had decided not to criminalize – for performing abortions, for example. Can the desirability of preventing this state of affairs possibly show that the conduct may be criminalized under the harm principle? This cannot be the result that Gardner and Shute intend. But such questions indicate how their interpretation of the harm requirement has the potential to expand the scope of the criminal law exponentially.

I hope to have shown that the foregoing three accounts – which award a central place to economics, utility, or harm – produce inadequate theories of criminalization. Still, the theory actually in place in the United States today is no better and probably worse. Legal practice has provided little help in developing rationales to narrow the scope of the criminal law. In the United States, legislators have nearly unlimited authority to enact new crimes. Although the Constitution imposes many significant constraints on law enforcement, its provisions are seldom interpreted to give rise to restrictions on the power of states to create criminal offenses. In what follows, I will describe what passes for a theory of criminalization under constitutional law at the present time. I recount this theory not only to demonstrate its inadequacies, but also to build a better account of criminalization upon its foundations.

Most laws burden (that is, limit or restrict) liberties. When the constitutionality of these laws is challenged, courts respond by dividing liberties into two kinds: fundamental and nonfundamental. Some liberties (e.g., speech) are fundamental because they are explicitly enumerated in the United States Constitution. Other liberties (e.g., marriage) are fundamental because they are said to be "implicit in the concept of ordered liberty." The constitutionality of legislation that burdens a fundamental liberty is subjected to "strict scrutiny" and is evaluated by applying the onerous "compelling state interest" test. Under this test, the challenged law will be upheld only if it is necessary to achieve a compelling government purpose. In other words, the government's purpose must be essential, and the law must be the least restrictive means to attain it. The constitutionality of legislation that burdens a nonfundamental liberty, on the other hand, is evaluated by applying the much less demanding "rational basis" test. Under this test, the challenged law will be upheld only if it is substantially related to a legitimate government purpose. The legitimate government purpose need not be the actual objective of the legislation – only its conceivable objective. Since only those laws that lack a conceivable legitimate purpose will fail this test, courts almost never find a law to be unconstitutional when nonfundamental liberties are burdened.

The vast majority of criminal laws burden nonfundamental liberties and thus are assessed by the rational basis test. As a result, the state needs only some conceivable legitimate purpose to enact most of the criminal laws on our books today. Persons who break these laws can be punished simply because the state has a rational basis to do so. Moreover, punishments can be (and often are) severe, since courts refrain from applying a test of proportionality to ensure that the severity of the punishment reflects the seriousness of the offense. Applications of the rational basis test produce a startling departure from what should be demanded before punishment can be imposed. People's lives can be ruined – they can spend their remaining years in prison – simply because they engaged in conduct the state had only a rational basis to proscribe.

Of course, the state needs an extraordinary rationale to punish persons who exercise fundamental liberties. The United States Constitution effectively precludes the state from criminalizing travel, prayer, or political speech, for example. Outside the narrow range of fundamental liberties, however, it is only a slight exaggeration to say that the state can decide to criminalize almost anything. A hypothetical case may help to dem-

onstrate the extent of state power in the criminal arena – and the potential injustice of this power. Suppose that legislators become alarmed by the fact that too many persons are unhealthy and overweight. Initially, they decide to facilitate the efforts of consumers to eat a better diet by enacting legislation requiring distributors of fast foods to display nutritional information on their packaging. If the constitutionality of this law were challenged, it would seem appropriate for courts to defer to legislators by invoking the rational basis test. Suppose, however, that legislators came to believe (as is probably the case) that better information would have little impact on the problem of obesity. Imagine that they decided to prohibit – on pain of criminal liability – the consumption of designated unhealthy foods. Suppose that sausage were placed on this list. Once again, the rational basis test would be applied to assess the constitutionality of this law. This hypothetical crime is almost certainly constitutional, since the liberty to eat sausage does not seem to qualify as fundamental. The state has an uncontested interest in protecting health, and it is at least conceivable that proscribing the consumption of sausage would bear a substantial relation to this interest. Admittedly, many foods are more detrimental to health than sausage, and not all sausages are especially detrimental to health. But the fact that a criminal law is underinclusive and/or overinclusive is not regarded as a constitutional impediment under the rational basis test. In other words, a statute need not proscribe each instance of conduct that contributes to the statutory objective, and may proscribe some instances of conduct that do not contribute to the statutory objective.

I have briefly surveyed four theories of criminalization. Although inadequate, each makes a valuable contribution to our understanding of the conditions that must be satisfied before the state can subject persons to punishment. It is hard to believe that criminal liability may be imposed if civil liability would suffice to achieve the statutory objective. No sensible person would believe a criminal statute should be enacted that creates more disutility than it prevents. The penal sanction should be used only to prevent harm. Even though it is evident that all criminal laws must have a rational basis, contemporary constitutional law may seem to offer the least help in constructing a viable theory to limit the reach of the penal sanction. Nonetheless, I will try to correct the deficiencies of this account in order to build a better theory of criminalization upon its foundations.

A Better Approach to Criminalization

What is most remarkable about the last approach surveyed is its complete indifference to the distinction between criminal and noncriminal legislation. It is one thing for the Constitution to evaluate noncriminal laws that burden nonfundamental liberties by the rational basis test. But it is quite another when criminal legislation is assessed by that same standard. The criminal law is different – importantly dissimilar from other kinds of law. The extraordinary procedural protections surrounding the criminal sanction are sensible only on the assumption that the criminal law is unlike other bodies of law (Stuntz 1996). The criminal law is different in that it subjects persons to punishment. By definition, punishment includes both hard treatment and censure, each of which is a clear violation of rights in the absence of a compelling justification. Contemporary constitutional law provides an inadequate theory of criminalization because it fails to offer a justification sufficient to override these rights.

The key to constructing a better theory of criminalization is to understand how the criminal law is different – that is, why it should be evaluated by a higher standard of justification than other kinds of law. The criminal law burdens interests not implicated when other types of law are employed. When persons become subject to punishment, more important interests are at stake than the liberty to perform whatever conduct has been proscribed. These interests can be illustrated by returning to my earlier example. Suppose that the liberty to eat sausage is not especially valuable. If so, the state would need only a minimal reason to dissuade persons from exercising this liberty. This reason might support noncriminal means to discourage consumption – increased taxation, bans on advertising, educational programs, and the like. But the interest burdened by a *criminal*

law against eating sausage is much more important. Persons not only have an interest in eating sausage, but also have an interest in not being punished when they violate the law by eating sausage. This latter interest can be far more significant than the former. The state needs a much better reason – more than a mere rational basis – to justify deprivations of this valuable interest. Even though the state may have a good reason to discourage the consumption of sausage, it may lack a good reason to subject persons who eat sausage to the hard treatment and stigma inherent in the penal sanction.

This point is crucial, and I want to elaborate on it. Proscriptions in a possible world in which the legislature could effectively prevent conduct without resorting to punishment would be easier to defend. In such a world, the only substantive consideration that would be relevant to criminalization would be the value of the liberty that is lost when conduct becomes an offense. But that world is not our world. We should avoid the common mistake of supposing that the criminal law operates by preventing given forms of conduct. In reality, the criminal law proscribes, but does not always prevent. We can safely predict that some people will engage in the prohibited behavior, whatever the law may say. If the law in question is indeed a criminal law, these offenders will become subject to punishment – which has proved very difficult to justify. Punishment involves hard treatment and censure, both infringements of rights that should not be permitted in the absence of compelling reasons. Hence a more stringent test of justification applies to criminal laws.

Perhaps attempts to justify punishment can provide an important source of limitations on the reach of the penal sanction. In stark contrast to their neglect of the topic of criminalization, legal philosophers have written countless volumes about the justification of punishment. Remarkably, few of these philosophers have shown much interest in the content of the substantive criminal law. They have tried to theorize about punishment as though they could afford to ignore the issue of what punishment is imposed for. Despite this tendency, theories about the justification of punishment might prove enormously useful in generating constraints on the kinds of conduct that may be criminalized. Before legislators enact a criminal law, they must be confident that the state would be justified in punishing persons who violate it. In other words, the state should not draft statutes that will subject offenders to hard treatment and reprobation unless it has good reason to believe that the punishment to which such persons will become subject would be justified. If we are relatively sure that our theory of punishment is correct, but we cannot apply it to justify the punishment of those who commit a given offense, we should not have made that offense criminal in the first place. The existence of such an offense would require the state to impose unjustified punishments, or to renege on its classification of that law as criminal.

Of course, this strategy will not generate limitations on the scope of the criminal law unless we are reasonably confident in the cogency of our theory of punishment. Although philosophers disagree vehemently about what justifies punishment, none disagree that a justification is needed. An adequate theory will have two dimensions. Understandably, most of the focus is on the conditions under which punishment is justified. But a given theory must also identify the conditions under which punishment is not justified. As long as we are talking about rape, theft, murder, or other cases of core criminality, virtually all theorists agree that punishment is justified; they only disagree about why. As we have seen, however, the criminal law has expanded far beyond its core. When new examples of criminality such as walking dogs on federal property are involved, reasonable persons should doubt that punishment is justified at all. Still, persons who commit these offenses, no less than those who commit crimes within the core, become subject to punishment. Can their punishments possibly be defensible?

Clearly, a better theory of criminalization is needed to answer this question – a theory that demands a higher standard of justification for criminal than for noncriminal laws. What standard of justification should be applied to infringe our interest in not being subjected to hard treatment or reprobation? Fortunately, we have ample experience in answering questions of this kind. The conditions that should be satisfied before a criminal law is enacted can be drawn from that

body of constitutional law that protects interests acknowledged to be as valuable as our interest in not being punished. Our liberties in speech and religion are foremost among these interests. The body of law applicable to deprivations of these liberties can be readily adapted to limit impositions of the criminal sanction (Colb 1994).

Recall that current constitutional law in the United States requires the state to have a compelling interest before it will allow important fundamental interests to be burdened. Why should we concede that our fundamental liberties to speak or to exercise our religious beliefs are more important and thus entitled to a greater degree of protection than our interest in not being punished? If forced to choose, reasonable persons might be less willing to be punished than to sacrifice many of the liberties deemed fundamental under contemporary constitutional law. If we agree that our interest not to be punished is equally valuable, all criminal laws should be required to satisfy the same justificatory test that applies to deprivations of our fundamental liberties. By examining what counts as a persuasive reason to burden fundamental liberties such as speech or religion, we can begin to develop standards for subjecting persons to criminal liability and punishment.

The implications of this theory of criminalization are radical and profound. Applying the same standard of justification that already pertains to infringements of speech and religion would require the state to strictly scrutinize all criminal laws. In other words, the state would need to have a compelling interest before it subjects any conduct to punishment. Of course, this theory cannot be implemented without criteria to decide which state interests are compelling; attempts to identify these interests are bound to generate enormous dispute. Moreover, determining that a statutory objective is compelling is only the first step in applying a more demanding standard of justification to criminal legislation. The law must also be necessary to achieve this objective. That is, the state must show that its legislative objective would be harder to achieve without resorting to punishment. The criminal law must be a last resort – a condition not imposed on the criminal law by the rational basis test. Applying this criterion to the criminal law would open up an entirely new area of research. Deciding whether and under what circumstances noncriminal alternatives are as effective as criminal sanctions would often require empirical investigation that criminal theorists have seldom recognized the need to undertake (Ashworth 1995).

An equally important step in the justificatory process is the determination that the criminal law is narrowly tailored to serve the compelling state interest. The requirement of narrow tailoring has two dimensions. First and perhaps more importantly, criminal laws must not be overinclusive, proscribing instances of conduct beyond those that serve the compelling state interest. Desert is individual; punishment must be justified for each and every person on whom it is imposed. In addition, the requirement of narrow tailoring precludes the enactment of criminal laws that are underinclusive. To be justified, a criminal law must apply equally to each type of conduct the state has the same compelling interest to proscribe. The state must treat us as equals in our interest in not being punished; it should not punish some while sparing others if it has the same compelling reason to punish both. A principle against underinclusive legislation would help to ensure that the state is really aiming toward the interest it alleges to be promoted by the statute.

The foregoing account simply begins the extraordinarily difficult task of providing an adequate theory of criminalization. Further details would borrow from that body of law that protects interests of equal importance as our interest in not being punished. Applying the principles I have described requires normative judgments that are immensely controversial. But far greater controversy *should* surround the enactment of criminal laws; the state needs excellent reasons to deprive us of our interest in not being subjected to hard treatment and censure.

How would this theory apply to the proliferation of new offenses outside the so-called core of criminality? Can the state possibly have a compelling interest in punishing persons who include a member of the armed forces in a voter preference poll, or exhibit deformed animals? The answer seems obvious. Still, we should not be too quick to decide until the state has had an opportunity to justify these laws by applying the demanding criteria I have described. One advantage of this theory of criminalization is that the state would be required to articulate a rationale in favor of the criminal laws it enacts. Today, no such requirement exists, and judges and citizens alike must guess about the objectives of given laws.

I do not discuss the enormous difficulties in implementing the theory I have described. I doubt that judges should be given the power to declare a criminal statute unconstitutional if it fails the justificatory test I have sketched. The judiciary almost certainly lacks the competence to apply my theory of criminalization, which is addressed primarily to legislators. I am confident, however, that applications of my theory would help to make the criminal law more just. The theory would go a long way toward retarding the current trends to criminalize too much and to punish too many. But a better account of criminalization would also have obvious advantages for criminal theory as traditionally construed. The doctrines in the general part of criminal law – the area on which theorists have tended to focus – are derived by generalizing from offenses in the special part. A better theory of criminalization can only improve the normative content of criminal theory generally.

References

Abrams, N. 1989. The new ancillary offenses. *Criminal Law Forum* 1: 1–39.

Ashworth, A. 1995. *Principles of Criminal Law*, 2nd edn. Oxford: Clarendon Press.

Ashworth, A. 2000. Is the criminal law a lost cause? *Law Quarterly Review* 116: 225–56.

Bilionis, L. 1998. Process, the Constitution, and substantive criminal law. *Michigan Law Review* 96: 1269–1334.

Calabresi, G. and Melamed, D. A. 1972. Property rules, liability rules, and inalienability: One view of the cathedral. *Harvard Law Review* 85: 1089–1128.

Coffee, J. 1991. Does "unlawful" mean "criminal"? Reflections on the disappearing tort/crime distinction in American law. *Boston University Law Review* 71: 193–246.

Colb, S. 1994. Freedom from incarceration: Why is this right different from all other rights? *New York University Law Review* 69: 781–849.

Dubber, M. 2001. Policing possession: The war on crime and the end of criminal law. *Journal of Criminal Law and Criminology* 91: 829–996.

Feinberg, J. 1984. *Harm to Others*. New York: Oxford University Press.

Feinberg, J. 1986. Harm to others – a rejoinder. *Criminal Justice Ethics* 5: 16–29.

Gardner, J. and Shute, S. 2000. The wrongness of rape. In J. Horder (ed.), *Oxford Essays in Jurisprudence*, 4th series. Oxford: Oxford University Press, 193–217.

Hart, H. 1958. The aims of the criminal law. *Law & Contemporary Problems* 23: 401–41.

Husak, D. 1995. The nature and justifiability of non-consummate offenses. *Arizona Law Review* 37: 151–83.

Kadish, S. and Schulhofer, S. 2001. *Criminal Law and its Processes*, 7th edn. New York: Aspen Law & Business.

Kleinig, J. 1986. Criminally harming others. *Criminal Justice Ethics* 5: 3–10.

Lacey, N. 1998. Contingency, coherence, and conceptualism. In A. Duff (ed.), *Philosophy and the Criminal Law*. Cambridge, UK: Cambridge University Press, 9–59.

Logan, W. 1998. The ex post facto clause and the jurisprudence of punishment. *American Criminal Law Review* 35: 1261–1318.

Marshall, S. and Duff, R. A. 1998. Criminalization and sharing wrongs. *Canadian Journal of Law and Jurisprudence* XI: 7–22.

Moore, M. 1997. *Placing Blame: A General Theory of the Criminal Law*. Oxford: Clarendon Press.

Nozick, R. 1974. *Anarchy, State, and Utopia*. New York: Basic Books.

Posner, R. 1985. An economic theory of the criminal law. *Columbia Law Review* 85: 1193–1231.

Robinson, P. 2001. Punishing dangerousness: Cloaking preventive detention as criminal justice. *Harvard Law Review* 114: 1429–56.

Simester, A. P. and Sullivan, G. R. 2000. *Criminal Law: Theory and Doctrine*. Oxford: Hart.

Stuntz, W. 1996. Substance, process, and the civil-criminal line. *Journal of Contemporary Legal Issues* 7: 1–41.

Stuntz, W. 2001. The pathological politics of criminal law. *Michigan Law Review* 100: 505–600.

Von Hirsch, A. and Jareborg, N. 1991. Gauging criminal harm: A living-standard analysis. *Oxford Journal of Legal Studies* 11: 1–38.

Williams, G. 1961. *Criminal Law: The General Part*, 2nd edn. London: Stevens & Sons.

Further Reading

Alexander, L. 2000. Insufficient concern: A unified conception of criminal culpability. *California Law Review* 88: 931–64.

Alexander, L. 2002. The philosophy of criminal law. In J. Coleman and S. Shapiro (eds.), *Oxford Handbook of Jurisprudence and Philosophy of Law*. Oxford: Oxford University Press, 815–67.

Coffee, J. 1992. Paradigms lost: The blurring of the criminal and civil law models – and what can be done about it. *Yale Law Journal* 101: 1875–93.

Coleman, J. 2000. Crimes and transactions. *California Law Review* 88: 921–30.

Dressler, J. 1995. *Understanding Criminal Law*, 2nd edn. New York: Matthew Bender.

Duff, A. 1996. *Criminal Attempts*. Oxford: Clarendon Press.

Dyer, J. 2000. *The Perpetual Prisoner Machine*. Boulder, CO: Westview Press.

Feinberg, J. 1985. *Offense to Others*. New York: Oxford University Press.

Feinberg, J. 1987. *Harmless Wrongdoing*. New York: Oxford University Press.

Fletcher, G. 1978. *Rethinking Criminal Law*. Boston: Little, Brown.

Fletcher, G. 1993. Blackmail – the paradigmatic crime. *University of Pennsylvania Law Review* 141: 1617–38.

Fletcher, G. 1998. *Basic Concepts of Criminal Law*. New York: Oxford University Press.

Gainer, R. 1998. Federal criminal law reform: Past and future. *Buffalo Criminal Law Review* 2: 45–159.

Green, S. 1997. Why it's a crime to tear the tag off a mattress: Overcriminalization and the moral content of regulatory offenses. *Emory Law Journal* 46: 1533–1615.

Hart, H. L. A. 1968. *Punishment and Responsibility*. New York: Oxford University Press.

Husak, D. 1987. *Philosophy of Criminal Law*. Totowa, NJ: Rowman & Allanheld.

Husak, D. 1992. The serial view of criminal law defenses. *Criminal Law Forum* 3: 369–400.

Katz, L. 1987. *Bad Acts and Guilty Minds*. Chicago: University of Chicago Press.

Klein, S. 1999. Redrawing the criminal-civil boundary. *Buffalo Criminal Law Review* 2: 679–721.

Michaels, A. 1998. Acceptance: The missing mental state. *Southern California Law Review* 71: 101–83.

Norrie, A. 1993. *Crime, Reason and History*. London: Weidenfeld and Nicolson.

Robinson, P. 1997. *Structure and Function in Criminal Law.* Oxford: Clarendon Press.

Schauer, F. 1991. *Playing by the Rules.* Oxford: Clarendon Press.

Schonsheck, J. 1994. *On Criminalization.* Dordrecht: Kluwer Academic Publishers.

Shute, S., Gardner, J., and Horder, J. (eds.) 1993. *Action and Value in Criminal Law.* Oxford: Clarendon Press.

Shute, S. and Simester, A. P. (eds.) 2002. *Criminal Law Theory: Doctrines of the General Part.* Oxford: Oxford University Press.

Simester, A. P. and Smith, A. T. H. (eds.) 1996. *Harm and Culpability.* Oxford: Clarendon Press.

Simons, K. 1992. Rethinking mental states. *Boston University Law Review* 72: 463–554.

Stephen. J. 1883. *A History of the Criminal Law of England.* New York: Burt Franklin.

Chapter 8

Philosophy of Tort Law

Benjamin C. Zipursky

The string of words, "Philosophy of tort law" may seem like a random conjunction of academic topic nouns selected from columns in a word game. If the phrase has a comical ring, it is because tort law is among the most practical and least high-falutin' areas of law. Tort law deals with car accidents, medical malpractice, and defective lawn mowers, matters seemingly far from the celestial concerns of the philosopher. And so, like the lobster ice cream sold in a sea-faring tourist town, the existence of philosophy of tort law as a subject may seem to be proof that people will swallow just about anything that can be served up.

The decision to write this chapter indicates that I do not share the perspective articulated above. And yet the question raised – "Is philosophy of tort law intellectually unmotivated?" – provides a valuable backdrop for thinking about the topic. I shall suggest in what follows that the subject actually covers a number of different kinds of inquiry, each kind motivated by a set of practical or intellectual concerns. By probing these diverse motivations we will not only address the reasons why there is such a subject (philosophy of tort law), we will also get a better sense of the substance of ongoing debates within tort law, and we will have greater reason to hope that further development in philosophy of tort law will lead to valuable contributions to our legal system and academic culture. Rather than setting forth several leading tort theories as if the subject had an uncontested subject matter over which different scholars had different theories, we shall look at several different kinds of questions that have led

to the development of philosophically rich answers.

Philosophy/tort questions will be presented in three sections. The first section pertains to problems in the development of the black-letter law of torts within the twentieth century, which have spurred the development of philosophical tort theories. The second looks to broader debates within legal theory in which tort theory has been a singularly important domain. Third, and finally, there are debates within moral and political philosophy that have again displayed tort theory as a domain within which particularly rich philosophical ideas have been generated. Philosophical work in tort law has emerged from, addressed, pushed forward, and been shaped by, developments in all of these debates.

Pushed by Problems in Law and Policy

Negligence versus strict liability

In a number of different domains of tort law during the twentieth century, judges, lawyers, legislators, and academics engaged in a debate over whether companies and individuals should be held strictly liable for the injuries they cause. Workers' compensation for workplace injuries, no-fault automobile insurance for car accidents in some jurisdictions, and strict liability for manufacturing defects in products are prominent examples of domains in which the advocates of strict liability have prevailed. A wide variety – probably the vast preponderance – of areas of accident law remain negligence-based, but there has been and continues to be a significant range of areas in which debates between a negligence principle and a strict liability principle remain energetic and nuanced. This includes, for example, liability for suboptimal designs and unknown hazards in products, liability for automobile accidents, and a significant number of dangerous activities.

While the strict-liability-versus-negligence debate has benefited from major, and in some cases, central, contributions from economists, historians, and other analysts within the social sciences, it has from its inception presented a significant philosophical aspect. At first appearance, one might suppose that the philosophical question at issue has been: *ought a person who has caused injury to another person be held liable for the cost of compensating the victim's injury, regardless of whether the one who caused injury acted in a faulty manner?* In fact, this bald normative question has not been the primary target of philosophical analysis. Rather, the primary philosophical question has been one that presupposes a setting within legal doctrine, and an interpretive slant: *to the extent that the imposition of liability under Anglo-American tort law embodies a set of legal principles that displays a defensible normative structure, does that normative structure permit the imposition of liability without fault, and if so, when?*

The results of this broad inquiry fall into a spectrum running from strict liability to negligence. Richard Epstein's straightforwardly titled "A Theory of Strict Liability" (1973) is a libertarian case for strict liability in accident law; by contrast, Ernest Weinrib's corrective justice theory advocates a fault principle across the board, and Arthur Ripstein largely shares this position. Several views fall in between – including those of George Fletcher, Gregory Keating, Jules Coleman, and Stephen Perry.

Epstein's strict-liability corrective justice theory

Richard Epstein has taken the view that, just as each person who infringes upon another's prop-erty right is required by the law to compensate the property owner for the infringement, so each who causes injury to another's body is also liable to the other for the costs of the injury inflicted – at least where there is not a specific showing of excuse or justification (Epstein 1973: 203–4). The purpose of this body of law is not to provide compensation to accident victims, nor to deter wrongdoers (although it does, and not unimportantly, have those consequences); the purpose of the law is to protect each person's holdings against the infringements of others. Whether those infringements are deliberate or negligent or without fault is largely irrelevant, just as it generally is for property infringements. One's body is as precious as one's real property, so invasions of bodily integrity trigger a right to compensation.

The key to the interpretive success or failure of Epstein's account is whether he can recast what would otherwise seem to be a conception of fault in many cases as an aspect of the causation requirement; Stephen Perry's widely respected critique of Epstein (based on the idea that he must smuggle normative notions into his conception of cause) suggests that he cannot (Perry 1989: 404–12). From a normative point of view, the view requires adherence to an almost visceral Nozickian libertarianism – a view to which Epstein appears to remain loyal, albeit for a different set of reasons than he initially endorsed.

Weinrib and Ripstein: Fault-based conceptions of corrective justice theory

Weinrib, like Epstein, embraces a corrective justice framework in which restoring an equilibrium that was disturbed by tortious conduct is a central feature of tort law (Weinrib 1995). Unlike Epstein, however, Weinrib openly states that the equilibrium disturbed (and then ideally restored) is not simply the status quo distribution of entitlements. It is, Weinrib argues, a "normative equilibrium," which is disturbed only where people have acted in a manner that they were not entitled to act, outside of their rights. Where the defendant has so acted and the conduct ripens into an invasion of the plaintiff's right, that invasion is a disturbance that needs to be rectified. When the tort law obligates the tortfeasor defendant to pay the plaintiff, it is making sure that the rectification occurs and normative equilibrium is restored; things are set right, so far as possible. Because the trigger of liability is an action in breach of duty, or outside of a defendant's right, this is not strict liability. The defendant has injured the plaintiff, but the liability for the injury is not generated by that fact alone, but by the wrongfulness of the defendant's injuring of the plaintiff. Hence, fault is essential to liability in tort, under Weinrib's view. This is not to say that insurance or administrative law frameworks could not justifiably be created that would impose strict liability, but such structures could not properly come from within the judiciary purporting to apply tort law, and could not appeal to the supposed normative bases of tort law.

Arthur Ripstein's powerful book, *Equality, Responsibility and the Law* (1998), takes Kantian strands in Weinrib and weaves them into a contemporary, constructivist, Rawlsian defense of tort law. His basic idea is that security and liberty are goods that it is the domain of law to shape and constrain for citizens on equal terms. Tort law does this by declaring that when people act in a manner that takes more liberty than a generalized scheme of liberty could permit – when they unreasonably risk harm to others, for example – then the risked harm, if it comes to pass, will be their responsibility. In that manner, tortious conduct in effect creates a domain of responsibility for injuries caused. Because it is essential to Ripstein's view that the injury only becomes the defendant's responsibility under the tort law because he or she acted beyond the limit of liberty designated, negligence or fault is critical to liability.

Fletcher's reciprocity theory

Two pioneers of the philosophical study of tort law – George Fletcher and Jules Coleman – have offered accounts that expressly leave room for both strict liability and negligence within tort law. Fletcher's 1972 article, "Fairness and Utility in Tort Theory," asserts that a single principle accounts for both strict liability and negligence: a principle that the creation of nonreciprocal risks generates liability for the realization of those risks. In risky activities that are widely engaged in and are taken as part and parcel of modern life

in a given community – such as driving – each of us accepts a certain degree of risk as a form of vulnerability that we must tolerate in light of our own production of similar risks to others. Therefore, when those risks are realized, the generator of realized risks need not bear the liability. However, when people do not use reasonable care in engaging in those activities, they generate a nonreciprocal risk and must therefore take responsibility if the risk is realized in an injury. That is negligence-based liability. Similarly, if people engage in abnormally risky activities, the reciprocity of risk does not apply, and they should be held liable for the results of those realized risks. That is strict liability. Recent work by Gregory Keating has expanded Fletcher's theory in illuminating ways (Keating 1996, 1997, 2001).

Mixed corrective justice theories: Coleman and Perry

Coleman has offered at least two quite different models aimed at capturing both strict liability and negligence. In his early work, Coleman depicted the tort law as a system fundamentally aimed at annulling unjustifiable losses (which, he argued, is consistent with strict liability) (Coleman 1976). At the same time, Coleman recognized that the legal system may choose particular modes of rectifying those losses, and some modes (e.g., a fault principle) may serve other social goals or implement other principles (Coleman 1983). Those crafting the tort system presumably need to decide which principles they think should be treated as primary if they want to ascertain the propriety of strict liability.

A second incarnation of Coleman's thinking – which displays a stimulating conversation with Stephen Perry's work – is found in *Risks and Wrongs* (Coleman 1992). Like both Perry and Weinrib, Coleman urges a corrective justice view that treats plaintiffs and defendants in an interlocked relationship, within which their rights and duties are correlative. Tort liability is imposed where defendants have a duty of repair running to the plaintiff, and they have this duty of repair where they are responsible for the plaintiff's injury. They are responsible for injuries where they have violated a right not to be injured tortiously. For the most part, such rights are cor-relative to duties not to injure another wrong-fully. To this extent, they are negligence-based. However, Coleman also suggests that some rights are defined such that infringement can occur without wrongdoing; land rights are a good example, for a trespass need not be negligent or wrongful (Coleman 1992: 371–4). Hence, a rights violation is either a wrongful injuring or an infringement of a predefined interest in not being injured through a certain sort of conduct and as to a particular sort of entitlement. Negli-gence liability is the first sort, strict liability is consistent with the second.

Perry grounds corrective justice in a notion of responsibility – one that he labels (following Honoré) "outcome responsibility" (Honoré 1988; Perry 1992). The assignment of liability in tort is, in effect, a recognition that the defend-ant is responsible for the plaintiff's injury. The implication of such a finding of responsibility, as a moral matter, is the recognition of a duty of con-duct toward the plaintiff to rectify the injury in some manner. Perry offers a detailed analysis of the moral principle underpinning the assignment of responsibility, arguing that the notion of out-come responsibility is part and parcel of a social practice in which certain outcomes are linked to, and associated with, a person's agency. Typically, an accidental injury is not simply within one per-son's agency, but within more than one person's agency. The question therefore arises as to which should be deemed responsible for the outcome, given that both are linked with it causally, and possibly both (or several) could have foreseen the outcome (Perry 1992: 509). Our notions of corrective justice offer a principle of distribution localized to the few who are outcome-respon-sible, imposing a duty of repair upon the one whom we judge most fairly bears the burden among those who are outcome-responsible (Perry 1992: 512–13). Normally, a notion that one of the parties was at fault is necessary to a judgment that that person should fairly bear the burden of the injury, but in a certain class of cases, the comparative judgment may not require any actual judgment of fault (Perry 1992: 510–11). To that extent, Perry argues, a fragment of strict liability may be cogent, notwithstanding the gen-eral preference for fault.

Revisiting the doctrinal and policy arenas

It is not necessarily easy to say what the precise contributions of these philosophical accounts have been to the development of legal doctrine, but that is not to say that they have been inert. A variety of economic, political, social, and intel-lectual forces pushed toward strict liability in products and more generally in the 1950s through the early 1970s. Philosophical theorists of tort law at first added to this pressure, by depicting tort as aimed toward – or at least con-strained by – the notion of responsibility and by analyzing responsibility in a manner that permit-ted strict liability. However, since Epstein's views were rejected and an analysis of responsibility in terms of fault gained prominence, philosophical and justice-based accounts of tort law have tended to support at least a strong presumption that fault or negligence is required in the theory of tort liability, with strict liability remaining a fragment of exceptions. At the same time, courts, legislatures, and tort doctrinalists have greatly retreated from the movement toward strict liabil-ity. Indeed, the American Law Institute's *Restate-ment (Third) of Products Liability* has expressly advocated negligence over strict liability in both the products context and more generally, in part citing philosophical reasons. The directions of the causal link among these academic, political, and legal developments – if there be any links – would require much greater analysis; suffice it to say that there is no *a priori* reason to assume that the causal link traveled in only one direction.

A somewhat subtler, but perhaps even more significant effect has involved the issue of caus-ation more than the issue of fault. During the 1970s, courts began experimenting with the relaxation of proof requirements for cause in fact and for tortfeasor identification. Hence, in the DES context, plaintiffs in jurisdictions that permit market-share liability can recover from a drug company that produced the same sort of drug that injured them, without proving that the manufacturer produced the particular brand that injured them (Ripstein and Zipursky 2001: 215). A spate of commentators asserted that this sort of innovation should be followed in a wide variety of tort cases, and in fact provided a more sound basis for tort law than actual doctrine.

Philosophical analysts of tort law, particularly corrective justice theorists, presented an account of tort law in terms of responsibility for injuries that provided a powerful and cogent justification for the central role of causation, roughly as traditionally understood. In combination with a number of other intellectual and political forces, it would appear that the principled defense of causation has seriously stalled the efforts of enterprise liability revisionists.

To summarize: legal scholars and courts seem to be near consensus on the view that to assign responsibility for a defendant without deeming its conduct to be either a *prima facie* wrong or an extraordinary taking of a risk runs against the grain of the principles embedded in the tort law, and is therefore disfavored unless there are particularly forceful reasons of policy or equity for doing so. Hence, there is strict liability for ultrahazardous activities – those involving extraordinary risks – and there is strict liability in worker's compensation as a policy-motivated legislative choice during the inception of the last century, and there is strict liability on a restitutionary basis in a narrow range of cases. But otherwise there is not. And to the extent that, for example, product liability has moved toward strict liability, scholars have favored a return to the negligence-based idea, unless particularly strong policy-based justifications can be demonstrated.

At a broader level, the richness of philosophical theories of tort law over the past few decades should not seem either mundane or rarified. Questions about the basis of our tort liability push lawyers and citizens to think philosophically. Inquiry into the basic concept of responsibility and what role fault plays within it cuts deeply into both moral and political theory, and is hardly banal; exploration and modification of the contours of liability on the border of negligence and strict liability raise the bar on the importance of crafting intelligent answers to such questions, an activity that is hardly inert or esoteric.

Concepts within tort doctrine

Commentators on tort theory – even those who recognize an important link between theory and open questions in legal doctrine – typically assume that philosophy of tort law is largely exhausted by grand philosophical theories of the domain of tort law. It would be odd if this were true in torts, for it is not true in those areas of law where philosophical work has been most prominent – constitutional law and criminal law. In those areas, while grand theories such as fundamental rights theory or retributivism have been prominent, philosophers and philosophically oriented legal scholars have probed a variety of narrower questions. In constitutional law, for example, important scholarship has focused on questions such as (simply to name a few) the nature and scope of free speech, the right to privacy, the proper scope of judicial review, the role of framers' intent in constitutional interpretation. Similarly, in criminal law, scholarship has focused not only on the justification of punishment, but on (for example) the nature of criminal intent, the distinction between justification and excuse, and defenses such as insanity and self-defense. See CRIMINAL LAW THEORY. We should not expect, therefore, that theories over whether fault or strict liability is the basic principle of tort would take up the space in philosophy of tort law. And that is just what we find.

Philosophers and philosophically oriented scholars of tort law have provided serious and interesting work on a variety of broad but defined legal issues. Thus, for example, philosophers have investigated the nature of the cause-in-fact and the proximate cause requirements for tort liability; the meaning of the "prudent person" standard or the "reasonable care" standard in negligence law (Feldman 2000; Keating 1996); the relation between intent and knowledge in intentional torts (Finnis 1995; Sebok 2001); the concept of foreseeability (Perry 2001: 88–101); and the nature of duty in negligence law (Goldberg and Zipursky 1998; Weinrib 1995), just to take a few examples. The areas are far too numerous even to survey here, but it may be useful to explore an example of this phenomenon. Like the broader debate between fault and strict liability, the theoretical issues that revolve around more defined doctrines have tended to arise out of ongoing practical debates within actual types of legal disputes that courts are trying to resolve in a coherent, just, and beneficial manner.

Let us take the example of "duty" in negligence law. The meaning and nature of the "duty" element in negligence law is equally inviting to the skeptic and the moralist. This is immediately evident in Holmes's famous anticipation of legal realism in "The Path of the Law" (1897), where he states that: "a legal duty so called is nothing but a prediction that if a man does or omits certain things he will be made to suffer in this or that way by judgment of the court; – and so of a legal right" (1897: 458–9). Holmes the scholar was above all a tort theorist and so it is fair to take this largely jurisprudential statement as a commentary on duty in torts as well. Legal realism in torts in particular was advanced by Leon Green in the early part of the twentieth century in work that expressly asserted that "duty" in negligence law was largely a procedural device for shifting classes of cases to the court from the jury (Green 1928). See AMERICAN LEGAL REALISM. These theoretical statements then made their way into hornbook statements of law, and from there, they entered into the lexicon of the California Supreme Court of the 1960s and 1970s, as if they were black letter law. Essentially, Holmes's blend of realism, moral skepticism, and reductive instrumentalism as attached to the pivotally important "duty" in negligence law had prevailed within the legal academy and within certain avant garde courts. The result was quite real as well: large bodies of well-settled law, such as landowner liability, professional liability to third parties, emotional harm doctrine, and economic harm doctrine, as well as limitations on the duty to rescue, became targets of sustained critique purporting to display the rules as arbitrary limitations based on philosophically naïve interpretations of the concept of duty.

In the context of a near landslide of support for a philosophical (and reductive) analysis of a central element of the main tort, negligence, it is not surprising that a philosophical opposition began to emerge. Weinrib's articles, and those of several of his students, began to take a harder look at the question of what role the duty element plays in negligence law. Weinrib's Kantian and Hegelian account of the correlativity of right and duty within negligence law is fundamental to his account of torts. And it is critical, on Weinrib's view, that the term "duty" refers to a relation of moral significance between two parties. Weinrib's moralization – or remoralization – of torts anticipated a broader philosophical investigation of the meaning of "duty" within negligence law (Weinrib 1983, 1989, 1995).

In a series of articles, my coauthor John Goldberg and I have depicted the debate over duty as, in part, a philosophical debate over the structure of the concept of duty within certain kinds of normative systems (Goldberg and Zipursky 1998, 2001, 2002). Quite apart from the interpretive question of what concept the law of negligence is best understood as displaying, there is an analytical question of whether a nonreductive conception of duty in negligence law can be articulated in such a way that it is not equivalent to the question of whether reasonable or ordinary care was used by the defendant. According to what is now the academically dominant account, to say that there was unreasonable conduct by the defendant but that there was no duty to use such care running to the plaintiff is simply to say that notwithstanding breach of duty causing injury, there shall be no right of action available to this particular plaintiff. That is because, according to this conception, the only genuine obligation of conduct within negligence law is an obligation to use due care, and this obligation does not run to any person or class of persons; it just exists as the standard of reasonable conduct, full stop. And hence, once one has concluded that reasonable conduct was not used, one has decided that the only genuinely duty-like aspect of the situation – the obligation to use reasonable care – existed and was breached. If the court then turns around and says that the plaintiff must lose because there was no duty *to him or her*, the court can only be interpreted to mean that there is a class of cases involving a plaintiff situated a particular way and a defendant situated a particular way, which for some reason should not be actionable even where there is unreasonable conduct causing injury, and that this case belongs to that class.

The analytical challenge is therefore the puzzle of explaining how there could be a form of obligation to use due care that is not simply a duty to use reasonable care owed to no person or class of persons: why, as we have put it, it might be possible to think of duties of due care as *relational* in a nonquestion-begging sense. The answer offered is that it is possible to think of norms of conduct as either monadic (or simple) or dyadic (or relational). Monadic norms direct or enjoin a class of persons not to behave in a certain way (or to behave in a certain way). Dyadic norms of conduct are norms that direct or implore a class of persons not to treat members of some class some way. It is possible to ask whether one person has violated the norm with respect to some particular person, if the norm is understood as having a dyadic structure, but not otherwise (Zipursky 1998b: 61–3). It is possible to think of a norm of due care as a dyadic norm, not a monadic norm. Insofar as the obligation's existence is constituted by or identical with the existence of a norm, it is possible to think of an obligation to use due care as a relational obligation, an obligation that it is coherent to think is owed to a person or class of persons, and coherent to say has been violated with respect to one person but not to another. It is therefore possible to think of duties of due care as owed to persons or classes of persons (and, correspondingly, to think of a breach of the duty of due care as a breach of a duty owed to a person or a class of persons). And – so long as one can think of legal norms as directing or enjoining conduct – it is possible to conceptualize all of this without begging the question of whether the right to sue for negligence is limited by whether one is among the class of persons to whom a duty is breached.

Of course, even if it is possible to understand duties of care in this manner, it does not follow that tort law's duties of due care are best understood in this manner, or that a body of law so constituted would be more desirable than what "simple duty" theorists would advocate. We and others have addressed these questions in detail elsewhere (Goldberg and Zipursky 1998: 1826–42). What I wish to point out here, however, is that the question of the structure of duties is really only the beginning of a domain of philosophical debate that can and should inform ongoing legal controversies. Later in this chapter, I shall comment on the role of philosophical analysis of the concept of duty in tort to moral philosophy more broadly.

Jurisprudence and Legal Theory

The philosophical literature on tort law has been at least as important within jurisprudence as it has within tort law itself. Broadly speaking, tort theorists have contributed to jurisprudential debates in at least two ways. The first looks to the nature of the value system to be utilized in explaining or justifying bodies of law. The second looks to the nature of the analytical process to be used in breaking down and understanding the law.

Fairness versus utility

Drawing from Mill and Bentham, Oliver Wendell Holmes Jr. thought that the measure of a legal system was its contribution to overall well-being of the community it served. The point of the law was to improve concrete human functioning. It did this by compensating those wrongfully injured and by giving teeth to the norms of prudent conduct that our society needs. Holmes's pioneering work was followed, in different ways, by doctrinalists such as *Prosser and Keeton* and by economic theorists such as Richard Posner (Posner 1972), Guido Calabresi (Calabresi 1970), and Ronald Coase (1960), and, of course, by many leading courts. By the end of the 1960s, tort law as a domain in which we seek out the most commendable system for compensating accidental injury was well entrenched. Indeed, a general view of the law as aimed toward producing human happiness was flourishing in constitutional law, contracts, and criminal law. This was not surprising, since utilitarianism and its offshoots had achieved extraordinary prominence in America during the twentieth century. Partly because of Holmes's leadership, and partly because of its practical importance within a quickly industrializing nation, tort law was the exemplar of the utilitarian approach.

But moral and political philosophy in the English-speaking world was altered in the 1950s and 1960s by the publication of important papers by John Rawls, culminating in his *Theory of Justice* in 1971. Rawls, of course, revitalized social contract theory and used it as a foundation from which to construct a critique of utilitarianism. Moreover, after generations of skepticism about the notion of justice, Rawls confidently offered a grand theory of justice, deploying a notion of fairness in a central role. Given that jurisprudence has historically and conceptually enjoyed a sibling-like relationship with moral and political philosophy, one would expect these changes to be reflected in legal theory.

In 1972, less than a year after Rawls's book, George Fletcher published a landmark article in the *Harvard Law Review* entitled "Fairness and Utility in Tort Theory." Fletcher expressly cited Rawls as foundation and inspiration for his ideas in the philosophy of tort law. Unlike constitutional law, where others (most notably Dworkin) had cited the significance of Rawls, and where utilitarianism was unlikely to have achieved unquestioned superiority, tort law was an area in which utilitarian theorizing reigned supreme. Fletcher argued that a notion of fairness was better than a notion of utility for understanding tort law, both from an interpretive and from a normative point of view. He urged that even strict liability, which was famously advocated from a utilitarian point of view, was in fact better interpreted in terms of a notion of fairness. And he used this notion of fairness as means for casting in relief how dogmatically utility-based legal theory in America had become.

Fletcher's article is emblematic of a now-familiar paradigm battle between economically oriented legal theorists and deontologically oriented ones, both within torts and elsewhere. And tort law has been viewed as a field over which these two paradigms should properly do battle. Fletcher's reciprocity-based approach is no longer the dominant model for the antiutilitarians in torts (corrective justice theory is); but, again, the philosophy of tort law remains the centrally contested forum within which broadly speaking utilitarian theories are challenged by nonutilitarian ones: Libertarian Strict Liability (Epstein 1973), Aristotelian Corrective Justice Theory (Gordley 1995; Stone 2001; Weinrib 1995), Constructivist Corrective Justice Theories (Coleman 2001; Ripstein 1998); Social Contract-based Theories (Fletcher 1972; Keating 2001). To the extent that such theories have provided

fertile and plausible insights into tort law and tort policy, they have fortified the plausibility of an entire paradigm of legal theorizing. This broader plane of theorizing has spread across contract, property, criminal law, tax, and a variety of other areas once almost entirely dominated by the utilitarian framework.

Instrumentalism versus conceptualism

The debate described above, between utilitarian and nonutilitarian theories, is related to another legal theory debate: that between instrumentalist analysis of law and legal concepts and conceptualistic analysis. The instrumentalist took the key to understanding law and legal concepts to be an appreciation of the capacity of pieces of doctrine to serve as instruments for the realization of social ends (Summers 1982: 20).

Examples of this sort of analysis abound within twentieth-century legal theory, both inside and outside of torts. Take the example of "unconscionability" within contract law. The doctrine that unconscionable contracts are unenforceable superficially appears to be a moralistic requirement that bargains that are so extremely one-sided as to be grossly oppressive or unfair should not be enforced. An instrumentalist analysis would eschew this superficial interpretation – at least insofar as it aimed to resurrect some justifiable aspect of the doctrine – and read unconscionability as a doctrine aimed to ferret out bargains that were made in a context of such disproportionate bargaining power that the usual presumption that freely agreed to bargains are efficient no longer holds. "Unconscionable" is just a rhetorically effective label for such contracts. The propriety of refusing to enforce them has nothing to do with the superficial meaning of the term, and is really just a disguise for one of the law's means of adhering to a program of promoting efficiency. Similar examples exist through virtually all areas of the common law and constitutional law. Instrumentalism has thrived in torts as much, or more, than in other parts of the law – famously, for terms such as "proximate cause" and "duty," and for fundamental principles, such as the requirement that defendant's conduct actually caused plaintiff's injury.

Instrumentalism and utilitarianism are by no means identical, even if adherence to one often accompanies adherence to the other. It is entirely possible for an instrumentalist to believe that rights and duties are not simply a matter of utility, but have a thoroughly deontological foundation, and that the legal terms and concepts are best viewed as instruments for promoting such rights and duties. Justice Brennan's First Amendment decisions could be viewed in such light, for example. Conversely, it is possible to think of the legal system as a whole as justified within a utilitarian framework, but to think that understanding of legal concepts requires a noninstrumentalist approach; H. L. A. Hart's treatment of the criminal law arguably falls within such a description (Hart 1968) and, from quite a different point of view, a variety of neoformalist approaches to statutory interpretation and constitutional law do so as well.

Ironically, philosophy of tort law has fueled the attack on instrumentalism, even though torts was probably the field in which instrumentalism enjoyed the greatest dominance. Above all, Ernest Weinrib has advanced a rich and intricate theory of tort law that is profoundly anti-instrumentalist (Weinrib 1995). The jurisprudential core of his view is that the distinctive form of legal justification is one in which concepts play a particular role that is essentially distinct from that of *promoting* certain ends. Part of what makes tort law a form of law, on Weinrib's view, is that the concepts within it fit one another in an integrated manner, and this cluster of integrated concepts manages to realize a certain kind of normative order, rather than advancing one. The concept of a "juridical structure" within tort law, examined with great philosophical subtlety by Weinrib, suggests an entirely different model of how law gets content and meaning, if not by its role in a system aimed at promoting certain goals.

Among the most powerful arguments made against instrumentalism has been the "bipolarity critique" of instrumentalist accounts of tort law, an attack offered in slightly different forms by Weinrib and Coleman (Weinrib 1989, 1995; Coleman 1988, 2001). Briefly, both of these thinkers point out that instrumentalists must view it as a contingent matter, from a normative point of view, that defendants in tort are presumptively required to pay an amount equal to the magnitude of the plaintiff's injury. For if the tort law is viewed as aiming at efficient deterrence, it is an entirely open question whether the correct amount will match the plaintiff's injury; conversely, if it is aimed at efficient compensation. The system is a truly magnificent coincidence if it is aimed at both, and the precise magnitude of the injury from these respective parties is what would be required. By contrast, Weinrib and Coleman have each insisted that the concept of a duty to make whole is central both to corrective justice and to tort law. To seek to dig underneath this concept in favor of finding an independently specifiable social goal that is reached is to flush away the core of the justification of the system.

Weinrib has understandably been criticized for riding the pendulum too far from instrumentalism all the way to the sort of Langdellian formalism that was rejected in the early part of the last century (Rabin 1996). Whether or not that is a fair criticism, there is no doubt that Weinrib demands a level of sympathy for Hegelian and Aristotelian metaphysics that law professors cannot always muster. And yet similar ideas have emerged from Jules Coleman (Coleman 1988, 2001), Stephen Perry (Perry 1997), Martin Stone (Stone 1996, 2001), and by me (Zipursky 1998a, 2000, 2003) and by my coauthors, John Goldberg (Goldberg 1999; Goldberg and Zipursky 1998, 2001, 2002) and Arthur Ripstein (Ripstein and Zipursky 2001). Coleman was never a formalist, and yet by contemporary legal academic standards, his patience for the analysis (rather than the reduction or elimination) of legal concepts has always been remarkable. I have coined the term "pragmatic conceptualist" to connote a form of anti-instrumentalism that is open to late twentieth-century legal practice as we know it (Zipursky 2000). This view borrows from Cardozo on the one hand (Goldberg and Zipursky 1998; Goldberg 1999) and from contemporary philosophers of language on the other. Its point is that concepts and principles within a given domain are grasped by those who interact in that domain, and that their content is, in a sense, just the network of "moves" with those concepts and principles. To understand these concepts is not to adopt the right theory of the concept, from a normative point of view, but to learn what it means and be able to apply it. And the pattern of results that would flow out of these "moves" constitutes the relevant domain of law.

Moral and Political Philosophy

Thus far, I have articulated a number of debates within which the turn to philosophical ideas and philosophical analysis is natural, and has been fruitful. In these areas, law, or at least legal theory, have drawn from philosophy. In the remaining discussion, I shall (following Bernard Williams) turn the arrows around, and ask what other areas of philosophy have learned or could learn from the philosophy of tort law (Williams 1995).

Contextualism in moral thinking

In the roughly 25 years that have elapsed since Alasdair MacIntyre published his celebrated book *After Virtue*, moral philosophy has undergone several different changes. MacIntyre (1981) argued that the concepts that comprised moral and ethical thinking as a coherent whole depended upon a teleological backdrop that enlightenment thinking rendered untenable, certainly as a practical matter and possibly as a theoretical matter too. The result was the paradox of modern moral philosophy, which inevitably would be unstable and unsatisfactory because its cogency depended on a metaphysical backdrop that had been rejected. If the modern world had moved too fast for our metaphysics and morals to catch up, the unfortunate consequence was that a whole world of concepts, although basic, would not endure in any cogent, comprehensible, and transmissible form.

I suggest that philosophy of law, particularly philosophy of the private law, has retained the vitality it has as a philosophical area in part because the common law has proved itself, for better or worse, to be driven by and controlled by genuine moral concepts. Moreover, the law is durable – sometimes maddeningly so – and consequently the disintegration of moral concepts bemoaned

by MacIntyre and others need not be accepted as a foregone conclusion in the law. If these conjectures are true, at least two felicitous features are enjoyed by the philosophy of tort law. First, philosophical examination of moral concepts in tort law is particularly valuable as a form of moral anthropology. Like the cooking implements that outlast the food and drink of ancient peoples, and thereby provide valuable information about them, the enduring common law provides valuable understanding of the morality of prior cultures. Second, if MacIntyre is correct that moral concepts of a commendable and vital form are difficult to retain and reconstruct, then it is not merely a historical curiosity, but a valuable guide to affirmative normative efforts to reconstruct aspects of our moral conceptual framework, and revitalize it.

The first part of this chapter, which explored the contributions of philosophy to tort law itself, provides a useful framework within which to illustrate these points. Some concepts – like the concept of responsibility – figure pervasively within the content and structure of tort law. Other concepts – such as the concept of the duty of due care – figure within tort law in a more doctrinally structured way. Philosophy of tort law has, I believe, the potentiality to further thinking within moral theory more generally both on the level of pervasive principles, and on more focused concepts.

Consider first the concept of responsibility. To begin with, there are of course multiple distinctions corresponding to forms of liability, culpability, and obligation. To be criminally responsible for an act is different from being held liable for damages in tort. Both of these are forms of liability that can be defeated if certain features of responsibility (or their more doctrinally structured counterparts in law) are missing. In addition, there is an important way of discussing responsibility that pertains not to liability *ex post*, but to the allocation of duties, *ex ante*. Thus, for example, an assistant teacher might be responsible for the reading practice of the N-Z students, while the principal teacher was responsible for the A-M students. Or maintaining safe conduct in the swimming pool might be a camp counselor's responsibilities. Or identifying automobile models that have had significant defects and recalling them might be among a manufacturer's responsibilities. The concept of responsibility here not only mirrors morality, but is intertwined with legal concepts. Not only does the law incorporate morality in such concepts. Morality also incorporates legal concepts.

Stephen Perry's excellent work on outcome responsibility, discussed above, provides an illuminating account of the sense in which legal responsibility in torts for outcomes has a prelegal foundation in ideas pertaining to moral responsibility and fault (Perry 1992, 1997, 2001). I think that there is much to this suggestion, and do not mean to undercut it by suggesting that the opposite is probably also true; that there is a domain of moral attributions of responsibility whose origin and interpretation requires an understanding of institutional – and perhaps legal – arrangements that allocate blame and liability for bad outcomes. As Arthur Ripstein and Jules Coleman have argued, there are domains in which the allocation of liability and the shifting of costs are probably not prelegal, where our moral judgment is relatively amorphous and there is a more probing political and institutional account of how responsibility judgments are constituted (Ripstein 1998; Coleman and Ripstein 1995; Coleman 2001). I would suggest that accountability for injuries caused by defective products, and a broader range of enterprise liability falls into this category, for example. Yet in these areas we certainly deploy moral concepts of responsibility too. Here, I would be inclined to think the legal concepts will play a role in understanding the moral ones.

More generally, what it means to hold someone responsible, how responsibility for groups works, what the relation between state of mind and responsibility is, and how responsibility relates to freedom and voluntariness are all questions that have both moral and legal aspects. If contemporary moral philosophers are right to suggest that the abstractness and acontextuality of the framing of moral problems often plays a large role in their evolution into conundrums – and I think they are – then philosophical examination of legal aspects of these problems will also illuminate their moral aspects.

For a variety of broad, but somewhat more pigeon-holed concepts, such as intent, duties of care, injury, and negligence, the river between moral and legal understanding flows in both directions. Duty within negligence law again provides a strong example. An important debate over the past 25 years in moral philosophy is whether all duties are universal, and essentially require of moral agents impartiality among all persons as obligees, or whether the superficially attractive idea that some duties are agent-relative is in fact morally defensible (even apart from contractual obligations). There is little doubt that, according to common-sense morality or folk morality, or late twentieth- and early twenty-first-century Western morality, agent-relative duties exist and are fairly prominent on our moral landscape (Nagel 1986; Scheffler 1994). There is also little doubt that the law of torts and beyond are rife with agent-relative duties, even apart from contract. The questions in both morality and law is whether such duties are defensible, and if so, what their range, nature, content, and ground of justification is.

These are obviously complex questions that I am not about to answer here. What I am commenting upon is, however, one of the reasons that philosophy of tort law makes sense as a subject, and more particularly, the idea that moral philosophy more broadly can learn from philosophy of tort law – now in the context of whether agent-relative duties are defensible. What tort law teaches us, John Goldberg and I have argued, is that those who think in terms of duties of care, by virtue of the structure of the concept of duty, highlight a domain of persons and a domain of goods for those persons as ones on which a certain kind of focus and vigilance and responsiveness is of the highest priority. The nature of the vigilance, the responsiveness, and the prioritization are all sensitive to the institutional context and the ramifications for liability and courts. Agent relativity simultaneously emerges from this context as a rather appropriate kind of link, and also serves a certain function by permitting vigilance to develop and play a role where certain kinds of bonds exist. The concepts and institutions of the law solidify and perpetuate these roles and bonds.

If this picture of the duties in the law of negligence is correct, then it suggests a possible route for understanding agent-relativity in morality too. Moral duties of care that are recognized by folk morality tend to relate to family, friendships, and groups of social organization. To some degree they relate to expectations, but there is a circularity here that will be vicious if we do not offer an explanation of why the expectations are what they are. The legal account suggests that, as Mill and Sidgwick recognized, the sanctions of conscience ingrained through folk morality structure our patterns of vigilance, care, and responsiveness, so that we prioritize those with whom we have certain kinds of relationships over others. Just as patterns of legally recognized duties of care within, say, hospitals or governments, make those institutions possible, so patterns of moral duties within friendships and families play a role in making these possible (Raz 1994). The scope, content, and nature of these patterns of care and vigilance within ordinary morality are less structured and perhaps more intuitive than on the legal level. But the legal case – the case within negligence law – provides a powerful analytical framework for thinking about the moral level. I would argue that theories of intent, causation, fault, reasonableness, restitution – even the concepts of fact and opinion – could provide similar illumination to debates within substantive moral and political philosophy.

Distributive justice and corrective justice

Finally, philosophy of tort law has made a substantial contribution to philosophical theorizing about justice. The previous section on 'Jurisprudence and Legal Theory' discussed legal theory's building upon Rawls in the philosophy of tort law. Here I shall discuss the possibility that political theory can break out of a Rawlsian conception of the subject matter of theories of justice by building upon tort theory.

John Rawls's *A Theory of Justice* (1971) is probably the most important piece of political theory in the English-speaking world of the past century. While its scope is remarkable, Rawls's theory of justice is ultimately an account of only certain aspects and forms of justice, sometimes lumped under the heading "distributive justice." I am doubtful that this is really just one large form of justice – considering that Rawls addresses not

only the distribution of goods and posts but also the basic structure of a just society. Putting that question to one side, Rawls's own title and a generation of scholars have taken Rawls's work to demarcate boundaries of the subject of justice. As discussed above, this was notable not only because of the depth and quality of Rawls's own theory of justice, but also because it developed a philosophical approach that, both in plan and in execution, displayed justice as a different, and in some ways superior, value to social welfare.

Tort theory has brought an entirely different aspect of justice to the forefront of political philosophy. "Corrective justice" is of course the label used, and it is distinguished from "distributive justice." There are other forms of justice that have been interestingly developed, most notably "retributive justice" within the criminal law. But the depth and philosophical breadth of corrective justice theory have made it a uniquely important foil of and complement to distributive justice within political theory. Moreover, the pedigree of this pair of forms of justice comes from Aristotle's *Nicomachean Ethics* (1962) leading many to suspect that a full philosophical theory of justice would have to reckon with both halves. If constitutional law, property law, and tax policy are the legal domains that most usefully accompany theoretical examination of issues in distributive justice, tort law is the legal domain that most usefully complements theoretical examination of issues in corrective justice.

Aristotle distinguished corrective justice from distributive justice using mathematical metaphors. Distributive justice is geometric and involves proportionality in the allocation of goods among members of society. Corrective justice is arithmetic, and involves adding back what has been taken away, or subtracted, from someone. The one who adds back is the one who gained from a transaction or activity more than he or she should have. The rendering even between the two parties is corrective justice, on the Aristotelian account.

This distinction between "corrective justice" and "distributive justice" has been criticized on numerous grounds; I suggest, simply for purposes of demarcating a domain of study, a different basis of distinction. What is remarkable about the Rawlsian domain of justice is that justice is an attribute of a state or system, in the first instance. Relatedly, justice is like beauty or fairness or transparency: it is an attribute that, as a matter of logical form, is enjoyed or not enjoyed by an entity at a time. Distributive justice is, in this sense, *static*.

Corrective justice is a different sort of thing, I suggest, following Weinrib (Weinrib 1995). The phrases "justice is done" or "let justice be done" connote the idea that justice is something that is done in certain processes or transactions. Now certainly distributive justice could be done, in the sense that changes could occur that transform a state that is unjust from a distributive point of view into one that is just. But here, the nonstatic sense of justice is derivative of the static sense. The idea of justice being done contemplates, I believe, a primary sense of justice at the level of the doing, or the event, or the transaction. A court's doing justice or a private party's doing justice is not usually conceived of as the reestablishment of a state of affairs that is incontrovertibly distributively just. The opinion of whether justice has been done is surely sensitive to the past and the context; indeed, the judgment of whether justice has been done cannot be made until we know in response to what a court or private party has acted. The point, however, is that as a matter of form the sort of justice we are considering now pertains in the first instance to acts or events or doings – all of which occur through time and are processes. The noun "justice" is not simply a conjugation of the adjective "just," referring to the static attribute of being just. And "doing justice" is not simply putting things into a state of affairs that enjoys the attribute of being just. In this sense, the concept of justice is capable of being nonstatic, or what I would call *dynamic*.

If these remarks are plausible then corrective justice theory can be viewed, most broadly, as the philosophical examination of the dynamic aspect of justice, while distributive justice theory is the philosophical examination of the static aspect of justice, particularly of the state. Not all of those who would call themselves "corrective justice theorists" would accept this characterization, but even the attempt to avoid dynamic conceptions of justice is itself extraordinarily illuminating. Thus, for example, to return to the exploration of responsibility, Perry conceives of corrective justice as a form of distributive justice in which losses are allocated fairly by considering fault and the connections between conduct and consequence that constitutes "outcome responsibility" (Perry 1992). Ripstein conceives of tort law in terms of "risk ownership" within a system that involves fair and equal terms in the distribution of risk ownership (Ripstein 1998). It is a subtle question whether corrective justice, for Perry or Ripstein, involves a dynamic conception of justice or merely a static conception, applied to a very different sort of good and equality than we usually think.

Weinrib is a corrective justice theorist in precisely the sense I have described, and, indeed, is largely responsible for the reinvigoration of this branch of political philosophy emanating out of Aristotle. Corrective justice involves *rectification* or, more colloquially, *setting things right*. The idea of justice being done is an idea of rectification being done. Various philosophers of tort law have offered different theories of what constitutes rectification. Weinrib himself analyzes rectification as a restoration of a normative equilibrium, and argues that a synthesis of Aristotle, Kant, and Hegel yields an understanding of normative equilibrium. A larger group of scholars, including Epstein, Wright, and Gordley (the latter two, purporting to follow Aristotle), understand rectification in a manner that tracks property rights more closely (Epstein 1973; Gordley 1995; Wright 1995). Margaret Radin understands rectification in communicative terms, as the sending of a countermessage that negates the message of the wrongdoer (Radin 1993). Hampton explored a parallel variation of retributive justice in criminal law (Hampton 1988). Ripstein's book has interestingly synthesized a number of aspects of these views (Ripstein 1998).

In my own work, I have offered what is, in an important sense, a more subjective interpretation of the dynamic form of justice that acts as a foil to distributive justice, an idea sufficiently different from corrective justice to merit a different name: "civil recourse" (Zipursky 1998b, 2002, 2003). I have argued that a domain of justice involves *response* to wrongdoing (indeed, the word "responsibility" connotes the idea of who is properly the object of a response). However, what our modern political state offers, at least in common law systems, is not necessarily an approximation to an objective form of setting things right. Rather, it offers those who have been wronged a means of responding to those wrongdoings, and both defines and constrains the nature and magnitude of permissible response to wrongdoing. The law of torts embodies what I have called a "principle of civil recourse": in denying individuals the raw liberty to respond aggressively to having been wronged, it is incumbent upon the state to provide each person an avenue of civil recourse against the wrongdoer. A right of action is an artificial, civil, means of redress with which the state empowers each citizen, in order to provide an avenue of recourse. Yet a right of action in tort is simply an individual's legal power to seek redress; its exercise does not necessarily, or even in principle, entail that justice will be done. Corrective justice is perhaps what we individually and socially aspire to as a regulative ideal. But the structure of our tort law is better understood as affording and constraining an individual's opportunity to pursue justice, than as comprising society's effort to do so.

These philosophical theories of tort law are underdeveloped, particularly in comparison with the philosophical riches that enlightenment thinkers and Rawls and his critics have provided in the theory of distributive justice. But what they have contributed, which is surely of enormous importance in political and legal philosophy, is a recognition of an entirely different aspect of justice, one that likely equals distributive justice in its importance for understanding and evaluating our legal system and our aspirations to realize and apply the more primitive sense of justice upon which we rely to guide our social and political world. For once we see this form of justice in tort theory, we see that a wide range of public and private law do appear to seek a form of justice quite different from distributive justice, even if they also appear to seek that.

Conclusion

Tort law is in many ways the simplest area of law. In this sense, it stands to the legal philosopher as the ball of wax does to the epistemologist or the metaphysician.

Its simplicity ironically invites the deepest inquiries. It invites basic questions about what justice is, how morality and justice are intertwined, how legal concepts shape conduct but also constitute forms of thinking, and how deontic and utilitarian notions share the playing field in the arena of law. Philosophers of tort law have probed in these areas and proceeded to deeper levels than philosophers of law have previously reached.

At the same time, tort law is not only quotidian at a conceptual level, its problems touch almost every area of conduct in daily life. It is therefore not surprising that the relatively comfortable concepts with which the tort law began, and which, because of the place of precedent in the common law, constitute tort law, have provided an almost dizzying array of conceptual puzzles as we have forged ahead with new sorts of activities, problems, injuries, and torts. Here too, philosophical inquiry has offered the means to continue on our framework of concepts, reflectively pruning that framework so as to retain an intelligible form that we are willing to stand by.

References

Aristotle. 1962. *Nicomachean Ethics,* trans. M. Ostwald. New York: Bobbs-Merrill, Book 5.4.

Calabresi, Guido. 1970. *The Costs of Accidents.* New Haven, CT: Yale University Press.

Coase, R. H. 1960. The problem of social cost. *Journal of Law and Economics* 3: 1–44.

Coleman, Jules L. 1976. The morality of strict tort liability. *William and Mary Law Review* 18: 259–86.

Coleman, Jules L. 1983. Moral theories of tort: Their scope and limits: Part 2. *Law and Philosophy* 2: 5–36.

Coleman, Jules L. 1988. The economic structure of tort law. *Yale Law Journal* 97: 1233–53.

Coleman, Jules L. 1992. *Risks and Wrongs.* Cambridge, UK: Cambridge University Press.

Coleman, Jules L. 2001. *The Practice of Principle: In Defense of a Pragmatist Approach to Legal Theory.* Oxford: Oxford University Press.

Coleman, Jules L. and Ripstein, Arthur. 1995. Mischief and misfortune. *McGill Law Journal* 41: 91–130.

Epstein, Richard A. 1973. A theory of strict liability. *Journal of Legal Studies* 2: 151–204.

Feldman, Heidi Li. 2000. Prudence, benevolence, and negligence: Virtue ethics and tort law. *Chicago-Kent Law Review* 74: 1431–66.

Finnis, John. 1995. Intention in tort law. In D. Owen (ed.), *Philosophical Foundations of Tort Law.* Oxford: Clarendon Press: 229–47.

Fletcher, George P. 1972. Fairness and utility in tort theory. *Harvard Law Review* 85: 537–64.

Goldberg, John C. P. 1999. The life of the law. *Stanford Law Review* 51: 1419, 1436–55.

Goldberg, John C. P. and Zipursky, Benjamin C. 1998. The moral of MacPherson. *University of Pennsylvania Law Review* 146: 1733–1847.

Goldberg, John C. P. and Zipursky, Benjamin C. 2001. The Restatement (third) and the place of duty in negligence law. *Vanderbilt Law Review* 544: 657, 658–9.

Goldberg, John C. P. and Zipursky, Benjamin C. 2002. Unrealized torts. *Virginia Law Review* 88: 1625–1719.

Gordley, James. 1995. Tort law and the Aristotelian tradition. In D. Owen (ed.), *Philosophical Foundations of Tort Law.* Oxford: Clarendon Press, 131–58.

Green, Leon. 1928. The duty problem in negligence cases (part I). *Columbia Law Review* 28: 1014–45.

Hampton, Jean. 1988. The retributive idea. In Jeffrey G. Murphy and Jean Hampton, *Forgiveness and Mercy.* Cambridge, UK: Cambridge University Press, 111–61.

Hart, H. L. A. 1961. *The Concept of Law.* Oxford: Oxford University Press.

Hart, H. L. A. 1968. *Punishment and Responsibility: Essays in the Philosophy of Law.* New York: Oxford University Press.

Holmes, Jr, Oliver Wendell. 1897. The path of the law. *Harvard Law Review* 10: 457–78.

Honoré, Tony. 1988. Responsibility and luck. *Law Quarterly Review* 104: 530–53.

Keating, Gregory C. 1996. Reasonableness and rationality in negligence theory. *Stanford Law Review* 48: 311–84.

Keating, Gregory C. 1997. The idea of fairness in the law of enterprise liability. *Michigan Law Review* 96: 1266–1380.

Keating, Gregory C. 2001. A social contract conception of the tort law of accidents. In G. Postema (ed.), *Philosophy and the Law of Torts.* Cambridge, UK and New York: Cambridge University Press, 22–71.

Macintyre, Alasdair. 1981. *After Virtue.* London: Duckworth.

Nagel, Thomas. 1986. *The View From Nowhere.* New York: Oxford University Press.

Perry, Stephen R. 1989. The impossibility of general strict liability. *Journal of Product Liability.* 383–419.

Perry, Stephen R. 1992. The moral foundations in tort law. *Iowa Law Review* 77: 449–514.

Perry, Stephen R. 1997. Two models of legal principles. *Iowa Law Review* 82: 787–819.

Perry, Stephen R. 2001. Responsibility for outcomes, risk, and the law of torts. In G. Postema (ed.), *Philosophy and the Law of Torts.* Cambridge, UK and New York: Cambridge University Press, 72–130.

Posner, Richard A. 1972. A theory of negligence. *Journal of Legal Studies* 1: 29–76.

Rabin, Robert. 1996. Law for law's sake. *Yale Law Journal* 105: 2261–83.

Radin, Margaret Jane. 1993. Compensation and commensurability. *Duke Law Journal* 43: 56–86.

Rawls, John. 1971. *A Theory of Justice.* Cambridge, MA: Harvard University Press.

Raz, Joseph. 1994. *Ethics in the Public Domain: Essays in the Morality of Law and Politics.* Oxford: Oxford University Press.

Ripstein, Arthur. 1998. *Equality, Responsibility and the Law.* New York: Cambridge University Press.

Ripstein, Arthur and Zipursky, Benjamin C. 2001. Corrective justice in an age of mass torts. In G. Postema (ed.), *Philosophy and the Law of Torts.* Cambridge, UK and New York: Cambridge University Press, 214–49.

Scheffler, Samuel. 1994. *The Rejection of Consequentialism*, revised edn. Oxford: Clarendon Press.

Sebok, Anthony. 2001. Purpose, belief, and recklessness: Pruning the *Restatement (Third)'s* definition of intent. *Vanderbilt Law Review* 54: 1165–86.

Stone, Martin. 1996. On the idea of private law. *Canadian Journal of Law and Jurisprudence* 9: 235–77.

Stone, Martin. 2001. The significance of doing and suffering. In G. Postema (ed.), *Philosophy and the Law of Torts.* Cambridge, UK and New York: Cambridge University Press, 131–82.

Summers, Robert S. 1982. *Instrumentalism and American Legal Theory.* Ithaca, NY: Cornell University Press.

Weinrib, Ernest J. 1983. Toward a moral theory of negligence law. *Law and Philosophy* 2: 37–62.

Weinrib, Ernest J. 1988. Legal formalism: On the imminent rationality of law. *Yale Law Journal* 97: 949–1016.

Weinrib, Ernest J. 1989. Understanding tort law. *Valparaiso University Law Review* 23: 485, 494–526.

Weinrib, Ernest J. 1995. *The Idea of Private Law.* Cambridge, MA: Harvard University Press.

Williams, Bernard. 1995. Afterword: What has philosophy to learn from tort law? In D. Owen (ed.), *Philosophical Foundations of Tort Law.* Oxford: Clarendon Press, 487–97.

Wright, Richard. 1995. Right, justice and tort law. In D. Owen (ed.), *Philosophical Foundations of Tort Law*. Oxford: Clarendon Press, 159–82.

Zipursky, Benjamin C. 1998a. Legal malpractice and the structure of negligence law. *Fordham Law Review* 67: 649–90.

Zipursky, Benjamin C. 1998b. Rights, wrongs, and recourse in the law of torts. *Vanderbilt Law Review* 51: 1–100.

Zipursky, Benjamin C. 2000. Pragmatic conceptualism. *Legal Theory* 6: 457–85.

Zipursky, Benjamin C. 2002. The philosophy of private law. In Jules Coleman and Scott Shapiro (eds.), *The Oxford Handbook of Jurisprudence and Philosophy of Law*. New York: Oxford University Press, 623–55.

Zipursky, Benjamin C. 2003. Civil recourse, not corrective justice. *Georgetown Law Journal* 91: 695–796.

Chapter 9

Contract Theory

Eric A. Posner

Introduction

Contract law governs a range of behavior loosely connected by the idea of promising. When X proposes to Y an exchange of money, goods, or services, and Y accepts, we say by convention that X and Y exchange promises. If X or Y subsequently breaks that promise, contract law determines whether the victim of the breach is entitled to a remedy. The victim will be denied a remedy if a valid offer and acceptance were not exchanged, or if the promise was not supported by consideration or reasonable reliance, or if the promisor has an excuse, or if the promise is indefinite; and so forth. Contract law also determines the nature of the remedy, and provides background interpretive presumptions for use when the terms of the contract are vague or incomplete. Sometimes courts push interpretive presumptions aggressively, so that parties can be bound to promises that they did not make – treated as if they made a certain promise – as when a warranty is implied for a sale of goods by a seller who had no such intention and said no such thing. Because promises are not enforceable when formal requirements like consideration are not satisfied, and because nonpromissory representations can generate liability under the principles of contract law, the idea of promise can be only a starting point for understanding contract law: the two are not co-extensive.

Theories of contract law purport to show that contract law has an internal logic and that the logic is normatively attractive or, in the case of

critical theories, grounded in historical contingency or struggles for power among competing groups. See CRITICAL LEGAL THEORY. The first group of theories divides into welfarist and nonwelfarist approaches. The welfarist approach comprehends only one theory: the law and economics theory. The nonwelfarist approaches come in many flavors, but can be conveniently divided into "liberal" or "promissory" theories, and "corrective justice" or "reliance" theories.

My focus is the philosophical justification for contract doctrine (welfarist, nonwelfarist, etc.), and not the analytic question of whether contract doctrine can be unified conceptually (contract as promise, as reliance, as transfer, etc.) (see Smith 2000; Kraus 2002). To be sure, the latter question is the topic of much writing; and it has been the practice of nonwelfarists to try to find the central unifying idea of contract law as well as a philosophical justification for it. For these reasons discussion of both topics is unavoidable. But I am less interested in the second question and will not give it the attention that some philosophers think it deserves.

Welfarism: Law and Economics

The economic theory of contract law holds, minimally, that economic concepts can be used to illuminate contract law. A more aggressive version of the theory holds that contract law has an economic logic. Not all scholars within law and economics hold this view – indeed, most criticize contract law for failing to meet economic criteria – but the extreme view lends itself to expository crispness, and for that reason I will focus on it.

This "economic theory of contract law" assumes that (1) individuals conform to the rationality assumptions of economic theory; and (2) contract law promotes "efficiency." The first premise is that individuals have preferences over states of the world; that people's behavior conforms to their preferences; that these preferences are consistent and transitive; and that they can be represented as utility functions. In addition, people have high enough discount factors and find it worthwhile to invest in legal advice. Otherwise, the law would not affect people's behavior. See ECONOMIC RATIONALITY IN THE ANALYSIS OF LEGAL RULES AND INSTITUTIONS.

The second premise might seem to invite standard criticisms about the normative force of efficiency, which also infect the descriptive project to the extent one doubts that judges would enforce normatively unattractive rules. From an *ex post* perspective, the court takes money from one person and gives it to another, and it might seem difficult to make the proper welfare comparisons. But economists think of contract law from an *ex ante* perspective: as an institution that parties voluntarily invoke in order to arrange their affairs. When the rules are *ex post* inefficient in the Kaldor–Hicks sense – that is, when they result in an obligation that costs the obligor more than it benefits the obligee – then the parties will either avoid contracts, or use elaborate and costly contracts in order to avoid the inefficient rules. When the rules are *ex post* efficient but also seem to impose a hardship on one party, the parties can arrange *ex ante* for a transfer that compensates expected losers. The economic project assumes that judges would enforce efficient rules because the judges see themselves as minimizing the cost of contracting for all parties, and thus making all parties, in an *ex ante* sense, better off.

To understand what efficiency requires, one must first see that contract-related behavior occurs along many margins. A person must decide how much to invest in finding a contract partner; how vigorously to negotiate; whether to reveal private information during bargaining; whether to make a promise or not; whether to "rely" on the promise made by someone else;

whether to perform a promise or not; whether to renegotiate the promise or not; and so forth. Each of these decisions constitutes a separate dimension of efficiency: contract law could, for example, provide optimal incentives to search for a partner, but not to gather information prior to entering the contract. The literature has investigated all of these decisions, but the two decisions that have received the most attention are the decision to perform or breach, and the decision to rely. (For surveys, with citations, see R. A. Posner 1998; Kaplow and Shavell 2001.)

Let two parties, S and B, enter a contract for a trade that will take place at some future time. Prior to the trade B can make an investment that would increase the value which he attaches to performance. If transaction costs were zero, they would enter a "complete" contract that specifies that trade will occur only when B's valuation exceeds S's cost. The contract would also specify the level of B's investment – that is, the optimal amount of investment given the probability of trade. But because transaction costs are positive, the parties might enter an "incomplete" contract that does not identify "good" and "bad" states in which trade should and should not occur, and that does not specify the level of investment, but instead simply says that at the future time there will be a trade.

Contract law produces the same outcome as the complete (efficient) contract by providing the optimal terms in the form of default rules. Expectation damages produce *ex post* efficiency by giving the promisor the option to pay the promisee's valuation or perform. If, for example, S's cost is higher than B's valuation, S will pay damages; if not, S will perform. Thus, S will perform if and only if S's cost is less than B's valuation – and *ex post* efficiency is satisfied. Therefore, expectation damages are efficient with respect to the decision whether to perform or breach.

However, expectation damages also make B indifferent between performance and nonperformance – he gets his valuation in both cases. Thus, B will "overrely" in the sense of investing as though the efficiency of performance were certain, rather than stochastic, if such is the case. Thus, expectation damages are not efficient with respect to the incentive to rely.

These standard arguments have been qualified in many ways. Expectation damages are not likely to be efficient even with respect to the breach decision if, as seems likely in many cases, courts cannot determine B's valuation and thus fix an equivalent monetary sum. In that case, specific performance is likely to be more efficient than expectation damages, as specific performance does not require an independent valuation by the court. The standard explanation for the superiority of expectation damages to specific performance – that expectation damages do not require renegotiation of the contract when performance is inefficient – is questionable. S has the motive, and usually will have the opportunity, to pay B to release her from the contract when cost exceeds valuation, and B has no reason to resist, though the two parties might haggle over the division of the surplus.

Indeed, the consensus today is, I think, that the doctrines of contract law are not necessarily the most efficient rules. There are several reasons for this consensus (Posner 2003).

First, as we have seen, contract doctrines do not appear to conform to the predictions of simple economic models of the contracting promise. Specific performance is likely to be superior to expectation damages, yet expectation damages are the rule. Even if the cost of renegotiation is high, it is not clear that expectation damages produce optimal incentives. Other models have trouble explaining other doctrines – mistake, impossibility, and so forth.

Second, more complex models usually make indeterminate predictions about the doctrines of contract law. Models of asymmetric information in contract negotiations (e.g., Ayres and Gertner 1989) make the optimality of default rules turn on a range of variables – including the distribution of valuations in the populations of buyers and sellers – that cannot plausibly be measured or estimated by scholars or judges. This conclusion has led to a resurgence of the view that courts should enforce contracts formalistically (e.g., Schwartz 1998), but that view is itself based on an unverified and probably unverifiable empirical conjecture about the abilities of courts and the complexity of contracting behavior.

Third, the central motivating concept of the economic approach to contract law – that of

transaction costs interfering with optimal contracts – is ambiguous. Transaction costs make judicial creativity – and the various doctrines of contract law – necessary. If transaction costs were zero, parties would enter complete contracts and courts would have the task of specifically enforcing all terms (except when the contract harms third parties). However, even if transaction costs are high, parties could enter relatively simple (in the sense of short), albeit complicated (in the sense of cognitively challenging), contracts that would produce optimal results, or results that are superior to those that courts could impose through the creation of default rules. Contractual incompleteness is likely the result of bounded rationality, rather than transaction costs, but then the behavioral premises of the economics of contract law are violated. If parties are not rational enough to design optimal contracts, then they might not be rational enough to respond to legal incentives to act efficiently (Posner 2003).

None of these criticisms denies the value of economics for shedding light on contract law, but the criticisms do suggest that an "economic theory of contract law" is likely to be coarse-grained. A market economy produces greater wealth than plausible alternatives, and any market economy needs an institution for enabling people to make commitments. Contract law is, at the most general level, the institutional form that gives people the power to make commitments when reputation and other nonlegal sanctions are insufficient (Posner 2000). But many alternative doctrines might serve this purpose equally well, in which case economic theory will not distinguish between them, or at best provide partial explanations or rationalizations.

Another possible reason for the descriptive weaknesses of the economic model is that contract law does not reflect welfarist premises, and instead reflects other norms, the topic of the next section.

Nonwelfarist theories

Many legal philosophers reject the welfarist approach to contract law and argue that contract law reflects nonwelfarist commitments. Two views have received the most attention. The first is that contract law reflects corrective justice by forcing the breacher to return a wrongful gain to the victim. The second is that contract law respects the autonomy of promisor and promisee by forcing promisors to keep their promises. (A very useful survey is Benson 1996.)

Corrective justice

The corrective justice theory is often called the reliance theory because of its focus on the reliance of the promisee (Fuller and Perdue 1936; Gilmore 1974; Atiyah 1981). A person B promises that if S produces a widget, B will buy it. S invests in new machinery (thus, "relying" on the promise), and then B announces that he will not keep his promise. S has incurred a sunk cost which she cannot recover by producing and selling the widget to someone else.

To explain why S should recover her reliance cost, reliance theorists liken B's actions to a tort. Just as a driver wrongs pedestrians by negligently running over them, so does B wrong S by failing to perform after inducing reliance. If, as reliance theorists assume, corrective justice demands that the pedestrians recover from the tortfeasor for the injury, then corrective justice also demands that S recover from B for the reliance loss. B's action has made S worse off than she was in the status quo; B ought to compensate S for the harm.

The theory does not on its own terms explain much about contract law. It does not explain why victims of breach of contract can recover damages even if they do not rely. The theory suggests that promissory estoppel should be the basis of liability, not the consideration doctrine; but promissory estoppel remains a subsidiary doctrine. The theory implies, according to Fuller and Perdue, that reliance damages are the appropriate remedy, not expectation damages or specific performance. Fuller and Perdue point out that in a market the reliance loss will include opportunity cost, so expectation damages and reliance damages will be equal; and expectation damages might otherwise be a reasonable, because more measurable, proxy for reliance. But the fact is that expectation

damages are the routine measure of damages, and reliance damages are reserved for unusual cases, or cases where the profit cannot be calculated.

Another problem with the theory is its invocation of corrective justice. In tort theory, the status quo is taken to be existing property rights. The tortfeasor causes harm by violating these rights. In contract theory, the status quo is more difficult to specify. The "reliance interest" – the expected return on the investment that the promisee makes in anticipation of performance – could be considered a kind of property interest, deprivation of which justifies a remedy. But it need not be so considered; it could be thought of as a gratuitous act by which the promisee voluntarily risks disappointment. By contrast to tort, where the victim is (in the standard case) a passive recipient of the wrongdoer's act, promisees voluntarily make an investment in the hope that the promisors will keep their promise. To say that corrective justice obliges the promisor to compensate the victim, one must first show that the right to the return on this investment is part of the victim's background entitlements (Craswell 1991, 2000).

The problem could be solved in two ways. The first would be to revert to welfarism and argue that the reliance interest should be protected because otherwise optimal investment would not occur. This approach explains why contract law protects reliance, but does away with corrective justice. The second would show that reliance, or some kinds of reliance, are protected by conventional practices or understandings, and for that reason should be thought of as part of the promisee's entitlements. This argument would preserve a role for corrective justice, but it depends on empirical premises that would be difficult to establish.

Defenders of the reliance theory have argued instead that the failure of contract law to conform to the requirements of the reliance theory shows that contract law is unjust. Atiyah and Gilmore argue that contract law has served an ideological purpose: it promotes the market, and reflects laissez faire prejudices. For that reason, their project becomes one of excavating the historical record for evidence of a purer contract law at an earlier stage of development, subsequently compromised by judges with ideological blinders. (See also Gordley 1991.) But in the absence of a reason for thinking that the reliance theory itself reflects moral commitments grounded in corrective justice or other concepts, their arguments cannot be accepted.

Liberal theory

The second type of nonwelfarist theory derives contract law from the morality of promising or cooperating. Fried (1981) argues that people have a natural or moral right to alienate their property. They do so by exchanging it for other things, and this inevitably involves making promises. If the law did not enforce promises, people would have difficulty making binding promises, and so an important aspect of their freedom would be lacking.

Barnett (1986) argues that the law concerns itself with protecting people from nonconsensual takings of their property. Tort law is a prominent example. But if people consent to alienation, then the law should permit that alienation. Contract law enforces promises because by making a promise people consent to its enforcement by the law.

Scanlon (2001) emphasizes the perspective of the promisee. Just as individuals have a right not to be deceived by the representations of others, they have the right not to be misled by the promises of others. Contract law protects this right by giving the promisee a remedy when a promise is broken. (For yet another theory, see Raz 1994.)

These theories share the premise that the law should respect individual autonomy. Autonomous people have the freedom to arrange their lives in any way that they see fit, as long as they do not violate the autonomy of others. If people consent to the transfer of their property through a promise, then legal enforcement of that promise is unobjectionable. If people make promises, then they seek to bind themselves, and legal enforcement of those promises can only enhance their autonomy. And if people rely on the promises of others, then the law can help protect their autonomy from violation through opportunistic promise breaking by the others.

Autonomy is a significant value but it is also a complex idea and has ambiguous implications for the law. People exercise autonomy by making binding promises, but, arguably, they also exer-

cise autonomy when they choose not to keep a promise. Thus, the law might violate their autonomy if it compels them to pay damages or perform the promise. A more complex view is that promisors should not be compelled to perform extremely burdensome promises when expectations are disappointed by remote events (cf. Kronman 1983). The implications for the law, in any event, are obscure.

Fried avoids these problems by focusing on the promise; Barnett, by focusing on consent at the time of contracting. But even taken on their own terms, the theories do not explain doctrine very well. Fried acknowledges that under his theory gratuitous promises should be enforced, when in fact they often are not. But the real problem for his theory is that it does not tell us whether gratuitous promises should be enforced or not. Liberal courts could reasonably believe that the gratuitousness of a promise is an adequate proxy for the parties' desire or expectation that the promise not be legally enforced (Fuller 1941). Craswell (1989) points out in another context that Fried and Barnett's theories are compatible with any remedy that penalizes the promisor for violating a promise. The bare fact that a promise should under general conditions be enforced does not tell us whether expectation damages, reliance damages, or specific performance should be the remedy. (For a defense of Fried's theory against Craswell's criticisms, see Kraus 2002.)

For this reason, Scanlon's argument is of interest, as he asserts that his theory justifies expectation damages or specific performance, as opposed to reliance damages. He says, suppose that X wants Y not to reveal information about X. X promises to pay Y $100 in five years if Y does not reveal this information to someone else. Under the reliance measure, X cannot commit to paying Y the $100 – for if X breaches and Y does not "rely" in the sense of giving up the opportunity to exchange the information for a benefit, Y would not recover anything. But then Y might not agree to the contract in the first place.

Scanlon's argument does not so much justify expectation damages (or specific performance) over reliance damages, as explain why courts should defer to parties' arrangements. A default rule of reliance damages would be unobjectionable as long as the parties can opt out of it by agreeing to an enforceable liquidated damages provision (cf. Craswell 1989).

Related ideas are Benson's (2001) argument that a contract should be considered a transfer of an interest from promisor to promisee, and Smith's (2000) argument that a contract should be seen as akin to the creation of a new property interest. Neither scholar makes a purely promissory argument. Promises by themselves do not give promisees the right to enforcement under liberal premises because promisees are not injured by nonperformance of a promise unless they rely, and reliance by itself cannot be the basis for a right because it is freely chosen. Both scholars thus argue that the promisee has a property right in the enforcement of the promise. For Benson, this property right exists because the promisor transfers it, just as the owner of a good can transfer it to a buyer or donee; for Smith, the property right exists because the promisor creates it in the same way that a person can create a property interest by catching a wild animal or inventing a new product.

Benson and Smith are more interested in producing an internally consistent analysis of contract doctrine than (especially in Benson's case) providing a moral justification for it. But one is entitled to be skeptical about the likelihood that these redescriptions of the interests at stake can be given a philosophical defense. Autonomy, as we have seen, is an insufficiently determinate notion; and corrective justice requires an explanation for the baseline property entitlements. An appeal to the common good needs to be distinguished from welfarism, which can do without the analytic distinctions that Benson and Smith propose.

Historical Explanations

Contract law has changed over the years. In the eighteenth century and before, courts enforced all kinds of agreements, but a recognizable system of "contract law" did not come into existence until the nineteenth century, both in England and the United States. This system became increasingly formal, abstract, and unified over the course of the century, with disparate areas of the law – sales, insurance, debtor–creditor – being stripped of their idiosyncrasies and merged into a single general contract law. Conventional wisdom places the apogee of this system in the second half of the nineteenth century. At the same time, laissez faire ideology was at its height, and there has been since then a persistent identification of formal contract law and market morality. The twentieth century is seen as one of a decline of contract law, in both senses: the decline of the formalism of contract law; and decreasing government deference to voluntary agreements (see, e.g., Gilmore 1974, Friedman 1985, Atiyah 1979).

The historical variation – and for that matter, variation across jurisdiction – poses questions for those who seek a theory of contract law. If contract law reflects a single moral structure, what accounts for its variation across time and place? There are many possibilities. First, morality changes across time and place; or, the deep moral commitments (like corrective justice) remain constant, and embodied in the law, even as more superficial commitments change. Second, morality remains constant, but empirical conditions change. Thus, economics at one time was thought to offer a general theory – welfare maximization – that predicts different laws in different jurisdiction where empirical conditions vary. Or political conditions change, with courts and other government institutions, for their own reasons including the amount of prestige they hold, becoming more or less willing to bend contractual behavior to the demands of morality. Third, contract law does not reflect general moral commitments, but is a hodgepodge, reflecting not just moral ideas, but politics, mistakes, ideologies, general institutional developments, and so forth.

The third view has attracted historians and critics of market institutions. Indeed, we have seen that welfarists are more likely to criticize contract law than defend it, and in their criticism is the implicit concession that contract law has over history deviated from proper welfarist premises. Gilmore, Atiyah, and others think that contract law was distorted by the laissez faire craze of the nineteenth century and today reflects more humane commitments. Other scholars have emphasized the relationship between contract law and changes in legal institutions such as the jury and the court system. Simpson (1987), for example, argues that the modern hostility to penalties can be traced to a trend from private enforcement to public enforcement of the law, before which penalties were enforced.

These theories, and others as well, fall into the trap of mistaking correlation for causation. Gilmore (1974) cannot resist connecting changes in contract law (which he hyperbolically calls its death) to the rise of the welfare state (on which see below), but there is no reason to think that traditional contract law cannot operate within the constraints imposed by taxation and welfare. Simpson identifies just one of many trends to which the legal change could be connected; and this connection does not make any sense on its own terms. Parties relied on courts to enforce contracts both before the rise of the penalty doctrine and after; the courts and related government institutions retained at all times the exclusive power to use force in order to extract damages from breachers.

None of these observations is meant to imply that history does not matter. Indeed, history surely does matter, and in two ways. First, it matters as a fund of data that any good theory of contract law must explain. A theory of contract law must be general enough to "predict" differences across time (and place), or else explain why its inconsistency with the law in other jurisdictions should not count against it. Second, history can stand in for the idea that elements of contract law at a particular time and place might be the product of chance, decisions that had unforeseen consequences, local political institutions, and inertia – in which case ambitions for a comprehensive or satisfying theory of contract law should be avoided.

Topics in Contract Theory

Contract disputes often raise theoretical questions common to other areas of law but that interest contracts scholars because of their importance in contract doctrine. I will discuss some of these questions because of their significance in the contracts literature but I will do so briefly in order to avoid redundancy with other chapters in this volume.

Formalism

Many scholars have been struck by the "formalism" of contract doctrine. Many rules seem, by the standards of other areas of the common law, rigid and simple; as a result, considerations of justice may be excluded from the evaluation of a contract dispute. Under traditional contract doctrine, for example, a promise is enforceable if supported by bargained-for consideration, which could mean any giving up of a legal right, no matter how small. Reasonable reliance on a gratuitous promise would not create liability even if justice would seem to require it. The rise of promissory estoppel, which makes the reasonableness of reliance and the justice of enforcement relevant considerations, reflects the decline of the formalism of contract law, though contract law remains more formalistic than tort.

The standard explanation for formalism in contract law is that contract law, like testamentary law, is facilitative, and the law best enables people to accomplish their goals by making the legal consequences of alternative actions as clear as possible (Fuller 1941). Hence Gilmore saw the decline of the formalism of contract law as an expression of the decline of laissez faire. The problem with these views is that formalism also interferes with people's ability to accomplish their goals: a rigorous consideration doctrine prevents a promisor from inducing reliance; rigorous offer/acceptance doctrines make it harder to enter contracts. Markets stumble over rigid procedural formalities: people want to know that informal handshake quasi-agreements will receive legal protection when warranted by the fluidity of circumstances. The optimal level of formalism is distinct from the substantive values of contract law, and turns on such factors as judicial competence and the complexity of the contractual environment (Posner 1999).

Redistribution

A number of scholars have discussed whether contract law reflects principles of distributive justice (e.g., Kennedy 1981; Kronman 1980). Contract law does redistribute wealth *ex post*, of course, from the breacher to the victim. The expectation measure puts the victim in the position he or she would have been if the promisor had performed; the reliance measure returns the victim to the status quo. But neither measure treats the promisor's or victim's wealth as a relevant factor in the determination of damages.

Nonetheless, certain defenses appear to have a more explicit redistributive purpose. The unconscionability doctrine, for example, has sometimes been used to release impoverished buyers from bad deals. The poverty of the buyer and the wealth of the seller, often a business rather than a person, are sometimes mentioned by the court, though rarely are they made dispositive factors.

The problem with releasing poor people from contracts is that although such a policy helps the particular individuals *ex post*, it can harm the poor as a class *ex ante*. Sellers and creditors will raise their prices, or withdraw products, in markets that serve poor people if unconscionability doctrine gives poor people excuses that others lack. The poor as a class, therefore, will be harmed. Within that class, some poor people might benefit at the expense of others. If doctrine makes it harder for creditors to discriminate among bad and good risks by demanding high levels of security, then the doctrine might enable some marginal bad risks to obtain credit even as the total amount of credit is reduced. These distributive consequences are, except in special cases, unlikely to be desirable, or to be superior to more direct methods for redistributing wealth (see Craswell 1991; Kaplow and Shavell 2001).

Paternalism

Courts usually defer to the terms of the contract, and in this way make parties responsible for their own mistakes, but a few doctrines are in tension with the norm of deference. Doctrines such as mistake and impossibility release promisors from liability under narrow conditions. Interpretive presumptions against insurers, drafters, and other experienced parties are probably more important if less overt examples of judicial protection of unsophisticated parties. And the unconscionability doctrine is sometimes invoked when the promisor is less sophisticated than the promisee.

All of these doctrines are possible examples of paternalism; but alternative interpretations are available. The impossibility doctrine, for example, might shift risk away from risk-averse parties. The mistake doctrine and related doctrines like the duty to disclose might provide informed parties with the incentive to disclose private information to uninformed parties, and in certain conditions these incentives can be efficient. The strategy pursued by economics is to deny that "sophistication" refers to levels of cognitive ability, and instead assert that when courts talk about sophistication, they refer to the amount of information possessed by one party, or the cost of obtaining additional information. The success of these explanations is disputed (Posner 2003).

Within the noneconomic contracts literature most scholars agree that paternalism plays a role in the doctrine, albeit quite a small role against a general presumption in favor of freedom of contract. Shiffrin (2000) has recently argued instead that the unconscionability doctrine does not reflect paternalism, but rather the unwillingness of the state to take part in the "exploitation" of one person by another. That is why a buyer can escape enforcement of an unconscionable contract but has no grounds for suing a seller who does not seek to enforce it.

But however one interprets the unconscionability doctrine and related doctrines, one must take care to understand the nature of the transactions that are labeled "unfair" or "exploitative" by courts or commentators. Many of these transactions – such as security arrangements, the subject of many cases – have straightforward economic interpretations: poor buyers who want credit from a seller will receive it only if they pay a high interest rate and supply security (Epstein

1975). If the buyers understand that onerous terms are the price for credit, they do not necessarily exercise bad judgment in entering the contract, and refusing to enforce the contract on the basis of paternalism is unwarranted.

Conclusion: Whither Contract Theory?

The contracts literature has for a long time suffered from a mismatch between theory and doctrine. The theories on which scholars rely are too coarse-grained to permit evaluation of particular rules and case outcomes. A similar hazard has been observed in other areas of legal scholarship, where authors rely on an abstract idea like "democracy" to criticize particular laws and institutions. The meaning of democracy is vague and contested, so it cannot be used, by itself, to compare the merits of, say, parliamentary and presidential systems, or independent and politically accountable courts. Similarly, a commitment to liberalism does not entail a particular view about the mirror image rule, specific performance, or the consideration doctrine.

Skepticism about the overtly philosophical approaches to contract law is not, then, skepticism about the commitments that underlie them, but skepticism about their methodological value. For a while it seemed that the economic approach to contract law escaped the indeterminacy of the philosophical approaches. The economic approach was based on a methodological bargain in which philosophical rigor was exchanged for analytic tractability. Uneasiness about the normative assumptions underlying the economic approach was the result, but it could be suppressed for plausible reasons. Distributional and paternalistic concerns did not need to be denied, and instead could be shuttled outside contract law, where they would be lodged in other institutions: the welfare system, the educational system, and so forth. The remaining body of contract law could be explained and evaluated under the efficiency criterion, which seemed to promise the tractability that the philosophical approaches lacked.

Has economics delivered on this promise? On the one hand, the reorienting of scholarship around the incentive effects of the doctrines has been valuable, and now it is hard to think about contract rules without also thinking about how they affect incentives to perform or breach, gather or conceal information, and invest in reliance. On the other hand, definite conclusions about the efficiency of contract rules have proven to be will-o'-the-wisps. The models needed to evaluate contract-related behavior turn out to be complex, and the empirical correlates to the models' variables hard to determine. The literature has lost its coherence, and has become an aggregation of propositions of the form "If the facts are X, then a particular doctrine will cause Y," with no clear explanation of how these propositions can be brought together into a coherent guide for courts and legislatures.

An alternative view of contract law is that the rules simply do not matter very much from the larger normative perspectives used in the literature. Efficient allocation of resources in modern societies almost certainly requires a market economy, and a market economy relies on laws and institutions that enable the movement of resources from one person to another. But as long as the rules together provide sufficiently strong sanctions – whether they be expectation damages or something else – for those who break promises in a sufficiently wide range of settings, then efficiency is probably satisfied. The rules of contract law might be like the rules of the road: adequate, as long as everyone agrees on what the rules are, within very broad constraints that can be identified without rigorous analysis.

References

Atiyah, P. S. 1979. *The Rise and Fall of Freedom of Contract*. Oxford: Clarendon Press.

Atiyah, P. S. 1981. *Promises, Morals, and Law*. Oxford: Clarendon Press.

Ayres, I. and Gertner, R. 1989. Filling gaps in incomplete contracts: An economic theory of default rules. *Yale Law Journal* 99: 87–130.

Barnett, R. E. 1986. A consent theory of contract. *Columbia Law Review* 86: 269–321.

Benson, P. 1996. Contract. In D. Patterson (ed.), *A Companion to Philosophy of Law and Legal Theory.* Cambridge, MA: Blackwell, 24–56.

Benson, P. 2001. The unity of contract law. In P. Benson (ed.), *The Theory of Contract Law.* Cambridge, UK: Cambridge University Press, 118–205.

Craswell, R. 1989. Contract, default rules, and the philosophy of promising. *Michigan Law Review* 99: 489–529.

Craswell, R. 1991. Passing on the costs of legal rules: Efficiency and distribution in buyer-seller relationships. *Stanford Law Review* 43: 361–98.

Craswell, R. 2000. Against Fuller and Perdue. *University of Chicago Law Review* 67: 99–162.

Epstein, R. 1975. Unconscionability: A critical reappraisal. *Journal of Law and Economics* 18: 293–315.

Fried, C. 1981. *Contract as Promise.* Cambridge, MA: Harvard University Press.

Friedman, L. A. 1985. *A History of American Law.* New York: Simon & Schuster.

Fuller, L. L. 1941. Consideration and form. *Columbia Law Review* 41: 799, 800–1.

Fuller, L. L. and Perdue, Jr., W. W. 1936. The reliance interest in contract damages. *Yale Law Journal* 46: 52–96.

Gilmore, G. 1974. *The Death of Contract.* Columbus, OH: Ohio University Press.

Gordley, C. J. 1991. *The Philosophical Origins of Modern Contract Doctrine.* Oxford: Clarendon Press.

Kaplow, L. and Shavell, S. 2001. *Fairness Versus Welfare.* Cambridge, MA: Harvard University Press.

Kennedy, D. 1981. Distributive and paternalistic motives in contract and tort law, with special reference to compulsory terms and unequal bargaining power. *Maryland Law Review* 41: 563–658.

Kraus, J. S. 2002. Philosophy of contract law. In J. Coleman and S. Shapiro (eds.), *The Oxford Handbook of Jurisprudence and Philosophy of Law.* New York: Oxford University Press, 687–751.

Kronman, A. T. 1980. Contract law and distributive justice. *Yale Law Journal* 89: 472–511.

Kronman, A. T. 1983. Paternalism and the law of contracts. *Yale Law Journal* 92: 763, 778–84.

Posner, E. A. 1999. The decline of formality in contract law. In F. H. Buckley (ed.), *The Fall and Rise of Freedom of Contract.* Durham, NC: Duke University Press, 61–78.

Posner, E. A. 2000. A theory of contract law under conditions of radical judicial error. *Northwestern University Law Review* 94: 749–74.

Posner, E. A. 2003. Economic analysis of contract law after three decades: Success or failure? *Yale Law Journal* 112: 829–80.

Posner, R. A. 1998. *Economic Analysis of Law.* New York: Aspen Law and Business.

Raz, J. 1994. *The Morality of Freedom.* New York: Oxford University Press.

Scanlon, T. M. 2001. Promises and contracts. In P. Benson (ed.), *The Theory of Contract Law.* Cambridge, UK: Cambridge University Press, 86–117.

Schwartz, A. 1998. Incomplete contracts. In P. Newman (ed.), *The New Palgrave Dictionary of Economics and the Law,* vol. 2. London: Macmillan, 277–83.

Shiffrin, S. V. 2000. Paternalism, unconscionability doctrine, and accommodation. *Philosophy and Public Affairs* 29: 205–50.

Simpson, A. W. B. 1987. *A History of the Common Law of Contract.* Oxford: Clarendon Press.

Smith, S. A. 2000: Towards a theory of contract. In J. Horder (ed.), *Oxford Essays in Jurisprudence,* 4th series. New York: Oxford University Press, 107–29.

Chapter 10

The Commons and the Anticommons in the Law and Theory of Property

Stephen R. Munzer

Introduction

There is something new under the sun. What is new is careful and insightful analysis of the commons and the anticommons as they relate to the middle ground of private or state ownership of resources.

Briefly, a commons is a resource which all have a liberty-right to use, from which no one has a normative power to exclude others, and which no one has a duty to refrain from exploiting. The term "commons" includes, somewhat confusingly, two different arrangements: open-access resources and commons property. Under open access, anyone may come in and take out units of the resource, but no person or set of persons may sell or manage the resource. Under commons property, the members of the group individually have rights of entry and withdrawal and collectively have rights to manage or sell the resource and to exclude nonmembers (Eggertsson 2003: 73–4). Many accounts of the commons – notably Demsetz (1967) and Hardin (1968) – refer to both arrangements, but some refer exclusively either to open access or to commons property. Commons property is "the first step on the long and complex path from open access to individual exclusive ownership" (Eggertsson 2003: 73). By contrast, an anticommons is, preliminarily, a resource from which each person has a normative power to exclude others and which no one has a liberty-right to use without the permission of others. The concept of private property lies midway between the concepts of a commons and an anticommons. Less obviously, the concept of state property also lies between them. If an individual, a corporation, or the state has property rights in a resource, the property holder can step in to use the resource and can exclude others from using it.

The chief aims of this chapter are to explain how commons and anticommons analysis illuminates property law as well as property theory, to show why the analysis is novel, to explore some further developments of the analysis, and to venture a critical appraisal of it. Although Buchanan and Yoon (2000) identify economic symmetries between the commons and the anticommons, to my knowledge no general combined legal and philosophical examination of them yet exists, so this chapter tries to fill a gap in the literature. If God alone can create something out of nothing, anything new developed by humans must be constructed out of materials that are already available. Thus, the first order of business is to sketch the components out of which this assertedly new analysis is built.

Familiar Analyses of the Concept of Property

Philosophers, academic lawyers, and some economists frequently analyze property in one or the other of two related and ultimately compatible ways. Each way is a tool for clear thinking. Neither is designed to resolve justificatory issues about property, except insofar as thinking lucidly conduces to a better understanding of such issues. One may call these ways the *bundle-of-rights analysis* and the *rule-governed entitlements analysis*. Both analyses can make room for the lay view that property is *things* – whether material things such as automobiles and land or immaterial things such as copyrights and patents. A point of each analysis is to clarify what is going on when various things are referred to as property.

The bundle-of-rights analysis views property as a package of rights among persons with respect to things. The word "rights" is used in a broad fashion that includes the following normative modalities, which were mapped out systematically by Hohfeld ([1919] 1978): claim-rights, liberty-rights, powers, and immunities. According to Hohfeld, each of these modalities has a "correlative" – that is, a counterpart modality held by a different individual. If *A* has a claim-right to $50 from *B*, then *B* has a duty to pay $50 to *A*. If *A* has a liberty-right to walk across the lawn, *B* has a "no-right" to interfere with *A*'s walking across the lawn. (Perhaps Hohfeld's characterization is overinclusive, as lawyers might say that a liberty-right exists only if the law affords *A* a penumbra of legal protection to walk across the lawn.) If *A* has a power to bequeath jewelry to *B*, *B* has a "liability" (that is, a susceptibility to having *B*'s legal position altered with respect to the jewelry) to receive the jewelry upon *A*'s death. If *A* has an immunity against the government's inundating *A*'s farm without the payment of just compensation, the government has a "disability" (or "no-power") with respect to flooding *A*'s farm unless it pays *A* just compensation. These eight normative modalities – claim-right, liberty-right, power, and immunity, with their respective correlatives of duty, no-right, liability, and disability – are Hohfeld's "fundamental legal conceptions." See THEORIES OF RIGHTS.

To shed light on property, however, the bundle-of-rights analysis must explain *which* rights are somehow peculiar to property. Hohfeld's analytical vocabulary is as applicable to tort and contract and civil procedure as it is to prop-

erty. He never thought that his fundamental legal conceptions were limited to property.

The next step was taken by Honoré (1961). He sought to specify the standard "incidents" of ownership common to Western legal systems. His list of incidents, with minor adjustments, includes the claim-rights to possess, manage, use, and receive income; the liberty-rights to consume or destroy; the powers to sell, give, transfer, exclude, and abandon; the immunities from forced sale and government expropriation; the duty not to use harmfully; and the liability for execution to satisfy a court judgment. Thus, Honoré in effect builds on Hohfeld by taking the fundamental legal conceptions and making them more specific by indicating certain actions or events – for instance, to use, to sell, to exclude – in relation to other persons with respect to things.

The bundle-of-rights analysis facilitates further clarification of the concept of property. If someone has all or almost all of the incidents with respect to a given thing, one can speak of *ownership*. If someone has rather less than the full package of incidents – as with easements or bailments – there is *limited property*. The term *property rights* can be reserved for incidents that are advantageous to the property holder. The claim-right to possess and the powers to sell and exclude, for example, are advantageous to the property holder, whereas the duty not to use harmfully is disadvantageous to the holder. It is possible to identify different sorts of property depending on the identity of the right-holder. Thus, an individual person or a corporation has *private* property, a tribe has *communal* property, and a government has *public* or *state* property. These and related distinctions form the core of the bundle-of-rights analysis (Munzer 1990: 15–36).

The rule-governed entitlements analysis was proposed in Calabresi and Melamed (1972). An entitlement is, roughly, an interest that the law does or should protect. The law can do so by using one or more different sorts of rules: "property rules," "liability rules," and "rules of inalienability." A property rule protects an entitlement if anyone who wishes to remove it from its holder must buy it from the holder in a voluntary transaction at a price agreed upon between the buyer and the holder-seller. A property rule so defined applies only to *market*-alienability; an owner could always give an entitlement away, provided that the donee accepts the gift. A liability rule protects an entitlement if and only if anyone who takes or lessens the value of the entitlement must pay a collectively determined (for example, by a judge or a jury) amount to its holder. A rule of inalienability protects an entitlement if and only if its transfer is not permitted between a willing buyer and a willing seller – for instance, the attempted sale of one's left kidney to someone else. A property rule, in this analysis, involves a collective decision about who gets an initial entitlement but not as to its value, whereas a liability rule involves collective decisions on both who gets an initial entitlement and what it is worth. A rule of inalienability not only protects an entitlement but also limits or regulates it; it involves the most state intervention. Most entitlements are protected by a *combination* of property rules, liability rules, and, to a lesser extent, rules of inalienability.

To bring this analysis down to earth, consider the following example and restrict attention to property rules and liability rules. *A* owns land that *A* is developing into a retirement community. *B* owns a cattle feedlot close to *A*'s land. The feedlot creates unpleasant odors and draws flies. These conditions would not affect *A*'s land in its raw state but reduce its value as a retirement community. However, *B*'s feedlot was in operation when *A* purchased the nearby land from a prior owner. The rule-governed entitlements analysis generates four possible rules.

Rule 1: *A* has an entitlement, protected by a property rule, to be free from pollution.
Rule 2: *A* has an entitlement, protected by a liability rule, to be free from pollution.
Rule 3: *B* has an entitlement, protected by a property rule, to pollute.
Rule 4: *B* has an entitlement, protected by a liability rule, to pollute.

Which rule would be best in the circumstances? Under Rule 1 *A* could extract a high price from *B* or get an injunction against the feedlot, and under Rule 3 *B* could extract a high price from *A* or continue to operate. Rule 2 would allow *B* to operate but require *B* to pay damages to *A*. The

court that faced this case (*Spur Industries, Inc. v. Del E. Webb Development Co.* 1972) in effect opted for Rule 4 – but out of a sense of which outcome would be most appropriate rather than economic modeling. It held that *A*'s retirement community was entitled to be free from pollution, but that, because *B* was there first, *A* had to pay *B* for the cost of shutting down or relocating.

The bundle-of-rights analysis and the rule-governed entitlements analysis of property are intertranslatable and compatible. The sorts of rules distinguished by Calabresi and Melamed can be stated in Hohfeld's vocabulary. If *A*'s entitlement is protected by a property rule, then others have a disability (a no-power) in regard to obtaining the entitlement except by paying a price acceptable to *A*. If *A*'s entitlement is protected by a liability rule, then others have a disability in regard to obtaining or reducing the value of the entitlement unless they pay *A* a collectively determined amount. If *A*'s entitlement is protected by a rule of inalienability, *A* has a no-power to transfer the entitlement to others save as permitted by law. There is a veritable industry of law-and-economics scholars who use the rule-governed entitlements analysis to examine existing law and possible changes to it. The enduring value of this analysis rests on the light it throws on the interconnections between property, tort, and contract; on its sensitivity to both distributional and efficiency considerations; and on the choice between civil and criminal sanctions for violations of property rights.

The Commons and its Tragedy

In the language of Hohfeld and Honoré, a commons is a resource that each has a liberty-right to use and a no-power to exclude others and which no one has a duty to refrain from exploiting. In the language of Calabresi and Melamed, a commons is an entitlement protected by neither property rules nor liability rules, save a liability rule that forbids each from interfering in specified ways – say, by the use of force – with others in the use of the entitlement. Examples of commons – often called common pools – fall into two classes: open-access resources owned by no one, such as ocean waters for fishing and some groundwater basins; and commons property, such as communally owned fields and a swimming pool owned by a large homeowners' association. Classification can be difficult because rules and practices change over time and there are mixed cases (cf. Eggertsson 1990; Ostrom 1990; Smith 2000). Commons differ from public goods, such as national defense, because each person's use of a commons lessens the amount available to others. *The* commons typically refers to open-access resources or commons property as a subject for academic investigation. *A* commons applies to any of a broad range of these resources or entitlements, such as fisheries, grazing lands, and mining territories. Occasionally a commons sprouts a capital, loses an "'s'", and gets a proper name – for instance, Clapham Common in South London. The study of common-pool resources goes back at least to Jens Warming in the early twentieth century (Smith 2000: 138 n.18).

The "tragedy of the commons" is a term introduced by Hardin (1968) to describe the effects of overusing a commons. The leading examples include not only depleted fisheries and overgrazed fields but also overpopulation and air pollution. But why should such effects be tragic? They need not involve a calamity that results from a single character flaw in one individual. Indeed, for Hardin all or most who have access to a commons must succumb to the temptation to overuse it. Anyway, though overuse is suboptimal, it need not be so grave as to be calamitous. Hardin is using the word "tragedy" in a specialized way. Its essence lies "in the solemnity of the remorseless workings of things" (1968: 1244). Hardin thought that individuals with access to a commons would fail to consider the full social costs of actions that give them private benefits. Their failure results in an inevitable working out of the costs of their decisions.

> Therein is the tragedy. Each man is locked into a system that compels him to increase his herd without limit – in a world that is limited. Ruin is the destination toward which all men rush, each pursuing his own best interest in a society that believes in the freedom of the commons. (Hardin 1968: 1244)

Subsequent literature pursues both cause and cure. As to the cause of Hardin's asserted tragedy of the commons, economists have treated manifold aspects of common-pool resources. They have explored uncertainty, force, and so-called prisoner's dilemmas in the use of these resources. They have supplied empirical studies of various commons. Above all, they have argued that the value of common-pool resources declines because the lack of property rights limits exchange. Occasional voices stress the virtues of common ownership (for instance, Rose 1986). To the extent that these voices are correct, the ruin that Hardin claims to be inevitable sometimes does not occur. If so, not all commons are tragic in Hardin's own sense. Still, "the tragedy of the commons" is a label that, though histrionic, has stuck and will be used here.

As to cure, the chief mantra is "Create rights of private property!" Hardin himself favored "mutual coercion, mutually agreed upon by the majority of the people affected" (Hardin 1968: 1247). Private property rights along with taxes were, he thought, useful "coercive devices to escape the horror of the commons" (ibid.). A similar message lies in Demsetz (1967). Demsetz is not, however, wedded to the word "coercion," and good reason exists for employing a richer vocabulary (Munzer 2001: 46–52). Krier (1992: 337–9; cf. Rose 1990: 50–3) claims that Hardin's endorsement of coercion harbors a "contradiction." Krier's claim is that if people can agree to a program of mutual coercion, then they could agree on other ways to restrain themselves. The consequent does not logically follow from the antecedent; just because people can agree on *x* it hardly follows that they can agree on *y* or *z*, which are closely related to *x*. Still, Krier has a point: Any solution that Hardin is likely to come up with involves cooperation, but the absence of cooperation is the root of the problem. This point is not, however, a contradiction – a statement of the form that both *p* and not-*p* are true. At most, Krier can find Hardin guilty of begging the question. Krier identifies a tension in Hardin's argument but not a contradiction. Also, some scholars suggest that those with access to a commons can cooperate to regulate its use rather more successfully than Hardin and Demsetz allow (for example, Cronon 1983; Ostrom 1990). Although some nongovernmental rules limiting access to a commons may increase its value, they can, however, run afoul of laws such as the Sherman Act (for example, *Gulf Coast Shrimpers and Oystermans Association v. United States* 1956 (antitrust violation)).

The Anticommons and its Tragedy

The term "anticommons" was defined preliminarily in the introductory section above. Michelman (1982: 6) specified the concept but did so in a highly speculative way and did not introduce the term. Heller (1998: 668) was among the first to use the term and supplied a helpful definition of it: Anticommons property is "a property regime in which multiple owners hold effective rights of exclusion in a scarce resource" (italics omitted). His favorite example is storefront property in postsocialist Russia, where different persons or other entities have rights to occupy, sell, lease, determine use, and receive revenue from the storefront, and each entity has a power to exclude others (1998: 637–40). Only those familiar with storefronts after the collapse of the Soviet Union can vouch for the accuracy of Heller's account of them, but if his description is accurate it is an apt example.

In four respects Heller improves on prior efforts to think about the anticommons. First, he does not require that everyone has a power to exclude. His definition applies to real-world situations in which a limited number of persons or other entities have a power of exclusion. Second, in contrast with earlier scholars, who tried to come up with examples in which anticommons property would be efficient, Heller points out that such property is usually suboptimal. Third, multiple powers of exclusion need not all derive from the legal system. If state authority is weak, as it was in postsocialist Russia, mafia groups may have nonlegal but effective powers to exclude. Fourth, anticommons property may not prevail throughout an entire property system but only with respect to certain resources, such as storefronts or apartments (Heller 1998: 668–9).

What is supposed to be tragic about the anticommons? Heller understands tragedy differently from Hardin. For Hardin, the tragedy of the commons is the solemn, remorseless working out of things to a ruinous destination (1968: 1244). For Heller, the tragedy of the anticommons is the result of rational individuals who hold powers of exclusion acting separately so as collectively to "waste the resource by underconsuming it compared with a social optimum" (Heller 1998: 677). Heller carefully points out that an anticommons is not necessarily tragic (673–6). Still, some readers might regard his conception of tragedy as too inclusive, for slightly suboptimal underconsumption of a resource is, though perhaps not ideal, hardly "tragic." Only if the underconsumption were severely or gravely suboptimal might one justifiably regard the result as tragic or at least highly unfortunate. Although Hardin and Heller use the word "tragic" in somewhat different ways, the tragedies of the commons and the anticommons are economically symmetrical in several respects (Buchanan and Yoon 2000). Symmetries are unsurprising, for in each case seemingly rational individual action leads to irrational collective action.

A significant worry is that, even granting Heller's rather expansive understanding of tragedy, he might too readily conclude that the rights affecting the use of a resource could issue in anticommons property. For example, Heller and Eisenberg (1998: 699) claim that if the US Patent Office were to issue patents on the gene fragments known as expressed sequence tags (ESTs), that could "create ... an anticommons." Although transaction costs and other factors can inhibit or block optimal bundling of property rights, Heller and Eisenberg's discussion does not address the difference between a patent on an EST itself and a patent on the full-length gene of which the patented EST is a part; the former does not, without more, create anticommons property as Heller defines it, though the latter might. Heller and Eisenberg provide almost no empirical evidence to back up their concern about the tragedy of the anticommons in the area of biotechnology. Even if anticommons patent rights create collective-action difficulties, these difficulties can in turn yield an opportunity for wealth creation in the form of bundling services

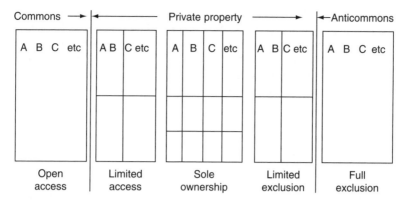

Figure 1 The boundaries of private property
Source: Heller 1999: 1167

(Holman and Munzer 2000: 802–3; cf. Hansmann and Kraakman 2000).

The worry just described, however, invokes a single example. Plainly Heller is on to something new in his theory of the tragedy of the anticommons. It remains to explore further developments and applications of the anticommons analysis and its use in conjunction with the earlier analysis of the commons.

The Accounts of Commons and Anticommons Property Elaborated and Applied

Two notable areas in which these analyses have been extended and applied are the metes and bounds of private property and the law of governmental takings of private property. In a third area – the *numerus clausus* principle (namely, that the number of forms of property is closed and limited) – anticommons analysis has proved less useful.

The boundaries of private property

To some degree the law allows property owners to subdivide their interest. The owner of a mountain cabin, for instance, can transfer it to his or her five children as tenants in common. Yet the law also discourages owners from breaking their

property into wastefully small fragments. If a great deal of fragmentation were allowed, people might find it much easier to splinter property than to reassemble it because of transaction costs and strategic behavior. As Heller (1999: 1166) puts it, "If too many people gain rights to use or exclude, then bargaining among owners may break down. With too many owners of property fragments, resources become prone to waste either through overuse in a commons or through underuse in an anticommons" (footnotes omitted).

Heller argues that private property is, and should be, bounded on both sides. On one side is the right of all or many to gain access to a commons. On the other side is the power of some or many to exclude others from an anticommons. The effect of legal doctrines that separate commons, private property, and anticommons is to promote an efficient allocation of resources for productive use. Figure 1 illustrates his boundary principle.

Heller's boundary principle has substantial explanatory power, a good deal of theoretical interest, and at least some normative bite. First, as to explanation, he develops the boundary principle in relation to physical things, legal things, and legal relations. In the category of physical things, for example, the boundary principle explains some salient features of early English land law, such as the barring of subinfeudation and allowing property owners to transfer their holdings for value. So far as legal things are concerned, Heller makes a case that the forms of ownership in a given legal system must not be too numerous. Here Heller has a useful discussion of reverter acts and the rule against perpetuities. Some limitations on its usefulness are examined below in connection with the *numerus clausus* principle. The treatment of relational boundaries is also interesting. Still, Heller might have made his task more challenging by discussing *Local 1330, United Steel Workers of America v. United States Steel Corp.* (1980), a plant-closing case which held that the steel company was not legally required to keep the plant open or sell it to the union. Singer (1988) argues that the manifold relations among the company, the union, the workers, the town, and its inhabitants could create a property right in the plant for the plaintiffs. Munzer (2001: 63–5, 67) identifies problems with and alternatives to Singer's argument.

A second dimension of Heller's contribution lies in the significance of the boundary principle in the theory of property. The fact that metaphors (for instance, "metes and bounds") can mislead those who work in the theory of property is an old point but still is worth making. The real contribution that Heller makes here is to emphasize that most theorists of property have tended to overlook anticommons property. As to commons property, however, more needs to be said about intellectual property. Shiffrin (2001) identifies different Lockean understandings of the intellectual commons, though to assess the ultimate merits of these understandings requires looking at the full range of theories of intellectual property (Fisher 2001). Furthermore, the vertical dividing lines in Figure 1 do not mark a sharp separation between the commons and private property on the one hand or between private property and the anticommons on the other. Open access shades into limited access, and limited exclusion shades into full exclusion. Yet the point is not just that, at the margins, intermingling of elements occurs. It is also that different elements can interact. Smith (2000) uses the term "semicommons" for a mix of common and private rights in which each set of rights has a significant impact on the other. The leading example is the open-field system of medieval and early modern England which combines common rights for grazing and private rights for growing crops on scattered strips of land.

Third, Heller's argument not only sheds light on the discordance of the Supreme Court's decisions in takings cases but also gives some hints for grappling with those cases in a more promising fashion. For example, in *Hodel v. Irving* (1987), the Court held unconstitutional a federal statute providing that highly fractionated low-value Indian allotments would escheat to the tribe upon the owner's death instead of being devisable. Heller argues convincingly that the *Hodel* Court ignored the boundary principle and in trying to strengthen a stick (namely, the power to devise) in the bundle of rights called property it entrenched a tragedy of the anticommons (Heller 1999: 1213–17). Still, the normative discussion is not as thoroughly articulated as it might be in terms of exactly how the Court can decide takings cases better than it has. He "notes several issues that the Court could consider in constructing a practical test for bounding private property" (1999: 1217, footnote omitted), but the ensuing treatment is more suggestive than systematic (1217–22).

Takings

Whatever the shortcomings of Heller (1999) on takings, Heller and Krier (1999) try to make up for them. Their article does not build entirely on Heller's earlier work and in fact is more reminiscent of the modeling exercise in Calabresi and Melamed (1972). Heller and Krier attack the standard view that it is possible to decide every takings case in one of two ways: either there is no taking at all and hence no compensation is due, or there is a taking and the government must compensate the property owner. If the chief purposes of the takings clause are efficiency and justice, and if these purposes sometimes conflict, one may need four possible decisions rather than just two. One can get a four-box grid by uncoupling takings and compensation. Heller and Krier associate efficiency with deterrence (whether general or specific) and justice with distribution (whether general or specific), though they acknowledge deterrence and distribution are sometimes dependent on each other (1999: 998–1003). Figure 2 displays the resulting grid.

	Should there be payment by the government?	
	No	Yes
No	Box 1 Ordinary regulation	Box 2 Taking/no compensation
Yes	Box 3 No taking/ compensation	Box 4 Ordinary taking

Should there be specific distribution to claimants?

Figure 2 Uncoupling deterrence and distribution, takings and compensation
Source: Heller and Krier 1999: 1002

In this four-box drawing, Boxes 2 and 3 signal the innovation of Heller and Krier's approach – namely, that sometimes a taking should be declared but no compensation should be paid, whereas in other circumstances no taking should be declared but compensation ought to be paid anyway. Boxes 1 and 4 capture ordinary regulations (for which no compensation is due) and ordinary takings (for which compensation should be paid), respectively. So, what goes in the interesting boxes? Heller and Krier argue that *Loretto v. Teleprompter Manhattan CATV Corporation* (1982) (state-authorized cable television wires and junction boxes on leased property) goes in Box 2. They also argue that *Hadacheck v. Sebastian* (1915) (municipal closure of an existing brickyard in a newly residential area) belongs in Box 3. *Loretto* and *Hadacheck* are old chestnuts among takings scholars. But Heller and Krier use their approach to illuminate a more recent case – *Phillips v. Washington Legal Foundation* (1998). The question in *Phillips* was whether the interest on client funds individually incapable (because nominal or short-term) of earning interest net of expenses was, when pooled into an account under an Interest on Lawyer Trust Account program, "private property" under the Fifth Amendment. The Supreme Court upheld a Court of Appeals decision that it was under the

rule that "interest follows principal." Heller and Krier criticize the Court's decision. Although they see that there is a case for putting *Phillips* in Box 2, they conclude tentatively that it fits best in Box 1.

Insightful as Heller and Krier's pithy article is, four reservations are in order. First, it seems doubtful that the Supreme Court will accept Boxes 2 and 3 in light of the *language* of the takings clause of the Fifth Amendment to the US Constitution. The clause states that "nor shall private property be taken for public use, without just compensation." The very words of this clause couple something taken with just compensation. So it is rowing upstream to suggest that the Court may uncouple them. There is no constitutional warrant for Box 2 – a taking without compensation – except in rare cases in which "just compensation" amounts to zero (when, for example, the benefits and burdens to an owner whose property has been taken are, if monetized, mathematically equal) (cf. *Phillips*: 172). There is, moreover, no constitutional warrant for Box 3 – compensation without a taking. The takings clause does not authorize a compensatory payment in the absence of a taking. Nor should it, for in the context compensation has to be recompense for a takings-related loss. True, the Court has enlarged or changed the meaning of some constitutional phrases – such as "interstate commerce," "cruel and unusual punishments," and "equal protection." But it will take a benchful of Houdinis to escape the grammatical and conceptual chains of the takings clause as a whole. Even if a legislature could adopt some of Heller and Krier's suggestions (1999: 1012–13), the takings clause of the Constitution would not justify their adoption.

Second, Heller and Krier take it as obvious that efficiency and justice are the purposes of the takings clause. Yet they present no historical or other arguments for this position. Instead, they say, "there appears to be virtual consensus that the purposes of just compensation are essentially [these] two" (1999: 998). Even if everyone agrees on a particular proposition, agreement does not establish the truth of that proposition. Heller and Krier ignore disputes over the origins and meaning of the takings clause of the Fifth Amendment (cf. Treanor 1995). They also ignore issues of constitutional interpretation pertaining to that clause – for instance, whether its original meaning, if recoverable, should bind judges today.

Third, Heller and Krier not only elide differences between efficiency and utility (1999: 998–9), they also pass over radically different understandings of justice as a principle of distribution (998–1003). As usually understood, efficiency does not rest on or even allow interpersonal comparisons of individual welfare and at best yields only ordinal rankings of alternatives, whereas utility (at least as understood by philosophers) sometimes allows interpersonal comparisons and in principle can yield cardinal rankings of alternatives. The association of justice with distribution, though common, leaves almost everything up in the air as to what justice requires in a theory of property and, within that, a theory of takings. Does it require a strictly equal distribution, or a distribution that is in the long-range best interests of the least well off, or something else?

Fourth, Heller and Krier do not acknowledge how much more complicated an approach to takings must be if it recognizes a principle of desert based on labor. Justice as understood so far rests on patterned distributions that ignore the labor-desert of individuals. If one broadens justice to include desert based on labor, justice becomes vastly more complex. If one regards a labor-desert principle as distinct from a principle of justice, the structure of takings law and theory becomes reticulated and requires more than the four boxes provided (Munzer 1990: 419–68).

The numerus clausus *principle*

This principle, it will be recalled, states that the number of forms of property is closed and limited. By far the ablest and most thorough treatment of it in Anglo-American law is Merrill and Smith (2000; cf. Rudden 1987). The law of contracts allows the parties enormous freedom to create legally enforceable promises to suit their needs. The law of property, however, gives a limited menu. The land law recognizes a handful of present estates (fees simple absolute, fees tail (now abolished), several types of defeasible fees, life estates, and leaseholds) and a handful of

future interests (reversions, possibilities of reverter, rights of entry, several types of remainders, executory interests, and, perhaps, powers of appointment). These estates and future interests can be owned individually, in joint tenancy or tenancy in common or tenancy by the entirety, as community property or as marital property, or held in trust. There are a few nonpossessory interests in land, such as easements. The law of personal property has an even briefer catalogue. Patents and copyrights are the most important types of intellectual property. With rare exceptions the courts do not allow consenting adults to create new forms of property.

What explains the *numerus clausus* principle? Heller (1999: 1176–82) suggests that his anticommons analysis gives a reason to limit the excessive fragmentation of property. If property in legal things is split across space, time, or individuals, then the productivity of resources may decline. Merrill and Smith (2000: 6, 51–4) question this explanation. They stress that the *numerus clausus* principle limits the *types* of property rights. It does not limit the number of rightholders or the size of parcels, which are the main concerns of antifragmentation theories such as Heller's anticommons analysis.

Merrill and Smith advance a different explanation: information costs to third parties. Property rights are *in rem* – that is, good against all the world, not just against parties to a particular transaction. When property rights are created or transferred, third parties must discover what exactly the rights are, who holds them, whether there are exceptions to or limitations on them, and so on if the third parties wish to purchase them or to avoid violating them. Thus there are many sorts of pertinent information. The *numerus clausus* principle, Merrill and Smith contend, holds down the number of forms of property and thereby cabins the costs to third parties of finding out about them. If, instead, people could create a large number of types of property to suit their own situation, the resulting property rights could be idiosyncratic. It would require much time and resources to inform oneself about these rights. Moreover, those creating specialized forms of property rights might well lack sufficient incentive to take these increased information costs into account and thereby create external diseconomies. Hence, the *numerus clausus* principle holds down the information costs to third parties by confining property rights to a limited number of standard forms.

Yet Merrill and Smith do not, as their title might suggest, provide a complete account of "optimal standardization in the law of property." Optimality requires not only a limit on the number of types of property. It also requires that the types be individually well crafted and that they hang together well as a whole. Scattered passages suggest that Merrill and Smith are aware of this and kindred points (2000: 40, 67). One should not expect that either the *numerus clausus* principle or Heller's antifragmentation analysis, or both, suffice even for a general theory of which legislatively standardized forms of property are optimal. And once one inspects the operation of these forms in practice, some judicial adjustment of them may be desirable.

Furthermore, the position of Merrill and Smith may be open to a different criticism. Hansmann and Kraakman (2002) agree that third-party information costs are key to the way the law regulates property rights, but deny that the law restricts the sorts of property rights individuals can create. "Just using the ordinary tools of contract, it is possible with sufficient effort to fashion nonpossessory rights in an asset that will bind third-party purchasers" (2002: S419). Hence, they argue, the law does not impose the limits on property rights, or categories of property rights, that Merrill and Smith claim. "Rather, it is more accurate to say that there are only limited kinds of property rights whose creation the law affirmatively facilitates" (Hansmann and Kraakman 2002: S419). One may venture that the last word on explaining the *numerus clausus* principle has yet to be uttered.

The Liberal Commons

The general account

Dagan and Heller (2001) argue that no need exists to elect between the benefits of the cooperative use of scarce resources and the commitments of political liberals to the values of autonomy and exit. Rather, they contend, their account of the *liberal commons* enables people to have these benefits and honor these commitments at the same time. Their article excludes open-access resources and focuses solely on commons property. The goals of the account are to observe the liberal value of exit, to secure gains from cooperation, and to employ the law to catalyze trust. With respect to each goal, Dagan and Heller suggest ways of mediating between extremes and resolving tensions. Next, they specify three spheres of a liberal commons: individual dominion, democratic self-government, and exit that enhances cooperation. For each sphere, Dagan and Heller offer ways of mediating between extremes and reducing conflicts. Figure 3 displays their theory.

A salient virtue of their ambitious article lies in its melding of critical and constructive components, legal and political theory, and historical and comparative contributions to the study of law. The article has critical bite in its reasoned opposition both to overly aggressive privatization and to illiberal communitarian proposals. On the plane of theory, Dagan and Heller draw on the rich vein of contemporary legal speculation about property as well as the importance of exit in economic and political thought (for example, Hirschman 1970). They also reorient the debate over commons property, which traditionally concentrated on efficiency and economic benefits, by including social as well as economic gains. Their contributions to law-on-the-ground include an historical explanation for the decline of black farmland ownership over the last 125 years; a penetrating critique of co-ownership in the United States; and a comparison of American law with that of foreign legal systems (especially British, German, and Israeli) on various aspects of the law of property.

As with any proposal that tries to occupy a middle ground and smooth over tensions, Dagan and Heller's proposal can be peppered with doubts and objections on many points. (1) It is difficult for the law to foster trust within large, heterogeneous groups of individuals. Given the propensity of many individuals to act in their own self-interest, a serious problem of opportunistic behavior remains, especially when the costs

A Identifying the Goals		
1 Preserve the liberal value of exit	Recognize the link between exit and autonomy	
	Accept reasonable limits on entry	
2 Achieve gains from cooperation	Maximize economic gains from resource use	
	Strengthen social and interpersonal values	
3 Use law to catalyze trust	Recognize the limits of direct legal control	
	Deploy law as a safety net to strengthen social norms	
B The Three Spheres of a Liberal Commons		
1 The sphere of individual dominion	Deter opportunistic overuse and underinvestment	
	Help create fruits and revenues and divide them fairly	
2 The sphere of democratic self-governance	Use default rules to promote well-tempered voice	
	Enable broad majority rule, yet protect the minority	
3 The sphere of cooperation-enhancing exit	Create deterrent and protective exit mechanisms	
	Protect exit decisions that are informed and sincere	

Figure 3   A theory of the liberal commons
Source: Dagan and Heller 2001: 602

of detection and enforcement are high. (2) The foregoing difficulty may explain why almost all of Dagan and Heller's examples are confined to small groups whose members have shared values. To have liberal commons in cotenancies, marriages, homeowners' associations, and close corporations is one thing. To have it as a general model for property in a large, diverse society is quite another. (3) In turn, an explanation of the absence of large-scale liberal commons lies in Demsetz (1967): the perceived gains of such liberal commons do not exceed the costs of trading an existing private-property system for them. More radically, even if it were costless to move from private property to a large-scale liberal commons, some may argue that a private-property system remains preferable. Such a system arguably gives greater scope to autonomy, allows economies of scale through bargaining, and facilitates risk spreading through insurance contracts. (4) At all events, Dagan and Heller's discussion of exit is wanting. They dwell on "artificial" costs such as exit taxes and penalties and slight the fact that leaving a commons carries many "natural" costs – for instance, relocating geographically, losing friends and having to make new ones, or disrupting settled patterns of life. Sometimes

these natural costs might be high enough to lessen the need to impose artificial costs on exit.

Something else is wanting: a thorough discussion of entry. To their credit, Dagan and Heller display a keen interest in the freedom and autonomy of individuals and hence in their liberty-right to leave. But those who exit have to go somewhere, which prompts the question of whether they have a claim-right to come into another socioeconomic system with a correlative duty on that system to allow them to enter. In fact, the question has an even broader scope, for it applies not only to those who leave voluntarily. It applies also to those who are driven out by civil war, political force, religious persecution, or failed governmental institutions that plunge people into poverty or keep them there. Two dimensions of this broader question merit isolation. One has to do with *immigration*: are other nations that have a modicum of civil concord, religious tolerance, well-functioning governmental institutions, and material well-being under a political duty to allow immigrants and, if so, on what terms? The other dimension concerns *economic access*: do other nations that make available public education, old-age benefits, welfare payments, health services, and other financial benefits to their own citizens have a political duty to provide them to new immigrants? No hope exists of answering these questions here but the need to grapple with them is plain.

Marital property

Frantz and Dagan (2004) extend the liberal commons, with minor adjustments, to marital property. They begin with the premise that marriage is, or ought to be, an egalitarian liberal community. Such a community rests on the equality, nonsubordination, autonomy, and "plural identity" of the spouses. In an ideal marriage, and in many actual marriages, spouses perceive themselves at least partially as a "we" – a "plural subject" – that is, in turn, also a constitutive feature of each spouse's identity as an "I." This conception of marriage has implications for assets acquired during marriage. It implies, argue Frantz and Dagan, that both spouses have a right to control them, and that, upon divorce, each spouse has an equal right to them. Because marriage as a liberal community carries with it a liberty-right of exit, divorce is allowable without regard to fault. Permanent alimony is not justified, but under some circumstances time-limited ("rehabilitative") alimony is justifiable.

Several features and limitations of Frantz and Dagan's proposed marital property regime merit comment. First, their account seeks both to explain and to justify. Because their conception of marriage accords with many features of actual marriages in the United States, it reflects and illuminates current marital property law. Yet because their conception is also an ideal, it provides normative grounds for revising current law in some respects. Second, their account sets forth what academic lawyers call default rules: rules that will apply unless people do something to avoid them. The most obvious avoidance mechanisms are prenuptial agreements and cohabitation. Third, autonomy has to do with legally free exit, not individual desert. Frantz and Dagan suggest, plausibly, that although a desert for labor principle is attractive in many other property settings, this principle is an anathema to the

fundamental communitarian maxim of sharing if it is assumed that the deserving unit is an individual spouse. In fact, they contend, a labor-desert principle could select the marital community as the deserving unit in the context of marriage. Fourth, the assets subject to division upon divorce do not, with a few exceptions, include property acquired before marriage. Still, Frantz and Dagan make significant inroads into the general rule that property acquired by one spouse by gift or inheritance during the marriage is separate property. They also maintain that earning capacity – for example, professional degrees and business or celebrity goodwill – gained during the tenure of the marriage is part of the marital estate.

As to critical evaluation, Frantz and Dagan's account works in practice only if, upon divorce, the division of marital property is clearly separable from the award of alimony. In fact, sometimes no clear separation is possible, especially in the case of increased earning capacity. The usual maneuver is to reduce the increased capacity to present value and give one spouse half of that. Frantz and Dagan complicate this maneuver by making earning capacity subject to division only when it is realized, that is, when the money is actually made in the years after divorce. The complication may preserve postdivorce autonomy (by not penalizing choices that fail to realize some earning capacity). But it pushes up accounting costs, enforcement costs, and postdivorce wrangling. Especially in marriages of modest duration – four to eight years, for example – the realization rule interferes with the ability of former spouses without children to make a clean break from each other.

Part of Frantz and Dagan's response to the clean-break objection is that if a couple has children, a clean break is neither possible nor desirable. This response, however, points up the artificiality of omitting the care and support of children from their account. Often the having and raising of children form a dominant motivation for marriage. The need to care for children is vital within marriage and in the event of divorce. It is questionable for Frantz and Dagan to push children offstage at the beginning of their article only to wheel them onstage to respond to the clean-break objection.

The introduction of children destabilizes Frantz and Dagan's proposal, even if there are analytical reasons for separating an interspousal dimension (spouses *qua* spouses) from a parental dimension (spouses *qua* coparents). (1) Those who hold a (noneconomic) traditional view of marriage and gender roles will claim that Frantz and Dagan's ideal of marriage ignores or deforms the different functional contributions of men and women. (2) Those who espouse an economically oriented traditional view of marriage will make a similar claim. For them no-fault divorce without generous rules pertaining to property division and alimony will disadvantage women, because biology and culture usually suit women better than men to childrearing and homemaking; absent adequate legal protection some women will not enter traditional marriage (Becker 1991: 14–19, 30–79, 324–41; Landes 1978: 48–51, 58–63). Cohen (1987: 278–87) contends that men gain more than women early in marriage and women more than men later on. He traces the asymmetry to differences in childbearing, childrearing, mortality rates, and age-related sexual attractiveness. In language that some might read as a parody of economic discourse, he says that "women in general are of relatively higher value as wives at younger ages and depreciate more rapidly than do men" (1987: 278). The long-term asymmetry or "imbalance provides the opportunity for strategic behavior whereby one of the parties, generally the man, might find it in his interest to breach the [marriage] contract unless otherwise constrained" (287). (3) Some feminist scholars of family law believe that the legal system should support a feminine lifestyle during marriage and after divorce that accepts cultural differences between men and women. They favor, variously, a stronger role for alimony (O'Connell 1988: 492–506), using an investment-partnership model to achieve equal standards of living after divorce (Singer 1989: 1114–21), and even giving wives *more* than half of the property acquired during marriage if that is needed for an equal financial outcome after divorce (Fineman 1991: 47, 49, 50, 52). (4) Therefore, though some scholars (for example, Kay 1987) might endorse Frantz and Dagan's emphasis on liberal equality, thinkers who have radically different political and empirical beliefs may support, for different reasons, traditional gender roles (see generally Carbone and Brinig 1991: 987–1010). If the law protects these roles when married couples have children, Frantz and Dagan's proposal will require radical revision.

Yet these four criticisms are hardly decisive. A salient virtue of Frantz and Dagan's analysis is that they consider manifold objections to their position. They endeavor, with admirable resourcefulness and even-handedness, to parry objections without sacrificing the distinctiveness of their central claims.

A final worry about their proposal is more general: the resistance of marriage to being governed by *any* single top-down ideal or model. If the last two centuries of legal and social change and efforts to craft reforms show anything, they show that the complexity of marriage, the family, gender roles, and economic behavior stubbornly resist management by any single vision. No doubt the intensity of Frantz and Dagan's partial vision throws new light on marital property and its reform. Yet devising a legal framework that solves all problems will remain elusive.

Retrospect and Prospect

Hardin (1968) and Heller (1998) point out disadvantages of the commons and the anticommons, respectively. Their novel analyses shed light on the law and theory of property. Yet each analysis, when extended beyond sensible limits, reveals flaws.

Not all commons are tragic. Although the commons and the anticommons, as extremes on a spectrum, illuminate the boundaries of private property, anticommons analysis helps only modestly with governmental takings of private property and the *numerus clausus* principle. The further account of the liberal commons by Dagan and Heller (2001) runs into general difficulties and its extension to marital property encounters pitfalls.

The next several decades will reveal much about the intellectual staying power of the commons, the anticommons, and related ideas. For the present it suffices to be grateful for work,

much of it published within the last six years, that
pushes forward speculation about the theory of
property and helps to solve real-world problems
in property law.

References

Becker, G. S. (1981)1991. *A Treatise on the Family*,
enlarged 2nd edn. Cambridge, MA and London:
Harvard University Press.

Buchanan, J. M. and Yoon, Y. J. 2000. Symmetric tragedies: Commons and anticommons. *Journal of Law
and Economics* 43: 1–13.

Calabresi, G. and Melamed, A. D. 1972. Property rules,
liability rules, and inalienability: One view of the
cathedral. *Harvard Law Review* 85: 1089–1128.

Carbone, J. and Brinig, M. F. 1991. Rethinking marriage: Feminist ideology, economic change, and divorce reform. *Tulane Law Review* 65: 953–1010.

Cohen, L. 1987. Marriage, divorce, and quasi rents: Or,
"I gave him the best years of my life." *Journal of Legal
Studies* 16: 267–303.

Cronon, W. 1983. *Changes in the Land: Indians, Col-
onists, and the Ecology of New England.* New York:
Hill and Wang.

Dagan, H. and Heller, M. A. 2001. The liberal commons. *Yale Law Journal* 110: 549–623.

Demsetz, H. 1967. Towards a theory of property rights.
American Economic Review, Papers and Proceedings
57: 347–59.

Eggertsson, T. 1990. *Economic Behavior and Institutions.* Cambridge, UK: Cambridge University Press.

Eggertsson, T. 2003. Open access versus common
property. In T. L. Anderson and F. S. McChesney
(eds), *Property Rights: Cooperation, Conflict, and
Law.* Princeton, NJ and Oxford: Princeton University
Press, 73–89.

Fineman, M. A. 1991. *The Illusion of Equality: The
Rhetoric and Reality of Divorce Reform.* Chicago
and London: University of Chicago Press.

Fisher, W. 2001. Theories of intellectual property. In S.
R. Munzer (ed.), *New Essays in the Legal and Political
Theory of Property.* Cambridge, UK: Cambridge Uni-
versity Press, 168–99.

Frantz, C. J. and Dagan, H. 2004. Properties of marriage. *Columbia Law Review* 104: 75–133.

*Gulf Coast Shrimpers and Oystermans Association v.
United States.* 1956. 263 F.2d 658 (5th Cir.).

Hadacheck v. Sebastian. 1915. 239 U.S. 394.

Hansmann, H. and Kraakman, R. 2000. The essential
role of organizational law. *Yale Law Journal* 110:
387–440.

Hansmann, H. and Kraakman, R. 2002. Property, contract, and verification: The *numerus clausus* problem
and the divisibility of rights. *Journal of Legal Studies*
31 (2, pt. 2): S373–420.

Hardin, G. 1968. The tragedy of the commons. *Science*
162: 1243–8.

Heller, M. A. 1998. The tragedy of the anticommons:
Property in the transition from Marx to markets.
Harvard Law Review 111: 621–88.

Heller, M. A. 1999. The boundaries of private property.
Yale Law Journal 108: 1163–1223.

Heller, M. A. and Eisenberg, R. S. 1998. Can patents
deter innovation? The anticommons in biomedical
research. *Science* 290: 698–701.

Heller, M. A. and Krier, J. E. 1999. Deterrence and
distribution in the law of takings. *Harvard Law
Review* 112: 997–1025.

Hirschman, A. O. 1970. *Exit, Voice, and Loyalty: Responses to Decline in Firms, Organizations, and States.*
Cambridge, MA: Harvard University Press.

Hodel v. Irving. 1987. 481 U.S. 704.

Hohfeld, W. N. [1919] 1978. *Fundamental Legal Conceptions as Applied in Judicial Reasoning*, ed. W. W.
Cook. Westport, CT: Greenwood Press.

Holman, M. A. and Munzer, S. R. 2000. Intellectual
property rights in genes and gene fragments: A registration solution for expressed sequence tags. *Iowa
Law Review* 85: 735–848.

Honoré, A. M. 1961. Ownership. In A. G. Guest (ed.),
Oxford Essays in Jurisprudence. Oxford: Clarendon
Press, 107–47.

Kay, H. H. 1987. Equality and difference: A perspective
on no-fault divorce and its aftermath. *University of
Cincinnati Law Review* 56: 1–90.

Krier, J. E. 1992. The tragedy of the commons, Part
two. *Harvard Journal of Law & Public Policy* 15:
325–47.

Landes, E. M. 1978. Economics of alimony. *Journal of
Legal Studies* 7: 35–63.

*Local 1330, United Steel Workers of America v. United
States Steel Corp.* 1980. 631 F.2d 1264 (6th Cir.).

Loretto v. Teleprompter Manhattan CATV Corp. 1982.
458 U.S. 419.

Merrill, T. W. and Smith, H. E. 2000. Optimal standardization in the law of property: The *numerus clausus* principle. *Yale Law Journal* 110: 1–70.

Michelman, F. I. 1982. Ethics, economics, and the law
of property. In J. R. Pennock and J. W. Chapman
(eds.), *Ethics, Economics, and the Law.* New York:
New York University Press, 3–40.

Munzer, S. R. 1990. *A Theory of Property.* Cambridge,
UK: Cambridge University Press.

Munzer, S. R. 2001. Property as social relations. In S. R.
Munzer (ed.), *New Essays in the Legal and Political*

Theory of Property. Cambridge, UK: Cambridge University Press, 36–75.

O'Connell, M. E. 1988. Alimony after no-fault: A practice in search of a theory. *New England Law Review* 23: 437–513.

Ostrom, E. 1990. *Governing the Commons: The Evolution of Institutions for Collective Action.* New York: Cambridge University Press.

Phillips v. Washington Legal Foundation. 1998. 524 U.S. 156.

Rose, C. M. 1986. The comedy of the commons: Custom, commerce, and inherently public property. *University of Chicago Law Review* 53: 711–81.

Rose, C. M. 1990. Property as storytelling: Perspectives from game theory, narrative theory, feminist theory. *Yale Journal of Law & the Humanities* 2: 37–57.

Rudden, B. 1987. Economic theory v. property law: The *numerus clausus* problem. In J. Eekelaar and J. Bell (eds.), *Oxford Essays in Jurisprudence*, 3rd series. Oxford: Clarendon Press, 239–63.

Shiffrin, S. V. 2001. Lockean arguments for private intellectual property. In S. R. Munzer (ed.), *New Essays in the Legal and Political Theory of Property.* Cambridge, UK: Cambridge University Press, 138–67.

Singer, J. B. 1989. Divorce reform and gender justice. *North Carolina Law Review* 67: 1103–21.

Singer, J. W. 1988. The reliance interest in property. *Stanford Law Review* 40: 611–751.

Smith, H. E. 2000. Semicommon property rights and scattering in the open fields. *Journal of Legal Studies* 29: 131–69.

Spur Industries, Inc. v. Del E. Webb Development Co. 1972. 108 Ariz. 178, 494 P.2d 700.

Treanor, W. M. 1995. The original understanding of the takings clause and the political process. *Columbia Law Review*, 95: 782–887.

— Chapter 11 —

Legal Evidence

Alvin I. Goldman

Scope of the Topic

The topic of evidence in the law can be approached either narrowly or broadly. The narrow construal restricts the topic to decisions about admitting or excluding evidence at trial. Evidence textbooks tend to focus on rules governing admission or exclusion and the ramifications of these rules. Research on rules of evidence tackles at least two other issues: the historical question of how and why the extant rules came into being and the policy question of whether current rules are in need of reform. The question of which evidence rules *ought* to be adopted is related to epistemology, a branch of philosophy that does not figure prominently in other parts of philosophy of law.

A broader construal of the evidence topic is also possible. Such a construal would go beyond questions of admissibility at trial by including pretrial evidence-handling procedures such as the collection of evidence during criminal investigation or the pretrial taking of depositions and the disclosure of evidence from one party to another during the "discovery" phase of litigation. The latter topics are usually treated under the headings of "criminal procedure" and "civil procedure." Even more expansively, the topic of evidence can address the general adequacy of the common-law adversary framework. Is the adversary format the best institutional structure for conducting legal adjudication? The present chapter adopts the broad construal, devoting a fair bit of space to issues outside the narrow scope of "rules of evidence." Later segments of the chapter, how-

ever, cleave to the core concern of the law of evidence.

The theory of legal evidence primarily concerns the resolution of matters of fact, which the "trier of fact" (a jury, judge, or magistrate) is responsible for determining. Other important determinations are also made in courts, for example, determinations about the content or applicability of the law. These decisions fall outside the scope of the theory of evidence as usually understood, mainly because they address the nature of law, or what exactly makes statements of law true, false, or indeterminate (lacking in truth value). These questions belong to jurisprudence, which is addressed elsewhere in this volume. See CAN THERE BE A THEORY OF LAW?

A Unified Theory: The Search for Truth

A theory of legal evidence can take a more unified or a less unified shape. A pluralistic theory would say that a multiplicity of irreducibly different aims and standards underlies the choice of evidence-handling procedures, no one of which is central or dominant. A unified theory, by contrast, would explain all or most procedures of evidence collection and utilization in terms of a single overarching rationale, or a single hierarchy of nested rationales. A pure version of the unity thesis would say that every practice concerning evidence is subsumable under a single dominant aim, with

163

no appeal to any independent elements. An impure version would highlight a single rationale (or hierarchy of rationales) but also acknowledge assorted side-constraints that exist alongside the dominant rationale. This chapter begins by developing the case for an impure unity thesis.

A unity thesis is a thesis about the (dominant) *aim* or *rationale* of evidence-handling procedures. Such a thesis does not claim that present procedures actually achieve the posited aim. It merely holds that institutions of legal adjudication (or enforcement) are best understood in terms of this aim, however successful or unsuccessful the currently chosen means may be. What is meant here in speaking of an institutional aim or rationale is a rationale that best explains and justifies official policies and statements offered in behalf of those policies. Identifying one or more rationales for current procedures is important for the theory of evidence because it provides some standards by which to evaluate both existing and proposed procedures.

A widely endorsed unity thesis is that a principal aim of evidence-handling procedures, and the aim most pertinent to the theory of evidence, is the aim of promoting the *accurate* or *truthful* determination of facts relevant to the case at hand (Twining 1984: 261, 272). However, the search for truth is not the highest level, or overarching, aim of adjudication. The overarching aim is securing *substantively just* treatment of individuals. Substantive justice is a matter of treating individuals in appropriate ways given (1) the content of the law and (2) the genuine, or true, facts concerning the actions they (and others) performed and the circumstances of those actions. Given this characterization of substantive justice, especially element (2), it is clear that determining the truth about a person's actions (etc.) is a crucial *means* to just treatment. Thus, truthful determination of facts becomes a derivative aim of the legal system, but the paramount aim in matters of evidence handling.

Substantive justice should be distinguished from procedural justice. Procedural justice is treatment that results from the correct application of proper procedures or processes. If people are convicted by wholly proper procedures of crimes they did not commit, what is done is procedurally just but substantively unjust. The search for truth is a means to substantive justice, and many if not most evidence-related procedures are selected with an eye to truth determination. But some procedures in the domain of evidence are not designed to promote the search for truth, and are even known to have a countervailing tendency. They are chosen for such purposes as safeguarding certain rights and relationships, and of keeping the length and cost of litigation within reasonable bounds.

The thesis that evidence-handling procedures are primarily dedicated to the search for truth is most clearly supported in the core domain of evidence theory: the rules of evidence. Rules of evidence in the American legal system vary from jurisdiction to jurisdiction, but federal rules are at the center of the judicial system and heavily influence ones adopted at the state level. Support for the truth goal is found in many places, including central statements of the Federal Rules of Evidence (FRE) and several Supreme Court holdings. FRE 102 says that the "end" of the development of the law of evidence is "that the truth may be ascertained and proceedings justly determined." FRE 611 (a) says: "The court shall exercise reasonable control over the mode and order of interrogating witnesses and presenting evidence so as to (1) make the interrogation and presentation effective for the ascertainment of truth...." In one holding the Supreme Court observed that "[t]he basic purpose of a trial is the determination of truth" (*Tehan v. U.S. ex. rel. Shott* 1966).

Another evidence-handling domain in which the truth goal seems critical is the arena of "discovery" or "disclosure." At the pretrial stage of a civil legal proceeding, parties are required to disclose relevant evidence in their possession to the other side, and each side is entitled to make "discovery" requests to their opponents which the latter are obliged to honor. In civil actions this subject-matter is treated under the heading of "civil procedure" rather than "rules of evidence," but it still concerns the handling of evidence. This stage of a proceeding does not yet concern presentation of evidence to a trier of fact, only to an opposing party. However, if evidence disclosed to a party is helpful to its case, the party will present that evidence to the trier at the appropriate juncture. Thus, discovery procedures are designed to help get relevant facts before the court. The ultimate aim of these discovery requirements is substantive justice, to be achieved by means of truth determination by the trier of fact. These ideas are conveyed in the following passage by Charles Alan Wright:

[The federal civil discovery rules are] based on a philosophy that prior to trial every party to a civil action is entitled to the disclosure of all relevant information in the possession of any person, unless the information is privileged.... Victory is intended to go to the party *entitled* to it, *on all the facts*, rather than to the side that best uses it wits. (Wright 1983: 540; emphasis added)

That victory should go to the "entitled" party speaks to the aim of substantive justice. That substantive justice depends on "all the facts" speaks to the desirability of bringing all relevant truths to the attention of the factfinder.

It is clear that not all rules of evidence handling have a truth-oriented rationale. First, the (constitutional) exclusionary rule that bars the admission of illegally obtained evidence obviously has a different rationale from truth, and can certainly conflict with the truth aim. Second, the various "privileges" allow potential testimonial evidence to be kept out of court, despite the fact that this undoubtedly militates against the search for truth. Prominent among these privileges are the attorney–client privilege, the physician–patient privilege, and the marital privilege. Each of these rules permits people who have reliable, relevant information to keep secret what they know. These exclusions contrast with other types of exclusions, such as hearsay and character evidence, which are thought to enhance the search for truth because they exclude evidence that is believed to be prejudicial, unreliable, or otherwise prone to interfere with truth determination. The existence of non-truth-promoting exclusionary rules speaks to the system's acceptance of other values or aims in addition to truth-determination. Exactly what these values or aims are, however, is controversial.

It is also controversial which privileges have truth aims and which do not. Consider the privilege against self-incrimination, an injunction of the Constitution (the Fifth Amendment) rather than of the congressionally enacted federal rules

of evidence. The Fifth Amendment clause, which reads "No person...shall be compelled in any criminal case to be a witness against himself," is also the basis for *Miranda* rights that govern police interrogations (*Miranda v. Arizona* 1966). What is the rationale for the privilege against self-incrimination? The dominant view is that the rationale is unrelated to truth, but what value does the privilege protect?

One proposed rationale is that the self-incrimination clause protects a special zone of mental privacy (*Murphy v. Waterfront Commission* 1964: 55). But is our legal system committed to such a special zone? Akhil Amar (1997: 65–6) argues in the negative. Civil litigants are often called to testify concerning intensely private matters, for example, in divorce cases. Even in criminal cases, witnesses granted immunity from prosecution can be forced to testify about anything in their private mental enclave. This suggests that preserving a private zone is not a fundamental requirement of the legal system. See PRIVACY.

Another possible foundation of the self-incrimination clause is "noninstrumentalization," the idea that government must respect individuals as persons, which implies not using them as a means of their own destruction. But the noninstrumentalization rationale proves too much. The government "uses" persons as witnesses all the time, whether they are willing or not. It is a general duty of citizenship to serve as a witness when necessary to enforce the laws, and the government is allowed to force arrestees to submit to photographing, fingerprinting, and voice tests whose results may be used against them in criminal court (Amar 1997: 66–7).

Amar's explanation of the self-incrimination clause is a truth-based one. Truth is said to be a preeminent criminal procedure value in the Bill of Rights; most procedures were designed to protect innocent defendants from erroneous conviction (1997: 84). Especially when pressured, people may confess – or seem to confess – to crimes they never committed. As Sir William Blackstone put it, confessions "are the weakest and most suspicious of all testimony; ever liable to be obtained by artifice, false hopes, promises of favor or menaces; seldom remembered accurately, or reported with due precision; and incapable in their nature of being disproved by other negative evidence"

([1765–9] 1979: 357). Notice that well into the twentieth century many innocent defendants in noncapital cases could not afford lawyers and were not furnished lawyers by the government. If forced to take the stand, timid or nervous witnesses will often embarrass themselves to such a degree as to increase rather than remove prejudices against them (*Wilson v. United States* 1893: 66). Thus, the privilege of not bearing witness against oneself in a criminal case serves the goal of reliability. Despite these considerations, the truth-based interpretation of the Fifth Amendment is quite controversial (cf. Luban 1988).

Apart from the matter of privileges, the truth rationale is very powerful as a unifying rationale for a broad array of rules, principles, and policies in the evidence arena. Are there other contenders for the role of unifying rationale? One possibility is fairness or impartiality. According to this approach, evidence should be handled in a way that treats all parties fairly or impartially. The main question about this approach is whether fairness can be satisfactorily unpacked without covertly appealing to the truth rationale. One way to unpack fairness is to say that each party to the litigation should have an equal chance of winning, and evidence-handling procedures should be designed to preserve that equality. But if the prime rationale is equal chance of victory, why not exclude all evidence entirely and simply flip a coin? Obviously we don't want a system in which an innocent defendant has only a 50–50 chance of acquittal, or in which someone who causes no harm or damages stands a 50–50 chance of being held liable in a civil suit. An equal chance of winning or losing is not a desideratum of evidence-handling procedures. The proper desideratum is that parties who *merit* victory in virtue of the material facts should wind up favored by the evidence-handling system (favored in the sense of being more likely to win), and parties who deserve to lose should be disfavored by it. This is just another way of saying that a good system should yield evidence-related activity that generates merit-reflecting judgments, judgments that accord with the facts of the case, which is precisely what the truth-oriented approach holds (Goldman 1999: 280–1).

Perhaps there is another way to understand the fairness proposal. Perhaps it means merely that the *same* evidence-handling procedures should apply equally to opposing parties. One problem with this proposal is that certain evidential asymmetries between plaintiff and defendant are unobjectionable in fairness terms. For example, plaintiff and defendant shoulder different "burdens of proof" at trial. Second, equal application of evidence-handling procedures is not sufficient for satisfactoriness. As before, suppose an adjudication system required each party to simply state its view of the case (just make its "pleading") without presenting any evidence of the normal kind at all. This would treat the two parties symmetrically but the system would be grossly unsatisfactory, precisely because there is no reason to expect truth to emerge.

The fairness approach might be linked to the notion of procedural justice. Many people would insist that procedural justice is a crucial aim of the legal system, the content of which is not wholly traceable to truth maximization. Examples of such content might include notice, the right to be heard, and the right to confront witnesses. It is not entirely clear, however, exactly what notion of fairness would rationalize desiderata of procedural justice. Nor does it seem likely that either fairness or procedural justice could replace truth determination as the overarching aim of evidence-handling procedures.

Another contender for the role of unifying rationale is acceptability of the adjudication system, either acceptability to the litigants or acceptability to the public at large. Other things equal, it is certainly a good-making feature of an adjudication system that it be acceptable to all parties. But is this either a necessary or sufficient condition for its deserving high marks? It is not a necessary condition because guilty defendants accused of crimes might find fault with any effective and accurate system, but that should not disqualify such a system as a worthy one. It is not a sufficient condition because parties might be prepared to accept an adjudication system, warts and all, out of despair of doing better outside the system or of improving upon it (Goldman 1999: 282). What about acceptability to the public at large? Again, this is a good-making feature of an adjudication system, but hardly a satisfactory standard. A majority of the public might accept a system that ignores minority rights.

Furthermore, the public might accept a system because they are *ignorant* of its real consequences, for example, how often it yields convictions of the innocent, including the frequency with which it places innocent people on death row. In 2002 Governor Ryan of Illinois pardoned a number of death row inmates precisely because of decisive evidence of factually wrongful convictions. The mere fact that most people in Illinois had found the system acceptable does not show that it really passed muster. Relatively few citizens were sufficiently aware of the full facts of these cases, especially prior to findings by extrajudicial investigative bodies and belated DNA tests.

In sum, truth determination is the most plausible aim or rationale of evidence-handling procedures, though it is subsidiary to the desideratum of administering substantive justice.

The Adversary System and the Search for Truth

The American system of handling evidence prominently features the adversary form of litigation. Partisan lawyers for the two sides prepare all evidence and initiate and conduct the case at trial, while a largely passive judge acts as referee. This system descends, of course, from the English common-law tradition. In Western legal history it stands in contrast to the civil-law tradition of Continental Europe, in which a group of neutral judges gather all evidence (on both sides of the case), organize the evidence, and serve as trier of fact (akin to a jury). In the civil-law tradition, there is no "battle" between opposing sides of the sort found in American trials.

How good is the adversary system from the vantage point of truth? How does it compare in this respect with the civil-law tradition? One strong point of the adversary system is the marshalling of evidence. Zealous advocates are highly motivated to pursue lines of investigation thoroughly, and that seems to augur well for evidence collection. Presumably, when each side does this energetically, fewer items of potentially relevant evidence go undiscovered or unutilized than would happen under a different system. If neutral judges serve as investigators, for example, they

may not have a comparable level of motivation or dedication.

A second *prima facie* virtue of the adversary system, in regard to truth determination, is the dialectical argumentation of the trial. When lawyers criticize their opponents' inferences and cross-examine their witnesses, there is a better chance of pinpointing false or misleading statements, thereby revealing where the truth lies. At least this is a plausible conclusion if critical argumentation is indeed a good method of searching for truth.

Nonetheless, there are many weaknesses in the adversary system as judged by the standard of truth determination. First, given the influence assigned to lawyers, disparities in legal representation between opposing sides become a serious liability. The usual rhetoric in support of the adversary system assumes that the two sides are represented with equal strength, but that assumption is often dramatically inaccurate. Many capital cases are ones in which indigent defendants are represented by public defenders who lack time, skill, and/or motivation to conduct a satisfactory defense. In Texas and Illinois, underqualified or inattentive public defenders have resulted in a shocking number of death sentences, often where subsequent evidence demonstrates or strongly suggests the innocence of the defendants. Civil litigation provides other examples in which disparities in legal resources rather than the merits of the cases seem to explain the outcomes. In complex civil litigation, the number of hours a legal team devotes to a case can make a huge difference to the outcome, so the side that can afford larger billings has a much better chance of winning, other things being equal. The same applies to lead attorneys with exceptional skill or persuasive power. Victory is likely to go to litigants who can afford those attorneys, a feature unlikely to be highly correlated with truth.

Second, even if adversarial argumentation is generally truth-enhancing, not everything partisan lawyers do consists in argumentation. In cross-examination, for instance, an experienced lawyer can make a perfectly honest witness appear to be concealing significant facts. In such an activity, the lawyer is not merely arguing over a fixed body of evidence, but is in effect engaged in "molding" or "modifying" the evidence by producing actions or expressions in the witness that convey an impression at variance with the facts. If highly partisan cross-examination were not an integral part of the litigation process, this scenario would happen less often.

Third, partisan lawyers can tilt evidence in another way, by their selection, preparation, and payment of expert witnesses. The common-law system gives wide latitude to lawyers to select an expert who will testify to the desired proposition, even if it is not true (Gross 1991:1113–14). On many matters of professional expertise, there are stables of people who make careers of testifying on one or another side of a recurring set of issues. These expert witnesses are often described by judges and lawyers as "prostitutes," that is, people who live by selling services that should not be for sale (Gross 1991: 1115). Lawyers choose witnesses who are good at persuading jurors of the kind of proposition that favors the represented party, even if it isn't true. Of course, a similar thing occurs on the other side. This situation tends to confront the factfinder with two well-prepared but staunchly opposed positions, and it is very difficult to determine which one is right. Even a substantial consensus among experts in the field can easily get submerged or ignored in the partisan battle. None of this is conducive to truth determination. These problematic features of the common-law system are absent in the civil-law tradition, where experts are appointed by judges rather than lawyers, and contact between lawyers and experts (commonly called "judges' aides") is strenuously discouraged.

Legal adjudication is an interesting example of "social epistemology" (Goldman 1999), because it is devoted to an epistemic end – finding the truth – and many of its practices are social in the sense of involving interactions among multiple participants. The question addressed in this section is whether the adversary system, with its emphasis on a contest between zealous advocates, is an optimal institutional way of finding the truth. A good test case involves the "discovery" of evidence, especially documentary evidence, in the pretrial phase of civil litigation.

If, in a civil action, one litigant possesses documentary evidence that favors its case, it will, of course, introduce that evidence in court. If it possesses evidence that disfavors its case, it won't introduce that evidence in court and will prefer that it remain undisclosed to the opposition. Let us call the first kind of evidence "positive" and the second kind "negative" (Talbott and Goldman 1998). The 1938 Federal Rules of Civil Procedure incorporated procedures for obtaining pretrial disclosure of potential evidence, both positive and negative. One purpose was to solve the problem of "trial by ambush," in which a litigant keeps its positive evidence secret until it actually introduces it at trial, preventing the opposition from developing effective rebuttal evidence in a timely manner. A second purpose was to prevent a party from keeping its negative evidence altogether secret and never introduced in court.

The 1938 discovery rules were pretty successful in preventing "trial by ambush," but not very successful in getting parties to disclose negative evidence. Parties and their lawyers can be quite skillful at avoiding the extraction of negative evidence that the opposition would like (but may not antecedently know to exist). The federal discovery rules were amended in 1993 to require mandatory disclosure of relevant information, including known negative evidence. But it is unclear how effective these amendments are. If a party has in its possession a "smoking gun" document that threatens to doom its case, and if a loss of the case might cost millions of dollars in damages, the party may be prepared to go to extremes to keep the nature and existence of the document secret. A vivid example of this occurred in *Washington State Physicians Insurance Exchange & Association v. Fisons Corp.* (1993).

The problem of discovery is enmeshed in the adversary-advocacy system. If an attorney knows that his or her client in a civil suit possesses evidence that is potentially damaging to its case, what is the attorney's responsibility under the law and the professional rules of conduct for lawyers? This is a delicate matter. Talbott and Goldman (1998) argue that the adversarial tradition fosters a "Fair Fight" ethos in litigation, in which each side is supposed to do their best to win and nobody is expected to do anything that "helps" the other side. This might encourage the notion that it is legitimate for attorneys to assist their clients in "ducking and dodging" when an opponent tries to extract negative evidence, but this conception is inconsistent with the truth rationale for a litigation system. Talbott and Goldman (1998) propose amendments to discovery procedures that would impose stiff sanctions on attorneys for failing to assist the overall determination of truth (and hence justice), even if it means some dilution of a pure and unadulterated version of the adversarial ethos.

If the analysis of these matters is an exercise in social epistemology, then social epistemology departs from traditional epistemology's exclusive focus on the mental life of believers. Pursuit of truth does depend on what transpires in the heads of individuals, but some information that *reaches* those heads does so because of institutional practices. An institution can influence the performance or nonperformance of information-transmitting acts by people under that institution's aegis, and such information-transmitting acts are often critical to other people's ability to determine the truth.

Truth, Reliability, and Bayesianism

Whatever the virtues and vices of the adversary system, discussions of evidence in the American legal system generally take it for granted. Most discussions also take for granted the basic precepts of the rules of evidence, and proceed to consider possible reforms and fine-tuning of more specific rules. There remain, however, some fundamental philosophical problems about the basic precepts, and these deserve scrutiny.

At the heart of the Federal Rules of Evidence is the concept of relevant evidence. Relevant evidence is generally admissible, whereas irrelevant evidence is not admissible. FRE 401 defines "relevant evidence" as evidence having "any tendency to make the existence of any fact that is of consequence to the determination of the action more probable or less probable than it would be without the evidence." How are the phrases "more probable" and "less probable" to be interpreted? One possibility is to interpret them in terms of *rational degrees of belief.* On this interpretation, FRE 401 says that relevant evidence is evidence such that rational people would assign a

higher or lower degree of belief (or subjective credence) in the existence of the fact if they were given the evidence than they would assign without the evidence. But what determines what it is rational to do? According to Bayesianism, the most prominent theory of probability and evidence, it is rational to conform one's degrees of belief to the probability calculus. But according to Bayesianism what makes it rational to raise, lower, or maintain one's degree of belief in a hypothesis depends on one's prior degrees of belief about the likelihood (conditional probability) of getting the evidence if the hypothesis is true versus the likelihood of getting that evidence if the hypothesis is false.

Bayesian agents use the following formula to update their degree of belief in hypothesis H if given evidence E:

$$P(H/E) = \frac{P(E/H)\,P(H)}{P(E/H)\,P(H) + P(E/\sim H)\,P(\sim H)}$$

Bayesian agents who receive a new piece of evidence E and use this formula will increase their degree of belief in a hypothesis H if their subjective estimate of $P(E/H)$ exceeds their subjective estimate of $P(E/\sim H)$, will decrease their degree of belief in H if their subjective estimate of $P(E/H)$ is less than their subjective estimate of $P(E/\sim H)$, and will leave their degree of belief in H unchanged if their subjective estimate of $P(E/H)$ equals their subjective estimate of $P(E/\sim H)$. So, under orthodox Bayesianism, whether a given piece of evidence increases, decreases, or leaves unchanged the degree of belief in a factual hypothesis depends on their subjective likelihood ratio, that is, $P(E/H)$ divided by $P(E/\sim H)$. Since different people might have different subjective likelihood ratios, whose subjective likelihood ratio should be used in deciding whether evidence meets the relevance test? In practical terms, of course, judges will use their own subjective likelihood ratio. But is that the proper *standard* that FRE 401 means to present? What if a judge has a wildly inaccurate subjective likelihood ratio? It may be replied that the judge has the duty of being well enough informed that his or her likelihood ratio is accurate. But "accuracy" suggests that there is also, independently of the judge's opinion, an *objective* (true) likelihood ratio against which subjective likelihood ratios can be measured for accuracy. This would quickly resolve the interpretation of FRE 401 – evidence makes a hypothesis more probable or less probable as long as the objective likelihood ratio is not 1.0. But most Bayesians do not accept the assumption of objective likelihoods and likelihood ratios. Orthodox Bayesianism is purely subjectivist, or "personalistic."

If objective likelihoods are assumed, however, that would help make sense of other requirements of the Federal Rules of Evidence, and the entire truth rationale to which it is committed. Consider FRE 403, which says that relevant evidence may be excluded if, among other things, its "probative value" is outweighed by the danger of misleading the jury. What does it mean for evidence to "mislead" a jury? A plausible interpretation is that jurors are misled if they make a (serious) mistake about the *real* probative value of the evidence. In Bayesian terms, this happens if jurors associate with the evidence a different subjective likelihood ratio than its true likelihood ratio, and hence are prone to revise their degree of belief in the hypothesis inappropriately, for example, revising it upwards or downwards excessively, not in accord with the true likelihood ratio. This is just what Richard Lempert suggests, that a "misled" juror might be a juror who *misestimates* the likelihood ratio (Lempert 1977; Lempert, Gross, and Liebman 2000: 232–3). Lempert also suggests that the courts may have been concerned with precisely this danger in excluding evidence of character traits or withdrawn guilty pleas. Jurors may have a tendency to magnify the import of character traits or withdrawn guilty pleas. "Misestimation" or "magnification" of a likelihood ratio must involve making an estimate that is too high or too low relative to the *objective* likelihood ratio. Thus, assuming objective likelihoods would make sense of the Federal Rules of Evidence.

Other reasons also make it hard to interpret the federal rules in purely subjectivist Bayesian terms. The federal rules heavily invoke the truth aim, but there is no tight connection between subjective Bayesianism and truth determination, because subjective Bayesianism gives no guidance on how to form one's "priors" (i.e., one's prior assignments to the target hypothesis) or one's likelihood estimates. The absence of a tight connection with truth determination is candidly acknowledged by Joseph Kadane and David Schum, coauthors of one of the most sophisticated treatments of Bayesianism in the legal domain (Kadane and Schum 1996). They admit that subjectivist methods cannot promise objectivity or truth-conduciveness. "Should persons adopting an ... approach [like ours] ... believe that his approach leads us closer to 'the truth' ...? The answer is *no*" (1996: 197). If Bayesianism is to mesh with the truth rationale, it cannot be accomplished via the usual subjectivist variety of Bayesianism.

Another prominent term in the judicial literature on evidence is "reliability." In many arenas of testimony, the Supreme Court has appealed to reliability as the crucial element for admissible testimony. In the landmark *Daubert* case, concerning testimony by scientific experts, the Court held that under the Federal Rules of Evidence "the trial judge must ensure that any and all scientific testimony or evidence admitted is not only relevant, but reliable" (*Daubert v. Merrell Dow Pharmaceuticals* 1993: 589). Testimony is considered reliable if it is likely to be true or accurate. So truth-conduciveness again seems to be paramount. If Bayesianism is to be serviceable as a general theory of legal evidence, it must be extended beyond purely subjectivist forms of Bayesianism.

In considering Bayesianism in the context of legal evidence, two things might be meant. First, one might propose that triers of fact (jurors) should use Bayesian methods, and therefore should be instructed in these methods by suitable experts. Second, one might propose Bayesian methods as a tool for legal *theorists*, who seek to analyze the impact of various rules. As regards the first proposal, a Court of Appeal in Britain has rejected the notion that jurors should be encouraged to use Bayesian methods. It contended that precise numbers conceal the element of judgment, and claimed that discrete numerical assignments cannot be given to separate items of evidence, as is required under Bayesianism. Broadly similar criticisms have been made by Lawrence Tribe (1971). But should expert witnesses give no numbers at all to juries? Ian Evett (1987), a British forensic scientist, has suggested that expert witnesses could translate likelihood ratios into verbal equivalents of how much support the evidence provides for the proposition. They could say that the evidence "slightly increases," "increases," "greatly increases," or "very greatly increases" the support for the proposition. This might induce juries to exploit the concepts behind Bayesian methods without being burdened with the mathematics.

Can Bayesianism legitimately be used by legal theorists, as is proposed here? Theorists will usually make statements like, "If a factfinder reasons in a Bayesian fashion, then such-and-such results will ensue." The problem with this is whether the antecedent is ever satisfied, or even approximated. Are ordinary jurors capable of reasoning in a Bayesian fashion? An influential research program on "heuristics and biases" maintains that lay reasoning violates Bayesian norms (Tversky and Kahneman 1982), and this constitutes a serious challenge to its application in the legal context. Other psychologists, however, find evidence that laypersons are capable of making roughly Bayesian use of probabilities if they are presented in a frequency format (actually, Tversky and Kahneman were the first to notice this, but did not emphasize it). Casscells, Schoenberger, and Grayboys (1978) had found that Harvard medical faculty gave wildly incorrect answers to a probabilistic inference problem in medical diagnosis. But when the same problem was presented in a frequency format – using the language of sampling, such as "8 out of 10" or "1 out of 100" – correct Bayesian answers rose from 18 to 76 percent (Cosmides and Tooby 1996). So perhaps laypersons are capable of approximating Bayesian reasoning when they understand the probabilistic information better.

Returning to our earlier question, how can Bayesian reasoning advance the cause of truth? An explanation of this requires an approach that I call "quasi-objective Bayesianism" (Goldman 2002). This theoretical approach studies what will transpire if agents reason in a Bayesianism fashion *and* their subjective likelihood estimates bear certain relationships to the objective values of these likelihoods. In a legal case, a target hypothesis might be H = "Brown shot Jones," and the evidence might be E = "a gun with fingerprints matching Brown's fingerprints was found near Jones's body." The likelihoods of interest are $P(E / H)$ and $P(E / \sim H)$. The distinctive feature of quasi-objective Bayesianism is the assumption that these conditional probabilities have objective as well as subjective values. Given this assumption, the use of subjective likelihoods that match the objective likelihoods will, on average, lead a reasoner closer to the truth. This follows from the following theorem:

Theorem on Expected Increases in Truth-possession: If an agent uses new evidence to update his degree of belief in a hypothesis by Bayesian methods, and if his subjective likelihoods match the objective likelihoods (and his prior probabilities are neither 0 nor 1.0 and the likelihood ratio does not equal 1.0), then there is an objective expectation that he will increase his degree of truth-possession with respect to this hypothesis (Goldman and Shaked 1991; Goldman 1999: 115–21).

Ignoring details, the theorem says that the Bayesian use of new evidence together with accurate subjective likelihoods entails an objective expectation of a positive increase in degree of truth-possession with respect to a hypothesis H.

What is meant here by "degrees of truth-possession"? If one believes a true proposition outright, one "possesses" that truth completely, to degree 1.0. More generally, if one's degree of belief in a true proposition is n ($0 \leq n \leq 1.0$), then one's degree of possession of that truth is n. To increase one's degree of truth-possession vis-à-vis the question of H vs. $\sim$H, one must increase one's degree of belief vis-à-vis the true member of that pair. The theorem stated above says that, no matter what one's prior degree of belief vis-à-vis H (except 0 and 1.0), if one's subjective likelihoods match the corresponding objective likelihoods, and if one reasons by Bayesian conditionalization, then one enjoys an objective expectation of increasing one's degree of truth-possession with respect to H vs. $\sim$H when moving from priors to posteriors. In particular, the objectively expected change in truth-possession is positive *whether H or $\sim$H is the true member of the pair*.

How does this theorem relate to a juror's ability to make true, or accurate, factual judgments? If jurors receive new evidence relevant to a hypothesis that bears on the case, and if their subjective likelihoods match the objective likelihoods, the theorem says they are in a position to get an expected increase in truth-possession by engaging in Bayesian inference from that evidence. Even if there are objective likelihoods, of course, it is far from easy to match those likelihoods. But the theorem says only that likelihood matching is *sufficient* for expected increases in truth-possession, not *necessary*. And there are good prospects for increasing truth-possession even when exact matching does not occur (Goldman 2002). Moreover, when an expert explains the methodology used to link a target hypothesis with evidence that has been presented, and when that methodology is reliable, this generally helps a juror make a more accurate estimate of the objective likelihoods. This is what occurs, or should occur, when an expert explains the significance of DNA evidence.

A theorem on the relative discriminatingness of an item of evidence is also instructive:

Theorem on Relative Discriminatingness: Other things being equal, the more extreme the objective likelihood ratio associated with a given item of evidence, the greater is the expected increase in truth-possession that comes from conditionalizing on that evidence (Goldman and Shaked 1991; Goldman 1999:121–3).

The more "decisive" or "probative" the evidence, the greater is the expected increase. Suppose a juror's prior degree of belief vis-à-vis H is 0.50, and he or she receives evidence E that bears on H vs. ~H. If the objective likelihood ratio = 0.60 / 0.20 = 3, and if the juror's subjective likelihood ratio matches the objective one, then the expected change in truth possession = +0.083. If the likelihood ratio = 0.80/0.10 = 8, then the juror's expected change in truth possession = +0.247. In general, more extreme likelihood ratios help an investigator make bigger expected jumps in the direction of truth, other things being equal.

The significance of these theorems depends, of course, on the existence of objective conditional probabilities, a problematic matter. Objective conditional probabilities – especially when applied to probabilities about a particular event occurring at a particular time, as is standard in the law – are not simply a function of actual base rates,

that is, observed relative frequencies. One proposal to interpret objective likelihoods (Goldman 2002) adopts a *modal* approach to the problem, invoking nonactual possibilities in the manner developed in philosophical treatments of counterfactual conditionals (Lewis 1973). The details of this proposal cannot be pursued here. It does appear, however, that the law of evidence *needs* an account of objective likelihoods quite apart from the specific theorems introduced above, because objective likelihoods are invoked in central uses of evidence, such as DNA evidence.

Applications of Quasi-objective Bayesianism

Can quasi-objective Bayesianism be applied to standard issues in legal evidence? As we have seen, FRE 403 gives judges discretion to exclude relevant evidence when it is likely to mislead the jury, for example, via misestimation of the probative force of the evidence. But should a court follow this advice whenever the expected misestimation will be large? Lempert et al. (2000) argue to the contrary: "[I]f the [objective] likelihood ratio for the evidence is 100:1 and the factfinder misperceives it as 1000:1, the error is unlikely to be critical because the evidence whether properly weighed or overweighted will usually lead to the same conclusion: that the favored hypothesis is established by the appropriate standard of proof" (2000: 233). Notice that this discussion presupposes the fundamental feature of quasi-objective Bayesianism: the existence of objective likelihoods. Although their point is basically a good one, it needs some qualification. Caution is in order with inflated likelihoods because inflated likelihoods, unlike perfectly accurate ones, have the property of expected decreases in truth-possession for *some* priors. However, even inflated likelihoods can lead to expected increases in truth-possession for a very extensive range of priors, although, unlike accurate likelihoods, they do not yield such increases across the entire range of priors (see Goldman 2002 for an illustration).

Next let us ask whether quasi-objective Bayesianism can help clarify a standard of legal proof, the standard in criminal cases of "beyond a reasonable doubt." Although the courts have acknowledged that the reasonable doubt standard is itself probabilistic, they have steadfastly declined to assign any particular probability to it, such as 90, 95, or 99 percent. Even if a particular probabilistic threshold were selected, would that solve the entire problem? Presumably, a body of evidence does not constitute sufficient "proof" simply because it elicits a level of confidence on the part of the factfinder that crosses the selected threshold. Such confidence might be elicited by extremely flimsy evidence, where the factfinder indulges in prejudice in arriving at its level of confidence. The level of confidence *per se* would not show that the evidence constituted proof beyond a reasonable doubt. Goldman (2002) proposes that what the legal system really wants is that the body of evidence be such that *were* the triers of fact to apply impeccable reasoning to it, they would reach the appropriate level of confidence. What conception of "impeccable" or "ideal" reasoning is appropriate? Here is where quasi-objective Bayesianism might be helpful. Part of ideal reasoning (in the legal context) is to start from a presumption of innocence. So the initial degree of belief the factfinder attaches to the factual allegations should be suitably low. Another part is that the factfinder should reason from the total evidence presented at trial in accordance with correct probabilistic reasoning, that is, Bayesian reasoning. Third, the reasoning should employ likelihoods that match, or at least approximate, the objective likelihoods. The proposal does not say the factfinder must actually satisfy these conditions in order for a body of evidence to meet the "beyond reasonable doubt" standard. It says that this standard is met only if the appropriate threshold confidence would be attained by the factfinder *if*, hypothetically, it engaged in ideal reasoning of the type specified. This approach bears a resemblance to other philosophical attempts to explain ordinary notions in terms of ideal procedures, for example, John Rawls's (1971) attempt to explain the notion of justice in terms of the hypothetical results of an ideal procedure.

Another illustration of quasi-objective Bayesianism concerns the selection of expert witnesses. For reasons explained earlier, partisan selection of expert witnesses has a number of drawbacks, and court appointment of expert witnesses seems to be a promising solution to some of these problems. Court appointment is permitted under FRE 706, but rarely used. Here is a quasi-objective Bayesian analysis of why court-appointed experts could solve one problem associated with lawyer-appointed experts. As noted earlier, attorneys commonly choose experts from stables of witnesses who make a living by testifying in a standard way on a recurring issue. In a given case, jurors may be confronted with two such witnesses for opposing sides. One testifies to H and the other to ~H. Each is very likely to testify to the same conclusion whether H or ~H were true. In other words, for the first witness, who in fact testifies to H, the conditional probability that he or she would testify to H if H were true is very close to the conditional probability that he or she would testify to H if ~H were true. And for the second witness, who testifies to ~H, the conditional probability that he or she would testify to ~H if H were true is very close to the conditional probability that he or she would testify to ~H if ~H were true. Thus, the conditional probability that they *both* would testify as they do if H were true is very close to the conditional probability that they both would testify as they do if ~H were true. If jurors had accurate estimates of these likelihoods, they would make very small changes, at most, as the result of hearing these witnesses. Thus, they have little expectation of increasing their degrees of truth-possession very much for H versus ~H by hearing the testimonial evidence of these two witnesses. If a neutral witness were selected, however, that witness's testimony is much more likely to be sensitive to, that is, to vary with, the truth of H versus ~H. The neutral witness is not so committed to one of these propositions by virtue of his or her professional reputation. This is the sort of witness that a court is more likely to appoint, and this is just the sort of witness whose testimonial evidence offers better prospects for expected increases in truth possession. First of all, the objective likelihood ratio associated with the neutral witness's testimony will be more extreme than the corresponding objective likelihood ratio associated with the paired testimonies of the first two experts described above. As we know from the Theorem on Relative Discriminatingness, such evidence offers the prospects for greater expected increases in truth possession. There is no guarantee, of course, that jurors will make accurate estimates of the likelihoods associated with this expert's testimony. But the least that can be said is that mildly accurate estimates offer reasonably good prospects for truth-possession increases, and nothing comparable can be said for pairs of partisan experts of the sort we have described. This is one reason to prefer court-appointed to party-appointed experts.

A large chunk of scholarly commentary on the rules of evidence concerns rules requiring the exclusion of certain types of evidence. There are rules requiring the exclusion of both character evidence (to prove conduct in accordance with character) and hearsay evidence, though both rules are heavily qualified by an abundance of exception clauses. In the case of hearsay, the exceptions practically nullify the fundamental exclusion rule. Scholars frequently criticize these rules and offer replacements. Since many of the criticisms have a truth-oriented rationale, quasi-objective Bayesianism may be helpful in evaluating such criticisms. Another domain in which it might be helpful is the treatment of cross-examination. Rules of evidence place great weight on cross-examination because it is traditionally thought that triers of fact can discriminate witnesses' credibility by their demeanor, in other words, can assign, on the basis of demeanor, fairly accurate likelihoods of the testimony being true or false. But experimental evidence suggests that laypersons are not very good at inferring truthfulness from demeanor, and that undercuts the traditional insistence on cross-examination (Wellborn 1991).

In many cases it is not clear whether, or to what extent, exclusions are based on the truth rationale. For example, FRE 410 declares inadmissible (for use against a defendant) evidence of pleas, plea discussions, and related statements made in the context of plea bargaining. The rationale for this exclusion may be partly truth-based, because triers of fact may overweight the probative value of statements made in a plea-bargaining context. A different rationale is also possible, however. The system may simply seek to encourage plea bargaining because of its efficiency, and to admit plea-bargaining statements in evidence at trial

may substantially reduce defendants' willingness to plea bargain. We should not exaggerate the role of the truth-rationale in the general theory of legal evidence. Where it is the governing consideration, however, quasi-objective Bayesianism may be a helpful analytical tool to evaluate rules of evidence.

References

Amar, A. R. 1997. *The Constitution and Criminal Procedure*. New Haven, CT: Yale University Press.

Blackstone, W. [1765–9] 1979. *Commentaries on the Laws of England*. Chicago: Chicago University Press.

Casscells, W., Schoenberger, A., and Grayboys, T. 1978. Interpretation by physicians of clinical laboratory results. *New England Journal of Medicine* 299: 999–1000.

Cosmides, L. and Tooby, J. 1996. Are humans good intuitive statisticians after all? Rethinking some conclusions from the literature on judgment under uncertainty. *Cognition* 58: 1–73.

Daubert v. Merrell Dow Pharmaceuticals. 1993. 509 U.S. 579.

Evett, I. W. 1987. Bayesian inference and forensic science: Problems and perspectives. *The Statistician* 36: 99–105.

Goldman, A. I. 1999. *Knowledge in a Social World*. Oxford: Oxford University Press.

Goldman, A. I. 2002. Quasi-objective Bayesianism and legal evidence. *Jurimetrics* 42: 237–60.

Goldman, A. I. and Shaked, M. 1991. An economic model of scientific activity and truth acquisition. *Philosophical Studies* 63: 31–55.

Gross, S. R. 1991. Expert evidence. *Wisconsin Law Review* 1991: 1113–1232.

Kadane, J. B. and Schum, D. A. 1996. *A Probabilistic Analysis of the Sacco and Vanzetti Evidence*. New York: Wiley.

Lempert, R. O. 1977. Modeling relevance. *Michigan Law Review* 75: 1021–57.

Lempert, R. O., Gross, S. R., and Liebman, J. S. 2000. *A Modern Approach to Evidence*, 3rd edn. St. Paul, MN: West Group.

Lewis, D. K. 1973. *Counterfactuals*. Oxford: Blackwell.

Luban, David. 1988. *Lawyers and Justice*. Princeton, NJ: Princeton University Press.

Miranda v. Arizona. 1966. 384 U.S. 436.

Murphy v. Waterfront Commission. 1964. 378 U.S. 52.

Rawls, J. 1971. *A Theory of Justice*. Cambridge, MA: Harvard University Press.

Talbott, W. J. and Goldman, A. I. 1998. Games lawyers play: Legal discovery and social epistemology. *Legal Theory* 4: 3–163.

Tehan v. U.S. ex. rel. *Shott*. 1966. 382 U.S. 406.

Tribe, L. H. 1971. Trial by mathematics: Precision and ritual in the legal process. *Harvard Law Review* 84: 1329–93.

Tversky, A. and Kahneman, D. 1982. Judgment under uncertainty: Heuristics and biases. In D. Kahneman, P. Slovic, and A. Tversky (eds.), *Judgment Under Uncertainty: Heuristics and Biases*. New York: Cambridge University Press, 3–20.

Twining, W. 1984. Evidence and legal theory. *Modern Law Review* 47: 261.

Washington State Physicians Insurance Exchange & Association v. Fisons Corp. 1993. 122 Wn 2d 299.

Wellborn, O. G. 1991. Demeanor. *Cornell Law Review* 76: 1075–1105.

Wilson v. United States. 1893. 149 U.S. 60.

Wright, C. A. 1983. *The Law of Federal Courts*, 4th edn. St Paul, MN: West.

Further Reading

Cohen, L. J. 1977. *The Probable and the Provable*. Oxford: Oxford University Press.

Damaska, M. 1997. *Evidence Law Adrift*. New Haven, CT: Yale University Press.

Earman, J. 1992. *Bayes or Bust?* Cambridge, MA: MIT Press.

Frank, J. 1949. *Courts on Trial*. Princeton, NJ: Princeton University Press.

Friedman, R. D. 1998. Truth and its rivals in the law of hearsay and confrontation. *Hastings Law Journal* 49: 545–64.

Friedman, R. D. 1998. *The Elements of Evidence*, 2nd edn. St. Paul, MN: West Group.

Gigerenzer, G. 2000. *Adaptive Thinking: Rationality in the Real World*. New York: Oxford University Press.

Howson, C. and Urbach, P. 1989. *Scientific Reasoning: The Bayesian Approach*. La Salle, IL: Open Court.

Jeffrey, R. C. 1983. *The Logic of Decision*, 2nd edn. New York: McGraw Hill.

Kaye, D. 1979. The paradox of the gatecrasher and other stories. *Arizona State Law Journal* 1979: 101–43.

Langbein, J. H. 1985. The German advantage in civil procedure. *University of Chicago Law Review* 52: 823–66.

Park, R. C. 1998. Character at the crossroads. *Hastings Law Journal* 49: 717–79.

Posner, R. A. 1999. An economic analysis of the law of evidence. *Stanford Law Review* 51:1477–1546.

Tillers, P. and Green, E. D. (eds.). 1988. *Probability and Inference in the Law of Evidence: The Uses and Limits of Bayesianism*. Boston: Reidel.

Part III

Perennial Topics

Chapter 12

Legal and Moral Obligation

Matthew H. Kramer

Questions pertaining to legal and moral obligation divide roughly into three main groups. For many legal and political philosophers, the central questions in this area concern the extent to which legal obligations – simply by dint of the fact that they are legal obligations – give rise to moral obligations. Inquiries of this first sort constitute what is often designated as the problem of political obligation; that is, someone who seeks to answer those inquiries is attempting to determine whether each citizen of a nation is morally obligated to obey the nation's legal requirements precisely because of the status of those requirements as laws.

Addressing a second array of questions on this topic, philosophers of law ask whether legal norms inherently purport to impose moral obligations in the course of imposing legal obligations. When the officials in a legal system state people's legal duties, do their statements carry the implication that the people bearing those duties are morally obligated to comply therewith? Regardless of whether the duty-imposing laws do in fact engender moral obligations of obedience, and regardless of whether the jural officials believe that such laws engender such obligations, do the officials' authoritative pronouncements on legal requirements imply that those requirements are morally binding? Or, more mildly, do those pronouncements at least imply that the officials' activities of enforcing the requirements are morally legitimate?

A third set of questions is of interest to moral philosophers as well as to legal philosophers. What are the basic characteristics of obligations,

and do those characteristics differ between the moral realm and the legal realm? Are there formal or structural differences as well as substantive differences, or does a high degree of similarity in the structural features account for the fact that the terminological and conceptual framework of law overlaps so strikingly with the terminological and conceptual framework of morality? Are all obligations correlated with rights, or do some obligations exist independently of anyone's rights?

These medleys of questions, which cut across the domains of legal, political, and moral philosophy, are the subject of this chapter. Though the third group of questions intersects with each of the other two in certain respects, the three can undistortively be expounded as separate sets of debates. (Throughout this chapter, the words "obligation" and "duty" are used interchangeably.)

The Obligation-to-Obey-the-Law

For centuries, political and legal theorists have pondered whether each person is under a general obligation of obedience to the legal norms of the society wherein he or she lives. The obligation at issue in those theorists' discussions is usually taken to be *prima-facie*, comprehensively applicable, universally borne, and content-independent. It is *prima-facie* in that it is subject to being exceeded in importance by countervailing considerations that are morally more weighty. Very few theorists have sought to argue that the obligation-to-obey-the-law is absolute and is thus insusceptible to being overridden by competing concerns. The obligation under discussion is *comprehensively applicable* in that it attaches to every one of a society's duty-imposing legal norms, rather than only to some subset of those norms. When we ask whether each person is under an obligation-to-obey-the-law, we are asking whether each person is under a *prima-facie* moral duty to abstain from violating any of the mandates established by the prevailing legal-governmental system. If such an obligation exists, then it is *universally borne* in the sense that absolutely everyone who is subject to the laws of any given jurisdiction must abide by that obligation and therefore must abide by those laws (unless the demands of those laws are overridden by some weightier countervailing factors). Also warranting a description of the obligation-to-obey-the-law as universal is the fact that it partakes of *content-independence*. That is, the applicability of the obligation does not depend on the morally worthy tenor of a legal system as a whole or on the morally worthy substance of any specific laws within the system. Instead, the obligation applies across the board to the norms of every functional legal regime.

Although many contemporary legal and political philosophers deny the existence of any moral obligation-to-obey-the-law of the sort recounted above, there have been numerous attempts – both past and present – to specify the grounds for such an obligation (Harris 1997: ch. 16; Horton 1992; Wolff 1996: ch. 2). Perhaps most famous are the attempts which focus on the idea that people consent in some fashion to the operations of their legal-governmental systems. Theories concentrating on consent generally present the obligation-to-obey-the-law as a species of promissory obligation. Having implicitly or explicitly undertaken to support the prevailing institutions of government, people are consequently bound to comply with the requirements laid down by those institutions. So, at least, a consent-focused account of political obligation maintains. Among the difficulties besetting any such account is the implausibility of the notion that people do in fact consent in any morally significant way to the matrices of laws within which they live. Moreover,

even if we could credibly establish such consent on the part of everyone, it would not be sufficient to undergird a comprehensively applicable and content-independent obligation of obedience. An implicit or explicit undertaking would not encompass absolutely every legal mandate that might be introduced; the consent involved in such an undertaking would be consent within limits. Much the same can be said in connection with the overall character of a regime. Should a regime decline into corrupt odium, any binding force previously conferred on its directives by undertakings of obedience would dissipate.

Thus, although theories of political obligation focused on consent have not altogether vanished, they have largely lost favor among political and legal philosophers. An alternative principle that became prominent in the second half of the twentieth century, the principle of fair play, was given expression by H. L. A. Hart: "When any number of persons conduct any joint enterprise according to rules, and thus restrict their liberty, those who have submitted to these restrictions when required have a right to similar submission from those who have benefited by their submission" (Hart 1955: 185). In this context, of course, the "joint enterprise" is an overall system of legal governance, which benefits people greatly by enabling them to enjoy orderliness, stability, and coordination. That is, the principle of fair play is combined with a view about the morally estimable functions performed by any operative legal system (even any legal system that may fall far short of moral worthiness in many other respects). Given the importance of those functions and the elementary demands of fairness, everyone is under a *prima-facie* moral duty to abide by the laws of his or her society simply because they are laws within a genuine legal regime. Such is the conclusion which the proponents of the principle of fair play seek to uphold.

As sketched above, the argument focused on fair play is clearly of enormous significance for legal philosophy as well as for political philosophy. After all, if the basic functions of law in combination with the principle of fairness were sufficient to generate a moral obligation of obedience that is comprehensively applicable, universally borne, and content-independent, then law and morality would be integrally connected in a far-reaching way. *Every* genuine legal system would not simply produce moral consequences – as natural phenomena like earthquakes also do – but would additionally partake of some degree of moral worthiness just by dint of existing and functioning as a system of law. The criteria for apprehending the existence of any legal system as such would not be separate from the criteria for ascribing *prima-facie* moral obligatoriness to every mandate in such a system. Legal positivism's insistence on the separability of law and morality would accordingly be subject to some major qualifications. Hence, a defense of legal positivism must extend into the realm of political philosophy to engage with the issue of the obligation-to-obey-the-law (Kramer 1999: 204–9, 254–308).

In fact, however, a host of problems afflict both the principle of fair play and the broader argument encompassing that principle. Some of the shortcomings in the principle of fair play relate to its presupposition that the burdens and benefits of general obedience with legal requirements will be equally distributed among people over the long term, while other shortcomings consist in the inapplicability of the principle to many ordinary situations that should be covered by it (Kramer 1999: 279–85). Although those difficulties cannot be explored here, they call into question the sustainability of any argument which draws on that principle as a ground for the obligation-to-obey-the-law. Furthermore, the argument that dwells on the basic functions of law is vulnerable in a number of other respects. Chief among its inadequacies is its assumption that the relevant baseline for comparison in an assessment of any legal system's moral bearings is a situation of anarchic tumult. Although the existence of law is essential for the viability of a civilized way of life in any society larger than a handful of families – and although a comparison between virtually any system of legal governance and a situation of anarchy will therefore reveal the former in a favorable light – the pertinent baseline for comparison when we gauge the merits of this or that particular legal system is not usually a situation of lawlessness but is instead any alternative legal system that could realistically be attained. Anarchic disorder is very seldom the lone feasible alternative to an existent legal regime; very often a worthier

regime is a feasible alternative. Consequently, no legal system's directives are endowed with obligatory force simply because the absence of all such directives would be worse (probably far worse) than the system as a whole.

Various other attempts to demonstrate the existence of a blanket obligation-to-obey-the-law have emerged from time to time. For example, some theorists have put forth arguments broadly similar to those just examined, but have concentrated on the desideratum of gratitude rather than on fairness. Other theorists have tried to base a blanket obligation-to-obey-the-law on utilitarian concerns, combined with an emphasis on the limitedness of human foresight (specifically, foresight concerning the salutariness of departing from the law's requirements). However, many contemporary legal and political philosophers have abandoned the effort to demonstrate the existence of a blanket obligation. Some have sought to argue instead in favor of a *prima-facie* obligation of obedience that is neither comprehensively applicable nor entirely content-independent (e.g., Gans 1992). Ronald Dworkin's focus on associative obligations, which obtain only in societies characterized by equal and substantial concern for the well-being of the people who belong thereto, is an example of such an approach (Dworkin 1986: 176–216). Others have striven to shift attention to alternative moral consequences that might follow from the basic functions of law, such as the *prima-facie* impermissibility of interfering with officials' endeavors to give effect to legal norms (e.g., Edmundson 1998). Still others have maintained that, although no one is under a *prima-facie* moral obligation to comply with every legal norm, the law through its official formulations and pronouncements nonetheless claims in effect that everyone is under such an obligation. It is to this last-mentioned line of argument, which distinguishes between obligatoriness and purported obligatoriness, that we now turn.

What the Law Claims

The distinction between the authority which the law possesses and the authority which the law professes to possess is most prominently emphasized in the work of Joseph Raz. He has presented several sophisticated lines of argument to underpin the view that officials' authoritative statements of legal obligations are perforce statements of moral obligations as well. Even when an authoritative pronouncement declaring the existence of some legal duty is made by an official who does not believe in the moral bindingness of the duty, the pronouncement necessarily implies that the duty is indeed morally binding. Such is the conclusion for which Raz argues (Raz 1979: 153–7, 1984, 1990: 123–9, 162–77).

His central line of reasoning in support of that conclusion is as follows. When judges or other officials authoritatively proclaim that some legal norm requires people to act in a certain way, they are declaring that people ought to act in that specified way. Now, because every "ought" statement in favor of a person's adoption of some particular mode of conduct is logically equivalent to a statement affirming the existence of some reason(s) for the person to adopt that mode of conduct, the proclamations of legal officials implicitly or explicitly assert that people have reasons to act in accordance with the terms of the prevailing legal mandates. That is, authoritative statements of legal obligations implicitly or explicitly presuppose the existence of reasons for people to perform the acts which the obligations require or to eschew the acts which the obligations forbid. Those reasons must be independent of anyone's interests, since the legal obligations themselves are independent of anyone's interests; because legal duties frequently require individuals to act against their own interests and their preferred objectives, the reasons-for-action constituted by the duties must be independent of those interests and objectives. Thus, statements of legal duties explicitly or implicitly affirm that people have interest-independent reasons to comply with the duties. In short, such statements imply that there are *moral* reasons for people to conduct themselves in conformity with the law's requirements.

The foregoing argument rests on the dubious premise that official declarations concerning what the law requires are necessarily declarations concerning how people *ought* to behave. To buttress that premise, Raz has offered a number of ancil-

lary lines of reasoning. For example, he highlights the justificatory tenor of the statements made by officials when they invoke legal obligations in order to explain their decisions. Their explanations are not purely informative but are also vindicatory, in that they attempt to show that their decisions and the mechanisms of enforcement which implement those decisions are morally legitimate and morally binding. In the course of contending that their determinations give effect to legal duties, judges and other officials establish or purport to establish the fundamental correctness of what they have done. They present those determinations as morally obligatory by presenting them – implicitly if not expressly – as grounded on moral reasons-for-action.

> While one can accept the law as a guide for one's own behaviour for reasons of one's own personal preferences or of self-interest one cannot adduce one's preferences or one's self-interest by themselves as a *justification* for holding that other people must, or have a duty to, act in a certain way. (Raz 1986: 92–3, emphasis added)

Another claim put forward by Raz in furtherance of his general position is that a denial of the ineluctably moral tenor of official legal pronouncements is tantamount to a denial of the distinction between law and the brute coercion of gangsters. As he states the matter in one of numerous relevant passages: "[T]he law – unlike the threats of the highwayman – claims to itself legitimacy. The law presents itself as justified" (Raz 1979: 158). In many respects, this new line of argument is a means of reinforcing the previous line, since it adduces a strong reason for thinking that the character of the authoritative assertions by legal officials is indeed morally justificatory. Unless we acknowledge that those assertions are justifications or purported justifications of the officials' decisions and actions, we shall have blinded ourselves to the very feature of any genuine legal regime that distinguishes it from the nakedly violent sway of thugs. We shall have returned to the model of a legal system as a gunman-writ-large – the very model, put forward by nineteenth-century legal positivists, from which Hart and other modern writers in the positivist tradition have endeavored to distance themselves. (See LEGAL POSITIVISM.) To avoid such a regressive step, we have to allow that legal systems invariably claim moral authority. While arguing as much, Raz does not suggest that such systems invariably partake of moral authority. On the contrary, he is alert to the potential for a gap between what is professed and what is actual. Still, while duly noting that potential gap, he submits that every veritable legal system does indeed profess to be morally authoritative.

A third argument which Raz propounds is focused on the inextricability of judges' actual or ostensible belief in a duty's legal bindingness and their actual or ostensible belief in the duty's moral bindingness. Given that those two facets of the judicial outlook are not credibly disseverable, an authoritative statement expressive of the former facet is likewise expressive of the latter. Hence, when judges invoke a legal mandate as a basis for a ruling, they are adverting to what they actually or apparently take to be a moral reason that requires the ruling. As Raz writes, in a rejoinder to a contrary view articulated by Hart:

> It is possible that while judges believe that legal obligations are morally binding this is not what they say when they assert the validity of obligations according to law. It may be that all they state is that certain relations exist between certain people and certain legal sources or laws. Their belief that those relations give rise to a (moral) obligation may be quite separate and may not be part of what they actually say when asserting obligations according to the law. But such an interpretation seems contrived and artificial. (Raz 1984: 131)

In short, according to Raz, a judge who invokes a legal duty actually or ostensibly believes that it is morally binding and that it derives its moral force partly or wholly from its status as a legal duty.

A final line of reasoning to be found occasionally in Raz's work and more often in the work of other theorists is premised on the distinction between moral legitimacy and moral obligatoriness. A legal norm is morally *legitimate* insofar as it does not require or authorize conduct that violates anyone's moral rights. The formulation and the implementation of such a norm do not involve the commission of any moral wrongs; the officials introducing and administering that norm are morally at liberty to engage in such courses of action. A legal norm is morally *obligatory* insofar as its addressees are morally required to comply with its terms or to acquiesce in what it authorizes. The formulation and the implementation of such a norm impose duties on the people subject to it, who are not morally at liberty to disregard its demands.

Although Raz often uses the term "legitimacy" when writing of the law's claim to authority, he generally has in mind the law's claim to be morally binding. In his view, official statements which assert legal obligations are statements which assert or purport to assert moral *obligations*. Occasionally, however, he appears to suggest instead that what is presupposed by the statements of legal officials is a claim to moral legitimacy:

> Given that the courts are manned by people who will act only in ways they perceive to be valuable, principles of adjudication will not be viable, will not be followed by the courts, unless they can reasonably be thought to be morally acceptable, even though the thought may be misguided. (Raz 1994: 317–18)

Other legal philosophers, such as Philip Soper, have more clearly and emphatically declared that the central presupposition of the law is its own moral legitimacy. Soper submits, for example, that an essential tenet of any legal system is "that the State does no wrong (is not morally culpable) in acting on (enforcing) the norms which, in good faith, it believes are necessary to govern society" (Soper 1995: 375). In such passages as these, then, we encounter the thesis that the law invariably presents itself and its requirements as morally unexceptionable.

Raz's views concerning officials' invocations of legal obligations, intimately connected with his views concerning the law's general claim to moral authority, have been broadly influential but have recently come under sustained challenge (Kramer 1999: ch. 4). Each of the four lines of reasoning sketched above has been impugned. The first, pertaining to the justificatory tenor of officials' authoritative pronouncements, is doubtful even if we grant that publicly accessible explanations of official decisions are an integral feature of anything that counts as a full-fledged legal system.

In a wicked legal system, both the actual purpose and the avowed purpose of those explanations can consist in the reinforcement of incentives for compliance with evil dictates, rather than in the ascription of moral authority to the decisions that apply the dictates. Officials within such a regime may well explain their heinous decisions by reference to people's legal obligations, but their purpose in doing so will not necessarily be to demonstrate the decisions' moral warrantedness; rather, their purpose might be to make clear that violations of applicable legal requirements will indeed trigger punishments. In emphasizing the connection between the breaching of duties and the incurring of penalties, the officials need not be aiming to establish that their decisions are fair. They may simply want to sustain people's incentives for submission to the law's evil demands. After all, if the imposition of punishments manifestly bears very little relation to the legal culpability or innocence of each person, then the inclination of the law's addressees to abide by its requirements will dwindle. Thus, faced with the task of providing strong inducements for people to behave in accordance with repugnant legal norms, the officials who administer those norms in a malevolent regime are well advised to explain their decisions credibly by reference to people's legal duties. Their highlighting of the correlation between nonfulfillment-of-duty and subjection-to-punishment is a means of fostering a pattern of incentives that will promote the efficacious functioning of directives which are highly distasteful to the people called upon to abide by them. Within such a regime, official explanations of decisions play a role in a ruthless process of securing obedience, rather than in a process of moral justification.

Hence, a defender of Raz's position cannot rely on the notion that the authoritative pronouncements of judges and other legal officials are invariably justificatory. Equally vulnerable is the thesis that legal officials must claim moral authority for the workings of their regime if those workings are to differ at all from the undisguised thuggishness of gangsters. The decisive difference between law and raw coercion lies not in a claim to moral authority, but in the sway of norms. Whereas the ascendance of a gunman over his victims typically involves situation-specific orders rather than any general mandates or standards, a regime of law must involve a framework of operative general norms if it is to be properly classifiable as a regime of law. Even in an evil legal regime where officials impose requirements upon citizens that are starkly in the officials' own interests, the means by which the officials impose the exploitative requirements are distinctively jural. Whereas a highwayman almost always issues his orders to an extremely limited set of people for an extremely limited stretch of time, a system of governance that counts as a full-fledged regime of law will have imposed its mandates through various sorts of norms (statutes, regulations, general decrees, judicial principles, and so forth) that typically apply to indefinitely numerous people for long periods of time. Those norms together cover a far, far wider range of behavior than do the usual instructions of a highwayman.

The dictates uttered during a heist by a gunman are narrowly focused on certain specific instances of conduct to be undertaken by a small group of people who are temporarily in proximity with him; moreover, those dictates are hardly ever intended to be applicable to the victims after the brief period during which the heist is carried out. Laws, by contrast, extend to general classes of people and to general modes of conduct, and they typically last for long periods (often for indefinitely long periods). All or most laws have the general applicability and standing durability of norms. A gunman's instructions, contrariwise, are almost always occasion-specific through and through. Furthermore, because the formulation and implementation of the gunman's orders are less systematic than the formulation and implementation of legal norms, the likelihood of a close correspondence between the stage of formulation and the stage of implementation is considerably greater in a legal system than in a heist. Unless a gunman intends to prey on future victims who will probably recognize him and who will know about his treatment of his current victims, he does not have to worry about impairing the incentives for his future victims to submit. A legal regime, even a monstrous legal regime, is quite different. Officials have to be concerned about the effects of their current actions on the motivations of people in the future. If officials do not sustain a high correlation between disobedience and punishment, then the incentives for citizens to comply with repellent laws will greatly diminish. Hence, given that wicked rulers will doubtless want their malign mandates to channel people's behavior effectively, they will have good grounds for enforcing those mandates substantially in accordance with the terms thereof. Unlike a robber's fleeting encounter with his victims, the reign of repressive officials is a long-run enterprise whose success depends on the cultivation of long-run incentives for compliance. The temporal extendedness of an evil legal regime's existence is a factor which helps to ensure that the regime operates in the manner of a system of law. Its continuousness promotes the regularity of its workings – which is to say that one distinctive feature of law (i.e., one feature that differentiates legal norms from a gunman's commands) promotes the existence of another indispensable feature.

Raz's third strand of argument, which concentrates on the inextricability of a judge's beliefs concerning the legally binding force and the morally binding force of any obligation, is even more plainly susceptible to challenges. On the one hand, we should accept the point about the inseparability of the specified beliefs. When judges announce that somebody is obligated to comply with a legal mandate, and when they view the mandate as morally obligatory for anyone to whom it applies, they almost certainly do not see themselves as making a statement about a purely legal requirement – a requirement that might or might not partake of moral significance. On the other hand, the intertwinedness of the legal judgment and the moral judgment in such a situation does not obtain when we shift our attention to heinous legal regimes wherein judges neither believe nor pretend to believe that the obligations which they enforce are morally worthy. When the officials in such a regime invoke the vile directives thereof in order to explain their decisions, they do so (or might well do so) exclusively to reinforce incentives for compliance, rather than to justify the decisions as fair. Such officials make statements of legal obligations without committing themselves implicitly or explicitly to the notion that those obligations are morally binding. In other words, Raz's third line of argument would be suitable for his purpose only if legal officials

must always believe or profess to believe that the legal requirements which they invoke and enforce are morally obligatory. Because such an actual or professed outlook on the part of officials is by no means inevitable, Raz's argument is of limited applicability. A line of reasoning that is sound when applied to benevolent legal regimes – and also to some woefully misguided legal regimes – is unsound when applied to legal regimes that are undisguisedly exploitative.

Equally unavailing is the focus on moral legitimacy (as opposed to moral obligatoriness) that turns up occasionally in Raz's work and much more frequently in the work of Soper and others. Arguments that adopt such a focus tend erroneously to assume that someone who does not claim to be acting legitimately is thereby necessarily claiming to be acting *illegitimately.* Even if we agree that the officials in any genuine legal system are exceedingly unlikely to advance a claim of the latter sort, we are not obliged to accept that those officials must be expressly or implicitly advancing a claim of the former sort. If they are running a vile regime, they may simply display complete indifference to questions about the moral legitimacy or illegitimacy of their actions. Here the analogy between such officials and a group of gunmen is illuminating, despite the imperfections of that analogy in several other respects. The gunmen are exceedingly unlikely to announce: "We hereby issue a reprehensibly unjust demand for your money!" However, the improbability of that self-accusatory assertion should not lead us to infer that the gunmen's orders explicitly or implicitly present themselves as morally worthy. Instead, the gunmen and their behests will very likely exhibit a thoroughgoing lack of concern with the moral status of their conduct. If the immorality of their conduct were pointed out to them by one of their victims, they would very likely not respond by denying the charge. Their response, rather, would be "So what?" Their dictates to their victims carry (or, at any rate, might well carry) the moral indifference of the "So what?" response, rather than the pretended moral sensitivity of an implicit claim-to-legitimacy.

Officials in a wicked legal regime may show the same unconcern about even purporting to be morally conscientious. On the one hand, to be sure, the officials face some constraints and pressures which gunmen typically do not face. As has already been discussed, the persistence and regularity of the officials' interaction with citizens are not usually characteristic of a gunman's inter- action with his victims. As a result, the officials may feel a greater need than do gunmen to depict their own actions as morally acceptable. On the other hand, there is no basis for thinking that officials in a monstrous legal regime will invari- ably commend their actions in such a fashion. Though they are highly unlikely to describe the norms of their regime candidly as evil, they may simply exhibit indifference to the moral status of those norms. Each official might deal with ques- tions of the immorality or morality of his or her conduct by contemptuously ignoring them. A brusquely dismissive wave of the hand, rather than a negative shake of the head, may be the gesture which each official deems to be most suitable. Of course, a reticent disdain for ques- tions about the morality or immorality of insti- tutions and decisions is not the only posture which evil officials might adopt; but it is certainly not an outlandish posture that can never be at- tributed to them without ludicrousness.

Hence, by failing to distinguish adequately between indicating-moral-disapproval and not- indicating-moral-approval, and thus by suppos- ing that the only alternative to an indication of moral disapproval is an indication of moral ap- proval, the arguments propounded by Soper and others have wrongly concluded that we must ascribe to every official utterance a tacit or explicit seal of moral self-approbation. We should recog- nize the credible possibility of a contrary state of affairs. An iniquitous legal system might not ad- vance any claim to legitimacy, precisely because the absence of such a claim can be due to contemptu- ous indifference rather than to an overt disavowal.

In sum, we can detect weaknesses in all four of the principal lines of reasoning that have been put forward to support the view that official pro- nouncements on people's legal duties ineluctably ascribe moral obligatoriness or moral legitimacy to those duties. No such ascription of moral obli- gatoriness or legitimacy is necessarily presup- posed by any such pronouncement. Officials in perfectly believable circumstances might invoke people's legal duties without tacitly or expressly

claiming that those duties are morally binding, and without even tacitly or expressly claiming that the enforcement of those duties is morally permissible. Although virtually anyone participat- ing in the running of a morally commendable system of law will generally believe that the duties imposed by the system's mandates are a subset of people's moral duties, the officials in a monstrous regime might neither harbor nor profess to harbor such a belief. Their invocations of the obligations imposed by the vile directives of their regime would not implicitly or explicitly presuppose that those obligations constitute moral reasons-for-action on the part of the direct- ives' addressees.

Of course, nothing in this rejoinder to Raz is meant to suggest that an extreme variant of the monstrous regime just mentioned – a variant in which *all* the officials are *always* too cynical and self-assured to engage even in hypocritical affirm- ations of the moral obligatoriness of the mandates which they enforce – is itself credible. It is highly unlikely that all the officials in a vile regime on all occasions of law-application would decline to maintain that their legal requirements are morally obligatory. However, what is much more likely is that *some* of those officials on *some* occasions of law-application will dispense with any pretense of moral obligatoriness or moral legitimacy even while they justify their decisions by reference to the general directives of their regime. The highly credible possibility of such occas- ions is sufficient to falsify Raz's claim that officials' assertions of legal obligations are neces- sarily assertions of moral obligations.

Matters of Form

In discussions about the moral consequences of legal obligations and about the tenor of the offi- cial pronouncements which affirm such obliga- tions, theorists largely take for granted the basic characteristics of obligations in law and morality. This chapter closes by probing some of those characteristics, in order to explore the fundamen- tal similarities and dissimilarities between legal and moral duties. An obligation in either the moral realm or the legal realm is a requirement directly or indirectly laid down by a general norm. A duty imposed by a general norm can be applicable to everyone at all times, or it can ensue from some occurrence that has rendered a norm applicable to a certain person or set of persons; an example of the former sort is the duty of each person to abstain from committing murder, while an example of the latter sort is the duty of some person to carry out a promise which he or she has made. (A small number of philosophers, known as "moral particularists," would dissent from the emphasis here on general norms. However, most of the points in this discussion do not depend on a rejection of moral particularism.)

Now, although an obligation consists in mandatoriness, it does not consist in physical prevention or compulsion. Its constraining effects are normative rather than physical. An obligation-to-abstain-from-X does not in itself render any action impossible or even difficult; rather, it renders X impermissible. A duty borne by some person requires that person to do something or forbids that person to do something, but does not *per se* physically preclude the person from doing anything. People obligated to behave in a certain manner can usually behave in a contrary manner – though their doing so is legally or morally wrong (or both legally and morally wrong).

When people do not comply with a duty, they have *pro tanto* behaved wrongly. They have done something impermissible or have failed to do something mandatory, and have thereby acted at odds with some moral norm(s) or legal norm(s). If their noncompliance with the duty is not due to their having been under an even more pressing obligation that cut in the opposite direction, then the noncompliance is an outright violation of the norm that imposes the duty. On the other hand, if the noncompliance is indeed due to the presence of an even more pressing obligation, then it is merely an infringement of the aforementioned norm.

Even an infringement must be remedied, albeit perhaps solely through an apology. Indeed, though legal obligations are sometimes viewed as distinctively connected with remedies, only moral obligations are invariably connected therewith. Some legal duties are purely nominal, in that the norms which establish them do not provide for any means of giving effect to them

(Kramer 2001: 65–78). Although such legal duties instruct people to act in specified ways, the instructions receive no backing whatsoever from any legally authorized penalties or punishments. Those duties exist purely as formulations, and are not only unenforced but are also unenforceable. Within conventional or positive morality (that is, within prevailing moral codes that emerge as such by dint of being widely accepted), there is similarly a potential for nominal duties. However, within the domain of critical or transcendent morality – that is, within the domain of moral norms whose status as binding requirements does not depend on their being accepted – there is no room for nominal duties. Within that domain, if a person P owes an unwaived moral duty-to-do-x to some other person Q, then P will have committed at least a *prima-facie* moral wrong against Q if he fails to do x. What this means in turn is that P will have placed himself under a remedial obligation to Q if he fails to do x. In other words, P owes Q a moral duty-to-do-x if and only if P's failure to do x will have placed P under a moral obligation to Q to remedy the resultant situation in some way. Duties are integrally and invariably connected to remedies in the domain of critical morality. Precisely because the norms in that domain are independent of conventional formulations, they do not give rise to duties that exist only as formulations. (Note that the argument in this paragraph leaves entirely open the nature of the appropriate remedy in each case. In some circumstances, the fulfillment of P's remedial duty might consist simply in his acknowledging the correctness of chastisement from Q or from someone else. See PRIVACY.)

Both in the realm of morality and in the realm of law, obligations amount to reasons-for-action with a special force. Exactly how that force should be understood is a matter of controversy among legal and moral philosophers, however. Perhaps most common among the approaches to this topic is the construal of moral duties and morally justified legal duties as especially weighty nonprudential reasons-for-action. Any such reason is virtually insusceptible to being overridden, except by an even more pressing moral or legal obligation. Other considerations remain operative reasons-for-action that should be taken into account during any process of practical deliberation, but they will generally be outweighed insofar as they clash with people's duties.

A rival approach has been developed by Geoffrey Warnock and Joseph Raz, among other theorists (Raz 1990; Warnock 1971). Instead of viewing moral and legal obligations as simply weightier than all or most other factors on which people's deliberations might be focused, the adherents of this alternative perspective maintain that such obligations partake of exclusionary or peremptory force. In other words, the obligations not only are themselves reasons-for-action, but they additionally are reasons for not acting on the basis of other reasons. They are first-order reasons that directly enter people's deliberations as considerations to be taken into account, and they are also second-order reasons that affect people's deliberations by depriving certain other considerations of their status as operative reasons-for-action. (The excluded considerations are divested of that status because decisions and actions ought not to be based on them, even if the decisions and actions are in accordance with those considerations. However, the excluded factors are still reasons-for-action in other respects; courses of conduct that tally with them are *ceteris paribus* better than courses of conduct that run contrary to them.)

Proponents of the second approach to analyzing the special force of moral and legal duties have sought to distance it from the first approach. As Raz contends: "If [exclusionary reasons such as obligations] have to compete in weight with the excluded reasons, they will only exclude reasons which they outweigh, and thus lose distinctiveness" (Raz 1990: 190). However, because the supporters of the first approach regard obligations as especially weighty reasons, and because the supporters of the second approach accept that the exclusionary sway of just about any exclusionary reason is restricted in its scope, the two perspectives are by no means as clearly divergent as they might at first seem to be. Indeed, some prominent recent models of norm-based deliberation, such as Frederick Schauer's account of "decision-making by entrenched generalization" (Schauer 1991: ch. 5), are largely combinations of the two lines of analysis.

Whatever may be the best way of explicating the special force of moral and legal obligations, that force confers a significant degree of normative protectedness on the people to whom the obligations are owed. The position of normative protectedness that consists in being owed a moral or legal duty is a moral or legal right. Rights and duties are thus correlative – that is, mutually entailing – in that a duty owed by P to Q requiring P's nonperformance (or performance) of some action x is a right held by Q against the performance (or nonperformance) of x by P. The existence of the duty entails the existence of the right, and vice versa. (See THEORIES OF RIGHTS.)

A question that has generated considerable controversy among legal philosophers – not all of it very illuminating – is whether every right correlates with a duty and vice versa. Four broad stances on this topic are possible: (1) every right is correlated with a duty, and every duty is correlated with a right; (2) every duty is correlated with a right, but some rights are uncorrelated with duties; (3) every right is correlated with a duty, but some duties are uncorrelated with rights; and (4) some duties are uncorrelated with rights, and some rights are uncorrelated with duties. The first of these four theses will be briefly examined here.

That first thesis has received its most rigorous formulation in the analytical framework developed by the American jurist Wesley Hohfeld in the early twentieth century (Kramer 1998). Within the Hohfeldian analysis, the correlativity of rights and duties is axiomatic; every duty is owed to a right-holder, and every right is held against a duty-bearer. Just as a slope's downward direction is not prior or posterior to its upward direction – either logically or temporally – a duty is not prior or posterior to the right with which it is correlated. The existence of each is a necessary and sufficient condition for the existence of the other. (Although all of the points below are consistent with the Hohfeldian analytical framework, one or two of them will go beyond anything stated by Hohfeld himself.)

On the one hand, the Hohfeldian analysis is stipulative and purificatory rather than empirical. That is, it explicates the concepts of "right" and "duty" in such a way as to ensure that its proposition affirming the correlativity of rights and duties is true by definition. That proposition is not an empirical generalization or a refutable hypothesis, but is instead a fundamental axiom (often designated as the "Correlativity Axiom"). Hence, the adducing of empirical counterexamples is an endeavor as pointless as the adducing of empirical counterexamples to the proposition that all bachelors are unmarried. Moreover, the Hohfeldian analysis aims to refine ordinary patterns of thought and discourse rather than simply to chart them. Although inevitably its points of departure are some of those numerous inconsistent patterns – which are highlighted in a "rational reconstruction" – it seeks to introduce a much greater degree of precision and clarity than can usually be found in discussions of rights and duties. On the other hand, notwithstanding its stipulative and purificatory nature, it enables descriptions of right–duty relationships that are not at all far-fetched or misleading. So long as the content of each right and each duty is specified precisely, and so long as the right-holder and the duty-bearer are identified appropriately, any relationship involving a right and a duty can be characterized accurately and uncontrivedly in accordance with the Correlativity Axiom.

An insistence on the correlativity of rights and duties, furthermore, is entirely consistent with a recognition that the domain of morality extends beyond right–duty relationships. Although all obligatory reasons-for-action are covered by the Correlativity Axiom, supererogatory reasons-for-action – which constitute the sphere of the virtues – do not similarly involve right–duty relationships. A supererogatory deed or forbearance is commendable precisely because it goes beyond what is morally required. It exhibits a degree of heroism or solicitude that is more than the mere fulfillment of one's obligations. Failures to engage in such deeds or forbearances would warrant the withholding of special praise or admiration but would not warrant the leveling of condemnation. Such failures would indicate not that people are guilty of some moral faults, but instead that they are only modestly endowed with some virtues. Though they decline to do more than is owed by them to others, they do not omit to do what is owed (unless they are breaching moral obligations in addition to shrinking from supererogatory courses of conduct). In short, to assess the virtuousness of their behavior – as opposed to its mere acceptableness – we have to move beyond the categories of duty and right.

To acknowledge as much is not to endorse anything incompatible with the Correlativity Axiom. After all, that axiom simply specifies what must be the case when a duty exists or a right exists; it does not in any way suggest that all morally significant facts involve the existence of rights and duties.

Likewise, the Correlativity Axiom in itself leaves open the substance and distribution of various duties and rights, and it also leaves open the nature of various right-holders. It does of course affirm that a right with a certain content is held by P against Q if and only if a duty with the same content is owed by Q to P, but it does not *per se* preordain the contents and locations of particular right–duty relationships. Similarly, it does not preordain the identities of P and Q. This last point is of particular importance for proponents of the Correlativity Axiom who wish to parry putative counterexamples to that axiom. Among the ostensible counterexamples that are most frequently adduced, some so-called public duties figure prominently. (For discussions of some other types of ostensible counterexamples, see Kramer 1998: 24-49, 2001: 52–7, 93–4.) Public duties, such as the duty to pay taxes or the duty to engage in mandatory military service, are not correlated with any rights held by discrete individuals. Opponents of the Correlativity Axiom have thus concluded that such duties are not correlated with any rights at all. An inference along those lines mistakenly presupposes that the Correlativity Axiom pertains only to rights held and obligations borne by individuals. In fact, that axiom encompasses collective duties and rights, which are quite as real as individuals' legal positions (Kramer 1998: 49–60, 2001: 45–7). Hence, any public duty is owed to a collectivity (the state, the nation, the community) which holds the correlative right. A strict right–duty correlation does indeed characterize every public duty along with every private duty; the only difference is that each public duty correlates with a collective right, whereas each private duty correlates with an individual right. The party wronged by a breach of a public obligation is the political grouping that holds the correlative right. In sum, when the right-holder and the duty-bearer in a right–duty relationship are correctly identified, the Correlativity Axiom proves to be comprehensively applicable. Because it accommodates collective rights and obligations as well as individual rights and obligations, it is hardly belied by obligations that are not owed to separate individuals. Not all obligations are correlated with individual rights, but all obligations are correlated with rights.

References

Dworkin, Ronald. 1986. *Law's Empire*. London: Fontana Press.

Edmundson, William A. 1998. *Three Anarchical Fallacies*. Cambridge, UK: Cambridge University Press.

Gans, Chaim. 1992. *Philosophical Anarchism and Political Disobedience*. Cambridge, UK: Cambridge University Press.

Harris, J. W. 1997. *Legal Philosophies*. London: Butterworths.

Hart, H. L. A. 1955. Are there any natural rights? *Philosophical Review* 64: 175–91.

Horton, John. 1992. *Political Obligation*. London: Macmillan.

Kramer, Matthew H. 1998. Rights without trimmings. In Matthew H. Kramer, N. E. Simmonds, and Hillel Steiner, *A Debate Over Rights*. Oxford: Oxford University Press, 7–111.

Kramer, Matthew H. 1999. *In Defense of Legal Positivism*. Oxford: Oxford University Press.

Kramer, Matthew H. 2001. Getting rights right. In Matthew H. Kramer (ed.), *Rights, Wrongs, and Responsibilities*. Basingstoke, UK and New York: Palgrave, 28–95.

Raz, Joseph. 1979. *The Authority of Law*. Oxford: Clarendon Press.

Raz, Joseph. 1984. Hart on moral rights and legal duties. *Oxford Journal of Legal Studies* 4: 123–31.

Raz, Joseph. 1986. The purity of the pure theory. In Richard Tur and William Twining (eds.), *Essays on Kelsen*. Oxford: Clarendon Press, 79–97.

Raz, Joseph. 1990. *Practical Reason and Norms 2nd edn*. Princeton, NJ: Princeton University Press.

Raz, Joseph. 1994. *Ethics in the Public Domain*. Oxford: Clarendon Press.

Schauer, Frederick. 1991. *Playing by the Rules*. Oxford: Clarendon Press.

Soper, Philip. 1995. Legal systems, normative systems, and the paradoxes of positivism. *Canadian Journal of Law and Jurisprudence* 8: 363–76.

Warnock, G. J. 1971. *The Object of Morality*. London: Methuen.

Wolff, Jonathan. 1996. *An Introduction to Political Philosophy*. Oxford: Oxford University Press.

Further Reading

Beran, Harry. 1987. *The Consent Theory of Political Obligation*. London: Croom Helm.

Feinberg, Joel. 1961. Supererogation and rules. *Ethics* 71: 276–88.

Green, Leslie. 1988. *The Authority of the State*. Oxford: Clarendon Press.

Greenawalt, Kent. 1989. *Conflicts of Law and Morality*. Oxford: Clarendon Press.

Harris, Paul (ed.). 1990. *On Political Obligation*. London: Routledge.

Hart, H. L. A. 1961. *The Concept of Law*. Oxford: Clarendon Press.

Hohfeld, Wesley. 1923. *Fundamental Legal Conceptions as Applied in Judicial Reasoning*. New Haven, CT: Yale University Press.

Kamm, Frances. 1985. Supererogation and obligation. *Journal of Philosophy* 82: 118–38.

Klosko, George. 1992. *The Principle of Fairness and Political Obligation*. Lanham, MD: Rowman & Littlefield.

Rawls, John. 1964. Legal obligation and the duty of fair play. In Sidney Hook (ed.), *Law and Philosophy*. New York: New York University Press, 3–18.

Simmons, A. John. 1979. *Moral Principles and Political Obligations*. Princeton, NJ: Princeton University Press.

Soper, Philip. 1984. *A Theory of Law*. Cambridge, MA: Harvard University Press.

Williams, Bernard. 1985. Morality, the peculiar institution. In Bernard Williams, *Ethics and the Limits of Philosophy*. Cambridge, MA: Harvard University Press, 174–96.

Chapter 13

Theories of Rights

Alon Harel

Introduction

Imagine a world very much like ours, except that nobody has any rights. A world with no rights is not necessarily evil or cruel. People's lives, possessions, and well-being may be well protected in this imagined world, for instance, through the charitable behavior of others, or even through the imposition of sanction-backed duties on others (Feinberg 1970: 243). How would this world be different from ours? Would such a world be (other things being equal) worse or perhaps better than ours? A theory of rights can help in pointing out what, if anything, would be missing in this imagined world.

A theory of rights should satisfy two methodological requirements: first, it should be able to accommodate a range of plausible accounts of what rights we have. A theory which identifies as rights only rights advocated by libertarianism or progressive liberalism is thus defective. The question of what rights are should be answered in a way that "illuminates the entire tradition of rights discourse, in which a variety of different theories have offered incompatible views as to what rights there are and why" (Raz 1986: 166). This does not mean that a theory of rights is completely devoid of normative content. It does mean, however, that such a theory must explain the role of rights in different moral and political theories.

Secondly, a theory of rights must be attentive to some (or all) of the attributes traditionally associated or presupposed in the discourse of rights (be it legal, moral, or political). "Being attentive" implies either that the theory explains why these attributes are constitutive of the concept of rights, or that it explains why a particular attribute is unjustifiably associated with rights.

The attributes associated with rights are diverse. Rights are perceived as requirements with great importance – overriding the public good or utilitarian considerations. To say that one has a right is different from saying that it would be good, nice, or noble that one is provided with the good in question or with what one desires to have. More particularly, stating that one has a right implies an imperative, nondiscretionary requirement. Rights are also associated with individuals and their special worth; they protect the individual against the consequences of uninhibited pursuit of collective or social goods. Their individualistic flavor is often explained by reference to values such as dignity or autonomy – values which are closely related to one's personhood. Finally, rights are often characterized as having a certain legalistic and even antagonistic character. Right-holders do not merely request their rights; they claim or demand them!

A skeptic could argue that there is no unified theory that can accommodate the different uses of the term "rights." Rights can be legal, that is, protected by legal rules; social, that is, backed by societal conventions; institutional, that is, acknowledged and enforced by institutions; they can be negative, that is, rights to other person's omissions or forbearances; or positive, that is, rights to other person's actions. The term "rights" has been used in ancient legal documents of Roman law as well as in contemporary reports of Amnesty International. Arguably, it is doubtful that a unifying theory could explicate a concept which has been used in different times, different institutional settings, and for different purposes (Hohfeld 1919: 35; McCloskey 1965: 119; Kagan 1998: 170; Sumner 1987: 9).

This is indeed a valuable critique of the very enterprise of developing a theory of rights. Perhaps the theorist of rights needs to be more modest and aim at providing a partial account of rights. The following discussion presupposes that rights have different facets and that a theory of rights only needs to highlight certain aspects of rights without pretending to provide a single characterization which would serve equally the legal theorist of Roman times and the political activist of the twenty-first century.

The discussion is divided into two sections: the first section discusses the nature of rights and the second section investigates the role of rights within moral theory and its relations with other components of moral theory. The first section explores the nature of rights from three different perspectives: their formal or logical structure, their substance, and their special strength and importance in practical reasoning. The first sub section is devoted to the influential work of Wesley Hohfeld who analyzed the logical structure of rights. The second subsection characterizes rights on the basis of the concerns they protect. Two competing theories purporting to identify these concerns are examined: the choice and the interest theory of rights. The third subsection investigates the special strength of rights in practical reasoning, in particular, their overriding nature.

The second section explores the role of rights in moral theory. The first subsection asks whether the value of rights is derivative or foundational. The prevalent conviction, that the value of rights is derived from more fundamental values, which dictate the scope of protection of rights and their stringency, is shown to be based on questionable foundations. The second subsection investigates the accusation that the discourse of rights promotes a sectarian normative agenda, which is overly individualistic, masculine, and Western.

The Nature of Rights: Logic, Substance, and Strength

The logic of rights: Hohfeld's analytical framework

Statements ascribing rights often include a subject, an object, and content. A typical statement ascribing a right could therefore be of the type: "A has a right to X against B." A – the subject of rights – is termed the right-holder, the entity possessing the right. B – the object – is (typically) a duty-holder, the person against whom the right is held. X – the content of the right – specifies what the right is about, that is, what B is obliged to do, or to refrain from doing, or what A is entitled to do.

The classical account of Hohfeld shows that phrases ascribing rights, which seem superficially similar, are used in different ways. The superficial similarity of different statements ascribing rights often leads to conceptual confusions (Hohfeld 1919: 35). Hohfeld's task was to prevent such conceptual confusions by analyzing four different meanings of the phrase "A has a right to X" in judicial reasoning.

1 *Claim Rights*: "A has a right to X" may mean that an individual B has a duty towards A, that is, that A has a claim against B – the duty-holder – to the provision of X. *Claim rights* (as they are termed by Hohfeld) may imply the existence of negative duties – duties not to act in ways which impede the realization of X, as well as positive duties – duties to act in ways which facilitate the realization of X.

2 *Liberty Rights (Privileges)*: "A has a right to X" may mean that A has no duty towards a particular person B (or towards anybody) to refrain from X. Affirming that A has a right in the sense of *liberty*, or a *privilege* to do X, does not imply that B, or anybody, has any duties to facilitate the provision of X. "Naked liberties," that is, unprotected liberties, are the only rights recognized in a Hobbesian state of nature, where all people have a liberty right to kill, hurt, and take the possessions of others for the sake of promoting their own interests.

3   *Powers (Abilities)*: "A has a right to X" may mean that A is capable of changing an existing legal arrangement and can consequently change the legal (or moral) rights of others. This type of right is called by Hohfeld *power* or *ability*. For instance, in many legal systems one has a power to acquire ownership of an unowned object (by taking possession of it) and thus extinguish other people's liberties to take possession of the same object. By taking possession of a coat, for example, one unilaterally changes the legal duties of others. But even prior to the act of taking possession of the coat, others are subject to a "liability," that is, they are exposed to the possibility of an exercise of a power, which, if exercised would change their rights and duties. Other examples of such a unilateral normative change include the power of a legislature to impose new duties on the citizens, the power of people to bequeath their property (which is beneficial to those who are subject to the corresponding liability), the power of a person to accept an offer and thus create a binding contract, or the power to appoint an agent who is authorized to conduct legal transactions on one's behalf.

4   *Immunities*: "A has a right to X" may mean a lack of power, that is, "*an immunity*" against the possibility that others alter one's legal (or moral) rights. If A has an immunity right against B (or everybody) with respect to X, it follows that B (or everybody) cannot alter A's rights or duties concerning X; that is, A – the holder of the immunity – is not subject to B's power. Enshrined constitutional rights often include immunities, which deprive the legislature of powers which it would otherwise have. The legislature, which is incapable of exercising power, is subject to a "disability." For instance, one has an immunity right to freedom of expression, which bars the legislature from enacting legislation that extinguishes one's liberty to speak. In private law, a party to a contract has an immunity against the risk that the other party unilaterally changes the terms of the contract.

Typically, Hohfeldian rights do not operate alone, but in conjunction with each other. What is often termed "the right to free speech" is, within Hohfeld's scheme, a conjunction of diverse claims, liberties, and immunities. The claim rights consist of duties of others not to censor or interfere in one's exercise of the right to free speech; liberties include the liberty to express oneself in different ways (or not to express oneself at all); and immunities stand guard against the alteration of these claim rights and liberties.

Hohfeld's analytical structure is purely conceptual and definitional. Thus, it is not subject to empirical or moral refutation (Kramer 1998: 22). Yet Hohfeld's analytic scheme can be criticized on the grounds that some of its most fundamental concepts are underdefined. Hohfeld believes that "A has a claim right to X" means that there is a person B who has a duty towards A with regard to X, that is, a duty which is owed to A. Yet Hohfeld leaves unspecified the concept of a duty *owed to* A, that is, the concept of a claim right possessed by A. It is unclear whether, and in what ways, a duty *owed to* an entity A (e.g., the duty not to trespass on A's land) differs from a duty merely *concerning* an entity A (e.g., the duty not to destroy unowned works of art – a duty which, presumably is not owed to anybody). Hohfeldian rights and duties are relational or directional, that is, they are owed to somebody and it is thus necessary to supplement Hohfeld's conceptual scheme and explain what it means for a duty to be owed to somebody (Waldron 1984: 8; Sumner 1987: 24), or for a right to be possessed by somebody.

The substance of rights: What concerns do rights protect?

Two theories, the choice (or will) theory and the interest (or benefit) theory of rights, address the question of what concerns rights protect. One important by-product of addressing this question is clarifying the gap within Hohfeld's theory, that is, explaining what it means for a right to be possessed by somebody (and for a duty to be owed to somebody). Moreover, both the choice and the benefit theories demonstrate the relation between conceptual analysis of rights and particular moral or political visions. The choice theory and the interest theory are competing conceptual frames that reflect more foundational moral disagreements.

The choice theory of rights regards rights as protecting the exercise of choice (Hart 1982: 184). Right-holders are agents who are given control over another person's duty and can thus be analogized to a "small-scale sovereign" (Hart 1982: 183). Rights, under this view, can be identified as *protected choices* – protection which is conducive to the autonomy and self-realization of right-holders.

The choice theory inevitably emphasizes liberties and powers since it is only these Hofeldian rights which directly facilitate the exercise of choice. Yet the choice theory is not oblivious to claim rights. "Naked liberties," that is, liberties not accompanied by duties of others to respect or facilitate effective choices, are not sufficient to protect meaningful choice. The effective protection of choice requires that liberties and powers be protected by a "protective perimeter" of obligations (Hart 1982: 172). In order to demonstrate the impotence of "naked liberties," Hart presents the following example. Two people walking see a purse lying on the pavement. Each has a liberty, so far as the law is concerned, to pick it up and each may prevent the other from doing so (for instance by rushing to pick it up first). Yet, if the liberty to pick up the purse was a "naked liberty," each person could assault and even kill the other in their effort to get the purse. If one's liberty to pick up the purse were not protected by a "protective perimeter" of obligations (consisting, in this example, of the general obligations of criminal law), it would be worthless. In this case the relevant duties are general duties, which protect a person's body and are not specifically aimed at protecting one's liberty to pick up the purse. At other times, the duties are specifically designed to protect a particular liberty, such as when the law requires municipalities to provide a space for political protests in order to protect one's liberty to express oneself. Hence, under the choice theory, rights consist primarily of liberties and powers that are fortified by a protective perimeter of obligations.

Choice theorists often focus their attention on private law. Private law is distinguished from criminal law in that, typically, the victim of a tort, or breach of contract, is granted many powers, which facilitate ample choice on the part of the right-holder. The choices protected by private law consist of three elements: (1) right-holders may waive or extinguish the duty owed to them by others; (2) right-holders can leave the duty unenforced, or alternatively, enforce it; (3) right-holders may waive or extinguish the obligation to pay compensation to which the breach gives rise (Hart 1982: 183–4).

The choice theory explains why rights are often regarded as fundamental to one's personhood, individuality, and self-determination. By exercising choice one manifests one's individuality and personhood. Admittedly, conceptually one could argue that rights are protected choices and then deny the significance of autonomy and conclude on the basis of this that people have no rights. Yet choice theorists typically share a particular moral vision – a vision stressing the importance of self-determination and autonomy (Kramer 1998: 75; Sumner 1987: 47).

It is precisely the affinity of the choice theory with this moral vision that is responsible for some of the deficiencies in the choice theory of rights. The political vision, which animates the choice theory, is too narrow to provide a basis for a comprehensive theory of rights. Hence, the choice theory fails to give an account of some of the paradigmatic cases central to the discourse of rights. For instance, it cannot account for the very conceptual possibility of inalienable rights – rights that cannot be waived. Ironically, the most fundamental protections granted by law, namely the protection of one's inalienable right to life and liberty, would not be classified as rights while the protection of lesser interests – interests which can be alienated – such as property, would be recognized as such (MacCormick 1977: 197–9). The choice theory also cannot assign rights to entities that are not agents, that is, those incapable of exercising choice. Infants, senile people, and comatose people are, thus, under the choice theory, incapable of being right-holders (Kramer 2001: 29). Moreover, the choice theory distorts the commonsensical understanding of the relative importance of different rights. Under the choice theory, one's right not to be assaulted consists primarily of three liberties: the liberty to waive or not to waive the duty of others not to assault; the liberty to sue or not to sue for compensation; and the liberty to waive or not to waive the right to the payment of compensation. This description reverses the commonsense priority between the different Hohfeldian rights. While traditionally the claim right not to be assaulted is the most central component of the right to bodily integrity – a component protected by various peripheral liberties, powers, and immunities; under the choice theory, it is the liberties and the powers which are the key component of this right (Wellman 1985: 75). Lastly, there is a mismatch between the choice theory of rights and the political vision animating it. The liberties highlighted by the choice theory are not the most central to one's self-determination. For instance, one would not be appalled by a legal system which would deprive individuals of the power to waive their rights to compensation (Jhering 1915). But, under the choice theory, such deprivation would necessarily deprive a person of the right.

The interest theory of rights holds that the point of rights is to protect and promote (some of) the right-holders' interests. The dominating picture here contrasts with the choice theory in that it characterizes rights as *protected choices* and consequently emphasizes the status of right-holders as the *passive beneficiaries* of protective and supportive duties imposed on others (Sumner 1987: 47). Facilitating individual choice can be classified as an interest, and that interest can be protected by rights; but it does not have the privileged status that it has within the choice theory of rights. Moreover, in contrast to the choice theory, the interest theory protects choices only because, and to the extent, that they promote the right-holders' interests. Consequently, the interest theory is broader in the scope of concerns it protects and can acknowledge the existence of inalienable rights; it can also ascribe rights to entities which are not agents, as long as these entities have interests, that is, as long as they can be made better or worse off.

An early version of the interest theory of rights asserted that to have a right is simply "to be the *beneficiary* of another's duty or obligation" (Lyons 1994a: 23). Yet this version is clearly unsatisfactory and needs to be revised in at least two ways. First, right-holders do not necessarily bene-

fit from the fulfilling of duties owed to them; it is only typically or characteristically that the right-holder benefits from the fulfillment of these obligations. If I misuse my property in a manner detrimental to my interests, I do not benefit from the protection of my right to property. Yet I would still be regarded as having a right to my property for the reason that typically people benefit from the protection of their property (Raz 1986: 180; Lyons 1994a: 27).

Second, not all interests protected by duties give rise to a right on the part of the beneficiary of the duty. There are at least two types of interests which sometimes give rise to duties, but which cannot give rise to rights on the part of those who benefit from the fulfillment of these duties.

First there are the interests of entities which are incapable of having rights because the promotion of their interests or well-being is not of ultimate value, but only of instrumental value (Raz 1986: 166, 176–80). While the choice theory is too restrictive by insisting that right-holders must be agents (and thus denying the status of right-holders to infants and comatose persons), the simple unqualified interest theory is too generous in ascribing rights to entities whose interests are not of ultimate value. For instance, one may have a duty not to walk on nice well-attended lawns – a duty that enables the grass to flourish. Yet it would be preposterous to infer from this that the grass's interests generate rights or even can generate rights (Kramer 2001: 32–3). The grass does not belong to the type of entities whose interests are of ultimate value and consequently its interests cannot generate rights. The decision regarding which entities have interests that are of ultimate values depends on broader moral principles – principles which are not part of a theory of rights, but ones which must be presupposed by the theorist of rights.

Second, sometimes even entities whose interests are of ultimate value and whose interests are promoted by the existence of a duty cannot be characterized as right-holders. Suppose that John owes Mary $10 and that Mary decided to give Steven a present if and only if the debt is repaid. While Steven is a beneficiary of the duty, and while his interests are of ultimate value, he is not considered a right-holder.

One way to address this counterexample relies on identifying the intentions underlying the relevant norms. Right-holders are those beneficiaries, whom the norm is *meant*, or is *supposed to*, benefit. The qualified benefit theory limits the scope of right-holders to the intended beneficiaries only, those for whose sake obligations are imposed (Lyons 1994a: 28–9).

The reliance on intentions has been criticized on the grounds that intentions are often unclear and ambiguous (Kramer 1998: 85–7; Sumner 1987: 41). Questions may arise as to what the intentions really are and whose intentions count. An alternative suggestion is to identify as right-holders those entities whose interests are sufficient for holding other people to be under a duty (Raz 1986: 166). In our example it is Mary's interest which is sufficient to justify the imposition of duty on John; the duty would not be imposed merely in order to satisfy Steven's craving for a present.

Yet these attempts to select among the numerous beneficiaries the ones which are genuine right-holders is not free of difficulties. It is often the case that people speak of rights which are ascribed to the right-holder for the purpose of serving the interests of somebody else (Raz 1994: 37–40; Harel 1998: 233–43). The right to free speech is often ascribed to the speaker, or the potential speaker, but the justifications for protecting it are often grounded in the interests of other persons, or even the interests of the society as a whole. The "marketplace of ideas" is evidently a societal interest, which is often used to justify the protection of the right to free speech. Yet the speaker's interests in a vibrant discourse does not justify the imposition of the complex set of duties imposed for the sake of protecting the right to free speech. Moreover, the speaker's interests in the marketplace of ideas does not differ in any significant way from the interests of others. The usage of societal interest such as "the marketplace of ideas" to justify rights is a problem for the interest theory. The interest in the marketplace of ideas is shared equally by everybody in society. It seems, therefore, that the interest theory is bound to identify the society as the right-holder rather than the speaker. Yet both the discourse of rights, as practiced by judges and others, as well as normative considerations (which regard rights as protecting individuals against the society) suggest that it is the speaker, rather than the society as a whole, who is the real right-holder.

Many advocates of the interest theory believe that a right entails a corresponding duty and vice versa. A right exists if and only if a corresponding duty and, in particular, a corresponding duty-holder is specified. Recent advocates of the interest theory challenge this position and argue that rights are logically prior to duties (MacCormick 1982: 162). More specifically, rights provide the *grounds* for the imposition of duties (Raz 1986: 167). Consequently, one could assert the existence of a right, without specifying who the duty-holders are and even without specifying what the nature of the duties whose fulfillment is necessary for honoring the right are, as long as one is willing to assert that certain duties, yet unspecified, should be imposed if the right is to be honored. By stating that a child has a right to education, one need not commit oneself to identifying whether it is the state or the parents who have a corresponding duty; neither is one committed to saying whether this right is fulfilled by teaching the child languages, art, or biblical studies. Rights should be described therefore as grounds for duties (rather than be equated with duties). This view explains the "dynamic aspect of rights," that is, their inherent potential to create new duties or new duty-holders (Raz 1986: 171). It also explains the inherent ability of rights to maintain their identity even when the duties and the duty-holders are altered to accommodate new circumstances.

The difficulties of the choice theory on the one hand and those of the interest theory on the other hand led to a recent proposal to combine both theories into a "hybrid theory" (Sreenivasan forthcoming). The hybrid theory states that an entity X is a right-holder if and only if the question of who has some measure of control over a corresponding duty (i.e., who can waive the duty, enforce it, or not or who can waive or extinguish the duty to pay compensation in case of a breach) is determined by the balance of X's interests. If Y has control over a duty, Y is the right-holder if and only if Y was given control in order to promote Y's balance of interests while X is the right-holder if and only if Y's control over the duty is aimed at promoting X's balance of interests.

The hybrid theory overcomes many objections facing the choice and the interest theories of rights. Unlike the choice theory, the hybrid theory can attribute inalienable rights to an entity as long as their inalienability promotes the interests of that entity. I have an inalienable right to liberty because my own interests require that this right be inalienable. In contrast to the choice theory, it can also explain the attribution of rights to nonagents such as infants or comatose people. The power to control duties towards infants is typically given to third parties, for example parents, in order to promote the infants' interests. Hence, unlike the choice theory, the hybrid theory of rights classifies infants as right-holders. The hybrid theory also overcomes some of the difficulties faced by the interest theory. Consider again the case in which John owes Mary $10 and Mary decided to give Steven a present if and only if the debt is repaid. In contrast to the interest theory, the hybrid theory identifies Mary as the right-holder because it is Mary who can waive the duty if she so wishes and that power is granted to her not for the sake of promoting Steven's interests but for the sake of promoting her own interests.

Yet, the hybrid theory is not free of difficulties. Most importantly the hybrid theory lumps together two different types of interests, which determine who controls a duty. Sometimes an entity controls a duty in order to promote autonomy (typically its own autonomy); at other times control is granted to an entity because that entity is more capable of evaluating the well-being of itself or of another agent and promoting it. It seems therefore that unlike the choice theory that characterizes rights as protected choices, or the interest theory that characterizes right-holders as beneficiaries (irrespective of what the benefit consists of), the hybrid theory is grounded in interests whose nature varies from context to context. Sometimes, as in the choice theory, it is the value of autonomy or dignity that determines who controls a duty; at other time it is utilitarian or quasi-utilitarian considerations that determine who controls a duty. The hybrid theory lacks the unified normative foundations characterizing both the choice and the interest theory.

The choice and the interest theory of rights address the question of which concerns are pro-tected by rights. While doing so, they also fill a gap in Hohfeld's conceptual scheme. Most importantly, they clarify the concept of relational or directional duties, that is, they explain what it means for a duty to be owed to somebody, or for a right to be possessed by somebody. In the course of doing so, one learns about the intimate relation between rights and more fundamental principles of moral and political theory. Yet both the choice and the interest theory leave one important feature of rights unaccounted for. Why are rights considered to be so important in practical reasoning?

The strength of rights: Why should we take rights seriously?

The reason for the conviction that rights have special importance stems from the fact that there is a gap between the stringency or the weight attributed to a right and the degree to which this right promotes the right-holder's interests. The First Amendment of the US Constitution protects the right to free speech. It is often the case that expression which is detrimental to the interests of many and which, at least at face value, does not promote the speakers' interests, is stringently protected. Even when rights clearly promote an interest, it often seems that their protection is much more stringent than that which would be justified simply by weighing the relevant interests (Raz 1994: 30). A theory of rights should explain the exceptional strength rights have in practical reasoning – as a force greater than the importance of the interests it protects.

One influential theory states that when one has a right, the existence of the right provides right-holders with an "argumentative threshold" against objections, which could otherwise be addressed against them (Lyons 1994b: 152). The mere fact that not protecting one's right has some (however slight) beneficial outcomes is not sufficient to override this right. Dworkin coined the term "rights as trumps" to describe this phenomenon. Rights, in his view, should be understood as "trumps over some background justification for political decisions that states a goal for the community as a whole" (Dworkin 1984: 153). These background considerations are consequentialist in nature, that is, they specify certain goals, which the political community should strive towards. Rights disrupt the (otherwise justified) uninhibited pursuit of these goals. Rights-based reasoning should therefore be contrasted with the unqualified process of balancing competing interests and goals – a balancing which is most characteristically exemplified in the economically oriented method of decision making termed "cost–benefit analysis" or utility-maximization.

Two clarifications are necessary. First, although rights are understood as trumps over background justifications, they do not necessarily override the pursuit of every valuable social goal. If the gains in terms of the background justifications are large enough, rights can be overridden. Second, background justifications state goals that are not necessarily utilitarian. Equality could also function as a background justification. What characterizes social goals in contrast to rights is the willingness to trade off burdens and benefits "within a community in order to produce some overall benefit to the community as a whole" (Dworkin 1977: 91). Rights contrast with collective goals in that rights are individualistic, rather than collective, and consequently rights-based reasoning does not allow a trade-off of burdens and benefits between individuals and the society.

The "trumps theory" states a conceptual claim; it does not commit itself to any substantive normative presuppositions concerning what the trumps protect, or what collective interests they trump. It satisfies therefore the first methodological requirement specified earlier. It suffers, however, from two deficiencies. First, the "rights as trumps" theory can at most provide necessary, rather than sufficient, conditions for the existence of rights. After all, duties, as well as rights can override the community's goals. The retributivist conviction, which dictates that society has a duty to punish criminals (even if punishing them is detrimental to utility), is an example of such a duty. Second, it needs to explain the distinction between societal goals and individual rights. Making sense of this distinction requires using the dichotomy between consequentialist and deontological moral theories.

Consequentialist moral theories are moral theories which hold that:

> the right act in any given situation is the one that will produce the best overall outcome, as judged from an impersonal standpoint, which gives equal weight to the interests of everyone. States of affairs are ranked from best to worst from an impersonal standpoint and an action is right if and only if it will produce the highest ranked state of affairs that the agent can produce. (Scheffler 1988: 1)

In contrast, deontological theories posit that sometimes a person is permitted to act in a way which does not bring about the best consequences; or even, more typically, is prohibited from acting in a way which would bring about the best state of affairs. For instance, the deontologist, in contrast to the consequentialist, may maintain that it is sometimes immoral to kill one person, even for the sake of saving several people from death.

Deontological theories are not necessarily rights-based theories. They could assert the existence of duties without affirming that the beneficiaries of these duties have rights. Yet, many deontological theorists insist that the duties are indeed grounded in rights (Kamm 1996).

The "rights as trumps" theory seems to fall into the deontological camp since, within its framework, rights serve as constraints on the pursuit of desirable goals. Yet there is a way of framing its conclusions in consequentialist terms. If the value of states of affairs is determined not only on the basis of the overall utility, or well-being of individuals, but also on the basis of whether more or fewer rights are respected, then, arguably, the language of rights can be reconciled with consequentialism.

This view, termed "consequentialism of rights," can be explained by drawing a distinction between violation of rights and infringement of rights (Thomson 1986: 51-2). Violating a right is infringing it unjustifiably, while infringement of a right can be either justified or unjustified. An infringement is justified when the right is overridden by competing social goals, for example, when security concerns justify limitations of freedom of speech or when the right is overridden by competing rights, for example, when one's right to privacy justifies imposing limits on freedom of speech. Consequentialism of rights depicts the minimization of the infringement of rights as a collective goal, which competes with other goals, such as maximization of utility. Rights are, under this view, always justifiably infringed when their infringement prevents more infringements of the very same right.

Consequentialism of rights explains many commonsense moral judgments. It can, for instance, explain why a doctor is barred from killing a healthy person even when killing this person would save the lives of three patients who are waiting for an urgent transplant (as a result of natural illness). From the standpoint of consequentialism of rights, a state of affairs in which three persons die naturally (without infringing their right not to be killed) is (*prima facie*) a better state of affairs than a state of affairs in which even a single person is killed (provided other things are equal), because dying as a consequence of infringement of one's right not to be killed is a worse state of affairs than death which does not involve the infringement of this right, that is, natural death. In the former state of affairs, there is only death while in the latter, there is, in addition, a murder and disregard for human life. These intangible factors are given weight in the consequentialist evaluation of the various states of affairs.

In addition to solving moral puzzles such as barring the doctor from killing one person for the sake of saving several, consequentialism of rights can justify various institutional practices. The state often invests much more money in preventing a murder than in preventing a natural death, or in preventing theft than in preventing loss of property, which does not involve the violation of rights.

Nevertheless, orthodox deontologists reject "consequentialism of rights" and adhere to a stricter anticonsequentialist position (Nozick 1974: 28–30). Nozick holds that respect for rights sometimes requires an agent not to infringe a right even when infringing it would prevent the infringements of more rights of the very same type. Even if X, Y, and Z each have a right not to be killed, an agent may have a duty not to kill X (a duty which is grounded in X's rights) even

when killing X will save Y and Z from *being killed* (rather than from natural death). The characteristic of rights is that, in contrast to other considerations, an agent respects rights not by minimizing the infringements of rights, but by not infringing them, that is, by treating rights as deontological constraints.

Understanding rights in terms of deontological constraints explains some puzzling features of rights. For instance, many believe that human beings have a duty not to destroy valuable works of art, or not to exterminate certain species of animals. But these duties are rarely spoken of in terms of rights. The difference between the duty not to destroy valuable works of art and the duty not to kill people is that it seems that we are always morally permitted (or, perhaps, even required) to destroy a work of art for the sake of saving several equally valuable works of art, while it is not always the case that we are permitted to kill one person for the sake of preventing the killings of others (Kamm 1996: 241–2).

It may seem irrational not to infringe a right in order to prevent many infringements of the very same right. Some theorists argue that the reason why one agent may be barred from killing one person to save several people from being killed is grounded in the special status of the agent and, in particular, the agent's relation with the relevant action (Williams 1973: 93–100; Nagel 1986: 175–85). By killing, even if the killing prevents the killings of several other persons, the agent is guided by an evil intention which corrupts his or her agency. Nagel believes that by intentionally committing evil for the sake of preventing greater evil: "I incorporate that evil into what I do: it is my deliberate creation and the reasons stemming from it are magnified and lit up from my point of view" (Nagel 1986: 180). This type of explanation is labeled as "agent-focused" explanation; meaning that "some quality of agency not primarily concerned with the victim's properties and rights gives the agent a duty not to act" (Kamm 1996: 238).

Yet agent-focused explanation cannot provide a justification of deontological constraints in many of the circumstances in which they are thought to apply. More specifically, it cannot explain why an agent is barred from infringing the right of one victim for the sake of saving several victims from infringements of their rights committed by the very same agent. Take the case of a person who sent a trolley towards five people in order to kill them. After further consideration, the agent himself suddenly realizes to his horror that this is a violation of their rights not to be killed and decides to save the five. Unfortunately, the only way to save them is by pushing a sixth person into the path of the trolley. Such a rescue attempt (saving people from being killed by the agent) seems just as impermissible as the case in which the agent kills a person in order to save five people from being killed by somebody else (Kamm 1996: 242).

While this case seems to be an important counterexample, it can perhaps be resolved within the frame of agent-focused morality by conceding that while agents are responsible for their past actions, their agency is always more vivid with respect to actions they are now committing. Hence, *at any given moment* an agent has greater responsibility not to violate a constraint than *at that moment* to prevent its violation (Brook 1991: 198). This explanation may dictate giving greater weight to my not killing the sixth person (whose life depends on my future action) than to my saving the lives of the five people (whose lives depend on saving them from risks which have already been imposed, even if these risks were imposed by me).

Other objections, however, can be raised against agent-focused theories. Agent-focused explanations shift the concern from the victim whose rights are being infringed to the agent. This shift is plausible as long as one regards deontology as an exclusively duty-based moral theory, but it seems inappropriate when one justifies deontological constraints in terms of rights since rights in essence are designed to protect the basic concerns of victims rather than the purity of the soul of the duty-holder. The morality of rights is inherently a victim-focused rather than an agent-focused morality (Brook 1991: 201; Kamm 1996: 237–8).

One victim-focused explanation is based on the inviolability of persons where such inviolability is explained in terms of the separateness of persons (Nozick 1974: 33). There can be no moral outweighing of one life for the sake of others. People have a lesser moral status if their right to life can

be justifiably infringed in order to minimize overall infringement than if it were never permissible to infringe the right (Kamm 1996: 261). In the former case, the Kantian imperative to treat every person not merely as means is violated whereas, in the latter case, they are treated as ends.

But increased inviolability is bought at a great cost – the cost of "saveability" (Kagan 1991: 919–20). As our inviolability goes up, less and less harm can be done to us for the sake of saving others from violation of their rights. Nevertheless there is an inevitable corollary of our enhanced moral status, namely a decline in our "saveability" (Otsuka 1997: 204). The less harm that can be done to us for the sake of preventing infringements of the rights of others the less good can be done to us by way of preventing imminent infringements of our rights. Why does our humanity dictate greater inviolability rather than greater saveability?

One way of explaining the priority of inviolability over saveability is to draw a distinction between the societal goal of preserving life and the normative importance of respecting the value of life. Although such priority of inviolability over saveability may lead to more deaths, it is perhaps more respectful of the value of life. But establishing this claim requires a more thorough investigation of the moral foundations of deontological constraints.

Yet, despite the ingenuity, it would be hasty to characterize rights in terms of deontological constraints. Understanding rights in terms of deontological constraints is both underinclusive and overinclusive. It is underinclusive because not all rights are deontological constraints. My right not to be killed as the merely foreseeable, but unintended, consequence of the behavior of others is often subject to consequentialist reasoning. Suppose that someone has maliciously set a trolley towards two individuals. Another person can save the life of the two people at the expense of an innocent bystander by diverting the trolley into the path of this bystander. Here the common view is that the right of the bystander would be justifiably infringed by virtue of the fact that more of the same right will be protected if the right of the bystander is infringed. The analysis is also overinclusive because not all deontological constraints are rights. One may argue that one should not let one student whom one has caught cheating go unpunished, even if by letting that student off one can thereby uncover information about five other cheaters. Unless one believes that the cheater has a right to be punished, this phenomenon cannot be explained in terms of rights (Otsuka 1997: 205).

Last, while the trumps theory of rights is a conceptual frame, deontological constraints are too related to a particular Kantian moral theory to be regarded as an explication of the concept of rights. The theories which posit the existence of deontological constraints often rely on concepts such as dignity, autonomy, and agency. If indeed the concept of rights is identified with constraints grounded in these values, it is only the Kantian who would be legitimately using the concept. This does not detract from the validity of deontology as a moral theory; but it suggests that it cannot serve as a theory of rights since it does not explain the role of rights within a broad range of non-Kantian moral and political theories.

Rights and Their Role in Moral Theory

Are rights foundational?

Philosophers often argue that rights are not foundational; rather they are derivative of more fundamental values. Raz expresses this opinion when he states that: "Assertions of rights are typically intermediate conclusions in arguments from ultimate values to duties" (Raz 1986: 181). Raz holds what can be termed the reductionist hypothesis, namely the view that the values underlying rights are conceptually prior to rights and dictate their scope and strength.

A critical examination of the reductionist hypothesis requires a thorough investigation of the discourse of rights. Not all the reasons which justify the protection of speech, or religion, provide a reason to establish *a right* to free speech, or *a right* to freedom of religion. The protection of speech may, for instance, be conducive to economic prosperity. Such a contribution to economic prosperity provides reasons to protect speech, but the contribution of speech to economic prosperity is not used to justify the establishment of *a right* to free speech (Harel 1997: 104). A distinction should therefore be drawn between reasons which are intrinsic with respect to a right, namely reasons by virtue of which a certain demand is classified as a right, and reasons which are extrinsic with respect to a right – reasons which may justify protection of the object protected by a right, for example, speech, but not its inclusion within the scope of the right to free speech. Autonomy is an intrinsic reason relative to the right of free speech because it is used to justify the protection of a *right* to free speech, while economic prosperity is an extrinsic reason with respect to this right.

An advocate of the reductionist hypothesis faces two major challenges in explaining the way rights operate in legal and moral discourse (Harel 2003: 264). The right to free speech could be used as an example demonstrating the two challenges. First, the advocate of reductionism has to explain the *differential treatment of reasons*, namely why some reasons for protecting speech are classified as reasons which justify the *right* to free speech while others are merely used to justify the protection of speech. Arguably, in evaluating the desirability of censoring speech, it seems arbitrary to distinguish between autonomy, or the marketplace of ideas (classified as intrinsic) and other reasons, for example, economic prosperity (classified as extrinsic). Why should a dichotomy be drawn between reasons justifying the protection of speech and reasons justifying the establishment of *a right* to free speech, and why should the latter reasons enjoy such prominence in political discourse? Secondly, the advocate of reductionism has to explain the reasons for the *differential treatment of activities*, namely why are merely some activities protected, (e.g., speech) rather than all autonomy-enhancing activities. If speech, for instance, is protected only because its protection is conducive to autonomy, then, arguably, protection should be granted to any activity which is as autonomy-enhancing as speech (provided that protecting these activities does not conflict with other valuable objectives).

Explaining the differential treatment of activities is particularly difficult for the reductionist. If the value of rights is indeed derived from the values underlying these rights, one would expect that the scope of these rights and their strength would fully converge with the strength and the scope of the values underlying them. If what really counts is autonomy *per se* (or any other intrinsic reasons underlying the protection of the right), the very classification of rights in accordance with the protected activities seems capricious. Instead of classifying rights as rights to protected activities, for example, speech or religion, rights should be classified in accordance with the values underlying the rights, for example, autonomy, or dignity. By protecting speech, or religion, rather than all autonomy-enhancing activities, one fetishizes the protected activities and lessens the significance of the underlying values.

Could a nonreductionist theory of rights provide a useful explanation of the importance of activities such as speech or religion? One difficulty of reconciling nonreductionism with the practices governing the discourse of rights is that typically, in the case of a controversy concerning the scope of rights or their stringency, judges and philosophers examine the values underlying the rights. Free speech cases are often resolved by examining carefully the values justifying the protection of speech. It seems that resorting to these values in resolving disputes concerning the scope and stringency of the right to free speech is a testimony to the validity of reductionism.

This argument supporting reductionism is, however, based on a fallacy. The nonreductionist need not deny the importance of values or, more broadly, the importance of intrinsic reasons in dictating the stringency and the scope of rights. Nonreductionism, instead, asserts that the values underlying the protection of rights are dependent on the social practices aimed at protecting these values. This claim is part of a broader phenomenon, namely the social dependence of value on social practices sustaining it (Raz 1999: 204).

Raz points out that social practices have two important roles in facilitating the realization of values. First, access to value depends on the societal understanding of these values and the transmission of this knowledge and such transmission depends on the possession of concepts, which are sustained and created by social practices (Raz 1999: 204–5). Moreover, these social practices "thicken the texture" of societal goods and

"allow them to develop greater subtlety and nuance" (Raz 1999: 205). New socially created goods develop only once the practices sustaining them are created. These goods are not merely new manifestations of existing values; they are indeed new values, which emerge with the emergence of the practices sustaining them.

The social dependence of access to value and the social dependence of value itself can be applied to the context of rights and justify a nonreductionist theory of rights (Harel 2003: 269-75). In the context of speech and autonomy nonreductionism contends that the contribution of the right to free speech to the enhancement of autonomy depends on the societal convention of protecting speech *for the sake of autonomy.* This dependence can be justified on two grounds. First, in societies in which the right to free speech is protected for the sake of autonomy, people exercise their autonomy via speech rather than via other activities. Hence, the recognition that autonomy can be exercised via speech is internalized and people get accustomed to exercise their autonomy by exercising their right to free speech. Second, the very understanding of what it means to be fully autonomous is equated with the socially protected practices. More generally, nonreductionism insists on a close interdependence between values and practices reinforcing these values. Autonomy is dependent upon the existence and the reinforcement of conventionally recognized practices of exercising autonomy.

This nonreductionist theory of rights explains two central characteristics of rights. First, it explains why it is important to establish rights *for the sake of promoting the values underlying them.* Typically, in delineating the boundaries of the right to free speech, judges reiterate the values underlying the protection. The exercise of autonomy does not merely depend on the protection of value-enhancing activities, such as speech; it also depends on protecting these activities for the sake of promoting the relevant values. It is only the full awareness of the meaningfulness of these practices which facilitate access to these values, and such an awareness is nourished by the judicial reiteration of the role the values have in justifying the right and dictating its scope. Secondly, nonreductionism explains a very puzzling feature of the discourse concerning rights. On the one hand, human rights activists and courts often vigorously advocate the protection of certain rights and believe that their protection is crucial for maintaining the decency of their society. At the same time, these same human rights activists and courts are well aware that the very same rights remain unprotected or protected in different ways in other decent societies. Just look at the rigidity with which the United States protects the right to free speech and compare it to the more compromising protection prevailing within the European Union. The interdependence between values and practices provides an explanation founded on the conjecture that values are at least partially dependent upon societal practices and activities. This conjecture does not entail complete relativism, but it implies that different traditions can justify significant variations in the scope and the stringency of protection granted to rights in different societies.

This subsection established the hypothesis that values and rights are interdependent. Yet some moral theorists suggest that rights are at odds with values and sometimes even argue that a world with no rights is better in fundamental respects than a rights-based world. The next subsection explores this accusation.

Does moral theory need rights? The "progressive" opposition to rights

Moral theorists have conflicting attitudes towards rights. Some consider rights to be an essential and uncontroversial component of any morally acceptable social order, so that rebelling against rights is like rebelling against the moral order as such. Much of the international discourse concerning rights presupposes that, despite a fundamental disagreement with respect to what rights individuals have and how to balance them with other important values, every decent society protects certain rights. Others insist that rights reflect a partial or a biased understanding of morality – one which reflects legalism, formalism, individualism, and perhaps even masculinity and Eurocentrism, so that a moral conception governed by rights (or a legal order governed by rights) repre-

sents one sectarian conception of a moral or legal order.

There are numerous related features associated with rights, which explain the opposition to rights-based discourse. First, rights are perceived as barriers preventing the uninhibited pursuit of collective and social goals. Typically utilitarians are concerned that respecting rights comes at the expense of the rational pursuit of social prosperity. In his famous repudiation of the French Declaration of Rights, Bentham raised two major objections against rights. First, he argued that rights do not have an existence which is prior to their recognition by society, in particular, by the legal system, and speaking of them as if they existed independently of the law is nothing but "rhetorical nonsense – nonsense upon stilts" (Bentham 1987: 53). Secondly, he stated that "there is no right which, when the abolition of it is advantageous to society, should not be abolished" (ibid.). Second, rights are often accused of being too individualistic and disruptive of social solidarity. Marx expressed this accusation in the starkest terms by stating that: "Thus none of the so-called rights of man goes beyond egoistic man, man as he is in civil society, namely an individual withdrawn behind his private interests and whims and separated from the community" (Marx 1987: 147). Rights, in particular the "rights of men," as opposed to the rights of the citizens, protect the selfish desires of the acquisitive individual and presuppose an inherent conflict between independent individuals and the society which constrains their freedom. Society is perceived by the participants of the discourse of rights as a "framework exterior to individuals, a limitation of their original self sufficiency" (Marx 1987: 147).

Recently these accusations have shifted emphasis and focused on the claim that the discourse of rights is inherently sectarian, that is, it reflects a masculine or Eurocentric mode of reasoning. Feminist scholars have argued that women should think in terms of personal relationship rather than in terms of rights. Thinking in terms of rights evokes a picture of individuals as egoistic and asocial, which reflects a male way of thinking (Hardwig 1990: 61). Other scholars have accused rights of being a Western concept that does not leave sufficient room for the diversity of human cultures (Panikkar 1982). In contrast, other cultures put greater emphasis on duties as part of the moral order, perceive differently the relations between the individual and the society or community, or even deny the separability of individuals. The most extreme advocates of this view have described rights and, in particular, human rights as a form of cultural imperialism or even as a Western conspiracy (Tesòn 1985: 896–7) or as irrelevant, meaningless, or inapplicable to non-Western societies (Pollis and Schwab 1979: 9, 13).

The radical foes of rights resist rights as such. In contrast, the moderate foes of rights do not reject rights as such, but seek to limit the scope of rights-based reasoning and its applicability, or suitability to certain spheres. Thus, some feminist theorists advocate the exclusion of the sphere of the family from the reign of rights in order to preserve solidarity within the family (Hardwig 1990). Communitarians often suggest supplementing the language of rights with another discourse, for instance discourse which highlights the importance of obligations owed to the society without discarding the discourse of rights altogether (Taylor 1985: 187). Human rights theorists who concede the universal relevance of rights often argue that the manner in which rights are understood and implemented differs in practice and also ought to differ in order to fit with the local cultural traditions (An-Na'im 1992: 3–6). Some of the most fundamental provisions of the Universal Declaration of Human Rights, such as the protection of individual property (Article 17) and the perception of family and its importance (Article 16), conflict with local cultural perceptions and it is often implied that therefore they need to be revised accordingly (Pollis and Schwab 1979: 9). In addition, it is argued that the greater traditional emphasis on civil and political rights over economic rights is a Western phenomenon that ought not be applied universally. Under this view human rights ought to be interpreted in a way that is mediated through the web of cultural traditions and economic circumstances (Falk 1992: 45). Even some proponents of implementing one understanding of human rights globally – an understanding which is relatively independent of local variations – concede that the language of human rights is inappropriate in rare cases of societies that enjoy alternative mechanisms for protecting human dignity as some traditional societies do (Donnelly 1982: 312).

This moderate criticism is of immense value. It points out the importance of rights-free zones, in which spontaneity may flourish. It also points out the complexity in understanding and implementing rights in different societies. The more radical criticism of rights, however, is subject to a major difficulty, which is analogous to the difficulty faced by the more ambitious theorists of rights. At the outset, it was pointed out that it is perhaps too pretentious to aim at providing a unified theory of rights because of the immense diversity in the usages of this term. The very same diversity may frustrate the attempts at providing a radical critique of rights. A concept which is so multifaceted in its usages cannot, without being distorted or caricatured, be characterized as individualistic, masculine, or Western. Precisely as rights are too complex to be analyzed within the frame of a single theory, so they are too complex to be rejected in their entirety.

Conclusion

Rights can be characterized on the basis of their form, substance, and strength. Their role within moral theory is controversial and some even regard the discourse of rights as promoting a formal legalistic or sectarian moral agenda.

Developing a theory of rights requires a careful balancing of conceptual and normative considerations. The primary difficulty for the theorist is to develop a theory of rights which is sensitive to the way rights operate in practical reasoning and which accommodates diverse political and legal traditions. This consideration requires highlighting conceptual considerations at the expense of normative ones. Yet, to be meaningful for the participants in the discourse of rights, for example, for judges, political activists, and conscientious citizens, a theory of rights must have some normative commitments and ramifications. The theorist of rights needs therefore to preserve a very subtle balance between conceptual analysis and normative theorizing.

A world with no rights may not be as disastrous as some of the advocates of rights believe, but it would not be harmonious either (as some of the foes of rights suggest). In a world with no rights an intangible human sensitivity would be lost – sensitivity which highlights right-holders and their perspectives as central components of moral theory. People may be well protected in such a world but depriving them of the status of right-holders means that they are not protected for the rights reasons – reasons which highlight their central role in justifying that protection. Various theories of rights express this concern in different ways. The choice theory highlights agency while the interest theory focuses on the distinctive quality of right-holders as possessing "ultimate interests." Deontological theories stress the unwillingness to sacrifice individual rights even for the sake of promoting valuable interests. But even if one rejects this explanation as too metaphysical, it seems that some of the functions rights serve would, in such a world, be replaced by analogous conceptual tools. At the moment, rights are too entrenched in our moral and legal culture for us to comprehend how such a world would look.

References

An-Na'im, Abdullahi A. 1992. Introduction. In Abdullahi A. An-Na'im (ed.), *Human Rights in Cross-Cultural Perspectives: A Quest for Consensus.* Philadelphia: University of Pennsylvania Press, 1–18.

Bentham, Jeremy. 1987. Anarchical fallacies: Being an examination of the Declaration of Rights issued during the French Revolution. In Jeremy Waldron (ed.), *Nonsense Upon Stilts: Bentham, Burke and Marx on the Rights of Man.* London and New York: Methuen, 46–69.

Brook, Richard. 1991. Agency and morality. *Journal of Philosophy* 88: 190–212.

Donnelly, Jack. 1982. Human rights and human dignity: An analytic critique of non-Western conceptions of human rights. *The American Political Science Review* 76: 303–16.

Dworkin, Ronald. 1977. *Taking Rights Seriously.* Cambridge, MA: Harvard University Press.

Dworkin, Ronald. 1984. Rights as trumps. In Jeremy Waldron (ed.), *Theories of Rights.* Oxford: Oxford University Press, 153–67.

Falk, Richard. 1992. Cultural foundations for the international protection of human rights. In Abdullahi A. An-Na'im (ed.), *Human Rights in Cross-Cultural Perspectives: A Quest for Consensus.* Philadelphia: University of Pennsylvania Press, 44–64.

Feinberg, Joel. 1970. The nature and value of rights. *Journal of Value Inquiry* 4: 243–57.

Hardwig, John. 1990. Should women think in terms of rights? In C. Sunstein (ed.), *Feminism and Political Theory.* Chicago and London: University of Chicago Press, 53–67.

Harel, Alon. 1997. What demands are rights? An investigation into the relations between rights and reasons. *Oxford Journal of Legal Studies* 17: 101–14.

Harel, Alon. 1998. Revisionist theories of rights: An unwelcome defense. *Canadian Journal of Law and Jurisprudence* 11: 227–44.

Harel, Alon. 2003. Rights-based judicial review: A democratic justification. *Law and Philosophy* 22: 247–76.

Hart, H. L. A. 1982. Legal rights. In H. L. A. Hart, *Essays on Bentham: Jurisprudence and Political Theory.* Oxford: Clarendon Press, 162–93.

Hohfeld, Wesley Newcomb. 1919. *Fundamental Legal Conceptions as Applied in Judicial Reasoning,* ed. Walter Wheeler Cook. New Haven, CT: Yale University Press.

Jhering, Rudolph von. 1915. *The Struggle for Law,* 2nd edn., trans. from 5th edn. John Lalor. Chicago: Callaghan and Co.

Kagan, Shelly. 1991. Replies to my critics. *Philosophy and Phenomenological Research* 51: 919–28.

Kagan, Shelly. 1998. *Normative Ethics.* Boulder, CO: Westview Press.

Kamm, Frances. 1996. *Morality, Mortality: Rights, Duties, and Status,* vol. II. Oxford: Oxford University Press.

Kramer, Matthew H. 1998. Rights without trimming. In Matthew Kramer, N. E. Simmonds, and Hillel Steiner (eds.), *A Debate Over Rights: Philosophical Inquiries.* Oxford: Clarendon Press, 8–111.

Kramer, Matthew H. 2001. Do animals and dead people have legal rights? *Canadian Journal of Law and Jurisprudence* 14: 29–54.

Lyons, David. 1994a. Rights, claimants and beneficiaries. In David Lyons (ed.), *Rights, Welfare, and Mill's Moral Theory.* Oxford: Oxford University Press, 23–46.

Lyons, David. 1994b. Utility and rights. In David Lyons (ed.), *Rights, Welfare, and Mill's Moral Theory.* Oxford: Oxford University Press: 147–175.

McCloskey, H. J. 1965. Rights. *Philosophical Quarterly* 15: 115–27.

MacCormick, Neil. 1977. Rights in legislation. In P. M. S. Hacker and J. Raz (eds.), *Law, Morality and Society: Essays in Honour of H. L. A. Hart*. Oxford: Clarendon Press, 189–209.

MacCormick, Neil. 1982. Children's rights: A test case in legal right. In Neil MacCormick (ed.), *Legal Right and Social Democracy*. Oxford: Clarendon Press, 154–66.

Marx, Karl. 1987. On the Jewish question. In Jeremy Waldron (ed.), *Nonsense Upon Stilts: Bentham, Burke and Marx on the Rights of Man*. London and New York: Methuen, 137–50.

Nagel, Thomas. 1986. *The View from Nowhere*. Oxford: Oxford University Press.

Nozick, Robert. 1974. *Anarchy, State, and Utopia*. New York: Basic Books.

Otsuka, Michael. 1997. Kamm on the morality of killing. *Ethics* 108: 197–207.

Panikkar, R. 1982. Is the notion of human rights a Western concept? *Diogenes* 120: 75–102.

Pollis, Adamantia and Schwab, Peter. 1979. Human rights: A Western construct with limited applicability. In Adamantia Pollis and Peter Schwab (eds.), *Human Rights: Cultural and Ideological Perspectives*. New York: Praeger, 1–18.

Raz, Joseph. 1986. *The Morality of Freedom*. Oxford: Clarendon Press.

Raz, Joseph. 1994. Rights and individual well-being. In Joseph Raz (ed.), *Ethics in the Public Domain: Essays in the Morality of Law and Politics*. Oxford: Clarendon Press, 29–44.

Raz, Joseph. 1999. *The Value of Practice in Engaging Reason: On the Theory of Value and Action*. Oxford: Oxford University Press.

Scheffler, Samuel (ed.). 1988. *Consequentialism and its Critics*. Oxford: Oxford University Press.

Sreenivasan, Gopal. forthcoming. A hybrid theory of claim rights. *Oxford Journal of Legal Studies*.

Sumner, L. W. 1987. *The Moral Foundations of Rights*. Oxford: Clarendon Press.

Taylor, Charles. 1985. Atomism. In Charles Taylor, *Philosophical Papers: Philosophy and the Human Sciences*, vol II. Cambridge, UK: Cambridge University Press, 187–210.

Tesòn, Fernando R. 1985. International human rights and cultural relativism. *Virginia Journal of International Law* 25: 869–98.

Thomson, Judith Jarvis. 1986. Some ruminations on rights. In Judith Jarvis Thomson, *Rights, Restitution, and Risk: Essays in Moral Theory*, ed. W. Parent. Cambridge, MA: Harvard University Press, 49–65.

Jeremy Waldron (ed.). 1984. *Theories of Rights*. Oxford: Oxford University Press.

Wellman, Carl. 1985. *A Theory of Rights: Persons Under Laws, Institutions and Morals*. New York: Rowman and Allanheld.

Williams, Bernard. 1973. A critique of utilitarianism. In Bernard Williams and J. C. C. Smart, *Utilitarianism: For and Against*. Cambridge, UK: Cambridge University Press.

Chapter 14

A Contractarian Approach to Punishment

Claire Finkelstein

What is a Theory of Punishment?

Philosophical accounts of legal practices often proceed by showing the various rules associated with the practice as having a unified point or purpose. Tort theorists, for example, attempt to explain doctrines like assumption of risk or contributory negligence in terms of the overall point or purpose of mandating civil compensation for injuries. Criminal law theorists attempt to explain mental state requirements or the rules governing justifications and excuses in terms of the purpose of criminal prohibition. And contract theorists seek to explain the doctrine of consideration or rules like the prohibition on punitive damages in terms of the point of contract enforcement. Legal theorists thus often restrict themselves to the task of showing how particular legal rules cohere with the overall legal institution of which they are a part.

Philosophers seeking to offer a theory of punishment, however, cannot content themselves with this coherentist approach. For unlike compensation in tort, or the specific rules governing crimes or contract formation, the institution of punishment involves acts that are normally highly morally objectionable. While forcing people to pay compensation is admittedly a gross imposition, it is quite a different matter from controlling their bodies, inflicting physical suffering, or depriving them of their liberty.[1] For this reason, a theory of punishment must do more than show that the rules of the practice cohere with the purpose of the institution of which they are a part. A theory of punishment must first and foremost seek to *justify* the practice of punishment as a whole. Only then can the theory justify particular rules in terms of that institution.

In what follows, I shall suggest that the two prevailing approaches to punishment – deterrence and retributivism – fail at that task. On the one hand, deterrence theorists normally identify the fact that punishment deters others from committing offenses in the future as a sufficient condition for justifying the institution, and in turn for punishing a given offender under that institution. I shall argue, however, that while effective deterrence may weigh in favor of the practice of punishment, and in turn of particular punishments, that fact alone cannot overcome the presumption against the institution and the acts that fall under it. On the other hand, retributivists point to the fact that offenders *deserve* punishment as a sufficient basis for subjecting them to it. But I shall suggest that while desert may provide a reason in favor of the institution as a whole, it cannot by itself constitute an adequate justification for inflicting a certain punishment on a given offender. Thus while the rationale offered by each theory *tends* in the direction of a justification for the practices that constitute the institution of punishment, neither of the standard justifications offered is sufficient by itself to render the relevant practices morally permissible. I shall not attempt to canvass *all* possible theories of punishment. For example, I do not address the interesting expressivist and communicative alternatives to the traditional theories that have been offered in recent years.[2] But I suspect that such theories will suffer from the same difficulties as the traditional theories. The problem, I shall argue, is that no treatment of another human being as harsh as that which standard forms of punishment for serious crimes involve can be permissible if it is truly involuntarily imposed. For this reason, only a consensual theory of punishment holds out hope for a true justification for the institution.

I am *not* suggesting that consent is by itself a sufficient condition to justify the infliction of pain on an individual. That clearly is not the case. The criminal law, for example, rejects consent as an adequate defense to most crimes, most notably to murder. And although consent is sometimes a defense against some crimes, such as rape and assault, it is limited in its operation even in these cases to situations in which the consent offered signifies that the victim is not being harmed. A consensual theory of punishment, then, must be prepared to explain the relevance of consent in this context. I shall argue that it is not consent alone that justifies punishment, but consent coupled with the fact that the agent receives a benefit under the institution to which he consents. The result will be that deterrence and desert need not provide mutually exclusive foundations for a theory of punishment. Each has its place in a properly conceived consensual theory of that institution.

Deterrence Theories of Punishment

The most common deterrence-based approach to punishment maintains that punishment is justified just in case punishing an offender would deter other potential criminals from committing crimes in the future. Thus practices like incarceration are justified as applied to one person because they forestall wrongful acts on the part of others. The most significant limitation of such accounts is that deterrence as a rationale for punishment cannot stand alone. There are two quite obvious reasons for this. The first we might call the "problem of torture." Suppose it turned out that torturing offenders at various intervals during incarceration improved the deterrent efficacy of prison sentences substantially. Are deterrence theorists prepared to endorse torture? Of

course not. Deterrence theorists, like everyone else, believe there are restrictions on what it is permissible to do to another human being. But if torture deters, on what grounds will deterrence theorists rule it out? A second problem we might call the "problem of responsibility." Suppose a robber is on the loose and the police have been unable to catch him. Suppose further that the lack of detection is well-publicized, with the effect that the number of robberies in that community is increasing. May officials frame an innocent person in order to reap the deterrent benefits of a public conviction? Of course not. Deterrence theorists, like everyone else, would limit punishment to the guilty. But once again, if "punishing" the innocent deters, on what grounds will the deterrence theorist rule it out of bounds?

It should not be surprising that deterrence theorists encounter such difficulties. Deterrence is a utilitarian rationale for punishment, and the problem here is the same as that which utilitarians face when they try to account for the impermissibility of inflicting pain on one person for the sake of improving the welfare of a larger number of other persons. Philosophers of Kantian persuasion sometimes couch the objection by saying that utilitarian theories permit treating individuals as a means to benefiting other individuals, and that ordinary morality does not. The constraint on using, or some other similar constraint, is typically thought to provide a basis for establishing a system of rights (see Thomson 1990). Rights in turn constrain maximizing social welfare, and constrain it so thoroughly that it is not even permissible to violate one innocent person's rights in order to minimize a larger number of rights violations that would befall others.[3] The result is that there are *no* circumstances in which we may permissibly inflict pain or other physical hardship on one person in order to benefit a larger number of other people. How, then, can we justify a punishment involving severe physical hardship by pointing to the fact that others would be deterred from committing crimes if we use it?

One response deterrence theorists might make is to seek to explain the significance of conditions of personal responsibility in deterrence terms as well. They might argue that it simply would not be maximally efficacious from the standpoint of deterrence to punish innocents, children, the insane, and others who are not physically or morally responsible for crimes. For in this case, people would have no more reason to fear punishment in the wake of having committed a crime than they would if they had not committed a crime. Similarly, if punishment does not distinguish between those who can control their conduct and those who cannot, then punishment would not have special deterrent efficacy for those who *can* control their conduct.

But deterrence theorists have no reason actually to restrict the use of punishment to responsible agents. They only require the *perception* that the punishment is reserved for those responsible for their crimes. Deterrence theorists therefore must be ready to adopt punishment of the factually and morally innocent if that proves the most expedient deterrent, as in the example we considered above. A second problem is that it is simply not the case that punishing nonresponsible agents will have no deterrent efficacy. For example, it might well deter crime to punish those who violate the law under duress, inadvertently or involuntarily. For if it were well known that the state would not excuse someone who committed a crime under these circumstances, potential criminals would take precautions against ending up in situations where they might be forced to commit crimes. Thus even if wholly innocent agents were "punished" for crimes they did not commit, such punishment could well contribute to deterrence, as long as the individuals selected could plausibly be thought to have some connection to a past crime.

A second argument deterrence theorists might make is a conceptual one. They might say that harsh treatment inflicted on an innocent person would simply not be punishment. Thus, arguably, deterrence theorists need not offer an account that explains why incarceration and other forms of harsh treatment are only justified against the innocent, since they would be entitled on this account to treat "punishment of the innocent" as a logical impossibility. But this argument will not do, since any adequate justification for punishment must be able to account for why it is that acts otherwise strictly forbidden are permissible in this context. The fact that those acts will be directed toward someone guilty of a crime must itself be part of the justification offered for per-

forming them, and so it cannot be ruled out on conceptual grounds that such acts are only used in that way.

For the above reasons, most deterrence theorists do not assert a *pure* version of the deterrence argument. Instead, they will mostly restrict pursuing the aim of deterrence to situations that do not require violating basic principles of responsibility. They will claim that deterrence as a rationale operates on a range of punishments that satisfy various moral constraints in addition to deterrence, and that such punishment can only be permissibly inflicted if the offender meets the conditions of responsibility we discussed. A mixed theory of this sort would arguably be consistent with a deterrence rationale because deterrence would still be the *reason* for inflicting punishment. The additional constraints deterrence theorists might adopt would simply be limiting conditions on the circumstances in which it would be permissible to act on that reason. Is deterrence a compelling rationale for punishment when advanced in a mixed theory of this sort?

A primary difficulty is of course that deterrence theorists cannot simply help themselves to restrictions on permissible punishments or to background conditions of responsibility. They must advance a theory that explains why these limiting conditions should be incorporated into a general theory of deterrence. Such a theory will be difficult to come by, since the relevant conditions will conflict with the end of deterrence. This point has generally been well understood in the writing on deterrence. What has been less noticed, however, is that even once these conditions are defended in the context of a mixed theory, deterrence theorists' problems are not at an end. For it will turn out that the "mixed" deterrence theory is not able to escape the difficulties of the more obviously flawed pure theory. Let us see why this is so.

Begin by considering the following case. Suppose there is a terrorist holding eight innocent people hostage, and threatening to shoot them all within minutes. As it happens, he is listening to the radio, waiting for news of another man's execution. This other man is guilty of murder, but he has undergone a conversion in prison, and he is desperately hoping for a reprieve from the governor. If the governor grants clemency to the murderer, the terrorist will kill the eight hostages. If the governor denies clemency, so that the execution takes place, the terrorist will be intimidated into releasing the eight people. The governor is inclined to grant clemency, because he believes in the murderer's conversion, but he has become aware of the plight of the hostages, and knows they will be killed if he proceeds with his plan. Should he therefore deny clemency? Indeed, is he *obligated* to deny the request for clemency, as deterrence theorists would probably have it?

Notice that deterrence theorists must be prepared to assert that deterrence provides a basis for punishing in this case, given that the other conditions they impose as constraints on the deterrence rationale, such as reasonableness of punishment and guilt, are met. They must be prepared to say in this case that the fact that eight murders would be deterred, and hence eight lives saved, is a *reason* for the governor to proceed to execute an offender.[4] But I do not think deterrence theorists can say this. For the fact that killing one person would prevent another, different person from killing others does not seem to provide a valid reason for killing the one, despite the fact that he is guilty of a crime. That is, adding restrictions of the sort we have considered does not make deterrence itself a better reason for inflicting punishment. Deterrence is still supposed to do the work of justifying punishment, and it is still a rationale that permits the rights of one individual to be violated for the sake of benefit to others.

Notice that the situation would be different if granting clemency to this offender would result in *his* killing eight people immediately. In that case, the governor would have a strong preventive justification for incapacitating the offender by putting him to death. The killing would then be an instance of *defense of others* – clearly permissible as an extension of the self-defensive rights any one of the eight might have. But matters seem significantly different when the killings to be prevented are to take place at the hands of a person other than the one being executed. The reason for this can most simply be put by saying that *the preventive privilege does not travel across persons.* That is, while it may be permissible to make a person suffer in order to prevent future harm to

others, it is not permissible to do so in order to prevent *some other agent* from inflicting that harm.

The *no traveling across persons* restriction would appear to be a fundamental part of the way we think of personal responsibility. It stems from basic intuitions we have about the autonomy of persons and the way in which such autonomy grounds rights against interference by others. It also appears to be deeply ingrained in our responsibility-based practices. In the criminal law, for example, we have the doctrine of *novus actus interveniens*, according to which a person who causes a prohibited result is nevertheless not responsible for that result if the causal route by which the result was produced passes through the voluntary act of another human being.[5] A stabs B, who is rushed to the hospital where a doctor, C, performs a highly reckless operation on him in order to rescue him from A's stab wounds. B subsequently dies, although he would not have died from the stab wounds alone. A is not responsible for B's death, because the locus of responsibility shifts to C. We explain this by saying that agents are not responsible for the free, voluntary acts of other agents. They are responsible for their own acts alone. The problem with deterrence as a rationale for punishment, then, is that it is a preventive justification for punishment that travels across persons.

To see the importance of the *no traveling across persons* restriction, consider the following modification of our clemency case. As before, the terrorist is listening for news about the murderer on death row in order to decide whether to kill the eight hostages. The murderer is strapped to the electric chair, and all are awaiting word of the governor's decision. It turns out, however, that one of the hostages has a device that will activate the electric chair. He can surreptitiously press a button and the electric chair will electrocute its victim. If the hostage presses the button, he will cause the murderer to be killed, and since the terrorist will think the governor himself ordered the execution, he will be deterred. In this way, the hostage with his finger on the button will have saved his own life, along with the lives of the other seven hostages. If the hostage does not press the button, he strongly suspects that the execution will not take place, because he knows that the governor is inclined to grant clemency. May he press the button under these circumstances?

It is very tempting to say that he may. It seems, after all, to be an extension of the hostage's right to self-defense. If he presses the button, he can save his life. If he does not press the button, he will almost certainly be killed. How could it be impermissible for him to press the button? Nevertheless, I think there is little doubt he may *not* press it.

To see this, we need only suppose (contrary to our earlier assumption of guilt) that the person sitting in the electric chair is an innocent person dragged in off the street to serve as an example to others. Surely it would be impermissible for the hostage to kill him if he is not in any way the source of the threat. In general, it is not permissible to harm an innocent, uninvolved third party in order to prevent some sort of future harm to oneself or another. While the self-defensive privilege is a strong one – it will permit someone who only fears grievous bodily injury to use lethal force against an assailant, even if that assailant is a child or insane – it is sharply limited to those who are the source of the harm to persons defending themselves.[6]

The question we should now ask is: does it make any difference if the person in the chair is a murderer? The answer seems to be that it is irrelevant, since it does not make that person any more the source of the threat to the eight than if he were dragged in off the street to serve as a mock example to others. And if it is not permissible for one of the eight to push the button and execute the murderer in the chair, it is not permissible for the governor (in effect) to order the execution of that same person to deter the killing of the eight. The reason, once again, would seem to be that *the broad privilege granted to preventive killing does not travel across persons.* In this case, application of the principle would mean that neither the governor nor one of the hostages himself may put the murderer to death *just in order to deter someone else* from killing the hostages. Whether it is permissible for the state to order the execution of the person strapped to the electric chair, given that he is a murderer, is another matter. The point is simply that we may not justify putting him to death by the fact that killing him would have the desirable effect of saving the hostages, given that

the person in the electric chair is not himself the source of the threat to them. In Kantian terms, we might say that killing the murderer would be *using* him to save the hostages, in the case in which he is not the source of the threat. Where he *is* the source of the threat, by contrast, killing him would be justified because it would be repelling the attack.[7]

Thus the basic problem with deterrence as a rationale, even when combined with the requirement of guilt and other restrictions in a mixed theory, is that it is a justification for killing that travels across persons, since it purports to justify killing one person in order to deter someone else from killing in the future. This amounts to saying that deterrence is ineliminably utilitarian in that it permits using a person as an instrument to bring about a good to someone else. Killing one murderer on the ground that we can prevent another person from murdering in the future does not fall under the preventive privilege, then, because it impermissibly holds the first murderer responsible for a murder committed by another person.

In closing this section, it is worth noting that it might be possible to construct a form of deterrence that does not involve traveling across persons if we do not apply the deterrence rationale to punishment directly. Instead, an act of punishment might be justified just in case it follows from a threat it was legitimate to issue. We might in turn seek to justify the threat in terms of its deterrent benefits.[8] Without exploring this possible alternative form of deterrence in further detail here, let me briefly suggest that this account is unlikely to provide an adequate justification for punishment without violating the prohibition against traveling across persons. For the fact that on this account, the appeal to deterrence only supplies a justification for the *threat* to punish will make it difficult to justify actually following through on the threat. One would expect to have to appeal to something further, such as the need to establish the credibility of future threats or the benefits supplied by the institution of punishment as a whole. But once such an appeal is made, the account will involve traveling across persons, since the justification for punishing *this* offender would be established by reference to other, future offenders. We will see, however, that this version of the deterrence argument has some advantages over the standard version. Later in the chapter we will explore a contractarian alternative with a similar structure. But it will turn out that the consensual foundation for this account avoids the problem of traveling across persons.[9]

Retributivist Theories of Punishment

The objections we considered to a deterrence-based theory of punishment stemmed from intuitions we have about what it is morally permissible to do to people on which occasions. We saw that while deterrence theorists may try to incorporate core deontological intuitions into their theory by placing constraints on the applicability of the deterrence rationale, the account will still run afoul of those intuitions, even on a "mixed" version of the deterrence account. One might then be tempted to abandon concerns with deterrence, and to base one's theory of punishment entirely on deontological intuitions. The most common deontological account of punishment is a retributivist account. As we shall see, however, retributivist theories have problems of their own.

Retributivism is the theory of punishment that says that punishment is justified because, and only to the extent that, the criminal *deserves* to be punished. Traditionally, the core of retributivists' arguments for any specific penalty is the doctrine of *lex talionis*, the idea that offenders deserve to experience the suffering they inflicted on their victims. Taken literally, *lex talionis* is an absurd doctrine: no one would advocate raping rapists, assaulting assailants, or burgling the homes of burglars. And what would we do with those who write bad checks or engage in forgery? The difficulty making sense of *lex talionis* has accordingly led some retributivists to suggest that retributivism is most compelling as an abstract theory about desert and punishment, without its associated account of the measure of punishment (see Moore 1997: 205–6). But in the absence of its accompanying doctrine of *lex talionis* or some other way of giving content to the notion of desert, retributivists will be unable to justify any specific penalty. Given that retributivism is absurd if accompanied by a literal interpretation of *lex talionis* and vacuous if articulated without *lex talionis*, the only hope retributivists have for articulating a comprehensive theory of punishment is to try to advance a more approximate system for matching crimes with punishments that does not insist that the punishment exactly fit the crime.

Now this turns out to be quite difficult to do. Begin by considering just how approximate the doctrine must be to work. It is not only that we are presently unwilling to inflict one or two of the more extreme harms on criminals, like rape and torture, that criminals sometimes inflict on their victims. The prohibited list also includes more modest harms like forcing a member of a fraternity to imbibe too much alcohol, or requiring a rogue cop to remove his clothes and walk half a mile in winter along a public road, both harms that perpetrators have inflicted on their victims. Indeed, once one begins to consider all the deviant forms of behavior our criminal codes outlaw, it is clear that the vast majority of criminal acts are not ones we feel entitled to impose by way of punishment. There are really only a few criminal acts we regard as yielding acceptable forms of punishment: false imprisonment, theft, and in some states murder. Retributivists who wish to match crimes with punishments must come up with a theory that would limit the deserved penalty to the three forms of criminal conduct listed above.

There are two possible strategies available to retributivists to accomplish this. The first distributes punishments proportionately, so that the worst crimes are matched with the worst penalties, and so on down the line. We might call this version of retributivism the "proportionate penalty" theory. The problem with the proportionate penalty theory, whatever its other merits, is that it will not ultimately help retributivists to justify any particular penalty. For the method does not provide an argument to the effect that we *ought* to include any particular penalty on the list of acceptable penalties. It merely insists on taking available punishments – that is, punishments we are already willing to inflict – and imposing them on perpetrators in order of severity according to the severity of the criminal acts performed. Recall that we turned to retributivism from a deterrence approach in the hope of finding a way of identifying certain penalties as morally unacceptable. It does not look, however, as though the proportionate penalty theory can help us with that task.

The second, and more promising strategy is to attempt to establish a *moral* equivalence between crimes and permissible punishments in the following way: while the perpetrator deserves to suffer an amount equivalent to the amount of harm or moral evil inflicted on the victim, the *kinds* of harm or evil involved need not match. That is, instead of either assigning the same harms or evils as a punishment that the offender inflicted on his victim, or fixing penalties proportionately by making sure that the right intervals obtain between levels of punishments, we can match crimes with punishments on an absolute scale, but establish only a rough moral equivalence between the two. We would seek to inflict on the perpetrator by way of punishment the nearest match to his own act that it is morally permissible for us to inflict. Alternatively, we simply make a list of all the acceptable penalties, and a list of all the possible crimes, and assign the worst penalty to the worst crime, the least penalty to the least crime, and match penalties with crimes in between (Davis 1983). Let us call this type of retributivism, under either of the above formulations, the "moral equivalence" theory of justified punishment.

Unfortunately the moral equivalence theory does not solve retributivism's difficulties. For the theory, considered in and of itself, has no way of identifying which penalties are morally permissible and which are not. How do we know, for example, that locking a perpetrator in the trunk of a car and then killing him is not permissible under the theory, but that simply executing him is? Without an account of which penalties are permissible and why, we may as well argue that putting an offender to death is impermissible, but that locking him up in prison for his life is not, or even that lifetime incarceration is impermissible, but that a 20–year sentence is not. The moral equivalence theory would thus need to be supplemented by another moral theory, one that would tell us which penalties are morally permissible and which not. The theory of permissibility then becomes a side constraint on the penalties it is permissible to inflict. But since retributivists' theory of punishment was supposed itself to answer the question of which punishments are morally acceptable and which are not, the moral equivalence theory would now appear to be woefully incomplete.

Let us now suppose moral equivalence theorists do manage to supplement that account with an additional theory establishing when a penalty is too harsh to be permissibly imposed, and let us suppose we accept the theory in that form. It is still not clear that the moral equivalence theory can be made to justify specific penalties. There are at least two remaining problems with the moral equivalence theory. First, even in this modified form, there clearly are some penalties we think of as morally unacceptable that are less severe than other penalties we find acceptable. And if we wish to rule out those lesser penalties, we will be compelled to rule out the more severe penalties as well. Consider shame sanctions, such as forcing sex offenders to bear an identifying license plate or to undergo involuntary sterilization. Such penalties have been highly controversial, and many people think them beyond all moral bounds. But whatever their merits or demerits, they are clearly less severe than other penalties we currently think of as acceptable, such as lifetime imprisonment without parole. If we are to rule out some lesser penalty as morally unacceptable, however, we should perhaps be prepared to rule out any penalties more severe than it. And thus we would be forced to conclude that incarceration for long periods of time is morally unacceptable.

Second, the moral equivalence theorist's use of the notion of desert is unclear. What does it mean to say that a person "deserves" to suffer a certain harm but that it is not permissible for anyone to inflict that harm on him? We can surely make sense of the idea of a person deserving a certain penalty which, for some very local reason, it is not permissible for us to inflict. For example, a person revealed to be guilty who was once found innocent in a criminal trial might rightly be judged to deserve some penalty which the prohibition on placing a person's life or limb "twice in jeopardy" would prohibit. But can we apply this same logic to a punishment which it would never, under any circumstances, be permissible to inflict on a person? It seems strange, for example, to say that someone might "deserve" to be tortured, at the same time that we are prepared to say that it is not, and never has been, permissible for anyone ever to inflict torture as a penalty on another person. I do not, therefore, find this move a compelling alternative to the unmodified version of *lex talionis* that we saw was problematic in the beginning of our discussion of retributivism.

The above arguments at least show that retributivists have not met their burden of proof. Since I cannot meet that burden for them, I can only issue an invitation to retributivists to make their case in greater detail. In the next section, we shall see that the retributivist's core intuition – that there should be some kind of internal relation between crime and punishment – is essentially correct. But the history of attempts to build a theory out of that intuition alone makes apparent that any such theory will be dramatically incomplete.

The Contractarian Alternative

Our discussion in the preceding two sections suggests that both deterrence and retributivism provide only partial justifications for punishment. Each theory appears to raise considerations that would tend in the direction of a justification for any system of punishment organized around them. Thus the fact that inflicting sanctions would deter future crimes of a similar nature weighs in favor of the legitimacy of punishment as a general matter. But, as we saw above, the fact that inflicting *this* penalty on *this* offender would have a positive effect on deterrence cannot itself constitute a reason for inflicting it, even assuming the reason is invoked in the case of a guilty offender and for the sake of a reasonable penalty. And the fact that the severity of a given penalty bears some relation to the crime the offender committed also seems to make the sanction more defensible. But that fact alone cannot provide a theory of punishment, since this idea cannot be translated into anything like an absolute metric to establish the moral acceptability of specific penalties. We might suppose, then, that while each theory identifies relevant considerations, something is missing from each. My suggestion will be that it is the voluntary nature of the system of punishment that is required to give both deterrence and moral desert their proper

places. It is beyond the scope of the current chapter to articulate a complete consensual account of punishment. In what follows, however, I shall attempt to trace the outlines of one possible consensual theory. I do not claim this is the only possible consent-based approach to punishment, but only that it is a possible theory that yields quite definite, and I think, interesting results.

Let us begin with the assumption that society is itself, to use Rawls' phrase, "a cooperative venture for mutual advantage" (Rawls 1971: 4). One natural way to interpret this thought is that society is the product of agreement among rational agents who see themselves as advantaged under the terms of social interaction, using as a baseline how they would fare in its absence. Indeed, one might here depart from Rawls and treat this as something in the nature of a *requirement* for the basic institutions and practices that make up the fabric of social interaction: the basic institutions of society would not be agreed upon generally by rational agents unless each person whose agreement is required believes she will be better off under the terms of that institution than she would be in its absence. Furthermore, basic institutions like education, medical care, public transportation, national defense, and law enforcement might all be subject to the constraint that rational agents living under these systems would have consented to them, and would have been rational to do so, had they been offered the choice in advance. Our question would then be: would each rational agent involved in selecting the basic institutions of society regard it as advantageous to include punishment among those to which she gives her assent? If so, does the fact that such an institution must be voluntarily selected tell us anything about the form that such an institution must take?

Notice there are several ambiguities in the requirement I articulated above. What does it mean to say that each person must believe she would be better off under a given institution than she would be in its absence? Is it sufficient that each rational agent's expected utility is positive when she evaluates the institution from the *ex ante* point of view? In other words, is it sufficient if the agent regards the gamble on that institution as worth taking, even if the odds are actually low that her welfare will be improved under the institution? I suggest that rational agents entering into agreements for basic social institutions would require more than this. They would require that institutions to which they give their assent would *actually* improve their conditions, as compared with the lives they would lead in their absence. They would, in other words, eschew gambles where the basic elements of their well-being are concerned. This is a common theme in contractarian political writings. Locke builds such a condition into his account of initial distributions, when he maintains that a condition on removing goods or other benefits from the commons is that the agent leave "enough and as good" for others, a condition designed to protect each agent's basic welfare (Locke 1960: ch. V, §§ 27, 33). Rawls expresses a similar thought when he maintains that the parties to the original position would not trade basic liberties against any amount of social or economic benefit (Rawls 1971: §11). The no-gambling requirement is also built into Rawls's difference principle, in the condition that social and economic distributions must maximize the welfare of the least well-off (Rawls 1971: §13).

Let us call the principle that underlies the requirement that basic institutions leave individuals better off then they would be in its absence the "benefit principle." My suggestion is that the benefit principle supplies a helpful test for the rationality of a basic social institution from the standpoint of individual welfare. The benefit principle should not be treated as a general test for the rationality of all agreements, plans, or courses of action rational agents might adopt. For as a general condition of rationality, the principle would be much too strong: it would have the effect of ruling out much, although not all, insurance, gambling (no matter how favorable the odds), and stock market investment.[10] I am suggesting, however, that such a strong condition is not irrational with regard to the basic structure of society.[11] Since rational individuals seeking to reach agreement on the basic structure would be deciding before their actual positions under social institutions are known, they would not count on ordinary calculations of expected utility to adequately protect their interests.

I cannot here offer a fuller defense of the benefit principle, especially as compared with other contractarian principles that have been developed in greater detail by others. I offer the benefit principle in particular because it may provide something in the nature of a lowest common denominator, namely a test that any contractarian account is likely to meet. Nor am I suggesting that the benefit principle uniquely identifies the institutions that rational agents *would* adopt. There might be many possible legal regimes that satisfied the benefit principle. My suggestion is only that rational contracting agents would reject any basic institution that failed the benefit test. Satisfying the benefit principle thus provides a necessary, but not a sufficient condition for basic institutions. In a fuller contractarian account, one would need to specify further principles of selection that would allow the parties to choose from among the various eligible regimes. The various and more specific contractarian principles offered in other accounts might serve in this regard.

Does the institution of punishment pass the benefit test? There is reason to suppose that it does, and indeed, that the possibility of punishment is quite essential to a social order predicated on voluntary agreement. Members of a social contract must have some way of ensuring continued compliance with the terms of the agreement, given the temptation members will have to offer their initial consent and then free-ride on the compliance of others while silently defecting. Any voluntary agreement must therefore set out consequences for violators, along with a plausible enforcement mechanism for detecting violations and imposing the announced penalties. Thus a system of punishment will be part and parcel of the agreement that sets out substantive rules of compliance.

Let us now apply the benefit principle to the contract establishing the basic principles of punishment. Straightforwardly applied, the benefit principle requires that each member of society regard himself as faring better, under an institution that mandates punishment, than he would fare in the absence of such an institution. Thus each member of society must project himself into the position of someone who has violated the conditions of the more basic, substantive social contract, and ask himself whether, if he were to be punished for such violations, he would still fare better than he would had he never agreed to live under threat of punishment in the first place. For many sanctions the benefit test will be satisfied. A complete absence of any form of punishment for violations of the social contract would eliminate the possibility of social cooperation entirely, since an agreement would unravel without the threat of enforcement. And as Hobbes so vividly describes in Chapter XIII of *Leviathan*, life for most people would be calamitous in the absence of all society, surely worse than it would be to live with the benefits of society for most of one's life, and suffer some period of incarceration or other penalty later. Thus for most penalties, and most societies, even an offender who must suffer punitive sanctions will fare better under a punishment agreement than he would in the absence of all social enforcement.

Does this hold true for the worst violators, those who must suffer the worst penalties? Can a person who receives the death penalty or life in prison regard himself as better off under the terms of the penalty contract than he would have been had he never agreed to the contract in the first place? Certainly if Hobbes is to be believed, life in the absence of all social cooperation would be so brutal and insecure that no one could expect to live into old age. As compared with "continual fear, and danger of violent death" (Hobbes 1994: ch. XIII [9]), it is possible that a person receiving a very severe sentence like death or life in prison without parole would regard himself as benefited as compared with his life in the absence of such penalties. Whether this is so would depend on the marginal deterrent benefits of those penalties relative to more moderate penalties. It would also depend on a host of other factors, such as when in his life we conceive of the offender as receiving the penalty. A person who had had many years to reap the deterrence benefits of those penalties would be in a different position from a very young offender who had not, and who now could reap no further benefits from such rules if put to death or imprisoned for the rest of his life. It should also be noted, however, that the death penalty and life in prison without parole are likely to fare somewhat differently under the benefit test. If the death penalty has only very modest additional deterrent efficacy over life in prison without parole, it is unlikely to be incorporated into the punishment agreement,

as its detriment for the person suffering it is vastly greater than the nearest available alternative penalties.

A theory of punishment governed by the benefit principle has important advantages over both deterrence theories and retributivism. On the one hand, the contractarian approach solves the two problems associated with deterrence theories, namely the problem of torture and the problem of responsibility. With regard to torture and other severe penalties, the contractarian theory has a basis for rejecting extreme penalties, since these would normally fail the benefit test. And a contractarian theory organized around the benefit principle has no difficulty reconciling principles of responsibility with the goal of deterrence. Although deterrence is the reason for adopting an institution of punishment in the first place, no institution that inflicted punishment in the absence of conditions of responsibility would pass the benefit test. For a society that left individuals subject to "punishment" at random would be no better, and possibly worse, than a world in the absence of society. In a regime of terror, human beings are left just as defenseless as they are in their natural state, but matters are worse, since now they must protect themselves not just against lone individuals, but against an organized state. If the institution of punishment is to leave members of society better off than they would be in its absence, sanctions must be allocated predictably, fairly, and according to principles of control and individual responsibility.

On the other hand, the contractarian theory of punishment, as I have articulated it, would also have advantages over retributivism. Recall that the central problem of that account was its inability to justify particular penalties. The benefit principle gives us a way of justifying penalties with specificity, at the same time that we are able to preserve an intrinsic connection between the crime and the penalty. In particular, the specificity is provided by the aim of deterrence, in combination with the limitation the benefit principle provides. Let us see more specifically how this works.

Consider how the aim of deterrence, in combination with the benefit principle, would identify the appropriate punishment for a crime like burglary. The norms protected by a prohibition on burglary are norms of private ownership, and in the absence of any punishment for burglary (and like crimes) private ownership would be eliminated. Thus each person can ask himself: would I be better off under the terms of a contract that established penalties for burglary, assuming that I myself may end up subject to that penalty, than I would be if there were no private ownership at all? Notice that if the penalties for burglary are too low, the deterrent effect will be insignificant, and private property will not be protected. If the penalties are too high, however, agents receiving the penalty would be worse off than they would have been in the absence of private property, and the benefit principle would not be satisfied. Thus when we combine the benefit principle with the goal of deterrence, we are able to develop specific parameters for the punishment of each separate crime.

Notice furthermore that this theory also captures the greatest strength of the retributive principle in that it establishes something like a moral equivalence between crime and punishment. It does so because applying the benefit principle will require that we consider the importance of the underlying norm we are trying to protect, and compare it with the suffering the offender would experience under a given penalty. In the burglary example we implicitly compared the gravity of a violation of rights of ownership with the loss in welfare an individual would suffer who undergoes a term of imprisonment for that violation when we asked whether a rational agent would be better off suffering a given punishment for burglary than he would be abandoning protection for private property altogether. Since the importance of the underlying institution we are trying to protect establishes the gravity of the violation for which we are punishing, the benefit principle creates a metric whereby we can match offenses with appropriate penalties. But it is able to match crime and punishment without sacrificing the importance of deterrence as a guiding aim of a system of punishment. The complete rejection of deterrence as a legitimate aim of punishment is what dooms retributive theories to generality, since the notion of desert substituted in its place is ineliminably nonspecific.

One question that might arise, in view of the role the contractarian account assigns to deter-

rence, is why that account would constitute an improvement over the deterrence accounts we saw above with regard to the "traveling across persons" objection. The answer is that the consensual nature of punishment in this scheme defeats the concern with traveling across persons. Unlike in the deterrence accounts we saw above, each party to the social contract agrees that he will submit himself to punishment in the event that he would violate the conditions of the social contract. It is this self-imposed threat that he offers to his fellows as his assurance that he will not defect. And the willingness of each to subject himself to punishment should he choose to defect is the condition each party to the contract requires for his own compliance. The calculation of the required level of deterrence is a function of the threat necessary to induce compliance and to provide the assurance of compliance necessary for the agreement to be rationally entered into in the first place. The punishment itself is legitimate to inflict, not because it deters others, but because it has already been consented to by the offender himself. Thus the appeal to deterrence made by the contractarian theory of punishment does not travel across persons, since the deterrence is supposed to operate on the offender himself at the moment he enters into the original social contract. As in the alternative deterrence account we considered briefly at the end of the second section of this chapter, the punishment itself is only the follow-through on the threat made to the offender himself. But unlike in that account, there is here an independent justification for following through on the threat, namely that the offender consented to this scheme, thinking he would benefit himself thereby.

A final concern about the proposed account might be raised. Why should we care about whether the offender himself is benefited under the punishment scheme, since he has arguably chosen to place himself outside of the terms of the social contract anyway by violating social norms? Why not treat the offender as having exempted himself from society's protection, and as having entitled other members of society to discount his benefit altogether? This would be the usual approach to punishment in the contractarian tradition (see Morris 1991). That tradition treats violators of the social contract as permanently expelled from the contractual relationship that holds among members of society. The tradition thus denies that punishment is governed by the terms of the contract itself, and treats it as governed by norms that lie outside the contract. And from a certain perspective, this is quite a defensible approach. If society is a "cooperative venture for mutual advantage," it makes sense to think of criminals as having placed themselves outside the scope of all voluntary arrangements, since cooperating with *them* would not be to the advantage of members of society who are faithful to the terms of the agreement.

But I think such a view is to be rejected. For while it is true that the initial contract is made only among those who accept the conditions of cooperation, cooperators can become defectors after the basic contract has been entered into. It would be wrong to treat defection as though it were noncooperation at the outset. There are several reasons for this. First, defections can be large or small, and it may be that it is still advantageous to cooperate with those responsible for small defections. Second, it is not possible to address the problem of noncooperation at the outset in any way other than refusing to contract. But defectors are themselves subject to the terms of an antecedent agreement, and can therefore be dealt with contractually. Finally, it simply seems wrong to think of a defector as beyond the bounds of all social interaction, someone who deserves none of the protections or entitlements that those who enter into rational relations with others receive. Even the most heinous violations ought not to deprive their perpetrators of basic dignitary rights, such as the right to be free from torture, the right to speak in one's own defense, and the right to minimal bodily dignity and comfort. It is true that nonrational creatures are often thought of as possessing at least some subset of these same rights, and thus there may be a basis for affording protection to biological creatures outside the contractual context. But the protections afforded such creatures are thought to be significantly less than those afforded even the worst criminals. The higher protections afforded to rational life, even the least deserving rational life, is most plausibly explained as a product of at least a putative exchange of human wills. For these and other reasons, the conditions under which human beings may permissibly inflict sanctions for noncooperation on members of their own kind should be thought of as governed by an antecedent agreement such as humans make to enforce the terms of cooperative interaction.

It is in fact only by including potential violators in the terms of the social contract that the contractarian model can provide any practical guidance to a theory of punishment. And it is also in this way that we are able to capture within a contractarian framework the basic deontological intuitions that may have made retributivism seem initially attractive. As we have seen, these deontological intuitions are insufficient in and of themselves to produce a theory of punishment directly. It is only when combined with the aim of deterrence that they find their proper place. Normally the aim of deterrence and intuitions concerning desert cannot coexist in a theory of punishment.[12] These opposing elements complement without contradiction in the consensual approach I have proposed.[13]

Notes

1. I do not mean to suggest that every infliction of physical suffering or deprivation of liberty is worse than every order to pay compensation, but simply that as a general matter, bodily invasions are more morally suspect than financial ones.

2. For a clear statement of an expressive approach to punishment, see Feinberg (1970). For an interesting argument for a communicative approach, see Duff (2003). See also Finkelstein (2004) commenting on Duff.

3. There is some irony in this: one might suppose that if deontologists cared about rights violations, they would care about minimizing the number of rights violations in the world, and that therefore some trade-offs of the sort deterrence theorists contemplate would be permissible. But someone committed to deontological principles could not take that position without effectively abandoning the idea that there are restrictions on what human beings may do to one another in the name of utility, restrictions that cannot be traded off against other sorts of reasons. For a helpful discussion of this aspect of deontological morality, see Kamm (1993, 1996).

4. I am only assuming, for the sake of argument, that the death penalty is morally acceptable. I do not in any sense mean to be endorsing that conclusion.

5 The exception to this occurs in cases in which some special doctrine of the criminal law connects one agent with the free, voluntary acts of another. Felony murder, vicarious liability, and accomplice liability are examples.

6 There are admittedly some exceptions. It is often thought to be permissible to *redirect* a harm that threatens one group of people towards others who are fewer in number, despite the fact that the latter are not in any way the source of the threat. See Thomson (1985). It is also sometimes thought permissible to inflict a slight harm on one innocent (noninvolved) person in order to prevent a *dramatically* greater harm to another or to some vastly larger number of persons. See Moore (1997), defending what he calls "threshold deontology." But presumably neither of these exceptions would apply in this case. On the one hand, activating the electric chair would be initiating a new harm, and on the other, the hostage pressing the button would be saving his own life and the lives of only seven other hostages, which most threshold deontologists would not consider sufficient to justify killing the one.

7 This is a very rough and ready characterization. For one thing, it surely is not the case that every killing that is not a using is permissible. For another, there are possibly other principles at work here that may better capture the distinction we are seeking, such as the doctrine of double effect. It is beyond the scope of this chapter, however, to explore such alternative principles. I point to the prohibition on using simply to sketch, at the grossest level of generality, a standard contrast between utilitarian and deontological approaches.

8 David Gauthier has recently suggested such an account to me. It is also a version of Warren Quinn's approach in "The Right to Threaten and the Right to Punish" (Quinn 1985).

9 As I said at the outset, it is beyond the scope of this chapter to consider every possible theory of punishment. There is one I have thus far ignored, however, that may seem a particularly important omission in the context of our discussion of deterrence theories, namely a mixed theory of the sort that Rawls argued for in "Two Concepts of Rules" (Rawls 1955). According to a mixed theory of this sort, the rationale for having an institution of punishment in the first place is utilitarian, while the specific form the rules of such an institution take are themselves desert-based. Someone might argue that this is a form of deterrence that does not involve traveling across persons, since the reason for punishing any particular offender is that he deserves to be punished. The effect of his treatment on other, potential offenders is not particularly a reason for punishing *him*. It is simply part of the background conditions for having an institution of this sort in the first place. But it seems likely that a mixed account of this sort will still suffer from the same problems as the more generic mixed deterrence account we have considered. For the justification for the institution itself travels across persons. Whether this is objectionable would require further exploration, however. In addition, such an account will likely suffer from the difficulties with retributivist accounts, which I detail below.

10 I say "much" rather than "all" because I believe that the benefit principle is compatible with *some* risky agreements or plans. The reason is that there are conditions under which agents are benefited by losing gambles: they can sometimes receive a net benefit from the chance of benefit the gamble supplied. As long as the actual losses are not very great, and the *ex ante* chance of benefit is sufficiently large, it is possible for the *ex ante* chance of benefit to supply a net benefit, even in the face of losing gambles. See Finkelstein (2003).

11 I leave to one side here the question whether basic social institutions like punishment can be adequately justified if the only benefit they produce for a given individual is the benefit that individual received from exposure to a chance of benefit.

12 Some notable exceptions are Hart's approach in *Punishment and Responsibility* (1968), and Rawls' approach in "Two Concepts of Rules" (1955).

13 I wish to thank Michael Davis, Bill Edmundson, David Gauthier, Leo Katz, and Connie Rosati for comments on various drafts of this article or for conversations and advice on the issues it raises.

References

Davis, Michael. 1983. How to make the punishment fit the crime. *Ethics* 93: 726–52.

Duff, R. A. 2003. Penance, punishment and the limits of community. *Punishment and Society* 5: 295–312.

Feinberg, Joel. 1970. The expressive function of punishment. In Joel Feinberg, *Doing and Deserving*. Princeton, NJ: Princeton University Press, 95–118.

Finkelstein, Claire. 2003. Is risk a harm? *University of Pennsylvania Law Review* 151: 963–1001.

Finkelstein, Claire. 2004. Comments on Anthony Duff's "Penance, punishment, and the limits of community." *Punishment and Society* 6: 99–104.

Hart, H. L. A. 1968. *Punishment and Responsibility.* Oxford: Oxford University Press.

Hobbes, Thomas. 1994. *Leviathan*, ed. Edwin Curley. Indianapolis, IN: Hackett.

Kamm, Frances Myrna. 1993, 1996. *Morality, Mortality*, 2 vols. Oxford: Oxford University Press.

Locke, John. 1960. *Two Treatises of Government*, ed. Peter Laslett. Cambridge, UK: Cambridge University Press.

Moore, Michael. 1997. *Placing Blame: A General Theory of the Criminal Law*. Oxford: Oxford University Press.

Morris, Christopher W. 1991. Punishment and loss of moral standing. *Canadian Journal of Philosophy* 21(1): 53–80.

Quinn, Warren. 1985. The right to threaten and the right to punish. *Philosophy and Public Affairs* 14(4): 327–73.

Rawls, John. 1955. Two concepts of rules. *The Philosophical Review* 64: 3–32.

Rawls, John. 1971. *A Theory of Justice*. Cambridge, MA: Harvard University Press.

Thomson, Judith Jarvis. 1985. The trolley problem. *Yale Law Journal* 94: 1395–1415.

Thomson, Judith Jarvis. 1990. *The Realm of Rights*. Cambridge, MA: Harvard University Press.

Chapter 15

Responsibility

Martin P. Golding

> *Man blames fate for other accidents, but feels personally responsible when he makes a hole-in-one.*
> *(Martha Beckman)*

The philosophy of criminal law is concerned with two broad areas of inquiry. First, what harms or states of affair should the law seek to prevent or reduce by means of the criminal sanction and what acts should be designated as crimes? See CRIMINAL LAW THEORY. And second, what should be the criteria of culpability? This latter question concerns the theory of responsibility, and a main issue is the extent to which these criteria should track our ordinary moral views about responsibility and blame. That they should do so seems important for two related reasons. First, it is generally believed that law-breakers deserve to be punished. And, second, that the "moral license" of the state to inflict punishment exists only when the law-breaker is morally blameworthy, to some degree. How far a system of criminal justice can depart from these considerations without losing the community's confidence is a complex question. In any case, we shall not be concerned with the first of these reasons. See A CONTRACTARIAN APPROACH TO PUNISHMENT. The second one, however, is disputed by some legal theorists, as we shall see in the discussion of objective and strict liability.

In an important discussion of the different senses of "responsibility," H. L. A. Hart distinguishes four heads of classification: Role-Responsibility, Causal-Responsibility, Liability-Responsibility, and Capacity-Responsibility. *Liability-Responsibility*, which mostly concerns us here, is divided into moral liability-responsibility and legal liability-responsibility. Hart states that "moral liability-responsibility" refers to being "morally blameworthy, or morally obliged to make amends for the harm" (Hart 1968: 225). The differences between legal and moral responsibility, he says, "are due to substantive differences between the content of legal and moral rules and principles rather than to any variation in the meaning of responsibility..." (225–6). Yet, as Hart goes on to say, a person might be held legally liable although moral blameworthiness is absent. We should not suppose that there will be a perfect coincidence between ordinary moral views and the law, because the law has aims and methods that are not identical to the subjects of everyday moral discourse.

In this chapter we shall deal with a few typical accounts of the concept of responsibility, primarily in relation to the criminal law. In the course of the discussion some of the specific problems that they raise will be treated. The subject is so vast that there is no pretense to completeness here.

Questions About Responsibility

"I didn't mean to do it." How often do we say that in everyday life! From childhood on, we become adept at excuse-giving, in shifting blame, and in denying responsibility. Both in the law and in everyday moral discourse responsibility and excuses appear to be two sides of the same coin: an excuse is a way of relieving oneself, fully or partially, of responsibility for something. In recent years, there has been a proliferation of new excuses: drug and alcohol addiction, gambling addiction, brainwashing (undue influence); battered woman; premenstrual syndrome; post-traumatic stress disorder; genetic disorder; alien cultural beliefs; rotten social background. A man charged with a sex crime has even offered his being a sex addict as an excuse. Whether such excuses should be accepted depends on the criteria of culpability, how they are to be analyzed, and what the rationale of excuses is. Also important is the analysis of various "mental" concepts, such as voluntariness and intention, and of the language we use in characterizing various kinds of conduct, such as "knowingly," "mistakenly," and "accidentally," because of their bearing on blameworthiness.

In the legal tradition there is an old maxim: *actus non facit reum nisi mens sit rea*, which may be translated as "an act is not wrongful (guilty, obnoxious) unless the mind (the will, the intention) is wrongful (guilty, obnoxious)." As Paul Sayre writes, "*mens rea* doubtless meant little more than immorality of motive," a general notion of moral blameworthiness (cited in Robinson and Grall 1983: 685). In an article on the treatment of *mens rea* in the Model Penal Code, the late Professor Herbert Wechsler describes the field of penal law as consisting of procedural problems (jurisdiction, burden of proof, etc.), penological problems (sentencing, probation, administration), and issues of the existence and the scope of liability and the grounds of exculpation (Wechsler 1962). (The Model Penal Code was officially adopted by the American Law Institute in 1962, and published with a revised commentary in 1985. It has been highly influential in the United States.)

About these last issues Wechsler raises a number of questions: when conduct has the external attributes demanded by the definition of a crime, should further mental elements be required, and what are they? Should it suffice for exculpation that the actor was unaware of the offensive aspects of his or her conduct or believed them nonexistent because of mistake of fact or law? What bearing should age, mental disease or defect, intoxication, duress, or entrapment have? When is conduct that would otherwise be criminal be justifiable because it serves, or is believed by the actor to serve, a higher social purpose? We can deal here with only a few of these matters. An example will provide an entree into them.

The Holmesian Approach: Objective Liability

Our example is baby shaking, baby shaking that results in the serious injury or death of the infant ("shaken baby syndrome") – it occurs more often than one might think. (The courts in North Carolina deal with a number of such cases every year. See also the classic English case *R. v. Ward* 1956.) Suppose the death of the infant results. In all of these cases the actor claims that he or she "didn't mean to do it." The actor didn't even realize that death or a serious injury could result, and only meant to quiet the child. While there may be other charges that can be lodged, is there a theory of criminal liability on which the actor could be held guilty of murder? Apparently there is: the theory of "objective" or "external" criminal liability put forward by Oliver Wendell Holmes, Jr. (the future US Supreme Court Justice), in his book *The Common Law* (1923), first published in 1881. The traditional definition of "murder" is causing the death of a human being with "malice aforethought." To maliciously cause some harm is to bring it about intentionally, deliberately, on purpose. Although "malice aforethought" had come to be recognized by many as a technical legal term, Holmes is anxious to avoid any possible confusion of law and morality. "Malice" is a term from everyday morality, and Holmes wants to get rid of it in the law, or at least to give it, and some other legal terms that come from everyday moral discourse (e.g., "rights"), an interpretation that is consistent with the general purposes of the criminal law, as he sees them.

The term "malice" connotes a "vitious will," as Sir William Blackstone quaintly put it, a subjective state of the agent's mind, importing a high degree of moral blameworthiness. But on Holmes's view, in order to convict someone of murder it is not (usually) necessary that the actor "meant" to bring about a death or even that the actor contemplated or foresaw that a death or serious injury would result from his or her action. (Various conditions have to be fulfilled to secure a conviction: that the accused is not insane, not an infant, did not act in self-defense, besides some other considerations.) Holmes instead argues that it is sufficient to show that the accused's act would have been blameworthy if it had been performed by the "average member" of the community, the so-called "reasonable and prudent man." It doesn't matter what the actor foresaw; what matters is whether the result (e.g., death or serious injury) would have been foreseen by the "reasonable man." The reasonable man is the "objective standard" by which conduct is to be judged, rather than the subjective state of the agent's mind. According to Holmes, "[W]hile the terminology of morals is still retained, and while the law does still and always, in a certain sense, measure legal liability by moral standards, it nevertheless, by the very necessity of its nature, is continually transmuting those moral standards into external or objective ones, from which the actual guilt of the party concerned is wholly eliminated" (Holmes 1923: 38). It seems, then, that Holmes is rejecting the *mens rea* requirement, and it is not surprising that Holmes's theory should be called a "nonmoral" theory of criminal liability, because it ignores facts relevant to an individual's culpability (Hall 1960: 151; compare Hart 1968: 37–40).

How does Holmes arrive at this position? Aside from claiming that it is shown in the historical development of the law, he relies on basic philosophical considerations. "For the most part," he says, "the purpose of the criminal law is only to induce external conformity to rule" (Holmes 1923: 49), by threatening punishment for violations. The purpose of punishment is "preventive," that is, to deter the criminal and others from committing similar crimes. Against this deterrence theory there is the argument that it conflicts with the sense of justice, that it licenses the punishment of the innocent, that it overlooks the ill-desert of wrong-doing and treats man as a thing, not as a person (Kant is mentioned), that it denies the "dogma" of equality (as Holmes calls it). To all this Holmes replies: "No society

has ever admitted that it could not sacrifice individual welfare to its own existence. If conscripts are necessary for its army, it seizes them, and marches them, with bayonets in their rear, to death" (Holmes 1923: 43). This, then, is how Holmes justifies his doctrine of objective liability: it allows the punishment of a party who is not morally blameworthy, for the benefit of society. A similar argument is made in support of the principle that ignorance of law is no excuse. It is not because of the difficulty in proving that the accused did know the law that we have this principle, as John Austin maintains. Aside from the (presumed) fact that the excuse would encourage ignorance of the law, the "true explanation," says Holmes, is that "[p]ublic policy sacrifices the individual to the general good" (Holmes 1923: 48).

And there is a further crucial consideration in Holmes's argument. The criminal law sets up certain standards of conduct to which the individual must conform. These are "external" standards, defined in terms of patterns of behavior. Holmes assumes that since these standards are external, so also is the test of the individual's liability external, that is, behavioral. However, as Francis G. Jacobs writes: "[It] does not follow from the fact that the law is concerned with the prevention or promotion of certain external patterns of conduct, that it should not, still less that it could not, take into account the actual state of mind of the individual" (Jacobs 1971: 133). This point is especially important if we think of punishment as more than preventive or deterrent. If punishment is an expression of the blameworthiness of the offender, the actual state of mind of the offender cannot be overlooked.

Now it is of course the case that the law uses an objective standard whenever a person may be held criminally responsible for negligently causing a harm. In general, a departure from what the "reasonable man" would do in the given circumstance is what counts as negligence. "I didn't mean to do it," would not constitute an excuse in such a case. Nevertheless, objective liability fails to reflect the moral distinction between intentional and negligent wrongdoing, which may be subject to different dispositions. As Holmes himself recognizes, in everyday life it matters a great deal why people do things to us, whether, for instance, someone steps on one's toe deliberately, out of carelessness, or accidentally (see Strawson 1974). In each case, we judge the individual differently, as blameworthy in some degree or not, and these judgments may affect our future relations with that individual. Holmes apparently thinks that it is not entirely necessary that the law should track everyday moral notions. Yet, for the criminal law, it seems vital, as a matter of justice or fairness, even in the instance of negligent conduct, that the test of the individual's liability should include whether he or she had the opportunity and the capacity to conform to the established pattern of conduct.

With a little bit of pressing, Holmes's argument seems to support "strict liability," if the personal guilt of the actor is "wholly eliminated." Typical examples of strict liability offences are the selling of adulterated food and selling alcoholic beverages to a minor. It does not matter whether the grocer knew that the food was adulterated or that the bartender knew that the purchaser was a minor. In fact, the seller may have taken all possible care to determine that the food was not adulterated or that the purchaser was not a minor. The seller may be held criminally liable anyway: it is no excuse to say "I didn't know the food was adulterated" or "I didn't know the purchaser was underage." While many people find strict criminal liability in the criminal law to be generally unacceptable, they would allow it in such cases, for administrative efficiency and convenience, as long as the penalties are limited to fines, as they usually are. They might also add that in engaging in certain occupations the individual assumes the risk that his or her behavior might go awry and subject him or her to a penalty. (See the discussion of Wasserstrom 1959–60 and Ezorsky 1974, in Ten 1987: 106–10.) Still, most people find strict liability particularly objectionable when it comes to the "core" of the criminal law: homicide, assault, and theft. It is true that there is not complete agreement on these matters. Some people think that petty shoplifting or stealing from the wealthy is not a serious offense. However, as long as these matters are on the books as crimes, it seems important that "mental elements" be taken into account in assessing an offender's responsibility. (Of course, there are strict liability elements in some serious offenses, for instance, statutory rape.)

Holmes probably would allow having strict liability in the selling cases, but it is not clear how far toward strict liability his argument otherwise goes. While Holmes restricts the range of excuses, he does allow that a "mistake" might be an excuse in some contexts if it is the sort of mistake a "reasonable man" would make. This point brings us back to Herbert Wechsler's question: should it suffice for exculpation that the actor was unaware of the offensive aspects of his or her conduct or believed them nonexistent because of mistake of fact or law? What is the importance of the idea of mistake? Mistake, or something very much like it, is discussed by Aristotle.

Aristotle on Voluntary Action and Responsibility

Perhaps the most influential work on responsibility is Book III of Aristotle's *Nicomachean Ethics*. Aristotle does not sharply differentiate between legal and moral responsibility. He is concerned with the role of the *polis* in shaping the good person and the acquisition of the virtues, established dispositions. When, then, do we praise or blame a person; when do we pardon or pity? The central ideas are those of *hekousion* and *akousion* actions, usually translated as voluntary and involuntary actions, although there is no exact English equivalent of the Greek terms. In the background of his treatment is the Socratic notion that although virtue is voluntary, vice is involuntary, a notion that Aristotle disputes. Aristotle uses praise and blame, and reward and punishment, as evidence for voluntary activity. When an action is done involuntarily, it is a matter for pardon (exculpation) or pity.

Aristotle begins by asking what it is that we attribute to a person as a "begetter" of an action, or as we might say, as an agent? He immediately excludes actions (bodily movements) done under compulsion, for example, caused by an external force (a strong wind, a push) and actions that are due to ignorance. These factors negate voluntariness. Certain qualifications, however, are introduced. Sometimes one acts out of fear of a greater evil, as when one does something base because a tyrant has threatened one's parents or children with death unless the action is performed. In such cases there may be psychological pressures that a normal person cannot withstand, and Aristotle is in doubt as to whether they should be considered voluntary or involuntary. Another example is the jettison of a cargo to save the ship from sinking. While nobody voluntarily throws away property, in the circumstance it is what a sensible person would do. Such actions are "mixed." They are voluntary because the initiative in moving the body rests in the agent, though in themselves they are involuntary. In general, they are more like voluntary actions when they are worthy of choice at the moment of action. The notion of voluntary action here, then, involves a combination of descriptive and normative judgments, an idea that is endorsed by some recent writers (see Fletcher 1978: 802 ff.).

About actions due to ignorance, Aristotle makes some interesting remarks. All such actions are *nonvoluntary*, but they are *involuntary* only when they bring regret and sorrow in their train. For instance, hunter A thinks he is shooting at a deer but in fact shoots B, another hunter. A's act is involuntary if he feels regret and sorrow, otherwise it is merely nonvoluntary. We might put the matter differently: in neither case did A intentionally or knowingly shoot B. Aristotle's distinction may here reflect a judgment about the moral character of the actor. In the latter case ("I didn't mean to shoot B but I'm glad he's dead, anyway"), we can't say that A intentionally or knowingly shot B, but A is hardly a very nice fellow.

Although Aristotle does not explicitly say that all actions due to ignorance are excused, he does seem to suggest it. But what kind of ignorance is involved here? It is ignorance of the *particulars* that constitute the circumstances, or as we might say, ignorance or mistake of fact. Hunter A's ignorance or mistake about what he was shooting at negatives the voluntariness of his act. (Ignorance of a fact and mistake as to a fact are not quite the same thing. A mistake involves a mistaken judgment, while ignorance need not involve one. But they are close enough in this context.) However, there is a kind of ignorance that does not excuse:

Now every wicked man is in a state of ignorance as to what he ought to do and what he should refrain from doing, and it is due to this kind of error that men become unjust and, in general, immoral. But an act can hardly be called involuntary if the agent is ignorant of what is beneficial. Ignorance in moral choice does not make an act involuntary – it makes it wicked; nor does ignorance of the universal, for that invites reproach .... (Aristotle 1962: 1110b, 55)

By ignorance of the "universal" Aristotle means ignorance (or mistake) of the major premise of a practical syllogism, for example, "to remove by stealth another person's property is stealing." Ignorance of the minor premise, for example, "this horse is another person's property," is ignorance of a particular. Ignorance in the former respect is a moral defect; in the latter, taking the horse would not be voluntary.

Aristotle's distinction between ignorance of a particular and ignorance of the universal is parallel to the distinction implied in Wechsler's question: should it suffice for exculpation that the actor was unaware of the offensive aspects of his or her conduct or believed them nonexistent because of mistake of fact or law? Aristotle's position denies that a mistake (ignorance) of law excuses. On the other hand, Aristotle would say that a mistake (ignorance) of fact excuses (unless the agent is responsible for his or her ignorance, e.g., by getting drunk) because the agent's action is not voluntary. And, one might want to add, because of the agent's ignorance he or she had no opportunity to avoid the evil, so there was no "vicious will."

One issue discussed by later theorists is whether a mistake of fact has to be reasonable in order to excuse. According to Jerome Hall, to require that it be reasonable is to adopt objective liability, which he regards as odious. *Mens rea*, on his view, means that the criminal act was performed voluntarily, that is, according to him, it was performed intentionally or recklessly and the actor has made a choice. (Note, however, that an act can be performed intentionally without being voluntary, i.e., when done under duress.) With a few apparent exceptions (e.g., the defendant intended to kill A but killed B instead), he holds that "mistake of fact is a defense if, because of the mistake, mens rea is lacking" (Hall 1960: 365).

The basic issue here is culpability or blameworthiness. Therefore, on the other side, we find the position that if the defendant committed the *actus reus* (the material elements) of the offense, the defendant may be blamed if he or she deserves blame, is at fault, for making the mistake, which is already suggested in Aristotle. (For a detailed discussion of the varieties of mistake, see Fletcher 1978: ch. 9.)

The Model Penal Code and Voluntariness

The theoretical importance of the voluntary act requirement is brought out by the Model Penal Code. According to the Code, "[a] person is not guilty of an offense unless his liability is based upon conduct which *includes* a voluntary act or the omission to perform an act which it was physically possible to perform," that is, unless for an omission, a voluntary act is a necessary but not a sufficient condition for liability (American Law Institute 1985: 2, 2.01, emphasis added). The reason for these requirements is explained as follows:

> That penal sanctions cannot be employed with justice unless these requirements are satisfied seems wholly clear. The law cannot hope to deter involuntary movement or to stimulate action that cannot physically be performed; the sense of personal security would be short-lived in a society where such movement or inactivity could lead to formal condemnation of the sort that a conviction entails. People whose involuntary movements threaten harm to others may present a public health or safety problem, calling for therapy or even custodial commitment; they do not present a problem of correction. (American Law Institute 1985: comment to section 2.01)

It will be noticed that the Code has contrasted voluntary and involuntary acts. But what is a voluntary act? In the philosophical literature a number of possibilities are found: that the act would have been different had the agent willed or chosen otherwise (hypothetical analysis), that

voluntariness is a positive mental state (an act of will), that this state is indefinable, that a voluntary act is defined in terms of conditions that would defeat an act's being voluntary (the "negative" analysis). The Code's position is not entirely clear. It goes on to list acts that are *not* voluntary: a reflex or convulsion; a bodily movement during unconsciousness; conduct during hypnosis; a bodily movement that otherwise is not a product of the effort or determination of the actor, either conscious or habitual. This last item seems to be just a catchall, rather than a reference to a positive mental state. On the Code's approach voluntariness is a "negative" concept. (Other conditions usually treated as not voluntary are dealt with under different rubrics; for instance, duress is treated under the heading of extreme mental or emotional disturbance.)

Of course, voluntariness is just a minimal requirement of responsibility. The Code drops the old idea of a generalized *mens rea*, and in a sense substitutes for it *mentes reae*. Aside from a narrow allowance for offenses of strict liability, the Code insists that an element of culpability is requisite for any valid criminal conviction and that the four concepts of purpose, knowledge, recklessness, and negligence suffice to delineate the kinds of culpability that may be called for in the definition of specific crimes (American Law Institute 1985: explanatory note to section 2.02, 227). The four concepts in effect constitute the *mens rea* requirements, and a well-formulated substantive penal law will indicate which type of culpability has to be proved for each material element of the offense, for conviction.

Now it is quite clear that when a particular offense requires that the prosecution prove, beyond a reasonable doubt, that it was committed purposely or knowingly, a (relevant) mistake of fact will negate these elements and will excuse. So the prosecution will have failed to prove that the offense was committed. A mistake-of-fact defense, then, is what some recent writers have called a "failure-of-proof" defense, and not a genuine excuse, such as insanity and duress are (see Dressler 1988). While technically correct, this approach obscures the moral issue of what criterion of culpability should be attached to an offense and why a mistake of fact excuses. (This is not to say that theorists who take this approach ignore the question of the rationale of excuses.)

Responsibility as a Defeasible Concept: H. L. A. Hart

It was earlier noted that responsibility and excuses appear to be two sides of the same coin: an excuse is a way of relieving oneself, fully or partially, of responsibility for something. Does this mean that a positive account of responsibility cannot be given, that to say that someone is responsible for some harm is merely to say that the agent has no excuse, that responsibility is a "negative" concept in this respect?

Something like this view is found in an influential article by H. L. A. Hart, "The Ascription of Responsibility and Rights" (Hart 1949). His main terms are "ascription" and "defeasibility." According to Hart, the principal function of such past-tense statements as "He did it" is not descriptive but rather to *ascribe* responsibility for actions, just as "This is his" ascribes (a right of) property to someone. Clearly, the latter sort of statement does not describe anything; no quality or set of observable facts is perceived. Property is not a straightforwardly descriptive concept. It cannot be explained without reference to nondescriptive utterances, the laws or social rules by which rights are recognized.

Legal concepts have another feature. It looks as if the law contains a group of concepts (e.g., contract, trespass) and a judge must decide whether certain facts come within the scope of a formula defining when a given concept applies. However, says Hart, legal concepts are not definable in terms of a set of necessary and sufficient conditions, such that when the conditions are fulfilled the concepts apply. Hart uses the concept of "contract" to illustrate his point. No full account of the concept can be given without appending to it the word "unless." The "unless" is the beginning of a list of exceptions or negative examples, impossible to specify completely in advance, showing where the concept may not be applied or, in other words, when the application is defeated. Thus, contract is a *defeasible* concept.

Similar considerations obtain with respect to the concept of a human "action." Hart rejects the traditional and modern analyses: respectively, that an action is a willed muscular movement or a movement plus a hypothetical statement (that the act would have been different had the agent willed or chosen otherwise). Statements such as "He did it" ("He hit her") cannot be distinguished from "His body moved in violent contact with another's" *without* reference to nondescriptive utterances, the laws or social rules by which liability or responsibility is ascribed. Past-tense action statements are both ascriptive and defeasible (apparently) because ascriptions of responsibility are defeasible. There is an indefinite list of circumstances that may defeat such ascriptions. Hart maintains that the heterogeneous defenses available for defeating ascriptions of responsibility cannot be defined in terms of necessary and sufficient conditions. Moreover, the concepts involved in *mens rea* are defeasible. The purported positive mental elements (intention, foresight, voluntariness) must be treated as summaries of defenses or exceptions that defeat their attribution to the agent. (One reason some philosophers find this type of approach attractive is that it avoids metaphysical issues about the nature of mental states.)

It seems, then, that in this 1949 article Hart has something like a "negative" view of responsibility ("legal liability-responsibility," Hart 1968: 215), though he frames it in terms of defeasibility. A person is responsible for some harm, unless the attribution can be defeated by a defense or excuse. This approach makes general sense. We assume that almost all members of the community are responsible persons and that the individual citizen can be held responsible for what he or she does unless some kind of "out," a defense or exception, exists. What is questionable, however, is Hart's apparent view, here at least, that the mental elements relevant to blameworthiness are summaries of defenses or exceptions that defeat their attribution to the agent. (It should be mentioned that Hart later disowned the "Ascription" article, and in subsequent pieces he does present rich analyses of the various mental elements. See the articles in Hart 1968.) The fact, for instance, that an agent has intentionally rather than accidentally harmed someone ordinarily reflects on the agent's blameworthiness. (It may seem that Aristotle has a purely "negative" account of voluntary action, but this is not correct. For there is a form of voluntary action that involves forechoice (*prohairesis*), action chosen after deliberation as a means to an end (Aristotle 1962: 1111b5–13a14, 58–63).

Individual Responsibility: Antony Duff

The above mentioned assumption of responsibility has been attacked by Professor Alan Norrie on the grounds that it is "individualistic" (Norrie 1998, 2000). It rests on the idea that responsibility is always attached to individuals, in which the human agent is (falsely) conceptualized in isolation from the psychosocial connections that determine the person. We shall come back to Norrie's position after we consider some aspects of the views of Professor R. A. Duff. His work is important because of its rather full account of responsible agency and its stress on the idea of intention in relation to responsibility. Both authors support their points with numerous references to the reported cases. It will not be possible, though, to give a detailed, nuanced account of either writer.

Antony Duff maintains that the idea of responsible agency is a moral concept that should underlie criminal liability. According to Duff, intention is the "central species" of *mens rea* (Duff 1990: 99). This is not to say that only intentional criminal harms are subject to possible punishment. Rather, the centrality of intention derives from its centrality in ascribing moral responsibility for something. Responsible agency requires reference to the concept of intention, which he analyzes in elaborate detail. There is no unitary concept of intention, however; rather, it has two species: intending a result (acting in order to bring about that result) and bringing it about intentionally (where the result is an expected or foreseen side effect of one's action). I might play my trumpet at 3:00 a.m. in order to disturb my neighbor's sleep (intended result) or I might play it for personal enjoyment but with the expected

effect of keeping him awake (intentionally brought about result). UK writers follow Jeremy Bentham in designating the latter as "oblique intention." (These writers might have alleviated some confusion had they spoken of "knowingly" bringing about a foreseen but unintended harm, instead of obliquely intending it or intentionally bringing it about. Knowingly producing a harm can be as morally or legally objectionable as intending the result.) Duff discusses whether this latter species should be required for various criminal offenses. While the first species seems more fundamental, both "intended and intentional actions are paradigms of responsible agency" (Duff 1990: 100). "Now I am, of course, blamed for harm which I cause recklessly or negligently: but I am most culpable, because most fully responsible as an agent, for harm which I bring about with intent or intentionally" (Duff 1990: 102).

"Ascriptions of intentional agency," says Duff, "are, as a matter of meaning, ascriptions of responsibility..." (Duff 1990: 77). "Intentional agency" here covers both the narrower and the wider meanings of "intention." Still, one is not properly *held* responsible for *all* of the expected side effects of one's actions. "We are held responsible for effects for which we are liable to be *blamed*," and "[to] hold someone responsible for an effect, to portray it as the result of her intentional action, is to hold her *answerable* for it ... To ascribe responsibility is not yet to blame the agent ... " (Duff 1990: 78, emphasis in original). It is rather to say that the individual is called upon to explain or justify his or her action.

Norrie finds a problem in this account. Duff, he says, "appears to describe a preliminary situation prior to that of ascribing blame, in which the issue of blameworthiness is yet to be settled" (Norrie 1998: 125). Responsibility-as-answerability does not settle the issue of responsibility-as-blameworthiness, Norrie argues, and as a result raises other difficulties for Duff. Perhaps there is a tangle here. Responsibility, answerability, and blame do appear to be variously interrelated. "To respond" and "to answer" are sometimes interchangeable, and "to blame" is sometimes used descriptively, and so is "responsible for" ("The dry weather is to blame for – responsible for – the forest fire"). Still, Duff may be correct in holding that a justification of one's action is not a denial of responsible agency, though it does relieve one of legal or moral guilt.

Duff, as we have seen, distinguishes between the concept of intending a result and the concept of bringing it about intentionally, and he points out some complications in the latter. He gives the example of an examiner who fails a student's thesis, because he thought it bad, thereby ruining her career, a foreseen side effect. Ruining her career was not part of the examiner's reasons for his action, so this result was not an intended result. But was it brought about intentionally? The answer does not depend on what the examiner thinks but on what *we* think, and on this, disagreement is possible. "You and I disagree," says Duff, "about whether I intentionally ruin the student... because we have different normative views about the scope of an examiner's responsibilities [should an examiner have to take into account the side effects in grading the thesis?]; and we may be unable to resolve the disagreement" (Duff 1990: 84). (Note that the plural of "responsibility" is here being used somewhat in the sense of "duty." See Hart 1968: 212–14, on "Role-Responsibility.") Whether someone intentionally caused a harm is not a purely descriptive matter; it is in part a normative issue. There is, however, less scope for normative disagreement within the law, according to Duff.

In ascribing intentional agency to others we normally presuppose that they are rational agents. This is why, in the law, duress, necessity, and insanity may operate as excuses, insofar as the agent's rational competence is impaired.

> In holding someone responsible for his actions, we suppose that he is in some relevant sense a "free" agent; that he has, in traditional terminology, "free will." Now the meaning of "free will," as a precondition of responsibility, is a matter of long controversy. I think it can best be explained, however, in terms of the concept of rational agency: an agent is "free" in so far as his actions are guided by his understanding of good reasons for action. (Duff 1990: 102)

But should the law distinguish intended from intentional agency? Is the latter concept sufficient for legal purposes?

The answer to these questions, according to Duff, depends on what view is adopted on responsible agency. He discusses two such views: *consequentialist* and *nonconsequentialist* (Duff 1990: 105–15). The discussion is intricate and we shall have to pass over many details.

In moral philosophy consequentialism is the position that the rightness or wrongness of actions depends solely on the overall goodness or badness of their consequences. As applied to a legal system, the general approach is that the purpose of the criminal law is the prevention or reduction of incidents of harm. While there is some disagreement about the meaning of "harm," harms (e.g., death) can be identified as such without reference to human actions as their causes (see Feinberg 1984). Because a purely consequentialist approach leads to imposing punishment on some who do not deserve it (see Holmes, above), many consequentialists adopt a qualified consequentialism. There are side constraints on the imposition of punishment, which require that the offender should have had a fair opportunity to obey the law. "This," says Duff, "makes *knowledge* and *control* the two basic conditions of criminal liability: I have a fair opportunity to obey the law against homicide only if I know (or could easily realize) that my conduct will or might cause death, and only if I control that conduct – only if I could avoid acting thus" (Duff 1990: 107–8, emphasis in original). This consideration makes negligence a minimum condition of liability.

Duff proceeds to generate a hierarchy of degrees of criminal fault, going from intention (the most serious) to negligence (the least serious), with recklessness somewhere in between. While there are degrees of culpable fault, on the qualified consequentialist view it is the *intentional*, not the intended, causation of harm that is the paradigm of criminal fault. "[O]ne who acts intentionally as to some prohibited harm is," on this view, "just as culpably responsible as one who acts with the intention of causing that harm..." (Duff 1990: 110). As he additionally points out, consequentialists often claim in moral contexts that there is no difference between intention and foresight (of consequences). That claim, he says, applies equally to the law.

The nonconsequentialist view of responsible agency, which is initially expounded more briefly, finds an "intrinsic moral significance" in intended actions (Duff 1990: 111). It begins by asking whether certain kinds of harms (primary harms) can be identified in a way that makes no essential reference to a human action as its cause. Duff takes the example of rape. In a rape the victim suffers a serious *attack* on her sexual integrity and autonomy, whatever else she suffers. Similarly, murder is not just the consequential harm of death, but a willful *killing*, which the law seeks to prevent. On the nonconsequentialist view, then, the action is an attack on another person's rights or interests. Intending harm is fraught with moral significance:

> It is through the intentions with which I act that I engage the world as an agent, and relate myself most closely to the actual and potential effects of my actions; and the central or fundamental kind of wrongdoing is to *direct* my actions towards evil – to *intend* and to *try* to do what is evil. Intentional agency is parasitic on intended agency.... (Duff 1990: 113, emphasis in original)

With respect to many crimes, as Duff points out, it will not make any difference which view is adopted. For these crimes, *mens rea* is satisfied whether the agent acts with intention or intentionally. The distinction between them marks different kinds of culpability, but not necessarily different degrees of culpability. Although, as far as one can tell, Duff does not choose between the two views, he leans toward nonconsequentialism. But he is interested in how both play out. He discusses a number of crimes and how the two paradigms might be extended to deal with them. We cannot go into these matters of detail here.

The main conclusion for us is that in Duff we have an account of responsible agency that is highly "individualistic." Individual responsibility is the reference point of his theory of criminal law. In a later article, which deals with punishment, Duff's approach is more "communitarian," though individual responsibility is not abandoned (Duff 1996). There, Duff seeks to go beyond a retributivism that would give to the offender what he or she deserves. Instead, punishment should be communicative: the community needs to explain to the offender the nature of his or her wrongdoing and, through punishment, contribute to the offender's moral improvement and rehabilitation. All this is possible only under certain political and social conditions, and Duff is in doubt that they are currently realized.

Individual Responsibility: Norrie's Critique of Duff

Alan Norrie examines a variety of criminal law theorists (George Fletcher, Michael Moore, and others), but we shall narrowly focus on a few aspects of his criticisms of Duff. Norrie describes himself as sympathetic to "postmodern" approaches to criminal justice theory. But in contrast to other postmodernists he wants "to hold on to the sense of the 'first order' importance of legal subjectivity as reflecting human agency at the same time as...recognize its exclusionary role in safeguarding a particular social order" (Norrie 2000: ix). The target of his criticism is the *morality of form*, which he traces to Immanuel Kant, and which, he maintains is based on "formal, universal attributes of human agency, such as whether one had psychological control over one's actions. Such an approach systematically marginalizes questions about the moral substance of one's acts" (Norrie 2000: 8). It also separates the individual from the social relations of which he or she is a part. Such an individual is an abstraction. "Individualist juridical ideology," Norrie moreover says, "represented the social world as consensual, whereas in reality it was racked by social and political conflict" (Norrie 2000: 46, quoting Norrie 1993: 221).

The idea of a morality of form underlies the distinction between responsibility and the criteria of culpability (the general part of the criminal law), on the one hand, and the material content (offenses) of the criminal law, on the other (the special part). The function of this distinction in the ideology of the law, Norrie maintains, is to separate, even to isolate, questions of responsibility from the social context of crime and from substantive moral values. This is a false separation, but one which is also necessary to the maintenance of law as a social and historical practice. (See Norrie 2000: 80–1, 134.)

Norrie characterizes Duff as a "legal revisionist" (Norrie 2000: 132) who goes beyond a purely cognitive account of responsibility: culpability is infused with moral substance, as the nonconsequentialist view shows. This means, for Norrie, that the law cannot escape dealing with normative questions. Still, he thinks, Duff lapses into the morality of form in defending some legal doctrines. Consider "oblique intention." Duff allows that whether someone intentionally caused a harm is in part a normative issue about which disagreement is possible. There is, however, less scope for normative disagreement within the law, according to Duff. ("[The] law provides authoritative criteria which determine our legal responsibilities, the legal relevance of expected side-effects, and thus the scope (in law) of our intentional agency" (Duff 1990: 84).) What the law does, then, says Norrie, is to foreclose the issue of normative disagreement by imposing its unilateral declaration of "authoritative criteria."

Norrie takes up Duff's treatment of the famous Steane case (*R. v. Steane* 1947). Steane, an English citizen, was stranded with his family in Germany by the war. He broadcasted for the Germans under threat of death to his wife and children. He was acquitted of the charge of intending to assist the enemy in time of war. Did he *intend* to assist the enemy? Apparently yes, according to Duff. As he writes:

> If we deny that he intended to assist the enemy, because he intended to save his family, we must likewise deny that one who broadcasts for the enemy in order to earn money intends to assist the enemy; but it would be outrageous to acquit such a person of "doing acts likely to assist the enemy, with intent to assist the enemy." Mr. Steane's defense should have been duress, not lack of intent; . . . .(Duff 1990: 93)

To all this, Norrie raises a pointed objection, for there is a world of moral difference between Steane and a mercenary, a difference that should be reflected in Duff's consideration as to whether Steane acted *intentionally*. "In foreclosing the moral question of intentionality in Steane," says Norrie, "and sidelining it to the excuse of duress,

Duff does precisely what the law does to avoid contestable moral issues around its paradigm categories of intention and intentionality" (Norrie 2000: 137). In other terms, Duff has lapsed back into the neutral, "morality of form" approach. Once we see that normative questions are relevant to holding someone responsible, a more thoroughgoing critique of the criminal law becomes possible.

Norrie claims that the criminal law is beset by various contradictions or antinomies partly as a result of its purporting to require some kind of individual fault as a basis for blameworthiness, on the one hand, and the use of the criminal law as a means of social control and preservation of the existing social order, on the other (Norrie 1993, 1998). Such contradictions are especially shown in the law's treatment of "motive." To all this, Duff has an extensive response, to which the reader is referred (Duff 1998).

In his book, *Punishment, Responsibility, and Justice* (Norrie 2000), Norrie presents a so-called *relational* theory of responsibility, which is based on the rejection of the abstract, nonsocial individual of Kantian morality. Here he uses the philosophical concepts of person and self in the work of Roy Bhaskar and Rom Harré, into the particulars of which we cannot go. The upshot of his discussion is that blame is *shared* between the individual and the society. What kinds of reforms in the criminal law are implied by this conception is not entirely clear.

The Abandonment of Responsibility: Wootton

Why have excuses at all? Why not have a system of criminal law in which all (or nearly all) offenses are strict liability offenses, for which excuses are not accepted? Responsibility and excuses, as stated, appear to be two sides of the same coin: in asserting that someone is responsible for an offense we ordinarily imply that the malefactor has no excuse for it; and in proffering an excuse the individual is denying full responsibility for it. These questions are treated by H. L. A. Hart, who offers a general rationale of excuses (Hart

1968: 28–53). On the other side stands Lady Barbara Wootton, who would abolish excuses and allow responsibility to "wither away," as has been said (Wootton 1963). She is in the tradition of "social defense" theories, which aim at the prevention of socially unwanted events but which, however, do not emphasize the general deterrent effects of punishment. In fact, such theories would abolish punishment and instead focus on the treatment of individual offenders by psychosocial methods and by commitment when these fail. We shall begin with Wootton.

A good place to start is with her reaction to relaxations of the *M'Naghten Rules* laid down by an English court in 1843. According to *M'Naghten*:

> [T]o establish a defense on the grounds of insanity, it must be clearly proved that, at the time of the committing of the act, the party accused was labouring under such a defect of reason, from disease of the mind, as to not know the nature and quality of the act he was doing; or if he did know it, that he did not know he was doing what is wrong.

These Rules have been criticized on the grounds that they are too "cognitivist," relying as they do on what the accused knew or didn't know, while ignoring the volitional side of conduct. Various modifications therefore have been introduced. Thus, according to the Model Penal Code, "A person is not responsible for criminal conduct if at the time of such conduct as a result of mental disease or defect he lacks substantial capacity either to appreciate the criminality of his conduct or to conform his conduct to the requirements of law" (American Law Institute 1985: 2, 4.01). In addition, some jurisdictions have adopted the defenses of diminished responsibility and irresistible impulse. (These defenses are critically discussed in Wootton 1959.) Now, according to Wootton, traditional notions of punishment and blameworthiness presuppose the distinction between normal, responsible offenders and abnormal, nonresponsible offenders. However, once such modifications to M'Naghten are made, there is no resting place short of abandonment of responsibility. She in fact claims that "the crux of the whole matter lies in the inherent impossibility of

making valid decisions about other people's responsibility, in the sense of their capacity to act otherwise than as they have in fact acted; in the inherent impossibility of maintaining a reliable distinction between the wicked and the weak-minded" (Wootton 1960: 224).

As Wootton points out, the issue involved in these decisions and distinctions is not the debate between free will and determinism. It has to do rather with "the objectives of the criminal process, with the question whether the aim of that process is punitive or preventive, whether what matters is to punish the wrongdoer or to set him on the road to virtue ..." (Wootton 1963: 78). She thus contrasts punishment and "treatability." And it seems to be Wootton's view that the aim of the criminal process is *either* the backward-looking one of retribution for moral derelictions *or* the forward-looking one of prevention of antisocial behavior. She opts for the second alternative, which has certain consequences: the ascription of responsibility should be abandoned in favor of the idea of occasions for social interventions; the concept of guilt should no longer be necessary, and the purpose of the criminal trial solely should be to determine whether the accused was the author of the offense; the insanity defense should be abolished; the function of the criminal law should be to modify personality, and through that to modify behavior; sentencing should be indeterminate and the offender should be kept in a "house of safety" or under supervision until he or she is judged by psychiatrists or social workers ready (cured) to be returned to society. (See Packer 1968: 9–34, on the "dilemma of punishment.")

Much has been written in criticism of Wootton's approach (see Jacobs 1971 and Ten 1987, for extensive discussions). Some readers are likely to think that she has presented us with the "brave new world." For our purposes, however, it is a final apparent consequence of her position that is important: under her approach liability would be strict, and the usual mental conditions that are elements of offenses would be jettisoned. For either we have retribution for moral derelictions and, hence, allow for excuses, or strict liability, without the necessity of finding some kind of fault. After all, why exonerate or excuse an offender whose antisocial behavior may be a symptom of a treatable personality or behavioral defect? (One difficulty with Wootton's position is that the mental conditions of culpability do not disappear: they arise at the sentencing or disposition phase, if not at the guilt phase.)

The General Rationale of Excuses: H. L. A. Hart

While H. L. A. Hart is somewhat sympathetic to Wootton, he argues for the retention of excuses. More generally, he maintains that "the principle of responsibility, which may be sacrificed when the cost of retaining it is too high, has a value and importance quite independent of retributive and denunciatory theories of punishment which we may very well discard" (Hart 1968: 185). Hart rejects the idea that excuses make sense only if punishment is retribution for moral derelictions, and he offers a general rationale of excuses on other grounds. His position has been extremely influential.

The background of Hart's approach is the problem of the justification of punishment (see "Prolegomenon to the Principles of Punishment" in Hart 1968: 1–27). The issue of justification involves a few different questions, two of which are important here. The first question is: why have punishment at all? What is its "general justifying aim"? Basically, this asks: why have criminal law at all? Hart's own answer is in line with utilitarianism: certain unwanted acts are designated as punishable offenses in order to reduce their incidence, to deter people from committing them. The second question concerns the "distribution" of punishment: who is it who should be punished? Or to put it otherwise, who is it *fair* to punish? In broad terms, Hart's answer is, those offenders who have the capacity and fair opportunity to conform to the requirements of the law. This principle *qualifies* the deterrent aim of the criminal law, and it opens up the possibility of excusing conditions even though it might result in "deterrent losses."

Hart criticizes the "economy of threats" explanation of excuses proffered by Jeremy Bentham, a utilitarian theorist (Hart 1968: 40–3).

According to Bentham, punishment should not be threatened unless it is necessary in order to maintain the effectiveness and efficiency of the system. There are two cases in which the threat will not deter the individual from performing a kind of action: first, when the individual is mentally incompetent because of infancy or insanity; and second, where the individual lacks knowledge or control of the circumstances. On Bentham's view, says Hart, we inquire into the mental state of the offender to determine whether he or she belongs to a *class* of persons, such that if they are exempted from punishment, the general threat of punishment for others will not be weakened – excusing the offender will not harm society. Hart, however, finds an error in this approach. For the fact that the threat is useless against a given class (e.g., the insane) does not imply that it is not necessary for maintaining compliance from others. Punishing the insane may show how seriously the law is meant to be taken. Hart concludes

> that if we were to base our views of criminal responsibility on the doctrine of the economy of threats, we should misrepresent altogether the character of our moral preference for a legal system that requires mental conditions of responsibility over a system of total strict liability, or entirely different methods of social control such as hypnosis, propaganda, or conditioning. (Hart 1968: 43–4)

That moral preference is based on fairness to the offender.

But Hart also goes beyond fairness to the offender, and he shows the value of having a system of excuses (see the "principle of responsibility" above, and "Legal Responsibility and Excuses" in Hart 1968: 28–53). He rejects, however, the view that excuses make sense only for a retributivist theory of punishment that requires the culpable doing of a morally wrong act. An analogy is drawn between excusing conditions in the criminal law and invalidating conditions in civil transactions. In the law of contracts such mental factors as mistake, deception, and undue influence may invalidate or make voidable a contract. The mechanisms of law enable the individual to bring into operation coercive forces so that his or her chosen legal arrangements are carried into effect. Something of value to individuals could be lost if these invalidating conditions did not exist. For when the invalidating conditions are present the transactions do not represent one's "real choice." We should think of the law, Hart suggests, as a *choosing* system, in which individuals can find out, in general terms, the costs they have to pay if they act in certain ways.

Similarly, for the criminal law. In the criminal law, assuming it does diminish the frequency of antisocial behavior, allowing excuses (i.e., no total strict liability) has important consequences: (1) it maximizes the individual's power to predict the likelihood that sanctions will be applied to him or her; (2) it introduces the individual's choice as a factor in determining whether or not such sanctions will be applied to him or her; and (3) paying the penalty will, for each individual, represent the price of some satisfaction obtained from breach of the law. In this way, says Hart,

> the criminal law respects the claims of the individual as such, or at least as a *choosing being*, and distributes its coercive sanctions in a way that reflects this respect for the individual. This surely is very central in the notion of justice and is *one*, though no doubt only one, among the many strands of principle that I think lie at the root of the preference for legal institutions conditioning liability by reference to excusing conditions. (Hart 1968: 49, emphasis in original)

More than its value to the individual in protecting him or her from the claims of society, we see that Hart's rationale of excuses has its moral basis in justice to the individual.

We have called Hart's approach to excuses a "general rationale." This is because it leaves us with some unfinished business. Central to his account of responsibility are the concepts of capacity and fair opportunity. The latter concept is related to knowledge of circumstances and foresight of consequences, without which the actor presumably does not have a fair opportunity to adhere to the law. But what specific excuses does it thereby justify or require? For instance, does it justify or require an ignorance of law excuse? Or is this an excuse "which may be sacrificed when the cost of retaining it is too high..." (Hart 1968:

185). And what about all the "new excuses" mentioned near the beginning of this chapter? How would the argument on these matters proceed? A specific answer is not supplied. Nevertheless, the significance of Hart's general rationale of excuses cannot be gainsaid.

Conclusion

In this chapter we have examined some of the main issues involved in criminal responsibility and have looked at some of the approaches to it. A general thread running through the discussion is the relation between moral and legal responsibility as seen by different theorists. Implicated in the question of responsibility are problems of philosophical psychology which have occasionally been remarked on. Plainly, there are various empirical questions relevant to our topic. But these have not been treated here.

References

American Law Institute. 1985. *Model Penal Code*. Philadelphia, PA: American Law Institute.

Aristotle. 1962. *Nicomachean Ethics*, trans. M. Ostwald. Indianapolis, IN: Bobbs-Merrill.

Dressler, Joshua. 1988. Reflections on excusing wrongdoers: Moral theory, new excuses and the Model Penal Code. *Rutgers Law Journal* 19: 671–716.

Duff, R. A. 1990. *Intention, Agency and Criminal Liability*. Oxford: Blackwell.

Duff, R. A. 1996. Penal communications. In M. Tonry (ed.), *Crime and Justice: A Review of Research*. Chicago: University of Chicago Press, 1–97.

Duff, R. A. 1998. Principle and contradiction in the criminal law: Motives and criminal liability. In R. A. Duff (ed.), *Philosophy and the Criminal Law*. Cambridge, UK: Cambridge University Press, 156–204.

Ezorsky, Gertrude. 1974. Punishment and excuses. In M. Goldinger (ed.), *Punishment and Human Rights*. Cambridge, UK: Cambridge University Press, 99–115.

Feinberg, Joel. 1984. *Harm to Others*. New York: Oxford University Press.

Fletcher, George. 1978. *Rethinking Criminal Law*. Boston, MA: Little Brown.

Hall, Jerome. 1960. *General Principles of Criminal Law*, 2nd edn. Indianapolis, IN: Bobbs-Merrill.

Hart, H. L. A. 1949. The ascription of responsibility and rights. *Proceedings of the Aristotelian Society* 49: 171–94.

Hart, H. L. A. 1968. *Punishment and Responsibility.* Oxford: Clarendon Press.

Holmes, Oliver Wendell, Jr. 1923. *The Common Law.* Boston: Little, Brown.

Jacobs, Francis G. 1971. *Criminal Responsibility.* London: Weidenfeld and Nicolson.

Norrie, Alan. 1993. *Crime, Reason and History.* London: Butterworths.

Norrie, Alan. 1998. "Simulacra of morality"? Beyond the ideal/actual antinomies of criminal justice. In R. A. Duff (ed.), *Philosophy and the Criminal Law.* Cambridge, UK: Cambridge University Press, 101–55.

Norrie, Alan. 2000. *Punishment, Responsibility, and Justice.* Oxford: Oxford University Press.

Packer, Herbert L. 1968. *The Limits of the Criminal Sanction.* Stanford, CA: Stanford University Press.

R. v. Steane. 1947. KB 997.

R. v. Ward. 1956. 1 QB 351.

Robinson, Paul H. and Grall, Jane A. 1983. Element analysis in defining criminal liability: The Model Penal Code and beyond. *Stanford Law Review* 35: 681–762.

Strawson, P. F. 1974. *Freedom and Resentment.* London: Methuen.

Ten, C. L. 1987. *Crime, Guilt, and Punishment.* Oxford: Clarendon Press.

Wasserstrom, Richard. 1959–60. Strict liability in the criminal law. *Stanford Law Review* 12: 731–45.

Wechsler, Herbert. 1962. On culpability and crime: The treatment of mens rea in the Model Penal Code. *Annals of the American Academy of Political and Social Science* 339: 24–41.

Wootton, Barbara. 1959. *Social Science and Social Pathology.* New York: Macmillan.

Wootton, Barbara. 1960. Diminished responsibility: A layman's view. *Law Quarterly Review* 76: 224–39.

Wootton, Barbara. 1963. *Crime and the Criminal Law.* London: Stevens.

Further Reading

Austin, J. L. 1956–7. A plea for excuses. *Proceedings of the Aristotelian Society* 57: 1–30.

Boldman, Craig and Mathews, Pete. 1998. *Every Excuse in the Book.* Kansas City: Andrews McMeel.

Corrado, M. L. (ed.). 1994. *Justification and Excuse in the Criminal Law.* New York and London: Garland.

Feinberg, Joel. 1970. *Doing and Deserving.* Princeton, NJ: Princeton University Press.

Fitzgerald, P. J. 1962. *Criminal Law and Punishment.* Oxford: Oxford University Press.

Fletcher, George P. 1994. The individualization of excusing conditions. In M. L. Corrado (ed.), *Justification and Excuse in the Criminal Law.* New York: Garland, 53–94.

Hruschka, Joachim. 1986. Imputation. *Brigham Young University Law Review* 1986: 669–710.

May, Larry and Hoffman, Stacey (eds.). 1991. *Collective Responsibility.* Savage, MD: Rowman and Littlefield.

Moore, Michael S. 1993. *Act and Crime.* New York: Oxford University Press.

Moore, Michael S. 1997. *Placing Blame.* New York: Oxford University Press.

Morris, Herbert (ed.). 1961. *Freedom and Responsibility.* Stanford, CA: Stanford University Press.

Naffine, N., Owens, R., and Williams, J. (eds.). 2001. *Intention in Law and Philosophy.* Aldershot, UK: Ashgate.

Robinson, Paul H. 1984. *Criminal Law Defenses*, 2 vols. St Paul, MN: West.

Sher, George. 1987. *Desert.* Princeton, NJ: Princeton University Press.

Williams, Glanville. 1961. *Criminal Law: The General Part*, 2nd edn. London: Stevens.

Chapter 16

Legislation

Jeremy J. Waldron

Images of Legislation

Legislation is a practice whereby laws are made (or changed or repealed) deliberately by formal processes dedicated explicitly to that task. The first thing to consider in this definition is the idea of processes "dedicated explicitly" to law-making.

We know that legislation is not the only way law changes. Law is also changed by the decisions of common law judges. But though the lawmaking role of the courts is well known to legal professionals, judicial decision making does not present itself in public as a process for changing the law. Quite the contrary: any widespread impression that judges were acting as lawmakers, rather than law-appliers, would detract from the legitimacy of their decisions in the eyes of the public. And this popular perception is not groundless. Courts are not set up in a way that is calculated to make lawmaking legitimate. See ADJUDICATION AND LEGAL REASONING. Legislatures, on the other hand, exist explicitly for the purpose of lawmaking. Sure, they also have other functions, like approving appointments, deciding about taxation, and debating government policy. But lawmaking is their official *raison d'être*, and when we evaluate the structure and processes of legislatures and the basis on which their membership is determined, we do so with that function in mind.

Not only do they claim legitimacy as sources of new law, but most legislatures do so on democratic grounds. Unlike courts, modern legislatures are mostly elective institutions. Their membership is determined on some theory of fair representation and their members are held regularly accountable for the decisions that they make. This means that in the legislature our politics approximates something like self-government: here we lay down the law to ourselves and we deliberate together – or our elected representatives deliberate together – on the need for changing or restructuring the ground rules for our common life in society. When we want to alter the basis on which divorces are granted or social welfare provided or criminals punished or markets regulated, when we want to protect the environment or set up a national health system, we look first to the legislature, for only a legislature can furnish the sort of authority that is required for change or innovation on this scale. A new law may be drafted by civil servants; but as supporters of democracy we expect that the drafters will not simply impose their ideas on the basis of their own expert confidence in the merits of their proposal. However important the innovation is perceived to be, and however well-drafted the measure, we expect its sponsors to submit it to a large representative assembly – an assembly comprising hundreds of representatives, organized into parties perhaps, but facing one another as equals, elected by the people, and drawn from all sections of society. We expect the merits of the proposal to be debated freely, publicly, and comprehensively in that assembly; we expect the measure to be amended and modified in the course of debate; and we expect that, in its amended form, it will eventually be voted on by the members, and that it will acquire the status and dignity of *law* only in virtue of a final decision supported by a majority in an assembly of this kind.

That there should *be* a legislature, with this function of explicit lawmaking, is something which most people nowadays take for granted. Historically, however, the idea that law may be subject to regular modification in this way has often been disparaged. In ancient times, law was regarded as sacred and immemorial, changing (if it did) in the way that customs change, gradually over long periods of time. There is a long antipathy between custom and legislation stretching from Antigone's defiance of the edicts of King Creon in the name of the *nomos* governing human burial (Sophocles 2001) to Savigny's (1831) challenge to the Napoleonic codes at the beginning of the nineteenth century in the name of the organic expression in customary law of the common consciousness of particular European peoples (Kelley 1990).

Or even if the laws were not viewed as immemorial, even if they were understood as originating in the conscious work of great lawmakers, still in antiquity the results tended to be viewed rather in the way that modern Americans view the work of the Founding Fathers on the US Constitution – not as we view regular legislation, but as something extraordinary, which should be modified only very occasionally and then with the greatest trepidation. Aristotle observed in the *Politics* that "the habit of lightly changing the laws is an evil." Of course, he said, the laws could be improved: ancient customs are often primitive and absurd. Still, "when the advantage is small, some errors both of lawgivers and rulers had better be left.... For the law has no power to command obedience except that of habit, which can only be given by time..." (Aristotle 1988: 39). If the laws were changed every time a new idea occurred to some politician, they would forfeit their special place in public life and become little more than an evanescent and incoherent array of dicta and decrees.

Nor is this only ancient prejudice. Jurists in common law systems have long nurtured a snobbish antipathy towards legislation which survives to the present day. The difference in this regard between the views of legal scholars and the views

of democratic theorists is considerable. As I have already mentioned, theorists of democracy tend to see legislation as the focus of democratic values: they regard the legislature as a place where representatives of the citizenry engage in one of the most active and morally respectable forms of self-government. But the very thing that attracts democratic theorists – the involvement of ordinary people in lawmaking – tends to repel the legal professional. Sir William Blackstone observed in 1765 that a long course of reading and study is required to become a professor of laws, "but every man of superior fortune thinks himself *born* a legislator." As a result, he said, "the common law of England has fared like other venerable edifices of antiquity, which rash and inexperienced work-men have ventured to new-dress and refine" (Blackstone 2001: 7).

Many modern legal scholars echo Blackstone's concern. They argue that the character of common law systems is changing for the worse as the legislative impulse crowds out the more endogenous and traditional bases of legal growth (Calabresi 1982). To some extent, the growth of the modern science of legislative drafting has helped to solve this problem. It is no surprise that much of the jurisprudential antipathy towards legislation is heard in the United States, where standards of drafting are low (with most bills being drafted by politicians and their staffs, and then redrafted by conference committees in bicameral legislatures), where legislative proceedings make a mockery of debate (with legislators presenting speeches to an empty chamber in the middle of the night for the benefit of television cameras), and where the whole process is riddled with the worst sort of political maneuvering. It is all too easy to regard this as a basis of misgiving about legislatures and legislation as such. And we may be supported in what seems like a healthy skepticism by empirical political scientists who delight in debunking the dreams of democratic theory: they portray real-world legislatures as weak, quarrelsome, and corrupt institutions, whose "deliberations" consist in a series of unconvincing publicity stunts, whose procedures are riddled with contradictions from the point of view of rational decision theory, and whose formalities are most likely a cover for secret deals worked out among special interests in smoke-filled rooms.

A more thoughtful critique of the idea of legislation can be found in the later writings of F. A. Hayek (1973). Though the essence of good government, according to Hayek, is rule by general laws, and though he places a premium on predictability as necessary for individual freedom under the law, it is important for him that law be conceived of as impersonal norms implicit in the practices of a free society. If the laws are thought of as changing, their change should be gradual and spontaneous, rather than planned and orchestrated by politicians. Law, in the sense that Hayek favors, is quite different from legislation: it is independent of human purpose, for its function is to accommodate human purposes, and it is independent of human will, for its business is the coordination of free wills (Hayek 1973: 72–3). Legislation, by contrast, presents itself as the conscious work of particular individuals: bills are named for the politicians who sponsor them (the McCain–Feingold Act, for example, in the area of campaign finance law) or for the particular incidents that occasioned the rush to change the law in some regard (Megan's Law, for example, responding to outrage about particular incidents of child abuse and kidnapping). Both examples illustrate the extent to which, in Hayek's opinion, legislation deviates from the impersonality and universality that characterize true law. Historically, he says, the chief concern of legislative bodies has not been the coordination of independent purposes in a free society, but the structuring, financing and administration of government. Hayek identifies the legislative mentality with an essentially managerial vision of law:

> It was in connection with the rules of the organization of government that the deliberate making of "laws" became a familiar and every-day procedure; every new undertaking of a government or every change in the structure of government required some new rules for its organization. The laying down of such new rules thus became an accepted procedure long before anyone contemplated using it for altering the established rules of just conduct. But when the wish to do so arose it was almost inevitable that the task was entrusted to the body which had

> always made laws in another sense....(Hayek 1973: 91)

Hayek conceded that legislation might be useful for society at large when more implicit processes of legal adaptation ended up in a doctrinal *cul-de-sac* or when some area of law needed comprehensive clarification (Hayek 1973: 88–9). But often the results of legislative "clarification" were counterintuitive, and the tendency of modern "social legislation" is to project the mentality of state administration outwards and treat the whole of society as an organization to be "managed," with frightful consequences for liberty and the rule of law.

Now, a good jurisprudential theory of legislation need not be committed necessarily to rebutting all these criticisms (though some have tried: see Waldron 1999b). But it does need to offer something affirmative. Too often theories of legislation are nothing more than theories about what courts should do with legislative output: how statutes should be interpreted, and so forth. This is certainly important, but it is bound to remain a sterile enterprise as long as it is isolated from a normative account of what legislative institutions should be like and what we might reasonably expect from them in the real world.

Legislation in Legal Theory

One obvious place to look for a theory of legislation is in the jurisprudence of legal positivism. In the early positivist theories of Jeremy Bentham (1970) and John Austin (1913), law is conceived as a set of general commands issued by a sovereign and backed up with the threat of sanctions. See LEGAL POSITIVISM. On this definition, measures enacted by a legislature seem to be the very paradigm of positive law: parliaments are sovereign and statutes are their commands. This is not to say that the positivists denied the existence of judge-made law. But they saw it as a problematic form of lawmaking. The judge's "direct and proper purpose is not the establishment of the rule, but the decision of the specific case. He legislates *as properly judging*, and not *as properly legislating*" (Austin 1913: 315, emphasis in original; see also 266–27). Moreover the rules that judges lay down can be regarded as law in the positivist model only by virtue of some fiction of delegated authority or tacit acceptance by the sovereign. Normatively, too, the early positivists tended to privilege the more explicit work of legislatures. Discerning when courts have changed the law and what new legal rules they have put in place is a formidable task that challenges the talents of the most formidable lawyer, so that the ordinary layperson has virtually no way of getting reliable information about the state of judge-made law. Jeremy Bentham's critique of common law as a "cobweb of ancient barbarism" – confused and largely unknown to those who suffer under it – is perhaps the most striking example of the English positivists' hostility to laws made by "Judge & Co." (see Postema 1986: 266). Law made explicitly in legislatures, by contrast, is easily promulgated; indeed, the public will often be on notice that a debate about some aspect of law is taking place and that various reforms are being considered. Of course, no one denies that statute law also may be poorly expressed and insufficiently publicized:

> But there is this essential difference between the kinds of law. The evil [of obscurity and inaccessibility] is inherent in judiciary law, although it be as well constructed as judiciary law can be. But statute law (though it often is bulky and obscure) may be compact and perspicacious, if constructed with care and skill. (Austin 1913: 327)

Interestingly, these virtues of explicit command and clear exposition were emphasized by natural law theorists as well. For natural lawyers, the test of positive law is not simply whether it conforms to natural law; the test is whether positive law adds anything determinate and useful to such natural law reasoning as we might expect to take place in its absence. For example, natural law might tell us that we should exercise care when we are driving, but it will be positive law that gives us a determinate speed limit; or natural law may tell us that a man is entitled to the land he has cultivated, but it is positive law that will give us

determinate criteria of title and the incidents of ownership. To fulfill these functions (which natural lawyers refer to as *determinatio*), it is important that human law be public and predictable, because these are not matters that people can figure out for themselves on the basis of their own natural law reasoning (Aquinas 1988: 78). See NATURAL LAW THEORY. So, as John Locke (1988) put it, civil society will offer no improvement over the uncertainty that accrues from uncoordinated natural law thinking by individuals in the state of nature, if people are ruled by judges' or sovereigns' own personal interpretations of natural law. There will be no improvement unless we are governed under the auspices of "standing Rules," or as Locke sometimes put it, "declared and received Laws, and not by extemporary Dictates and undetermined Resolutions" (Locke 1988: 358–60). It was for this reason, along with its popular character, that Locke regarded the legislature as supreme among the established institutions of government (Locke 1988: 367).

In their more recent manifestations, however, theories of positive law have offered more complex and equivocal accounts of the role of legislation in a well-ordered legal system.

Let's begin with the modern legal positivists. It is not hard to place legislation at the center of the account of positive law developed by H. L. A. Hart (1994). Hart argued that it is "characteristic of a legal system that new legal rules can be introduced and old ones changed or repealed by deliberate enactment" (Hart 1994: 175). According to Hart, the ability to change rules deliberately is a striking feature of the contrast between "prelegal" societies and modern legal systems. A "prelegal" society is one governed by a set of conventional customs or moral practices. Norm change is possible for such a society, but it involves a slow process of evolution; there is no means whereby such a society can deliberately adapt existing rules to changing circumstances. According to Hart, the transition to distinctively *legal* governance involves the gradual institution of practices of more deliberate legal change. It involves the emergence of secondary rules which specify a basis on which new rules are to be enacted, and a basis on which duly enacted rules can be recognized as such (Hart 1994: 94–9).

The idea of secondary rules governing lawmaking represents the major innovation of Hart's jurisprudence, and it is the basis of his challenge to the sovereign command theories of Bentham's and Austin's accounts of lawmaking. The idea of command always seemed to Hart an inadequate basis for thinking about even the most explicit forms of legal enactment (Hart 1994: 20). It begged the question of the authority that lies behind the command and it left unexplained the fact that what Bentham and Austin described as sovereign legislatures actually operated themselves on the basis of rules constituting and regulating their ability to produce new law. Hart's hypothesis that a legal system exists only when secondary rules emerge helps us to understand how a lawmaking body may function *as an institution*, as opposed to a simple center of power. It also helps explain features like the electoral procedures that determine the membership of most modern legislatures, as well as the bicameral structure and the complex majoritarian procedures that characterize their internal operations. These are all minutely rule-governed aspects of the legislative process and they could not be explained on the Hobbesian assumption that the sovereign legislature was the source of all legal rules.

So Hart's positivism does have the potential to explain the distinctive features of modern legislation. On the other hand, it was always possible that a shift away from the simple "sovereign command" model of positive law would have the effect of de-emphasizing formal legislation, by allowing positivists to develop less tortured accounts of other sources of law. One obvious area is constitutional law. Hart's theory of secondary rules gives modern positivism the ability to explain what the theories of Bentham and Austin could never explain – the existence and operation of legal constraints on legislation such as those imposed by the US Constitution (Hart 1994: 66–71). See CONSTITUTIONALISM. Or, to take another example, secondary rules might be understood as a basis for understanding the growth of judge-made law, which would not require the old fiction of tacit adoption by the sovereign. A rule of recognition is a basis on which judges can identify and apply rules that have been properly enacted. But judges also share practices of recognizing and according authority to one another's decisions: recognition need not be confined to legislation, and actually most of the issues that interest modern positivists focus on the judiciary, not the legislature, as a major source of law

Indeed the idea of a legislative institution is dispensable in the modern positivist vision of a dynamic legal system. The argument here is due to Joseph Raz (1999: 132–8). Suppose the following two things are true of a legal system: (1) there are courts and it is their task to apply preexisting norms; but (2) any determination by a court as to what those preexisting norms amount to is binding on other courts. A system organized in this way might well develop a complex and evolving body of law, without any institution thinking of itself or being perceived as an explicitly legislative body. Law in such a system would change mainly by virtue of mistakes made by courts in the application of the task laid down in (1), mistakes which would nevertheless themselves acquire the status of authoritative legal norms by virtue of the doctrine of authority laid down in (2). Such a system would satisfy Raz's own "sources thesis" – that is, the proposition that law is valid in terms of its institutional origin rather than its content (Raz 1979: 47) – and it would involve the operation of a rule (or rules) of recognition. But it would not be oriented, as those ideas are often assumed to be oriented, towards a sovereign legislature as source, and towards criteria of valid enactment as the basis on which law is distinguished from nonlaw. Hence, Raz concludes that "the existence of norm-*creating* institutions, though characteristic of modern legal systems, is not a necessary feature of all legal systems, but that the existence of certain types of norm-applying institutions is" (Raz 1979: 105).

The relative importance of legislation also came under attack from another direction in twentieth-century legal theory. The Legal Realists were fond of quoting Bishop Hoadley's maxim to the effect that "whoever has absolute authority to interpret any written or spoken laws, it is He who is truly the Law Giver ... and not the Person who first wrote or spoke them" (Frank 1970: 132). If the rules as enacted are indeterminate verbal formulae, capable of supporting a multitude of interpretations in the courtroom, then the best that can be said for the legislative process is that it is sometimes a way of stimulating law-making by judges, but it is not itself a process of making law. See AMERICAN LEGAL REALISM. This critique was mitigated somewhat by the belief held by some of the Legal Realists (e.g., Cohen 1935: 809) that legislative procedures offered more open and intelligent possibilities for policy making than the arcane processes of appellate adjudication. But when the Legal Realists' critique of the indeterminacy of rules became unfashionable, that view became unfashionable too. Though the critics of Legal Realism rescued the idea of determinate rules, they certainly did not accept the view that legislatures rather than courts were the best places for formulating such rules. Henry Hart and Albert Sacks put this forward in the late 1950s in their famous *Legal Process* materials:

> A legislature has a primary, first-line responsibility to establish the institutions necessary or appropriate in the everyday operation of government. For example, it must create courts. . . . But in relation to the body of general directive arrangements which govern private activity in the society its responsibility is more accurately described as secondary in the sense of second-line. The legislature characteristically functions in this relation as an intermittently intervening, trouble-shooting, back-stopping agency. . . . The private lawmakers, the courts, and administrative agencies are . . . the regularly available continuously functioning agencies of growth in the legal system. (Hart and Sacks 1994: 164)

The marginalization of legislatures continued as legal positivism came under renewed attack in the second half of the twentieth century. In the 1960s, critics began attacking what they saw as an undue emphasis on formulated rules, on institutional sources of law, and on source-based tests of legal validity: they criticized Hart's positivism for neglecting the role of unenacted legal norms (principles) imbedded deep in the fabric of the legal system, and for denigrating the modes of moral argument that were necessary to uncover these principles (Dworkin 1977). For Dworkin it was not enough to regard judicial precedents as an alternative mode of enactment: what one had

to grasp was the "gravitational force" of precedents as opposed to their enactment force – that is, what one had to grasp was not what a holding *said* but the difference it might make to the arguments that would subsequently be appropriate in court. All this meant that the focus of debate shifted decisively from legislation and legislative proceedings to the way courts operate and the way judges make their decisions.

Analytics of the Legislative Process

Is it possible to do any better than this? Without pretending that legislation is the only source of law, or even that it is the most important, is it possible to say anything significant about the legislative process which might help us think more clearly about the authority of statute law and the basis on which it is interpreted and applied? Bismarck is reputed to have observed that a person with a taste for statutes, like a person with a taste for sausages, should not inquire too closely into the way they are made (see Waldron 1999a: 88). And it may seem that the rather unseemly – indeed, unsavory – scramble that characterizes the process of legislating, particularly in American legislatures, is not something we should approach too delicately or high-mindedly. But I think an affirmative theory of legislation does need to focus on some of the distinctive features of legislative procedure, and the way in which those procedures mediate between values like democracy and values associated with the rule of law.

I said earlier that legislation comes with democratic credentials. But now I want to emphasize the way in which those credentials are related to their structure and composition. Legislatures are large institutions, comprising hundreds of members: the voting membership of a typical legislature is one or two orders of magnitude higher than that found in a typical cabinet or Supreme Court panel (see Waldron 2000). This is not related in any simple way to democratic legitimacy: a single individual like a president might have democratic legitimacy by virtue of having won a popular election for the office. But it is interesting that in lawmaking, above all, we think it important that the people be represented by *people* rather than by just one person.

Why is the voting membership of our legislatures so much greater than our courts? One possible explanation might invoke Condorcet's "jury theorem," which establishes that the bigger a group is, the more likely it is to choose the right answer using majority voting (Condorcet 1976). But that is unsatisfactory, for two reasons. First, it fails to distinguish legislatures from courts. And secondly, the jury theorem holds only if the average member of the group is more likely than not to vote for the correct answer, and as Condorcet himself pointed out:

> A very numerous assembly cannot be composed of very enlightened men. It is even probable that those comprising this assembly will on many matters combine great ignorance with many prejudices. Thus there will be a great number of questions on which the probability of the truth of each voter will be below $\frac{1}{2}$. It follows that the more numerous the assembly, the more it will be exposed to the risk of making false decisions. (Condorcet 1976: 49)

Others have argued that, even if the individuals are competent, group dynamics will interfere with good decision making in a large group. As the authors of *The Federalist Papers* put it, "[i]n all very numerous assemblies, of whatever characters composed, passion never fails to wrest the scepter from reason. Had every Athenian citizen been a Socrates, every Athenian assembly would still have been a mob" (Madison, Hamilton, and Jay 1987: 336).

Evidently, large numbers are valued in the legislature not just because more is better, but because more gives us the opportunity to diversify the membership of the institution, to have legislators from a variety of places representing a diversity of interests and opinions. True, there is often political pressure to diversify the judiciary – a balance between men and women, for example, or liberals and conservatives. But alone among the great departments of state, legislatures are formally structured to ensure diversity. Of course there are disputes about what the axes of diversity should be. In almost all cases, the electoral system is set up to ensure geographical diversity; but political diversity is also valued in the sense that

there is supposed to be some sort of rough comparability between the proportion of (say) liberals and conservatives in the legislature and the proportion of liberals and conservatives in the community. Even if "proportional representation" is not a formal feature of the legislative structure (as it is almost everywhere except in the United States and in most elections in the UK), most observers would be very uncomfortable with a legislature that operated on anything like a comprehensive winner-takes-all basis. Normally we want one or two active opposition parties represented in the legislature and we want some assurance, too, that dissident voices commanding any sort of substantial support in the community will not be excluded. These features of modern legislative assemblies are very well known and widely discussed. Unfortunately, though, that discussion is seldom related in any systematic way to the status of the output of these institutions considered as law.

Why is this diversity particularly important for lawmaking? Partly it is informational. We want to ensure an adequate representation of the diversity of *interests* in society. We organize elections hoping that representatives will come from different parts of the country, and bring with them knowledge of the special needs and circumstances of different groups. Mostly, however, the value of diversity has to do with heterogeneity of opinions, not interests. The legislature is a place where our representatives argue and debate, and we want to ensure a hearing for the largest possible variety of opinions and political ideals concerning the issues that are raised when a change in the law is being contemplated. New law or modified law emerging from this institution is supposed to claim its authority not on the basis of any cozy consensus among like-minded people, but in the heat of opposition and in full public awareness that there are many opposing views about social justice and social policy in society. If citizens who disagree with the new law ask why they should obey it, we want to be able to say to them that disagreements (along the lines that they are expressing) were aired as fiercely and as forcefully as possible at the time the law was enacted, in a fair process of deliberation, and that a choice was made among the various alternatives (including views like theirs) on a basis that was fair to all the members of the community.

This brings us to the decision procedures used in the legislature. It is often said that legislatures arc majoritarian institutions. Now that is true: they make their legislative decisions by majority voting – often several tiers of voting for each bill. In itself, however, this fails to distinguish legislatures from supreme courts, where decisions are also characteristically made by margins of five votes to four, or three votes to two. I think we have to be careful about the relation between majoritarianism and democracy. An institution is democratic not in virtue of its use of majoritarian decision procedures but in virtue of its voting membership. What makes the decision procedures of legislatures fair from a democratic point of view is that a vote in the house is related to a notional vote in the country, by virtue of the elective credentials of each voting member. To be sure, the relation is very rough: a majority among the legislators may represent much less than a majority of the people, if some constituencies were won by large margins and others, whose representatives vote with the majority, were won by small margins. Too much of this, and there will be reason to adjust the electoral system or the system of representation to tighten up the correlation. Now it would make little sense to pursue similar adjustments in the case of institutions, like the US Supreme Court, that also use majoritarian procedures, for their use of these procedures is unrelated to norms of democratic fairness. In the case of legislatures, however, we strive for decision procedures that are fair to all the members of the society, and not just to the voting members of the legislature, precisely so that we are in a position to answer recalcitrant citizens who want to know why they should comply with this new law that they disagree with. For this case, then, the structural attributes of legislatures that I have been emphasizing – the use of fair decision procedures together with the representation in the legislative chamber of a diverse body of opinions – are indispensable for the legitimacy of the legislation that emerges.

In general we need to take seriously the "political" nature of legislation and legislative deliberation. Jurists sometimes try to resist the charge – made by various skeptics in the Critical Legal Studies movement – that law and legal decision making is political or "just politics." See CRITICAL LEGAL THEORY. What they mean (when they resist this charge) is that there are methods and techniques for interpreting and applying existing legal materials whose use does not depend on any particular set of political doctrines or commitments. Conservatives and liberals alike know how to identify the holding of a case, how to follow precedent, how to relate general words in one part of a statute to particular words in another part, and so on. But the existence of these techniques need not be oblivious to the politicized nature of the processes that generate the legal materials the jurists have to interpret. Confronted with a piece of legislation that poses a difficult problem of interpretation, the legal technician must bear in mind that the legislation has emerged from, and claims its legitimacy in relation to, proposals, deliberations, politicking, and voting that take place among a diverse body of opinionated representatives. Legal technicians should not put all that out of sight as a distasteful matter of political history. On the contrary the interpretive techniques that they use must be sensitive to the political structures and dynamics that we have been discussing.

Interpreting and Applying Legislation

A statute consists of an enacted form of words, and many of the problems involved in interpreting and applying legislation, are problems about relating a written text to persons, things, and events in the world. One could imagine a legal system that accorded "no particular respect to the verbal form in which legislative texts are cast, treating statutes simply as cases are treated in the common law system" (Atiyah and Summers 1987: 97). In fact, however, that is not the way we treat statutes, and there ought to be a reason for that. It is not enough to say that the legislature is an authoritative source of law, and that is why its *ipsissima verba* must be respected. For we do not treat all authorities in this way – hanging, as it were, on their every word.

Maybe textuality contributes to predictability in the community to which the legislation is directed, though some theorists are skeptical about this (Hayek 1973: 118). I suspect that the textual quality of legislation has more to do with the conditions of its production. I have described the legislature as a gathering of disparate individuals who do not necessarily sympathize with or understand one another particularly well. Whatever differences of ideology, value, culture, opinion, and interest are found in the community are also supposed to be represented in the legislature. So the potential for mutual misunderstanding in any interaction between them is great. No doubt it is mitigated to some degree by institutional collegiality and their common experience of a life in politics. But if there is too much of that, we start to lose exactly what we value about diversity, which is its reflection of the disparate beliefs and concerns among members of the community at large. How then is it possible for legislators to interact in the institutional mechanics of legislation? The answer lies in their highly stylized rules of procedure: these are rules, so to speak, for people who have very little else in common. Now there is an important connection between procedural formality and what we might call the output-formality of a deliberative body. The key to rules of procedural order is usually a tight focus on a particular resolution under discussion – a resolution which is formulated clearly, established as a criterion of relevance for a particular debate, amended only in a carefully controlled way, and subject in the end to formal voting. Without that textual focus, without this reference to a given form of words, a disparate body of representatives of the sort I have postulated will find it difficult to share a view about exactly what they have been debating, exactly what they have voted upon, exactly what they have done as a collective body acting in the name of the community. (See Waldron 1999a: 69–87 for this argument.)

One common mode of statutory interpretation is to attempt to recover the *intention* of the legislature in passing a particular bill, whose text now seems for some reason obscure or difficult to apply. We ask ourselves whether the legislature intended the text to apply in a particular way to a case like the one in front of us, or we speculate about what the legislators would have intended if

cases like the one in front of us had been brought to their attention. The quest for legislative intent is big business in the United States, where lawyers spend hundreds of billable hours combing the congressional record for any scrap of material, any speech or memo. (Since the decision in *Pepper v. Hart* 1993, it has become common also in England and in Commonwealth jurisdictions.) But it is a controversial practice: the quest for legislative intent has been described as something like searching for a friendly face in a crowd (Radin 1930: 863), and it is strongly opposed in America by devotees of what is called "the new textualism" (see Scalia 1997 and Manning 2001).

On the face of it, the idea of legislative intent makes sense. Legislation is an intentional activity, and if there is a question about *what change* has been effected by legislative action, the answer is surely: the very change that the legislature intended to effect (Raz 1996: 258–9). But this account of legislative intent does not take us beyond the intention conventionally associated with the language of the enactment, and it is the unclarity of the meaning – that is, of the intention conventionally associated with the language – that is supposed to be the problem here. In the case of individual speakers, when their words are unclear, we can ask them what they meant or we can consult what we know of the thoughts or ideas associated with their original utterances. And if the legislature were a single individual we might do exactly the same thing. Confronted with an ambiguous enactment, we would take the sovereign aside and ask him what he meant; or if he was unavailable, we would pore over what else we knew about the state of mind he was in at the time that he did his legislating. None of this makes sense, however, in the case of a legislature that is *not* a natural individual, a legislature that comprises hundreds of members with radically diverse opinions and states of mind. Such a body has intentions only in the performance of its formally specified acts – that is, only by virtue of the constitutive rules (about voting, etc.) that stipulate what is to count as an Act of Parliament or an Act of Congress. Beyond that, there is no question of our being able to attribute *to the legislature as such* any intentions, or thoughts, or beliefs, or purposes. Of course, individual legislators may have had their own individual views and hopes about the legislation expectations. But there is simply no authorized mechanism for bringing these particular mental states into relation with one another to define the views and hopes of the legislature as such.

It does not follow from this that it is always a mistake to associate a purpose with a piece of legislation. Sometimes the text of the legislation will state its purpose, or sometimes the ascription of purpose is just a straightforward exercise of common sense: everyone knows that the purpose of statute X must be to combat evil Y or promote benefit Z. But that is how the ascription must be defended – not in terms of what the legislature thought, but in terms of what seems obvious or sensible to us. Or if our ascription of a purpose is controversial, we might debate with one another about which ascription of purpose makes the text look best to us, who, for our sins, have been charged with administering it. These modes of "constructive" interpretation (Dworkin 1986: 65–8, 313–54) at least have the virtue of candor, whereas the appeal to some phantom of legislative intent is almost always fanciful.

Something similar may be said about doctrines of statutory "absurdity," in light of our reflections in the previous section on the disparate character of the membership of modern legislatures. I guess some things are literally absurd, and a court might want to interpret a statute in a way that is charitable, so far as typing errors and verbal slips are concerned. But one's sense of absurdity is also relative to one's values and ideological priorities. In *Church of the Holy Trinity v. United States* (1892), it seemed absurd to the Supreme Court that a statute aimed at restricting Chinese immigration should have the effect – which its text facially required – of excluding the recruitment of an English clergyman. Yet even in 1892 there will have been those who did not see the grouping of the one restriction with the other as "absurd" (Manning 2003: 2424). We must remember that we assemble legislators in their hundreds precisely because the values and priorities that affect our sense of the absurd are *not* the same; if they were, we could have a legislature of eight or nine individuals, solidly representative of the *shared* moral sense of the community.

In all of this, I have emphasized the point that legislatures are political institutions: they are places where law is politicized. The politics are not just in the deliberation and in the voting; they are also in the search for votes and in the compromises and adjustments that the formation of a majority often requires. It is sometimes said that courts have a responsibility to statutes in a way that is not blatantly overinclusive or underinclusive relative to their purpose. Thus an ordinance prohibiting dogs in restaurants for health reasons might be read in a way that admits clean dogs, so as to avoid overinclusiveness, while excluding filthy cats, so as to avoid underinclusiveness (Schauer 1991: 207–28). However, quite apart from the difficulty of discerning the purpose of the legislation in question, there are also issues about the respect that is due to the compromises that were necessary in the legislatures in order to get a particular bill enacted. It may have been the case that the bill would not have been passed without the support of the cat lobby, that is, unless it was (from a health point of view) underinclusive in this regard. In other words, provisions which seem arbitrary in the bill may seem nonarbitrary when the politics surrounding its enactment are taken into account. Certainly there are good reasons to avoid incoherent legislation, even when such incoherence is the price of political support in the legislatures: legislators should strive to enact laws which have integrity and which do not disturb the integrity of the legal system as a whole (Dworkin 1986: 167, 176–86, 217–24). But if a court takes it upon itself to clean up the statute, it is slighting the political process in virtue of which alone the statute has its legitimacy, as well as begging the important question – which any exercise in repairing inconsistency inevitably gives rise to – as to which cleaned-up version of the bill would have been enacted had the legislature been paying proper attention to its duty in this regard.

A Forum of Principle?

Many countries now have legal systems which allow for judicial review of legislation – that is, they empower courts to test a statute against a charter of rights or other constitutional restraints and refuse to apply the statute (or in some cases strike it from the statute-book) if it violates those rights and restraints. The acts of the national legislature can be judged *ultra vires* just as much as the acts of a subordinate rulemaker or the activities of an executive agency. In this way legislation itself becomes, in a sense, an activity subject to the rule of law. If one glosses over the human origin of the constitution or (more importantly) the latitude that the judges have in interpreting and updating the more abstract provisions of the constitution, one might almost say that a system of this kind fulfills the ancient promise of "*the rule of laws, not men,*" since it puts constitutional law and constitutional adjudication above what many have regarded as the ultimate human source of law in every society.

Justifications for this practice vary. In some systems, judicial review is thought necessary to maintain the federal structure of the legal system: the national legislature has competence in some areas and no others, and it must be prevented by the courts from encroaching on the jurisdiction of the state legislatures (and vice versa). Difficulties arise, however, when the constitutional rules determining federal structure are themselves vague or ambiguous or inappropriate for modern conditions. Then the question to be answered is not whether the legislature should be restrained from acting unconstitutionally, but why the courts, rather than an assembly comprising the people's representatives, should be the place where the federal structure is disambiguated or brought up to date.

The same can be said about judicial review based on individual rights. Suppose a society commits itself to a set of constitutional restraints on legislation, corresponding to certain individual rights. And suppose that the written text embodying those constraints is susceptible to several interpretations, and those interpretations correspond to firmly held rival opinions in the society as to what rights people have and what legislation ought to be required to respect. In these circumstances – which I believe are the circumstances of almost all constitutional adjudication (Waldron 1999a) – the question is not whether the legislature should be restrained, but which institution – the courts or the legislature – is the best institution for determining what the restraints should (now be taken to) be.

What we shouldn't say about this question is that it is a matter of pitting majoritarian against nonmajoritarian determinations. Courts are majoritarian institutions too, and the example of the United States has shown over and over again that disagreement among the people as to the interpretation of constitutional restraints are represented also in the highest court, and that Supreme Court justices have to vote – usually by margins of five-to-four – to determine what rights the members of the society should be taken to have. As I said earlier, the only difference is that this judicial majoritarianism represents and is accountable to no opinions other than those of the justices, whereas a majority decision on the matter in the legislature accords respect also to the millions of right-bearers who also have a view on what their rights should be taken to be.

It is sometimes said that a court is a more appropriate place for deliberation (and, if necessary, voting) on matters of rights, because a court is set up as "a forum of principle," and the arguments and reason-giving characteristic of judicial procedure is a more attractive basis for decision making about rights than the politicking and haggling that takes place in the legislature (Dworkin 1985: 33). We cannot resolve that issue here. But we can say that it is based on a remarkably limited experience of legislative deliberation. Defenders of judicial review will no doubt cite the great milestone victories in the United States – *Brown v. Board of Education* (1954), *Roe v. Wade* (1973), and perhaps now *Lawrence v. Texas* (2003) – as examples of what they have in mind. But the issue is not truly joined until we have also read and reflected upon the great debates in the British parliament and in legislatures around the world whereby race relations legislation was enacted and abortion and homosexuality decriminalized. Reading these materials, one becomes aware that there is in fact something attractive about a full and principled debate among the people's representatives, in which all the main voices in the society are heard on the great issue of rights under consideration, and in which (unavoidably) a vote is taken, but this time one that is calculated to be fair to rival views held in community in proportion to the strength with which they are held. Someone is always dissatisfied or aggrieved when one of these decisions is made – whether by court or by parliament. But the difference may be that there is something that can be said to a recalcitrant citizen about the legitimacy of a legislative vote on these matters, which cannot be said about the legitimacy of a judicial vote, in circumstances where everyone knows the law is ambiguous and the judges are just voting for the opinions they hold as nine citizens among millions.

References

Aquinas, Thomas. 1988. *Treatise on Law.* Washington, DC: Regnery Gateway.

Aristotle. 1988. *The Politics*, ed. Stephen Everson. Cambridge, UK: Cambridge University Press.

Atiyah P. S. and Summers, Robert. 1987. *Form and Substance in Anglo-American Law: A Comparative Study of Legal Reasoning, Legal Theory, and Legal Institutions.* Oxford: Clarendon Press.

Austin, John. 1913. *Lectures on Jurisprudence, or the Philosophy of Positive Law.* London: John Murray.

Bentham, Jeremy. 1970. *Of Laws in General*, ed. H. L. A. Hart. London: Athlone Press.

Blackstone, William. 2001. *Blackstone's Commentaries on the Laws of England*, ed. Wayne Morrison. London: Cavendish Publishing.

Brown v. Board of Education. 1954. 347 U.S. 483.

Calabresi, Guido. 1982. *A Common Law for the Age of Statutes.* Cambridge, MA: Harvard University Press.

Church of the Holy Trinity v. United States. 1892. 143 U.S. 457.

Cohen, Felix. 1935. Transcendental nonsense and the functional approach. *Columbia Law Review* 35: 809–49.

Condorcet, Marquis de. 1976. Essay on the application of mathematics to the theory of decision-making. In Keith Michael Baker (ed.), *Condorcet: Selected Writings.* Indianapolis, IN: Bobbs-Merrill, 33–70.

Dworkin, Ronald. 1977. *Taking Rights Seriously*, revised edn. London: Duckworth.

Dworkin, Ronald. 1985. *A Matter of Principle.* Cambridge, MA: Harvard University Press.

Dworkin, Ronald. 1986. *Law's Empire.* Cambridge, MA: Harvard University Press.

Frank, Jerome. 1970. *Law and the Modern Mind.* Gloucester, MA: Peter Smith.

Hart, Henry M. and Sacks, Albert. 1994. *The Legal Process: Basic Problems in the Making and Application of Law*, ed. William N. Eskridge and Philip P. Frickey. New York: Foundation Press.

Hart, H. L. A. 1994. *The Concept of Law*, 2nd edn. Oxford: Clarendon Press.

Hayek, F. A. 1973. *Law, Legislation and Liberty. vol. I – Rules and Order.* Chicago: University of Chicago Press.

Kelley, Donald R. 1990. *The Human Measure: Social Thought in the Western Legal Tradition.* Cambridge, MA: Harvard University Press.

Lawrence v. Texas. 2003. 539 U.S. 558.

Locke, John. 1988. *Two Treatises of Government*, ed. Peter Laslett. Cambridge, UK: Cambridge University Press.

Madison, James, Hamilton, Alexander and Jay, John. 1987. *The Federalist Papers*, ed. Isaac Kramnick. Harmondsworth, UK: Penguin Books.

Manning, John. 2001. Textualism and the equity of the statute. *Columbia Law Review* 101: 1–127.

Manning, John. 2003. The absurdity doctrine. *Harvard Law Review* 116: 2387–486.

Pepper v. Hart. 1993. A.C. 593.

Postema, Gerald J. 1986. *Bentham and the Common Law Tradition.* Oxford: Clarendon Press.

Radin, Max. 1930. Statutory interpretation. *Harvard Law Review* 43: 863–85.

Raz, Joseph. 1979. *The Authority of Law: Essays on Law and Morality.* Oxford: Clarendon Press.

Raz, Joseph. 1996. Intention in interpretation. In Robert George (ed.), *The Autonomy of Law: Essays in Legal Positivism.* Oxford: Clarendon Press, 249–86.

Raz, Joseph. 1999. *Practical Reason and Norms*, 3rd edn. Oxford: Clarendon Press.

Roe v. Wade. 1973. 410 U.S. 113

Savigny, Frederick Charles von. 1831. *Of the Vocation of our Age for Legislation and Jurisprudence*, trans. Abraham Hayward. London: Littlewood.

Scalia, Antonin. 1997. *A Matter of Interpretation: Federal Courts and the Law.* Princeton, NJ: Princeton University Press.

Schauer, Frederick. 1991. *Playing by the Rules: A Philosophical Examination of Rule-based Decision-making in Law and in Life.* Oxford: Clarendon Press.

Sophocles. 2001. *Antigone*, trans. Paul Woodruff. Indianapolis, IN: Hackett Publishing.

Waldron, Jeremy. 1999a. *Law and Disagreement.* Oxford: Clarendon Press.

Waldron, Jeremy. 1999b. *The Dignity of Legislation.* Cambridge, UK: Cambridge University Press.

Waldron, Jeremy. 2000. Legislation by assembly. *Loyola Law Review* 46: 507–34.

Chapter 17

Constitutionalism

Larry A. Alexander

Constitutionalism refers to the practice of establishing constitutions for social governance. Understanding the practice requires that one understand what constitutions are, what functions they perform, and whether they are on balance desirable. I take up these three topics in turn.

What Constitutions Are

Consider the following account of constitutionalism and the various philosophical problems that it entails (Alexander 1998; Grey 1979; Kay 1998). At step 1, I begin with my own current views about principles of justice and other aspects of political morality, about principles of wise governance, and about the institutional arrangements best suited to realizing these various principles. If I could impose these principles and institutions by myself, I would do so (unless they included principles, such as democratic side constraints, that prohibited their unilateral imposition). Because I do not have such power, however, I need the assistance of others, others who will not share all of my views about political morality, wise governance, and institutional arrangements.

At step 2, then, I seek wide agreement on rules of governmental behavior and rules defining governmental institutions that realize my own personal principles and views to a greater extent than any alternative set of such rules on which I can obtain wide agreement. In other words, under my own principles, it is better that they not be

fully realized than that anarchy prevail (because of lack of wide agreement), but preferable that they be realized as fully as possible consistent with wide agreement. Others who hold different principles and views will reason similarly, which will result in agreement on rules of governmental behavior and rules defining institutions that no one believes are optimal but that most believe are good enough – that is, superior to anarchy. (Obviously, not just any set of rules will be superior to anarchy according to everyone's principles of political morality and wise governance; the rules must be the best that can be widely agreed upon and above everyone's better-than-anarchy threshold of acceptability.)

Let me elaborate on how this agreement at step 2 can be achieved. For this is important in understanding how constitutions can change without formal amendment, how revolutions can be domesticated, how separate systems of authoritative rules can exist side by side in the same community (and why this happens less frequently than might be expected), and other mysteries of constitutionalism and of law more generally.

Let me begin with the simplest version of the story (Alexander and Sherwin 2001). Members of the community disagree about or are uncertain about how their common moral principles are to be applied concretely. They perceive the moral need for authoritative settlement of those disagreements and uncertainties. Jane prefers the rule "Let Jane decide." John prefers the rule "Let John decide." And so on for each member of the community.

Jane's second best rule is "Let Sarah decide." But although it is also Sarah's preferred rule, it must compete with John's second best rule, "Let Jim decide," which is, of course, supported by Jim and John.

Now let us suppose that everyone's third, second, or first-choice rule is "Let the majority decide." If everyone understands that other first-choice and second-choice rules will not command agreement – and if everyone believes that "Let the majority decide" is morally superior to the alternative of no authoritative decision maker – then everyone has a strategic reason for accepting "Let the majority decide" as the foundational authoritative rule. I say "strategic" to emphasize that perhaps everyone will view the rule, not as the best rule for settling moral controversies, but as the best rule that they can get others to accept. (In an important sense, of course, because the purpose of authoritative rules is to settle moral controversies, by being the best rule everyone can accept and the only rule that will actually perform the settlement function, this suboptimal rule becomes, for everyone, the optimal rule.)

Now as I complicate the story and move from the one basic rule, "Let the majority decide," to a complex set of rules regarding rights, procedures, and institutions, including perhaps supermajority institutions with the power to promulgate, repeal, and amend those rules, it becomes more and more likely that the resulting set of rules that must be agreed upon is far from anyone's ideal set of such rules. Some of the rules may be some members' first or second choices, but others will be further down on their list, and some may even be morally repugnant. Still, all have good reason to agree to the entire set, including the rules that they find morally repugnant, if that is the best set of rules to which they can get the others to agree, and if that set of rules is morally preferable to the absence of authoritative settlement. And again, because authoritative settlement requires agreement on authoritative rules, the morally best rules on which agreement can be obtained are in some sense the morally best rules. Rules that cannot command agreement cannot perform their moral function of settling what should be done and are thus undesirable, no matter how good those rules would be if they did command agreement.

We thus end up with the following picture. Our mythical community has reached agreement about certain foundational rules, rules that set up some institution (or person) as the basic rule promulgator and decision maker, that prescribe certain rights and procedures and set up certain additional institutions, and that set up a super-majoritarian institution for expanding or changing these basic rules. (I am assuming that this complex set of rules, with its distinctions between ordinary and "constitutional" rules, and its creation of various institutions and divisions of powers among them, is deemed morally preferable to the simple rule "Let the majority decide" in enough people's preference sets to have the complex set emerge as the coalescence point.) The members agree to this complex package of rules, but not necessarily because it is anyone's ideal, and not necessarily because there are no rules in the package that anyone finds morally repugnant as opposed to suboptimal. Rather, they agree to the package because it is from everyone's point of view both morally superior to the absence of authoritative settlement and also the morally best such package to which they can get others to agree. And because it meets those conditions, the package is in an important sense everyone's morally ideal package of rules.

The rules widely accepted at step 2 may be entrenched to various degrees. That is, it may be widely accepted that these rules may not be altered ever, may not be altered for a certain length of time, and/or may not be altered except by extraordinary procedures. We may believe that we have the best rules we can ever have, and that there is far more danger of loss of political wisdom or will or loss of moral concern than there is danger that wide agreement on better rules will be thwarted.

At the moment of agreement on the entrenched rules at step 2, the rules will mean what we who have agreed to them mean by them. In other words, we will have not merely agreed to certain symbols or sounds, but to particular meanings of those symbols and sounds. Our agreement can be memorialized only in symbolic form, however, which means that the symbols we have agreed upon and what we meant by them can come apart. Therefore, at step 2 we might agree not only on the rules of governmental behavior and institutions, but also on rules about who is to decide at later times what we meant by those rules.

It might be useful, then, to distinguish a constitution as a collection of agreed-upon symbols from a metaconstitution (or preconstitutional rules), with the latter consisting of agreed-upon norms – metarules – about which particular set of symbols is the constitution, who is to interpret those symbols, and whose semantic intentions shall count as the authoritative meaning of the symbols. The constitution and the metaconstitution are inseparable at the moment of agreement in step 2, but they can come apart at any time thereafter. Thus, although we may at some later time lack the earlier substantive agreement regarding the content of the rules that we had at step 2 – for example, we might now disagree about what freedom of speech should cover or about whether separation of powers is a good idea – we can still have wide agreement on the metaconstitution. And that agreement might still be sufficient under our principles of political morality to favor the constitution over anarchy.

This discussion of the metaconstitution and its relation to the symbolic constitution illustrates various ways that a constitution might change at the next stage, step 3. At step 3, three things might happen. First, the symbolic constitution might change without a change in the metaconstitution. Constitutional amendment in pursuance of the (original meaning of the) amending rules laid down in the symbolic constitution changes the original constitution organically.

Second, a constitutional revolution might occur in which agreement on the first metaconstitution is replaced by agreement on another metaconstitution that in turn picks out a different symbolic constitution. We may draft a brand new constitution, widely agree on what it means and that it is more desirable than the current constitution, and also agree that it, and not the current constitution, shall now be authoritative for us. (Arguably, the United States Constitution itself was the product of such a constitutional revolution.)

Third, the symbolic constitution might remain the same, but the metaconstitution might change. Thus, the original metaconstitutional agreement might be supplanted at step 3 by a new metaconstitutional agreement, one that deems some parts of the symbolic constitution to be nonauthoritative, that substitutes a new understanding of the symbols for their original meaning, or that "ratifies" otherwise improper interpretations of the symbolic constitution.

Just as it is understandable how people of differing moral and political views could nonetheless agree to entrench a set of constitutional rules and metaconstitutional rules, so it is understandable how they might come to agree on new rules and metarules and hence effect a constitutional revolution. Because it is only the agreement that these rules and metarules shall be supremely authoritative that makes them so, any subsequent agreement can supplant the original agreement to this effect. Of course, some who might have gone along with the original agreement and its constitution may not go along with the later one. For them, the new constitution will not be authoritative even if it purports to obligate them. At least, it will not be so if their political-moral beliefs favor anarchy or resistance to the new constitution. But that will be the case for any dissenters from a constitutional agreement as long as their acceptance of the constitution is not necessary to achieve the degree of effectiveness required to sustain the others' acceptance of the constitution.

Why should anyone at step 4 accept as authoritative a constitution or constitutional provision – whether in the original constitution of step 2 or a supplanting constitution of step 3 – if he or she does not view the constitution or the relevant provision hereof to be morally and prudentially ideal? The reason is the same one we had at steps 1 and 2: an effective set of relatively good entrenched rules, even if nonideal, may be ranked by our own ideal political morality as better than either anarchy or any other set of entrenched rules that has a chance of gaining wide agreement.

Finally, there is the question of why we should ever accept any rule as authoritative – that is, as providing us with a content-independent reason for action, a reason that does not derive from the merits of the rule's content but derives instead solely from the fact that we have accepted the rule or a higher-level rule that authorizes it. What I have argued thus far is that we can have content-*dependent* reasons – reasons derived from our political morality – to establish and entrench rules that others recognize as authoritative. But why should *we* recognize those rules as authoritative? Why should we not depart from them whenever our political morality marks disobedience as the preferable course? Of course, if our political morality supports these rules as the best we can get agreement upon, then our political morality will never dictate disobedience if that would undermine agreement. But it might well dictate secret or inconsequential disobedience.

This is the central dilemma of rule-following. Following a rule because it is a rule is what is meant by attributing practical authority to the rule. But if practical authority is impossible, claims of practical authority will be false, and hence rules *qua* rules will be undermined, which by hypothesis is morally nonoptimal. So it appears, paradoxically, that it is morally optimal to make claims on behalf of rules that one might know to be false. And what goes for rules generally applies equally to the entrenched rules of constitutional law.

Let us now look more closely at various aspects of this "just so" story of adopting a constitution. First, the story assumes distinctions between, on the one hand, the constitution and the metaconstitutional rules and, on the other hand, the constitution and ordinary law. But how are these distinctions to be drawn?

Take the distinction between the constitution and the metaconstitution. Recall that at step 2, we accepted a particular set of rules for making and changing valid laws (settlements of what we, as a society, should do), along with rules regarding how that first set of rules may be amended, how it should be interpreted, by whom, and with what degree of entrenchment if the interpretation is later thought to be wrong. Now suppose the rules for making and changing valid law (and perhaps the rules for amending these rules) are written, but the other rules (regarding the how, the who, and the effect of constitutional interpretation) are not. (This describes the United States Constitution on most understandings.) Are only the written rules "the constitution," with the unwritten rules being metaconstitutional or preconstitutional? All of these rules, written and unwritten, rest on acceptance. Moreover, the written rules could have been unwritten, and the unwritten rules could have been written.

Consider now the distinction between the constitution and ordinary law. Presumably, the constitution contains the rules governing how ordinary law is made and changed. But ordinary law may itself prescribe how other law is made and changed. (Consider legislation setting forth the rules governing the enactment and repeal of administrative regulations, or state legislation governing lawmaking by municipalities and counties.) Moreover, much of law consists of rules specifying how legal obligations can be created, modified, or expunged – the rules governing "private ordering." At which level in the hierarchy do the rules governing the making of other rules become "constitutional"?

One might be tempted to distinguish constitutions from ordinary law by subject matter. Constitutions, one might suppose, contain broad general rules establishing the basic procedures for governance and perhaps some individual rights and other limitations on governmental action. Ordinary laws, on the other hand, deal with more mundane matters or with temporary matters. But, of course, the preceding is not true of most existing constitutions as we understand them. The United States Constitution contains, in addition to the basic structural and empowering rules for the national government, and the magisterial rights in the Bill of Rights, several quite specific rules, many of which were responses to historical problems that have long since disappeared. And what is true of the United States Constitution is even more characteristic of other constitutions (Finer, Bognador, and Rudden 1995). The constitutions of France, Germany, and Russia, particularly the latter two, are chock-full of very specific rules addressing very limited problems or rooted in traditions and concerns that are closely bound to time and place. On the other hand, much ordinary law establishes basic structures (for example, the cabinet departments and administrative agencies) and basic individual rights (for example, those found in the 1964 Civil Rights Act and the 1965 Voting Rights Act in the USA).

What about "writtenness"? Does not the fact that constitutions are written distinguish them from metaconstitutional rules although not from ordinary statutory law? I would submit that "writtenness" is neither necessary nor sufficient for constitutions, nor does it distinguish them from metaconstitutional rules. The latter might all be memorialized in writing. What would then distinguish them from "the constitution" might be only the fact that the authority of the metaconstitutional rules rests directly on the fact of acceptance, whereas the "constitution's" authority would derive from the authority of the metaconstitutional rules and would rest on acceptance one step removed. One could dissent from the constitutional rules but accept them as authoritative, whereas that would not be possible with metaconstitutional rules. Of course, because the whole edifice rests on acceptance – and because acceptance of metaconstitutional rules is rational even if they are not ideal from anyone's perspective, but only ideal in the sense that they are the best rules that everyone can accept – the line between "the constitution" and "the metaconstitution" appears impossible to draw as a theoretical matter.

Perhaps then we should just say that when the authority of written rules rests on unwritten metaconstitutional rules, the written rules can be deemed "the constitution." Although "writtenness" would then distinguish constitutions from metaconstitutions, it would still not distinguish constitutions from other written laws.

Moreover, just as "writtenness" is not sufficient for identifying constitutions, neither is it necessary. Although it would be impractical in any society over a certain size, or in any legal system intended to last for many years, there is no logical impossibility in having all laws, including the constitution, be unwritten. Memorializing rules in writing is enormously useful, of course, because it averts controversies over just what rules were posited. It would be a mistake, however, to view "writtenness" as a necessary attribute of law or of constitutions.

Perhaps the most promising way of distinguishing constitutions from metaconstitutional rules and from ordinary law is by reference to degrees of entrenchment. One might argue that constitutions are rules that are more entrenched against change than ordinary laws. Thus, in the United States, the Constitution may be changed only by the supermajority requirements set forth in Article V – and the rule giving "equal suffrage" to the states in the Senate may not be changed at all – whereas ordinary legislation and its repeal is accomplished by majority votes in Congress.

The relative entrenchment story is, however, a more complicated one. Consider, first, that the existence of the Constitution of the United States itself depends on the public's acceptance now and from moment to moment of the authority of the document drafted in Philadelphia in 1787 and ratified according to the terms it set forth. That acceptance – the metaconstitution – is never entrenched, nor could it be. Even the most entrenched part of the Constitution – the "equal suffrage" rule – is authoritative only because it is accepted as such at any given time. (This point reflects the paradox of authoritative rules: we accept them as means of settling disagreements about what should be done; but because, to effect such settlements, they must be determinate and thus must diverge in a range of cases from what is morally optimal, we have reason to depart from what we have reason to accept, and these competing reasons cannot be weighed or balanced because they are aspects of the same reason and operate at different levels.)

In saying that even the most entrenched rules rest on moment-to-moment acceptance, I am not overlooking the possibility that at their inception, these rules were agreed to by the entire community. There are three points to make about such constitutional agreements. First, it is difficult to think of an existing constitutional regime that was founded on universal agreement. The Constitution of the United States surely was not. Not only were many of those subject to it disenfranchised, but also many of those who could vote on its ratification opposed it.

Second, for the same reason that a promise to commit a wrong is not morally binding, an agreement to be bound by a rule is not morally binding when the rule is later assessed to be morally iniquitous.

Third, however many founders agreed to the constitutional rules, and whatever force such an agreement might have for *their* being bound, the successor generations are not bound by virtue of an original agreement of the founders. The founders' rules are authoritative for successor generations only through the successors' acceptance of that authority. Of course, that does not mean that if they do not accept the rules, it is wrong for those who do accept them to impose those rules on the dissenters. See LEGAL AND MORAL OBLIGATION. Once the level of acceptance declines sufficiently, however, the rules will become ineffective in settling community disagreements over what to do, which means that those who accepted the rules will now themselves have no reason to do so. The community will need to coordinate around a new set of rules in order to settle controversies.

The point here is that even the most entrenched rule – a rule like the "equal suffrage" rule that cannot be amended – ultimately rests on acceptance of its entrenchment. On the other hand, even the least entrenched rule – say, one that can at any time be overturned by a majority – must be entrenched for some period of time for it to be effective as a rule. Consider a rule that can be reconsidered over and over at any time, and that is alternately enacted and repealed with retroactive effect again and again within a single day. Such a rule is, during its various enactments, too unentrenched to perform its function.

That example is, in terms of entrenchment, the polar opposite of the totally entrenched "equal suffrage" rule. But between the two are rules that are entrenched to varying degrees. For example, we typically distinguish the provisions in the United States Constitution that can be repealed only through the supermajoritarian processes of Article V from ordinary statutes passed by Congress, which can be repealed by subsequent ordinary statutes. The latter we deem to be ordinary law, whereas the former we deem to be constitutional law. And it is true that constitutional provisions are more entrenched than ordinary statutes. But notice that to enact or repeal a statute, the statute must receive a majority vote in the two houses of Congress and then be signed by the President. If the President refuses to sign, the statute or repeal requires a two-thirds vote of both houses. Surely, then, the status quo of "ordinary" law of the United States is entrenched a good deal more than it would be if laws were passed and repealed solely by majority vote in a unicameral legislature or in a plebiscite.

In addition to the two-house and presidential concurrence requirements of the United States Constitution, there are various additional rules in the United States and in other countries that entrench ordinary laws to varying degrees. There are usually numerous procedural rules about when and how issues may be raised that both entrench the status quo somewhat and avoid problems of cycling that Arrow's Theorem (Arrow 1951) would otherwise predict for simple majoritarianism and unentrenched rules. And as John McGinnis and Michael Rappaport illustrate in their exhaustive study of the topic, the United States Constitution has a number of rules that entrench ordinary laws against change, such as the two-thirds vote in the Senate required to approve a treaty or to convict a federal official in an impeachment trial (McGinnis and Rappaport 2002).

Thus, although constitutions might be distinguished by the degree to which their rules are entrenched, ordinary, nonconstitutional laws are always entrenched to some extent. And in constitutions such as that of the United States, many ordinary laws are highly entrenched due to the bicameralism and presidential concurrence requirements and to specific supermajority rules in the Constitution itself.

What Constitutions Do

If constitutions are laws that are more entrenched than ordinary laws – remembering that entrenchment is often a matter of degree, and that even the most entrenched laws ultimately rest on moment-to-moment acceptance – what functions do constitutions perform? Theoretically, a constitution could entrench a complete legal code, with no mechanisms for changing that code other than through constitutional amendment or revolution. In modern societies, however, such a static legal system would be highly dysfunctional. Therefore, realistically, at a minimum, constitutions entrench the rules governing the making and changing of ordinary (nonconstitutional) law. Those rules might do no more than establish a simple, unicameral parliamentary democracy. Even such a simple constitutional system would probably have rules regarding how the parliament is selected, who the eligible voters are, and so on, though it is possible that these rules might not be entrenched and could be altered by parliament itself in its ordinary lawmaking capacity. If the constitutional entrenchments are not absolute, then the constitution will normally contain entrenched rules about how the constitution can itself be altered.

Most constitutions go beyond entrenching a simple parliamentary democracy and procedures for constitutional amendment. They may entrench rules setting up more complex lawmaking procedures – for example, the bicameral and presidential concurrence requirements of the United States Constitution. They may entrench rules establishing executive and judicial departments and specifying their powers, procedures, and membership criteria. They may entrench federal systems of divided and limited lawmaking powers. And, of course, they may entrench certain rights held by individuals against the government or against other individuals.

Why entrench rules against repeal or amendment by current majorities? After all, no matter how wise and virtuous, constitutional founders know that they are fallible both morally and prudentially. What would motivate them to entrench rules that may well turn out to be suboptimal or even mischievous?

There are several reasons that might justify entrenchment. One is a reason that lies behind all attempts to guide behavior through posited, determinate rules, namely, settlement of controversies over what should be done. Such controversies produce moral and prudential costs in terms of decision-making time and expense, failure to coordinate decisions, and the inability to make optimal use of expertise. Determinate rules simplify decision making, make coordination possible, and, if posited by authorities selected for their expertise or their ability to utilize expertise, are more likely to be morally and prudentially optimal or near optimal than random decisions.

Determinate rules produce these settlement benefits to a greater extent the more they are entrenched against repeal. If such rules are subject to repeal at any moment upon a slight shift in majority sentiment, they are less reliable for coordination purposes, and more resources will be spent in attempting to repeal them (and fighting off such attempts). So although there is a danger in entrenching rules – the rules may be imprudent or iniquitous – there are settlement benefits derived from entrenchments.

Moreover, there are particular classes of rules that founders might think are particularly apt for entrenchment. Some rule entrenchments protect against predictable legislative shortsightedness. For example, the "contracts clause" of the United States Constitution in Article I, section 10, which forbids the states from impairing the obligations of contracts, was entrenched because in economic downturns, debtors, who greatly outnumber creditors, find it in their interest to have legislatures pass laws relieving them of their debts. Such laws benefit the current debtors, but because they make extension of credit risky, they raise the interest rates future debtors must pay and are ultimately economically disastrous. Legislative majorities cannot be counted on to protect future generations of debtors, who, of course, cannot currently vote.

The scenario that lies behind the contracts clause is a typical example of the type that is of interest to public choice theorists regarding when legislative majorities will predictably be untrustworthy and where an entrenched rule will be of benefit. Other examples in this vein are entrenched rules that are, in John Ely's words, "representation-reinforcing" (Ely 1980). Thus, rules that define who is eligible to vote for the legislature might be entrenched so that a momentary majority cannot freeze out those who favor the opposition by disenfranchising them. Similarly, rules that guarantee free speech might be entrenched to prevent momentary majorities from silencing their critics.

Another class of rules that might seem quite appropriate for entrenchment are those Adrian Vermeule calls "veil of ignorance rules," "eligibility rules," and "recusal rules," all of which find expression in provisions of the United States Constitution (Vermeule 2001). Veil of ignorance rules are rules, such as those requiring that laws be general and prospective, that prevent the predictable legislative abuses that occur when legislators are aware of the particular people whom their laws benefit and burden. Eligibility rules and recusal rules prevent predictable conflicts of interest from occurring. All of these types of rules are entrenched, when they are, because the dangers that self-interest will impair governmental judgment outweigh whatever dangers attend entrenchment itself.

Of course, the rules whose entrenchments in constitutions are often most controversial are those establishing certain rights. One source of controversy is over whether such constitutional rights should be restricted to rights against government action – rights ensuring that government not infringe various liberties, that government not take or excessively regulate property, or that government not discriminate along various axes, such as on the basis of race, sex, religion, or nationality – or whether constitutional rights should include claim rights *to* certain governmental actions, such as rights to employment or to a certain level of income, health care, and the like, or should include rights against private parties and institutions in addition to rights against the government. See THEORIES OF RIGHTS. Negative rights protecting liberty and property have the advantage of being easier to enforce judicially than affirmative claim rights to employment, health care, and income, particularly because they are frequently viewed as less sensitive to context, though this does not in itself make the latter unsuitable for constitutional entrenchment (Sunstein 2001). The prelegal (moral) existence of negative rights is also less controversial than the existence of affirmative ones.

The more important controversy regarding the constitutionalization of rights is whether there is sufficient justification for entrenching rights against democratic revision. On one view, rights are particularly apt for constitutional entrenchment because they represent limits on what majorities are entitled to do, and because majorities cannot be trusted to uphold rights when rights thwart their ambitions. On the opposing view, rights should be left to majority determination because the content of rights is frequently controversial, and no past determination of that content should constrain the current majority's view of it. This controversy is more fully elaborated and evaluated in the final section.

Are Constitutions Desirable?

Constitutions entrench rules so that they cannot be overturned by mere legislative majorities. For that reason, constitutionalism and judicial review – the practice giving courts the authority to overturn majoritarian decisions found by them to be inconsistent with constitutionally entrenched rules – have been attacked as antidemocratic and therefore morally illegitimate. Is such an attack warranted?

At the outset it will be useful to distinguish between attacking constitutionally entrenched rules because they cannot be *overturned* by current majorities, and attacking those rules because they are *interpreted* by nondemocratic bodies. The former attack is on the very idea of constitutional entrenchment. The latter is on the practice of judicial review. One can have a constitution of entrenched rules but leave the interpretation of those rules to democratic decision making, and many countries do just that.

Nonetheless, the two attacks are closely related in this sense. If the constitutional rules are quite determinate, so that a democratic majority will likely interpret them no differently from how a court would, that majority is still being bound by a decision made, not by the current majority, but by the constitutional founders. Judicial review does not change matters. The "despotism" is that of the founders. On the other hand, if the constitutional rules are indeterminate standards, judicial review essentially becomes rule by the courts or judicial despotism. Only the combination of an indeterminate set of constitutional standards "interpreted" by current majorities leaves those current majorities untethered. In other words, only if we are free to decide what to do based entirely on what the current majority deems best have we satisfied the pure democrat. Determinate constitutional rules legislatively interpreted are no less antidemocratic than indeterminate rules judicially interpreted.

Jeremy Waldron is well known for his defense of the supremacy of decisions made by democratic legislatures over the enforcement of written constitutional guarantees by judges (Waldron

1999, 1998). In other words, Waldron is firmly on the side of majoritarian decision making and against judicial review. See LEGISLATION. Because we live in what Waldron calls "the circumstances of politics" – we each hold different judgments regarding what we as a group ought to do, and what we as a group ought to allow individuals to do; and we each prefer that we adopt a single policy on these matters, even if it is not the one we favor, than that we each act on our own but differing judgments about what ought to be done – therefore, argues Waldron, we need a mechanism for collectively deciding upon such a single policy, and democratic legislation is the morally superior of the possible mechanisms. Moreover, for Waldron, a bill of rights, judicially enforced, that is supposed to trump any democratically made decisions inconsistent with it, is a morally inferior mechanism to democratic decision making, even with respect to protecting individual rights. For if we disagree, as we do and will, about what those rights are, how they are to be elaborated, and what weight they possess vis-à-vis other values, then we will need to reach a decision about these contested matters. And democratic decision making is morally superior to nondemocratic judicial review when the contested matters are individual rights and their contours, just as it is with respect to other policy disputes. In other words, the circumstances of politics apply to questions of individual rights as much as to other issues, and democratic decision making is morally mandated for all contested matters.

That is Waldron's position painted with a very broad brush. But the argument from the circumstances of politics to the moral superiority of democratic-majoritarian decision making is, I find, elusive. I shall examine what I believe are the three possible arguments that Waldron might make. In the end, I conclude that none of the three can get Waldron what he wants, namely, a knockdown moral case against constitutionalism and judicial review.

What are the three arguments that might be advanced to support the moral superiority of democratic decision making over constitutionalism with judicial review? One argument is epistemic. The decisions enacted by democratic majorities might be more likely morally correct than those enforced by judges in the name of rights endorsed at some point in the past. Present democratic majorities might be better informed than past majorities and their judicial agents, both because they can draw upon the wisdom of both the past and the present, and because they are better able to assess the interests of all who will be affected by their decisions. And, pace Condorcet, whom Waldron cites on this point, the more who support a decision as the morally correct one, the more likely the decision is to be correct, at least given the assumption that individuals are each more likely to decide correctly than incorrectly.

The epistemic argument for the superiority of democratic decision making over constitutionalism with judicial review is not rejectable on analytic grounds, but it is hostage to the facts. And the facts about democratic decision making do not establish its epistemic superiority across the board on those issues within its purview. Majorities are better informed on some moral matters than on others. They are more likely to deliberate thoughtfully on some matters than on others. The same goes for constitutional framers and for judges. The proof of the pudding here is whether unconstrained majoritarianism produces morally better legislation than the impure majoritarianism of, say, the American legal system, with its mix of bicameralism, executive veto, federalism, and, of course, constitutional rights, the constitutional amendment procedure, and judicial review. Conceivably, unconstrained majoritarianism might be epistemically superior at some times and places. But I doubt that it can be shown to be for all times and places. In the end, with respect to the epistemic argument, I conclude that even though the more people who oppose me on some moral issue, the more I should be aware of my own fallibility, in the end, numbers do not guarantee moral correctness, and those who swim against the moral current are not always wrong to do so. Although Waldron does not dispute it, I believe that this point ultimately undermines any epistemic argument for democracy. For the same epistemic reasons we exclude infants, the insane, and perhaps felons from the franchise, we might also establish bicameralism, the veto, and judicially enforced constitutional rights. We know we are subject to political weakness of will and other forms of cognitive and moral distortion.

And particularly if the constitutionally entrenched rules were adopted by a supermajority after full deliberation, we may have more confidence in the decisions of long-dead constitutional founders than in present-day bare majorities.

The second argument in favor of democratic decision making is a straightforward moral one. Where A believe morality dictates policy X, and B and C believe it dictates policy Y, B and C have a moral right to have policy Y prevail *even if* (from the God's-eye point of view) *policy X is morally correct and policy Y is morally flawed.* Assuming both X and Y affect the lives of those who oppose them, the moral right of B and C to have incorrect policy Y prevail is then a moral right to commit moral wrongs against others. The right to democratic decision making is, on this argument, a right to do wrong.

Now I believe there indeed are some rights to act immorally. See PRIVACY. But this argument goes far beyond that limited set of rights and applies to all moral wrongs so long as the democratic majority votes to permit or compel them. But such a right to do wrong is untenable.

To see this, imagine that for A, the circumstances of politics do not exist because A can enforce his will against B and C. (He is endowed with superior strength and technology.) And suppose A believes – we shall assume correctly – that what B and C propose is profoundly unjust. On the argument under consideration, A must let B and C have their way, despite the fact that what they propose is morally wrong and that A can prevent the immoral outcome. But such a moral must is quite implausible. Numbers do not, any more than might, make right.

Consider as an illustration a variation of the situation described in Walter Van Tilburg's *The Ox Bow Incident* (Van Tilburg 1940). A large posse has captured some suspected killers and cattle rustlers. Most of the posse wants, on moral grounds, to hang them on the spot rather than turn them over to the lawful authorities and lawful processes. A few on the posse dissent, however, and argue vigorously for the latter course. After lengthy discussion, the posse votes, and immediate hanging wins by a large margin. The dissenters, however, appalled at the decision, discuss whether they should employ the element of surprise, pull their guns on the majority, and force

it to hand over the suspects to the dissenters, who would see that the suspects received full due process. Waldron can be read as arguing that the dissenters would be acting morally wrongly in following their own rather than the majority's moral view of the matter.

Nor does the notion of "respect" morally dictate that A accede to B and C's immoral proposal. A's moral theory may hold that B and C must be respected as persons, or some such thing; but it would be a strange moral theory that contains a notion of respect that made the moral theory "self-effacing" (Alexander and Kress 1997).

Waldron sometimes appears to be making a moral argument on behalf of democratic decision making. But if suspension of the circumstances of politics does not leave A with a moral obligation to accede to the immoral B and C, it is difficult to see how placing A in the circumstances of politics creates a moral obligation to do so. The circumstances of politics do bear on what A is morally obligated to do, as I shall show. But they do not do so in the way this argument claims.

Waldron does not deal at length with control of the franchise. But such control affects the moral argument for democratic decision making. Suppose B, C, and D vote to exclude E from the franchise. (E is uneducated, and B, C, and D enact a franchise restriction excluding the uneducated.) A believes – correctly, we shall assume – that such an exclusion is unjust, and votes against the exclusion, along with E. Because the two of them are outvoted, E is excluded. Now B, C, and D vote for another measure (X) that A believes – again, correctly – is unjust. Is A bound by such an unjust measure passed by a democratic majority that has unjustly excluded some from the franchise? If unjust measures are morally obligating if democratically enacted, does that apply to democratically enacted limitations of the franchise (Christiano 2000)? (Remember, E did vote on his own exclusion; he just lost.) Again, it is difficult to see how one can distinguish the two types of unjust but democratically enacted measures. But it is also difficult to believe that democratically enacted but unjust measures are morally obligatory when the democratic franchise has been unjustly restricted.

Waldron also does not discuss Arrovian problems in defining the output of democratic majorities. Those problems are usually avoided by various rules controlling the agenda or privileging the *status quo ante*, rules that violate Arrovian conditions. With those rules, we do not have pure majoritarianism; without them, we would have trouble, because of cycling and so on, identifying the relevant democratically endorsed positions.

The third argument Waldron might make against constitutional entrenchment *does* take the circumstances of politics seriously. It is described near the beginning of the first section and is what I shall call a strategic moral argument. Suppose that A believes that moral theory T is correct. Were A all-powerful, A would impose T, even over the objection of everyone else. But A is not all-powerful.

The question then is what is the moral imperative that A faces given the circumstances of politics? More particularly, is that moral imperative to opt for majoritarian decision making? I believe that the answer goes something like this. A wants an outcome that is as close as he can get to the outcome dictated by correct moral theory T. He therefore wants that system of government that is (1) most likely to produce results closest to what T dictates and (2) most likely to be agreed upon by a sufficient number of people to eliminate the circumstances-of-politics problem. If either A and B or A and C are sufficiently powerful to impose their will, and B's moral views are closer to T than C's, A will join with B in whatever form of government they can agree to. Moreover, if C morally prefers the likely outcomes of the A-B system to anarchy, C will have a moral reason to accept the authority of that system. The system might turn out to be majoritarian democracy, *but it might turn out to be something else*. What each of us has a moral reason to accept is that form of government that is most likely to get it right from our point of view among those forms that we can get enough others to accept. Because the moral costs of anarchy are usually assessed to be quite high from most people's moral standpoints, many

governmental arrangements would be accepted over anarchy. Majoritarian democracy may be one of them. But so might constitutionalism and judicial review.

References

Alexander, L. A. 1998. Introduction. In L. A. Alexander (ed.), *Constitutionalism: Philosophical Foundations*. Cambridge, UK: Cambridge University Press, 1–15.

Alexander, L. A. and Kress, K. 1997. Replies to our critics. *Iowa Law Review*, 82: 923–41.

Alexander, L. and Sherwin, E. 2001. *The Rule of Rules*. Durham, NC: Duke University Press.

Arrow, K. 1951. *Social Choice and Individual Values*. New York: Wiley.

Christiano, T. 2000. Waldron on law and disagreement. *Law and Philosophy* 19: 513–43.

Ely, J. H. 1980. *Democracy and Distrust*. Cambridge, MA: Harvard University Press.

Finer, S. E., Bognador, V., and Rudden, B. 1995. *Comparing Constitutions*. Oxford: Clarendon Press.

Grey, T. C. 1979. Constitutionalism: An analytic framework. In J. R. Pennock and J. W. Chapman (eds.), *Constitutionalism*. New York: New York University Press, 189–209.

Kay, R. S. 1998. American constitutionalism. In L. A. Alexander (ed.), *Constitutionalism: Philosophical Foundations*. Cambridge, UK: Cambridge University Press, 16–63.

McGinnis, J. O. and Rappaport, M. B. 2002. Our supermajoritarian constitution. *Texas Law Review* 80: 703–806.

Sunstein, C. R. 2001. *Designing Democracy*. Oxford: Oxford University Press.

Van Tilburg, W. 1940. *The Ox Bow Incident*. New York: Random House.

Vermeule, A. 2001. Veil of ignorance rules in constitutional law. *Yale Law Journal* 111: 399–442.

Waldron, J. 1998. Precommitment and disagreement. In L. A. Alexander (ed.), *Constitutionalism: Philosophical Foundations*. Cambridge, UK: Cambridge University Press, 271–99.

Waldron, J. 1999. *Law and Disagreement*. Oxford: Clarendon Press.

Chapter 18

Adjudication and Legal Reasoning

Richard Warner

Legal reasoning is a special case of practical reasoning. Practical reasoning is reasoning about what one ought to do; legal reasoning is reasoning about what one ought to do given applicable legal rules. The distinctive feature of legal reasoning is precisely the role of "legal rules," where we understand "legal rules" very broadly to include statutes, common law doctrines, precedents, principles, and practices. An example illustrates the distinctive role of legal rules. On his deathbed, Franz Kafka wrested from his friend and literary executor, Max Brod, a promise to burn all of Kafka's manuscripts. Brod broke the promise – not only preserving the manuscripts, but publishing them – on the very plausible ground that the good achieved outweighed the promissory obligation. Now imagine Kafka's will directed Brod, as executor, to burn the manuscripts (it in fact contained no such provision). The will subjects Brod to a legal obligation to burn the manuscripts, so imagine that he goes to court to request that the "manuscript burning" provision be set aside. In court, it is not sufficient for Brod simply to appeal to the good achieved; he must also cite some legal rule that makes the good achieved a relevant ground for a legal decision.

Why do we insist that courts base their decisions on legal rules? And what is it to "base" a decision on legal rules? We begin by presenting a view – the Received View – that answers these questions. The view focuses exclusively on adjudication, on, that is, dispute resolution by judicial decision makers. Legal reasoning includes much more, of course. Legislators engage in such

reasoning when framing statutes, as do lawyers advising clients, business professionals trying to operate within the framework of the law, and the owners of Internet file-sharing networks claiming that the practice does not violate copyright law. Adjudication nonetheless merits close attention in its own right, and what we say about it generalizes to other forms of legal reasoning. The Received View sees adjudication as resting extensively, but not necessarily exclusively, on relativistic moral convictions. The convictions are relativistic in the sense that, insofar as they are true, they are true *only for this or that community or group*; they are not true *simpliciter*. On the Received View, the central practical and theoretical problem is justifying the imposition of judicial decisions on groups or communities that do not share the moral claims on which they ultimately rest. The Received View solves this problem in a way that reveals important aspects of the role of courts in modern democracies. This ultimate goal of this chapter is to delineate the key features of this role.

The Demands of Political Legitimacy

We present the Received View as arising out of criticism of another view, which we label the Mistaken View. This is an expositorily convenient fiction. We set aside the complex and interesting question of the Received View's historical antecedents. It bears emphasis that the following exposition of the Received View does not appear in the works of any of its adherents; the exposition is nonetheless consistent with the spirit and intent of the view's proponents.

Nonrepresentative decision makers

The Mistaken View arises out of a misconception of the role courts must play to qualify as legitimate decision makers in a democratic form of government. A brief consideration of the notion of legitimacy provides the necessary background. Three points are in order.

1 *The general concept of legitimacy.* A state is legitimate when (and only when) its citizens have a *prima facie* obligation to obey it. See LEGAL AND MORAL OBLIGATION. The idea is that the state may properly compel conformity only when those citizens who recognized and lived up to their obligations would voluntarily obey in the absence of state coercion (assuming that no other obligation outweighed the *prima facie* obligation to obey). Freedom is the rationale. The closer a state approximates the requirement of legitimacy, the less it intrudes on its citizens' freedom by compelling compliance that would not occur voluntarily. Legitimacy is an ideal to which actual states only approximate. States routinely attempt to compel conformity to their demands even when citizens would not otherwise voluntarily obey. In such cases, citizens may obey, but they do so for the prudential reason of avoiding coercion (or social censure from those who would disapprove of their behavior).
2 *Legitimacy and representative democracy.* It is a mainstay of democratic theory that citizens have a *prima facie* obligation to obey the state only when the state is appropriately responsive to its citizens' will. Appropriate responsiveness requires that citizens exercise personal sovereignty by electing decision makers who represent the views and preferences of their electorate. The claim (which we take for granted here) is that appropriately representative decision makers may legitimately impose obligations on those who elected them. (See LEGISLATION)

3 *The judiciary as nonrepresentative.* The second point would appear to have an immediate consequence for the judiciary, for the judiciary is *not* representative. It consists of *impartial* decision makers, where impartiality requires *not* improperly favoring the views and preferences of any distinct group. Even when judges are elected, they are not supposed to represent the preferences of their electorate in the way required of legislators. It would seem to follow that judicial decision makers may *only* impose obligations that have been encoded in laws through prior representative political processes. In Ronald Dworkin's words: "Law insists that force not be used or withheld, no matter how useful that would be to ends in view, except as licensed or required by individual rights and responsibilities flowing from past political decisions about when collective force is justified" (Dworkin 1986: 193). In short, legitimacy seems to require that courts confine themselves to imposing obligations originally ordained by representative decision makers. This "confinement claim" is the heart of the Mistaken View.

The mistaken view

To formulate the Mistaken View more fully, it is helpful to introduce the notion of *authoritative legal materials*. These materials include statutes and all (nonoverturned) decisions applying them, constitutional provisions and all (nonoverturned) decisions applying them, and all (nonoverturned) decisions and holdings generated by the common law (as it evolves within the institutional constraints to which the judiciary is subject; assume that these constraints ensure that the obligations evolve in a way that qualifies as representatively imposed). There is no need here for a precise definition; the examples are sufficient. Authoritative legal materials so conceived encode obligations ordained by representative decision makers. The Mistaken View is that legitimacy requires that courts decide *solely* on the basis of authoritative legal materials (plus, of course, the relevant facts, where "facts" include the various theories and assumptions to which courts help themselves; we suppress this qualification). The Mistaken View is mistaken because courts cannot decide cases solely on the basis of authoritative legal materials. They also appeal to moral principles.

An example illustrates the point. In *United States v. Escamilla* (1972), Escamilla killed Bernie Lightsey, his coworker at a research station located on T–3, a floating island of ice in the Arctic Ocean. The trial court held that Escamilla was criminally negligent in killing Lightsey and convicted him of involuntary manslaughter. The events that led to Lightsey's killing began with Lightsey's friend, David Leavitt. Leavitt, nicknamed Porky, habitually drank excessively and became violent as a result. Porky had a history of attacking others, including Escamilla, with butcher cleavers in attempts to get alcohol. On the day of the killing, Escamilla's roommate telephoned him at the research facility to urge him to return to help control Porky, who was drunk and had taken wine from their living quarters. On his way, Escamilla took a rifle from the common storage of firearms. The rifle was defective and would fire even if one did not pull the trigger. Escamilla was unaware of, and had no reason to be aware of, the defect. When Escamilla was in his living quarters Lightsey entered. Lightsey and Porky had been drinking 140 proof grain alcohol cut with grape juice, and Lightsey was very drunk. An argument ensued over whether Lightsey and Porky should have some of Escamilla's wine. Waving the rifle back and forth, Escamilla ordered Lightsey to leave. The rifle accidentally discharged; Lightsey was wounded and subsequently died.

Was Escamilla criminally negligent? Here is the relevant legal rule from the *Model Penal Code*, §2.02(2)(d):

A person acts [criminally] negligently when he should be aware of a substantial and unjustifiable risk that . . . will result from his conduct. The risk must be of such a nature and degree that the actor's failure to perceive it, considering the nature and purpose of his conduct and the circumstances known to him, involves a gross deviation from the standard of care that a reasonable person would observe in the actor's situation.

This does not tell us how to decide *Escamilla*. The rule tells us that criminal negligence involves a "gross deviation." Did Escamilla's behavior involve such a deviation? This is just to ask: was his behavior negligent enough to be a crime? And this is where we started. The rule does not provide a noncircular definition of criminal negligence. So how does one determine if Escamilla's behavior was sufficiently negligent? What are the relevant considerations?

The trial court and appeals court disagreed on the relevant considerations, or at least on the weight they should be assigned. The appeals court overturned the trial court's conviction of Escamilla for manslaughter on the ground that

[i]t would seem plain that what is negligent or grossly negligent conduct in the Eastern District of Virginia may not be negligent or grossly negligent on T-3 when it is remembered that T-3 has no governing authority, no police force, is relatively inaccessible from the rest of the world, lacks medical facilities and the dwellings thereon lack locks – in short, that absent self-restraint on the part of those stationed on T-3 and effectiveness of the group leader, T-3 is a place where no recognized means of law enforcement exist and each man looks to himself for the immediate enforcement of his rights.

Why do these differences matter?

The answer is that they matter to balancing a variety of competing moral concerns. To see the concerns involved, consider that it is far from obvious that Escamilla acted unreasonably. He had reason to think Porky – and Lightsey as well – might attack him with deadly force, and his intention in arming himself was presumably to deter an attack through a display of superior force; and, if necessary, to meet force with force. However, he could also have avoided an attack by simply giving up the wine, and some may think this the more reasonable course. However, law enforcement did not exist on T-3; consequently, if Escamilla were to surrender his property to avoid a confrontation, he would be unable to enlist law enforcement to recover his property or to extract compensation for it. Moreover, if unopposed, Porky's drunken demands might easily have grown more frequent, insistent, and irrational, and neither the law nor morality requires us to live at the mercy of the tyrannical whims of others, at least not when those whims subject us to genuine danger. But, even if it was reasonable for Escamilla to arm himself, was it also reasonable to point a loaded rifle with a released safety at Lightsey? Would a reasonable person have kept the safety on? Or perhaps even have unloaded the rifle, or at least not pointed it at another human being? Pointing the rifle at Lightsey made the threat to use it more credible and contributed more effectively to deterring attacks through a show of superior force; releasing the safety on the loaded rifle ensured that deadly force was immediately available to repel an attack that used deadly force. Was the threat sufficiently great that it was reasonable to proceed in this way?

This particular set of questions is unique to *Escamilla*, but the sort of balancing inquiry the questions illustrate is typical of self-defense cases. The pattern of decisions in those cases reveals the balancing principles the courts use. The pattern consists of a series of judgments of relevant similarity and dissimilarity to paradigm cases of self-defense. The underlying balancing principles which explain this pattern are moral principles (in the broad sense of "moral" in which a principle qualifies as moral provided it is a principle about what one ought or ought not to do). The principles are often – indeed, typically – complex, multidimensional structures incorporating a variety of evaluative strategies. As any first-year law student will testify, the principles can be frustratingly difficult to articulate explicitly and fully.

What is typical of self-defense cases is typical in general. Courts do not decide disputes solely on the basis of authoritative legal materials. They also appeal to moral principles. This conclusion is not controversial. While it arguably had adherents in the past, the Mistaken View has no serious advocates now. Consequently, if we cling to the view that legitimacy requires that courts operate entirely within the confines of authoritative legal materials, we must conclude that judicial decisions lack legitimacy. This conclusion is unpalatable. No state of any complexity can function adequately without a dispute resolution process backed by the state's enforcement powers. In short: states require courts. If theory compels us

to regard this essential function as falling short of the demands of legitimacy, that is a reason to look for an alternative theory. Given that the state and its courts are a necessity, it would be agreeable to be able to see them as legitimate.

If we wish to do so, we have only one option: hold that courts may legitimately appeal to moral principles. There are two ways to do this. The first preserves a key feature of the Mistaken View. The heart of the Mistaken View is the "confinement claim": courts must confine themselves solely to authoritative legal materials. The first approach broadens the confinement claim. It holds that the sole legitimate basis for judicial decisions is a combination of authoritative legal materials *and* a determinate, specifiable set of moral principles. The second option abandons any confinement claim. It concedes that it is impossible to specify a determinate set of relevant moral principles. The second option is the Received View. We motivate it by showing that the first option is untenable.

Dworkin (1986) offers a persuasive development of the first option. He asks us to imagine surveying the moral principles of a community and ranking various sets of those moral principles in terms of how well they justify the authoritative legal materials – most of those materials, that is. Some materials can be discarded as mistaken, but the principles one picks must fit with most. Dworkin assumes that the above process leads to *one and only one* best justification. Thus, the authoritative legal materials *uniquely determine* the set of moral principles that provide the best justification of those materials. Dworkin holds that legitimacy requires that court decisions be in principle justifiable solely on the basis of the (nondiscarded) authoritative legal materials *and* the moral principles that provide the best justification for those materials. The rationale for this requirement is Dworkin's conviction, which he shares with the Mistaken View, that judicial legitimacy requires that judicial decisions be based solely on past representative political decisions. Dworkin's point is that courts meet this requirement when they decide on the basis of authoritative legal materials *and* the moral principles that provide the best justification for those materials. They do so because the authoritative legal materials *uniquely* determine the set of moral principles.

Consequently, when courts decide on the combined basis of that set of moral principles and the authoritative legal materials, they impose obligations originally established by representative decision makers via the promulgation of authoritative legal materials.

Dworkin's approach faces insuperable problems. First, it is *extremely* unlikely that the collection of authoritative legal materials uniquely determines the set of moral principles that provides the best justification for those materials. The authoritative legal materials do not comprise a consistent set of rules. The common law on self-defense illustrates the point. Under the common law, it is a complete defense to a charge of murder that: (1) one reasonably believed that it was necessary to use force to repel a danger that was (or was reasonably believed to be) immediate; (2) the danger was (or was reasonably believed to be) unlawful; and (3) the force used was proportionate to the danger. Some courts add the requirement that one did not have (or reasonably believed one did not have) a sufficiently safe possibility of retreat. The difference is considerable. Imagine a mugger threatens Victoria with a knife. She kills him in a situation in which (1)–(3) are fulfilled. She could have safely retreated when he was still a few feet away, but she did not consider that option. Attitudes inculcated through years of self-defense classes took hold, and, confident that she could repel the attacker, she stood her ground. In courts that do not have a retreat requirement, Victoria has a valid self-defense claim. In "retreat" courts, her defense is more dubious. The question becomes whether the danger of retreat was sufficiently small that she should have risked it to avoid serious injury to the attacker. No such question arises in "no retreat" courts.

"Retreat" courts place greater moral weight on avoiding injury to attackers than "no retreat" courts, and the differing moral judgments lead to inconsistent legal rules. This is typical. Legal rules are the product of legislators and judges fashioning laws and decisions in light of various moral perspectives and social goals. Different perspectives and goals lead to different and conflicting rules. It would be astonishing if a set of competing and inconsistent authoritative legal materials uniquely determined the set of – consistent – moral principles that provided the best justification for those materials. Some may object that there is no real problem here. After all, the difference between "retreat" and "no retreat" courts is a difference between courts in *different jurisdictions*. As long as there are no inconsistencies within jurisdictions, inconsistency is not a barrier to constructing a unique best justification for the authoritative materials used in a given jurisdiction. In fact, however, it is crystal clear that inconsistencies occur within jurisdictions. (See Llewellyn 1931, 1950; Dewey 1924; see also AMERICAN LEGAL REALISM.)

The second objection assumes, for the sake of argument, that it is possible to find a set of moral principles that best justifies the authoritative legal materials. The objection to this is: if we can find one such set, why can we not find two or more? Why think there must be *just one* set that provides *the* best justification for the authoritative legal materials? Just as there can be two or more best performances on an examination, why can there not be two or more best justifications of the authoritative legal materials? Dworkin provides no reason to think that such ties are impossible. The existence of ties undermines Dworkin's treatment of legitimacy. That treatment rests on the claim that, when courts decide on the combined basis of that set of moral principles and the authoritative legal materials, they impose obligations originally ordained by representative decision makers via the promulgation of authoritative legal materials. This claim in turn rests on the claim that the authoritative legal materials *uniquely* determine *the* best justification for those materials, and this claim is false if different sets of moral principles can be tied as best justifications for the authoritative legal materials.

The third objection grants that *the unique* best justification (UBJ) exists. The objection is that the UBJ is simply irrelevant to assessing the legitimacy of judicial decisions. The reason lies in the fact that, as Dworkin grants, no one has, or ever will, even come close to formulating the UBJ. The task is enormous. We must survey the authoritative legal materials. That is, we must survey all statutes and all decisions applying them, all constitutional provisions and all decisions applying them, and all decisions and holdings generated by the common law. We must then identify the moral principles prevailing in the community and determine which combination of those principles best justifies the authoritative legal materials. The task (if possible at all) is the task of a lifetime, or – more accurately – of lifetime*s*. This means the UBJ is irrelevant to assessing the legitimacy of judicial decisions. To see why, imagine two exactly similar self-defense cases – one in a "retreat" court, the other in a "no retreat" court. The former disallows the self-defense claim that the latter countenances. Which decision is consistent with the requirements of legitimacy? For Dworkin, the answer is, "The decision that can in principle be justified solely on the basis of the authoritative legal materials and the moral principles identified in the UBJ." But we will never know which moral principles these are since no one will ever even come close to formulating the UBJ. We cannot therefore use the UBJ as a standard against which to assess the legitimacy of judicial decisions. To have a useable criterion of legitimacy, we must use some other independent standard. But if we have another independent standard, then the UBJ is irrelevant.

The conclusion to draw from the failure of Dworkin's approach is that one cannot *precisely delimit* the moral principles that courts may legitimately use in reaching legal decisions. The inadequacies of Dworkin's view do not show that is impossible to do so, but they do suggest that it is highly unlikely. If authoritative legal materials fail to uniquely determine the relevant set of principles, what else will?

The Received View

The Received View provides an alternative to Dworkin's failed approach. The Received View consists of four claims. First, courts employ both authoritative legal materials and moral principles in arriving at their conclusions. Second, the authoritative legal materials do not uniquely determine the moral principles used. Third, despite this lack of unique determination, judicial decision makers do *not* have a completely free hand in choosing moral principles. Their choices are highly constrained by a variety of factors. Fourth, legal decisions comply with requirements of legit-

imacy when appropriately constrained decision makers reach decisions based on authoritative legal materials and selected moral principles.

Much of the discussion of the Received View has focused on the third claim, on just what the relevant constraints are. Discussions of the third claim may be factual or normative. The factual inquiry asks why moral principles in fact constrain courts. The normative inquiry asks what principles should do so. Both inquires have generated controversy. On the factual side, some (e.g., Singer 1984) contend that judicial decisions are so unconstrained that they lack legitimacy; they are instead a self-serving exercise of power by the ruling elite. Others (e.g., Cardozo 1985, Burton 1992) see decisions as sufficiently constrained so as to achieve legitimacy. On the normative side, theorists – and judges – differ about what the constraints should be. (Wright 1999, for example, argues for a Kantian conception while Wells 1992 urges a pragmatist approach.) These controversies are important, but we may put them aside here. Our concern is with the claim that adequately constrained decisions comply with the requirements of legitimacy. Investigating this aspect of the Received View brings to the fore important aspects of courts in modern democracies.

Legitimacy issues arise for the Received View because, on that view, courts frequently decide open questions, questions not previously answered by any legislator or any other representative body. For example, prior to *Escamilla*, it was certainly an open and undecided question whether it was criminally negligent to kill someone in the precise circumstances in which Escamilla killed Lightsey. If we assume that such open questions can only be legitimately decided by appropriately representative decision makers, then judicial decisions by *nonrepresentative* judges must lack legitimacy. To avoid this conclusion, we must offer some ground for legitimacy other than representativeness.

It is not difficult to do so. We can regard judicial decisions as legitimate provided the courts issuing these decisions do so under constraints that ensure that they do not decide open questions any more than "necessary" (in a sense addressed below). The rationale for this claim is threefold. First, the point with which we began:

representative decision makers may legitimately impose obligations on their electorate. Second, as also emphasized earlier, the state cannot adequately function without courts, without, that is, nonrepresentative decision makers who interpret and apply obligations initially decreed by representative decision makers. Third, if you have voluntarily embraced the end of living under a legitimate government, you can hardly object to complying with the necessary means of administering that government. Therefore: if the legal rules courts apply are the product of adequately representative processes, the court decisions must themselves comport with the requirements of legitimacy – provided they do not go beyond what is "necessary" to administer the state. Call this the "necessary means" conception of judicial legitimacy.

Theorists – and judges – differ on what qualifies as necessary. Consider, for example, the common situation in which applying authoritative legal materials as required by their meaning and the relevant precedents leads to injustice in the particular circumstances before the court. Depending on the exact situation, some theorists and judges will see the court as bound to apply the materials while some will think that equity demands the court decide as justice requires. The question of what counts as "necessary" is indeed just the question of what the constraints on judicial decisions should be. As noted earlier, this is a matter of considerable controversy.

To summarize, the Received View's treatment of legitimacy comes to this: courts inherit their legitimacy from the legitimacy of the authoritative legal materials they apply; adequately constrained judicial decisions are legitimate provided those materials are the product of adequately representative processes. Is this an acceptable account of the legitimacy of judicial decisions? The answer is "yes," but with a serious qualification. Seeing why the answer is positive but qualified highlights key features of the role of courts in modern democracies.

An example is helpful. Consider *Wisconsin v. Yoder* (1972). Wisconsin criminally prosecuted Amish parents for not complying with a statute requiring children to attend school until age 16. The parents had withdrawn their children from school after the eighth grade. What reason did the parents have to comply with the statute? They had a reason to comply in order to avoid the adverse consequences of noncompliance, but legitimacy requires more than such a prudential reason; it requires that they have a reason that would lead them to comply voluntarily in the absence of coercion. Given their beliefs, the parents would appear to have had just the opposite. The Amish place paramount importance on religious salvation, which they believe requires living in a religious community isolated from worldly influences. They see high school education as a seriously corrupting influence that alienates children from God. These beliefs gave the parents a compelling reason not to comply with the statute. Continued education threatened both their children's eternal salvation and the continued existence of the church community necessary for salvation. That community will shrink and ultimately vanish if enough children desert Amish beliefs.

In light of these facts, should the parents be compelled to send their children to school? When the case came before the United States Supreme Court, the majority held that the free exercise clause of the Constitution gave the parents the right to withdraw their children from school. The opposite holding would also have been consistent with all applicable authoritative legal materials and precedents, and there was a dissent by Justice Douglas arguing for that result. He would have ordered the parents to send to school children who wished to attend (actually, he would have remanded the case to the trial court to investigate the children's attitudes, but it serves our expository purposes to suppose he would have ordered attendance). Justice Douglas's goal was to protect the freedom and self-determination of the children. Would it have comported with the demands of legitimacy to order that the children continue to attend school? The answer is a qualified "yes," and seeing why shows why a qualified yes is also the answer to the general question of whether the Received View's "necessary means" conception of legitimacy provides an acceptable account of legitimacy.

For our purposes, assume that the Wisconsin statute was the product of an adequately representative process. The Amish might have contended that their self-imposed isolation from society ensured that their views were not suffi-ciently represented, but put this issue aside. We are concerned with situations in which citizens do (or at least should) perceive the laws to which they are subject as legitimate; our focus is on the issues that arise when nonrepresentative *judicial* decision makers appeal to moral principles to in-terpret and apply laws legitimately decreed by representative decision makers. To this end, im-agine the Amish did obey the decision that they must let their children continue in school. They obeyed voluntarily and would have done so even without the threat of coercion. They obeyed because they had voluntarily embraced the end of living under a legitimate government, and they realized that, as long as they remained committed to that end, they must, insofar as they were ra-tional, comply with the necessary means of ad-ministering that government. In this situation, the Justice Douglas hypothetical version of *Yoder* does comport with the demands of legitim-acy. The demand is that the Amish have a reason sufficient to secure their voluntary compliance with the decision, and that they do have. This is one of the central points of the "necessary means" conception of legitimacy: judicial deci-sions can be legitimate even when those adversely affected profoundly disagree with the moral prin-ciples on which those decisions rest.

Now let us turn to the qualification. The prob-lem is that there is a crucial ambiguity in our initial explication of legitimacy, which was that the legitimate state compels conformity only in those cases in which those citizens who recog-nized and lived up to their obligations would voluntarily comply in the absence of coercion. We can use the hypothetical Justice Douglas vari-ant of *Yoder* to illustrate the ambiguity. In that variant, the Amish comply because – and *only* be-cause – they recognize that courts are necessary to the functioning of the government under which they are committed to living. They have no reason independent of this "necessary means" reason sufficient for voluntarily compliance. By way of contrast, imagine – implausibly – that the Amish parents were so committed to fostering the inde-pendence and self-determination of their adoles-cent children that they saw that commitment as a decisive reason to send their children to school if the children so wished. These parents would have

two reasons to send their children to school – the "necessary means" reason, and the reason arising from their commitment to their children. For both sets of parents, compliance is voluntary, and in both cases it is legitimate to order the Amish to send their children to school. Nonethe-less, the difference between the two sets of parents matters.

We should regard the situation of the first parents as a *second-best* realization of legitimacy. To see why, recall that promoting individual free-dom is the point of insisting that the state be legitimate (there are nonlibertarian conceptions of legitimacy (see Finnis 1980: 270–9), but these conceptions are difficult to square with the para-mount importance of individual freedom). The state intrudes on freedom when it requires a person to act contrary to his or her moral beliefs. The more important the beliefs, the more serious the intrusion. Therefore, it is best for the state to compel compliance only in cases of the sort illus-trated by our second set of Amish parents, the parents committed to fostering independence and self-determination in their adolescent chil-dren. These parents comply voluntarily for a reason *entirely independent* of their commitment to living under a legitimate government. It is a second best when citizens' only reason for com-pliance is that commitment. It is best to avoid second-best legitimacy. Respect for freedom demands that we do so whenever possible.

Even so, some may not think that the second-best legitimacy of judicial decisions is a very wor-risome problem. It will not appear as a serious problem to those who think: first, that whatever is truly of value is of value at all times, in all circum-stances, for all groups, communities, and cul-tures; and, second, that people disagree about values only because they make mistakes in identi-fying universal values or in applying and interpret-ing universal values in particular circumstances. So, where the law and citizens disagree, one side is right (or both are wrong). Consider our hypo-thetical *Yoder* in this regard. If the state is wrong, second-best legitimacy is the best available. Even where the law is morally wrong, the parents' commitment to living under a legitimate govern-ment may – at least in the eyes of some theorists – still be sufficient to provide them with a reason that should secure their voluntary compliance.

From a practical point of view, the solution consists in effective mechanisms to repeal or revise the law; for, if it is morally right to order the Amish to send their children to school, there is no second-best legitimacy worry. The Amish have a reason – the fact that it is the morally right thing to do – to send their children to school, and that reason is entirely independent of their commitment to living under a legitimate government.

Viewed from the darkness that dominates the beginning of the twenty-first century, this unqualified commitment to universal values is untenable. Rationally unresolvable disagreement on fundamental moral matters is an obvious fact of contemporary life. John Rawls makes the point:

> Long historical experience suggests, and many plausible reflections confirm, that reasoned and uncoerced agreement are not to be expected …Our individual and associative points of view, intellectual affinities and affective attachments, are too diverse, especially in a free democratic society, to allow of lasting and reasoned agreement. Many conceptions of the world can plausibly be constructed from different standpoints. Diversity naturally arises from our limited powers and distinct perspectives; it is unrealistic to suppose that all our differences are rooted solely in ignorance and perversity, or else in the rivalries that result from scarcity. [The appropriate view of social organization] takes deep and unresolvable differences on matters of fundamental significance as a permanent condition of human life. (Rawls 1980: 534)

It bears emphasis that to agree with Rawls is *not* to endorse a complete (and indeed untenable) relativism about values. It is consistent to contend, for example, that it is a universally valid moral truth that all persons, simply by virtue of being persons, are owed a certain degree or kind of respect. What widespread, rationally unresolvable disagreement shows is that such universally valid moral truths as there may be do not provide a sufficient basis for many of the decisions we face. In *Escamilla*, for example, we have to decide whether Escamilla was negligent when he released the safety and pointed the loaded rifle at Lightsey. The decision rests on the interpretation and application of various moral views about what counts as reasonable self-defense, adequate re-

spect for the lives of others, and reasonable care in the use of firearms. There are multiple acceptable ways to balance the various factors and considerations involved, and ways of doing so vary from culture to culture.

Even granting a considerable degree of moral relativism, however, second-best legitimacy may still strike some as an infrequent and isolated issue. Raising the issue in the context of *Yoder* contributes to this impression. The Amish, after all, are a small, isolated religious community far removed from the mainstream of contemporary life. In fact, however, many of us in that mainstream often find ourselves in similar situations. Such situations arise whenever the law enjoins an individual or a group to act contrary to moral convictions that provide a compelling reason to disobey. Gay men, for example, have certain attitudes and values about sexual and emotional relations, and, in light of those attitudes, they have no reason to comply voluntarily with sodomy laws, yet such laws were enforced until 2003 when the Supreme Court held they violated privacy rights in *Lawrence v. Texas*. See PRIVACY. The state also generally denies gay and lesbian couples the benefits of a legally recognized marriage as well as a variety of other benefits heterosexuals enjoy. To take another example, consider a community that opposes affirmative action as unjustifiable discrimination. Their opposition arises out of a deep commitment to equality among persons. The community does not deny that affirmative action may be a means to a greater good. Its objection is that the means is morally unacceptable. The state compels the compliance of members of this community with affirmative action laws. In general, modern nation-states attempt to govern a conglomeration of distinct communities committed to different values under a single set of laws, and it is, consequently, not uncommon for citizens to have only the "necessary means" rationale for obeying judicial decisions that require them to act contrary to deeply held values.

None of this is in any way an objection to the Received View's "necessary means" account of judicial legitimacy. Judicial decisions can achieve legitimacy – subject to the qualification that, across a significant range of cases, the legitimacy achieved may be only second best. This is just what judicial legitimacy is like in modern, massive nation-states. It would, however, be wrong to stop here as the Received View has more to reveal about the role of courts in modern democracies. The way to begin is to note that situations of second-best legitimacy divide into two types. To see how, return to *Yoder*, and imagine two types of Amish parents. The first sort have *no reason whatsoever* to send the children to school after the eighth grade – no reason, that is, apart from their commitment to living under a legitimate government. Compare the hypothetical but implausible Amish parents who are so committed to fostering the independence and self-determination of their adolescent children that they see themselves as having a reason to send their children to school until age 16 if that is what the children wish. Earlier we imagined that this reason was sufficiently strong that it led the parents voluntarily to send their children to school. This time, imagine that the parents find the reason weaker than the reason based on their concern for their children's eternal salvation. Thus, for *both* sets of parents we are imagining, there is only one reason, the "necessary means" reason, *sufficient* to lead them voluntarily to comply with the order to send their children to school, and consequently that order has only second-best legitimacy with regard to both sets of parents. Nonetheless, there is an important difference between cases: namely, the second parents share an important common ground with the Douglas-hypothetical *Yoder* Court that the first parents lack.

Both the Court and the second parents recognize a reason – and indeed, the *same* reason, the children's self-determination – to continue to send the children to school. They just differ as to the strength of this reason. Shared reasons are important even when the parties disagree as to their strength. It is typically easier to tolerate the state's telling you that you must act in a certain way if you already see yourself as having a reason to so act apart from any directive from the state. This is typically true even in those cases in which you think you have better reasons to act otherwise – as common sense suggests, and many practical experiences confirm. The importance of such a basis for toleration and compromise is difficult to overemphasize where the state consists of diverse communities that often harbor deeply conflicting values.

To generalize from this discussion, ask: what are "second-best" legitimacy situations usually like? Are they cases in which those adversely affected by the judicial decision share no relevant reason in common with the court? Or are they cases in which the adversely affected share relevant reasons with the court, even if they disagree with the court's decision? Given the importance of toleration and compromise, it would be ideal if most second-best situations were of the second "same shared reason" type. Fortunately, this ideal situation turns out to be the typical situation. In all (or most) second-best situations, those adversely affected by a judicial decision share a relevant reason with the state. The point matters to the role of the judicial decision makers in modern nation-states.

Persons

The concept of a person is the key to seeing why second-best legitimacy situations are typically situations in which relevant reasons are shared. William James captures the relevant concept of a person when he wrote:

> I am often confronted by the necessity of standing by one of my empirical selves and relinquishing the rest. Not that I would not, if I could, be both handsome and fat and well dressed, and a great athlete, and make a million a year, be a wit, a bon vivant, and a lady killer, as well as a philosopher, and a philanthropist, statesman, warrior, and African explorer, as well as a "tone poet"' and saint. But the thing is simply impossible. The millionaire's work would run counter to the saint's; the bon vivant and the philanthropist would trip each other; the philosopher and the lady killer could not well keep house in the same tenement of clay. Such characters may at the outset of life be alike possible to a man. But to make anyone of them actual, the rest must be more or less suppressed. So the seeker of his truest, strongest, deepest self must review the list carefully, and pick out the one on which to stake his salvation. All other selves thereupon become unreal, but the fortunes of this self are

real, its failures are real failures, its triumphs real triumphs, carrying shame and gladness with them. (James 1980: 309–10)

James describes a widely shared conception of the self. You make yourself the person you are by what you "stand by," by the commitments you strive to realize. This conception of personhood underlies political philosophy from John Stuart Mill to John Rawls and Joseph Raz, and we assume that it is uncontroversial that persons are typically just as James describes them. One important philosophical task is showing that what is typically true is also necessarily true, that our Jamesian nature is inescapable (see Warner 1987), but it is sufficient for our purposes to assume that we are just typically as James describes.

To see that situations of second-best legitimacy are typically "shared reasons" situations, we first need to establish this claim: to the extent that we find fundamental reasons for our attitudes and actions in the fact that we have self-defining commitments, we are constrained to acknowledge the similar reasons of others – *all* others. *Yoder* serves as a convenient example. The Amish commitment to a particular religious way of life provides the parents with a compelling reason to withdraw their children from school after the eighth grade. But what if the affected teenage children have conflicting commitments that provide them with a reason to continue in school? The Amish parents cannot claim that their commitments give them a reason to curtail schooling and then ignore conflicting claims from the children. If commitment to concepts one stands by is sufficient to generate reasons for the parents, it is also sufficient in the case of the children. There is no mystery here. The point follows from a simple fact about explanations. If A explains why B is true, and A' is relevantly similar to A and B' is relevantly similar to B, then A' explains why B' is true. The Amish assert that their self-defining religious commitment explains why they have a reason to withdraw their children from school. The teenage children assert (we are supposing) that their different self-defining commitments explain why they have a reason to continue in school. If the Amish parents are right in their claim, they must acknowledge that the children are right in theirs.

This means the Amish parents have two reasons – one, grounded in *their* commitment, not to send their children to school; and one, grounded in their *children's* commitments, to send them to school. The question is whether the parents or the children should prevail. This is the point of Justice Douglas's dissent. He complains that the majority improperly ignores the interests of the children. As Douglas emphasizes, "[w]here the child is mature enough to express potentially conflicting desires, it would be an invasion of the child's rights to permit such an imposition without canvassing his views" (*Wisconsin v. Yoder* 1972: 32). In general: where self-defining commitments give us a reason to do A, others' self-defining commitments give us a reason to allow others do a relevantly similar B.

These observations apply generally, not just to *Yoder*. Court decisions typically favor the self-determination of one individual or group over another. In *Escamilla*, for example, the question is to what extent Escamilla can defend himself against the threats and demands of his drunken coworkers; in a typical breach of contract case, to take another example, the issue is the extent to which one party must divert money from the pursuit of that party's plans to compensate the other party for damage. In all cases, the adversely affected party has a reason to comply with the decision in order to allow the other party to pursue that party's plans for self-determination. Thus, to return to Max Brod, he would have a reason to comply with the court if the court ordered him to burn the manuscripts as dictated by the (hypothetical) will. These points reveal a role for courts in modern democracies.

Courts and Persons

Courts interpret and apply laws. In doing so, they inevitably highlight differences among us. Legal decisions create winners and losers, and it is the court's task to draw principled distinctions between the two. This does not, however, preclude courts – and commentators – from also drawing attention to the ways in which our shared nature as persons gives us reason to respect others' plans, projects, and goals. Douglas illustrates how this can be done in his dissent in *Yoder* when he reminds us that:

> If a parent keeps his child out of school beyond the grade school, then the child will be forever barred from entry into the new and amazing world of diversity that we have today. The child may decide that that is the preferred course, or he may rebel. It is the student's judgment, not his parents', that is essential if we are to give full meaning to what we have said about the Bill of Rights and of the right of students to be masters of their own destiny.
> (*Wisconsin v.* Yoder 1972: 32)

Self-defense like *Escamilla* illustrates another way in which courts take into account our reasons to respect others. The pattern of decisions in those cases traces out the responses that we ought to make to violent interference by others, and they do so in vastly more detail and responsiveness to actual situations than any abstract philosophical discussion. Legal reasoning yields, to a remarkable extent, a life-like portrait of the intricate moral boundaries that define the relations that we ought to have with each other. In a world where toleration and compromise are so important, it is appropriate to insist that courts make as much an effort to articulate the ways which we are alike as they do in defining principled differences among us.

References

Burton, S. 1992. *Judging in Good Faith*. Cambridge, UK: Cambridge University Press.

Cardozo, B. 1985. *The Nature of the Judicial Process*. New Haven, CT: Yale University Press.

Dewey, J. 1924. Logical method and law. *Cornell Law Quarterly* 10: 17–27.

Dworkin, R. 1986. *Law's Empire*. Cambridge, MA: Harvard University Press.

Finnis, J. 1980. *Natural Law and Natural Rights*. Oxford: Clarendon Press.

James, W. 1980. *The Principles of Psychology*, vol. 1. New York: Dover.

Lawrence v. Texas. 2003. 539 U.S. 558.

Llewellyn, K. 1931. Some realism about realism – responding to Dean Pound. *Harvard Law Review* 44: 1222–64.

Llewellyn, K. 1950. Remarks on the theory of appellate decision and the rules or cannons about how statutes are to be interpreted. *Vanderbilt Law Review* 3: 395–406.

Rawls, J. 1980. Kantian constructivism in moral theory. *Journal of Philosophy* 77: 515–72.

Singer, J. 1984. The player and the cards: Nihilism and legal theory. *Yale Law Journal* 94: 1–70.

Warner, R. 1987. *Freedom, Enjoyment, and Happiness*. New York: Cornell.

United States v. Escamilla. 1972. 467 F.2d 341 (4th Cir.).

Wells, C. 1992. Improving one's situation: Some pragmatic reflections on the art of judging. *Washington and Lee Law Review* 49: 323–38.

Wisconsin v. Yoder. 1972. 406 U.S. 205.

Wright, R. 1999. Principled adjudication: Tort law and beyond. *The Canterbury Law Review* 7: 265–95.

Further Reading

Altman, A. 1990. *Critical Legal Studies: A Liberal Critique*. Princeton, NJ: Princeton University Press.

Dworkin, R. 1977. *Taking Rights Seriously*. Cambridge, MA: Harvard University Press.

Fuller, L. 1958. Positivism and fidelity to law – a reply to Professor Hart. *Harvard Law Review* 71: 630–72.

Hart, H. 1961. *The Concept of Law*. Oxford: Clarendon Press.

Singer, J. 1988. Legal realism now. *California Law Review* 76: 465–544.

Warner, R. 1989. Three theories of legal reasoning. *University of Southern California Law Review* 62: 1523–71.

Warner, R. 1993. Why pragmatism?: The puzzling place of pragmatism in critical theory. *University of Illinois Law Review* 3: 535–63.

——— Chapter 19 ———

Privacy

William A. Edmundson

As topics in legal and political philosophy, privacy and the *right* to privacy are closely intertwined. The expression "That's private!" typically serves as a shorthand way of saying that the matter or activity in question is protected by a privacy right. Accordingly, this chapter will focus upon the status of privacy as a moral right and as a candidate for protection as a positive legal or constitutional right.

There are several forms of legal protection of privacy. The earliest form to be recognized in the United States as a protection of privacy as such was a cause of action in tort for any of four distinct sorts of infringement: (1) appropriation of a person's name, likeness or identity for commercial purposes; (2) intrusion into the seclusion of another, whether or not trespassory; (3) publication of embarrassing information about another; (4) publication that casts a "false light" upon a person, although perhaps not defamatory (Prosser 1960). These tort protections were more or less novel extensions of much older property and private law doctrines. More recently, legislatures have by statutory enactment sought to restrict the collection and dissemination of data about persons, whether by the government or by nongovernmental actors. Both of these forms of protection – tort remedy and statutory regulation – are subject to wide variation across jurisdictions, and are also subject to enlargement, qualification, and repeal by ordinary legislation.

In contrast, there are also constitutional rights of privacy. In the United States, this form of protection originated in a reading of the Bill of Rights that located a constitutional right of privacy in "emanations" from a "penumbra" of protections found in the text, which itself does not enumerate a right of privacy as such (*Griswold v. Connecticut* 1965). This constitutional right of privacy has been held to protect such activities as the decision to possess contraceptives, to marry a person of another race, to educate one's children privately, to abort a pregnancy in the first trimester, and to engage in consensual homosexuality. The Universal Declaration of Human Rights forbids "arbitrary interference with ... privacy, family, home or correspondence" (Brownlie 1992), and international courts charged with the task of adjudicating human rights claims have recognized nontextual rights of privacy, much as the US Supreme Court has done (e.g., *Dudgeon v. United Kingdom* 1981; and see SOME CONTEMPORARY TRENDS IN CONTINENTAL PHILOSOPHY OF LAW). Because this is a form of legal protection of privacy determined by judicial construction, and which is not subject to change by ordinary legislation (see LEGISLATION), it is a subject of intense and continuing controversy. See ADJUDICATION AND LEGAL REASONING. The remainder of this chapter will locate the chief difficulties attending the task of giving a general theoretical account of privacy.

Dimensions of Privacy

Privacy as a legal and moral concept has at least three different dimensions, which have been referred to as the physical, the informational, and the decisional (Allen 1996; DeCew 2002). In its *physical* sense, privacy refers to an agent's enjoyment of spaces from which others may be excluded, and within which the agent's activities are not readily monitored without his or her knowledge and consent. Despite considerable cultural variation, it seems almost instinctive among humans to conduct certain activities (excretory and sexual functions, for example) in whatever physical seclusion their circumstances afford, and respect for privacy in this sense is nearly but not quite universal (Westin 1967; Whitman 2004). Fastidiousness in the use of the terminology of rights may counsel against speaking of, for example, a *right* to defecate in seclusion, for the seclusion is mandatory and not optional. See THEORIES OF RIGHTS. One's right to be left alone in one's own home is a clearer case of a right to physical privacy – a right that is waivable at one's option. Some have suggested that physical privacy encompasses a right generally to be free of exposure to environmental pollutants and offensive noises, odors, and displays (van den Haag 1971); but others have doubted that such a right is properly stated in terms of privacy (Beardsley 1971).

The second, *informational*, sense of privacy has to do with one's control over access to information about oneself, and not with physical seclusion *per se*. Although certain uses of sophisticated surveillance techniques, such as wiretapping and infrared imaging, might be classified both as breaches of physical and of informational privacy, the distinction between the two aspects of privacy remains useful despite the accelerating emergence of such borderline cases. Just as in the case of physical privacy, here too there are types of information about oneself that one is customarily forbidden to disclose (Benn [1971] 1984: 224), which should perhaps not be spoken of as the subject of a right, in all strictness. Even so, most of us will acknowledge that there is a significant range of information about ourselves that we are not forbidden to disclose, but would prefer not to, or at least not for general consumption. Much of the information within this range would embarrass us; but much is nothing to be ashamed of, such as our income levels, perhaps, or our Social Security numbers.

Informational privacy should not be confused with privacy in the epistemological sense of the term, which refers to the direct and supposedly privileged access all conscious subjects have to what occurs in their own minds (Alston 1971). Being private in the epistemological sense is neither necessary to nor sufficient for being private in the informational sense. One's income level is informationally but not epistemologically private, while what one thought one heard in the middle of the night may not be informationally private despite being epistemologically so. See LEGAL EVIDENCE. Informational privacy is perhaps less uniformly respected in different cultures and times than privacy in the physical sense (Whitman 2004), and it has seemed to be a more modern concern (e.g., Warren and Brandeis 1890; Spiro 1971). Roberts and Gregor (1971) speculate that physical and informational privacy arose in neolithic times with the transition from a hunter-gatherer to an agricultural way of life; but others point to the much later period when interior partitions and doors became standard in European domestic architecture (cf. Olsen 1998: 690-1).

In the third or *decisional* sense of privacy, what is at issue is the right to *do* something, period, as contrasted to the right to do it in seclusion, or the right to do it without the world knowing. Although decisional privacy is abstractly distinguishable from physical and informational privacy, conduct that is protected by a decisional privacy right will normally also be protected by physical and informational privacy rights. A legal illustration may be helpful here. Under US constitutional doctrine, the possession of an obscene photograph or the use of a condom in one's bedroom is protected by a physical privacy right, just as the possession of a hand grenade is – *in the sense that*, absent a judicial warrant, one's bedroom normally may not be entered and searched without one's consent. But it is a further question whether these physical privacy rights indicate the existence of a decisional privacy right to possess an obscene photograph or to use a condom: from the fact that one enjoys a physical privacy right to φ in one's bedroom (where "φ" stands for a verb), it does not necessarily follow that one has a decisional right to φ. Some commentators have criticized the *Griswold* opinion for fallaciously inferring a decisional right to use contraceptives from a physical right not to be disturbed in one's bedroom (Gross 1971; Ely 1973; Etzione 1999).

In *Stanley v. Georgia* (1969), the US Supreme Court held that "mere private possession" of obscene matter may not be criminalized. But the Court took care to note that the "mere private possession" of narcotics or firearms may be criminalized, as may private possession of obscene materials with intent to distribute them. These cases illustrate that physical and informational privacy rights are sometimes coupled with a decisional right (to view obscene materials or to use a condom, for example) but sometimes not (as in the case of private possession of hand grenades or narcotics). It is also noteworthy that although the decisional right to possess and use contraceptives encompasses a right to produce and distribute them, the right to view obscene materials does not.

Theories of Privacy

Despite its having at least these three different dimensions – the physical, the informational, and the decisional – some (e.g., Fried 1968: 475) have suggested that privacy is (or reflects) a distinctive, unary, and in some sense noninstrumental value. What is intended by such claims is perhaps not that privacy is itself an ultimate or intrinsic value, but that it contributes in a unique if complex way to the realization of further values – or perhaps is an essential component of valuable wholes. The range of further values said to be served is a wide one, including such values as individuality, dignity, and "inviolate personality" (Blioustein 1964; Warren and Brandeis 1890; Post 2001; Whitman 2004); liberty (Fried 1968; Gavison 1980; Whitman 2004); autonomy (Beardsley 1971; Benn 1971; Gavison 1980; Gross 1971); socialization (Freund 1971); inquiry (Weinstein 1971); liberal democracy (Gavison 1980; Rubenfeld 1989); learning, creativity, and relaxation (Gavison 1980); mental health and even sanity (Jourard 1966; Gavison 1980). It has also been argued that privacy is essential to personhood and moral ownership of one's body

(Reiman 1976) and to the human capacities for love, friendship, and trust (Fried 1968; Gerstein 1970; Rachels 1975, Rosen 2001).

These claims have been received with some skepticism (e.g., Frey 2000); and the case has been made that privacy and the right to privacy are a mere congeries of interests, values, and moral protections that can better be understood in terms of the right to property (including intangible property), the right not to be harmed, and the right to liberty (Thomson 1975), or – in legal terms – to protections of interests in reputation, in emotional tranquility, and in intellectual property (Prosser 1960). Other commentators (e.g., Post 2001) despair of a unified theory of privacy while offering less ambitious accounts of privacy in one of its aspects.

Some have suggested a connection between informational and decisional privacy, of the following description: there are certain actions we might wish to perform that would be essentially altered were they observed, and this essential alteration would occur whether or not the actor were conscious of being observed. Wasserstrom (1978) instances sexual intercourse; Gerstein (1978) prayer. Benn ([1971] 1984: 230) suggests that unconsented observation of an agent interferes with the agent's ability to perform a desired action, and accomplishes this interference by transforming the action into one which the agent cannot have reason to perform. For example, if one wishes to masturbate unobserved, a spy's mere surveillance transforms one's action into the quite different act of masturbating under observation. Such a transformation derogates from one's liberty in that it causes it to be the case that one acts contrary to one's own reasons and wishes.

Thus, there are areas of overlap between decisional and informational privacy. Nonetheless, the two concepts are distinct and useful to treat as such. There are many instances in which decisional and informational privacy do not overlap. For example, the decision not to wear a helmet while motorcycling on the highway might or might not be regarded as a private one in the decisional sense, even though in normal traffic conditions it obviously will not be private in the informational or in the physical sense.

Liberty and Decisional Privacy

Many commentators have noted that a *right to liberty* tends to overlap the right of privacy in the decisional sense. The US Supreme Court's recent opinion in *Lawrence v. Texas* (2003), invalidating a statute criminalizing homosexual sodomy (and overruling its 1986 decision in *Bowers v. Hardwick*) endorses the thought that there is more than an overlap but a conceptual linkage. The *Lawrence* Court discusses the right to privacy and the "liberty of the person both in its spatial and more transcendent dimensions" as interchangeable and equivalent. For purposes of this chapter (and of clarity), I will distinguish a right to decisional privacy and a right to liberty, in the following way. A right to φ is a "*liberty right*" just in case the right rests upon the fact that one is not morally forbidden to φ. In contrast, a right to φ is a "*decisional privacy right*" just in case the right rests upon the fact that interference with φ-ing is normally impermissible *regardless* of the moral permissibility of φ-ing itself. Whether there is a liberty right to abort a fetus, for example, turns upon the question of the moral permissibility of abortion itself. But whether there is a decisional privacy right to have an abortion turns instead upon the question whether it is permissible to interfere with abortion *whether or not* abortion is wrongful.

Decisional privacy rights, defined this way, are *rights to do wrong*, in the sense that an actor's privacy right to φ cashes out as a duty imposed upon others not to interfere with the actor's φ-ing *even though* it may be morally wrongful for the actor to φ. Notice that there need not be any *general* right to do wrong for there to be the possibility of privacy rights to do specific types of wrong action. Possible types of such actions could include selfish refusal to help others, having or performing an abortion, engaging in forbidden sexual practices, or voting on forbidden grounds for or against a candidate for office (Waldron 1981). For some, the very idea of a right to do wrong is an absurdity (Godwin [1793] 1976). For others, it is not (R. Dworkin 1978: 188; Raz 1979: 274). Because doing what is morally permissible – that is, what one has a liberty right to do – is not generally or as badly in need of protection from state and social pressures, some have argued that the most valuable of our rights are rights to do what may be not merely unpopular or unconventional but morally wrong (Waldron 1981; Gerstein [1970] 1984: 250). A defense of decisional privacy rights therefore crucially depends upon a defense of the cogency of rights to do at least certain types of wrong.

Rights to do wrong and sanction theories of duty

A wrong action is one that is contrary to a moral requirement. All persons have a moral duty not to do what is (all things considered) morally wrong. These assertions describe the logical relationship between the concepts of moral wrongness, moral requirement, and moral duty and, for present purposes, may be taken either as trivial truths or as stipulations. They are offered in order to clarify what have been termed *sanction theories of duty*: historically, many thinkers have held the view that there is a close conceptual relationship between the existence of a moral duty to φ and the existence of a sanction of some kind against failures to φ (Hacker 1973).

Sanction theories of duty may take various forms. One strong form would hold that the existence of a sanction of a certain type (flowing, for example, from God's wrath, or from social convention) against φ-ing is a sufficient condition of its being morally wrong to φ, and thus sufficient to impose a moral duty not to φ. A weaker form would hold merely that the existence of appropriate sanctions is a necessary but not sufficient condition of moral wrongness and moral duty. Sanction theory in its stronger form is open to the obvious and damaging objection that even God cannot make wrong actions right by commending or commanding them (Plato 1961, but cf. Kierkegaard [1843] 1941). Therefore, in what follows only the weaker form of sanction theory will be considered.

Sanction theory refers to the existence of sanctions as a necessary condition of moral duty, but this may misleadingly suggest that the relevant sanctions have been institutionalized or are inevitable consequences of a breach of moral duty. It would be more accurate to say that all moral requirements entail the existence of some *morally permissible* means of social enforcement – where by "means" it is intended to include such things as education, censure, and ridicule, insofar as these have a distinctively moral tenor, as well as more extreme means such as compulsion, punishment, and threats thereof. Although morally permissible, a suitable sanction may or may not be reliably applied or even practically possible. I will refer to this very weak version of sanction theory as the *Enforcement Thesis*. The *point d'appui* of the Enforcement Thesis is the fact that it is generally morally impermissible to employ the distinctive means of moral correction as a sanction against conduct that is neither morally wrongful nor sincerely thought to be so. A moral permission to employ such means is thus a significantly stronger product than the mere permission to entertain "reactive attitudes" (Strawson 1968) toward moral wrongdoing.

There is an obvious tension between the Enforcement Thesis and the existence of decisional privacy rights: for to say that there is a decisional privacy right to φ is to say that it is wrongful to interfere with another's decision to φ even in case that person's φ-ing is wrongful; but the Enforcement Thesis holds that an action φ is morally wrongful only if it is morally permissible to impose sanctions upon acts of φ-ing. If the Enforcement Thesis is correct, it does not necessarily mean that there are no decisional privacy rights; but it does mean that decisional privacy rights have to be explained in a way that is consistent with the Enforcement Thesis. Clarifying our understanding of the meaning of interference, and its relationship to sanctions, will be the key to resolving this conundrum (Edmundson 2004), if the Enforcement Thesis cannot be avoided.

The enforcement thesis examined

The better understanding of the Enforcement Thesis does not take it as a thesis about the meaning of the expressions "moral requirement" or "moral duty." If taken as a semantic claim, it would be vulnerable to the point that we can understand the idea of a *rational* requirement, for example, perfectly well in isolation from any idea of sanctionability. Because there is no general semantic linkage between requirements and sanctions, an argument would be needed to establish such a link in the special domain of ethics (Kagan 1994). There is a logical gap between having moral reasons to φ and there being a moral requirement of φ-ing; one may admit, for example, that one has a moral reason to give alms to a certain panhandler on the street corner, without thereby admitting that one is morally required to do so. It may be tempting to appeal to the idea of sanctionability as an (at least partial) explanation of what closes the gap between having moral reasons to φ and having a moral duty to φ. Kagan points out that we could say that what closes that gap, when it closes, is "*normative necessity*" – and have a less tendentious label for what it is that, added to moral reasons, yields a moral requirement (Kagan 1994: 339–46). The Enforcement Thesis, as it is intended here, holds simply that whenever, and *however*, the gap between moral reasons and moral requirements gets closed, a moral permission to sanction must *also* come into being – "must" not only in our world, but in all possible worlds that feature the phenomenon of morality. Unless such a permission were generally recognized in a society, its members would hardly be likely to form dispositions to sanction wrongdoing; and, as Christopher Kutz puts the point: "it is hard to imagine how a society could maintain its normative structure if its members were not disposed to monitor and censure each other for non-compliance" (Kutz 2002: 558).

Another possible misunderstanding of the Enforcement Thesis should be avoided. To say that a moral requirement entails the permissibility of some enforcement measure is not necessarily to say that anybody and everybody can do whatever it takes to see that the requirement is observed, and violations corrected. Permissible means of enforcement must respect physical and informational privacy rights; and this is so even though there is no obvious moral equivalent of the "exclusionary rule" in US constitutional jurisprudence, which generally forbids criminal sanctions to be based upon evidence gotten in violation of the Fourth Amendment prohibition of unreasonable searches and seizures (*Mapp v. Ohio* 1961). Morality itself limits its social enforcement by imposing moral constraints that dictate who may enforce, on what occasion, and by what means and degree. One is morally permitted, for example, to wrestle a bicycle thief to the ground to recover one's bicycle, but one is not morally permitted to shoot the thief. Some moral requirements are such that compliance can be compelled and violations punished. Other moral requirements are subject only to suasive enforcement: "an angry glare, rebuke, or other situational display," in the phrase of sociologist Donald Black (1993: 5) – but the "social pain" caused by such displays is, as suggested by brain studies, not merely metaphorical (Eisenberger, Lieberman, and Williams 2003). Some moral requirements are enforceable by all: this is consistent with John Locke's doctrine ([1690] 1952) that all possess a "natural executive right" to punish wrongdoing. But, *pace* Locke, some moral requirements seem – in the first instance, at least – to be enforceable only at the option of persons suitably related to the violator (Schoeman 1992). One may, for example, complain to one's pregnant spouse that she should not smoke, but others ordinarily may not. In short, there are what may be termed *standing* and *proportionality* norms that constrain the enforcement of morality in much the same way that the detection and exposure of moral transgressions is constrained by physical and informational privacy rights.

Standing norms take on a special importance with respect to the issue whether the state may permissibly enforce moral norms. Even if Mill is correct that all genuine moral requirements are enforceable (Mill [1859] 1956; Waldron 1994), it would not follow that the state is morally permitted to enforce, whether by legislative command or by common law remedy, any and every moral requirement. Although Mill suggests that the only issue is whether state enforcement is superior in utilitarian terms to social enforcement, many others have thought that the idea that certain types of moral wrongdoing are "not the law's business" goes deeper than that (Hart 1963; Committee on Homosexual Offenses and Prostitution 1957). But what that deeper restriction may be is not easy to say (G. Dworkin 1999; Edmundson 1998). Accordingly, the Enforce-

ment Thesis deserves careful scrutiny by those concerned to justify special restrictions upon the *legal* enforcement of morality.

Physical and informational privacy rights, together with standing and proportionality norms, may forestall but will not foreclose morally permissible correction of moral wrongdoing. Decisional privacy rights, in contrast, appear to present a moral *bar* to moral correction. The question arises whether it is possible to conceive of a moral requirement such that no one other than the actor has a moral permission to so much as censure an obvious violation (by "obvious violation," I mean one whose detection violated no physical or informational privacy rights). We may call such a moral requirement a *self-concerning* moral requirement. The truth of the Enforcement Thesis is logically tied to the nonexistence of self-concerning moral requirements. Accordingly, the most direct way to vindicate decisional privacy rights is to point to the existence of some self-concerning moral requirement and to explain how it came to be. If any such moral requirement can be justified, the Enforcement Thesis will have been refuted, and the existence of decisional privacy rights vindicated.

Are there any self-concerning moral requirements?

Moral requirements arise from and are justified by moral reasons; therefore the question arises: how can the set of relevant moral reasons justify *both* a moral requirement not to φ *and* a moral requirement that all abstain from enforcing the moral requirement not to φ? The question, if at first puzzling, is readily answered where worse consequences flow from enforcement than from nonenforcement; and it is easy to imagine cases in which this might be so. Suppose, for example, that Fagin credibly threatens to kill Oliver if anyone tries to discourage Oliver from picking pockets. Oliver is morally required not to pick pockets but all are morally required not to correct Oliver for doing this, if only in this extraordinary hypothetical case. Turning from particular cases to *types* of case, however, it is harder to understand how it can be true that φ-ing as an act-type can be a moral requirement while it is also morally forbidden for anyone to engage in any social enforcement measures directed toward conduct of that type. Thus, the Enforcement Thesis is better understood as asserting that no type of action is morally required unless failures to comply are at least *prima facie* subject to moral correction. To say that enforcement is "*prima facie*" permissible is to acknowledge that in extraordinary circumstances the permission may be overridden by other moral reasons.

One line of defense of self-concerning moral requirements holds that the existence of unresolved controversy about whether there in fact is a moral requirement to φ makes it morally impermissible to enforce any such requirement. But this response either casts doubt upon the supposition that φ-ing is a moral duty, or it does not. If it does, then it does not really challenge the Enforcement Thesis; if it does not, then a defender of the Enforcement Thesis will be entitled to ask how controversy surrounding an assumed moral requirement can foreclose even a merely *prima facie* moral permission to take measures to enforce that requirement.

An answer would seem to have to take the form of an assertion that enforcement in circumstances of controversy typically has worse consequences than the suspension and moral suppression of enforcement measures, perhaps because enforcement in circumstances of moral controversy expresses disrespect for the agent, or impairs the autonomy of the agent. In other words, the answer would be to assert that even where the set of all relevant moral reasons makes it a moral duty to φ, the existence of disagreement about this very fact gives rise to a moral requirement that failures to φ not be subject to correction. But this line of rebuttal to the Enforcement Thesis leaves mysterious the process by which failing to φ can be subject to a moral ban, while at the same time distinctively moralistic efforts to discourage and correct failures to φ are likewise subject to a moral ban. It is as though morality were disabling itself, to that degree. If the reasons for not interfering with omissions to φ are as important as this, how can they not also be vigorous enough to overthrow the supposed moral requirement of φ-ing? How can all other persons be categorically rendered morally unfree to correct my not φ-ing

unless there is nothing wrong with my not φ-ing? This is the puzzle.

It may be possible to establish self-concerning moral requirements upon some basis other than the balance of all moral reasons. Not all moral duties reflect – at least not directly – the balance of all morally relevant reasons. Sometimes our voluntary actions subject us to duties that are not compelled by the weight of relevant moral reasons. Such duties are quite commonly the product of choices; for example, X may have a duty to pay Y $5 because X has chosen to buy Y's Mel Tormé recording and there is a general (unchosen) duty to perform contractual promises. Of course, this chosen duty is not a self-concerning one; X owes Y the $5. But why could there not be a chosen duty that was self-concerning? Why could X not tailor the duty so that X was answerable for violating it only to what Oliver Wendell Holmes, Jr. (1897: 459) called "the vaguer sanctions" of X's own conscience?

Suppose for example that X agrees to pay $6 for the record, but on the condition that Y not remind X in any way (direct or indirect) of X's debt, even in case X fails to pay. This seems now to be a case in which X is morally required to pay Y, but Y, the person whom X owes, has no permission to complain if X fails; and if Y has no such permission, who else could possibly have standing to censure X for X's failing? No one, it seems. But the response to be made on behalf of the Enforcement Thesis is that X's promise to pay is vacuous. A promise not to complain of nonpayment is the functional equivalent of an anticipatory forgiveness of the debt. Y will have released X from the duty to pay.

Thus, if a self-concerning moral requirement is to come into being by the exercise of one's power of committing oneself, what has to be imagined is something akin to a promise to oneself, or an undertaking that is otherwise radically divorced from the involvement of others. Certain types of "identity-defining" choices have been advanced as core candidates for protection by rights of privacy (Tribe 1988: 1424; Karst 1980: 630–6), and the question arises whether such choices are self-concerning ones. Candidate identity-defining choices include, among others, the choice whether to take a person of another or one's own race or gender as a sexual or marital partner, and the choice whether to conceive a child or to take a pregnancy to term. Again, care should be taken to clarify whether identity-defining choices are being advanced as candidates for protection as a liberty right or as a decisional privacy right – only if taken as the latter are they germane to the present discussion, which is whether the notion of a decisional privacy right (understood as an outright ban on moral enforcement) is coherent.

In political discussion and in legislative debate, there is an apparent advantage to casting identity-defining choices as within the protection of a decisional privacy right, rather than a liberty right. To argue that an identity-defining choice whether to φ is a liberty right is to take the position that φ-ing is not morally wrongful: in other words, it is to take a position on the substantive moral issue. To argue instead that the identity-defining choice is protected by a decisional privacy right rather than a liberty right is to prescind from – or "bracket" – the (perhaps difficult and controversial) substantive moral question and to argue instead against the moral permissibility of enforcing the state's view of what is morally required of the actor, whether or not the state's view happens to be correct (Sandel 1989).

There is reason to doubt, however, that identity-defining choices can give rise to self-concerning moral requirements that would stand as counterinstances to the Enforcement Thesis. The difficulty is that identity-defining choices are such that the actor is, antecedently, morally at liberty to choose either way and, after choosing, is normally at liberty to reconsider and to choose anew with the same liberty (Rubenfeld 1989: 752-82). If, for example, the actor chooses to become intimate with a partner of his or her own race, that actor remains free to become intimate with partners of another race – subject of course to nonself-concerning moral requirements that may have arisen in consequence of the earlier choice. In short, identity-defining choices do not, by themselves, place agents under a moral duty to stick with their past identity-defining choices, and so do not furnish instances of self-concerning moral *requirements*.

One might object to this conclusion on the ground that it ignores the influence of a self-concerning moral *duty of integrity*, which requires

agents to remain committed to their prior identity-defining choices. The nature of such a duty is itself a matter of dispute, but in any case this sort of appeal to integrity is problematic (Calhoun 1995). In particular, if integrity possesses the moral decisiveness to place the agent under a moral requirement to φ, it is difficult to understand how it can be that all others are morally forbidden to correct the agent's morally wrongful failure to do as integrity requires. See LEGAL AND MORAL OBLIGATION. In other words, if lack of integrity is a moral vice serious enough to place the agent under a duty not to exhibit it, it is difficult to understand why that viciousness is immune from duly proportionate correction by suitably placed others who, we for present purposes assume, have violated no physical or informational privacy right of the agent's in coming to know of the agent's transgression.

Decisional privacy rights are rights against interference with making what may be a morally wrongful choice. So understood, they are problematic, but only because they entail a moral ban upon interference with morally wrongful conduct. They remain problematic even if the moral ban is subject to being overridden by competing reasons that exceed a sufficiently high threshold. The problem can, however, be relieved and perhaps removed altogether if the notion of interference is a reasonable one exploiting the standing and proportionality norms noted above (Edmundson 2004). The slogan "That's none of the law's business!" colorfully conveys the idea that there are standing norms that disqualify the state as a censor of morals. Nonetheless, it is more difficult than it may first appear to defend this common view, especially in the increasingly anonymous and anomic conditions of modern urbanism (see Edmundson 1998, ch. 9, for this argument).

Justifying a Right to Informational Privacy

Cultural and temporal variation is an oft-remarked feature of the norms of informational privacy, whether they pertain to what is forbidden to discover or to what is forbidden to disclose (Westin 1967). Accordingly, any account of a right of informational privacy will have to overcome a widespread suspicion that such a right is merely conventional rather than on a par with more fundamental moral rights (Weinreb 2000: 34–44). Such an account might invoke the deep resentment that many would feel were certain information about themselves discovered or disclosed; but, if so grounded, any defense of a right to informational privacy will have to confront the objection that the preferences, interests, and advantages of the putative right-holder must in some way be balanced against the preferences, interests, and advantages of those whose access to information would be curtailed (Posner [1978] 1984: 334).

A case for protecting intellectual property, such as trade secrets, can be made in terms of the incentive effects of such protection – as, indeed, can a case for physical privacy and property rights generally – but the analogous case for protecting personal information seems less compelling. Admittedly, the number and depth of intimacies, friendships, and trusting relationships might suffer in the absence of any moral norm protecting personal informational privacy, but it would be hyperbolic to suggest that they would disappear, and in any case the marginal loss might turn out to be made good by a coordinate increase in the availability of reliable information (Posner 1978; Brin 1998) and by the elimination of conventional safe harbors for hypocrisy and deceit and the needless emotional hangups they foster. To put the point differently, there is good reason to think that enterprises would stop investing in the production of valuable information if they were no longer granted proprietary rights in it; but there is much less reason to think that people will cease the production of personal information – in the form of deeds, expressions, and relationships – should the norms of informational privacy revert to those of the goldfish bowl of primitive society or of "open and honest" 1960s-style counterculture (Wasserstrom [1978] 1984: 329–32). Moreover, even if the balance of all preferences, interests, and advantages in our contemporary circumstances were to turn out to favor individual informational privacy in some form, that would not in itself establish a "natural"

moral right independent of that contingent balance and the conventional arrangements reflecting it (Frey 2000: 46–50).

Accordingly, a number of theorists have tried to ground the right to informational privacy on a surer footing. Benn, for instance, argues that a principle of respect for persons can provide better general support for a "claim not to be watched without leave" than can a rule-utilitarian duty not to cause harm. In Benn's view, such a principle grounds a *prima facie* duty not to observe or report upon anyone who desires that he or she not be an "object of scrutiny" (Benn [1971] 1984: 232; Gerstein [1978] 1984: 267). The ground of the duty is not the right-holder's desire, but rather "the relation between himself as an object of scrutiny and as a conscious and experiencing subject," which implicates "the very intimate connection between one's self and one's body." Benn's argument on this point is not pellucid, and Benn himself confesses that claims to any more extensive immunity are not universal but subject to cultural variation (Benn [1971] 1984: 232).

Some of the most prominent defenders of informational privacy rights make exception for cases in which the act the agent wishes not to be observed performing is one that is morally wrongful. Benn, for example, suggests that those who act wrongly have, *ipso facto*, a reason *not* to avoid observation ([1971] 1984: 230). Fried indicates that informational privacy rights serve to free us "to do or say things not forbidden by the restraints of morality, but which are nonetheless unpopular or unconventional" ([1968] 1984: 210) – suggesting that immoral doings and sayings are unworthy of protection by informational privacy rights. But it would appear that informational privacy rights, if so qualified, would afford protection only of acts which there was a liberty right to perform. Suppose, for example, that φ-ing is morally wrong, and that X would like to φ without being observed. It seems more plausible to say that X has an informational privacy right to φ unobserved than it is to say that X has a decisional privacy right to φ without correction or reproof if he is innocently detected.

Accordingly, a more plausible general account of privacy rights may be one featuring informational privacy rights whose protection is *not* restricted to morally permissible acts, rather than one that invokes decisional privacy rights. Many will agree that respect for our human dignity demands that we each be allowed some figurative if not literal space in which we may do as we please without detection (so long as what we do is without serious negative spillover effects upon others). Any space meeting this description will be one in which we may choose to do certain (not seriously harmful) wrongs. Respect for human dignity may coherently demand such spaces, but it is more doubtful that it can coherently demand that we have spaces in which we may do wrong with impunity even after that wrongdoing has legitimately been detected.

Moreover, a ban on punishing detected wrongdoing seems hard to reconcile with a permission to inculcate a disposition to feel guilt. Once an act-type has been judged to be wrongful, the institutions of moral education (formal and informal) normally endeavor to motivate compliance. Logically, the existence of a moral permission antecedently to instill in actors a disposition to feel badly if they φ is consistent with the nonexistence of a moral permission to chasten them proportionately, *post facto*, if they are innocently discovered to have φ-ed. Nonetheless, there is in this instance what one might term a pragmatic inconsistency – whereas there is neither a logical nor a pragmatic inconsistency involved in the combination of a moral permission to correct obvious wrongdoing with a ban on "intrusive" detection. Informational privacy rights thus are capable of being grounded in a way that does not implicate the perhaps more problematic notion of decisional privacy rights (Etzione 1999).

The recent decision of the US Supreme Court in *Lawrence v. Texas* appears to hold that a legislature may not rationally rely solely upon the perceived moral qualities of an act-type in determining to criminalize it. If a legislature does so, it fails to satisfy the requirement of the due process clause that disables it from restricting liberty irrationally. Read this way, the Court has tied its "fundamental rights" jurisprudence closely to the idea of a decisional privacy right. Accordingly, the task of giving a coherent account of decisional privacy rights becomes the primary challenge to the theory of privacy.

Secrecy and Authority

So far in this discussion the holders of privacy rights have tacitly been assumed to be individuals, couples, or small, intimate groups. But claims to physical and informational privacy on the part of larger, organized groups are also commonly made and recognized. Corporate businesses, for example, enjoy legal protection of privacy under a number of rubrics – such as intellectual property and trade secrets – although the rationales of such protection more typically invoke social welfare than is the case with individual privacy; and corporations and other merely "legal" persons do not, for example, enjoy such protections as the right against self-incrimination under US constitutional law.

One might ask whether the state itself might assert any rights to privacy. Privacy and secrecy are connected ideas (Freund 1971; Friedrich 1971); but it may seem incongruous to consider claims of official secrecy – such as executive privilege – as assertions of physical and informational privacy rights held by the state. Such claims seem to rest entirely upon *raisons d'état* and similar instrumental considerations rather than upon any thought that exposure of the workings of government would violate its dignity or autonomy – in fact, such a defense would seem inconsistent with democratic ideals. In contrast, as noted before, many have argued that a merely instrumentalistic construal of individual privacy rights misrepresents and disserves them.

With this contrast in mind, it may be illuminating to ponder the state's claim to exercise authority over its citizens. Governmental claims of authority could be considered as tantamount to assertions of decisional privacy rights held by the state. A decisional privacy right, after all, is a right to do, without interference, what may in fact be wrong – and this notion seems very much akin to the concept of political authority under recent analyses. See LEGAL AND MORAL OBLIGATION. The state, in other words, is typically represented by political theorists as asserting (if only implicitly) a right against interference with its prerogatives regardless of whether its exercise of those prerogatives happens to be morally correct. There is thus a kind of symmetry between the state's characteristic posture and the assertion of a decisional privacy right on the individual's behalf – at least insofar as both involve assertions of *authority* to do what may be wrong. Just as the state asserts a right to command regardless of the moral correctness of its edicts, individuals assert a right to choose by their lights and to act without interference regardless of the moral correctness of their choices.

The defense of political authority has long been troublesome and controversial (Simmons 1979); and this suggests that a compelling account of decisional privacy may prove to be similarly elusive. The analogy should not be overdrawn, however; for there are undeniable differences between the two cases. The democratic state possesses neither dignity nor autonomy except perhaps in a derivative sense – while individuals possess both originally, and the state's functions are typically intended to affect other actors – while the individual's private doings are not typically so. Such differences as these may point to resources for the defense of the individual's decisional privacy that are not readily available for the defense of political authority. Nonetheless, it remains to be seen whether such additional resources will prove adequate to the task.[1]

Note

1 I wish to thank Brian Bix, Martin Golding, David Lefkowitz, Michael Ridge, Ani Satz, and Eric Segall for helpful comments.

References

Allen, Anita. 1996. Constitutional law and privacy. In Dennis Patterson (ed.), *A Companion to Philosophy of Law and Legal Theory.* Oxford: Blackwell, 139–55.

Alston, William. 1971. Varieties of privileged access. *American Philosophical Quarterly* 8: 223–41.

Beardsley, Elizabeth L. 1971. Privacy: Autonomy and selective disclosure. In J. Roland Pennock and John W. Chapman (eds.), *Nomos XIII, Privacy.* New York: Atherton Press, 56–70.

Benn, Stanley I. 1971. Privacy, freedom, and respect for persons. In J. Roland Pennock and John W. Chapman (eds.), *Nomos XIII, Privacy.* New York: Atherton

Press, 1–26. Reprinted in Ferdinand David Schoeman (ed.), 1984, *Philosophical Dimensions of Privacy.* Cambridge, UK: Cambridge University Press, 223–44.

Black, Donald. 1993. *The Social Structure of Right and Wrong,* rev. edn. San Diego, CA: Academic Press.

Bloustein, Edward J. 1964. Privacy as an aspect of human dignity: A reply to Dean Prosser. *New York University Law Review* 39: 962–1007.

Bowers v. Hardwick. 1986. 478 U.S. 186.

Brin, David. 1998. *The Transparent Society.* Reading, MA: Perseus Books.

Brownlie, Ian. (ed.). 1992. *Basic Documents of Human Rights,* 3rd edn. Oxford: Clarendon Press.

Calhoun, Cheshire. 1995. Standing for something. *Journal of Philosophy* 92: 235–60.

Committee on Homosexual Offenses and Prostitution. 1957. *Report of the Committee on Homosexual Offenses and Prostitution,* CMD 247. London: Her Majesty's Stationery Office. [The "Wolfenden Report"].

DeCew, Judith. 2002. Privacy. In Edward N. Zalta (ed.), *The Stanford Encyclopedia of Philosophy* (Summer 2002 edn.). <http://plato.stanford.edu/archives/sum2002/entries/privacy>.

Dudgeon v. United Kingdom. 1981. 45 Eur. Ct. H. R. ¶52.

Dworkin, Gerald. 1999. Devlin was right: Law and the enforcement of morality. *William and Mary Law Review* 40: 927–46.

Dworkin, Ronald. 1978. *Taking Rights Seriously.* Cambridge, MA: Harvard University Press.

Edmundson, William A. 1998. *Three Anarchical Fallacies: An Essay on Political Authority.* Cambridge, UK: Cambridge University Press.

Edmundson, William A. 2004. *An Introduction to Rights.* Cambridge, UK: Cambridge University Press.

Eisenberger, Naomi I., Lieberman, Matthew D., and Williams, Kipling D. 2003. Does rejection hurt? An fMRI study of social exclusion. *Science* 302: 290–2.

Ely, John Hart. 1973. The wages of crying wolf: A comment on Roe v. Wade. *Yale Law Journal* 82: 920–49.

Etzione, Amitai. 1999. *The Limits of Privacy.* New York: Basic Books.

Freund, Paul A. 1971. Privacy: One concept or many. In J. Roland Pennock and John W. Chapman (eds.), *Nomos XIII, Privacy.* New York: Atherton Press, 182–98.

Frey, R. G. 2000. Privacy, control, and talk of rights. *Social Philosophy & Policy* 17: 45–67.

Fried, Charles. 1968. Privacy: A moral analysis. *Yale Law Journal* 77: 475–93. Reprinted in Ferdinand

David Schoeman (ed.), 1984, *Philosophical Dimensions of Privacy.* Cambridge, UK: Cambridge University Press, 203–22.

Friedrich, Carl J. 1971. Secrecy versus privacy: The democratic dilemma. In J. Roland Pennock and John W. Chapman (eds.), *Nomos XIII, Privacy.* New York: Atherton Press, 105–20.

Gavison, Ruth. 1980. Privacy and the limits of the law. *Yale Law Journal* 89: 421–71. Reprinted in Ferdinand David Schoeman (ed.), 1984, *Philosophical Dimensions of Privacy.* Cambridge, UK: Cambridge University Press, 346–402.

Gerstein, Robert S. 1970. Privacy and self-incrimination. *Ethics* 80: 87–101. Reprinted in Ferdinand David Schoeman (ed.), 1984, *Philosophical Dimensions of Privacy.* Cambridge, UK: Cambridge University Press, 245–64.

Gerstein, Robert S. 1978. Intimacy and privacy. *Ethics* 89: 76–81. Reprinted in Ferdinand David Schoeman (ed,), 1984, *Philosophical Dimensions of Privacy.* Cambridge, UK: Cambridge University Press, 265–71.

Godwin, William. [1793] 1976. *Enquiry Concerning Political Justice*, ed. Isaac Kramnick. Harmondsworth, UK: Penguin.

Griswold v. Connecticut. 1965. 381 U.S. 479.

Gross, Hyman. 1971. Privacy and autonomy. In J. Roland Pennock and John W. Chapman (eds.), *Nomos XIII, Privacy.* New York: Atherton Press, 169–82.

Hacker, P. M. S. 1973. Sanction theories of duty. In *Oxford Essays in Jurisprudence*, 2nd series, ed. A. W. B. Simpson. Oxford: Clarendon Press, 131–70.

Hart, H. L. A. 1963. *Law, Liberty, and Morality.* Stanford, CA: Stanford University Press.

Holmes, Oliver Wendell, Jr. 1897. The path of the law. *Harvard Law Review* 10: 457–78.

Jourard, Sidney. 1966. Some psychological aspects of privacy. *Law and Contemporary Problems.* 31: 307–11.

Kagan, Shelly. 1994. Defending options. *Ethics* 104: 333–51.

Karst, Kenneth. 1980. The freedom of intimate association. *Yale Law Journal* 89: 624–92.

Kierkegaard, Søren. [1843] 1941. *Fear and Trembling and the Sickness Unto Death*, trans. Walter Lowrie. Princeton, NJ: Princeton University Press.

Kutz, Christopher. 2002. Responsibility. In Jules Coleman and Scott Shapiro (eds), *The Oxford Handbook of Jurisprudence and Philosophy of Law.* Oxford: Oxford University Press, 548–87.

Lawrence v. Texas. 2003. 539 U.S. 558.

Locke, John. [1690] 1952. *The Second Treatise of Government*, ed. Thomas P. Peardon. Indianapolis, IN: Bobbs-Merrill.

Mapp v. Ohio. 1961. 367 U.S. 643.

Mill, John Stuart. [1859] 1956. *On Liberty*, ed. Currin V. Shields. New York: Liberal Arts.

Olsen, Frances. 1998. Privacy. In Edward Craig (ed.), *The Routledge Encyclopedia of Philosophy*, vol. 7. London: Routledge, 690–3.

Plato. 1961. Euthyphro. In *Plato: The Collected Dialogues*, eds. Edith Hamilton and Huntington Cairns. Princeton, NJ: Princeton University Press.

Posner, Richard A. 1978. An economic theory of privacy. *Regulation* (May/June): 19–26. Reprinted in Ferdinand David Schoeman (ed.), 1984, *Philosophical Dimensions of Privacy.* Cambridge, UK: Cambridge University Press, 333–45.

Post, Robert C. 2001. Three concepts of privacy. *Georgetown Law Review* 89: 2087–98.

Prosser, William. 1960. Privacy. *California Law Review* 48: 383–422.

Rachels, James. 1975. Why privacy is important. *Philosophy & Public Affairs* 4: 323–33. Reprinted in Ferdinand David Schoeman (ed.), 1984, *Philosophical Dimensions of Privacy.* Cambridge, UK: Cambridge University Press, 290–9.

Raz, Joseph. 1979. *The Authority of Law.* Oxford: Clarendon Press.

Reiman, Jeffrey H. 1976. Privacy, intimacy, and personhood. *Philosophy & Public Affairs* 6: 26–44. Reprinted in Ferdinand David Schoeman (ed.), 1984, *Philosophical Dimensions of Privacy.* Cambridge, UK: Cambridge University Press, 300–16.

Roberts, John M. and Thomas Gregor. 1971. Privacy: A cultural view. In J. Roland Pennock and John W. Chapman (eds.), *Nomos XIII, Privacy.* New York: Atherton Press, 199–225.

Rosen, Jeffrey. 2001. *The Unwanted Gaze.* New York: Vintage.

Rubenfeld, Jed. 1989. The right to privacy. *Harvard Law Review* 102: 737–807.

Sandel, Michael. 1989. Moral argument and liberal toleration: Abortion and homosexuality. *California Law Review* 77: 521–38.

Schoeman, Ferdinand David. 1992. *Privacy and Social Freedom.* Cambridge, UK: Cambridge University Press.

Simmons, A. John. 1979. *Moral Principles and Political Obligations.* Princeton, UK: Princeton University Press.

Spiro, Herbert J. 1971. Privacy in comparative perspective. In J. Roland Pennock and John W. Chapman (eds.), *Nomos XIII, Privacy.* New York: Atherton Press, 121–48.

Stanley v. Georgia. 1969. 394 U.S. 557.

Strawson, P. F. 1968. Freedom and resentment. In P. F. Strawson (ed.), *Studies in the Philosophy of Thought and Action*. Oxford: Clarendon Press, 59–80.

Thomson, Judith Jarvis. 1975. The right to privacy. *Philosophy & Public Affairs* 4: 295–314. Reprinted in Ferdinand David Schoeman (ed.), 1984, *Philosophical Dimensions of Privacy*. Cambridge, UK: Cambridge University Press, 272–89.

Tribe, Lawrence H. 1988. *American Constitutional Law*, 2nd edn. Mineola, NY: The Foundation Press.

Van den Haag, Ernest. 1971. On privacy. In J. Roland Pennock and John W. Chapman (eds.), *Nomos XIII, Privacy*. New York: Atherton Press, 149–68.

Waldron, Jeremy. 1981. A right to do wrong. *Ethics* 92: 21–39.

Waldron, Jeremy. 1994. Kagan on requirements: Mill on sanctions. *Ethics* 104: 310–24.

Warren, Samuel and Brandeis, Louis. 1890. The right to privacy. *Harvard Law Review* 4: 193–220.

Wasserstrom, Richard A. 1978. Privacy: Some arguments and assumptions. In Richard Bronough (ed.), *Philosophical Law*. Westport, CT: Greenwood Press, 148–66. Reprinted in Ferdinand David Schoeman (ed.), 1984, *Philosophical Dimensions of Privacy*. Cambridge, UK: Cambridge University Press, 317–32.

Weinreb, Lloyd. 2000. The right to privacy. *Social Philosophy & Policy* 17: 25–44.

Weinstein, W. L. 1971. The private and the free: A conceptual inquiry. In J. Roland Pennock and John W. Chapman (eds.), *Nomos XIII, Privacy*. New York: Atherton Press, 27–55.

Westin, Allen. 1967. *Privacy and Freedom*. New York: Atheneum.

Whitman, James Q. 2004. The two western cultures of privacy: Dignity versus liberty. *Yale Law Journal* 113: 1151–1221.

Part IV

Continental Perspectives

Chapter 20

Continental Perspectives on Natural Law Theory and Legal Positivism

Jes Bjarup

Continental and Noncontinental Perspectives

The title of this chapter suggests that continental and noncontinental perspectives on jurisprudential thinking about natural law or natural rights are as distinguishable as the landmasses themselves. Sir Henry Maine has described this distinction from the British viewpoint as

> [the] growing familiarity of Englishmen with the investigations of the so-called Analytical Jurists, of whom the most considerable are Jeremy Bentham and John Austin. Of this advantage we have a monopoly. Bentham seems to be exclusively known in France and Germany as the author of an unpopular system of morals. Austin is apparently not known at all. Yet to Bentham, and even in a higher degree to Austin, the world is indebted for the only existing attempt to construct a system of jurisprudence by strict scientific process and to found it, not on a priori assumption, but on the observation, comparison, and analysis of the various legal conceptions. (Maine 1897: 343)

Maine's characterization of Bentham and Austin's approach to jurisprudence is a useful starting point for a comparison of English and continental perspectives on what role natural law and natural rights play in establishing and evaluating positive laws and the duty to obey the law.

The English Perspective: The Rejection of Natural Law and Natural Rights

The English view of jurisprudence as expressed by Bentham and Austin is concerned with the analysis of such fundamental concepts as "the notions of Duty, Right, Liberty, Injury, Punishment, Redress; with their various relations to one another, and to Law, Sovereignty, and Independent Political Society" (Austin [1879]1996: 1108). As he puts it: "[W]e cannot imagine coherently a system of law (or a system of law as evolved in a refined community), without conceiving them as constituent parts of it." Writing from the continental point of view, Gustav Radbruch recognized that "Austin's necessary notions of law are in fact categories of legal thinking, forms of legal thinking without which legal phenomena cannot be conceived as phenomena of the law" (Radbruch 1936: 532). Maine's suggestion that continental jurists are not concerned with conceptual analysis is contradicted by Friedrich Carl von Savigny's *Das Recht des Besitzes*, which Austin recognized as "the most consummate and masterly of all books upon law" (Austin [1879]1996: 55).

This conceptual analysis is related to ontological and epistemological questions based upon the distinction, advanced by David Hume, between "is," or descriptive propositions, and "ought," or normative propositions. (Hume

1978: 469f). According to Hume, it is impossible to deduce a normative proposition from a descriptive proposition, and this is true as a matter of logic. His point is rather that the normative vocabulary cannot be defined in terms of reason, but only in empirical terms of the sensations of pleasure and pain.

Hume's philosophy underlies Bentham's distinction between expository jurisprudence concerned with law as it is and censorial jurisprudence concerned with the law as it ought to be, which Bentham asserts is confounded by theories of natural law (Bentham 1996: 293f). Theories of natural law are the foundation for the language of natural rights, which Bentham describes as "a perpetual vein of nonsense flowing from a perpetual abuse of words" (Bentham 1973: 261). Bentham replaces language and thinking in terms of natural law or natural rights with language and thinking informed by the principle of utility in order to give conceptual meaning to the normative vocabulary of "ought" or duty and right. The positive law is brought about by the will of the sovereign, which raises Plato's *Euthyphro* question: is an action right because the legislator approves of it, or does the legislator approve of it because it is right? The "intellectualist" answer assumes the latter, based upon an independent standard of what is right or wrong in terms of natural laws or natural rights. The "voluntaristic" answer, endorsed by Bentham and Austin, assumes the former: whether conduct is right or wrong derives from the will of the legislator with the constitutional and epistemic authority to make valid legal rules supported by sanctions in the sense of penalties resting on empirical facts of feelings of pleasure and pain that account for the conceptual meaning of the legal vocabulary.

For Bentham and Austin, the validity of the law depends solely upon the will of the sovereign – an imperative theory of law that conceives legal rules as commands. They reject Sir William Blackstone's view that "no human laws are of any validity, if contrary to the law of nature, dictated by God himself" (Austin [1879]1996: 220). The sovereign is the sole author of "all our positive law, and exclusively sets us the measure of legal justice and injustice" (Austin [1879]1996: 275). This is the positivist view – that the law is identi-

fied solely by reference to its source, rather than to its merits – expressed in Austin's famous dictum: "the existence of law is one thing; its merit or demerit is another" (Austin [1879]1996: 220). Whether a law exists is a legal question that is addressed within jurisprudence as an expository science to provide information about laws. But Bentham and Austin also hold that the merit of a law is an important question to be addressed within jurisprudence as deontology or moral science based upon the principle of utility, which Bentham justifies by reference to experience whereas Austin refers to the will of God as expressed in his commands to promote the end of "the greatest possible happiness of all his sentient creatures" (Austin [1879]1996: 112). The principle of utility also provides the framework for jurists' reasoned discussion of the law in relation to people's place in society. Maine rejects this aspect since "the jurist, properly so called, has nothing to do with any ideal standard of law and morals" (Maine 1897: 370).

The Continental Perspective: Kant on Natural Law and Natural Right

From the continental perspective, too, "is" and "ought" are fundamentally distinct, but the distinction is grounded in the work of Immanuel Kant. Because he looms so large in the background of continental thought, his position will be described in some detail. We shall find that it contains some strains of positivism.

Kant rejects the prevailing theories of natural law that locate the source of values in nature or the reason of the thing, since nature is devoid of values.

> [W]hen we have the course of nature alone in view, "ought" has no meaning whatsoever. It is just as absurd to ask what ought to happen in the natural world as to ask what properties a circle ought to have. All that we are justified in asking is: what happens in nature? What are the properties of the circle? (Kant [1787]1976: A547/B575)

Kant also rejects the notion that natural law is grounded in the will of God. Since God is not a possible object of experience, human beings have no cognitive access to God's will as the moral standard for their conduct. For Kant, the moral order is discoverable within us, through reason, which Kant sees as the source of value and motivation. It follows that, for Kant and other continental thinkers, the normative, "ought," vocabulary cannot be defined empirically (by what "is"), but only rationally (by what "ought"). Further, normative propositions cannot be justified in terms of empirical principles of utility or happiness, but only in terms of pure principles of the will or practical reason.

Kant presents a natural right theory grounded in human reason, respecting the dignity of human beings and their natural right to freedom as "the basis for any possible giving of positive laws" (Kant [1797]1996: 6:230). There is only one reason that can be used theoretically to determine what "is" – expressed descriptively by reference to natural laws – and practically to determine what "ought to be" – expressed in normative propositions grounded in laws of freedom. Reason in the practical sense is also called the will – the capacity to act according to representations of law – that constitutes the crucial distinction between human beings and animals. As autonomous and rational beings, humans are capable of transcending their instincts and initiating their own actions. They may choose to govern themselves, but only according to objective principles that are valid for every rational being as expressed in the "categorical imperative": "Act as if the maxim of your action were to become by your will a universal law of nature" (Kant [1785]1996: 4:421).

Thus autonomous agents can create laws that are binding for themselves and their own ends, but they must do so according to objective principles that are valid for other autonomous agents as expressed: "So act that you use humanity, whether in your own person or in the person of any other, always at the same time as an end, never merely as a means" (Kant [1785]1996: 4:429f). By virtue of their humanity, human beings have only one natural right: the right to freedom, defined as "independence from being constrained by another's choice, insofar as it can coexist with the freedom of every other in accordance with a universal law" (Kant [1797]1996: 6:237). This natural right rests upon an *a priori* principle of freedom that corresponds to a universal law of justice: "so act externally that the free use of your choice can coexist with the freedom of everyone in accordance with a universal law" ([1797]1996: 6:231). The principle of freedom implies that human beings are their own masters – not in the Lockean sense that they own themselves – but in the sense that they are accountable to the humanity of their own persons and thus cannot dispose of themselves or other human beings as they please. Further, the principle of freedom imposes a duty to respect the fundamental equality of all human beings, since every human being possesses a "dignity that is raised above all price and therefore admits of no equivalent" (Kant [1785]1996: 4:434).

The natural right to freedom is linked analytically to the authorization to use coercion to make effective one's choice of actions: a person can only coerce another person to perform an action but cannot coerce another person to act from a specific motive or set an end for other persons. This accounts for the difference between the area of legality, concerned with external freedom of actions in relation to legal duties that can be enforced, and the area of morality concerned with the internal freedom to act according to ethical duties of virtue in terms of a good will that cannot be enforced. Kant rejects the position that the positive law should enforce ethical duties and thus promote the citizen's morality. The positive law is only concerned with external freedom of actions and the determination and enforcement of duties of right.

Kant follows Hobbes's notion of the state of nature, in which human beings are not solitary individuals, but agents with the natural right to act freely (Hobbes 1991: 91). These agents interact according to permissive laws that allow them to acquire private rights in relation to contract, property, torts, and marriage. Thus, "there can certainly be society in a state of nature" (Kant [1797]1996: 6:242), which is not necessarily a "state of injustice," but it is a "state devoid of justice," since "each has [his] own right to do what *seems right and good to [him]* and not to be dependent upon another's opinion about this"

(Kant [1797]1996: 6:312, italics in the original). This condition of individual freedom may lead to war but war is not grounded in the evil nature of human beings, but in their moral disputes as to how to exercise permissive laws governing private rights and duties. "[W]hen [such] rights are in dispute, there would be no judge competent to render a verdict having rightful force" (Kant [1797]1996: 6:312). Kant holds that, when such moral disputes arise, people have a duty to leave the state of nature,

> in which each follows [his] own judgement, [and to] unite [him]self with all others (with [whom he] cannot avoid interacting), subject [him]self to a public lawful external coercion, and so enter into a condition in which what is to be recognized as belonging to [him] is determined by law and is allotted to [him] by adequate power (not [his] own but an external power); that is, [man] ought above all else to enter a civil condition. (Kant [1797]1996: 6:312)

The civil condition is brought about by humans in order to secure "the freedom of every member of the society as a human being, his equality with every other as a subject, and the independence of every member of a commonwealth as a citizen" (Kant [1793a]1996: 8:290). These human rights rest upon principles of practical reason, which can be known by everyone, to inform a constitution "providing for the greatest human freedom according to laws that permit the freedom of each to exist together with that of others (not providing for the greatest happiness, since that would follow of itself)" (Kant [1787]1976: A316/B373). The constitution is the authoritative framework for rightful conditions among citizens – rightful conditions established by making and promulgating public laws, which give determinate content to the provisional private rights held by people in the state of nature, and rightful conditions established in terms of positive rights secured through the courts by the use of coercive sanctions.

Kant follows the positivist view that the law can be identified by its source – for Kant, the will of the legislator. But Kant's positivism differs in important ways from that of Bentham and Austin: for them, rules are commands, and the relation between sovereign and citizen is explained as a form of subordination. In Kant's view, rules are normative propositions containing the categorical imperative of a partnership among free and equal citizens. The content of the law depends upon the approval of the will of the legislator, which again raises the *Euthyphro* question. Where Bentham and Austin endorse the voluntaristic position, Kant endorses the intellectualist position, perceiving the legislator's will as reason, which directs the legislator to comply with rational principles that determine what is right and what is wrong. Making law is a purposive activity relating to an end that for Bentham and Austin is the greatest happiness, whereas, for Kant, that end is the civil condition – the greatest freedom allowable for citizens living in a society.

For Kant, the positive law is related to legal science, having the task "to state what is laid down as right (*quid sit iuris*), that is, what the laws in a certain place and at a certain time say or have said," as opposed to "whether what these laws prescribed is also right, and what the universal criterion is by which one could recognize right as well as wrong" (Kant [1797]1996: 6:229). Kant thus subscribes to the distinction between what the law is and what the law ought to be. The former is a legal question, addressed by jurists within the faculty of law, whose books about law have no legal authority whatsoever, since their only task is to identify and present the law in order that people may grasp legal rules more easily and use legal concepts more safely (Kant [1798]1996: 7:22). Such descriptions of what the law is are distinct from positive laws, which proceed from and bear the authority of the legislator.

Whether the positive laws themselves are right or just cannot be neglected, but this task is for the faculty of philosophy to address according to a doctrine of right, or censorial jurisprudence grounded in practical reason. As Kant puts it, "like the wooden head in Phaedrus's fable, a merely empirical doctrine of right is a head that may be beautiful but unfortunately it has no brain" (Kant [1797]1996: 6:230). To be sure, the doctrine of rights cannot do without empirical elements but the justification of principles can only be grounded in practical reason. Kant holds that the only valid principle for making and evaluating positive laws is the principle of justice –

respect for the dignity and freedom of human beings as responsible and autonomous persons. This principle is sometimes expressed as "*fiat iustitia, pereat mundus,* or 'let justice reign, even if all the rogues in the world perish because of it.'" This is the fundamental principle of justice, provided that it is

> not misinterpreted and taken, as it might be, as a permission to use one's own right with utmost rigor (which would conflict with ethical duty) but is taken instead as the obligation of those in power not to deny anyone his rights or to encroach upon it out of disfavour or sympathy for others; and for this there is required, above all, a constitution organized in accordance with pure principle of right within a state. (Kant [1795]1996: 8:378)

The positive law can be just or unjust, depending on how it can be accepted or rejected by a people:

> [I]f a public law is so constituted that a whole people *could not possibly* give its consent to it (as, e.g. that a certain class of *subjects* should have the hereditary privilege of *ruling rank*), it is unjust; but if it is *only possible* that a people could agree to it, it is a duty to consider the law as just, even if the people is at present in such a situation or frame of mind that, if consulted about it, it would refuse its consent. (Kant [1793a]1996: 8:297, italics in the original)

Thus the test for a law has two forms: one is whether people can conceive the law as a universal law. If they cannot, then it is an unjust law. The other is that, if people can only *perhaps* see the law as universal, that is, whether they can *will* it as universal law. If they cannot, then, again, it is an unjust law. The results are exercised as rational discussion: citizens are entitled to publicly voice their opinions as to whether a law passes these tests. Nevertheless, the tests state only regulative, not constitutive principles, so an unjust law is still a valid law. No one has the right to resist a legislator, "since a rightful condition is possible only by submission to its general legislative will" (Kant [1797]1996: 6:320). A revolt against the legislator is wrong because it contradicts "a categorical imperative, *Obey the authority who has power over you* (in whatever does not conflict with inner

morality)" (Kant [1797]1996: 6:371, italics in the original). Room remains, however, for rightful disobedience: "when human beings command something that is evil in itself (directly opposed to the ethical law), we may not, and ought not, obey them" (Kant [1793b]1996: 6:100). Such were the commands of the Nazi state, which Kant would have said violated the dignity of human beings by treating them as "the class of domestic animals, which are used for any service as one wants and are kept in it without their consent as long as one wants" (Kant [1793a]1996: 8:293).

The Continental Perspective: The Critique of Natural Right and Natural Law

Georg Friedrich Hegel criticizes Kant's morality as "an empty formalism." The categorical imperative, he argues, can be used to justify any wrong and immoral conduct (Hegel 1991: §135). Hegel also attacks the natural right theory advanced by Kant and by Fichte (2000), since it depends upon an atomistic view of individuals living according to "the empty ethical law (the universal law of freedom of everyone)" as the foundation for the state. "The void of the Rights of Man" leads to a state that functions as a mechanical order based upon force, treating human beings as mechanical cogs (Hegel 1975: 84, 132). For Hegel, the state is a natural entity consisting of a rational system of institutions that preexist individuals and that direct them to exercise their will and personality in accord with the positive law, which expresses the will of the state. Hegel transforms the concept of natural law from an external standard to one embodied in the positive law as an expression of communal morality, which transcends private, individual morality. Hegel's theory of natural law is thus a version of legal positivism, dismissing philosophy of law or censorial jurisprudence as subjective fantasies and restricting jurisprudence to an expository, scientific analysis of legal concepts. Such a jurisprudence "has not only the right, but also the necessary duty to deduce in every detail from its positive data both the historical development and the applications and ramifications of the given determinations of right, and to follow up their consequences" (Hegel 1991: §212).

Based upon his theory that all law is positive law, Friedrich Carl von Savigny also rejects natural law in the sense of universal principles grounded in reason and applicable to all humankind. The positive law is found in the consciousness of the people as an inward necessity manifested in the historical development of a nation's legal institutions, to be elaborated and refined by jurists' conceptual analysis (Savigny [1840]1981). Savigny's position is not only a scientific but also a political stance, as opposed to that of Kant, since Savigny elevates the authority of the scientific textbook at the expense of the authority of the statute book.

Summarizing the impact of the historical school of natural law, Bernhard Windscheid wrote in 1854, "the dream of Natural Law is over." But 30 years later, he grumblingly admitted that the dream of a "universal, fixed and unchanging law grounded in reason" was extant (Windscheid 1904: 9, 105, my translation). This admission prompted Karl Bergbohm to present a comprehensive survey of natural law thinking so as to nullify its pernicious effects once and for all (Bergbohm [1892]1973). Bergbohm asserts that the concept of law must be a unitary concept. What matters is to replace "the idealistic doctrine of natural law" with "the realistic doctrine of positive law" (Bergbohm [1892]1973: 144, my translation). The latter is Austin's imperative theory of law, which Bergbohm, familiar with Austin's jurisprudence, follows, questioning only coercion as a necessary element in the concept of positive law. However that may be, the positive law may have any content whatsoever, depending upon the legislator's will. Thus Bergbohm endorses the voluntaristic answer, maintaining that the positive law can be identified solely by reference to its source, and quotes Austin's dictum – "the existence of law is one thing, its merit or demerit another" – with approval (Bergbohm [1892]1973: 398). For Bergbohm, the existence of the law is related to expository jurisprudence, whose task is to present a scientific account, grounded in experience. In contrast to Austin, Bergbohm makes no room for

censorial jurisprudence or philosophy of law, since ethical judgments are expressions of subjective feelings and belong to the area of *Rechtspolitik*, or legal politics. Legal politics are of no legitimate concern for jurists or for judges, whose duty is to apply the positive laws as they are to the facts before them. To this extent, the German jurists' view coincides with that of the British as described by Maine, that "ethical, political and economic considerations are not the business of the jurist as such" (Windscheid 1904: 112, my translation).

The Revival of Natural Law: The Thomistic Perspective

Despite Bergbohm's efforts to declare an end to natural law as a basis for legal reasoning, it survives in Catholic legal philosophy based upon the philosophy of Thomas Aquinas, represented in Germany by Viktor Cathrein (Cathrein 1909). Cathrein writes that natural law is immanent and manifested in the principle, evident and knowable to all as rational and social beings living together, that one should do good and avoid evil. Cathrein rejects the Kantian view that coercion is a necessary element in the concept of law and follows Aquinas's definition that law is "an ordinance of reason for the common good made by the authority who has care of the community, and promulgated" (Cathrein 1909: 323, my translation). Cathrein refers approvingly to the encyclical *Rerum Novarum* issued by Pope Leo XIII in 1891 concerning the duty of the legislator to pass laws that promote the common good and protect the natural rights of the citizens. In the encyclical, Pope Leo stresses, "man is older than the State. Wherefore he had to possess by nature his own right to protect his life and body before any polity had been formed" (*Rerum Novarum* §13).

This is an affront to some Catholic writers, who hold that the natural right to self-preservation is introduced by Hobbes and belongs to the modern world (d'Entreves 1965: 59). This has prompted an inquiry into the origins of the concept of natural rights, and Brian Tierney has shown that it is put forward by William of Ockham, informed by the canonist commentaries to Gratian's *Decretum*, printed around 1140.

> [T]he first natural rights theories were not based upon an apotheosis of simple greed or self-serving egotism; rather they derived from a view of individual human persons as free, endowed with reason, capable of moral discernment, and from a consideration of the ties of justice and charity that bound individuals to one another. (Tierney 1997: 77)

There is only scant evidence that Aquinas advances a theory of natural rights, but Ockham decidedly does, stating his position in terms of personal autonomy permitting individuals to act according to their will. This position coincides with that advanced by Pope Leo, who refers to the truth that human beings, born in God's image, are thus endowed, like God, with reason and will. Thus our natural right of self-preservation is a duty imposed by positive divine law – "Thou shalt not kill" – forbidding suicide. The fundamental right of self-preservation is, therefore, an inalienable right grounded in "the dignity of human personality" (*Rerum Novarum* §§ 31, 38). This is also Kant's position, although Kant grounds this right directly in practical reason, alone. By contrast, Cathrein considers natural rights to spring from God's natural law, since "a natural right without God is unthinkable" (Cathrein 1909: 248, my translation).

Natural law is the foundation for the validity of the positive law, and Cathrein approvingly quotes Blackstone's view that no human law is valid if it is contrary to the natural law (Cathrein 1909: 215). This is important for the duty to obey a law, since only a valid law binds the individual. Cathrein restates Aquinas's view that a law contradicting natural law is unjust and has no binding force, and "such offending articles are to be classified as corruptions of law, not as laws, and consequently it is not according to them that judgment should be passed" (Cathrein 1909: 205, my translation). Cathrein endorses the traditional understanding of Aquinas that an unjust law is not a valid law and thus imposes no duty of obedience. Cathrein takes issue with the Protestant jurist Otto von Gierke questioning this view by holding that an unjust law is formally a valid law although it lacks any moral force. John Finnis takes a similar position (Finnis 1980: 364f). Aquinas believes that unjust laws are corruptions of law, yet Cathrein sees Aquinas allowing for the possibility that there may be a duty of obedience, not because of the law, but because of the greater evil that will follow if the law is disregarded. A lawyer is not duty-bound to obey a constitutional but unjust law. Thus, Cathrein rejects Bergbohm's suggestion of the judicial duty to decide according to the positive law, whatever its content (Cathrein 1909: 258f). According to Cathrein, however, this is not an exercise of judicial duty, but rather signifies a lack of character and conscientiousness. Neither judge nor lawyer nor ordinary citizen has a duty to obey a law that violates the common good, even if it is passed in accordance with the constitution.

The importance of Aquinas's theory of law is recognized by Rudolf von Jhering, whose theory of law is grounded on viewing law's proper end as the promotion of the common good. Jhering, confessing his ignorance, asks "why Aquinas has been ignored among modern philosophers and Protestant theologians" (Jhering 1905: 125, my translation). Jhering's very question suggests its answer: Aquinas is a Catholic theologian; natural law is not a great subject of interest within Protestant theology. For Protestant lawyers, Aquinas is not a philosopher but a theological writer who can safely be ignored.

In modern times, Hans Kelsen follows this path and does not even mention Aquinas's theory when theories of natural law come before the tribunal of science, only to be rejected as unscientific, since such theories are not grounded in rational thinking but in nonrational volitions or desires (Kelsen 1957, and see George 2000).

The Transformation of Natural Law: Stammler's Doctrine of the Social Ideal

Kant's view that nature is devoid of values is the backdrop to Rudolf Stammler's doctrine of the social ideal. "Kant," Stammler writes, "did not carry through consistently in matters of law and justice the remarkable work which he accomplished for natural science and ethics" (Stammler 1923: 881). Stammler aims to remedy this perceived inadequacy, based upon the Kantian distinction between "concept" (*Begriff*) – the forms according to which objects of perceptions and volitions are structured to constitute objects of experience – and "idea" (*Idee*), which does not refer to objective experience, but functions as the standard for scientific research and the pursuit of human ends. The task of jurisprudence is to identify the concept of law that cannot be acquired experientially, but that preexists experience, in order to know what we mean by that concept and so have a criterion by which we can identify the positive laws. The concept of law must thus be constitutive, enabling us to distinguish between the legal rules and nonlegal rules regulating human conduct such as morality, conventions, and customs. It must also be a formal concept, whose elements are universal and necessary to thinking in legal terms. Stammler's concept of law is a version of the imperative theory of law: the law is stated as authoritative, normative propositions – commands – passed by a specific kind of volition: an inviolable, sovereign will, which regulates human conduct by means of coercive sanctions. Legal rules are generated by the purposive activity of human beings as means to promote various ends, but neither the ends nor their fulfillment are essential – universal and necessary – elements in the concept of law that is the focus of legal science.

In this respect, empirical laws relating cause and effect are fundamentally distinct from normative laws relating means and ends. The positive laws are to be observed as empirical, social facts, but they are not to be seen as empirical laws of human behavior in terms of causality. Rather, they must be viewed as normative laws for human conduct, since they are deliberately created as means to promote various ends. The same distinction differentiates the mechanical method of describing what "is" in terms of empirical laws relating cause and effect, used in the natural sciences, from the teleological method of describing the values expressed in terms of norms of human conduct relating means and ends, used in the social sciences. Stammler takes Karl Marx and

his economic interpretation of social life to task for overlooking this distinction between empirical and normative laws (Stammler 1924). For Marx, the development of material forces causes positive laws (the effect), whereas, for Stammler, it is rather the other way around: positive laws are the means used to bring about the production and distribution of goods among people as the end.

Stammler subscribes to the distinction between the empirical "is" and the normative "ought," calling the first "technical legal science," concerned with showing what the law is, and the second "theoretical legal science," concerned with what the law ought to be (Stammler 1925: 3ff). "Technical legal science" is not a natural science whose concern is to predict events, but a social science whose concern is to "make clear the meaning and real content of definite rules and regulations, apprehend them as a unit, and present them in systematic order." This "gives us the necessary foundation for building the doctrine of the content of justice" (Stammler 1925: 27).

Further, Stammler takes the positivist view that the law can be identified by reference to its source, as opposed to its merits. Yet, for Stammler, the question of the law's merit cannot be ignored. To the contrary, the need to address this question is vital. Savigny's and Hegel's confounding the historical origin of the positive law with its normative rightness and Windscheid's and Bergbohm's dismissing ethical judgments as legal politics have been inadequate answers. (Law is, nevertheless, undeniably related to politics: the proper standard for making and applying the law is a legitimate question for jurisprudence, as a theoretical science grounded in the idea of law, to address.)

Stammler rejects the traditional view that natural law provides the proper source for the development of positive law, like some "ideal legal code whose content shall be unchangeable and absolutely valid," for "there is not a single legal rule whose positive content can be fixed a priori" (Stammler 1925: 90). He also rejects Kant's theory of natural right fixed in reason as a standard, since "there are no innate rights of the individual which he brings with him upon his entrance into the sphere of law as inalienable and irrefragable as the stars" (Stammler 1925:

76). Stammler proposes that the proper standard is the regulative idea of a "natural law with a changing content" (Stammler 1924: 174, my translation). This commits Stammler to a version of moral relativism, expressed in his doctrine of the social ideal. Stammler's social ideal rests on the notion of a community of autonomous persons who subject themselves to the governance of the positive law in order to bring about a just society – one which permits autonomous beings to pursue their various, individual ends, yet to live together cooperatively and harmoniously. In this respect, Stammler rejects Jhering's theory of law because it is grounded in the principle of utility, which "stands in about the sharpest antagonism to the idea of justice of which it is possible to conceive" (Stammler 1923: 785). In Stammler's notion of the social ideal, the will of the legislator and judge is just when it "conceives of the persons united under the law as men who follow their particular aims [only insofar] as they accord with justice ... [such] that every individual absolutely respects the other and is respected by him" (Stammler 1925: 159).

Stammler's definition of a just society accords with Plato's view that "one cannot arrive at good social conditions if one builds the state simply on a sum total of individual interests" (Stammler 1923: 880). Thus, Stammler's doctrine of the social ideal may be adduced to support a communitarian understanding of the individual's place within the state, as opposed to a liberal understanding of the individual's relation to the state based upon Kant's theory of natural rights.

The idea of law is important to evaluating the law. But the idea of law is only a regulative idea, and this leads Stammler to question Cathrein's view that there can be no such thing as an unjust law since "the idea of a law whose content is unjust does not contain any logical contradiction" (Stammler 1925: 89). To the question whether an unjust law must be obeyed Stammler answers that a person is not justified "in setting aside an unjust legal rule by arbitrarily violating it" (Stammler 1925: 85). The political importance of Stammler's doctrine is evident: the call for revolution against unjust law based upon Marxism's social materialism is replaced with the call for reform of unjust law based upon social idealism.

Natural Law as a Worldview: Radbruch's Theory of Law and Justice

Stammler's theory has suffered from Max Weber's attack in a review dedicated to unraveling Stammler's ideas about social science as teleology (Weber 1977). Weber endorses the distinction between "is" and "ought," or facts and values, and maintains that it is impossible to prove the truth of any kind of normative judgment. Thus, Weber asserts, social science must be value-free: scientists cannot legitimately express normative judgments, but may study values only from the perspective of the agent – what the agent's actions mean to him or her. Gustav Radbruch follows Weber and claims that "Stammler posed rather than solved the problem of legal philosophy" (Radbruch 1950: 68), since Stammler is concerned only with form – the regulative idea of law – as opposed to content – what the law ought to be. But, Stammler would respond, the regulative idea of law may affect the content of the law. Stammler's relativism is based upon an evaluative attitude in terms of cognitive beliefs, expressed normatively, leading Radbruch to object that the evaluative attitude cannot be a matter of cognitive belief, but only a noncognitive attitude of faith: "statements concerning the Ought may be established or proved only by other statements concerning the Ought. For this very reason, the ultimate statements concerning the Ought are incapable of proof, axiomatic. They may not be discerned but only professed" (Radbruch 1950: 55). Thus, normative propositions, which can be conceived only as the expression of various preferences, have no epistemological foundation. Radbruch's relativism makes no room for any censorial jurisprudence or philosophy of law as a branch of knowledge. Radbruch follows Weber's view, rejecting Stammler's view that legal science is a social science; rather, it is a cultural science based upon a neutral but value-related attitude towards the idea of law, comprising the values of justice, purpose and security as manifested in the positive laws that set the public standards for what is right and wrong conduct that can be enforced, if necessary by coercive sanctions.

The law is brought about by the will of the legislator and Radbruch's answer to the *Euthyphro* question is voluntaristic: what makes actions right or wrong is approval by the will of the legislator. As Radbruch writes:

> If the enacted law is to fulfill the task of terminating the conflict of opposing legal views by authoritative fiat, law must be enacted by a will, which is able also to carry it through against any contrary legal view. He who is able to carry law through thereby proves that he is competent to enact law. Conversely, he who does not have enough power to protect every one of the people against anybody else has no right to command him, either (Kant). (Radbruch 1950: 117)

Radbruch refers to Kant, but for Kant, the legislator is bound to respect people's natural right to freedom, whereas this is not the case, or so it seems, with Radbruch's legislator.

Radbruch endorses the positivist view that the positive law can be identified by its source, as opposed to its merits. What matters is legal security, which is critical to the duty to obey the law.

> It is the professional duty of the judge to validate the law's claim to validity, to sacrifice his own sense of the right to the authoritative command of the law, to ask only what is legal and not if it is also just ... Even when he ceases to be the servant of justice because that is the will of the law, he still remains the servant of legal security. We despise the parson who preaches in a sense contrary to his conviction, but we respect the judge who does not permit himself to be diverted from his loyalty to the law by his conflicting sense of what is right. For the dogma is of value only as an expression of faith, while the law is of value not only as an expression of faith but also a guarantee of legal certainty, and it is preeminently as the latter that is entrusted to the judge. (Radbruch 1950: 119)

Radbruch lived in Germany during the period of the Nazi regime, and after the war he addressed the question of obedience to Hitler's laws. The imperative theory of law in terms of the will of the state rendered German lawyers helpless to do anything other than accept Hitler's decrees as valid law that must be obeyed. The blame, it however seems, lies not in the imperative theory of law, but Radbruch's view that the philosophy of law is not knowable by way of reason and experience, because a focus on moral questions – the proper standards for making and evaluating the positive laws and the duty to obey them – is not a matter of cognition but faith.

Radbruch still holds that the positive law must be defined in terms that realize the idea of law, which is justice, and he states this in what is known as the "Radbruch formula":

> Preference is given to the positive law, duly enacted and secured by state power as it is, even when it is unjust and of no benefit to the people, unless its conflict with justice reaches so intolerable a level that the statute becomes, in effect, "false law" (*unrichtiges Recht*) and must therefore yield to justice. It is impossible to draw a sharper line between cases of statutory nonlaw and statutes that are valid despite their flaws. One line of distinction, however, can be drawn with utmost clarity: Where there is not even an attempt at justice, where equality, the core of justice, is deliberately betrayed in the issuance of positive law, then the statute is not merely "false law," it lacks completely the very nature of law. (Radbruch 1970: 353, my translation)

Radbruch's formula has been used by German courts to hold laws of the Nazi-regime null and void as well as to decide cases concerning former East German border guards (Alexy 1999). Robert Alexy defends the Radbruch formula and holds that the formula raises a philosophical issue about the concept of law. Thus true laws have a just or unjust content in contrast to false laws that only have an unjust content and consequently lack the quality of law. Radbruch supports his view by reference to principles called "the natural law or the law of reason" established by "the work of centuries" that "have come to enjoy such a far-reaching consensus in the declarations of human and civil rights that only the deliberate skeptic can still entertain doubts about some of them" (Radbruch 1970: 336). Radbruch fails to address whether natural law principles are regulative or constitutive. For Kant and Stammler, they are only regulative principles for making and evaluating positive laws, not as law or nonlaw, but as just and unjust law. Thus, for Kant and Stammler, law and morality are necessarily related, although the positive law is not necessarily just. An unjust law is nevertheless a valid law by virtue of its source, as opposed to its merits. For Radbruch, an (extremely) unjust law is not a valid law – it is nonlaw – so it commands no duty to obey: "if laws lack validity, the people owe them no obedience, and even the jurists must find courage to deny their legal character" (Radbruch 1970: 336). Thus Radbruch's commitment to the declaration of natural law principles is not an attitude of cognitive belief but an attitude of noncognitive faith. Radbruch also confounds the legal question of whether a law is a valid law with the moral question of whether a valid law should be obeyed. Thus there is disagreement on whether Radbruch abandoned the basic postulates of his relativistic legal philosophy (Friedmann 1967: 194).

Conclusion

Since World War II, thinking in terms of natural law has been revived on all fronts. The fundamental distinction between those involved in its revival is not one between continental and noncontinental thinking, but between two approaches to natural law. On the one hand is an approach to a jurisprudence described in terms of natural rights (as exemplified by Kant) and one described in terms of natural law (as exemplified by Cathrein, following Thomas Aquinas). On the other is an approach to jurisprudence described in terms of *neither* natural rights or natural law, but in terms of Stammler's social ideal or in utilitarian terms as exemplified by Bentham and Austin. Contrary to the restricted positivist view held by Maine and Radbruch there is room for this debate in the legal education of lawyers.

References

Alexy, Robert. 1999. A defence of Radbruch's formula. In David Dyzenhaus (ed.), *Recrafting the Rule of Law: The Limits of Legal Order.* Oxford: Hart Publishing, 15-39.

Austin, John. [1879] 1996. *Lectures on Jurisprudence or the Philosophy of Positive Law*, vol. I–II. Bristol: Thoemmes Press.

Bentham, Jeremy. 1973. A critical examination of the declarations of rights. In Bhikhu Parekh (ed.), *Bentham's Political Thought.* London: Croom Helm, ch 20.

Bentham, Jeremy. 1996. *An Introduction to the Principles of Morals and Legislation*, ed. J. H. Burns and H. L. A. Hart, with a new introduction by F. Rosen. Oxford: Clarendon Press.

Bergbohm, Karl. [1892] 1973. *Jurisprudenz und Rechtsphilosophie. Kritische Abhandlungen.* Glashütten im Taunus: Detlev Auvermann.

Cathrein, Viktor. 1909. *Recht, Naturrecht und Positives Recht*, 2nd edn. Freiburg im Breisgau: Herdersche Verlagshandlung.

D'Entreves, A. P. 1965. *Natural Law. An Historical Survey.* New York: Harper Torchbooks.

Fichte, J. G. 2000. *Foundations of Natural Rights. According to the Principles of the Wissenschaftslehre*, trans. Michael Baur, ed. Frederick Neuhouser. Cambridge, UK: Cambridge University Press.

Finnis, John. 1980. *Natural Law and Natural Rights.* Oxford: Clarendon Press.

Friedmann, W. 1967. *Legal Theory*, 5th edn. London: Stevens & Sons.

George, Robert P. 2000. Kelsen and Aquinas on "the natural-law doctrine." *Notre Dame Law Review* 75: 1625–46.

Hegel, G. W. F. 1975. *Natural Law. The Scientific Ways of Treating Natural Law, Its Place in Moral Philosophy, and its Relation to the Positive Sciences of Law*, trans. T. M. Knox, introd. H. B. Acton. Philadelphia: University of Pennsylvania Press.

Hegel, G. W. F. 1991. *Elements of the Philosophy of Right or Natural Law and Political Science in Outline*, trans. H. B. Nisbet, introd. Allen W. Wood. Cambridge, UK: Cambridge University Press.

Hobbes, Thomas. 1991. *Leviathan, or The Matter, Forme, & Power of a Common-Wealth Ecclesiasticall and Civill*, ed. Richard Tuck. Cambridge, UK: Cambridge University Press.

Hume, David. 1978. *A Treatise of Human Nature: Being an Attempt to Introduce the Experimental Method of Reasoning into Moral Subjects*, ed. L. A. Selby-Bigge, 2nd edn., ed. P. H. Nidditch. Oxford: Clarendon Press.

Jhering, Rudolph von. 1905. *Der Zweck im Recht*, 4th edn., vol. II. Leipzig: Verlag von Breittkopf und Härtel.

Kant, Immanuel. [1787] 1976. *Critique of Pure Reason*, trans. Norman Kemp Smith. London: Macmillan.

Kant, Immanuel. [1785] 1996. Groundwork of the metaphysics of morals. In Immanuel Kant, *Practical Philosophy*, trans. and ed. Mary J. Gregor, introd. Allen Wood. Cambridge, UK: Cambridge University Press.

Kant, Immanuel. [1786] 1996.What does it mean to orient oneself in thinking? In Immanuel Kant, *Religion and Rational Theology*, trans. and ed. Allen W. Wood and Georgi di Giovanni. Cambridge, UK: Cambridge University Press.

Kant, Immanuel. [1793a] 1996. On the common saying: That may be correct in theory, but it is of no use in practice. In Immanuel Kant, *Practical Philosophy*, trans. and ed. Mary J. Gregor, introd. Allen Wood. Cambridge, UK: Cambridge University Press.

Kant, Immanuel. [1793b] 1996. Religion within the boundaries of mere reason. In Immanuel Kant, *Religion and Rational Theology*, trans. and ed. Allen W. Wood and Georgi di Giovanni. Cambridge, UK: Cambridge University Press.

Kant, Immanuel. [1795] 1996. Toward perpetual peace, a philosophical project. In Immanuel Kant, *Practical Philosophy*, trans. and ed. Mary J. Gregor, introd. Allen Wood. Cambridge, UK: Cambridge University Press.

Kant, Immanuel. [1797] 1996. The metaphysics of morals. In Immanuel Kant, *Practical Philosophy*, trans. and ed. Mary J. Gregor, introd. Allen Wood. Cambridge, UK: Cambridge University Press.

Kant, Immanuel. [1798] 1996. The conflict of the faculties. In Immanuel Kant, *Religion and Rational Theology*, trans. and ed. Allen W. Wood and Georgi di Giovanni. Cambridge, UK: Cambridge University Press.

Kelsen, Hans. 1957. The natural-law doctrine before the tribunal of science. In *What is Justice? Justice, Law, and Politics in the Mirror of Science*. Berkeley: University of California Press, 137ff.

Maine, Henry. 1897. *Lectures on the Early History of Institutions*, 7th edn. London: John Murray.

Radbruch, Gustav. 1936. Anglo-American jurisprudence through continental eyes. *The Law Quarterly Review* 52: 530–45.

Radbruch, Gustav. 1950. Legal philosophy. In Kurt Wilk (ed. and trans.), *The Legal Philosophies of Lask, Radbruch, and Dabin*, introd. Edwin W. Patterson. Cambridge, MA: Harvard University Press, 47–226.

Radbruch, Gustav. 1970. *Rechtsphilosophie*, ed. Erik Wolf. Stuttgart: K. F. Koehler Verlag.

Savigny, Friedrich Carl von. [1840] 1981. *System des heutigen römischen Rechts*. Aalen: Scientia Verlag.

Stammler, Rudolf. 1923. Fundamental tendencies in modern jurisprudence. *Michigan Law Review* 21: 623–54, 765–85, 862–903.

Stammler, Rudolf. 1924. *Wirtschaft und Recht nach der materialistischen Geschictsauffassung, Eine sozialphilosophische Untersuchung*, 5th edn. Berlin: Walter de Gruyter.

Stammler, Rudolf. 1925. *The Theory of Justice*, trans. Isaac Husik. New York: MacMillan.

Tierney, Brian. 1997. *The Idea of Natural Rights. Studies on Natural Rights, Natural Law, and Church Law 1150–1625*. Grand Rapids, MI and Cambridge, UK: William B. Eerdmans Publishing Company.

Weber, Max. 1977. *Critique of Stammler*, trans. Guy Oakes. New York: Free Press.

Windscheid, Bernhard. 1904. *Gesammelte Reden und Abhandlungen*, ed. Paul Oertmann. Leipzig: Dunker & Humbolt.

Further Reading

Alexy, Robert, Dreier, Ralf, and Neumann, Ulfried (eds.). 1991. *Rechts- und Sozialphilosophie in Deutschland Heute. Beiträge zur Standordbestimmung*. ARSP Beiheft 44. Stuttgart: Franz Steiner Verlag.

Höffe, Otfried (ed.). 1999. *Immanuel Kant, Metaphysishce Anfangsgründe der Rechtslehre*. Berlin: Akademie Verlag.

Maihofer, Werner (ed.). 1962. *Naturrecht oder Rechtspositivismus*. Darmstadt: Wissenschaftliche Buchgesellschaft.

Maihofer, Werner (ed.). 1973. *Begriff und Wesen des Rechts*. Darmstadt: Wissenschsaftliche Buchgesellschaft.

Messner, Johannes. 1984. *Das Naturrecht. Handbuch der Gesellschaftsethik, Staatsethik und Wirtschaftsethik*, 7th edn. Berlin: Duncker & Humblot.

Radbruch, Gustav. 1987. *Rechtsphilosophie I*, ed. Arthur Kaufmann. Heidelberg: C. F. Müller Juristischer Verlag.

Radbruch, Gustav. 1990. *Rechtsphilosophie III*, ed. Winfried Hassemer. Heidelberg: C. F. Müller Juristischer Verlag.

Stammler, Rudolf. 1923. *Lehrbuch der Rechtsphilosophie*, 2nd edn., Berlin: Walter de Gruyter.

Stone, Julius. 1965. *Human Law and Human Justice*. London: Stevens & Sons.

Tierney, Brian. 2001. Kant on property. The problem of permissive law. *Journal of the History of Ideas* 62: 301–12.

Tierney, Brian. 2001. Permissive natural law and property: Gratian to Kant. *Journal of the History of Ideas* 62: 381–99.

Welzel, Hans. 1962. *Naturrecht und materiale Gerechtigkeit*, 4th edn. Göttingen: Vandenhoeck & Ruprecht.

Wieacker, Franz. 1995. *A History of Private Law in Europe, with Particular Reference to Germany*, trans. Tony Weir, foreword Reinhard Zimmermann. Oxford: Clarendon Press.

Chapter 21

Some Contemporary Trends in Continental Philosophy of Law

Guy Haarscher

"Continental": Still Relevant?

The word "Continental" is not easy to define, and perhaps today even less than before. It seems that it captures some essential cultural differences between Western Europe (not including the United Kingdom) and the Anglo-Saxon world. It is a word that is used by the British and the Americans to characterize France, Germany, Italy, Spain, and so on, rather than by citizens of the latter states to characterize themselves. Approximately 30 years ago, the difference was apparently more clear-cut than it is today. Why? The short answer to this question is: "globalization." Contemporary cultures enter into many relationships, and the increasing number of exchanges creates the tendency to blur the distinctions that existed when people traveled and communicated less than they do today. But such an explanation, even if correct when maintained within certain reasonable limits, oversimplifies the process: Benjamin Barber, for example, has recently shown that the (or, more precisely, a certain type of) globalization process has a singular and in a sense perverse effect, in that in a certain way it strengthens or revitalizes communities which, in the worst scenario, are exclusive, illiberal, and aggressive. This is the famous thesis *Jihad vs. McWorld* (Barber 2001), which means that the universalization process ("McWorld"), instead of weakening particular and local cultures, antag-

onizes and reinforces them ("Jihad"). More precisely, if the process of globalization weakens the states (that is, also and maybe above all, the very conditions for the rule of law), it favors the (re)emergence of illiberal communities. The weakening of *Gesellschaften* (societies) would not take place in the interest of the *cosmopolis*, but of the *Gemeinschaft* (community) and maybe the worst aspect of it. This is the well-known distinction made by Ferdinand Tönnies in the nineteenth century, and reelaborated in the domain of the philosophy of law by Eugene Kamenka (Kamenka 1980). To the types of law that characterize, respectively, "community" and "society," Kamenka adds the "bureaucratic-administrative" type, which was dominant in the former communist countries, but also describes some essential traits of the European welfare states.

This already shows that the process of globalization must not be transformed into a contemporary catch-all explanation, as was formerly the case for the Marxist (materialist) conception of history (Haarscher 1980) . But it is at least likely that in the developed world, and particularly in the Western hemisphere – or the Western "civilization," as Samuel Huntington would put it (Huntington 1996) – some convergence processes related to the emergence of the "global village" (McLuhan 1989) have taken place during, say, the last quarter of the twentieth century and the first years of the twenty-first. Now what are the differences between the Continent and the

Anglo-Saxon world that are relevant for the philosophy of law and have presumptively diminished in the above-mentioned (complex) process?

First, let us briefly consider philosophy. Thirty years ago, and as far of course as only the main currents of thought were concerned, the differences between both "regions" were apparently dramatic. Continental philosophy was perceived by the Anglo-Saxons as being dominated by a certain number of broad conceptions and presuppositions. Spiritualism, that is, a reaction against the materialist, relativist, and potentially "nihilist" effects of the development of value-free science, was still in a strong position in the French and German universities; Marxism was very often simply dominant – that is, what has been called a "secular religion" (Aron 2002) promising ultimate redemption on this earth and not in an illusory afterlife. Also, what would later be called "postmodernism" was a dominant presence in the universities and in intellectual life – that is, the "deconstruction" of all claims to universal values, metaphysical foundations, and even scientific objectivity. In the other – Anglo-Saxon – "camp," Continental philosophers, in their turn, saw more prosaic philosophical currents at work: neopositivism and its heir, the analytic philosophy of language, related to a strong commitment to science and a correlative depreciation of metaphysics, objective values, and overambitious rationalist hopes. Even when there was a normative purpose in philosophy (as opposed to, for instance, "emotivist" or other subjectivist conceptions of morals), it seemed to be much more pragmatic and "want-regarding" than "ideal-regarding" (Rawls 1971) (this is characteristic of the long dominant philosophy of utilitarianism). So there were two antagonistic perceptions of the philosophical currents that were at work on the Continent and in the Anglo-Saxon world. Such a difference might be interpreted as being related to two opposed reactions to the advent of the technoscientific world. Generally speaking, Continental philosophy was – or was perceived to be – more hostile to the developments of modern science, at least as far as social sciences and the humanities were concerned. And Anglo-Saxon "pragmatism" (in a general sense, not in the particular sense given to the term in Dewey's and James's philosophies) was reputed to be more receptive to the advancement of technoscience, and at the same time more hostile to the ambitions of metaphysics, or – it goes without saying – to the Marxist "secular religion" that was often considered to be the old metaphysics in new post-Hegelian disguise.

Today, the situation may seem, at least at first glance, completely modified. Let us examine some indications and examples of this seemingly radical transformation. Postmodernism and "deconstructionism" have penetrated into the Anglo-Saxon (and particularly American) world, first through the French and English departments of the universities, then through the law schools. One might even say that this intellectual movement is today more present and more structured in the United States than in France (the word *déconstructionnisme*, forged on Derrida's "*déconstruction*," has never been widely used in France). An interesting characteristic of Anglo-Saxon deconstructionism is that it pays much more attention to law than the postmodernism of the 1960s and 1970s on the Continent did (before the concept was invented). Admittedly, such a role is (sometimes radically) negative, as can be seen in the Critical Legal Studies (CLS) movement, and for instance in Stanley Fish's works on the philosophy of law (Fish 1994). Neo-Marxism is present in Anglo-Saxon universities, even in the law schools, also for instance through the CLS movement. See CRITICAL LEGAL THEORY. The German philosopher Jürgen Habermas is very influential in some spheres of American academic activity. One of the main reasons for this is that he tries to give a convincing and philosophically elaborated synthesis of two main currents in the philosophy of law: the "liberal" current insists on the protection of individual liberty, while the "civic-republican" current emphasizes political participation. These two currents correspond to two ideas of liberty: individual autonomy (or independence from constraint), and collective autonomy (or democratic self-governance). Habermas tries to show, in a very sophisticated way, that both notions of liberty presuppose each other. He grounds such a synthesis in a theory of discourse which helps him to solve some classical difficulties in the philosophy of law, such as the opposition between legitimacy and effectiveness of the norms (see Habermas 1996). In the other direction, so to speak, things have also dramatically changed. Marxism is all but dead in French and German intellectual life. And, more to the point, American philosophers are now read and translated in the Continental countries. Rawls, Dworkin, the communitarians, the libertarian thinkers, and the "Law and Economics" movement are known and discussed on the Continent.

Admittedly, this has taken place in a specific context. Liberalism is now the dominant philosophy in the world. On the Continent, the global Marxist view of the world has all but disappeared. Metaphysics has been progressively superseded by more sober philosophical approaches. Habermas – certainly the most famous contemporary Continental philosopher – has criticized the neo-Marxist conceptions of the Frankfurt School in the intellectual context of which he had been philosophically educated. And law has become more and more a respectable, and even trendy, philosophical subject, this being undoubtedly related to the contemporary quasi-general consensus on democratic and liberal values. To be sure, such a dominance of the liberal "paradigm" has given rise to a lot of criticisms. But, generally speaking, the most interesting critiques of liberalism draw their intellectual resources from the liberal tradition itself. Communitarians, republicans, even Straussians, often criticize certain forms of liberalism with the aim of defending other forms of the same conception. For instance, Strauss opposes "ancient liberalism" to "modern liberalism" (Strauss 1968); Charles Taylor (1994) or Michael Walzer (1995) defend a form of "communitarian" or "republican" liberalism – and, for that matter, Habermas does the same (Habermas 1996). But deconstructionism and neo-Marxism are, as I suggested above, much less present on the Continent than in the Anglo-Saxon world.

If philosophy has become more and more globalized, what about the differences between the Continent and the Anglo-Saxon world as far as law itself is concerned? Here we have a well-known and well-documented difference, that is, between the civil law and the common law systems. But again, first modernization, then globalization, have forced, as it were, the systems to converge. Let us take just one example of this, which is eminently relevant for the philosophy of law. One often hears, particularly in formerly ultralegalistic France – the country of the *volonté générale* (general will) – of the contemporary "ascent of the judges" (Garapon 1996). Now this process is related to some major tendencies that give the judges a role and a power that they were not supposed to have in a system where, as Montesquieu put it in the eighteenth century, the judge can only be the "mouth of the law" (Montesquieu 1748, *De l'esprit des lois*, Book XI, chap. 6). (In the eighteenth and the beginning of the nineteenth century, "law" meant the codified statute.) The ascent of human rights and liberalism has the – sometimes controversial – effect that the fundamental regulation of society becomes, in a sense to be more fully explained later, less political and more legal. To summarize: liberal political and legal philosophy is dominant, and as such its perceived inner defects are criticized by many scholars. This debate about liberalism is common to both Continental and Anglo-Saxon countries. However, deconstructionism and neo-Marxism are paradoxically in a stronger position in Britain and America than, say, in France and Germany.

So how are we to treat the subject "contemporary Continental philosophy of law"? Does not such a title refer to an outmoded distinction, at a time when so many things have changed and the main debates take place in an intellectual space that transcends the "domain" of the West? In order to address this question, I would like to do two things. First, I shall give a critical assessment of the way in which certain transformations in law and the philosophy of law have been perceived and thought of in certain contemporary European works. I shall begin with a short analysis of a recent book, written by two Belgian scholars, on the subject. Then I shall try to show that certain basic differences of approach remain, particularly in the realm of human rights, and more particularly concerning freedom of expression (but also freedom of association, and the relations between church and state). One interesting element of such a debate is that, in a sense, it is taking place between Europe as a whole (thus including the United Kingdom) and the

United States – a phenomenon which we should not consider negligible. Then I shall try to relate these persistent differences with the "great transformation" diagnosed by many European scholars in recent years.

From Hierarchy to Equality: The Ascent of "Negotiated Law"

In 2002 François Ost and Michel van de Kerchove published a book entitled *De la pyramide au réseau?* (*From Pyramid to Network?*). The underlying basic idea of the book is as follows: law has been thought of, let us say, during the last two or three centuries, as essentially being related to the state. In order to obtain legal certainty, the conditions for free and coordinated activities in general, a guarantee of basic freedoms, a stable political order, and an efficient economy, a clear hierarchy of norms was deemed necessary. Hans Kelsen's *Pure Theory of Law* (Kelsen 1967) can be considered to be the paradigmatic embodiment of such a conception of the rule of law, ultimately based on the role of the state. See LEGAL POSITIVISM. The hierarchy could for instance be based on an "ultimate" command of the sovereign (first the monarch, later the people), or on a presupposed *Grundnorm* (basic norm), or else on a modernized and individualist conception of natural law. Now, the authors contend, such a "hierarchical" or, to use their own terminology, "pyramidal" conception of law has undergone fundamental changes that make it less and less relevant. The authors are very cautious as far as the positive or negative consequences of such a transformation are concerned (Ost and van de Kerchove 2002). They do not belong to the group of optimistic scholars that view in this a fundamentally and univocally positive change of "paradigm," to borrow Thomas Kuhn's term (Kuhn 1962). But they do not either take the pessimistic stance, that is, they do not think that such a supposedly basic transformation will lead to catastrophic results inasmuch as the ideals embodied in the "pyramidal" model would risk being forgotten (Taguieff 2002). They try to assess the transformation in a rather neutral way. We have to consider, the authors say, the problem from the point of view of the transformations of law, and then try to draw from it philosophical consequences in the domain of jurisprudence. From the first point of view, we shall see that the European context is particularly relevant, in that the construction of the European Union on the one hand, and the case-law of the Strasbourg European Court of Human Rights on the other hand, raise specific questions in the broader framework of what is summarily called "globalization" (or, in French, *mondialisation*).

Let us first try to schematize the transformation that law is supposed to have undergone. The pyramidal model of law is progressively (and partially) replaced by a "network" paradigm. The symptoms of such a more or less radical change are the following ones (Ost and van de Kerchove 2002: 43–96). The state is no more the only source of sovereignty: we are witnessing the ascent of other public authorities, be they regional ("infrastate") or supranational, and also of very powerful private powers. These powers deprive the "hierarchical" state of (sometimes fundamental) parts of its classical sovereignty. The statute (the law of the legislator), formerly the essential – and potentially the sole – source of valid law in civil law countries and particularly in postrevolutionary France, is no more considered a "dogma." The statutes are more and more *evaluated*, and such a process takes place, as it were, both upstream and downstream. This means that law enters a process of continued *negotiation* between, on the one hand, the executive and legislative branches of government, and, on the other hand, the various groups of citizens that represent the civil society, the importance of which has enormously grown in the last decades. "Upstream," the project of statute is discussed, negotiated, and modified before being passed and formally promulgated. "Downstream," the enacted statute is almost constantly evaluated, in order to see whether or not it is a good means to the stated purpose (the latter being also sometimes modified during the process of negotiation). This is probably the best example of the change that is supposed to be taking place today: from a hierarchical, "vertical" model of the norm that is "posited" by the sovereign (the people, as embodied by the liberal-democratic state) and has to be obeyed, to the model of the "horizontal" network. Such a network is composed of supposedly equal citizens discussing and negotiating, in the public arena, the norms they will freely accept to abide by, and monitoring downstream the adequacy of such norms to their commonly stated aims. But let us analyze now another "symptom" of the transformation.

In the legal positivist conception of law, such as the one developed by Hans Kelsen, norm and fact are supposed to be two different and separate things. Legal validity, that is, the formal validity of the norms in the legal system, is to be clearly distinguished from the effectiveness of the norms, that is, their general application by citizens and officials (their correspondence to "social needs," emphasized by the legal sociologist). And the third component of validity, that is, legitimacy, is supposed to flow from some very definite, limited, and "localized" actions by "the people" (in drafting a constitution, in electing representatives, in using their right to free speech to criticize – or approve of – the government, in litigating their rights in court, etc.). So I would insist that there is, in my opinion, a philosophically interesting relationship between the *hierarchy* of the norms and the principle of *equality* of citizens under the rule of law. Briefly, the argument can be stated as follows: equality of free individuals, that is, the principle of modern, postrevolutionary political philosophy, presupposes a clear hierarchy of norms.

Now hierarchy and equality might seem, on many fundamental aspects, to be quite opposite notions. A French scholar, Louis Dumont, captured the distinction very well when he successively wrote two books, one on premodern societies, the other on modern ones, called, respectively: *Homo Hierarchicus* (Dumont 1977) and *Homo Aequalis* (Dumont 1991). The main political trend of modern societies is a struggle for the ideal of free and equal citizenship. Of course, such an ideal – and the well-known potential tensions between freedom and equality – can be understood in various ways (purely liberal, liberal-communitarian, socialist, libertarian, liberal-republican, "classically liberal" in the Straussian sense, etc.). But it remains true that equality is a

commonly accepted goal, embodied in law, public policies, international treaties, and so on. And it is also true that societies have progressively put it into practice by dismantling the hierarchical elements that were dominant in the "*Ancien Régime*" and subsisted (or were sometimes much aggravated by the totalitarian experiences of the twentieth century) in contemporary times. Now the French historian François Furet rightly remarked (after Tocqueville) that equality is a goddess whose thirst seems never to be satisfied (Furet 1995). In the eyes of the egalitarian, any hierarchy is considered to be a remnant of the past. "Negotiated law," as briefly sketched above, commands the attention of the propagandists of equality inasmuch as it seems to *accelerate* the process of equalization. I have picked up, in some contemporary works dealing with the subject (and mainly in Ost and van de Kerchove's fundamental synthesis), the words and phrases that express such a conviction – namely, that "network" is more egalitarian than hierarchy, thus more "modern" and more democratic. Here are some characteristic examples that perhaps do not immediately draw the attention of the reader, but are in my opinion very meaningful when considered together.

Classical "vertical" hierarchy is supposed to be replaced with "horizontal" *heterarchy*, authority with consensus, obedience with negotiation: "We are in the process of moving from authoritarian, hierarchical, vertical forms of power to negotiated, network-oriented, horizontal, consensual forms, more civilized, but more complex" (Ramonet 2001: 7-8, quoted by Ost and van de Kerchove 2002: 13); the network paradigm is described in various ways as being related to creativity, flexibility, pluralism, lifelong learning, gentleness, conviviality, peaceful coexistence of frequently opposed values, relational and "cybernetic" ontology, pragmatics of intersubjectivity and communication, generalized interactivity (Van Hoecke 2002; Lenoble 1994; Timsit 1997; Delmas-Marty 1998; Teubner 1989, Luhmann 1983; de Sousa Santos 1987; see references in Ost and van de Kerchove 2002:19). Of course, such expressions betray a certain naïve euphoria about the changing world we live in. I shall particularly emphasize in this context some problems related to the philosophy of law. Admittedly, in the "paradigm" of the network, norm and fact are more and more intertwined, in that the above-mentioned process of negotiation that takes place upstream and downstream of the enactment of a statute involves a mixing of legality (the posited norm in the legal system) and effectiveness (the role of society in the elaboration and the monitoring of law through individuals and groups who are not formally representative of the nation, and thus do not belong to the process of validation of the norms that takes place within the state). But is this really a good thing? Such a porosity of the "frontiers" between norms and facts is of course an essential element of some philosophical criticisms that have been addressed since the nineteenth century to the strict, "Kantian," separation of the two domains, for instance in the name of Hegelian "dialectics." But the debate between Kant and Hegel is still open today, and some prominent legal philosophers are explicitly, at least in a certain sense, Kantian (Rawls and Dworkin, for instance). In order to assess the situation, it will be worthwhile distinguishing between *social-political* and *legal* hierarchy. The first one is related to distinctions and inequalities (one would say today – in a retrospective way – "discriminations") that have been progressively eliminated through the contemporary quest for equality. Even if there are normal divergences in democratic societies about the *scope* of equality (for instance in the economic domain, which is a classical matter of conflict between, say, libertarians and socialists), it remains that aristocracies, paternalism, and infinitely worse, racism, are generally considered incompatible with democratic values, and that dramatic progress has been made since World War II in that domain.

But we also know that hubris can transform any progressive idea into an absurdity, not to say a totalitarian nightmare. This was widely recognized after Nazism and Communism failed, even if, again, it is quite normal that some controversies exist in democratic societies about the problem of defining when hubris begins (while avoiding at the same time that prudence and reasonableness which constitute an excuse not to change anything in society and preserve the status quo). Among some hierarchical elements that have to be scrutinized before being hastily

abandoned is the *legal* hierarchy of norms. In the legal positivist conception, such a hierarchy is necessary to preserve the rule of law. It has been defined and embodied in various ways. The idea of a *system* of clear and well-defined laws, without inconsistencies and lacunae (Perelman and Forier 1978; Haarscher and Ingber 1986; Perelman 1968), is based on the requirements of legal certainty, which is undoubtedly at the very basis of the correct functioning of a legal system. Such an idea underpinned the theses of the nineteenth century *Ecole de l'Exégèse* (teaching and applying, in private law, the *Code Napoléon* and nothing else), and, in the twentieth century, Kelsen's *Pure Theory of Law*. Admittedly, such "paper rules" were criticized in various ways, in particular by the realist movements, first in Europe with François Gény in France, the *Interessenjurisprudenz* and the *Freirecht* movements in Germany, then the sociological jurisprudence and the realist movement in the United States; then, back on the Continent, with the Scandinavian realists and, in Belgium, Chaim Perelman and the School of Brussels. But it remains that these currents were – whatever their contributions to the analysis of the very nature of the process of judging and their awareness of the requirement of modern, complex societies – criticized from the point of view of the values (above all, legal certainty) that were associated with the concept of formal legality – and constituted at least a part of what Lon Fuller called the "inner morality of law" (Fuller 1964). Moreover, realism was – and still is – criticized by the defenders of natural law, that is, of a moral principle of legitimacy that is supposed to be superior to both the requirements of the legal system and of social "realities."

Now Ost and van de Kerchove rightly point out that such a debate about the validity of legal norms (systemic legality; social efficiency – not to say social engineering; natural law legitimacy) essentially took place in the last century in the framework of the state (Ost and van de Kerchove 2002: 307-84). But what will occur if – which seems to be the case – the state is definitely (and definitively?) weakened and becomes unable to fulfill its missions, in particular the guarantee of the rule of law? The globalization process today is associated with two major forces that, even if they are very often opposed to each other, embody a claim to equality that goes beyond – according to an idea of society that is perhaps naïve – what the state, so to speak, can "offer": market and civil society. The economy – at least for the exponents of free trade – has always had the tendency to transcend the borders of the states. The present "victory" of the market economy only strengthens such a tendency. Louis Dumont (1991) showed very convincingly that the market embodies some fundamental aspects of freedom and equality that are, at least *prima facie*, not easily put into practice by the hierarchical state (even taking into consideration that legal hierarchy is in a sense the precondition for social and political equality, that is, for nonhierarchy). Friedrich Hayek emphasized the merits of the *cosmos* (the spontaneous order of the market) over the – doomed to failure – "constructivist" attempts by the state to manage the economy from above (the order of *taxis*) well before the process of globalization took place (Hayek 1973). Civil society, for its part, has become international by benefiting in particular from the computer and Internet technological "revolutions." It appears that these two actors are essential today in the elaboration of the emerging "paradigm" of negotiated law. *Prima facie*, market and civil society are more adequate to the principle of equality than the states are: they seem to be more "horizontal" in their effective working, more consensual, more flexible, and so on. But the main thrust of Marx's critique of market capitalism consists in showing that the egalitarian "surface" of the markets hides a "vertical" process of exploitation (Haarscher 1980). At the same time, one immediately sees what can be lost in the ascent of these two actors (we shall speak later of two other actors who play an important role in the elaboration and application of law: the judges and the media). International civil society is not accountable to the people: it does not represent it in any verifiable and reliable way; and it is unable to arbitrate conflicts in ways that would be respectful of the principles of the rule of law, due process (in particular presumption of innocence), and so forth. As far as the market is concerned, one knows that an "invisible hand" can, in certain circumstances, transform the interaction of particular interests into something that promotes the common good. But the mechanism is only partially working in that direction, and

market efficiency has so far only been adequately "domesticated" and civilized by the action of the states in their capacity of representing the general interest.

So one can see that the conception of a presumptive radical change of "paradigms" in the philosophy of law must be considered in a critical way. Of course, this is done by many scholars, who definitely think that there is no rule of law without an active state and an informed and committed citizenry. In that sense, the contemporary so-called "ascent of the judges" has also to be assessed in a more philosophically sober way. Increasingly in Continental Europe there is talk of a new form of democracy, called "opinion democracy" (*démocratie d'opinion* in French), that is based on a sort of objective alliance between the judiciary (or, more exactly, the role of the judiciary as perceived by the people) and the media. Democracy is less than before considered to be essentially a *political* activity (Gauchet 1998): deliberative democracy, as Rawls would put it, is very often diagnosed as being on the decline. Television and the Internet revitalize the old ideal (or fantasy) of a direct democracy, which would be possible again today, even on the large scale of our mass societies (and potentially, via the global communication process, on the universal scale of the *cosmopolis*). According to such a conception, the local and the universal would be reconciled: international civil society and (virtual) "town hall democracy" would go hand in hand. Now law is supposed to play a fundamental role in this new arrangement of the world: the citizen increasingly considers society as being composed of negotiated interactions between free, equal, and voluntarily associated individuals. Law is there to regulate interactions and no longer embodies the imposition from above (in democratic societies: from the sovereign "people" as represented in the organs of the state) of (secularly) "sacred" rules that have to be obeyed because they are supposed to be the very embodiment of the general interest. Individuals litigate for the sake of their rights. The social fabric is on the surface more egalitarian. Only on the surface?

Why are European scholars so sensitive, be it in a positive or a negative way, to this kind of weakening of legal hierarchy by trends that supposedly "promise" a further step in the progress of freedom and equality? One obvious reason for this is that the building of the European Union has taken such a process to extremes. European legislation is today the very embodiment of "negotiated law," not only because the process of unification itself is taking place through European summits in which the heads of state and prime ministers reach (or do not reach) compromises. One should also emphasize that, in the context of EU law, there is *par excellence* no sovereign legislator, and – maybe essentially – that the European institutions (the Parliament, the Commission, and the Council of Ministers) do not play the strictly defined roles of the branches of government in democratic countries. So there is necessarily a continuous process of negotiation between the three instances, which involves also more and more lobbying and pressures by interest groups, as well as a strong influence of civil society and nongovernmental organizations. This accounts for the intricacy of European law – an intricacy that will probably diminish if the EU's Intergovernmental Conference that is supposed to adopt a Constitution for Europe succeeds in reaching a serious and viable agreement (the draft Constitution was elaborated by the Convention on the Future of Europe, under the presidency of former French President Valéry Giscard d'Estaing). But anyway, even if the European institutions are somewhat clarified, problems related to the hierarchy of norms and the priority rules will certainly subsist, at least for two reasons. First, the European Constitution will not, as such, dramatically modify the role played by noninstitutional actors (interest groups and civil society). Second, the judicial body of the European Union – that is, the European Court of Justice in Luxemburg – will not cease to pose problems of hierarchy. There are many examples showing that there is a basic uncertainty concerning the priority of European law over domestic law (and, in particular, domestic constitutions). Another problem is the relationship between the Strasbourg legal system (Council of Europe) and the Luxemburg legal system (European Union): if the Constitution of the EU is finally adopted, it will incorporate into EU law the European Charter of fundamental rights of the European Union that was adopted at the Nice summit in December 2000, but has so far only a moral-political

value in the system of the Union. So it is not sure at all that such a weakening of hierarchy in favor of a more collaborative and negotiated way of making law will lead to more democracy, more freedom, and more equality. And even if these problems were supposed to be resolved, what would happen? There would be a more or less clear hierarchy of norms in European law in general, and the "upstream" and "downstream" processes of elaboration of the law by nonrepresentative (in the institutional sense) groups would be, so to say, "domesticated" – which is not at all the case today: the trend goes rather in the opposite direction (Magnette 2000). But a fundamental ambiguity, related to the most essential values of the European polity – that is, human rights – would remain in place. My thesis is that at the level of the European Court of Human Rights, even if one supposes that this Court can become really supreme as far as human rights law is concerned, and can thus avoid falling prey to essential validity problems, the present role of the so-called "balance of interests" will continue to create uncertainties, and, worse, give the states and the "established" communities a power allowing them to threaten the fundamental conquests that have characterized (at least until recently) the jurisprudence of the Strasbourg Court.

Human Rights Law and the "Balance of Interests"

The ascent of human rights in theory but also, more and more, in practice, is of course one of the less controversial aspects of the progress that has been recently taking place in law. Nevertheless, here again, I shall not discuss the criticisms addressed to the human rights "ideology" by people who are hostile to such an ideal (who are unfortunately numerous in the contemporary world on the side of what Benjamin Barber calls "Jihad," which is, according to his analyses, the dark side of the supposedly egalitarian globalized "network"). More to the point are the critiques addressed by defenders of human rights who see the perverse effects, again, of a certain hubris and naïveté. There is a concern in Europe related to the fact that the defense of human rights might contribute, in the name of equality, to a weakening of law (Ost and van de Kerchove 2002: 319). This is very well documented by the ascent, in European Courts (the European Court of Human rights in Strasbourg, as well as the EU Court in Luxemburg), of the principles of "subsidiarity," "proportionality," and the "balance of interests." The principle of "subsidiarity" (decisions must be taken at the level of the states, except if there are good reasons to take them at the level of the Union) is defended in particular by European antifederalists, who want to preserve what remains of the sovereignty of the states (Verdussen 2000; Ost and van de Kerchove 2002; Van Drooghenbroeck 2001). In order to make this understood, I would like to briefly assess the consequences for the philosophy of law of the working of the latter principle. To do this, I shall briefly – and partially – examine the present status of freedom of expression in the case-law of the European Court of Human Rights.

The European Convention enunciates, in its Article 10, the right to freedom of expression. This right is subject to certain possible limitations by the member states. Such limitations must be scrutinized in a rather strict sense by the European Court in order to see whether a state has not gone beyond what is recognized to be its "margin of appreciation." On the subject, the Court has elaborated a case-law that is based on quite liberal presuppositions: in the famous 1976 *Handyside* case (*Handyside v. United Kingdom* 1976), the majority affirmed that freedom of expression covered ideas "that offend, shock or disturb the State or any sector of the population." This was an important statement (very often quoted in the later jurisprudence of the Strasbourg Court), in that it potentially established a standard by which European statutes, administrative regulations, and practices were to be assessed and reviewed. So it seemed that a superior law – the law of human rights – would be imposed on the member states in quite an efficient and "liberal" way. The European Court does not in general reason as the United States Supreme Court does, that is, by limiting the permissibility of restrictions of free speech to situations that present a "clear and present danger," or, more recently, to "fighting words" (Schweber 2003: 38 f., 46 f.). But the

statement in the *Handyside* case – and the interpretation it gave of Article 10 of the Convention – was as such very protective of freedom of expression. Actually, one can consider that such a liberal principle has sometimes been threatened, or at least weakened, by the Court's use of the notion of the "balance of interests" to decide important cases. The use of such a notion is unavoidable if one considers that there is no clear hierarchy between the rights protected by the Convention (Ovey and White 2002: 4 f.), and so, when a conflict takes place opposing two of the protected rights, they must be "balanced" against each other in the circumstances of the case. Now such a balancing process is clearly at odds with the idea of a hierarchy of norms or of what Rawls called priority rules that should in advance prescribe which norm applies in case of conflict. Of course, such a legal hierarchy is never all-encompassing, and there are always gray areas, as well as a certain scope for the discretion of the judges (and, for that matter, for the margin of appreciation of the states). But it remains that a hierarchy and the priority rule that goes with it are supposed to be present, at least in the clear cases. Now, in the jurisprudence of the European Court, there is not such a hierarchy between rights, except concerning nonderogable rights (in emergency situations), that is, the right to life, the prohibition of torture, the prohibition of slavery or servitude, and the principle "no punishment without law" (*nulla poena sine lege*), which are therefore hierarchically superior to "derogable" rights. But regardless of this, we are confronted with a situation in which, instead of having a preexisting norm being interpreted and applied to a particular case, we have two norms that are balanced against each other in the very process of judging.

One could observe that such a way of reasoning about and deciding legal cases is quite common in contemporary law. But we are dealing here with the basic values – human rights – of the system, and the balancing process has the probably perverse effect of creating a situation of legal uncertainty in the domain of the most fundamental values that underpin the legal order and confer on it its legitimacy. So we are confronted with at least two problems related to the so-called ascent of the judges (here the judges sitting in the principal international Human Right Court in Europe): first, some scholars, politicians, or activists would say, human rights do not make a politics (Gauchet 2002), and one of the consequences of their "ascent" is that the most important political debates are not decided by the assembled citizenry of the *res publica*, but by what some call an "aristocracy" of judges. Second, in the case of the European Court, such a so-called "aristocracy" does not apply "fixed" and fundamental standards but balances interests in a way that might make decisions rather unpredictable, and therefore generate legal uncertainty, although the case-law of the Court has shown so far remarkable results in the domain of the protection of human rights in the member states. The Court is composed of judges who are often very competent, but the philosophical problem raised by the use of the "balance of interests" as a way of deciding cases still remains.

Now an objection to such concerns seems to be self-evident: the Court does not balance rights against state needs and requirements, but essentially rights against rights. So the basic hierarchy between human rights and inferior norms is supposed to be preserved, although there are no clear priority rules *between* human rights (at least between the so-called "first generation" rights, that is, civil and political rights, and not taking into account nonderogable rights, that is, rights that must be guaranteed even in situations of war or national emergency). Now such an objection is controversial. First, there are the paragraphs 2 of Articles 8, 9, and 10 (concerning respectively the right to privacy, freedom of conscience, and freedom of expression). Concerning Article 10 (freedom of expression) for instance, §2 reads as follows:

> The exercise of these freedoms, since it carries with it duties and responsibilities, may be subject to such formalities, conditions, restrictions or penalties as are prescribed by law and are necessary in a democratic society, in the interests of national security, territorial integrity or public safety, for the prevention of disorder or crime, for the protection of health or morals, for the protection of the reputation or the rights of others, for preventing the disclosure of information received in confidence, or for maintaining the authority and impartiality of the judiciary.

This paragraph authorizes limitations to the relevant rights, that are related to state or communitarian requirements like "national security," "the protection of morals," and so on. Second – and this is in my opinion the most significant point – when a right is limited for the sake of protecting another right ("the rights of the others"), the reasoning of the Court sometimes conveys the impression that a state (or communitarian) "need" is translated into (and so disguised in) the language of a right. Let us briefly give an example that has created, in Europe, a heated controversy in the legal community and beyond.

In Innsbruck, Austria, the Otto-Preminger Institute, an association which promoted *art and essai* cinema, wanted to show a movie by director Werner Schröter about a nineteenth-century writer and playwright, Oskar Panizza (*Otto-Preminger Institute v. Austria* 1994). At the end of that century, Panizza had written a play entitled *Das Liebeskonzil* (translated as *Council in Heaven*), that was violently anti-Catholic. He had been tried and convicted on the basis of anti-blasphemy law, and the play was only shown for the first time in France in the 1960s. Schröter decided to make a movie about Panizza, thus showing the trial, and of course the play, that was the obvious central element of the prosecution. Catholic bishops in Innsbruck obtained the seizure and forfeiture of the film at the end of the 1980s, on the basis of a statute prohibiting blasphemy that was – and is – still in force in Austria. After having exhausted – as required by the European Convention – the domestic remedies, the Otto-Preminger Institute brought the case before the European Court of Human Rights. Many human rights activists in Europe were convinced that the Court would condemn Austria, and that such a decision would mean the end of all the antiblasphemy statutes that were still in force in the member states of the Council of Europe, as they would be declared incompatible with Article 10, guaranteeing freedom of expression, and particularly with the *Handyside* jurisprudence, protecting speeches – in a broad sense, including movies – that "offend, shock or disturb the state or any sector of the population." This was obviously the case for *A Council in Heaven*, in which Mary was portrayed as a whore kissing the Devil, Jesus as an impotent idiot, and so on. To the surprise of many students of European Court case-law, the majority of the Court declared that there had been no violation of Article 10. By doing so, the judges used the so-called "balance of interests" way of reasoning. The Austrian State had translated the blasphemy incrimination into the language of the Convention by saying that the Otto-Preminger Institute had violated the freedom of conscience (protected by Article 9 of the Convention) of the Catholic majority in Innsbruck by showing a movie that was undoubtedly offending, shocking, or disturbing (to use the *Handyside* terminology) for believers. So the case was reframed and reinterpreted in order to be presented as a classical problem of "balance of interests" between two fundamental protected rights, and not as a conflict between the human right of free speech and a statute that could reasonably be considered to be a remnant of the times when there had been an established church and an imposed "orthodoxy" in Austria. In the *Handyside* case, the protection of offending, shocking, or disturbing speech was justified by "the demands of that pluralism, tolerance, and broadmindedness without which there is no democratic society." Here, as even a dissenting judge said, "tolerance works both ways and the democratic character of a society will be affected if violent and abusive attacks on the reputation of a religious group are allowed." Which means that freedom of speech would be limited by what offended, shocked, or disturbed groups of people would consider to be an "intolerant" expression.

There is much to be said about such a decision. Let us just emphasize some deeply preoccupying questions. If tolerance works both ways, it seems that what has been gained in the difficult struggle against the dictatorship of opinions (be they religious or not) will be progressively lost. As I said before, there is no concept of "fighting words" in the case-law of the European Court, but the *Handyside* jurisprudence allows for a very liberal interpretation of Article 10 and its paragraph 2 (permitting some strictly defined restrictions to free speech). Now *Handyside* seems to have been radically deconstructed in *Otto-Preminger*, in that, instead of taking into account the nature of the situation (a classical example of free speech v. religious communities protected by antiblasphemy law), the majority of the judges curiously

"translated" it into the language of the balance of competing rights. If the fact of being offended, shocked, or disturbed by an expression becomes (by a legal conjuring trick, so to speak) "freedom of conscience," it seems that the "balance of interests" will have produced its worst perverse effects. Of course, this would enlarge the gap between Europe and the United States as far as a right protected by the First Amendment to the federal Constitution is concerned. So there is obviously a problem with such an idea of equal and competing rights claimed by individuals or groups, if such a "horizontal" relationship is simply, so to speak, the facade of surviving "vertical" relations between a still dominant church and the individual.

There is a final point I would like to make as a concluding remark. We are confronted today with very powerful social trends that might profoundly change the way law is thought of, in particular in Europe, for the reasons given above. These trends have undoubtedly a strong ideological appeal, in that they seem to embody substantial progress concerning the fundamental ideals – equality and freedom – that shape and orient contemporary democratic societies. It would be foolish not to acknowledge the fact that such trends are not only in a certain way irresistible, but contain the promise of certain positive effects. Nevertheless, we would also be imprudent – and, as intellectuals, we would not do our job – if we did not adopt a critical attitude towards these important transformations. The word "critical" must be understood in its Kantian sense, that is: defining the domain of the legitimate use of the antihierarchical notions that I have briefly listed in this chapter. In so doing, it is absolutely necessary to avoid what I would call the "ideological stance": in such a case, we would either demonize or naïvely welcome these trends, according to our prejudices and nonconsidered political judgments. I have perhaps insisted here more on the dangers related to the present trend than on their positive aspects. But I think it is one of the essential tasks of contemporary philosophy of law to make sense of what might appear as the new myth of the twenty-first century, that is, a blind acceptance of a presumptive "acceleration" of the implementation of the principles of freedom and equality. Critiques of the egalitarian claims made by market ideologues are numerous, as are the analyses of the nonrepresentative character of civil society and the danger of "special interests" dominating the polity. But one of the most difficult tasks of contemporary legal philosophy – a task that is perceived as being particularly urgent on the Continent for reasons I have tried to summarize above – consists in understanding when and how some supposedly self-evident notions, such as the balance of interests, could be, if not correctly analyzed and criticized, quite damaging to the very ideals that underpin contemporary law.

References

Aron, R. 2002. *L'opium des intellectuels*. Paris: Hachette.

Barber, B. 2001. *Jihad vs. McWorld*, 2nd edn. New York, Ballantine Books.

de Sousa Santos, B. 1987. Law: A map of misreading. *Journal of Law and Society* 14(3): 279–302.

Delmas-Marty, M. 1998. Introduction. In J. Clam and G. Martin (eds.), *Les transformations de la régulation juridique*. Paris: LGDJ.

Dumont, L. 1977. *Homo hierarchicus. Essai sur le système des castes*. Paris: Gallimard.

Dumont, L. 1991. *Homo aequalis. 1. Genèse et épanouissement de l'idéologie économique*. Paris: Gallimard.

Fish, S. 1994. *There's No Such Thing as Free Speech: And It's a Good Thing, Too*. New York: Oxford University Press.

Fuller, L. 1964. *The Morality of Law*. New Haven, CT: Yale University Press.

Furet, F. 1995. *Le passé d'une illusion: essai sur l'idée du communisme au XXe siècle*. Paris: Robert Laffont & Calmann-Lévy.

Garapon, A. 1996. *Le gardien des promesses: le juge et la démocratie*. Paris: Odile Jacob.

Gauchet, M. 1998. *La religion dans la démocratie*. Paris: Gallimard-Folio.

Gauchet, M. 2002. *La démocratie contre elle-même*. Paris: Gallimard.

Haarscher, G. 1980. *L'ontologie de Marx*. Brussels: Editions de l'Université.

Haarscher, G. and Ingber, L. (eds.). 1986. *Justice et argumentation. Essais à la mémoire de Chaïm Perelman*. Brussels: Bruylant.

Habermas, J. 1996. *Between Facts and Norms*. Boston: MIT Press.

Handyside v. United Kingdom. 1976. Judgment of 7 December 1976, Series A No. 24.

Hayek, F. A. 1973. *Law, Legislation, and Liberty, vol. 1, Rules and Order*. Chicago: University of Chicago Press.

Huntington, S. 1996. *The Clash of Civilizations and the Remaking of World Order*. New York: Simon and Schuster.

Kamenka, E. (ed.). 1980. *Law and Social Control*. New York: St. Martin's Press.

Kelsen, H. 1967. *Pure Theory of Law*. Berkeley: University of California Press.

Kuhn, T. 1962. *The Structure of Scientific Revolutions*. Chicago: The University of Chicago Press.

Lenoble, J. 1994. *Droit et communication*. Paris: Editions du Cerf.

Luhmann, N. 1983. *Rechtssoziologie*. Opladen: Westdeutscher Verlag.

Magnette, P. 2000. *L'Europe, l'Etat et la démocratie: le souverain apprivoisé*. Brussels: Editions Complexe.

McLuhan, M. 1989. *The Global Village: Transformations in World Life and Media in the 21st Century*. New York: Oxford University Press.

Ost, F. and van de Kerchove, M. 2002. *De la pyramide au réseau? Pour une théorie dialectique du droit*. Brussels: Facultés universitaires Saint-Louis.

Otto-Preminger Institute v. Austria. 1994. Judgment of 20 September 1994, Series A.

Ovey, C. and White, R. 2002. *Jacobs and White: The European Convention on Human Rights*, 3rd edn. Oxford: Clarendon Press.

Perelman, C. (ed.). 1968. *Le problème des lacunes en droit*. Brussels: Bruylant.

Perelman, C. and Foriers, P. (eds.). 1978. *La motivation des décisions de justice*. Brussels: Bruylant.

Ramonet, I. 2001. *Géopolitique du chaos*. Paris: Gallimard-Folio.

Rawls, J. 1971. *A Theory of Justice*. Cambridge, MA: Harvard University Press.

Schweber, H. 2003. *Speech, Conduct, and the First Amendment*. New York: Peter Lang.

Strauss, L. 1968. *Liberalism, Ancient and Modern*. New York: Basic Books.

Taguieff, P.-A.. 2002. *Résister au bougisme: démocratie forte contre mondialisation techno-marchande*. Paris: Mille et une Nuits.

Taylor, C. 1994. *Multiculturalism: Examining the Politics of Recognition*. Princeton, NJ: Princeton University Press.

Teubner, G. 1989. *Recht als autopoietisches System*. Frankfurt am Main: Suhrkamp.

Timsit, G. 1997. *L'archipel de la norme*. Paris: PUF.

Van Drooghenbroeck, S. 2001. *La proportionnalité dans le droit de la Convention européenne des droits de l'homme. Prendre l'idée simple au sérieux.*

Brussels: Facultés universitaires Saint-Louis/Editions Bruylant.

Van Hoecke, M. 2002. *Law as Communication*. Oxford: Hart Publishing.

Verdussen, M. (ed.). 2000. *L'Europe de la subsidiarité*. Brussels: Bruylant.

Walzer, M. 1995. *Pluralism, Justice, and Equality*. Oxford: Oxford University Press.

Part V
Methodological Concerns

Chapter 22

Objectivity

Nicos Stavropoulos

Objectivity: Reality and Thought

Philosophers usually discuss objectivity by reference to domains, to which objects or facts or
properties or notions belong. They may say that
the relative merit of ice cream flavors and other
matters of culinary taste are subjective, or that
physics is objective if anything is, and they are
split regarding morality. Some philosophers go
further: they say that different domains can be
objective in different ways, so that we cannot
usefully explain in a general way what makes a
domain objective. In this chapter we shall discuss
objectivity in law and shall leave open the question
whether the account of objectivity in law can
be generalized to other domains. Even so, we
shall initially look at what philosophers say
regarding objectivity elsewhere (or indeed objectivity in general) in order to get a better sense
of our subject and to deal with some threshold
issues.

Is there objectivity in law? It is often thought
that sensitive political issues such as the legitimacy
of adjudication turn on this question. But it is not
clear what the question comes to, that is, what it
would take for law to be objective. We need a
sharper formulation of the conditions that law
must fulfill if it is to come out objective, which
may help us decide the issue whether law is indeed
objective.

Two Approaches

In a classic approach, a domain is objective in case
the existence and character of the objects that
populate the domain is independent of the
mind, that is, of thoughts, beliefs, desires, and
other aspects of the mental. This approach puts
the emphasis on the world, and treats the standing of our thoughts or beliefs as derivative. It says
that our thoughts or beliefs about these objects
are capable of being objective in virtue of the fact
that reality contains the objects that it does, and
does so independently of minds. It is, however,
notoriously difficult to pin down what the required independence amounts to – precisely
what must be independent of what – and so to
design a test of objectivity. Among other difficulties, this approach to objectivity would quickly
raise too many fundamental issues in the neigh-
borhood, such as the character of reality, the indi-
viduation of objects, and the nature of reference
(cf. Raz 2001b: 196). Besides, a test of objectivity
should be such that thought itself and other
aspects of the nature and functions of the mind
are not ruled out from the outset. The test therefore cannot be that something should not be
constituted by the mind. Moreover, our test
should be subtle enough to allow not only for
constitution by the mind but also for causal or
historical dependence upon it. Consider domains

populated by things which would not exist at all were it not for human minds and the thoughts, beliefs, or desires that they entertain. It would be unhelpful to devise a test that things such as stars and rocks and chemical compounds would satisfy, but things such as trains and currency exchange rates would not. There seems to be a difference relevant to the nature of objectivity between questions such as whether travel by rail is romantic or whether speculating on forex is scary, on the one hand, and questions such as how best to design trains that satisfy certain design conditions (e.g., regarding speed, capacity, cost, or pollutants) or how currency volatility affects economic growth, on the other. Unlike the first, the second kind of question seems to belong to a domain where a great deal of objectivity is possible, so we need a more fine-grained test to capture the crucial distinction. A more promising test requires that *truths* in that domain be independent of thoughts or beliefs or desires. Specifically, the test requires that if p is an objective truth, it holds independently of people's thoughts or beliefs or desires that p (Nozick 2001: 76).

An alternative approach places the emphasis not on the world but on thinking subjects: instead of reality and its character, it focuses on the way we understand it and the intellectual norms that govern thought about it (cf. Nagel 1986; Raz 2001b). For example, Thomas Nagel says that objectivity is a method of understanding. In Nagel's view, objectivity is primarily a process or state of detachment, which is achieved by stepping back from an initial view formed from an individual or even generally human, perspective, and by coming to occupy instead a perspective that encompasses the initial view and its relation to the world. The new perspective allows us to consider the initial view as an appearance which can be assessed and corrected by reference to the detached perspective. The detachment, to the extent that it is achieved, makes the new perspective that much less dependent upon individual or generally human contingencies. Although Nagel concedes merit to the view that the existence of a larger reality underlies objectivity – the possibility of detachment, which for Nagel is distinctive of the objective perspective, presupposes that humans and how things appear to them are part of a larger reality – he argues that the connection

is derivative and often misleading: less detached (and therefore less objective, in Nagel's sense) perspectives and how things appear from them may themselves be part of reality: objective reality is incomplete (Nagel 1986: 4–7, 25–7).

Error

In spite of such differences, the two approaches have much in common. In this chapter we shall rely on a mark of objectivity that captures a key theme common to both approaches and shall leave open the question which approach focuses on the primary and which on the derivative sense of objectivity. We shall focus on the relation between how things are in the world and how subjects think of and understand it, and we shall try to test for objectivity by investigating whether the relevant domain is such that there is space for *error*. We should expect that for a domain to be objective there should be some logical space between how we understand or judge or perceive or believe things to be and what discriminations we make among different objects or properties in the domain, on the one hand, and what the case is, on the other. Availability of such space should be part at least of the domain's independence from the mind, on which the first approach focuses, and would suggest that in that domain there may be truths which are independent of our judgment. It would further make it possible to adopt the kind of perspective on which the second approach focuses, that is, one which is detached from and critical with respect to individual judgment, in order to pursue such truths, if any exist. We could then position a domain along a spectrum ranging from those where there is no such space at all – individual judgment and case necessarily coincide, so there is no genuine standard governing the former – on to domains where there is a standard by reference to which individual judgment may turn out to be mistaken, through to domains where even collective judgment or shared understanding can turn out to be mistaken. The precise position of a domain would of course depend on a great deal of refinement. For example, we may think that only unreflective judgment (individual or otherwise) or only judgment under certain other epistemic conditions may turn out to be mistaken in a certain domain, or we may think that even collective reflective judgment or fully articulated shared understanding could turn out to be wrong.

It should go without saying that the question what standard, if any, governs judgment in a certain domain is not to be referred back to the judgments made in the domain in question. This clarification is meant to allay any fears of making objectivity too easy, in the sense of allowing those who make the judgments to invent bogus "internal" standards which, instead of opening up any genuine space for criticism and correction, ensure that judgments in the domain are necessarily vindicated. First, to say that standards that make error possible are available in a domain is not merely to say that judgments in a domain are formulated in the cognitive idiom and purport to be about how things are in the world (cf. Raz 2001b). Second, the boundaries of the domain and hence the character of the relevant standard are matters open to critical evaluation. If astrologists or witchcraft specialists for example say that this is going to be one of these days because the stars are out of line or because a certain witch has cast a spell, their claims plausibly compete with ordinary scientific explanations, which involve causal relations governed by laws of nature. The claims, therefore, plausibly are to be assessed by reference to the usual scientific standard, and, we should hope, turn out false, and indeed objectively so.

Legal Objectivity

This no doubt is at best a partial conception of objectivity, but it should be helpful enough for the purpose of exploring the territory in respect of objectivity in law. We can formulate our problem as follows: are there objective legal facts? That is, is there an objective fact about what the law requires? We shall treat this question as roughly equivalent to the question whether the nature of law is such that our thoughts or beliefs or discriminations or judgments about what the law requires are subject to a (distinctively legal) standard by reference to which they can be corrected. For a standard to be capable of playing that role, it must be set at least in part by something external to that which it is meant to govern. This would require that the nature of law be such that there is space between lawyers' judgments, beliefs, and so on regarding what the law requires, on the one hand, and what it in fact requires, on the other, so that the larger the space, the stronger the objectivity that law can have.

Lawyers and judges seem to speak about the law in terms that presuppose a strongly objective standard. They often argue that received settled doctrines misrepresent the law, and may not treat the absence of a settled view regarding what the law requires as being in tension with their own view that it requires what they think it does. They seem, in short, to assume that some considerable distance exists between legal judgment and case. The fact that they often seem to make this assumption is not of course dispositive. Perhaps lawyers do not in fact make the assumption – it is possible that what they say is best explained otherwise – and they could certainly be wrong in making it even if they did – the law's objective or otherwise standing may after all be a purely philosophical, not a legal, question. We need therefore to scrutinize the apparent assumption by looking more closely at the character of the standard that governs judgment regarding what the law requires.

Determinacy

Our question ties objectivity with the possibility that lawyers mistake what the law requires. Some legal philosophers identify our question with another (see among others Brink 2001; Leiter 2001a, 2002); they ask: is the law determinate? This question is often put differently. Is there a fact of the matter regarding what the law requires? Are there right answers to questions of law? Or, more narrowly, are there right answers in hard cases?

These questions ask whether the law has determinate requirements at all, or whether it has determinate requirements in certain cases. Those who deny that it does may say that there is no fact of the matter regarding what the law requires, at least in some cases, or that there is no right answer to at least some questions of law. This approach has some appeal. After all, for lawyers to get legal requirements wrong there must be determinate requirements in the first place. Moreover, there is something important at stake when a certain subclass of lawyers, namely judges, rely or at least claim to rely on judgments about what the law requires in the resolution of disputes. Things would seem to be seriously amiss if there are no determinate legal requirements when they do so.

It would be wrong, however, to identify objectivity with determinacy. The fact that one has an experience of chocolate may have a determinate and subjective character at the same time: something may taste decidedly chocolaty to me, and I could not be wrong that it does. Judgments of color can also be determinate and subjective if certain explanations of the nature of color are right. If there is nothing more to something's being red than its being disposed to cause the occurrence of a certain qualitative experience in ordinary healthy subjects under normal conditions, it can be a determinate subjective fact that an object is red. Conversely, on a certain understanding, vagueness in predicates such as "bald" is not merely a consequence of our ignorance or failure to discriminate finely enough but rather a consequence of a feature of the world. On this view, it could be indeterminate whether Fred is bald. But if whether or not he is bald is determined by the actual number of strands of hair on his head, it can be an objective fact that it is neither true nor false that he is bald. Vague domains may include areas that are both indeterminate and objective. Determinacy is not necessarily tied to or even indicative of objectivity in law either, nor is indeterminacy so tied to or indicative of subjectivity. Suppose for a moment that what the law requires is fully determined by what individual judges decide regarding which party should win in a dispute. It would follow that the law could have determinate, albeit subjective, requirements. If a judge decided that plaintiff wins, it would be right to say that the law required that plaintiff win, and it could not turn out that the judge made a mistake about law's requirements. Conversely, if law's nature is such that we are all individually and collectively

fallible about what it requires – if even our shared understanding of what it requires can turn out to include mistakes – it can be an objective fact that the law is indeterminate on some question (compare Dworkin 1996: 134, regarding the question whether Picasso was a greater genius than Beethoven).

As we will see in a moment, philosophers who discuss the question of legal objectivity in terms of legal determinacy seem to rely on or at least to set aside further premises regarding the nature of law. By contrast, we have so far been addressing the question of objectivity with minimal or no reliance on controversial doctrines about the nature of law. We now need to consider how such alternative doctrines affect the issue. In this way, our investigation of objectivity may serve as a check of the plausibility of the doctrines. The question we then need to pose is not whether there are determinate legal requirements. Rather, we need to ask whether what determines what the law requires, and thereby defines the standard that governs judgments regarding what the law requires, is such that the relevant judgments can be mistaken and, if so, what precisely is the scope for error. We shall briefly survey some prominent substantive theories of the nature of law to see whether or not they imply that the law can be objective.

Conventions

H. L. A. Hart famously denied that judges are infallible, as some of the skeptics of his time suggested. On his and other legal positivists' view the nature of law and hence of the standard that governs judgment about the law is social in character, and consists of two components, one to do with *legality* and the other with *impact*. The first involves correct identification of the set of individual legal norms (or rules or laws), which stand in a systematic relation to each other and govern people's conduct in a community – the set of valid norms in the system. The second involves the conditions of correct application of the norms identified in the first stage to the facts of the cases in actual or hypothetical litigation. In classical positivism, both components are social, in the sense that both the identity of the set of valid norms and their correct application is determined by a social practice, conceived in terms of certain descriptive aspects of the collective behavior of a community. See LEGAL POSITIVISM. Different positivists explain the components differently and therefore each account entails a different precise sense in which the two components are social.

In Hart's original explanation, the set of valid norms is determined by a conventional practice of officials: it is the set of rules that officials apply in the resolution of disputes, as a matter of settled practice with which they consider it their duty to conform (Hart 1994: 100–23, 1982: 153–61). In that version of Hart's theory, the relevant officials identify these rules by origin: they are the rules which have either been expressly created by a person whose law-making authority is accepted by the officials by virtue of their practice, or are simply recognized by the officials as having the status of law.

The second component of the standard that governs judgment about the law consists in the part that governs how the rules are to be applied. This part, according to Hart, is also set by settled practice, albeit in respect of questions of classification. Correct application of the rules identified by the first component (which includes rules about the construction of other rules) is determined by correct application of the words in which the rules are formulated; and the latter is determined by judgments of classification actually made by lawyers or the community at large. Specifically, correct application is determined by general agreement in classificatory judgments. These include judgments that something is a paradigmatic instance of a term, or that it is (or is not) relevantly similar to the paradigms. Conversely, where "no firm convention or general agreement dictates [the word's] use or . . . its rejection by the person concerned to classify," there is no fact of the matter regarding the question whether or not a term applies (Hart 1994: 126–7).

In Hart's variant of positivism, the distance between legal requirement and legal judgment, in respect of both validity and impact, is small: while there is space between what the law requires and individual judgment about it, there is no space between what the law requires and settled collective judgment. Individual judges who

decide that the law includes a rule R may make a mistake as long as R is not in fact treated as such in judges' settled practice. But it would be incoherent to say that judges collectively made a similar mistake: the rules which judges have a settled disposition to consider legal just are – necessarily are – legal. And an individual judge who classifies Fs as Gs, where G is a term that figures in the formulation of a rule, may make a legal mistake by virtue of the fact that the settled practice of the community treats Fs as not-G. However it would make no sense to say that the community's settled practice of classification may incorporate mistake. What counts as G is determined by what we collectively classify as such (cf. Stavropoulos 2001).

In cases where there is no settled classificatory practice – some are disposed to classify Fs as G whereas others are disposed to classify Fs as not-G – the law becomes indeterminate for Hart. In such hard cases, judges must decide not in line with what the law requires – there is no determinate requirement for them to conform with – but rather by acting as legislators, extending the law in the hitherto indeterminate area. The choice they must make is unconstrained in a narrow sense: though of course it ought to be fair and just, and possibly to cohere with other parts of the law, it is a free choice insofar as, by hypothesis, the law as it stands does not dictate how they ought to choose.

Other variants of positivism may conceive differently of the components. For example, other accounts of legality may not accept that, conceived as purely conventional, the judicial practice of treating rules as legal suffices to determine the valid norms. For example, it may be necessary that the judiciary hold those who make norms to possess legitimate authority, in the sense that judges must either believe that they do possess it or at least merely adopt the perspective of someone who does believe they do (cf. Raz 1990: 170–7).

Further complications arise in respect of the question whether any moral conditions could ever be among law's determinants, granted that, if they are, this can only be in virtue of the contingent social fact that they are treated as such in judicial practice (which remains the ultimate, and itself purely social, foundation of law). This possibility is actually embraced by the so-called inclusive positivist view to which Hart eventually subscribed (Hart 1994: 238–76; Coleman 2001b). Drawing on a philosophical analysis of the concept of authority and cognate concepts, Joseph Raz suggests that this cannot be so. He argues that law's role in practical reason requires that norms that belong to a legal system must satisfy, among other conditions, the condition that they be created by someone who at least claims or is held to have legitimate authority over the norm's purported subjects. He argues that it would be inconsistent with the norms' role if their existence and content were not identifiable by reference to facts alone (see Raz 1995: 230).

Positivists may further conceive of the second component, which governs correct application of valid norms, in a way that is not dependent on strict linguistic conventions governing correct application of words in formulations of rules. For example, a positivist may accept that more than correct application of words in rules' formulations determines correct application of the rules; yet draw on an account of vagueness that is more sophisticated than Hart's to conclude, with him, that correct application of the rules is ultimately determined by similarity of putative instances to paradigms (cf. Endicott 2002). Like Hart's, such a view would limit the possibility of mistake in our classificatory practice, at least in this respect: what we treat as a paradigmatic instance of a term could not turn out to be not a genuine instance at all.

Law and its Application

In spite of differences among them, positivist theories of the nature of law seem to share two important implications in respect of the question of legal objectivity. First, by virtue of splitting the question what determines legal requirements in two – one about validity and another about application – they split the question of objectivity into two, relatively independent components.

Some of those who find the combined positivist explanation of the nature of law implausible may be tempted not to question the first part, thinking that it is only the second part that generates the implausibility. Grant for the sake of the argument that "the law" stands for a set or system of norms whose legality is distinct and prior to the question what the law requires: it follows that identifying law's requirements consists in applying the norms, which may necessitate interpretation, in the weak sense of a method for subsuming the facts of a case under the norms. The premise that we just granted then implies that the question of objectivity is equivalent to the question whether the law so conceived determines a uniquely correct outcome in disputes. If we are tempted by this line of thought, our discussion of objectivity should be accordingly focused on consideration of alternatives regarding the nature not of law but of legal interpretation (cf. Brink 2001; Leiter 2001b, 2002).

Even if we accept, either categorically or *arguendo*, the first part of the positivist explanation of the nature of law, we need not accept the second. For example, some skeptics grant the positivist that the law consists in a system of rules. They may then argue that since anything can be interpreted to accord with the rules (possibly because they agree with Hart and others that only settled practice could conceivably determine correct application of the rules, but think that anything could be made to accord with *that*), the law does not impose any determinate requirements. This view may be elaborated in different ways, which cannot be considered in this chapter.

Alternatively, one may argue both that legal interpretation includes more than the application of the words in the formulation of rules and that the further resources are not conventional or otherwise social in character. Moreover, one may argue that correct application of words is not (or not fully) determined by conventions or judgments of similarity practitioners are disposed to make, or generally by individual or social practice (cf. Moore 1985; Brink 2001; Stavropoulos 1996). In this way the law could come out that much more determinate and objective than Hart's model implies.

Social Practices

The second implication of positivist explanations of the nature of law flows from the thesis that social practices constitute both aspects of the standard which, according to this view, determines what the law requires. This has important consequences in respect of objectivity, since social standards restrict the scope of mistake. We already saw that Hart's theory only allows for a restricted kind of objectivity, limited by the understandings, judgments, and discriminations that judges collectively make as a matter of their settled practice. It is harder to assess conceptions of positivism that rely on more sophisticated conceptions of social standards. For example, Raz's explanation of such standards attempts to make more room for mistake, drawing on the notion of incomplete understanding.

According to Raz, a standard which governs social practices is constituted by the shared understanding of the practice, and provides the links among different judgments of practitioners by virtue of the fact that the judgments include implicit commitment to the shared understanding. However, although practitioners implicitly try to conform to the shared understanding, everyone may be mistaken about what that is – no one need fully understand what the shared understanding and hence the practice comes to, so everyone's judgment is subject to correction by reference to the standard, properly specified, to which they are all implicitly committed (compare Raz 2001a, 2001b, 2003). This account implies that, in spite of its social character, a standard can have critical bite in respect of each and every individual understanding and judgment, or even in respect of an amalgamation of all such understandings and judgments. Such an account may avoid crude reductions of social standards to statistical compilations of individual understanding and behavior, even supplemented by devices such as surveys of intuitions regarding hypothetical cases. In this way, it may serve to allow for considerable room for error and thereby objectivity in law: all judges may mistake what the standard they try to conform to requires in respect either of validity or correct application of norms.

It may still be argued that, since on this view the shared understanding of a practice constitutes the standard that governs it, law's objectivity is correspondingly limited. It would be incoherent on this view to say that the law has a certain requirement, even though a full and accurate specification of the shared understanding of the practice regarding conditions of validity and application (and of any other conditions that figure in the determination of law's requirement) in fact entails that it does not have it.

Values

Things may be otherwise if we accept that values are among law's determinants. On one version of such a view, what the law requires is determined by the principles that best justify certain political practices including the practices of lawyers and judges (Dworkin 1986). On this view, judges and other lawyers share a commitment, not to their shared understanding of their practice, but rather to the values or principles, if any, which in fact justify their practice. This means that they keep an open mind about which values or principles, if any, do so, and it is this tacit commitment that provides the link among the understandings and judgments of individual lawyers. This view introduces a determinant that is external to lawyers' shared understanding of legal practice (cf. Stavropoulos 2003). Now if we assume that something similar holds in respect of *evaluative* practices – that the domain of value is strongly objective in the sense that our shared understanding of values could be at least partly mistaken – law would have at least one determinant that lies at some considerable distance from the judgments, beliefs, and shared understandings of lawyers. This view then opens up the possibility not only of each judge or lawyer but of all judges and lawyers taken together, including any conception of their shared understanding, being mistaken about what the law requires.

Finally, the availability of such a strongly objectivist conception of value implies that inclusive positivists, who accept that values can figure among the conditions of legality, may run the risk of introducing instability to their view. For if what the law requires may turn, not on what lawyers and judges take it to require as a matter of their shared understanding of what it does, but rather on the correct understanding of some value, which may not match their understanding – if their shared understanding may turn out to be wrong – it is unclear how the character of law can still be conceived as fundamentally social (cf. Dworkin 2002: 1655–65).

Inclusive positivists such as Coleman acknowledge the apparent tension and introduce a distinction between the identity or content of rules and their application in order to eliminate it. They argue that values, to the extent that they figure in the determination of legal requirements, are pertinent only to application: the identity or content of the standard to which lawyers are committed can be on this view social and indeed conventional in character, even where its application turns on evaluative matters that go beyond any convention (Coleman 2001b). This implies that an evaluative fact, for example that a certain contract is in fact unfair, may in part make it the case that the law requires that the contract not be enforced, whether or not there exists a convention regarding what makes a contract unfair. But it can still be a conventional fact that the law requires nonenforcement of the contract, in virtue of the fact that there exists a convention of treating fairness, whatever it comes to, as a condition of enforceability.

The difficulty with this argument is that, on the usual understanding of convention, a standard is conventional just in case a certain kind of reason applies to those who are governed by it: the fact, itself, that there exists a certain settled behavior or judgment, itself constitutes a reason for conforming to it. But given that by hypothesis settled behavior or judgment may fail to track what the law requires, or none may exist, no such reason for doing as the law requires need be available. Since it need not be the case that other lawyers treat contracts such as the one in our example as unfair, a lawyer's reasons for considering it unfair need not include the reason that it is so treated by others.[1]

Note

1   I am grateful to William Edmundson and especially to Mark Greenberg for detailed written comments and discussion on an earlier draft.

References

Brink, D. 2001. Legal interpretation and morality. In B. Leiter (ed.), *Objectivity in Law and Morals*. Cambridge, UK: Cambridge University Press, 12–65.

Coleman, J. (ed.). 2001a. *Hart's Postscript*. Oxford: Oxford University Press.

Coleman, J. 2001b. *The Practice of Principle*. Oxford: Oxford University Press.

Dworkin, R. 1986. *Law's Empire*. Cambridge MA: Harvard University Press.

Dworkin, R. 1996. Objectivity and truth: You'd better believe it. *Philosophy and Public Affairs* 25: 87–139.

Dworkin, R. 2002. Thirty years on. *Harvard Law Review* 115: 1655–87.

Endicott, T. 2002. Law and language. In J. Coleman and S. Shapiro (eds.), *The Oxford Handbook of Jurisprudence & Philosophy of Law*. Oxford: Oxford University Press, 935–68.

Hart, H. L. A. 1982. *Essays on Bentham*. Oxford: Oxford University Press.

Hart, H. L. A. 1994. *The Concept of Law*, 2nd edn. Oxford: Clarendon Press.

Leiter, B. (ed.). 2001a. *Objectivity in Law and Morals*. Cambridge, UK: Cambridge University Press.

Leiter, B. 2001b. Objectivity, morality, and adjudication. In B. Leiter (ed.), *Objectivity in Law and Morals*. Cambridge, UK: Cambridge University Press, 68–98.

Leiter, B. 2002. Law and objectivity. In J. Coleman and S. Shapiro (eds.), *The Oxford Handbook of Jurisprudence & Philosophy of Law*. Oxford: Oxford University Press, 969–89.

Moore, M. 1985. A natural law theory of interpretation. *Southern California Law Review* 58: 277–398.

Nagel, T. 1986. *The View from Nowhere*. New York: Oxford University Press.

Nozick, R. 2001. *Invariances*. Cambridge, MA: Harvard University Press.

Raz, J. 1990. *Practical Reason and Norms*. Princeton, NJ: Princeton University Press.

Raz, J. 1995. *Ethics in the Public Domain*. Oxford: Oxford University Press.

Raz, J. 2001a. Two views about the nature of law. In J. Coleman (ed.), *Hart's Postscript*. Oxford, Oxford University Press, 1–37.

Raz., J. 2001b. Notes on value and objectivity. In B. Leiter (ed.), *Objectivity in Law and Morals*. Cambridge, UK: Cambridge University Press, 194–233.

Raz, J. 2003. *The Practice of Value*. Oxford: Clarendon Press.

Stavropoulos, N. 1996. *Objectivity in Law*. Oxford: Clarendon Press.

Stavropoulos, N. 2001. Hart's semantics. In J. Coleman (ed.), *Hart's Postscript*. Oxford, Oxford University Press, 59–98.

Stavropoulos, N. 2003. Interpretivist theories of law. In E. Zalta (ed.), *The Stanford Encyclopedia of Philosophy*, Winter 2003 edition <http://plato.stanford.edu/archives/win2003/entries/law-interpretivist/>.

Chapter 23

Can There Be a Theory of Law?

Joseph Raz

"Why not?" you may ask. And indeed few challenge the possibility of theorizing about the law, if that is taken to mean "engaging in theoretical debates" about the law. Yet the thought that there can be a theory of law, that is, a set of systematically related true propositions about the nature of law, has been challenged, and from several directions. None of the challenges is entirely successful. But through examining some of them we gain a better understanding of what a theory of law can be, and how its success can be established.[1]

I will be using "a theory of law" in a narrow sense, as referring to *an explanation of the nature of law.* It is a sense central to philosophical reflection about the law throughout its history. But in choosing this narrow understanding of "theory of law" I do not mean to dispute the appropriateness of other theoretical investigations about the law, some of which I have dabbled in myself on other occasions, nor to deny them the title of theories of law.[2] My choice to use the term in the narrow sense explained here is purely a matter of terminological convenience.

Therefore, as here understood a theory of law provides an account of the nature of law. The thesis I will be defending is that a theory of law is successful if it meets two criteria: first, it consists of propositions about the law which are *necessarily* true, and, second, they *explain* what the law is.

All theories aim to be successful, or at least to be more successful than their rivals. To understand what theories are we need to understand what it would be for them to be successful, that is, what it would be for them to be what they aim

to be. When discussing what a legal theory is I will assume that we are concerned with understanding the character of wholly successful theories, that is, of theories which meet the two conditions. The second and third sections of this chapter will discuss the two conditions. The first section aims to clarify the relationship between the thesis as stated above and the traditional way of understanding the task of legal theory as explaining the concept of law. The remaining sections (fourth to sixth) examine several difficulties with the idea that there can be a theory of law in general, a theory which since true is necessarily true of the law wherever and whenever it is to be found. The problems there examined arise out of the changing nature of concepts, out of the dependence of law on concepts, and out of the alleged impossibility of understanding alien cultures, using alien concepts.

Essence and Concept

What is the relation between the concept of a thing and its nature?

Concepts, as objects of philosophical study, as the target of conceptual analysis or elucidation, are a philosophical creation (Raz 1998: 254–5). Here is an example of one nonphilosophical use (quoted from the *Oxford English Dictionary*): " 'Techniques of testing product concepts in advertising could conceivably become as important as new physical research techniques have been to the chemical and metals industries' (*1970*

C. Ramond in R. Barton *Handbk. Advertising Managem.* xxii. 19).'' Here "product concepts" means something like ideas about possible products. There is, however, a common core to the philosophical and nonphilosophical uses. They relate to how people conceive certain objects or phenomena.

Metaphorically speaking, concepts (and from now on I will confine myself to the philosophical use of the term, and will feel free to suggest emendations of it) are placed between the world, aspects of which they are concepts of, and words or phrases, which express them (the concepts) and are used to talk about those aspects of the world. Some writers exaggerate their proximity to words and phrases and identify them with word – or phrase – meaning. Others associate them closely with the nature of their objects, the nature of what they are concepts of. When Ryle wrote about *The Concept of Mind*, or Hart *The Concept of Law* they meant, in advancing explanations of the concepts of mind and of law, to offer explanations of the nature of mind and of the law. Ryle opens his book by saying: "This book offers what may with reservations be described as a theory of the mind" (Ryle 1949: 9). Hart opens with: "My aim in this book has been to further the understanding of law, coercion, and morality as different but related social phenomena" (Hart 1961: v). For them, as for many other philosophers, there was no difference between an explanation of concepts and of the nature of things of which they are concepts. Some may even claim that there is no conflict between these two ways of understanding concepts, a view which dates back at least to the beginning of the twentieth century and the growth of "conceptual analysis" as a prime method of philosophical inquiry, which was often equated with analysis of the meanings of words and phrases.

The view I will advance allows that there is some truth in both approaches. But both are mistaken and misleading. Concepts are how we conceive aspects of the world, and lie between words and their meanings, in which they are expressed, on the one side, and the nature of things to which they apply, on the other.

The law offers an easy illustration of the non-identity of concepts and (word) meanings. Hart's *The Concept of Law* does not explain, nor does it aim to explain, the meaning of the word "law." It has nothing to say about divine law, mathematical or logical laws, laws of nature, nor many others. Nor do I think that it is a partial explanation of the meaning of the word. "Law" is not ambiguous, and *The Concept of Law* does not explain one of its meanings. When used in legal contexts "law" bears the same meaning as in other contexts. Nor is it plausible to think that its univocal meaning is explained by a list of alternatives, as if saying that "law" means what it means in legal contexts, *or* what it means in religious contexts, *or* what it means in mathematical contexts, and so on. The word is used in all these contexts to refer to rules of some permanence and generality, giving rise to one kind of necessity or another.

Those who offer explanations of the concept of law usually do mean, as Hart did, to explain the nature of a familiar social institution. It would have been possible for a language to contain a word which refers to this social institution and to nothing else. It may be mere accident that we do not have such a word, though there are good historical-intellectual explanations why "law" has the meaning it has. But things being as they are the meaning of the expression "the law" is not (identical with) the concept of law which Hart, and other philosophers of law, sought to explain.

Of course we express the concept, use it, and refer to it by using words. But we need not use the word "law" or "the law" to refer to it. We could talk of the law by talking of the system of courts and legislature and the rules they endorse in a state, for example. And we could do so in a large number of other ways. Most importantly, we rely on context, linguistic and nonlinguistic, to determine whether we are talking of the right sort of law when talking of law, or whether we are talking of scientific or other laws. The availability of context to determine reference establishes that there is no need for concepts to be identified by the use of specific words or phrases.

I will make two assumptions about concepts: first, I will assume that we can explain what they are by explaining what it is to have and understand them. That is, we explain a particular concept by setting out the conditions under which it is true of people that they have and understand that concept. Second, I will assume that concepts differ from each other by the information required to have and understand them, and by the skills and abilities involved in their possession. I call these assumptions, for in making them I am deviating from the ordinary meaning of "concepts," narrowing it down, and fashioning it in accordance with the way it is normally used in philosophical writings. Normally, rather than always, for the philosophical use is not uniform, and because in any case we should keep the freedom to deviate from philosophical usage where it would make sense to do so.

Those who, like Hart and Ryle, emphasize the close connection between concepts and the nature of things can be said to be implicitly committed to the view that a complete understanding of a concept consists in knowing and understanding all the necessary features of its object, that is, of that of which it is a concept. I will follow them in equating complete mastery of a concept with knowledge and understanding of all the necessary features of the objects to which it applies. Thus, complete mastery of the concept of a table consists in knowledge and understanding of all the essential properties of tables, and so on.

Is it an objection to this view that complete mastery of one concept can be identical with complete mastery of another without the two concepts being identical? Not necessarily. It is an objection only if we individuate concepts by the conditions for their complete mastery. Let me explain.

The concepts of an equilateral triangle and of an equiangular triangle are not the same concepts, but the necessary features of equilateral triangles are the same as those of equiangular ones. The necessary features of the one kind of triangle are the same as the necessary features of the other. We can accept that complete mastery of these concepts involves knowing that they apply to the same triangles, knowledge that the conditions for their complete mastery are the same. But they apply to the same triangles in different ways, for different reasons, the one because they are equilateral, while the other because they are equiangular.

How does this difference manifest itself? Primarily by the fact that concepts are individuated not merely by the conditions for their complete mastery, but also by the minimal conditions for having them. One may have the concept of an

equilateral triangle without realizing that it is part of the nature of such triangles to be equiangular. Admittedly, one's understanding of the concept will then be incomplete. But then the notion of complete understanding, as explained above, is very demanding. Most of the concepts we have and understand we master and understand incompletely. What one cannot fail to know, if one has the concept of equilateral triangles, is that the concept applies only to triangles with equal sides. This is where the two concepts (of equilateral and equiangular triangles, in the example) differ. They differ in the minimal conditions for their possession. For, of course, someone who does not know that the concept of equiangular triangles applies only to triangles with equal sides may still have (an incomplete mastery of) that concept. But if someone does not know that they apply to all and only triangles of equal angles then that person does not have the concept at all.

Following this line of thought I will maintain that an explanation of a concept has four parts:

1　Setting the conditions for the knowledge involved in complete mastery of the concept, which is the knowledge of all the essential features of the thing it is a concept of.
2　Explaining the understanding involved in complete mastery of the concept.
3　Explaining the conditions for minimal possession of the concept, that is, those essential or nonessential properties of what the concept is a concept of, knowledge of which is necessary for the person to have the concept at all, however incomplete his or her mastery of it may be.
4　Explaining the abilities required for minimal possession of the concept.[3]

The first condition determines what the concept is a concept of. But all of them together determine the identity of the concept.

As with other aspects of this inquiry my use of "minimal conditions for the possession of a concept" is partly responsive to our normal notions, and partly a stipulative regimentation of these notions. It allows that people may know things about concepts, while not having these concepts. One may know that N is an animal without having the concept of N. One may know that mauve is a color without having the concept, or that snakes lay eggs without having the concept of a snake. As this last example shows, knowledge that is inadequate for even minimal possession of a concept may be knowledge those who have mastered the concept (incompletely) may not have.

The mention of knowledge of nonessential properties as among the possible conditions for minimal possession of the concept is meant to allow that people may have knowledge which is sufficient to enable them to use the concept correctly in the circumstances of their life, but which is not true of it in all conditions. They may rely on the fact that swans that they have come across are white as crucial to their ability to identify swans. That may be part of what would justify judging them as having the concept.[4]

These considerations allow that people can refer to concepts which they do not possess. But this seems obvious for independent reasons as well. Reference to a concept need not employ any of its necessary features. For example, given that yesterday my friends discussed the concept of cruelty I can refer to it as the concept my friends discussed yesterday. I need know nothing more about it to successfully refer to it. They also allow that people may possess a concept and yet fail to recognize that it is identical with another, or think that there is only one, where there are two (the minimal conditions for the possession of the concepts of "water" and of "twater" are the same,[5] though the concepts are not identical since the conditions for their complete mastery differ).

It is possible for any person to invent or develop a new concept. Some concepts which emerge in that way make their way into the general culture, usually more or less modified along the way. But for the most part concepts exist independently of any one of their users. For the most part, we learn concepts, rather than invent or develop them. It must be so. Given the richness of our concepts and the limits of our abilities it is not possible for anyone to invent or modify more than a fractional margin of them. Given their role in communication it would be self-defeating to do so. The fact that for the most part concepts are there independently of any one of us does not mean of course that they are independent of us collectively. The conditions fixing the identity of particular concepts are idealizations constructed out of our conceptual practices, that is, out of the use of those concepts in general. They need not reflect any individual's practice. While it is impossible for a concept that no one knows anything about to exist, it is possible that no one has a completely correct understanding or knowledge of a concept, or indeed of any concept, including the concept of a concept.

Furthermore, while the conditions for concept possession are what they are because of our conceptual practices, it does not follow that we can identify the concept an individual uses, or intends to use, except by reference to our knowledge of what concepts there are. In part this is due to the fact that, with rare exceptions, when people use a concept, or try to, they intend to use a concept that is there (the one normally expressed by the word they use, etc.). Identification of intentions generally depends on (defeasible) presumptions of normality invoked by their manifestations (if you walk to the door then you intend to do so, unless some circumstances defeating the presumption obtain; if you say "I will open the door" then you mean what is normally meant when the sentence is uttered in like circumstances, unless some circumstances defeating the presumption obtain). Similarly, when you utter words to express a concept you express the concept that would normally be used when those words are uttered in those circumstances, unless defeating conditions obtain. Knowledge of the concept is presupposed in identifying the use of a concept. The speaker's intention to use the concept is identified by reference to presumptions of normality which presuppose such knowledge.

The preceding remarks show (1) how people can have incomplete understanding of concepts they possess, (2) how they can make mistakes about such concepts, including (3) mistakes about the identity of the concepts they possess and use.

These sketchy and rather dogmatically stated remarks were meant to explain why explaining a concept is close to explaining the nature of what it is a concept of (see the first condition of concept identity above), and yet why the two tasks differ (see the other conditions). They also explain why I regard the explanation of the nature of law as the primary task of the theory of law. That the explanation of the concept of law is one of its secondary tasks is a result of the fact that part of the task of explaining the nature of law is to explain how people perceive the law, and therefore, where the law exists in a country whose population has the concept of law, it becomes relevant to know whether the law is affected by its concept.

Can the Law Change its Nature?

A theory consists of necessary truths, for only necessary truths about the law reveal the nature of the law. We talk of "the nature of law," or the nature of anything else, to refer to those of the law's characteristics which are of the essence of law, which make law into what it is. That is those properties without which the law would not be law. As the *Oxford English Dictionary* explains, the nature of a thing consists of "the essential qualities or properties of a thing; the inherent and inseparable combination of properties essentially pertaining to anything and giving it its fundamental character."

Naturally, the essential properties of the law are universal characteristics of law. They are to be found in law wherever and whenever it exists. Moreover, these properties are universal properties of the law not accidentally, and not because of any prevailing economic or social circumstances, but because there is no law without them. This does not mean that there are no social institutions, or normative systems, which share many of the law's characteristics, but do not have the essential properties of the law. When surveying the different forms of social organization in different societies throughout the ages we will find many which resemble the law in various ways. Yet if they lack the essential features of the law, they are not legal systems.

This way of looking at the question may give rise to the suspicion that something has gone wrong right at the beginning of the inquiry. It seems to presuppose something which is plainly false. It presupposes that law has – indeed that it must have – an unchanging nature. But is not that a mistake? Surely – the objection runs – the nature of the law changes. Think of the law and the legal cultures of the Roman Empire, of European countries during feudalism, or in the age of absolutism. "Law" had different meanings during these different periods, and the modern Western notion of law differs from all of them. What was essential to the law of one period was absent in the law of another period. A theory of law which overlooks these facts cannot be a good theory.

But can the law change its nature? No doubt the law of any country can change, and does change. Moreover the institutions and practices of a country which constitute its law may lose the properties which are essential to the law. If that happens the result is not that the law changes its nature, but that the country no longer has a legal system (though it may have an institution which is not unlike the law in some or even many respects).

How do I know that the nature of law cannot change? That is a misconceived question. Following a well-established philosophical practice, I am using the term "the nature of law" and related terms such as "essential properties" to designate those properties which any (system of) law must possess to be law. This practice deviates from the way "the nature of" is sometimes used in nonphilosophical English. But it is important not to get hung up on terminological questions. The question is whether the law has essential properties, thus understood. And if it does, does understanding them enjoy a special role in understanding what the law is?

This reply to the objection that the inquiry is based on a false presupposition is not the end of the matter. It leads directly to a new criticism. It leads to a charge of arbitrariness, a charge of arbitrary verbal legislation which obscures important points. The use of "essential properties" and of "nature" which I propose to follow obscures the fact that in reality the nature of law changes with time, and therefore it obstructs rather than helps the development of a theoretical or philosophical account of law.

There is something right, as well as something wrong, in this objection. As has already been admitted, the use of "essential properties" and of "the nature of . . . " which I briefly delineated is not the only use these terms have. It is perfectly in order, indeed true, to say that with the rise of capitalism the nature of the state has undergone a profound change. Or to say that the absolute protection of property and contract has become an essential function of the state. "The nature of X," in other words, is often used to refer to properties of X which are taken to be of great importance, even though they are not definitive of the identity of X, that is, even though X will not cease being what it is without them. It will merely undergo radical change.

When Jeremiah asks "Can the Ethiopian change his skin or the leopard his spots?" (Jeremiah 13:23) is he assuming that the change is metaphysically impossible or conceptually inconceivable (for he thinks that a spotless leopard is no leopard, etc.) or just that it is impossible as a matter of fact? There is no answer to the question. In most communication and thought the distinction is rarely drawn, nor is there any reason to draw it. It is not surprising, however, that the distinction is of philosophical importance. Therefore it is not surprising that philosophers have established a technical meaning for the terms, and I will follow it. Doing so does not prejudge the questions: does the law have a nature, in that sense of the word? And if so, is it illuminating to investigate it? It is true, of course, that there is no point in using this philosophical terminology unless the answer to these questions is affirmative. The only point I have been arguing for so far is that the fact that the notions of essential properties, and of the nature of something, are philosophical notions does not in itself disqualify them, nor does it in itself impugn the enquiry into the nature of law.

Does the Law Have Essential Properties?

It is time to return to the argument: defining the object of a theory of law as a search for an explanation of the nature of law threatens to lead to its immediate abandonment, for it raises an obvious objection to the enterprise. I have conceded that it is part of our common understanding of the law that its nature (when that word is understood as it usually is) changes over time, both with changes in social and political practices, and with changes in culture, in philosophy, or more generally, in ways of understanding ourselves and our societies. Does not that show not only that the philosophical notion of the nature of a thing or of its essential properties is absent from our common discourse, but also that it has no application, or at least that it does not apply to the law? If this is so then by setting itself the goal of accounting for the nature of law legal theory condemns itself to inevitable failure. The argument that this is indeed the fate of legal theory so understood is simple: over time we have been happy to operate without the philosophical distinction between essential and nonessential properties, so that whenever changes in the character of the law or in our ideas or ways of understanding it so required we changed our concept of law. And this was true of any changes, however great. Does this not show that the thought that the law has a fixed nature is an illusion?

As it happens this argument is not a good one. It is not generally the case that belief that something has essential properties is a precondition of it having such properties. If being made of H_2O is of the nature of water then this is so whether or not people believe that it is so, and whether or not they believe that water has essential properties. More specifically, what counts is not the common understanding of expressions like "the nature of law," nor even the fact that the concept of law changes over time. What counts is the nature of the institution which the concept of law (i.e., the one we currently have and use) designates. To make its case the objection has to show that our concept of law (as it is at the moment) does not allow for the application of the (philosophical) notion of essential properties to the law, that is, that the law has no essential properties.

Prima facie the evidence points against the objection. It is part of our understanding of the law that certain social institutions are instances of law whereas others are nonlegal.[6] The distinction between the legal and the nonlegal is part and parcel of those of our practices which determine the concept of law. We know that the regulations of a golf club are not a legal system, and that independent states have legal systems. I know that an Act of the British Parliament is legally binding, but a resolution of my neighbors to deny any nonresident access to our street has no legal validity. And so on. Moreover, while the distinction is not marked by the presence of the same linguistic cues, it is fairly stable, used by lawyers, politicians, bureaucrats, and lay people, in a whole variety of contexts, always in the same way, always referring to the same set of practices and institutions. Indeed some may add that the very talk of "changes occurring in the concept of law" shows that once such changes occur it is no longer the same concept. It is a case of a new concept replacing the old one though they happen to share the same term.[7] Rather than challenging the thought that the law is marked by essential properties, talk of a change in the concept seems to confirm the thought – it seems to presuppose it.

This can be seen, of course, as a trivial point. The understanding of a concept includes an understanding of what determines what falls under the concept and what does not. In itself this does not show that the law has essential properties, that is, properties without which there can be no law. As we are often reminded, the concept of law may be a family resemblance concept.[8] Not all the items designated by a family resemblance concept share a common property, and *ipso facto* they do not have essential properties.

I believe that the news of family resemblance concepts has been much exaggerated. A family resemblance concept is meant to be an unstructured concept. It applies to some instances in virtue of their possession of a set of features, say A, B, C; it applies to other instances in virtue of a different, partly overlapping, set of features, say B, C, D; to others still in virtue of a set of features still further removed from the instances we started with, say C, D, E, and so on. I doubt that many concepts are of this kind. Elsewhere I have argued that the concept of a game, a paradigm of a family resemblance concept, is not a family resemblance concept after all (Raz 1999: ch. 4). While the meaning of many terms in natural languages cannot be given by a set of properties essential to their application, they usually have a core meaning with a structured set of extensions. This is why "root" can be used to refer to the root of the question, or "school" to a school of thought.

To some extent this debate is beside the point, beside our point. The notion of a family resem-

blance was developed by Wittgenstein in an argument against too regimented a way of accounting for the meanings of words and expressions. But the essential properties of law which legal theory is trying to give an account of are not invoked to account for the meaning of any term or class of terms. We are inquiring into the typology of social institutions, not into the semantics of terms. We build a typology of institutions by reference to properties we regard, or come to regard, as essential to the type of institution in question.

The distinction between inquiring into the meaning of terms and into the nature of institutions is often lost on legal theorists, perhaps in part because social institutions depend on the existence of complex practices including practices which can be broadly called linguistic, that is, practices of discussing certain matters by reference to aspects of these institutions. By coincidence it could happen that there are terms which derive their meanings exclusively from their employment to designate a central aspect of a particular social institution. In such a case the tasks of explaining the nature of the institution and explaining the meaning of the terms will be closely allied. Fortunately this is not the case with "law." While legal scholars sometimes write as if they think that the term is exclusively used to refer to the law of states, and courts, and so forth, the truth is otherwise. "Law" is employed in relation to sciences, grammar, logic, language, and many other areas. Moreover, while the law, that is, the law as we are interested in it, is replete with technical terms (e.g., "fee simple," "intestate") and other ordinary terms are used within the law with a technical meaning (e.g., "shares," "bonds," "equity") these are terms specific to one legal system or to a type of legal system. The general terminology of the law is no more specific to it than the word "law" itself. It consists of terms like "person," "status," "property," rights," "duties," which are part of the common terminology of practical discourse in general.[9]

Not only is the general terminology used to talk about the law common to practical discourse generally, but there is no single way in which we always mark that it is the lawyer's law that we have in mind when we talk of people's rights and duties, about what they are entitled to do or required to do, of benefits they enjoy or liabilities or risks they are subject to. Sentences of these kinds and many others can be used to assert how things are according to law, or how they are morally, or by the customs of the place, and so on. It is always possible to clarify which statement is made by prefacing one's words with "according to law" or by other devices. But most commonly we leave it to the context to clarify what exactly is being stated (and, of course, often we prefer not to disambiguate our meaning). It follows from these observations that while in the course of giving an account of the nature of law one may well engage in explaining the meaning of certain terms, the explanation of the nature of law cannot be equated with an analysis of the meaning of any term.

What then is an account of the nature of law, of its essential properties? We are trying, I have suggested, to explain the nature of a certain kind of social institution. This suggests that the explanation is part of the social sciences, and that it is guided or motivated by the considerations which guide theory construction in the social sciences. In a way this is true, but this way of making the point may encourage a misguided understanding of the enterprise. It makes it sound as if some abstract theoretical considerations determine the classification of social institutions, considerations like theoretical fruitfulness, simplicity of presentation, deductive or computational simplicity, or elegance.

Considerations like these may indeed be relevant when a classification, a typology, or a concept is introduced by academics for the purpose of facilitating their research or the presentation of its results. The notion of law as designating a type of social institution is not, however, part of the scholarly apparatus of any learned discipline. It is not a concept introduced by academics to help with explaining some social phenomena. Rather it is a concept entrenched in our society's self-understanding. It is a common concept in our society and one which is not the preserve of any specialized discipline. It is used by each and all of us to mark a social institution with which we are all, in various ways, and to various degrees, familiar. It occupies a central role in our understanding of society, our own as well as other societies.

In large measure what we study when we study the nature of law is the nature of our own self-understanding. The identification of a certain social institution as law is not introduced by sociologists, political scientists, or other academics as part of their study of society. It is part of the self-consciousness, of the way we conceive and understand our society. Certain institutions are thought of as legal institutions. That consciousness is part of what we study when we inquire into the nature of law.

But why should we? Is it not our aim to study the nature of law, rather than our culture and its concept of law? Yes and no. We aim to improve our understanding of the nature of law. The law is a type of social institution, the type which is picked up – designated – by the concept of law. Hence in improving our understanding of the nature of law we assume an understanding of the concept of law, and improve it.

Parochial or Universal?

At this point a new objection may be raised. Does not the fact that we study the nature of an institution which is picked out by *our* concept of law make the inquiry parochial rather than universal? Talk of *the* concept of law really means *our* concept of law. As has already been mentioned, the concept of law changes over time. Different cultures have different concepts of law. There is no one concept of law, and when we refer to the concept of law we just mean our concept. Therefore, to the extent that the inquiry is limited to the nature of law as understood in accordance with our concept of it, it is a parochial study of an aspect of our culture rather than a universal study of the nature of law as such. Far from coming together, as has been suggested above, the study of the nature of law as such and of our self-understanding (in as much as it is encapsulated in our concept of law) are inimical to each other. Some people may develop the point further to the conclusion that there is no such thing as "the nature of law as such." To claim otherwise is to commit the mistake of essentialism, or of objectification. Others would merely conclude that the study of the nature of the thing (the law) and of our concept of it are not as closely related as has been suggested above, and that one must choose which one to pursue.

Common though this line of thought is, it is misguided. Think of it: we and other cultures have different concepts; not only different concepts of law. What makes some of them alternative concepts of law, whereas others are concepts of government, religion, tribes, or whatever but not of law? What accounts for the difference? What makes a concept "the so-and-so concept of law" (e.g., "the medieval concept of law")? Ignoring the occasions on which "the concept of . . . " is used to refer to the common opinions which people held about the law (the medieval concept of law being the views about the law, its role and function, common in medieval Europe), different *concepts* of law are concepts of *law* in virtue of their relations to our concept of law. Most commonly these are relations of similarity (X's concept of law is a concept of a social institution very much like, though not quite the same as, what we understand by law), or of a common origin (our concept of law developed out of the medieval concept, etc.). The point to note is that it is our concept which calls the shots: other concepts are concepts of law if and only if they are related in appropriate ways to our concept.

Let us accept that what we are really studying is the nature of institutions of the type designated by the concept of law. These institutions are to be found not only in our society, but in others as well. While *the concept* of law is parochial, that is, not all societies have it, our inquiry is universal in that it explores *the nature* of law, wherever it is to be found. Even so the charge of parochialism is liable to reappear in a new form. Is it not the case that the institution of law is to be found only in societies which have the concept of law (i.e., our concept of law)? Since it has been allowed earlier that the concept of law as we know it has developed in the West in modern times, and is certainly far from a universal feature of human civilization, a theory of law which concentrates on the nature of law, in the sense explained above, is relevant to modern Western societies only. It may be universal in a formal sense. In the philosophically stipulated sense of "the nature of law" the inquiry applies to all the legal systems which ever existed or that could exist. But this way – my imagined objector goes on to say – of rebutting the charge of parochialism is a pyrrhic rebuttal. The inquiry, when successful, is universally valid

for a narrow concept of law, the modern Western concept of law. It is relevant not to all legal systems, as the term is usually – and nonphilosophically – understood, which include the law of the Aztecs, of the countries of medieval Europe, of the Roman Empire, or of China in the fifth century BC and so on. The philosophical inquiry would have to exclude those, as they do not conform to the modern, capitalist, or postindustrial, concept of law.

Put in this form the objection is based on a mistaken understanding of our concept of law. One way in which it has been changing over the last two or three centuries is to make it more inclusive and less parochial. As our knowledge of history and of the world has expanded, and as our interest in history, and our interaction with other parts of the world, have become more extensive, the concept of law has developed to be more inclusive. Admittedly, it responds not only to our interest in other societies, but also to our understanding of ourselves and our society, and the two may conflict. Features which seem to us central in ourselves and in our society may be lacking in other societies. Their importance to us in our societies tends to encourage forging more parochial concepts. To some this factor appears to be the only or the dominant factor influencing our concepts. This leads to further (or reformulated) objections to the universalist ambition of philosophical theories.

Some theorists take parochialism in their stride and allow it to fashion their theories. The outstanding example of a legal theory of this kind is R. M. Dworkin's. From the beginning he saw his theory as a theory of the law of the United States and of the United Kingdom. Of course it may be true of other legal systems as well. But it is not its declared ambition to be universal.[10] One reason elaborated by Dworkin in justification of this modest ambition is the fact that the concept of law is part of the practice of law (Dworkin 1986: ch. 1). Dworkin has pointed out that courts of law are sometimes confronted with issues which force them to reflect about the nature and boundaries of the law. They may refer to philosophical theories in answering these questions, and their answers and arguments buttressing them are on a par with philosophical discussions of these issues. This is not to say that their answers and discussions are as good as philosophical theories. They may be better or worse. The point is that they are engaged in the same enterprise as philosophers. Their conclusions rival philosophical conclusions: if they disagree then one is wrong and the other may be right.

It is tempting to reinforce the point just made by adding that while often courts will not attend to theoretical disputes about the nature of law since nothing in contention between the parties turns (or was claimed to turn) on disagreements about the nature of law, nevertheless any court's decision presupposes some view or other about the nature of law. This seems to me to go beyond what the evidence warrants. The fact that if challenged to defend an action of mine I will have to advance theoretical arguments does not establish that I already have a theoretical view of one kind or another. I may have none, not even implicitly, and I may not be committed to any.[11] One cannot infer that people have certain beliefs, or beliefs of a certain description, just because they should have them. And while the courts may be committed to the view that there is some way of justifying their decisions, they are not committed to any view about which way justification lies.

It is wiser, therefore, not to reinforce the observation that the courts sometimes engage in a theoretical argument about the nature of law with the further point that all their decisions presuppose a view about the nature of law. The observation itself, however, is correct and beyond dispute.[12] What lessons should we learn from them? Dworkin suggests that this establishes that law and legal philosophy are part of the same, self-reflective, practice. This implies that American legal philosophy is part of American law, that legal philosophy when studied in an American university is related to legal philosophy as studied in Italy in the same way that property law studied in an American university relates to property law studied in Italy. They are studies of analogous parts of the law, but are basically very different enterprises: an account of property law, or an aspect of it, may be true of Italy and false of the USA. Similarly a theory about the nature of law may be true of the USA, but false of Italy. If it is true of both countries this is a contingent result of some historical developments which could

have been otherwise. Theories of law, in other words, are necessarily parochial.

Whether or not they are parochial, this argument does not prove that they are. Perhaps it is no exaggeration to say that any issue, from astrophysics to economics to biblical exegesis, can be relevant to some legal decision or another. This would not show that any of those studies are part of American law in America and of Chinese law in China. The fact that a certain theoretical issue is material to a court's decision would only show that the court should aim to get the matter right, to learn from the discipline concerned how things stand in the matter at issue. It does not show that by engaging in economic, sociological, or biblical arguments courts can change the conclusions of those disciplines, that the fact that they come to some conclusion in these areas makes those conclusions true in economics or sociology, and so on. Nor will this conclusion change if in some country or another once a court has taken a decision based on such grounds it would not be open to challenge on the ground that it got its economics, and so forth, wrong.

All this is plain enough, but is it not different with legal theory? While the courts have no special authority in economics or political science, do they not have special authority regarding the concept of law? The answer is that it depends. Consider, by way of analogy, the same question raised about the notion of an undertaking. A case may turn on whether or not one person undertook to perform a service for another. Has the law authority to decide what counts as undertaking to do something? Yes and no. The courts have authority to decide when the law of their country would view an action as a binding undertaking. But the notion of an undertaking has life outside the law. And the court has no authority to decide what is an undertaking in that sense. I do not mean to say that it is precluded from forming a view on the matter, or from relying on that view. It may be required by law to form such a view since the plaintiff in a case may be entitled to relief only if the defendant has undertaken (in the ordinary sense of the word) to perform a service for him or her. The point I am urging is that if the court gets this wrong its decision would not change the nature of undertakings, any more than if it gets an economic argument wrong its decision can change economic theory.

If things look differently in the case of an undertaking than in economics this is because a mistaken decision of the court may be the first step towards the emergence of a special technical sense of undertaking in the legal system concerned. That may be so even if the court did not mean it that way, even if it meant simply to find out what is an undertaking in the ordinary sense of the word. It is the same with the concept of law as it is with the concept of an undertaking. Of course, unlike the concept of an undertaking the concept of law applies only to the law. But like the concept of an undertaking it is a common concept in our culture which applies not only to our law but to the law of other countries, now as well as in the past or the future. It also applies to law in fiction, and in hypothetical cases. In short it is not a concept regarding which the courts have special authority. When a decision turns on a correct elucidation of the concept the courts try to get it right, as they do when it is about an undertaking, or about an economic argument. If they fail this may lead to the emergence of a technical sense for the term in that legal system. But it will not lead to a change in the notion of law. The claim that a theory of law is parochial because legal theory is part of legal practice is misguided. Legal theory is not part of legal practice, at least not in the sense required to establish its parochial nature.

Can There be Law Without the Concept of Law?

Another argument for the parochial nature of legal theory turns on the claim that there is no law in a society which does not have the concept of law. Since I have admitted that the concept of law (i.e., our concept of law) is parochial and that not all societies which had law also had our concept of law, it follows that not all of them had institutions recognized as law by our concept. A theory of law which aims to explain the nature of the institutions and practices which our concept of law recognizes as law is therefore only

nominally universal. It applies to all that our concept recognizes as law, but our concept fails to recognize as law many legal systems for the reason that they did not have our concept of law, and there is no law without the concept of law.

We have to distinguish two versions of the argument. One claims that there cannot be law in a society which does not have a concept of law. According to it societies which do have some concept of law can have institutions and practices which are clear instances of the concept of law (as we have it). The other, more radical version claims that only societies which have our concept of law can have institutions and practices which are instances of the concept of law that we have. To make its conclusion good the radical version of the objection has to show that no society which does not have our concept of law can have a legal system, as that institution is understood by our concept. That is an unlikely claim, which can be easily refuted by example, by simply pointing to some faraway society, say that of Egypt in the fourth century BC, which did not have our concept of law, but had the institutions which that concept recognizes as legal.

Even the weaker claim – that there cannot be law in a society which does not have some concept of law – is probably mistaken. The rest of this section is devoted to an examination of this weaker claim. Remember the following three theses:

First, that the concept of law (our concept) is local in the sense that while some societies have it, others do not.

Second, that there is no law in a society which does not have a concept of law (though it need not have our concept).

Third, that a successful theory of law, being a correct account of a type of institution designated by a concept of law, applies only to institutions which prevail in cultures which possess the concept of law which designates the type of institution the theory explains.

Together they lead to the conclusion that there are many valid theories of law, each applicable to a different type of social institution, picked out by a different concept of law. A theory of the institutions picked out by our concept of law applies only to the law in societies which have (or had) our concept of law.

I have already endorsed the first of these propositions. We undermine the strong version of the argument by rejecting the third premise. To refute the weak version one has to show that there is no reason to accept the second premise. Undermining the second premise also undermines the third, which presupposes it. So let us examine the second premise, and with it the conclusion that legal theory understood as the study of the nature of the institutions identified as law by the (i.e., our) concept of law is valid only of legal systems equipped with some concept of law. I will argue that it is not the case that only a society with a concept of law can be governed by law.

What would it be like for law to exist in a society which does not have a concept of law? It would mean that they would not think of its law as law. It is true that we have law and that we think of it as law. But is it not possible for a society which has a legal system not to be aware of it as a legal system? I will argue that it is.

This means that in legal theory there is a tension between the parochial and the universal. It is both parochial and universal. On the one hand it is parochial, for it aims to explain an institution designated by a concept that is a local concept, a product of modern Western civilization. On the other hand it is a universal theory for it applies to law whenever and wherever it can conceivably be, and its existence does not presuppose the existence of its concept, indeed it does not presuppose the existence of any legal concept.

H. L. A. Hart, in *The Concept of Law*, argued that it is necessary for a satisfactory account of law to explain how the law is perceived and understood by the people who live under it. To use his terminology – which in general I will avoid as it is open to diverse and confusing interpretations – he argued that a legal system cannot exist in a country unless at least part of its population has an internal attitude to the law, regards the law from the internal point of view, or accepts the law as a guide to its behavior – these being alternative descriptions of the same attitude. This claim of Hart, perhaps the central claim of his theory of law, has since been widely accepted. But its meaning is much in dispute. I think that

Hart was right to insist that it is in the nature of law that in general its existence is known to those subject to it, and that normally it plays a role in their life.

I say "normally" for it is of course possible for people to disregard the law, to be mindless of its existence. But that condition is abnormal not only, if at all, in being rare. It is abnormal because it is of the essence of law that it expects people to be aware of its existence and, when appropriate, to be guided by it. They may not be. But that marks a failure in the law. It shows that it is not functioning as it aspires to function.

I find nothing amiss in personalizing the law, as I just did in the previous paragraph. We do refer to the law as imposing requirements and duties, conferring rights and privileges and so on. Such expressions are unexceptional. The law's actions, expectations, and intentions are its in virtue of the actions, expectations, and intentions of the people who hold legal office according to law, that is, we know when and how the actions, intentions, and attitudes of judges, legislators, and other legal officials, when acting as legal officials, are to be seen as the actions, intentions, and expectations of the law. They, acting as officials, express the demand and the expectation that people be aware of the law and that they be guided by it.

Hart, in describing the internal attitude which legal officials necessarily have, and which others are expected to have, strove to identify only those aspects of their attitude to the law which are essential to its existence. He saw no conflict between the fact that officials and others in every society with law adopt the internal point of view towards the law and the universal character of the law. And in a way he was right. There is no contradiction between the two. But I think that while his views are compatible with my emphasis on the parochial nature of the concept of law he was unaware of these implications.

The question is: does people's awareness of rules of law mean an awareness of them as rules or an awareness of them as rules of law? Need they, in other words, possess the concept of law in order to be members of a political community governed by law? Hart assumed, and surely he was right, that in our cultures the concept of law is available to all, that most people have a fairly good general grasp of it. He has identified certain features as the uncontroversial core of the common understanding of the concept of law. His own account of the concept merely deepens our understanding by drawing out some of the implications of the concept as it is commonly understood, the concept of law as we have it.

But our possession of the concept is logically independent of the fact that we live in a political community governed by law. We could have had the same concept had we lived in a state of nature. We might then have used the concept to understand the difference between the law-free society we inhabit and the condition of other countries which do live under legal systems, and the difference between the current state of our society and what it might have been or may become. Contrariwise it would seem that Hart is not committed to the view that to live in a society governed by law we need be aware of the concept of law, beyond an awareness of the rules which in fact constitute the law of our society.

I am, of course, asserting here that the concept of a rule, or a variant of it, is not a concept of a type of the social phenomena we take the law to be, that it is not any kind of concept of law. Of course, the word "law" designates, among other things, rules or norms, and the concept of a rule probably emerged from a concept of a law which did not separate natural law from customary practices, nor either of them from a normative law. But these features are not sufficient to make it *a* concept of law, of the family that "our" concept of law is a paradigm of, for I take it to be paradigmatic that a family of concepts designates types of normative systems, and of social institutions rather than a single norm or rule. Once we accept that concepts of law are concepts of normative systems/social institutions, it is easy to see that the fact that individuals in such societies did possess the concept of a rule does not show that they had a rudimentary grasp of some concept of law, unless the concept existed at the time. True, one cannot have the concept of a legal system without having the concept of a rule, and the latter concept can feature in a rudimentary grasp of the nature of a legal system. But individuals can have a rudimentary grasp of a concept only if it exists. Incomplete mastery is incomplete mastery of something there can be complete mastery of at

that time. Hence, in establishing that there can be no law without its subjects having the concept of a rule Hart has not shown that there can be no law without the concept of law.

By way of contrast Dworkin's theory of law assumes that an awareness of the concept of law is necessary for the existence of law in any society. For him the law is an interpretive practice which exists only in societies which are aware of the nature of that practice and of its interpretive character, and thus possess the concept of law.[13] In this, however, Hart's position is the correct one. Our concept of law does not make an awareness of it in a society a precondition of that society being governed by law. I will illustrate this point with one example only.

Jewish religious rules and practices are rich and diverse. They did, at an earlier stage of their development, govern the life of independent Jewish communities, and, in more recent times, they governed many aspects of life in Jewish communities in many parts of the world. Whenever theocratic autonomous Jewish communities existed or may exist they would be subject to law, that is, Jewish religious law. But the concept of law is not part of the Jewish religion, and where such communities existed in the past they often existed in societies whose members did not possess the concept of law. Jewish religious thought and doctrine encompasses much more than law. It encompasses what we regard as comprehensive systems of law, ethics, and religion, areas which though overlapping are also, in our eyes, distinct. To the Orthodox Jew of old there is no division within Judaic doctrines which captures the divisions indicated by "our" concepts of law, religion, and ethics. Yet beyond doubt theocratic Jewish communities did have a legal system even though they lacked the concept of law, or at any rate some of them (those which had not learnt it from other cultures) lacked it.

I believe that much the same is true of some other religious systems. "Our" concept of law is probably alien to the culture of Islamic theocracies, but it would be absurd to think that Iran, for example, does not have a legal system, or that its having a legal system depends on Iranians having acquired the concept of law before their Islamic revolution, or through their acquaintance with the law of other countries. Rather, the correct conclusion is that while the concept of law is itself a product of a specific culture, a concept which was not available to members of earlier cultures, this does not show that those cultures did not have law. The existence of law requires awareness by (at least some) members of the society of being guided by rules, awareness of disputes regarding the meaning of the rules, and regarding claims that they have been breached, being subject to adjudication by human institutions, and – in many, though not necessarily all cases – awareness that the rules, or some of them, are the product of deliberate rule-creation by some people or institutions. But none of these features is unique to the law. They are shared by it and many other social structures, such as religions, trade unions, and a variety of associations of many kinds. Therefore, awareness of these features does not presuppose awareness of them as aspects of a legal system. And there is nothing else in the concept of law which requires that people be aware of their institutional structure as a legal system in order for their institutions to constitute a legal system. Notice, however, that there is a discrepancy between my use of the example of Jewish religious law and the more abstract argument I provided. The argument rejected the second premise mentioned above, that is, the premise that law can exist only in a society which has some concept of law, on the ground that (1) the correct proposition that law can exist only in a society in which at least part of the population accepts its rules and is guided by it does not yield the second premise as a conclusion; and (2) that the example of Jewish law shows that our concept of law does apply to legal systems which do not have our concept of law. The example is not sufficient by itself to show that our concept of law identifies as legal systems practices existing in societies which had no concept of law whatsoever. That would be more difficult to show by example. The case rests on the absence of a reason to think otherwise, given the rest of the argument.

We can therefore conclude that the charge, or the ready admission, that a theory of law must be parochial, for it can apply only to countries which possess our concept of law, or to countries which possess some concept of law, is mistaken. The law can and does exist in cultures which do not think of their legal institutions as legal, and a theory of law aims to give an account of the law wherever it is found, including in societies which do not possess the concept of law.

On the Alleged Impossibility of Understanding Alien Cultures

I have argued that while the concept of law is parochial, legal theory is not. Legal theory can only grow in cultures which have the concept of law. But its conclusions, if valid at all, apply to all legal systems, including those, and there are such, which obtain in societies which do not have the concept of law.

This conclusion has been criticized from a slightly different direction. The fact that concepts emerge within a culture at a particular juncture is often seen as a vindication of some radical philosophical thesis such as relativism, or postmodernism, or ethnocentrism. In particular it is taken to show our principled inability to understand, or at any rate to understand completely, alien cultures. In fact it shows little, certainly not that concepts can only apply to phenomena which exist in cultures which have those concepts. Consider, for example, the notion of "the standard of living." It may well not have been available to people in medieval Europe. But there is nothing in this fact to invalidate discussions of the effect of the Wars of the Roses on the standard of living in Lancashire. People would enjoy the same standard of living whether or not they were aware of the notion, or of the measurement of their own standard of living. The same is true of many other economic notions.

Some concepts are different. Arguably since gifts are gifts only if intentionally given *as such* there cannot be gifts among people who do not possess the concept of a gift. As we saw, something like this is true of rules. People are not guided by rules unless they are aware of them as rules. But, and that is the crucial point, they need not be aware of rules as legal rules in order to be guided by rules which are in fact legal.

On reflection there is nothing surprising in this. Of crucial importance is the fact that concepts like that of the law are essential not only to our understanding of the practices and institutions of our own societies, but also to our understanding of other societies. In our attempts to understand societies with cultures radically different from ours we encounter a conflict. On the one hand, to understand other societies we must master their concepts, for we will not understand them unless we understand how they perceive themselves. But, on the other hand, we cannot understand other cultures unless we can relate their practices and customs to our own. Their concepts will not be understood by us unless we can relate them to our own concepts. How can this conflict be resolved? It seems to land us in an impasse which forces us to admit the impossibility of truly or completely understanding alien cultures.

This pessimism is, however, unjustified. We can meet both conditions for understanding alien cultures. While there may be a tension between the need to understand them in terms of some of our concepts, even though they do not have those concepts, and the need to understand how they understand themselves, that is, in terms of concepts which we do not have, there is no contradiction here. Both conditions can be fully met. Far from being irreconcilable they are interdependent. That is, the understanding of alien cultures requires possession of concepts which apply across the divide between us and them, concepts which can be applied to the practices of other cultures as well as to our own. Reliance on such concepts is necessary to make the alien cultures intelligible to us. They are required to enable us better to understand their concepts which we do not share.

Let us examine the argument to the contrary, the pessimistic argument. The fact that some cultures do not possess all of our concepts, and that they possess concepts which we do not have, makes them alien. If we need to rely on concepts which they do not possess in our attempt to understand them, as we commonly do, then our attempts are doomed to failure. They fail, the argument goes, to satisfy the other condition of understanding a culture, that is, that one must understand how its members understood themselves. This condition requires, so the argument continues, understanding the alien culture from inside, that is, using only concepts which were available to its members, only concepts that they used in understanding themselves.

Where does the pessimistic argument go wrong? It overlooks the ways in which we acquire many of the concepts that we muster. Concept acquisition often results from a combination of establishing, through explicit explanation or by observing how they are used by others, relations between them and other familiar concepts on the one hand, and learning their use by osmosis, by using them or observing their use, being set right by others when one makes a mistake, or, more commonly, observing through the reactions of others that one's use of the concept was not altogether happy. Let us call those two ways, often interrelated and not clearly distinguished in practice, learning by definition and learning through imitation. It is sometimes thought that some concepts are learnt one way and some another. Color concepts are thought to be examples of concepts acquired by imitation, by ostension. Mathematical concepts, and generally abstract concepts, are thought to be learnt through definitions. In fact it is reasonable to suppose that all our concepts which have use outside narrowly delimited groups of users and purposes of use[14] are learnt through a combination of both methods. To acquire the concept of red one needs to know that it is a color concept, that it is a perceptual concept, that nothing can be both red and green all over, and other matters one is likely to learn partly through definitions. To acquire the number concept "two" one needs to know that when two drops of water merge there is only one drop of water there, and to have other knowledge likely to be acquired partly by imitation.

I am not arguing that any single stage in the process of acquiring the concept, like the ones I mentioned, depends on only one or the other of the two methods. Most, perhaps all, of them can succeed through either method. I am saying, however, that it is humanly impossible to acquire concepts generally except through a combination of both methods.

Some people who share these views about concept acquisition may find in them further argument for the pessimistic conclusion about our alleged inability to understand alien cultures. But this seems to me to overlook the role of imagination and thought experiments in the process of learning and understanding. In principle we can understand alien cultures because we can acquire their concepts, provided we have a substantial enough body of data to allow learning by imitation, either real imitation of one who visits or joins the alien culture, or through imaginative and sympathetic engagement with and reflection on reports of the nature of the culture and its habits, and other historical data. Naturally the material available about that culture may be insufficient. It may leave gaps in our mastery of its concepts and our understanding of its ways. But these are practical, not principled, limitations.

Our understanding of alien cultures will, however, remain incomplete until we can relate their concepts to ours. Why is this a necessary condition of understanding? After all, it may well be that none of the members of the alien culture understands our culture. If they can understand their own culture, as surely they can, without relating it to ours why cannot we do the same? The short answer is: because we, unlike them, know and understand our culture. Given our situation we cannot understand the alien culture without relating it to ours. Here is an analogy: native French speakers have complete mastery of French, even if they have no knowledge of English. But native English speakers who study French as a foreign language cannot understand it if they do not know what "*un homme*," "*une maison*," "*plaisir*," and so on, mean in English.[15]

There is an asymmetry here between one's knowledge of French and one's knowledge of English. Only when the English speakers' command of French and its relations to English reaches very high levels of subtlety and expertise, or when it is reflective knowledge leading them to reflect about the similarities and the differences between the languages, does it become appropriate to say that their understanding of English is improved by their deep knowledge of French. For ordinary English speakers who study French for practical purposes and are not inclined to reflect on its nature, no such benefit occurs: that is, their knowledge of French is improved by their growing ability to translate French into English. But their knowledge of English is not affected. This asymmetry is the main manifestation of what I will call "the route-dependence" of understanding in general. We understand new things by relating them to what we already understand, even though had we started somewhere else we could have gained an understanding of those things without understanding how they relate to what we in fact know. Moreover, while in some ways, and under some conditions our newly acquired understanding can deepen or improve what we understood already, it need not do so.

The route-dependence of understanding is sometimes stated by saying that we understand whatever we understand from our personal "point of view." While there is nothing wrong in applying this overused expression in this context, it can have unfortunate connotations. For some people it carries associations of blinkers, of limitations, and distortions. If we can understand alien cultures *only* from our point of view it shows – or so it is alleged – that we do not understand them as they really are, that our understanding is imperfect and distorted. After all, we understand the alien cultures through *our* modern Western perspective, relying on *our* notions and on *our* knowledge of history and of many cultures not known to members of the cultures which we are studying. So our understanding of their cultures differs from their own understanding of their own cultures, and cannot be altogether objective, or perfect, or something like that.

The example of a native English speaker acquiring French was meant to disprove that thought. To be sure, it is difficult to acquire perfect command of a second language, which is learnt after one has acquired one's first language. But it is possible in principle, and in practice as the examples of people like Conrad and Nabokov show. To master a second language one has to relate it to one's first language, whereas a native speaker of that second language need know no other. Nevertheless, in principle both can have perfect command of that language. I have explained the fact that while they arrive at the same destination only one of them must, to get there, know how what is to that person the second language relates to his or her first language by saying that understanding (and explanation) are route-dependent. But until we understand why this is so we cannot be confident that route-dependence does not affect the possibility of perfect knowledge, or its objectivity. This is a topic for another occasion. Let us take stock of the conclusions tentatively arrived at so far.

We have already traveled some way from the goal of establishing the possibility of legal theory. That was made necessary because the challenge to the possibility of theory depends on assumptions with much wider ramifications. Now we have to travel even further afield. To establish the possibility of a theory of law, a theory which explains the nature of law, we need to examine some issues concerning the function of explanation. The aim of the examination would be to vindicate the conclusion tentatively arrived at in this chapter (at the end of the previous section), namely, that legal theory has universal application, that it – when successful – provides an account of the nature of law, wherever and whenever it is to be found. The objectivity and universality of the theory of law is not affected by the fact that the concept of law (which is our concept of law) is parochial and not shared by all the people nor by all the cultures which live or lived under the law.

That conclusion was based on the claim that to understand an alien culture and its institutions we need to understand both how its members understand themselves, and how their concepts, practices, and institutions relate to ours. This means that to understand alien cultures we must have concepts whose application is not limited by the boundaries of our culture, which apply to alien cultures as well as to our own. I neither have argued nor will argue that our culture has the intellectual resources which make it possible, with good will and sympathetic imagination, to understand alien cultures. I take it for granted that that is so. I have argued that if we have these resources, and if such understanding is possible, then the concept of law is one such concept. I have argued for that by the use of the example of theocratic societies, and the fact that we apply the concept of law to their institutional arrangements. The concept of law is among the culture-transcending concepts. It is a concept which picks out an institution which exists even in societies which do not have such a concept.

That does not establish that a theory of law is in principle possible, or that if it is possible it can achieve objective knowledge, rather than provide a blinkered way of understanding those alien cultures, albeit the best understanding which can be achieved from our subjective point of view. To positively establish the possibility of a theory of law we need to examine the nature of explanation and of objectivity. The reflections here offered do, however, remove some misunderstandings which sometimes lead people to doubt the possibility of such a theory.

Notes

1 This chapter uses material and ideas included in "On the Nature of Law" (Raz 1996) and in "Two Views of the Nature of the Theory of Law" (Raz 1998).

2 Notable among them are theories about the appropriate form or content that legal institutions should have, and theories about the concepts and principles which govern various legal areas (property, commercial law, torts, contract, etc.).

3 In the present chapter I will not dwell on the role of understanding ability in concept possession. My assumption is that understanding consists in knowing important relations among the essential properties of the things the concepts apply to, and among them and some other properties. I mention skill and abilities to indicate that for possession of a concept the verbal or conceptual abilities which manifest themselves in giving explanations of the concept or its use are not sufficient. It requires some nonverbal skills or abilities as well, abilities which manifest themselves in its correct use, rather than in any explanation of it.

4 Note that not all essential properties are used in identifying instances or occurrences of the things they are essential properties of. Some essential properties are useless for identificatory purposes. It may be an essential property of real tennis that it is the ball game first developed in France in the fourteenth century, but normally you cannot identify a game of real tennis as being that by reference to that property. Furthermore, properties which can be used for identification often are not essential properties. Possibly the only essential property of water is that it is H_2O. But few people use that to identify water. Finally, often we rely on nonessential properties to identify instances of concepts. They may be reliable marks of instances of the concept in all normal circumstances. Note also that there is no reason to suppose the same property is used to identify items falling under the concept by everyone who has the concept. Some essential properties may be used in this way by some people, and not be used, indeed

not be even known to others who nevertheless have mastered the concept some other way.

5 On these concepts see Putnam (1985).

6 Here and in what follows I will use "law," as it is often used, to refer sometimes to a legal system, and sometimes to a rule of law, or a statement of how the law is on a particular point. Sometimes I will use the word ambiguously to refer to one or the other of these, as it does not matter for the purposes of the discussion of this chapter which way it is understood.

7 Compare a different case: the way the meaning of "knight" changed in the Middle Ages. "Knight," the *Oxford English Dictionary* explains, means (among other things):

3. . . . : A military servant or follower (of a king or some other specified superior); later, one devoted to the service of a lady as her attendant, or her champion in war or the tournament; . . .

This is logically the direct predecessor of sense 4, the " 'king's knight" having become the "knight" par excellence, and a lady's knight being usually one of knightly rank.

4. Name of an order or rank. a. In the Middle Ages: Originally (as in 3), A military servant of the king or other person of rank; a feudal tenant holding land from a superior on condition of serving in the field as a mounted and well-armed man. In the fully-developed feudal system: One raised to honourable military rank by the king or other qualified person, the distinction being usually conferred only upon one of noble birth who had served a regular apprenticeship (as page and squire) to the profession of arms, and thus being a regular step in this even for those of the highest rank.

No one would deny that changes of meaning of this kind occur, but while there is no harm in referring to them as changes in the concept of a knight there is no reason to regard them as anything other than a case in which one concept has replaced another.

8 Some regard the fact that law is a vague concept as another reason for denying that it makes sense to talk of the essential properties of law.

9 It is not clear whether any philosopher of any stature ever supposed otherwise. Bentham's account is accompanied by a penetrating analysis of the semantic explanation of normative terms (see Bentham 1970; Hart 1982). But its purpose is to show that his account of the law is semantically legitimate. It does not establish that he thought of it as an explanation of the meaning of the word "law" in English. Clearly Hart never meant to offer a semantic analysis

of the word law (Hart 1961: ch. 1). It is strange that R. M. Dworkin, who did not make the mistake himself, thought that Hart and many others were guilty of it. For my own previous repudiations of this view see Raz (1995) among other places. Many other philosophers of law were less sensitive to the issue and did not discuss it directly. Yet the general character of their work would suggest that they did not think of themselves as providing a semantic analysis of the word "law." It would be strange to attribute such a view to Hobbes, or to Locke, or Kant or Hegel, for example.

10 These comments are offered as an interpretation of a point on which Dworkin's views are not altogether clear.

11 This matter turns in part on the pragmatic character of explanation (including justificatory explanations) which cannot be discussed here.

12 During the 1960s countries of the British Commonwealth saw a series of decisions regarding the validity of *coup d'état*, secession, and the like which took the courts deep into theoretical disputes, leading in turn to a spate of theoretical discussions in the journals.

13 Though it is possible that all his theory requires is that those living in a society subject to law regard the law as instantiating some interpretive concept or another rather than the concept of law specifically.

14 Such as the names of widgets in the building trade. Or some theoretical terms in science.

15 These are examples, which do not imply that our native English speakers must have a perfect ability to translate French into English to qualify as French speakers. Only that they need to have some such ability.

References

Bentham, J. 1970. *Of Laws in General,* ed. H. L. A. Hart. London: University of London, The Athlone Press.

Dworkin, R. 1986. *Law's Empire.* Cambridge, MA: Harvard University Press.

Hart, H. L. A. 1961. *The Concept of Law.* Oxford: Oxford University Press.

H. L. A. Hart (ed.). 1982. *Essays on Bentham.* Oxford: Oxford University Press.

Putnam, H. 1985. The meaning of "meaning." In H. Putnam, *Philosophical Papers, Vol. 2: Mind, Language and Reality.* Cambridge, UK: Cambridge University Press, 215-71.

Raz, J. 1995. The problem about the nature of law. In J. Raz, *Ethics in the Public Domain*. Oxford: Oxford University Press, ch. 9.

Raz, J. 1996. On the nature of law. *Archiv für Rechts und Sozialphilosophie* 82: 1–25.

Raz, J. 1998. Two views of the nature of the theory of law: A partial comparison. *Legal Theory* 4: 249–82.

Raz, J. 1999. *Practical Reason and Norms*, 2nd edn. Princeton, NJ: Princeton University Press.

Ryle, G. 1949. *The Concept of Mind*. London: Hutchinson.

Index

abortion
  in critical legal theory 86, 87
  in feminist legal theory 93
accident law, and negligence 123
action, voluntary 107
  in Aristotle 8, 224–6, 228
  in Model Penal Code 226–7
adjudication **259–70**
  and persons 9–10, 269–70
  and legal rules 259, 263
  and legitimacy 259–68
  Mistaken View 259, 260–4
  naturalized 57–8
  and obligation 77
  and persons 10, 268–9
  Received View 9, 259–60, 262, 264–8
  and substantive justice 6
  see also decision making; judicial review
adversary system 6, 98, 163, 167–9
affirmative action 86, 267
  in feminist legal theory 90–1, 100–1
agency, and responsibility 199–200, 228–30
Alexy, Robert 21, 296
alimony 159, 160
Amar, Akhil 165
American Law Institute 53, 60, 94, 125, 222, 226
American Legal Realism *see* Realism, Legal
Anand, P. 74
anticommons, tragedy 5–6, 152–3, 156, 160
Aquinas, St. Thomas
  and legal positivism 29
  and natural law theory 1, 15–22, 292–3, 297
  and natural rights 293
  and obligation 15–16, 20
  and unjust laws 293
Aristotle
  and distributive justice 5, 133
  and legislation 237
  and voluntary action 8, 224–6, 228
Arnold, Thurman 51
Arrow, K. 253
Atiyah, P. S. 5, 141, 143
Atiyah, P. S. and Summers, Robert 243

Augustine of Hippo, St. 19
Austin, John 10, 287
  and command theory 32–3, 34, 35, 39, 238, 240, 288, 290, 292
  and customary law 40
  and ignorance of the law 223
  and legal positivism 2, 22, 23, 29–31, 32, 34, 38, 238–9, 297
  and natural law theory 19–20, 29
authority
  and concept of law 333
  of constitution 249–52
  in governance 44, 182–4
  of law 7, 18, 26, 40–1, 43, 181–6, 240, 294, 296
  service conception 36–7
  of state 280–1
autonomy
  and contract law 142, 143
  individual/collective 301–2
  and morality 289
  and positive law 295
  and privacy 273
  and property rights 157–8, 159
  and rights 7, 191, 194, 201–2, 293
  sexual 95, 96, 230
  of state 280–1
  see also liberty

Barber, Benjamin 300, 307
Barnett, R. E. 5, 142
Bayesianism
  and evidence 6, 169–72
  and probability 6
  quasi-objective 6, 171, 172–4
Beckman, Martha 221
Bedau, Mark 25
behavior
  and male responsibility 97
  modification 232–3
  and obligation 73, 75–8, 139
  and policy analysis school 69–70
  and political economy school 70–1, 75–9
behaviorism, and Legal Realism 50, 54, 56–8
Benn, Stanley I. 273, 279